The Merovingians in Historiographical Tradition

The Merovingian centuries were a foundational period in the historical consciousness of western Europe. The memory of the first dynasty of Frankish kings, their origin myths, accomplishments, and failures were used by generations of chroniclers, propagandists, and historians to justify a wide range of social and political agendas. The process of curating and editing the source material gave rise to a recognizable "Merovingian narrative" with three distinct phases: meteoric ascent, stasis, and decline. Already in the seventh-century *Chronicle of Fredegar*, this tripartite model was invoked by a Merovingian queen to prophesy the fate of her descendants. This expert commentary sets out to understand how the story of the Merovingians was shaped through a process of continuous historiographical adaptation. It examines authors from across a millennium of historical writing and analyzes their influences and objectives, charting the often-unexpected ways in which their narratives were received and developed.

Yaniv Fox is Associate Professor of History at Bar-Ilan University. He is the organizer of the 2021–2022 Israel Institute for Advanced Studies research group "Purity and Pollution in Late Antique and Early Medieval Culture and Society" and the author of *Power and Religion in Merovingian Gaul: Columbanian Monasticism and the Frankish Elites* (2014).

The Merovingians in Historiographical Tradition
From the Sixth to the Sixteenth Centuries

Yaniv Fox
Bar-Ilan University, Israel

Shaftesbury Road, Cambridge CB2 8EA, United Kingdom

One Liberty Plaza, 20th Floor, New York, NY 10006, USA

477 Williamstown Road, Port Melbourne, VIC 3207, Australia

314–321, 3rd Floor, Plot 3, Splendor Forum, Jasola District Centre, New Delhi – 110025, India

103 Penang Road, #05–06/07, Visioncrest Commercial, Singapore 238467

Cambridge University Press is part of Cambridge University Press & Assessment, a department of the University of Cambridge.

We share the University's mission to contribute to society through the pursuit of education, learning and research at the highest international levels of excellence.

www.cambridge.org
Information on this title: www.cambridge.org/9781009285018

DOI: 10.1017/9781009285025

© Yaniv Fox 2024

This publication is in copyright. Subject to statutory exception and to the provisions of relevant collective licensing agreements, no reproduction of any part may take place without the written permission of Cambridge University Press & Assessment.

First published 2024

A catalogue record for this publication is available from the British Library.

Library of Congress Cataloging-in-Publication Data
Names: Fox, Yaniv, 1975– author.
Title: The Merovingians in historiographical tradition : from the sixth to the sixteenth centuries / Yaniv Fox, Bar-Ilan University, Israel.
Description: Cambridge ; New York : Cambridge University Press, 2023. | Includes bibliographical references and index.
Identifiers: LCCN 2023028786 | ISBN 9781009285018 (hardback) | ISBN 9781009285063 (paperback) | ISBN 9781009285025 (ebook)
Subjects: LCSH: Merovingians – Historiography. | Merovingians – History. | Civilization, Medieval – Historiography. | Civilization, Medieval. | France – History – Medieval period, 987–1515 – Historiography. | France – History – To 987 – Historiography.
Classification: LCC DC65 .F68 2023 | DDC 944/.02–dc23/eng/20230630
LC record available at https://lccn.loc.gov/2023028786

ISBN 978-1-009-28501-8 Hardback

Cambridge University Press & Assessment has no responsibility for the persistence or accuracy of URLs for external or third-party internet websites referred to in this publication and does not guarantee that any content on such websites is, or will remain, accurate or appropriate.

Contents

Acknowledgements	*page* vii
List of Abbreviations	ix
Introduction	1

Part I: Lions and Unicorns   27

1 Trojans, Sea-monsters, and Long-haired Kings: From Priam to Childeric   29
    1.1 Gregory of Tours's *Histories* and the Unknowable Origins of the Franks   33
    1.2 The *Chronicle of Fredegar*: The Ethics of an *origo*   41
    1.3 A Carolingian Interlude: The Trojan Comment in the *Gesta episcoporum Mettensium*   57
    1.4 An Evolving Royalism: Dionysian Historiography and Its Influences   62
    1.5 Conclusions   82

2 *Capud victuriarum vestrarum Chlodovechus*   84
    2.1 *Adora quod incendisti*: Gregory of Tours   88
    2.2 An Officer and a Gentleman: Paolo Emilio's *De rebus gestis Francorum*   99
    2.3 Conclusions   118

Part II: Bears and Wolves   121

3 *Taedit me memorare*: The Middle Merovingians   123
    3.1 Frechulf of Lisieux's *argumentum ex silentio*   129
    3.2 *Pro multis sceleribus*: Ado of Vienne's Tales of Woe   140
    3.3 Conclusions   168

4 *Omni ecclesiastica dignitate nobilitavit*: "Good King Dagobert"   170
    4.1 *Fredegar* and the *Gesta Dagoberti*   174
    4.2 Regino and the Rehistoricized Dagobert   206
    4.3 Conclusions   220

Part III: Dogs and Lesser Beasts 223

5 *Regibus solo nomine regnantibus*: The Late Merovingians 225

    5.1 Eighty-eight years of *fainéance*: Sigebert of Gembloux's Late Merovingians 229
    5.2 Yosef Ha-Kohen's Late Merovingians 256
    5.3 Conclusions 270

Conclusions 272

Bibliography 280
Index 318

Acknowledgements

The idea for this book came to me in 2017, as an attempt to remedy my unease with the way I was teaching the Merovingians, hopping from Clovis to Dagobert to their "do-nothing" successors. In the six years it took to complete, friends and colleagues have helped me think through my often-simplistic ideas, offering their guidance, encouragement, and experience at every turn. I have also received material and emotional support from a long and diverse group of institutions, friends, and family. Their generosity and insight have been crucial and, while offering my gratitude here is perhaps insufficient compensation for their efforts, I can only hope to be able to repay them in the future. As always, the flaws that remain in this work are mine alone.

This research was supported by the Israel Science Foundation (Grant 1417/18). The four years during which this grant was made available have been invaluable, and I am very grateful for their support. I would also like to acknowledge the University of Tübingen's Center for Advanced Studies project "Migration and Mobility in Late Antiquity and the Early Middle Ages," and to thank especially Steffen Patzold and Mischa Meier, for offering me a fellowship in February 2020. The time spent there was both insightful and delightful, especially since the world ground to a halt precisely as I returned home to the first of many lockdowns. I am also very grateful to the Israel Institute for Advanced Studies for the year I spent in Jerusalem in 2021–2022 as a member of the research group "Purity and Pollution in Late Antique and Medieval Society and Culture." The community and friendships forged there remain strong, even though we have all since dispersed. I would especially like to thank Iris Avivi, Keren Rechnitzer, and Anat Yagil for their kindness, patience, and humor.

I am especially thankful to my home institution of Bar-Ilan, to the Faculty of Humanities, and to the staff and faculty at the department of general history; to Hilda Nissimi and Doron Avraham for their assistance as department heads; to Revital Yitzhaki and Oriyan Yehezkel for their administrative help; and to my research students for their inquisitiveness.

But mostly I am indebted to my friends there for their engaging company and generous spirit: Yosef Liebersohn, Dov Stuczinski, Daniela Dueck, Yaakov Mascetti, and Tal Tovy. A special thanks is due to Myriam Greilsammer, not only for the kindness and guidance she has afforded me since I arrived at Bar-Ilan, but also for her assistance in translating Old French.

The generosity and camaraderie I found in the community of Late Antique and Early Medieval historians has been overwhelming. I would like to thank Stefan Esders, Rob Meens, and Carmela Vircillo Franklin for their efforts on my behalf and for their valuable guidance and advice. Laury Sarti has read and commented on early versions of this book and her friendship has been unwavering. To Éric Fournier and Daniella Talmon-Heller for their friendship, hospitality, and advice; to Robert Wiśniewski who welcomed me in Warsaw; and to Jerzy Szafranowski, whose gesture of friendship I will not forget, I am forever grateful.

My utmost gratitude to Yitzhak Hen, who has been a guiding light in matters big and small, academic and personal. It is to him that I came with my worries and ideas, setbacks and triumphs. Yitzhak was the first person I consulted about this book. He has since read many of its iterations and his input, as always, has been invaluable. Working alongside him at the Israel Institute for Advanced Studies was a rare privilege, which made a wonderful year that much better.

I am grateful for the editorial acumen of Sara Tropper, who often knew what I meant better than I did; to the team at Cambridge University Press for their diligence and professionalism–Elizabeth Friend-Smith, Elizabeth Hanlon, Victoria Phillips, and Laheba Alam; and to Mary Morton for her copy editing during the manuscript's final stages of production.

Finally, thank you to my family: for the many Sabbath dinners spent talking and lovingly arguing with my in-laws, the Naim family; to my parents, Michael and Leah, for their persistent support and encouragement; to my brother Yaron for his indefatigable optimism; to Lital, my wife and closest companion, with whom I shared my difficulties and my joys; and to my dear children, Yahav, Ouria, and Ivri. This book is dedicated to you.

Abbreviations

AASS	*Acta Sanctorum*
AMP	*Annales Mettenses Priores*
ARF	*Annales regni Francorum*
BECh	*Bibliothèque de l'École des chartes*
Bede, HE	Bede, *Ecclesiastical History of the English People*, ed. B. Colgrave and R. A. B. Mynors (Oxford, 1969)
CCCM	Corpus Christianorum Continuatio Medievalis
CCSL	Corpus Christianorum Series Latina
DRG	*De rebus gestis Francorum ad christianissimum Galliarum regem Franciscum Valesium, eius nominis primum, libri decem, ex postrema authoris recognitione. Additum est de regibus item Francorum Chronicon, ad hæc usque tempora studiosissime deductum, cum rerum maxime insignium indice copiosissimo*
HL	Paul the Deacon, *Historia Langobardorum*
LHF	*Liber historiae Francorum*
MGH	Monumenta Germaniae Historica
AA	Auctores Antiquissimi
Conc.	Concilia
DD	Diplomata
Merov.	Die Urkunden der Merowinger
Arnulf.	Die Urkunden der Arnulfinger
LdK	Die Urkunden der deutschen Karolinger: Ludwig das Kind
Epp.	Epistola
LL Nat. Germ.	Leges nationum Germanicarum
Poetae	Poetae Latini Medii aevi
QQ zur Geistesgesch.	Quellen zur Geistesgeschichte des Mittelalters
SRG	Scriptores rerum Germanicarum, in usum scholarum separatum editi

SRG n.s.	Scriptores rerum Germanicarum, nova series
SRL	Scriptores rerum Langobardorum
SRM	Scriptores rerum Merovingicarum
SS	Scriptores (in folio)
PL	Patrologiae cursus completus, series Latina, ed. J.-P. Migne, 221 vols. (Paris, 1844–1864)

Introduction

In 1274, a monk by the name of Primat from the Parisian monastery of Saint-Denis completed his *magnum opus*, a chronicle in Old French titled the *Roman des rois*. As its name suggests, this composition dealt with Frankish and French history from the perspective of its kings. It worked its way from the Franks' earliest origins in ancient Troy, through three royal dynasties, concluding with the reign of the great Capetian monarch, Philip Augustus (d. 1223). One of its earlier chapters contains this unusual story about the Merovingian king Childeric I (d. ca. 481) and his new wife, Basina:

When Queen Basina, wife of Bissinus king of Thuringia to whom the king [i.e., Childeric] escaped, learned that Childeric was reconciled with his barons and that he was accepted in his realm, she left her master, and came after Childeric to France, because it was said that he had known her when he lived with her lord.[1]

He asked her why she had followed him and left her lord. She responded to him: "I came to you", said she, "because I had known you and recognized your temperance and your virtue, and if I thought I could find someone better than you in any part of the world, neither the hardships of the road, nor any torture of the body could prevent me from going to search for him." When the king heard this response, he took her in marriage like the pagan that he was; indeed, he did not remember the presents and benefices that Bissinus, the king of Thuringia, her first husband, gave to him when he was chased out of France.

When they were lying down together at night and were in the privacy of the bed, the queen admonished him to refrain that night from approaching her. Then she said to him that he should get up and go in front of the palace door and should know to tell her what he sees. The king got up and obeyed her command. When he was in front of the exit, it seemed to him that he saw large forms of beasts, such as unicorns, leopards, and lions,

---

[1] On Philip Augustus and his magnates, echoing scenes reminiscent of those in which Primat placed Childeric and his "barons," see J. Bradbury, *Philip Augustus: King of France, 1180–1223* (London and New York: Routledge, 1998), pp. 226–234; J.W. Baldwin, *The Government of Philip Augustus: Foundations of French Royal Power in the Middle Ages* (Berkeley, CA: University of California Press, 1991), pp. 28–36; C.W. Hollister and J.W. Baldwin, "The Rise of Administrative Kingship: Henry I and Philip Augustus," *The American Historical Review* 83, 4 (1978), pp. 867–905; R.H. Bautier, ed., *La France de Philippe-Auguste: Le temps des mutations* (Paris: Centre National de la Recherche Scientifique, 1982).

1

which came and went in front of the palace. He returned very frightened and told the queen what he had seen. She told him that he should not be afraid, and that he should go back. When he did come back, he saw large forms of bears and wolves, as though they wanted to run one towards the other. He came back to the queen's bed and told her the second vision. She said to him again that he should go back once more. When he did return, he saw figures of dogs and small beasts that were all tearing each other to pieces.

When he returned to the queen and told her all that he had seen, he requested from her to make him understand what the meaning of these three visions was, because he knew well that she did not send him for nothing. She told him that they should remain chaste that night, and that she would explain to him in the morning the meaning of the three visions.

So they were, until morning, when the queen called the king, who, she saw, was very deep in thought. Thus, she said the following: "My lord, leave the thoughts of your heart, and hear what I am about to say. You should know with certainty that these visions are not so much signs of present things as harbingers of things to come.

So, you should not pay attention to the form of the beasts you saw, but to the deeds and the habits of the lineage that will issue from us. Because the first heir that will be born to us will be a man of noble prowess and of great power; and this is signified by the form of the unicorn and the lion, which are the most noble and the most courageous beasts there are. The meaning of the second vision is the following, that in the form of the bear and the wolf are signified those that will issue forth from our son, who will be as rapacious as those beasts are. The meaning of the third vision is the following, that in the form of the dog, a lecherous beast of no virtue that can do nothing without man's help, is signified the wickedness and idleness of those who, towards the end of the era, will hold the scepter and the crown of this kingdom.

In the rabble of the small beasts who were fighting each other are signified the common people who will kill each other because they will be without fear of a prince. My lord," said the queen, "understand that this is the explanation of the three visions, which is the certain demonstration of the things to come." So, this is how the king let go of the mood brought about by these visions, and he was elated by the noble line and by the great number of worthy men that were to issue from him.[2]

---

[2] *Grandes Chroniques de France*, ed. J. Viard, 3 vols. (Paris: Société de l'histoire de France, 1920), 1, ch. 10, pp. 34–37: "Quant le roine Basine, fame Bissine le roi de Toringe à cui li rois s'enfui, sout que Childeris se fu acordez à ses barons et que il fu receuz en son regne, ele guerpi son seigneur, et s'en vint après Childeric en France, car l'on disoit que, il l'avoit cogneue tandis com il demoiroit ovec son seigneur. Il li demanda porquoi ele l'avoit sui et son seigneur guerpi; ele li respondi: 'Je sui, dist ele, à toi venue pour ce que je ai cogneue et esprovée ta temprance et ta vertu, et se je cuidasse meilleur de toi trover en nules des partie dou monde, nus griés de voie ne nus travaus de cors ne me tenist que je ne l'alasse requerre.' Quant li rois oï ceste response, il la prist par marriage comme païens que il estoit; si ne li sovint pas des bontez et des benefices que Bissines, li rois de Toringe, ses premiers mariz, li out fez quant il out esté chaciez de France.

Quant il furent le soir couchié ensemble et il furent ou secré dou lit, la roine l'amonesta que il se tenist cele nuit d'abiter à li, puis li dist que il se levast et alast devant la porte dou palais, et li seust à dire ce que il auroit veu. Li rois se leva, et fist son commandement. Quant il fu devant la sale, il li sembla que il veist granz forms de bestes, ausi comme d'unicornes, de lieparz et de lyons, qui aloient et venoient par devant le palais. Il retorna touz espoentez et raconta à la roine ce que il avoit veu. Ele li dist que il n'eust pas paor,

Introduction

By Primat's day, the Merovingians and their Carolingian successors had long since come and gone, having supplied material for countless histories, songs, and legends. Writing during the zenith of the Capetians, Primat was doubtless sensitive to the ups and downs of dynastic fortune. In this, of course, he was not alone. The waxing and waning of dynastic fortune was a central motif of Frankish and French historiography. For chroniclers interested in the Merovingians, Basina's prophecy proved especially alluring. We might imagine them peering over Childeric's shoulder at the scenes unfolding outside the palace window, offering their own appraisals and justifications for how and why the Merovingians fared as they did. In a way, it is even possible to detect in their own periodizations traces of Basina's three-part schema. To paraphrase Patrick Geary, "These differing tripartite visions of the past provided the frames within which to place the past, a past remembered through texts, through people [...]."[3] The various interpretations, explanations, and narrative solutions they provided are the subject of this book. It will follow the parable through its three distinct phases—lions and unicorns, bears and wolves, and finally, dogs and lesser beasts—tracing the narration of Merovingian history from its murky beginnings to its conclusion in 751 in a select group of histories and chronicles.

et que il retornast arrieres. Quant retornez fu, il vit grandes ymages d'ours et de leus ausi com s'il voisissent courre sus li uns l'autre. Il retorna au lit la roine, et li raconta la seconde avision. Ele li redist que il retornast encore une foiz. Quant retornez fu, il vit figures de chiens et de petites bestes qui s'entredepeçoient toutes.
    Quant il fu retornez à la roine et il li out tout raconté quanque il out veu, il li request que ele li feist entendre que ces III avisions senefioient, car il savoit bien que ele ne l'i avoit pas envoié pour noient. Ele li dist que il se tenist chastement cele nuit, et ele li feroit au matin entendre la signification des III avisions.
    Ensi furent jusques au matin, que la roine apela le roi, que ele vit moult pensif. Puis li dist ensi: 'Sire, ostez ces pensées de ton cuer, et entent ce que je dirai. Si saches certeinement que ces avisions ne sont pas tant significations des choses presents comme de celes qui à avenir sont.
    Si ne prens pas garde aus forms des bestes que tu as veues, mais aus faiz et aus mours de la lignie qui de nous doit eissir. Car li premiers hoirs qui de nous naistra sera hons de noble proëce et de haut puissance; et ceste senefie en la forme de l'unicorne et dou lyon, qui sont les plus nobles bestes et les plus hardies qui soient. La signification de la seconde avision se est tele, car en la forme de l'ours et dou leu sont segnefié cil qui de nostre fil istront, qui seront rapineus ausi com les bestes sont. La segnefiance de la tierce avision se rest tele, que en la forme dou chien, qui est beste lecherresse et de nule vertu, ne ne puet sanz l'aide d'ome, est segnefié la mauvestié et la parece de ceus qui vivront à la fin dou siècle tendront le ceptre et la corone de cest roiaume. En la torbe des petites bestes qui s'entrabatoient est senefiez li menuz poples qui s'entrociront, pour ce que il seront sanz paor de prince. Sire, dist la roine, vez ci l'exposition des III avision qui est certaine demostrerresse des choses qui sont à avenir.' Ensi fu li rois hors de la pensée en quoi il estoit chaüz pour les avisions, et fu liez de la noble lignie et dou grant nombre des preudomes qui de lui devoient eissir."
[3] P.J. Geary, *Phantoms of Remembrance: Memory and Oblivion at the End of the First Millennium* (Princeton, NJ: Princeton University Press, 1994), p. 123, speaking here about the chronologies of foundation and destruction of the monastic communities of Novalesa and Benediktbeuern.

Childeric's vision and Basina's prognostication, related so vividly in the *Roman des rois*, were not the invention of Primat. The scene was a rendition of a tale first told in the third book of the *Chronicle of Fredegar*, composed *ca.* 660.[4] There, we find a similar, albeit less elaborate, version of the one found in the *Roman des rois*. The *Chronicle of Fredegar* was a composite text, made up of several earlier works, interpolated and reworked by an anonymous chronicler. The result was a new history, a "chain chronicle," whose main emphasis was on events taking place in Merovingian Gaul.[5]

Book III of *Fredegar*, in which we meet Childeric and Basina, was adapted from the work of Gregory of Tours. The bishop completed his *Ten Books of History* in the early 590s, some seventy years before the *Fredegar* chronicler put down his pen.[6] After Gregory's death and against his express wishes,[7] his work was re-edited and revised to produce a six-book abridgement, which formed the kernel of *Fredegar*'s Book III. The fourth and final book of the *Fredegar* chronicle was an original addition, composed as a continuation, until *ca.* 642, of the events covered in Book III. The *Fredegar* chronicler built on Gregory, but he was not committed to the bishop's style, nor to his narrative interests and overall agenda. Indeed, the *Fredegar* chronicler gazed on his world from a very different perch.[8]

Childeric's visions and Basina's prophetic interpretations, absent from Gregory,[9] were novel elements introduced by the *Fredegar* chronicler. At various points in the text, the chronicler would interrupt Gregory's prose

---

[4] *Chronicarum quae dicuntur Fredegarii scholastici libri IV cum continuationibus*, MGH (*Monumenta Germaniae Historica*) SRM 2, ed. B. Krusch (Hanover: Hahnsche Buchhandlung, 1888), III.12, pp. 97–98 [hereafter, *Fredegar*]. For a recent treatment of Fredegar's *origo* rendition, see H. Reimitz, "The Early History of Frankish Origin Legends, c.500–800 C.E.," in *Origin Legends in Early Medieval Western Europe*, eds. L. Brady and P. Wadden (Leiden and Boston: Brill, 2022), pp. 156–183.

[5] On the structure of *Fredegar*, see R. Collins, *Die Fredegar-Chroniken*, MGH Studien und Texte 44 (Hanover: Hahnsche Buchhandlung, 2007), pp. 8–81. On chain chronicles, see I. N. Wood, "Chains of Chronicles: The Example of London, British Library ms. add. 16794," in *Zwischen Niederschrift und Wiederschrift: Hagiographie und Historiographie im Spannungsfeld von Kompendienüberlieferung und Editionstechnik*, eds. R. Corradini and M. Diesenberger (Vienna: Verlag der österreichische Akademie der Wissenschaften 2010), pp. 67–78.

[6] On the six-book version of the *Histories*, see H. Reimitz, "The Early Medieval Editions of Gregory of Tours' *Histories*," in *A Companion to Gregory of Tours*, ed. A.C. Murray (Leiden and Boston: Brill, 2016), pp. 519–565.

[7] Gregory of Tours, *Libri Historiarum X*, MGH SRM 1.1, ed. B. Krusch and W. Levison (Hanover: Hahnsche Buchhandlung, 1951), X.31, p. 536 [hereafter, Gregory of Tours, *Histories*].

[8] H. Reimitz, *History, Frankish Identity and the Framing of Western Ethnicity, 550–850* (Cambridge: Cambridge University Press, 2015), pp. 166–239; S. Esders and H. Reimitz, "Legalizing Ethnicity: The Remaking of Citizenship in Post-Roman Gaul (Sixth–Seventh Centuries)," in *Civic Identity and Civic Participation in Late Antiquity and the Early Middle Ages*, eds. C. Brélaz and E. Rose (Turnhout: Brepols, 2021), pp. 295–329, at pp. 301–302.

[9] Gregory of Tours, *Histories*, II.12, pp. 61–62.

Introduction 5

to present the reader with relevant information. These interpolations had the effect of recontextualizing the actions of the *dramatis personae*. *Fredegar*'s Book III was also drastically reduced in size compared with the six-book version. In a very real sense, then, Book III was no longer Gregory's creation. It was something new. In the late eighth century, *Fredegar* was continued and reworked, and in this form—commonly known as the *Historia vel gesta Francorum*—it became a staple of Carolingian historiography.[10] Carolingian chroniclers also relied on *Fredegar* for information about the sixth and seventh centuries when writing their own compositions. Here, too, the material *Fredegar* supplied was modified to meet the needs of new ideologies.

Another chapter in the story of Basina's prophecy was ushered in with the *Gesta Francorum* by Aimoin of Fleury, a monk and historian working in the late tenth century.[11] In terms of its breadth and innovativeness, the historiographical composition produced in the monastery, famous in Francia for housing the remains of St. Benedict lifted by its monks from the temporarily abandoned Monte Cassino,[12] was the institutional forbear of twelfth- and thirteenth-century Saint-Denis.[13] The views expressed in Aimoin's work were none other than those of his abbot, Abbo of Fleury, and were, it seems, the product of a cumulative effort by a team of monks, compiling and reworking the material for a chronicle at Abbo's behest.[14]

Abbo's career began under the last Carolingian ruler of West Francia, Louis V, also known as Louis le fainéant.[15] In 987 Louis was killed in a riding accident and was replaced by Hugh Capet, whose reign signaled the beginning of the centuries-long Capetian hold on the French throne. Abbo ruled from 987 until his own murder in 1004 by a group of rebellious monks at Fleury's Gascon priory of La Réole.[16] This traumatic event brought to an unexpected end Aimoin's work on the *Gesta Francorum*,

---

[10] Reimitz, *History*, pp. 295–334.
[11] Aimoin of Fleury, *Historia Francorum libri quattuor*, PL 139, cols. 627–802 [hereafter, Aimoin of Fleury, *Gesta Francorum*].
[12] See P.J. Geary, *Furta Sacra: Thefts of Relics in the Central Middle Ages* (Princeton, NJ: Princeton University Press, 1978), pp. 120–122.
[13] Geary, *Phantoms of Remembrance*, p. 26.
[14] K.F. Werner, "Die literarischen Vorbilder des Aimoin von Fleury und die Entstehung seiner *Gesta Francorum*," *Francia* 45 (1999), pp. 192–226, at pp. 209–210.
[15] E. Dachowski, *First Among Abbots: The Career of Abbo of Fleury* (Washington, DC: The Catholic University of America Press, 2008), pp. 15–16. For historiography linking Louis's *fainéance* to that of the late Merovingians, see Bernard de Girard du Haillan's 1615 *Histoire générale des Roys de France* (Paris: Sebastien Cramoisy, 1615), pp. 283–286; E.M. Peters, "*Roi fainéant*: The Origins of an Historians' Commonplace," *Bibliothèque d'Humanisme et Renaissance* 30, 3 (1968), pp. 537–547, at pp. 542–543.
[16] Aimoin of Fleury, *Vita sancti Abbonis*, in *L'Abbaye de Fleury en l'an mil*, ed. and trans. R.-H. Bautier and G. Labory (Paris: Centre national de la recherche scientifique, 2004), ch. 20, pp. 118–126; Dachowski, *First Among Abbots*, p. 2.

prompting him to divert his attention to the composition of the *Life of St Abbo*, a hagiographical piece dedicated to his abbot,[17] whom Aimoin accompanied on the fateful trip to Gascony. Aimoin also added his own chapters to the corpus of miracles attributed to St. Benedict that was being recorded at Fleury.[18] Abbo's sudden death was thus the reason Aimoin's *Historia* cut off at 654, although it was doubtless meant to continue until his own day. As it stands, it already bears the traces of Abbo's complex views on institutional power, developed through his dealings with the late Carolingians, the early Capetians, and their regional representatives, both lay and ecclesiastical. Most of the Merovingian period was nevertheless covered in Aimoin's work, and with it the story of Childeric and Basina.[19] Since the work was not beholden to the tenets of Carolingian historiography, the Merovingian material could be revisited and reframed to suit Abbo's views on royal power and its relationship with the Church and particularly with Fleury. From Aimoin, the story made its way to the *Roman des rois* and then on to its countless medieval variations.[20]

This extensive borrowing from previous works was, by no means, an anomalous phenomenon in the historiographical treatment of Merovingian history up to the sixteenth century, when the present study terminates. As successive generations of chroniclers and historians turned their attention to the first royal dynasty of the Franks, each shaded the story to reflect a unique set of priorities. Some changes were semantic or stylistic; others, more comprehensive, still conserved the narrative core; still others opted to forgo entire blocks of plot that did not fit the authorial aims of the new composition.

Paolo Emilio, a humanist historian working in the sixteenth century, turned to Gregory's *Histories* as his guide to the affairs of fifth- and sixth-century Gaul when he wrote his great history, *De rebus gestis Francorum*.[21] So, while he probably knew the Childeric story from Aimoin and Primat,

---

[17] For the *Vita sancti Abbonis* as a martyrology, see Dachowski, *First Among Abbots*, p. 4.
[18] See E. de Certain, *Les miracles de Saint Benoît écrits par Adrevald, Aimoin, André, Raoul Tortaire et Hugues de Sainte Marie, moines de Fleury* (Paris: Mme. Ve. Jules Renouard, 1858).
[19] Aimoin of Fleury, *Gesta Francorum*, ch. 8, cols. 643–644; B. Guenée, "Chanceries and Monasteries," in *Rethinking France: Les Lieux de mémoire, vol. 4: Histories and Memories*, ed. P. Nora (Chicago and London: University of Chicago Press, 2001), pp. 1–26, at pp. 12–14.
[20] Werner, "Die literarischen Vorbilder," p. 224; G. Spiegel, *The Chronicle Tradition of Saint-Denis: A Survey* (Brookline, MA, and Leiden: Brill, 1978), esp. pp. 103–126.
[21] P. Emilio, *De rebus gestis Francorum ad christianissimum Galliarum regem Franciscum Valesium, eius nominis primum, libri decem, ex postrema authoris recognitione. Additum est de regibus item Francorum Chronicon, ad hæc usque tempora studiosissime deductum, cum rerum maxime insignium indice copiosissimo* (Paris: M. Vasconsanus, 1550).

Introduction   7

his reliance on Gregory dictated that he omit it. *The Merovingians in Historiographical Tradition: From the Sixth to the Sixteenth Centuries* engages with stories like this and with the authorial choices that governed their transmission, reception, and adaptation. It charts the evolution of Merovingian storylines from almost a millennium of historiography, tracing the often intriguing, sometimes serpentine, ways in which the narratives were adjusted to reflect new ideas and attract new audiences.

* * *

In medieval chronicles, prophecies have a way of becoming reality, and Basina's was no exception. The trajectory of her royal descendants over the course of the next three centuries was one of meteoric rise to power, then of stasis and internal conflict, and finally of decline and infamy. Or at least, that is how the story was conventionally told. Basina's explosive admonition was realized not so much by the historical Merovingians, which, it seems, were much more impressive than her vision foretold.[22] Rather, it became the canon of their portrayal in the compositions that set out to cover early Frankish history. The *Fredegar* chronicler, writing 100 years before the Merovingians were unceremoniously ushered offstage, could scarcely have foreseen how exquisitely useful his metaphor of decline would be. In the centuries to come, it informed, however indirectly, the process of retelling the history of the Merovingian era as a play in three acts, embodied in the three categories of beasts laid out in Basina's prophecy.

That this process received a major push under the Carolingians comes as no surprise. The Carolingians were preoccupied with legitimation and one way to allay their status anxiety was to denigrate their predecessors. This strategy is neither new nor disputed. The critical appraisal of the recent past in Carolingian historiography has been widely noted in the literature.[23] That does not mean, however, that ninth-century authors

---

[22] For recent assessments of the Merovingians and their world, see S. Esders et al., eds., *East and West in the Early Middle Ages: The Merovingian Kingdoms in Mediterranean Perspective* (Cambridge: Cambridge University Press, 2019); B. Effros and I. Moreira, eds., *The Oxford Handbook of the Merovingian World* (Oxford: Oxford University Press, 2020).

[23] For a very partial sampling, see P.J. Geary, *Before France and Germany: The Creation and Transformation of the Merovingian World* (Oxford and New York: Oxford University Press, 1988), pp. 221–231; R. McKitterick, *History and Memory in the Carolingian World* (Cambridge: Cambridge University Press, 2004); R. McKitterick, "Paul the Deacon and the Franks," *Early Medieval Europe* 8, 3 (1999), pp. 319–339; Y. Hen and M. Innes, eds., *The Uses of the Past in the Early Middle Ages* (Cambridge: Cambridge University Press, 2000); C.B. Bouchard, "Images of the Merovingians and Carolingians," *History Compass* 4, 2 (2006), pp. 293–307; C.B. Bouchard, "The Carolingian Creation of a Model of Patrilineage," in *Paradigms and Methods in Early Medieval Studies*, eds. C. Chazelle and F. Lifshitz (New York: Palgrave Macmillan, 2007), pp. 135–152; P. Fouracre, *The Age of Charles Martel* (New York: Routledge, 2000), p. 6; D. Kempf,

agreed on how to scapegoat the Merovingians or whether they even should do so. The truth is that the Carolingian response to the Merovingian past was neither orderly nor uniform. Instead, it was an ongoing literary experiment with a wide range of results.

When evaluating the nature of this experiment, for the Carolingian centuries and after, there is a tendency to focus on the changes in content, style, and emphasis introduced by a new author working with older material. Interpolations, omissions, and other interventions in the text are what made it a new creation, worthy of our attention. Yet it is equally important to appreciate the profound conservatism that underlay the medieval practice of writing history. We can only recognize the changes because they are embedded in familiar storylines.[24] There is certainly a long tradition of perceiving the repetitive and "derivative" nature of medieval historiography as an obstacle, limiting its usefulness.[25] Recent scholarship on the innovativeness of medieval chronicles has convinced us to rethink this notion, undoubtedly correctly. It is then worth reiterating that change can be appreciated only against the backdrop of what was conserved. This is an important point, because it demonstrates that authors were sensitive not only to the need to substantiate a range of proprietary or political claims by intervening in the plot. Pressure to conform to stylistic traditions, ideas about what the craft of writing history entailed, and even good storytelling might well have pushed the author to conserve components that otherwise might have changed, and *vice versa*.

Finally, we should bear in mind that, like us, medieval chroniclers and early modern historians were working with texts composed at considerable chronological remove from their own time. Their ability to understand their sources fully might thus be called into question. Geary has famously raised the possibility that eleventh-century historiography was forced to piece together its version of the past from "disjointed and

"Introduction," in Paul the Deacon, *Liber de episcopis Mettensibus*, ed. and trans. D. Kempf (Paris, Leuven, and Walpole, MA: Peeters, 2013), pp. 10–21; P.S. Barnwell, "Einhard, Louis the Pious and Childeric III," *Historical Research* 78, 200 (2005), pp. 129–139; T. Kölzer, "Die letzten Merowingerkönige: rois fainéants?," in *Der Dynastiewechsel von 751: Vorgeschichte, Legitimationsstrategien und Erinnerung*, eds. M.Becher and J. Jarnut (Münster: Scriptorium, 2004), pp. 33–60; R. Collins, "Frankish Past and Carolingian Present in the Age of Charlemagne," in *Am Vorabend der Kaiserkrönung: Das Epos "Karolus Magnus et Leo papa" und der Papstbesuch in Paderborn 799*, eds. P. Godman, J. Jarnut, and P. Johanek (Berlin: Akademie Verlag, 2011), pp. 301–322.

[24] On the conservatism of royal French histories, see O. Ranum, *Artisans of Glory: Writers and Historical Thought in Seventeenth-Century France* (Chapel Hill, NC: The University of North Carolina Press, 1980), pp. 15–16.

[25] On this see W. Pohl, "History in Fragments: Montecassino's Politics of Memory," *Early Medieval Europe* 10, 3 (2001), pp. 343–374; J. Lake, "Authorial Intention in Medieval Historiography," *History Compass* 12, 4 (2014), pp. 344–360, at p. 345, cites the different text sizes common to MGH editions.

Introduction 9

isolated" vignettes, on which it looked as one would on a foreign landscape.[26] All of these considerations directly affect the dynamics of change and conservation. Deciphering them becomes especially pressing when the editorial choices seem at odds with the stated purposes of the composition.

In this context it is useful to mention the concept of "literary shards," which Scott Bruce has recently coined to describe textual bundles that traverse time and genre, having been adapted for purposes "far removed from their ancient source."[27] The Byzantine emperor Heraclius's (d. 641) forced conversion of the Jews is one such example.[28] Echoes of the story are found in a variety of western and eastern sources, aimed at Jewish, Christian, and Muslim readers. The sources that report this event are diverse and cannot be traced to one original text. Their independence from each other should even encourage us to reconsider its historicity.[29] At least for the western material, however, there seems to have been a clear channel of transmission, which ran through key texts such as *Fredegar*, Aimoin of Fleury's *Gesta Francorum*, and the *Roman des rois*. When, in the sixteenth century, Yosef Ha-Kohen turned the story into a scathing indictment of the emperor's anti-Jewish policies, he was using it in a way that ran counter to its previous iterations. As instructive as such examples may be, in most of the works examined in this book we find more than the occasional shard. Thematic fragments could indeed be usefully cut and pasted into new historiographical works. Nonetheless, the composite result was always more than the sum of its parts. Each of the works I will discuss used the Merovingian period to make a historical claim about legitimacy, or power, or the vagaries of human affairs. Whatever the argument, the framing of the Merovingian period was part of it. We see this in the ways authors chose to begin and to end the Merovingian story, and in the thematic subdivisions they imposed on it to make it more clearly understood.

That the Merovingians were used to make such claims is hardly surprising given the foundational nature of their rule. The legitimacy of medieval

---

[26] Geary, *Phantoms of Remembrance*, p. 9.
[27] S. Bruce, "The Dark Age of Herodotus: Shards of a Fugitive History in Early Medieval Europe," *Speculum* 94, 1 (2019), pp. 47–67, at p. 49.
[28] For a discussion of this story, see Chapters 4 and 5.
[29] On this see S. Esders, "The Prophesied Rule of a 'Circumcised People': A Travelling Tradition from the Seventh-Century Mediterranean," in *Barbarians and Jews: Jews and Judaism in the Early Medieval West*, eds. Y. Hen and T.F.X. Noble (Turnhout: Brepols, 2018), pp. 119–154; T.J. MacMaster, "The Pogrom that Time Forgot: The Ecumenical anti-Jewish Campaign of 632 and Its Impact," in *Inclusion and Exclusion in Mediterranean Christianities, 400–800*, eds. Y. Fox and E. Buchberger (Turnhout: Brepols, 2019), pp. 217–235.

institutions and traditions of governance rested, to a large degree, on their antiquity. And indeed, many of the columns on which the organization of the Frankish and French state rested were erected under the Merovingians, while many others were expediently retro-projected onto this earlier period. The concept of reform, applied especially but not exclusively in an ecclesiastical context, made use of the corresponding notions of a pristine remote past and a deficient recent one to push ambitious social agendas, introducing innovation under the guise of traditionalism. Here, too, creatively reimagining Merovingian history proved uniquely advantageous. We immediately think of the Carolingians,[30] but this trope was used to great effect already in 643, when Jonas of Bobbio described Columbanus's underwhelming encounter with the religious life of Gaul: "Leaving the coast of Brittany behind them they enter Gaul. At that time, whether due to the numerous foreign enemies or through the negligence of the bishops, the fervor of the religious life had almost been extinguished there. All that remained was the Christian faith."[31] Themes of ascent, stasis, decline, and *renovatio* are integral to this type of treatment. They are commonly presented in a way that divides historical durations along reformational lines to highlight the need for change, in response to culturally deferential attitudes toward conservatism.

Periodization thus plays an important role in this book. As we shall see, the Merovingian period was perceived as a distinct historical moment by those who wrote about it. Some authors also broke it up into smaller thematic blocks, which corresponded to what they perceived as important shifts or junctures in Merovingian history. Certainly, these divisions were not uniformly accepted by all the authors considered in this book. Some were explicit about their rationale for dividing the period as they had, while others were more subtle, hinting about their intentions by introducing suggestive pauses into the narrative or by changing their tone. Identifying these *caesurae* is hardly straightforward and, admittedly, this is where much of what I say is speculative. Still, we are not dealing here only with remote hypotheticals. The reigns of Clovis I and Dagobert I were regularly regarded as zeniths of royal power, followed by an abrupt

---

[30] Particularly the activities and rhetoric of Boniface. On this, see M. Glatthaar, "Boniface and the Reform Councils," in *A Companion to Boniface*, eds. M. Aaij and S. Godlove (Leiden: Brill, 2020), pp. 219–246.

[31] Jonas of Bobbio, *Vita Columbani abbatis discipulorumque eius libri II*, MGH SRG 37, ed. B. Krusch (Hanover: Hahnsche Buchhandlung, 1905), I.5, p. 161: "A Brittanicis ergo sinibus progressi, ad Gallias tendunt, ubi tunc vel ob frequentia hostium externorum vel neglegentia praesulum religionis virtus pene abolita habebatur. Fides tantum manebat Christiana ... ." Trans. in Jonas of Bobbio, *Life of Columbanus, Life of John of Réomé, and Life of Vedast*, trans. A. O'Hara and I. Wood (Liverpool: Liverpool University Press, 2017), pp. 105–106.

Introduction 11

downturn in royal fortune. In the former case, this expressed itself primarily in the preoccupation with internal strife, while in the latter, the blasphemous acts of Clovis II against the relics of St. Dionysius signaled a shift into a phase of royal decadence and lethargy.

Since much of the material examined in this book was written with the benefit of hindsight, Merovingian decline cannot be discussed without the complementary theme of Carolingian ascent. The two topics are intertwined. The ways in which authors approached the task of fading out the Merovingians and fading in the Carolingians hold clues for how we should decipher their periodization models. Some authors sought to push the rise of the Carolingians deeper into the past, looking for clues of Merovingian decadence from the very beginning. Others emphasized regnal continuity and downplayed the obscure division of power between the late Merovingians and their Pippinid mayors. Still others sought to link the Carolingians and, through them, the Capetians, to the Merovingian *stirps* by blood. These choices illuminate how chroniclers in the Carolingian and post-Carolingian centuries relied on contemporary cultural sensibilities and political ideologies to introduce and justify certain thematic divisions in the period in question. Invariably, however, they tell a story of meteoric ascent, internal fracture, and eventual decline through the lives and deeds of a small number of key figures.

* * *

Throughout this book, we will encounter compositions drawn from centuries of retelling. Our guides will be ecclesiastical histories and chronicles from Late Antiquity and the early Middle Ages, episcopal *gesta*, high medieval French royal chronicles, and humanist and early modern Jewish histories. These are very different works, which naturally approached the task of storytelling with very different models in mind. All, however, partake of at least a little of Basina's determinism.

Yet the question arises: what binds these works together, and what justifies their examination as a coherent historiographical whole? They are not, of course, whole in any real sense, apart from their selection for the purposes of this study. Other choices could have been made, which would not have been any more or less justified. Indeed, this study makes no pretentions of exhaustiveness. The works contained herein are a consciously partial sample, ultimately chosen because they offer lucid examples of a certain development in the narrative.

Another important point is the degree to which the narrative approaches analyzed in the following represent a wider trend in contemporary historiography, or, alternatively, aim to subvert it. Clearly, the authors discussed were consciously selecting their material in a way that echoed their narrative programs, personal circumstances, institutional pressures, and stylistic proclivities. More than one of these reasons could have applied at any given time. Other authors writing at about the same period and preoccupied with similar topics might have selected differently. When the examples I offer are the fruit of a prolonged institutional effort, it is perhaps easier to reconstruct the range of options available to the author. In this context, the most obvious example is Saint-Denis, which, from the time of its abbot Suger (d. 1151) until Primat's day and beyond, boasted an impressive literary output with a consistent ideological bent. Dozens of works were authored in the monastery during these centuries, from which Primat could have drawn inspiration and knowledge. Fleury is another center of learning whose record of literary production affected the style and topic of Aimoin's *Gesta Francorum*, although there the emphasis was more on hagiography and miracle collections than on historiography proper.[32] However, compositions such as Yosef Ha-Kohen's *Divrei Hayamim* or the *Gesta Dagoberti* do not lend themselves so naturally to comparison, primarily because they are difficult to categorize in terms of genre, a problem to which I shall return shortly. When possible, I attempt to discuss the texts in question together with other contemporary compositions, drawing out their unique responses to the challenges posed by the sources.

As the title of this book implies, I view the works that appear here as historiographical, an assertion that warrants some explanation. While I use the term historiography as shorthand for several criteria I will outline shortly, these map only partially onto any conventional attempts to define medieval historiography.[33] As I have mentioned, works differ from one

---

[32] See R.-H. Bautier, "La place de l'abbaye de Fleury-sur-Loire dans l'historiographie française du IXe au XIIe siècle," in *Études ligériennes d'histoire et d'archéologie médiévales: mémoires et exposés présentés à la Semaine d'études médiévales de Saint-Benoit-sur-Loire du 3 au 10 Juillet 1969*, ed. R. Louis (Paris: Publications de la Société des Fouilles Archéologiques et des Monuments Historiques de l'Yonne, 1975), pp. 25–33.

[33] For a comprehensive review of these attempts and suggestions for rethinking genre as an analytical category for medieval historiography, see R. Markevičiūtė, "Rethinking the Chronicle: Modern Genre Theory Applied to Medieval Historiography," *The Medieval Chronicle* 13 (2020), pp. 182–200. See also D. Dumville's foundational paper, "What Is a Chronicle?," *The Medieval Chronicle* 2 (2002), pp. 1–27. For the problems of distinguishing *fasti*, annals, and chronicles, see Burgess and Kulikowski, *Mosaics of Time: The Latin Chronicle Traditions from the First Century BC to the Sixth Century AD, Volume I: A Historical Introduction to the Chronicle Genre from Its Origins to the High Middle Ages* (Turnhout: Brepols, 2013), pp. 1–63; G. Dunphy, "Chronicles (terminology)," in *Encyclopedia of the Medieval Chronicle*, ed. G. Dunphy, 2 vols. (Leiden, Boston: Brill, 2010), vol. 1, pp. 274–282; E. Breisach, *Historiography: Ancient, Medieval, & Modern*, 3rd edition (Chicago and London: University of Chicago Press, 2007), pp. 77–105 (framed as "Christian historiography").

Introduction 13

another in topic, style, and structure. Sigebert of Gembloux's *Chronicle* reads very differently from the *Liber historiae Francorum* [hereafter *LHF*] even though the former drew on the latter as a source.[34]

Genre stands at the heart of any attempt to define historiography, especially as it was understood across a thousand years of literary tradition. In the context of the present discussion, this takes the form of classifying the compositions I examine into such categories as "histories," "chronicles," "hagiographies," though recent discussions about genre have shown how misleading these categories often are.[35] Our inability to effectively distinguish between histories and chronicles also spills over into hagiographical, cartulary, and visionary literature. Any definition one might propose for historiography would thus land short of its mark. While Burgess and Kulikowski insist on the instrumentality of genre for understanding the text, they also point to the variations between early medieval and present-day genre taxonomies, and even concepts of genre more broadly.

Modern genre theory has sought to rehabilitate itself by distancing the term genre, as an analytical category, from a methodology of hierarchical classification. Relying on notions of family resemblance and prototype theory, Klaus Hempfer has recast genre as a network rather than a taxonomy. In this model, compositions can simultaneously inhabit several generic categories, interrelating along lines of shared similarity, influence, and authorial intent.[36] Importantly, this approach also allows for gradations of belonging to certain genres.

For the purposes of this book, genre is interesting insofar as it can shed light on the forces that regulate the handling of source material. Sigebert of Gembloux considered Frankish history as one element in a larger historiographical effort, which limited the amount of attention he could devote to each character. Naturally, this accounts for much of the difference between his work and that of his source, the *LHF*. Sigebert likewise differed from humanists such as Paolo Emilio, who were devoted to

---

[34] *Liber historiae Francorum*, MGH SRM 2, ed. B. Krusch (Hanover: Hahnsche Buchhandlung, 1888), pp. 215–328; Sigebert of Gembloux, *Chronica*, MGH SS 6, ed. G.H. Pertz (Hanover: Hahnsche Buchhandlung, 1844), pp. 300–375.
[35] F. Lifshitz, "Beyond Positivism and Genre: 'Hagiographical' Texts as Historical Narrative," *Viator* 25 (1994), pp. 95–114 [repr. in F. Lifshitz, *Writing Normandy: Stories of Saints and Rulers* (London and New York: Routledge, 2021), pp. 3–25]; B. Guenée, "Histoires, annales, chroniques: Essai sur les genres historiques au Moyen Âge," *Annales, Économies, Sociétés, Civilisations* 28 (1973), pp. 997–1016.
[36] K.W. Hempfer, "Some Aspects of a Theory of Genre," in *Linguistics and Literary Studies*, eds. M. Fludernik and D. Jacob (Berlin: De Gruyter, 2014), pp. 405–422. For a comparable approach, see now C. Taranu, *Vernacular Verse Histories in Early Medieval England and Francia: The Bard and the Rag-Picker* (New York and London: Routledge, 2021).

rationalizing the actions of the characters in the historical drama and to downplaying its ecclesiastical flavor. Different authors thought about their work in different ways, which led them to exclude some episodes and to amplify others, for reasons that will be discussed. All the texts examined in this book were susceptible to pressures of this sort, but each of them is unique in terms of its resulting structure, scope, and style. In this sense, then, it is perfectly natural to make observations about genre.

However, we know that there were countless narrative elements that carried over intact from one work to the next, traversing generic borders with ease. In other words, intertextual relations between compositions were largely unconstrained by genre. When we peel off one layer of the Dagobert narrative in Regino of Prüm's *Chronicle*, we find the *Gesta Dagoberti*. If we peel off another, we encounter the *Chronicle of Fredegar*. This channel of transmission is invaluable, because it is evidence of the permutations undergone by the narrative. While the three compositions fall into different generic categories, on this point at least their similarities matter more than anything one could hope to uncover by comparing them to works that are closer in aim, style, and structure. The dictates of genre taxonomy tend to obscure this fact.

We are still left with the question of what makes these works "historiographical." Notwithstanding their many differences and the problems of genre I just described, the works examined in the following chapters share important characteristics. It is these similarities that qualify them as historiographical. Firstly, they all employ a method of regulating the passage of time. In the closing remarks to Book I of his *Chronicle*, Regino of Prüm tells us how he approached his task: "Let us see, furthermore, if we can reconcile the same years of the Lord with the eras of the Roman popes, and consider how the spans of the secular rulers and the prelates correspond."[37] Regino was interested in ordering time by harmonizing chronologies extracted from competing traditions. Comparable statements can be found in Gregory of Tours, Ado of Vienne, Paolo Emilio, and others, although obviously in the service of dissimilar agendas.

Secondly, the works all portray a long historical era or process rather than the deeds of a single person. I looked for texts that approached the Merovingian period as a coherent narrative unit in a way that encouraged

---

[37] Regino of Prüm, *Chronicle*, MGH SRG 50, ed. F. Kurze (Hanover: Hahnsche Buchhandlung, 1890), at a.740, pp. 37–38: "Discernamus etiam, si placet, eosdem annos Domini per tempora pontificum Romanorum et videamus, quomodo sibi tempora principum et presulum adinvicem comparata respondeant." Trans. in S. Maclean, *History and Politics in Late Carolingian and Ottonian Europe: The Chronicle of Regino of Prüm and Adalbert of Magdeburg* (Manchester: Manchester University Press, 2009), p. 119.

Introduction 15

the emergence of periodization models.[38] Finally, I preferred works that took a syntactic, cause-and-effect view of history. Narrativity is obviously a spectrum, and I had to decide where to draw the line. Marius of Avenches was left out, while Sigebert of Gembloux was included. As a rule, I opted for more highly narrative compositions, because the stories that make up the Merovingian historiographical tradition are, in the end, the subject of this book.

The works that were chosen are also a partial subset of the available evidence. For some of the compositions, such as Yosef Ha-Kohen's *Divrei Hayamim* or the *Gesta Dagoberti*, no close narrative parallel survives, making them generic isolates.[39] The availability of sources, however, tended to grow as time progressed. Gregory of Tours's *Histories*, the *Chronicle of Fredegar*, and the *LHF* represent all of the narrative history produced in the Merovingian period, which is why they could all be considered. The farther along we are in history, the richer and more diverse the evidence becomes.

Eighth- and ninth-century compositions are especially interesting because they developed innovative solutions to the problems posed by the Merovingian past. Paul the Deacon, Frechulf of Lisieux, the author of the *Gesta Dagoberti*, and Ado of Vienne all interpreted it differently and ended up with different results. Carolingian-era historiography is thus heavily represented, although the surge in historiographical interest under the Carolingians also resulted in more works than can be usefully examined in this book. This is truer still for post-Carolingian chronicles, of which a very small proportion is represented in the following chapters. It would have been impossible to exhaust the richness of the medieval historiographical tradition, yet each of the works that were included had something important and original to say about early Frankish history.

In the group of works analyzed in the book, the *Gesta Dagoberti* is an anomaly. Something other than a work of historiography, it successfully resists definition. Perhaps it is a biography, although some of its characters and events were not drawn from any identifiable source and were likely narrative concoctions. It places heavy emphasis on proprietary and

---

[38] On changing concepts of time, see J. Le Goff, "Au Moyen Âge: temps de l'Église et temps du marchand," *Annales* 15, 3 (1960), pp. 417–433; J. Le Goff, "Le temps du travail dans la crise du XIVe siècle: du temps médiéval au temps moderne," *Le Moyen Âge* 69 (1963), pp. 597–613. Both are translated into English in *Time, Work and Culture in the Middle Ages*, trans. A. Goldhammer (Chicago and London: The University of Chicago Press, 1980), pp. 29–52. For "dynastic time," see J. Aurell, "From Genealogies to Chronicles: The Power of the Form in Medieval Catalan Historiography," *Viator* 36, pp. 235–264; Ranum, *Artisans of Glory*, pp. 6–8.

[39] *Divrei Hayamim* is a generic isolate only in the sense that no comparable work was available to a Hebrew readership.

donative topics, for which it unquestionably relied on charters and replicated their language.[40] Some of its chapters read like a will, while others feel as though they were taken straight from the visionary literature playbook. But it is also important to recognize that the narrative backbone of the *Gesta Dagoberti* is historiographical. More to the point, it embedded its protagonist in a broader Merovingian history, to which it loosely applied a model of periodization. I have thus placed the *Gesta Dagoberti* not in a section of its own, but alongside its main source, the *Chronicle of Fredegar*. It is crucial to understand the relation between *Fredegar* and the *Gesta Dagoberti* in order to grasp the next stage in the process, Regino of Prüm's *Chronicle*, which used the *Gesta Dagoberti* as a source.

One feature of the selected works is that they either used another work from the group as a source or were themselves such a source. Some works, like the *Gesta Dagoberti*, were both. It is this, more than anything else, that connects these works to each other. I also tried to choose works that were well known and often copied or, during the later period, printed. The compositions discussed in this book were, by contemporary standards, bestsellers. Gregory's *Histories* was a successful and influential work, albeit primarily in its six-book form. *Fredegar* and the *LHF* had a long career in Carolingian *scriptoria* and continued to be influential for centuries to come. The *Roman des rois* or, as it later came to be known, *the Grandes Chroniques de France*, is possibly the most conspicuous case, but Sigebert of Gembloux's *Chronicle* was also immensely popular.

Many of the chapters include hagiography. I use it sparingly, and only to the extent that it can complement information extracted from the historiographical corpus, as previously defined. As Felice Lifshitz has argued, for the task of telling apart historiography from hagiography "the categories themselves are hopelessly inadequate."[41] Authors such as Gregory of Tours, Ado of Vienne, and Sigebert of Gembloux used their own hagiographies as sources for their historiographical projects and *vice versa*. We might argue that there were certain differences in tone and emphasis between works considered hagiographical and works deemed historiographical, yet it is doubtful that the authors understood the two projects as essentially dissimilar. Recent work on Gregory of Tours's *Lives*

---

[40] For the construction of memory through the charter record, see the indispensable study by C. Bouchard, *Remembering Saints and Ancestors: Memory and Forgetting in France, 500–1200* (Philadelphia, PA: Pennsylvania University Press, 2014).
[41] Lifshitz, "Beyond Positivism," p. 102. See also A. Diem, "*Vita vel regula*: Multifunctional Hagiography in the Early Middle Ages," in *Hagiography and the History of Latin Christendom, 500–1500*, ed. S. Kahn Herrick (Leiden: Brill, 2019), pp. 123–142, esp. p. 126. See also M. van Uytfanghe, "Hagiographie: un 'genre' chrétien ou antique tardif," *Analecta Bollandiana* 111 (1993), pp. 135–188, with the problem of generic spillover discussed in pp. 146–147.

Introduction   17

and miracle collections has insisted on the close links these works had with his *Histories*, in both aim and methodology.[42] The same may be said of Ado of Vienne and Sigibert of Gembloux, both of whom appear in this book as chroniclers *and* hagiographers.

Interestingly, Ado of Vienne and Sigebert of Gembloux penned hagiographies about protagonists who lived in the Merovingian period. For Ado, these were Theudarius and Desiderius, an abbot and a bishop from sixth-century Vienne; for Sigebert, it was an actual Merovingian king, Sigibert III. Theudarius was a local celebrity, but his life did not intersect with events unfolding on the greater historical stage. The hagiographical portrayals of Desiderius of Vienne and Sigibert III were worlds apart from the tranquil scenes of the *Vita Theudarii*. If anything, the two *Lives* would have been incomprehensible without an excursus on broader regnal and political dynamics. So, the hagiographical corpus enables us to determine by comparison which details available to the author were deemed worthy of inclusion in the chronicles, and which were not (and *vice versa*). Even more importantly, it contains clues about periodization models that can supplement the analysis of the historiographical evidence, reflecting how the author thought about these questions at different stages in his life. All of this, I believe, can be achieved without dwelling overmuch on generic distinctions.

Finally, a word on the chronological scope of this book. Gregory of Tours's *Histories* mark the beginning of a narrative tradition covering the Merovingian era, and in this sense his usage as a *terminus post quem* is expected. The decision to choose Paolo Emilio's *De rebus gestis* and Yosef Ha-Kohen's *Divrei Hayamim* as the book's *terminus ante quem* less so. As the only post-medieval authors considered herein, Emilio and Ha-Kohen play a unique role in my inquiry into Merovingian representation. I use the two to bracket from both ends the Merovingian period—from Clovis, the conqueror of Gaul and *paterfamilias* of the dynasty in my discussion of Emilio to its final members in Ha-Kohen. One might say that Emilio was much less impressed by Carolingian and medieval models of thinking about the Merovingian period than was Ha-Kohen a generation or so later, and this has to do with the different nature of the sources they were using and the different aims of their histories. The two are interesting precisely because they were dealing with questions of source criticism at a historical period in which new narrative directions and methods of engagement with the source record were emerging. That they ended up

---

[42] T. Rotman, *Hagiography, Historiography, and Identity in Sixth-Century Gaul: Uncovering the Miracle Collections of Gregory of Tours* (Amsterdam: Amsterdam University Press, 2022).

18   Introduction

with such dissimilar results is surely revealing. While scholarship on Ha-Kohen has demonstrated his indebtedness to humanist methodology, his reliance on the *Grandes Chroniques* informed his views about periodization in ways that were much more in line with conventional medieval historiography. Emilio, as we shall see, took a different route. Their prose, then, is an example of the ways in which historiographical traditions about the rise and fall of the first Frankish dynasty were received during this critical stage in the development of historical thought, all the while serving a moralistic end for their contemporary readers.

This book ends about a century before the monumental efforts undertaken by the Bollandists and the Maurists in the seventeenth and eighteenth centuries to set church history in order. The Bollandists and Maurists were scholarly associations of monks in Belgium and France dedicated to the study and systematization of historical, primarily ecclesiastical, knowledge extracted from the many thousands of manuscripts they examined. From the early seventeenth century, the Jesuit Bollandists began to compile, edit, and harmonize the scattered and often contradictory information on the various saints venerated by the Church. Independent investigations conducted by Rosweyde (d. 1629), and later systematized under Bolland (d. 1665) and Henschen (d. 1681) into what became the *Acta Sanctorum*, originated with manuscripts procured initially from Belgian church libraries.[43] The Bollandists worked with saints, the record of whose cult emerged from ecclesiastical institutions located in what were once core regions of the Merovingian kingdom, a connection worth bearing in mind.[44] Ultimately, however, the Bollandists were dedicated to the *study* of saints' *Lives*—they suggestively referred to themselves as hagiographers[45]—, which is different from what the compositions examined in this book set out to do. That said, this book often uses hagiography and martyrological calendars to understand historiography, something that would have been impossible if not for the foundational work undertaken by such enterprises as the *Acta Sanctorum*.

Work done by the Bollandists influenced the Benedictine Maurists. In his six-book *De re diplomatica* (1681, later expanded), the great scholar

[43] See Hypolyte Delahaye's now century-old yet indispensable *L'Oeuvre des Bollandistes 1615 à 1915* (Brussels: Bureaux de la Société des Bollandistes, 1920), translated two years later by Princeton University Press.
[44] Although their later inquiries took Papenbroeck and others much farther afield, to the Vatican and elsewhere. See E. Dubois, "The Benedictine Congregation of Maurists in Seventeenth-Century France and Their Scholarly Activities," *Seventeenth-Century French Studies* 14, 1 (1992), pp. 219–233.
[45] See the helpful discussion in the introduction to J. Kitchen, *Saints' Lives and the Rhetoric of Gender: Male and Female in Merovingian Hagiography* (Oxford and New York: Oxford University Press, 1998).

Introduction 19

and engine of Maurist erudition Jean Mabillon (d. 1707) was reacting to the methods proposed by the Bollandist Papenbroeck six years earlier.[46] Unlike their Bollandist predecessors, the Maurists' literary project was meant to include, alongside an ambitious plan to produce exegetical, conciliar, and patristic editions, also studies of a secular nature, including history. The *Histoire littéraire de la France*, which they began publishing in 1733, is a great encyclopedic endeavor containing numerous entries on various historical—mostly ecclesiastical but some political and scholarly— personages throughout the centuries.[47]

Royal histories composed at the time of the Bollandists already signal the beginnings of a departure from humanist methodologies, anticipating the kind of critical scrutiny and interest in social and cultural institutions one finds fully developed in Enlightenment historiography. Seventeenth-century histories, even ones with a pronounced royalist bent, began to shift their interest from the deeds of kings to the evolution of the nation, its traditions, and institutions.[48] This is especially apparent in the works of court-appointed and pensioned "royal historiographers," as well as those of men of letters working in the court's orbit and hoping to curry its favor, all of whom expressed an interest in dynastic history.[49]

François Eudes de Mézeray's (d. 1683) three-volume opus, *Histoire de France depuis Faramond jusqu'à maintenant*, published between 1643 and 1651, was a detailed account of the military and political deeds of France's kings. An enterprise of unprecedented lavishness, it was intended to arouse public interest and secure institutional support with its reproductions of portraits and coins issued by each monarch. At least the latter objective was accomplished no later than 1645, when the second volume, dedicated to the Chancellor of France Pierre Séguier (d. 1672), identified its author as *historiographe de France*, a title that came with a pension and living accommodations.[50] Initially, Mézeray consciously adhered to a style developed by humanist court historians such as Paolo Emilio.[51] Yet, in his 1668 *Abrégé chronologique de l'histoire de France*, and increasingly in the

---

[46] In particular, to remarks made in D. Papenbroeck, *Propylaeum antiquarum circa veri discrimen in vetustis membranis* (Antwerp, 1675).
[47] On the composition and its history, see B. Neveu, "*Histoire littéraire de la France* et l'érudition bénédictine au siècle des Lumières," *Journal des savants* 2 (1979), pp. 73–113.
[48] See P.K. Leffler, "From Humanist to Enlightenment Historiography: A Case Study of François Eudes de Mézeray," *French Historical Studies* 10, 3 (1978), pp. 416–438; P. K. Leffler, "French Historians and the Challenge to Louis XIV's Absolutism," *French Historical Studies* 14, 1 (1985), pp. 1–22.
[49] The history of whose position is discussed in Ranum, *Artisans of Glory*, pp. 58–70.
[50] Ibid., pp. 208–209.
[51] T. Maissen, *Von der Legende zum Modell: Das Interesse an Frankreichs Vergangenheit während der italienischen Renaissance* (Basle and Frankfurt-am-Main: Helbing und Lichtenhahn, 1994), pp. 209–210.

1685 reissue of the first volume of the *Histoire de France*, his disillusionment with the court and the humanistic style used to praise it were becoming evident. The fact that his pension was reduced and, in 1673, apparently cut off altogether, goes some way in explaining this new approach, now unencumbered by the expectations that came with royal patronage. As always, the Merovingians were drawn into the fray, marshalled to prop up Mézeray's criticism of Louis XIV's Dutch war in the 1682 *Histoire de France avant Clovis*, which undermined the popular notion of the Franks as the liberators of the Gauls from the Roman yoke.[52]

The Maurist *Histoire littéraire de la France* brings us to the days of the early writers of French Enlightenment, discussed so thoughtfully in Ian Wood's *The Modern Origins of the Early Middle Ages*, who were already at work theorizing about the underlying causes of the Fall of Rome.[53] Engagement in the seventeenth and eighteenth centuries with late-antique and medieval historiography is, however, entirely beyond the scope of the present book. Emilio's and Ha-Kohen's *oeuvres* are its terminus because they constitute a reaction to late medieval traditions while still essentially dependent on royal history as their narrative backbone. Writing in a world only now becoming cognizant of the questionable historicity of many of these traditions, they are a good place to end.[54]

* * *

This book is divided into three parts, named after the beasts that appeared to Childeric on his trips to the palace window. Each of the visions reflects a distinct phase of Merovingian history—*ascent* (from the origins of the Franks to the death of Clovis), *stasis/conflict* (from Clovis's direct heirs to the death of Dagobert I), and *decline* (from the reign of Clovis II to the deposition and tonsure of Childeric III). By arranging the book this way, I assume that enough authors working on this history employed a periodization model along these lines. While this is certainly not universally true, compositions that engage seriously with this question usually came up with a similar division.

The roots for this division are, as is always true about periodization, to be found more in the literary tradition than in the actual historical events. Let us consider, in this regard, Clovis II. Clovis's infamy stemmed from

[52] Ranum, *Artisans of Glory*, p. 221.
[53] I. Wood, *The Modern Origins of the Early Middle Ages* (Oxford: Oxford University Press, 2013), esp. pp. 20–36.
[54] See the comments about the *Grandes Chroniques* and its paradigm-changing critique in Etienne Pasquier's 1599 *Recherches de la France* in P. Nora, "Between Memory and History: *Les Lieux de Mémoire*," *Representations* 26 (1989), pp. 7–24, at p. 21.

his desecration of the relics of St. Denis, not from his performance as a king.[55] In fact, he managed to enact a sweeping monastic reform and to intervene successfully in Austrasia, ending the questionable reign of Grimoald and Childebert "the Adopted." Clovis's designs on inheritance were also successful overall in sidelining his brother's branch of the Merovingian family, so one might say that he was a capable king. But his notorious trespass against Denis was not forgotten by chroniclers from Saint-Denis. It was portrayed as a gross abandonment of the ideals that guided his father, Dagobert I, in his relationship with the monastery. Given the outsized influence of Dionysian works on the historiographical tradition, Clovis invariably became a failed king, a *rex inutilis*, even in works that originated outside Saint-Denis. Perhaps the best-known example is the *Fredegar Continuations*, which chose Dagobert's death and Clovis's unremarkable tenure as their point of departure.[56] Clovis's importance becomes apparent when we realize that his failure was perceived as the opening scene in the Merovingians' last act.

The chapters in this book proceed along the storyline of Merovingian history, from its prehistory in Troy, through the highpoints that were the reigns of Clovis I and Dagobert I and through the lows that invariably followed. Within each chapter, the discussion will move from the earlier to the later evidence, although in each, a different set of works that deals with a different historical period is examined. I use the *Grandes Chroniques* to talk about Merovingian history before Clovis, although they had much to say about later events as well. I examine Sigibert of Gembloux's treatment of the late Merovingians, though he too wrote about the earlier ones. Moreover, while a particular composition's agenda is often alluded to in the Merovingian section, the author may have divulged his intentions elsewhere. To the greatest extent possible, I attempted to contextualize the discussion by referencing stories from non-Merovingian chapters.

Part I of the book will cover Merovingian history from its earliest origins to the end of Clovis I's reign. It will discuss the role played by ecclesiastical historiographers such as Gregory of Tours in determining Clovis's baptism as a turning point. Part I will also outline the crystallization, as a distinct "unit" of storytelling, of the first thematic block of Merovingian history, bounded, in later compositions, by the death of Clovis.

Chapter 1 is dedicated to the earliest phase in Merovingian history and to the origin stories and mythologies that depicted the birth of the Franks and their leading family. Gregory of Tours, as our foremost source of

[55] See especially *LHF*, ch. 44, pp. 316–317.
[56] *Fredegar*, Cont. 1, p. 168; Reimitz, *History*, p. 295, also for the influences of the *LHF* on the *Continuationes*.

information about the period, declined to offer a coherent origin story for the Franks or for the institution of Frankish kingship. As a historian of the Christian community of Gaul, Gregory was certainly aware of the Franks' impact on the world he inhabited. He was nevertheless reluctant to discuss them in any detail, privileging other axes of identity, such as religion, class, and civic status, over ethnicity.[57] While he chose to downplay the importance of Frankish identity, his treatment of this period in Gaul's history—namely, the arrival and establishment of the Franks and their kings—betrays an understanding of the existence of distinct phases of Frankish history.

The Trojan origin myth, which made its first appearance in the *Chronicle of Fredegar*, will also be discussed. This myth was accompanied by another, equally intriguing, fable about the Quinotaur, a mysterious sea-monster possibly responsible for fathering Merovech, who thereafter gave his name to the dynasty. This creature was not mentioned by the *LHF*, nor by any of the numerous later compositions that wrote about the origins of the Franks. I will discuss the Trojan myth in *Fredegar* and the *LHF*, as well as the possible reasons for its inclusion and for the rejection of competing origin myths. The Trojan story makes a brief appearance in Paul the Deacon's *Gesta episcoporum Mettensium*. Paul's work, which I also examine, offered a streamlined and idealized ancestry for Charlemagne, as well as a curious reworking of late Merovingian history. Perhaps unexpectedly, the Trojan origin story, which was acknowledged by Paul, was not subordinated to the Carolingian stemma he formulated. Finally, the discussion will turn to the highly developed articulation of the Trojan story found in the thirteenth-century *Roman des rois*. I will then turn to the portrayal of Childeric, and the various interpolations made by the *Fredegar* chronicler to the narrative presented by Gregory. The chapter will conclude with a discussion of Childeric's character, which Primat used to explore the Capetians' relations with their aristocracy.

Chapter 2 will focus on the depiction of Clovis I, the first Christian king of the Franks. The inflation of the Clovis myth in the medieval chronicle tradition has been treated exhaustively, primarily in French historiography, which is why this chapter proceeds along an alternate route.[58] Instead of interrogating the evolution of Clovis from *Fredegar* and the *LHF* to high and late medieval works of history, it will compare the story found in Gregory of Tours with that found in the sixteenth-century

[57] See G. Halsall, "Transformations of Romanness: The Northern Gallic Case," in *Transformations of Romanness: Early Medieval Regions and Identities*, ed. W. Pohl et al. (Berlin: De Gruyter, 2019), pp. 41–58.

[58] See the various chapters in M. Rouche, ed., *Clovis, histoire & mémoire: la baptême de Clovis, son écho à travers l'histoire*, 2 vols. (Paris: Presses de l'Université de Paris-Sorbonne, 1997).

Introduction 23

De rebus gestis Francorum [hereafter, *DRG*] by Paolo Emilio. The reason for this choice is that Emilio largely bypassed the intermediate sources, relying mainly on Gregory for this section of his opus. The *DRG* is thus only once removed from the *Histories*, although the two works diverge with respect to the subject of character-building and stylistic approach. Moreover, Emilio's distance from Carolingian historiography makes his work valuable for ascertaining to what extent eighth- and ninth-century periodization models, particularly those that confront themes of ascent and decline, endured into early modernity.

Part II of the book is concerned with the "middle Merovingians," from Clovis's heirs to the death of Dagobert I (d. 638). Current scholarship sees this as a vibrant and productive period, on every level of social and cultural life. Its narrative correlate, however, is another matter entirely. There, one finds violent conflict and moral atrophy, a point that was particularly emphasized by Carolingian authors, for whom the early onset of Merovingian *fainéance* was a narrative boon.

In Chapter 3, two universal chronicles will be presented—Frechulf of Lisieux's *Histories* and Ado of Vienne's *Chronicle*. Both men composed ambitious works in which Frankish history played only an ancillary role. The Franks make a fleeting appearance in the final chapters of Frechulf's *Histories*, which cut off unexpectedly in the seventh century. The motivations for this choice are not entirely clear, and yet they seem to have more to do with Frechulf's overarching structure of Christian history than with any assessment of the Merovingians. It is nevertheless possible to demonstrate that Frechulf was reticent about the Franks, to whom he devoted less space than to other early medieval *gentes*. This is surprising, considering Frechulf chose to end his *Histories* with the displacement of Romans and Goths by Franks and Lombards, signifying that they were important elements of his authorial program. Ado of Vienne's *Chronicle* took a different approach, highlighting the violent and discordant aspects of Merovingian history in the period 511–638. Ado thus presented a pessimistic appraisal of the entirety of the dynasty's tenure, not only its so-called *rois fainéants*.

Of all the Merovingian kings who succeeded Clovis, none has received more accolades than Dagobert I, who is the hero of Chapter 4. For a long time, Dagobert was considered to have been the last effective Merovingian. He was undoubtedly a successful king, although not so successful as to mar everything that came after him. The legend of Dagobert took time to mature, a process we can trace with the help of a small group of compositions. The source closest to Dagobert's day that attempted to narrativize his life was the *Chronicle of Fredegar*. *Fredegar*'s portrayal is favorable up to a point, beyond which the chronicler singled out the king for special reproof. The *LHF* did not share *Fredegar*'s acrimony, providing an image of Dagobert as a strict and honest judge, a fearsome warrior, and a magnanimous patron of the Church. The idealization of Dagobert reached new heights with the ninth-century *Gesta Dagoberti I regis Francorum*, which accentuated the king's monastic patronage, particularly of the monastery of Saint-Denis, where the composition was penned. In the early tenth century, Regino of Prüm used the *Gesta Dagoberti* as the sole source for narrating the life of King Dagobert in his *Chronicle*. As always, Regino remolded the character he extracted from the *Gesta Dagoberti* to serve a different set of aims.

Part III will explore the final episode of Merovingian history, the decline and displacement of the dynasty. The discussion will be limited to one chapter, spanning the death of Dagobert I to the deposition of the final Merovingian king in 751. It will consider the ways in which themes of decline were conceptualized and how they were transmitted. Views developed in the Carolingian period, in Saint-Denis and elsewhere, persevered relatively intact in much later compositions. The two sources discussed in Chapter 5, the twelfth-century *Chronica* of Sigebert of Gembloux and the sixteenth-century *Sefer Divrei Hayamim leMalkei Tzarfat uVeit Otoman Hatugar* [*The Chronicle of the Kings of France and the Turkish House of Ottoman*] by Yosef Ha-Kohen provide some evidence for this. Both were composed at considerable remove from the Carolingian period, yet they bear the traces of its historiography's far-reaching influence. This is especially noticeable in their periodization of the Merovingian era. The two authors saw the decline of the Merovingian line as a process precipitated by the disastrous reign of Clovis II (d. 657), and this shaped their view of his successors.

* * *

Although the narrative solutions discussed in this book are diverse, we are dealing with a concrete historical period that had a beginning, a middle, and an end. Any retelling of Merovingian history was constrained by this fact, and it is not my intention to question the historicity of Merovingian ascent and decline. Moreover, since historiographical narratives took a processual approach to their topic, it is only natural that they attempt to link the various stages of Merovingian history through causal rationale. Actions mattered in the present and the future, especially when kings and queens were involved.

For this reason, it is not impossible to imagine that an incompetent king living at the wrong time could destroy the legitimacy of an entire dynasty. Gazing across the three centuries of Merovingian history, however, no clear culprits emerge. There is no shortage of authors who wrote contemptuously about particular kings. Gregory fumed at Chilperic I (d. 584), whose branch of the family ended up as the clear winner in the dynastic struggles of the early seventh century. *Fredegar* was highly critical of Dagobert's Neustrian career, yet none would contest its success. The depiction of Clovis II in the *LHF* is another obvious example. In short, the moralizing protestations of historians and chroniclers cannot confirm deeper trends, such as the decline of the Merovingians, or even of blunders in their exercise of power.

In determining the contours of Merovingian ascent, internal fracture, and decline, it is authorial intent that set the tone. Events were harnessed to tell stories that exemplified the morals that a writer wished to impart. Even apparently non-negotiable events such as Clovis's baptism or Childeric III's deposition could be reframed or even ignored in the service of the author's agenda. In 751, Merovingian history was not a matter of hard fact. Supple still, it could be reimagined, reshuffled, and recast to meet the needs of a host of historiographers to come.

Part I

Lions and Unicorns

1 Trojans, Sea-monsters, and Long-haired Kings: From Priam to Childeric

The appearance of the Franks on the historical stage and the emergence of Frankish kingship are inherently joined historiographical themes; it is never quite clear where one ends and the other begins. Teasing apart the genesis of a *gens* from the origins of its rulers was as captivating for chroniclers working in the sixth century as it was for those working in the sixteenth. Origin stories, and their attendant claims about both aspects of this issue of ethnic origins versus royal origins, stand at the heart of this chapter. It will chart the continuous process of adaptation of material that deals with the formative period of Frankish history, from its very origins to the end of Childeric I's rule, ca. 480. Origin stories are populated by heroes, and it is to these heroes that royal lineages often attempted to trace their ancestries. Still, these stories are significant not just for the legitimacy they lend to dynasties, but also for the broader claims they can make about communities at large. In fact, they can most usefully be read against what we know about the communities for which they were written.

Frankish and French historiographical works used origin stories to express an ever-changing set of narrative constraints. As the product of a particular historical context, each composition had its own vision of the community for which it was intended, whether political, religious, ethnic, or an intersection of the three. Origin stories would have been an opening gambit in the longer game of delineating the contours of a specific community. Since these stories tend to be situated at the very beginning of historiographical treatments, they not only set the tone for what follows, but also frame the discussion and define its terminology. The best among them express an entire ideology in a few short passages. A royal history might place its emphasis on succession, continuity, and heroism. A composition that considers the development of a religious community might prefer to see kings as defenders of the faith or, alternatively, as its enemies. One that focuses on the formation of a *gens* or a political class could adopt a utilitarian outlook on kings, appraising them as either beneficial or detrimental according to their ability to promote certain agendas. Yet, historiographical compositions tend to defy such neat categorization. Instead, they show a medley of perspectives, reflecting a composite and layered historical vision.[1]

Despite the many differences among the historiographical accounts of the Franks and their origins, the birth of Frankishness as a recognizable category of identity and the consolidation of political power around the royal family are present in all such texts. These elements present as an imperative of any narrative that purports to contain a comprehensive history of the Franks. Although chroniclers had different aims when writing about this topic, their narrative choices were bound by earlier traditions, oral as well as written.[2] Even the earliest compositions at our disposal claim to be speaking on the authority of no longer extant, older sources.[3] Certainly, all the later texts bear the marks of an intensive, purposeful quarrying of source material. More importantly, they were engaged in continuous dialog with the ideological programs developed by their predecessors.

The degree to which a chronicler was dependent on sources available to him or her is especially pertinent to the question of origin and authority, which was entwined with communal notions of legitimacy. To explain a community's origin and networks of authority, and especially to employ it in the service of a broader authorial agenda, was to define its role as a force in history. Chroniclers were thus naturally drawn to offering new interpretations of the events, and, indeed, each of the compositions included in the family of texts discussed here—and many that are not—present some version of an origin story.[4] This is why chronicles, even ones making revisionist historical claims, needed to negotiate an ideological terrain already populated by earlier compositions. The basic structure of Frankish history, origin stories included, emerged not from an abrupt rejection or wholesale adoption of previous historiographical compositions, but rather from a delicate process of interpolation and rearticulation. Chroniclers

---

[1] H. Reimitz, "Historiography and Identity in the Post-Roman West: An Introduction," in *Historiography and Identity II: Post-Roman Multiplicity and New Political Identities*, eds. G. Heydemann, H. Reimitz (Turnhout: Brepols, 2020), pp. 1–26, at pp. 2, 5–8.

[2] See H. Reimitz, "Genre and Identity in Merovingian Historiography," in *Historiography and Identity II: Post-Roman Multiplicity and New Political Identities*, eds. G. Heydemann and H. Reimitz (Turnhout: Brepols, 2020), pp. 161–211, at pp. 181, 196–197.

[3] Gregory of Tours's forays into the origin question are reliant on the accounts of previous historians, as are *Fredegar*'s. On this, see pp. 33–57. While the *LHF*'s origin story is mostly original, it was based not only on oral traditions, but also on circulating, throughout the Carolingian period and beyond, under the name of Gregory. See N.K. Yavuz, "From Caesar to Charlemagne: The Tradition of Trojan Origins," *The Medieval History Journal* 21, 2 (2018), pp. 251–290, at p. 258.

[4] On origins and their functions, see P. Bourdieu, "Rethinking the State: Genesis and Structure of the Bureaucratic Field," in *State/Culture: State Formation after the Cultural Turn*, ed. G. Steinmetz (Ithaca and London: Cornell University Press, 1999), pp. 53–75, at pp. 56–57.

broaching the topic built on and adjusted the material they extracted from their sources in ways that allowed them to forward new claims while still adhering to a narrative structure recognized by their prospective readership.

While the motivations and chronologies ascribed to characters and events could be adjusted to conform to new narrative models, the deeper foundations were not so easily unsettled, even when the underlying aims of a composition were quite different from those of its source.[5] Historiography is cumulative, in the sense that it is creatively constrained by what already exists. This is why the story of the Franks' earliest beginnings, and the emergence of their kings could not be invented anew with each composition. One especially recognizable component of this narrative is the Trojan storyline, which has been among the most extensively studied aspects of Frankish and French historiography. Trojan origins are an important feature of the chronicle tradition, but they are not the whole story. In fact, in most of the compositions that rehearse some version of the Frankish origin story, it is possible to identify three distinct thematic blocks: first, the escape from Troy and the emergence of the Franks as a recognizable group; then, the Franks' interaction with the Romans and their advance into territories previously occupied by the Western Empire; and finally, their settlement in Gaul and the rise of the Merovingian family. Each of these phases has its own cast of characters, most of whom make appearances in several chronicles, and each plays an indispensable role in the larger story. Taken together, this schema sets the Franks against a wider backdrop of other *gentes* and entities, about whose historical role the origin story's author often had much to say.

From the very start, the Frankish origin story exhibits tension between several narrative poles. One strand of the narrative is concerned with the birth of the Franks from the Trojan parent-group. It chronicles the wanderings of peoples, their subsequent divisions into *ethne*, and the constitutive acts by which they merited their ethnonyms. Another strand is preoccupied with the emergence of Frankish political power and its structures, manifestations, and governing principles. One of these governing principles was genealogical, and many of the chronicles I will mention attempt to provide a coherent ancestry for the contemporary ruling dynasty that stretches back to Troy. At least one composition, the thirteenth-century *Roman des rois*,

---

[5] For an excellent example of this process in the *Fredegar* chronicler's treatment of source material from Gregory of Tours' *Histories*, see G. Schwedler, "Lethe and 'Delete' – Discarding the Past in the Early Middle Ages: The Case of Fredegar," in *Collectors' Knowledge: What Is Kept, What Is Discarded / Aufbewahren oder wegwerfen: wie Sammler entscheiden*, eds. A.-S. Goeing, A.T. Grafton, and P. Michel (Leiden and Boston: Brill, 2013), pp. 71–96, at p. 74.

stakes much of its argument on the claim that the royal families of the Franks were linked to each other by kinship, and that the earliest of these families—the Merovingians—could trace its origins to the refugees of fallen Troy, thereby providing a Trojan ancestry for France's kings.[6]

It is this that makes the line separating the history of the Franks from that of their kings so difficult to draw. In the case of the *Roman des rois*, the constraints of patronage and its effects on authorial tone are perhaps better understood than they are for the *Chronicle of Fredegar* or the *Liber historiae Francorum*, the latter written before 727 in either Soissons or Saint-Denis. The *Chronicle of Fredegar* is also not as confined, thematically, to the topic of French kingship. Frankish origins only appear in the abridged version of the Eusebius-Jerome world chronicle found in Book II, and not as they do in the *Roman des rois* and the *LHF*, as an organic point of entry into the whole text. To complicate things further, the *Chronicle of Fredegar* also presented several, possibly conflicting, origin stories, making its position on the question all the more elusive.

Yet all three see the evolution of kingship as a natural outgrowth of ethnic creation and are especially interested in both aspects. Moreover, to these two perspectives one must surely add a third, which prioritizes religion as the most salient criterion for defining the community, focusing on the Church's role as a legitimizing agent for the Franks and their kings.[7] This is obviously a strand that becomes more prominent after Clovis, but that does not mean that the pagan Franks had no role to play in the overarching agenda of Gregory of Tours writing in the sixth century, Paul the Deacon writing in the eighth, or Primat writing in the thirteenth. As we shall see, the perspective of the chroniclers could shift depending on historical circumstance. By the end of the chronological timeframe defined by the present chapter, the pendulum will have rested squarely at the royal end of its arc, although throughout Frankish history, it could be found at different points along its continuum.

---

[6] On this, see, for instance, G.M. Spiegel, "The *Reditus Regni ad Stirpem Karoli Magni*: A New Look," *French Historical Studies* 7, 2 (1971), pp. 145–174; repr. in *The Past as Text: The Theory and Practice of Medieval Historiography* (Baltimore, MD: Johns Hopkins University Press, 1997), pp. 111–137; idem, "Genealogy: Form and Function in Medieval Historiography," *History and Theory* 22, 1 (1983), pp. 43–53.

[7] See Aimoin of Fleury's explanation in *Gesta Francorum*, proemium, *PL* 139, cols 637C–638C. J. Lake, "Rewriting Merovingian History in the Tenth Century: Aimoin of Fleury's *Gesta Francorum*," *Early Medieval Europe* 25 (2017), pp. 489–525, at pp. 501–502. For an instructive comparison with Romanness, see Y. Hen, "Compelling and Intense: The Christian Transformation of Romanness," in *Transformations of Romanness: Early Medieval Regions and Identities*, ed. W. Pohl et al. (Berlin and Boston: De Gruyter, 2018), pp. 59–69.

1.1 Gregory of Tours's *Histories* and the Unknowable Origins of the Franks

The tale of King Priam of Troy as the progenitor of the Franks is a common feature of the compositions I survey in this book. Yet Gregory of Tours's *Histories*, which was the first attempt to write a broad historical narrative culminating in Merovingian Gaul, did not mention Trojan origins at all.[8] The omission is perfectly understandable, given that Gregory did not set out to recount a Frankish *origo gentis* story.[9] He preferred to circumvent the question by presenting any historical inquiry into the matter as futile, given the paucity of available information on the emergence of Frankish kingship. We cannot say with certainty whether the elements of the Trojan story found in later chronicles were simply unknown to Gregory, or whether he purposefully chose to ignore them. The latter seems more probable.[10] Certainly Gregory's friend Venantius Fortunatus drew on this textual tradition when he alluded to the marriage of Aeneas and Lavinia in his poem celebrating the union of Sigibert and Brunhild.[11] Incidentally, Gregory's city of Tours was itself tied to Trojan traditions in the ninth-century *Historia Brittonum*, although this was not a tradition that would have been familiar to him, writing in the sixth.[12] As we shall see later in this chapter, however, Geoffrey of Monmouth's adaptation of the Brutus storyline from the

---

[8] Gregory does mention Troy in *Histories* IV.30, likening the men of the Auvergne caught in the Rhône's current to the Trojans in the Simois. See Reimitz, *History*, p. 86, possibly echoing Sidonius Apollinaris, *Epistulae*, ed. W.B. Anderson (Cambridge, MA and London: Harvard University Press, 1936), vii.7.2, ii, 324–326.

[9] Reimitz, "Genre and Identity in Merovingian Historiography," pp. 173–175.

[10] See Ammianus Marcellinus's mention of Trojans on the Rhine in *Res gestae*, ed. and trans. J.C. Rolfe, 3 vols. (Cambridge, MA: Harvard University Press, 1935–1939), 1, xv.9.4–5: "Drasidae memorant re vera fuisse populi partem indigenam, sed alios quoque ab insulis extimis confluxisse et tractibus transrhenanis, crebritate bellorum et adluvione fervidi maris sedibus suis expulsos. Aiunt quidam paucos post excidium Troiae fugitantes Graecos ubique dispersos loca haec occupasse tunc vacua." For a discussion of other Trojan traditions on which the Franks could have drawn, see J. Barlow, "Gregory of Tours and the Myth of the Trojan Origins of the Franks," *Frühmittelalterliche Studien*, 29 (1995), pp. 86–95.

[11] Venantius Fortunatus, *Carmina*, MGH AA 4,1, ed. F. Leo (Berlin: Weidmann, 1881), vi.1, pp. 124–29; Reimitz, "Genre and Identity in Merovingian Historiography," p. 169.

[12] *Historia Brittonum*, in J. Morris, ed. and trans., *British History and The Welsh Annals* (London: Philimore, 1980), ch. 10, p. 6: "Et expulsus est ab Italia, et arminilis fuit, et venit ad insulas maris Tirreni, et expulsus est a Graecis causa occisionis Turni, quem Aeneas occiderat, et pervenit ad Gallos usque, et ibi condidt civitatem Turonorum, quae vocatur Turnis"; T. Summerfield, "Filling the Gap: Brutus in the *Historia Brittonum*, Anglo-Saxon Chronicle MS F, and Geoffrey of Monmouth," *The Medieval Chronicle VII* (2011), pp. 85–102; L. Mathey-Maille, "Mythe troyen et histoire romaine: de Geoffroy de Monmouth au 'Brut' de Wace," in *Entre fiction et histoire: Troie et Rome au Moyen Âge*, eds. E. Baumgartner and L. Harf-Lancner (Paris: Presses de la Sorbonne Nouvelle, 1997), pp. 113–125.

Historia Brittonum did make its way into the *Roman des rois*, impacting its handling of the Trojan narrative.

Yet we should not take all of this to mean that by choosing to omit Troy from his account, Gregory was resisting an established narrative tradition. Helmut Reimitz has noted that there need not have been only one Trojan story in circulation when he wrote. In other words, it would have been possible for Gregory to offer a vision of his imagined community without resorting to the Trojan narrative, which in any event was probably not yet formalized as a literary convention when he was writing.[13] The differences between *Fredegar* and the *Liber historiae Francorum*, the two earliest compositions to attempt an articulation of the myth, suggest as much.

As an ecclesiastical historian of Gaul, the establishment of royal power there would have been a significant point of interest for Gregory. Nine books out of the *Histories*' ten cover Gaul under the Merovingians. Gregory interacted with Frankish kings and their regional and local proxies often, and even the ecclesiastical structure he so cherished was structured around centralized royal power. The king was an important force in authorizing the convocation of Church councils and in the appointment of bishops; Gregory himself owed his nomination to the See of Tours to the intervention of Sigibert I (d. 575).[14] Gregory therefore had an accommodating view of Merovingian power and, while he was certainly conscious of its vagaries and shortcomings, he never questioned the Merovingians' right to rule. In fact, much of his political ideology used the Merovingians as templates of good (and not-so-good) kingship.[15] The moral lessons that readers were to draw from the *Histories* were nested in a history of Gaul and the kings who ruled it.

Yet the Merovingians in the *Histories* only emerge as a later feature of the Frankish storyline, preceded by a section devoted to the Frankish invasions of the Roman province of Germania and the attack on Cologne in 388. The *Histories*' coverage of this period of Frankish history relied primarily on three historians—Sulpicius Alexander, Renatus Profuturus Frigeridus, and Orosius—all of whom yield little in the form of resolution. The bulk of

---

[13] See Reimitz, "The Early History of Frankish Origin Legends," pp. 163, 166.
[14] M. Heinzelmann, *Gregory of Tours: History and Society in the Sixth Century* (Cambridge: Cambridge University Press, 2001), pp. 38–41; M. Heinzelmann, "Gregory of Tours: The Elements of a Biography," in *A Companion to Gregory of Tours*, ed. A.C. Murray (Leiden and Boston: Brill, 2016), pp. 7–34, at pp. 24–26.
[15] Y. Fox, "Revisiting Gregory of Tours' Burgundian Narrative," in *Les royaumes de Bourgogne jusque 1032 à travers la culture et la religion*, eds. A. Wagner and N. Brocard, Culture et société médiévales 30 (Brepols: Turnhout, 2018), pp. 227–238; G. Halsall, "Nero and Herod? The Death of Chilperic and Gregory's Writings of History," in *The World of Gregory of Tours*, eds. K. Mitchell and I. Wood (Leiden and Cologne: Brill, 2002), pp. 337–50.

information came from Sulpicius Alexander, who tells that the Franks, led by three leaders, named Marcomer, Sunno, and Genobaud, collided with a Roman military contingent under the command of Nanninus and Quintinus that was dispatched from the provincial administrative center of Trier. A Roman victory over a small Frankish detachment ensued. Encouraged, the Romans mounted a punitive expedition across the Rhine but fell prey to an elaborate trap set by the Franks and were cut to pieces. Gregory quotes Profuturus's equally intricate story of imperial politics, and Orosius's terse account of Stilicho's victory over the Franks, but ultimately concludes that neither Sulpicius Alexander, nor any of the others, knew much about the emergence of Frankish kingship.[16] We might surmise from Gregory that Marcomer, Sunno, and Genobaud played a central role in the incursions into Roman territory during the late fourth century, and that at one point the Franks may have been led by a king whose name has not survived.[17]

Gregory used these earlier historians as sources for more than just the origin (non-)story. They were critical to his work on the early chapters of Book II, which he devoted to the persecutions endured by Catholic churches and their communities. In the prologue to Book II, Gregory announces his intent to record the deeds of the saints, through whom he proposes to show how these antithetical, yet complementary, forces of saintliness and persecution have ruled history since biblical times.[18] It is within this framework that he discusses the misfortunes that befell the religious community of Tours, the invasions of Gaul by various barbarians, and the persecutions that followed in their wake. The cruelties inflicted on Catholic Christians by the heretical Vandals and Goths provide a preamble to the arrival of the Huns from Pannonia and the destruction they wrought on Metz and Orléans. The Battle of the Catalaunian Plains shifts the discussion to the Roman general Aëtius (d. 454), and it is here that Renatus Profuturus Frigeridus is first introduced as a source. The advent of the Franks is recounted not long afterwards, supported by the same material.

---

[16] See Reimitz, "Genre and Identity in Merovingian Historiography," p. 163; Reimitz, *Frankish Identity*, pp. 54–55.
[17] On the fates of Sunno and Marcomer, see Claudian, *De consulatu Stilichonis libri IV*, in *Carmina*, ed. J.B. Hall, *Bibliotheca scriptorum Graecorum et Romanorum Teubneriana* (Leipzig: Teubner, 1985), 1, lines 239–252: "Ultro quin etiam devota mente tuentur victorique favent. quotiens sociare catervas oravit iungique tuis Alamannia signis! nec doluit contempta tamen, spretoque recessit auxilio laudata fides. provincia missos expellet citius fasces quam Francia reges, quos dederis. acie nec iam pulsare rebelles, sed vinclis punire licet; sub iudice nostro regia Romanus disquirit crimina carcer: Marcomeres Sunnoque docet; quorum alter Etruscum pertulit exilium; cum se promitteret alter exulis ultorem, iacuit mucrone suorum: res avidi concire novas odioque furentes pacis et ingenio scelerumque cupidine fratres."
[18] Gregory of Tours, *Histories*, II.prologue.

Readers of Gregory have observed that he did not regard the pre-Christian Franks as essentially different from other barbarians.[19] At least as far as the three Frankish *regales* were concerned, Gregory clearly did not mean for them to function in the plot as the direct forerunners of the Merovingian kings of his day. If anything, when the Franks make their first appearance in Gregory, they are depicted as being like the Huns. Tellingly, the two scourges that descend on the population of Gaul, the Huns and the Franks, had their origins in Pannonia. But of course, so did Martin of Tours, foremost among Gaul's myriad saints.[20] Assuming that neither mention is coincidental,[21] one wonders which of these prototypes— Attila or Martin—the advancing Franks were meant to evoke in the mind of the reader.[22] In the beginning, it is likely to have been the former, since Gregory reports that under Marcomer, Sunno, and Genobaud, the Franks proceeded to plunder Cologne and Trier just as the Huns had terrorized Metz and other Gallic cities under Attila only a few chapters earlier.[23] All of this must be understood in the moralistic context of Gaul's invasions which undergirds the beginning of Book II.

Yet there is much in the story of the Franks that speaks to their resemblance to Martin. Notably, this is where Gregory switches from his written sources to a different body of evidence, which seems to have been primarily oral.[24] Like the Franks, Martin was a pagan in Pannonia, but it was his life as a Christian in Gaul that mattered to Gregory. Martin's journey, measured in miles but also in terms of spiritual growth, was a process of astonishing personal evolution. The Franks ended up retracing the footsteps of Martin as he made his way from Pannonia to Gaul and from

---

[19] R. Gerberding, *The Rise of the Carolingians and the* Liber Historiae Francorum (Oxford: Clarendon Press, 1987), p. 13.

[20] Gregory of Tours, *Histories* I.36; X.31. See E. Zöllner, *Geschichte der Franken bis zur Mitte des sechsten Jahrhunderts* (Munich: Beck, 1970), p. 4; E. James, *The Franks* (Oxford and Cambridge, MA: Blackwell, 1988), p. 235.

[21] Gregory's account is the only one to posit a Pannonian component. On this, see A. Plassmann, *Origo gentis. Identitäts- und Legitimitätsstiftung in früh- und hochmittelalterlichen Herkunftserzählungen* (Berlin: Akad.-Verl, 2006), p. 126, n.55.

[22] On the possible connections intended by Gregory, see J.D. Niles, "Myths of the Eastern Origins of the Franks: Fictions or a Kind of Truth?," in *Origin Legends in Early Medieval Western Europe*, eds. L. Brady and P. Wadden (Leiden and Boston: Brill, 2022), pp. 385–404, at pp. 394–395.

[23] Huns attack Metz: *Histories* II.6; Franks raid Cologne, Trier: *Histories* II.9. Plassman, *Origo gentis*, p. 153. On some interesting uses of Attila and Clovis in Napoleonic-era historiography, see Wood, *The Modern Origins*, p. 81.

[24] Gregory of Tours, *Histories* II.9: "Tradunt enim multi, eosdem de Pannonia fuisse degressus, et primum quidem litora Rheni amnes incoluisse, dehinc, transacto Rheno, Thoringiam transmeasse, ibique iuxta pagus vel civitates regis crinitos super se creavisse de prima, et, ut ita dicam, nobiliore suorum familia." For the continued salience of orally transmitted information in Gregory's world, see Reimitz, "Genre and Identity in Merovingian Historiography," pp. 176–178.

paganism to Catholic Christianity, although they did not know it at the time: "At first the Frankish people did not understand this; they would understand later, as the Histories will narrate in what follows."[25]

From Pannonia, the Franks travelled to Thuringia, where they began to elect "long-haired kings" from their most noble families.[26] This comment seems to have been a nod to an established tradition, although, if anything, the disjointed series of details that follows Gregory's statement makes the story even more difficult to understand.

Gregory remarks, for instance, that the son of Ricimer, whom he identified as Theudemer, was executed alongside his mother and that Clodio came to power around Duisburg at about the same time. Theudemer is otherwise unknown, although, if his father can be identified as the Richomeres who was appointed consul of 384 and held a long line of senior military commands, the context of the family's activity becomes slightly clearer. Richomeres's ranks are mentioned in the consular annals;[27] his battles against the Goths and his imperial appointments are mentioned by Ammianus.[28] While this is useful information, it does not support his identification as the figure from the *Histories*. In any event, Ricimer, his wife Ascyla, and their son Theudemer appear out of nowhere and disappear just as quickly. This obscure interjection suggests that Gregory relied on a particular unmentioned source in which these details were included, but it contributes very little to our understanding of early Frankish leaders and the establishment of royal power.

Notably, the *Histories* make no attempt to link Theudemer to Clodio by succession or kinship. The two are presented as ruling separate regions, and Clodio's ancestry and the circumstances of his coming to power are not disclosed. The relationship of Clodio to Merovech, the next named king of the Franks, is similarly ambiguous. Though Gregory reports that some claim that the two were of the same family, he is not willing to commit on this point.[29] Gregory's reticence to contextualize the earliest Frankish kings could have stemmed from faulty sources, but he clearly preferred to leave the matter unresolved. Recounting ancient royal ancestries would have shifted focus away from the Franks' paganism and ferocity, as well as from the parallels he was attempting to draw with

---

[25] Ibid. II.10: "Haec autem generatio Francorum non intellexit primum; intellexerunt autem postea, sicut sequens historia narrat."
[26] Ibid. II.9.
[27] Flavius Richomeres, in J.R. Martindale, *The Prosopography of the Later Roman Empire*, 4 vols. (Cambridge: Cambridge University Press, 1992), 1, pp. 765–766 [hereafter, *PLRE*]. Ricomer, father of Theudemer, see Richimer 1, *PLRE* 2, p. 942.
[28] Ammianus Marcellinus, *Res gestae*, XXXI.7.5–16, 8.2, 12.4, 12.14–17, 13.9.
[29] Gregory of Tours, *Histories* II.9: "De huius stirpe quidam Merovechum regem fuisse adserunt, cuius fuit filius Childericus."

Martin. These, more than any royal origin story, were the real point of this section of the narrative. Like Clodio, Merovech is essentially a nonentity in the *Histories*, whose sole purpose is to move the plot along to the rule of Childeric.

It is quite likely that Gregory saw the rule of Childeric as belonging to another thematic section. The story of Childeric appears after a lengthy segue, which begins with a drawn-out admonition of the Franks' cartoonish paganism in chapter 10 and is followed by the installation of Aegidius (d. 464/5) as *magister militum (per Gallias)*. Aegidius, who ruled a Roman enclave centered on the city of Soissons after the assassination of Majorian (d. 461), becomes a central figure for understanding Childeric's (and Clovis's) career.[30] He seems to have commanded Roman as well as Frankish troops, and was the one who deposed Childeric, according to the *Histories* on account of his womanizing. While in Gregory's account Childeric was eventually restored after the Franks tired of Aegidius, this had more to do with the machinations of his ally than with any repentance on his part. Historically, Aegidius's position *vis-à-vis* the Franks was probably more complicated, but in the *Histories* he, and later his son Syagrius, were there primarily to illuminate certain aspects in the careers of the earliest Merovingians.[31] To add insult to injury, Childeric took as his wife Basina, once the wife of the Thuringian king Bissinus, with whom Childeric found shelter during his eight-year-long exile. Hardly an impressive portrait.[32]

Much has been said about the *Histories*' intentional juxtaposition of Clovis and Constantine, which likened the newly christened Frankish king to the first Christian emperor of Rome.[33] Gregory's vigorous claim

---

[30] See W. Liebeschuetz, "Warlords and Landlords," in *A Companion to the Roman Army*, ed. P. Erdkamp (Malden, MA, and Oxford: Blackwell, 2007), pp. 479–494, at p. 487; R. W. Mathisen, *Roman Aristocrats in Barbarian Gaul: Strategies for Survival in an Age of Transition* (Austin, TX: University of Texas Press, 1993), pp. 83–85, 129.

[31] On Childeric's Hunnic entanglements and Roman realignment following the death of Attila, see H.J. Kim, *The Huns, Rome and the Birth of Europe* (Cambridge: Cambridge University Press, 2013), pp. 80–83 and the corresponding notes in pp. 220–224 for a comprehensive bibliography. See also S. Lebecq, "The Two Faces of King Childeric: History, Archeology, Historiography," in *From Roman Provinces to Medieval Kingdoms*, ed. T.F.X. Noble (London and New York: Routledge, 2006), pp. 272–288.

[32] See comments in Niles, "Myths of the Eastern Origins of the Franks," pp. 389–393.

[33] Gregory of Tours, *Histories*, II.31: "Procedit novos Constantinus ad lavacrum, deleturus leprae veteris morbum sordentesque maculas gestas antiquitus recenti lattice deleturus." See E. Ewig, "Der Bild Constantins des Grossen in den ersten Jahrhunderten des abendländischen Mittelalters," *Historisches Jahrbuch* 75 (1956), pp. 1–46, at pp. 28–29. Ian Wood ascribes it to a Reims tradition. See I. Wood, "Gregory of Tours and Clovis," *Revue belge de philologie et d'histoire* 63, 2 (1985), pp. 249–272, at p. 261; Y. Hen, "Clovis, Gregory of Tours, and Pro-Merovingian Propaganda," *Revue belge de philologie et d'histoire*, 71, 2 (1993), pp. 271–276, at pp. 271–272 agrees. See also K. Sessa, "Constantine and Silvester in the Actus Silvestri," in *The Life and Legacy of Constantine: Traditions*

for Clovis as a *novus Constantinus* leaves one wondering whether he also meant for Childeric to function as a Frankish mirror-image of Constantine's predecessor and polar opposite, Diocletian. The *Histories* do not have very much to say about Diocletian.[34] The emperor is charged with carrying out extensive persecutions, resulting in thousands of fatalities. He is also blamed for the martyrdom of Bishop Quirinus of Siscia. This snippet was almost certainly lifted from the *Chronicle of Jerome*, where it appears in the fifth year of the persecution, and three years after Diocletian had "laid down the purple" (i.e., 308).[35] If Gregory had access to the late fourth-century *Passio sancti Quirini*, he would have learned that the riverine martyrdom scene, which is mentioned in Jerome, took place in Sabaria (Szombathely, modern-day Hungary).[36] Quite the coincidence, given that in the very next chapter, Gregory relates that Martin was born in Sabaria during the reign of Constantine. Unlike the *Chronicle of Jerome*, the *Passio* cast Diocletian as the persecutor instead of Licinius, which coincides with Gregory's chronology, although this could simply be a matter of better storytelling. Diocletian was the archvillain of numerous works, Eusebius-Jerome included, and would have made for a more dramatically pleasing persecutor.[37] Gregory discusses the structure of the Eusebius-Jerome chronicle in chapter 36, so we must assume that this was his main

---

Through the Ages, ed. M.S. Bjornlie (London and New York: Routledge, 2017), pp. 77–91, and for the parallel with Clovis, M.S. Bjornlie, "Constantine in the Sixth Century: From Constantinople to Tours," in *The Life and Legacy of Constantine: Traditions Through the Ages*, ed. M.S. Bjornlie (London and New York: Routledge, 2017), pp. 92–114, at pp. 106–107. For additional discussion about this and other antithetical couplets, see A. Cain, "Miracles, Martyrs, and Arians: Gregory of Tours' Sources for His Account of the Vandal Kingdom," *Vigiliae Christianae* 59, 4 (2005), pp. 412–437, at pp. 421–422; W. Goffart, *The Narrators of Barbarian History (A.D. 550–800): Jordanes, Gregory of Tours, Bede, and Paul the Deacon* (Princeton, NJ: Princeton University Press, 1988), pp. 173–174.

[34] Nor, really, about the historical Constantine. See Wood, "Gregory of Tours and Clovis," p. 251. For the account of Diocletian, see Gregory of Tours, *Histories* I.35. For Gregory's coverage of emperors preceding Constantine, see Reimitz, "Genre and Identity in Merovingian History," pp. 168–169.

[35] Eusebius-Jerome, *Chronicon*, eds. R. Helm and T. Mommsen, *Eusebius Werke*, vol. VII.1: *Die Chronik des Hieronymus* (Leipzig: Teubner, 1913), p. 229 a.308, 2e: "Quirinus episcopus Sisciamus gloriose pro Christo interficitur: nam, manuali mola ad collum ligata, e ponte praecipitatus in flumen, diutissime supernatavit et cum spectantibus collocutus, ne sui terrerentur exemplo, vix orans ut mergeretur, obtinuit." Gregory would have accessed Eusebius primarily through Rufinus's translation and continuation, although the Quirinus martyrdom originated with Jerome. See Krusch's introduction to Gregory of Tours, *Histories*, pp. xix–xx; M. Heinzelmann, "The Works of Gregory of Tours and Patristic Tradition," in *A Companion to Gregory of Tours*, ed. A.C. Murray (Leiden and Boston: Brill, 2016), pp. 281–336, at pp. 282–286.

[36] *Passio Quirini*, ed. and trans. P. Chiesa, in *Le passioni dei martiri aquileiesi e istriani*, vol. 2, ed. E. Colombi (Rome: Istituto storico Italiano per il medio evo, 2013), pp. 499–583.

[37] See J.K. Zangenberg, "*Scelerum inventor et malorum machinator*: Diocletian and the Tetrarchy in Lactantius, *De mortibus persecutorum*," in *Imagining Emperors in the Later*

source, which, other than wrongly identifying the emperor, resembles his account in every detail.[38] But the temptation to read intent into Gregory's pairing of Diocletian with the martyrdom of a bishop and Constantine, in the subsequent chapter, with such meaningful events as the discovery of the True Cross and the birth of "Gaul's new light," seems almost too good to pass up.[39] Given the consciously antithetical treatment of Diocletian and Constantine, and Clovis's comparison with the latter, we should consider how Diocletian informed Gregory's handling of Childeric. In any event, as Book II structurally mimics Eusebius-Jerome's model of prolonged persecution capped by triumphant imperial conversion, this comparison seems justified.

All of this surely has bearing on Gregory's understanding of Childeric's narrative role as an exemplum of corrupt rule and moral bankruptcy.[40] As a character, Childeric is not well developed. We hear of his philandering, exile, and return in chapter 12, but the five subsequent chapters have to do with cities that held special importance for Gregory—Clermont, Autun, Tours, and their bishops. Childeric next appears as an actor in the regional reshuffling that followed the death of Aegidius. This chapter presents substantial difficulties, no matter how one chooses to explain its events.[41] The *Histories* wrap up this episode and return to the episcopal history of the Auvergne, focusing on the episcopacy of Sidonius. Coverage of Childeric is concluded in chapter 27 with the report of his death and succession by Clovis. His anticlimactic portrayal was perhaps meant to serve as an inverted version of Clovis's, but in this he was not

---

Roman Empire, eds. D.P.W. Burgersdijk and A.J. Ross, Cultural Interactions in the Mediterranean, vol. 1 (Leiden: Brill, 2018), pp. 39–62; C.S. Mackay, "Lactantius and the Succession to Diocletian," *Classical Philology* 94, 2 (1999), pp. 198–209; T. Africa, "Worms and the Death of Kings: A Cautionary Note on Disease and History," *Classical Antiquity* 1, 1 (1982), pp. 1–17; For the abiding legacy of Diocletian as the persecutor *par excellence*, see E.A. Castelli, *Martyrdom and Memory: Early Christian Culture Making* (New York: Columbia University Press, 2004), pp. 194–195; A. Papaconstantinou, "Historiography, Hagiography, and the Making of the Coptic 'Church of the Martyrs' in Early Islamic Egypt," *Dumbarton Oaks Papers* 60 (2006), pp. 65–86.

[38] Gregory of Tours, *Histories* I.36: "Usque hoc tempus historiographus in chronicis scribit Eusebius. A vicessimo primo enim eius imperii anno Hieronimus praesbiter addidit [...]."

[39] For this phrasing, Gregory of Tours, *Histories* 1.39: "Tunc iam et lumen nostrum exoritur, novisque lampadum radiis Gallia perlustratur [...]."

[40] However, see the narrative pairing of Childeric with Avitus in G. Halsall, "Childeric's Grave, Clovis' Succession, and the Origins of the Merovingian Kingdom," in *Cemeteries and Society in Merovingian Gaul: Selected Studies in History and Archaeology, 1992–2009* (Leiden: Brill, 2010), pp. 169–187, at p. 172.

[41] For a discussion of Childeric's takeover of Angers and its circumstances, see D. Frye, "Aegidius, Childeric, Odovacer and Paul," *Nottingham Medieval Studies* 36 (1992), pp. 1–14; P. MacGeorge, *Late Roman Warlords* (Oxford: Oxford University Press, 2002), pp. 95–100ff.

alone. Gregory had many Diocletians that could play the heel to his "new Constantine." Since his Clovis was a model of kingly conduct, he could be compared favorably not only to his ancestors,[42] but also to his contemporaries, most commonly to Gundobad, king of the Burgundians.[43]

Helmut Reimitz has termed Gregory's overall approach to the question of the Franks' origins an anti-*origo*, for its refusal to engage with any coherent origin story. This was, of course, intentional, since neither the Franks nor their Merovingian kings were the heroes of Gregory's opus. In the *Histories*' narrative architecture, they had an important role to play, but only insofar as they served a broader agenda—to focus on Gaul against the wider backdrop of Church history.[44] The Trojan origin story had several unappealing elements as far as Gregory was concerned. Firstly, it rested on a classical mythology that stood in opposition to the biblical reading Gregory brought to bear on history. Secondly, it made a strong identitarian argument that undercut Gregory's own ideas about the crystallization of a Christian community in Gaul. The Trojan story sidestepped Christianity entirely, in fact, and thus could not be harmonized with Gregory's authorial objectives. Historians of later generations did not follow Gregory in this regard; the Trojan origin story would become a mainstay of Frankish historiography for a millennium.

1.2 The *Chronicle of Fredegar*: The Ethics of an *origo*

The fall of Troy is a prodigiously popular textual motif featured in a wide range of western compositions, secular as well as ecclesiastical.[45] For late-antique and early medieval authors, it was an especially useful point of reference for events that carried unique symbolic weight, such as the Visigothic sack of Rome in 410, or that reordered regional geopolitics, such as the Muslim conquest of Spain in the early eighth century.[46]

---

[42] Gregory of Tours, *Histories* II.9: "Quod postea probatum Chlodovechi victuriae tradiderunt, itaque in sequenti diregimus," speaking of the nobility of the elected long-haired kings.
[43] Fox, "Revisiting," pp. 229–231.   [44] Reimitz, *History*, p. 87ff.
[45] See M. Coumert, "La mémoire de Troie en Occident, d'Orose à Benoît de Sainte-Maure," *Actes des congrès de la Société des historiens médiévistes de l'enseignement supérieur public, 36ᵉ congrès: Les villes capitales au Moyen Age* (2005), pp. 327–347.
[46] Jerome, *Letter* 127.12, quoting Virgil, *Aeneis* II, 361–365: "Quis cladem illius noctis, quis funera fando/ Explicet aut posit lacrimis aequare dolorem?/ Urbs antiqua ruit multos dominata per annos;/ Plurima perque uias sparguntur inertia passim/ Corpora perque domos et plurima mortis imago"; *Mozarabic Chronicle of 754*, in *Corpus scriptorium muzarabicorum*, ed. J. Gil, 2 vols. (Madrid: Instituto Antonio de Nebrija, 1973), vol. 1, ch. 45, p. 33: "Sed ut in brebi cuncta legenti retenem pagella, relictis seculi inumerabilibus ab Adam usque nunc cladibus, quas per infinitis regionibus et civitatibus crudelis intulit mundus iste immundus, quidquid historialiter capta Troia pertulit, quidquit Iherosolima predicta per prophetarum eloquia baiulabit, quidquid Babilonia per

The Trojan origin of the Franks famously makes its debut in the *Chronicle of Fredegar*, first as an interpolation of the excerpts of Eusebius-Jerome and the continuations of Hydatius that make up the second book, and then again in the early chapters of the third book. Not much can be said about *Fredegar*'s treatment of the Trojan material that has not already been covered by the voluminous literature on the topic.[47] It is nevertheless possible to offer some remarks on the relationship between ethnic formation and kingship in the Frankish case. In the *Fredegar* chronicle, the discussion of the emergence of kingship remains ancillary to the one concerned with the formation of the Franks, and this fact accords with the chronicler's overall assessment of contemporary and near-contemporary Merovingians.

scripturarum eloquia substulit, quidquid postremo Roma apostolorum novilitate decorate martialiter confecit, omnia et toth ut Spania condam deliciosa et nunc misera effecta tam in honore quam etiam in dedecore experibit." On Jerome's usage, see E. Fabbro, "'*Capitur urbs quae totum cepit orbem*': The Fates of the Sack of Rome (410) in Early Medieval Historiography," *The Medieval Chronicle* 10 (2015), pp. 49–67.

[47] The foundational work on *Fredegar* and the Trojans is František Graus, "Troja und trojanische Herkunftssage im Mittelalter" in *Kontinuität und Transformation der Antike im Mittelalter*, ed. W. Erzgräber (Sigmaringen, 1989), pp. 25–43. Also, H. Hommel, "Die trojanische Herkunft der Franken," *Rheinisches Museum für Philologie* 99, 4 (1956), pp. 323–341; H.-H. Anton, "Troja-Herkunft, origo gentis und frühe Verfasstheit der Franken in der gallisch-fränkischen Tradition des 5. und 8. Jhs," *Mitteilungen des Instituts für österreichische Geschichtsforschung* 108 (2000), pp. 1–30; Plassmann, *Origo gentis*, esp. pp. 150–192; R. Waswo, "Our Ancestors, the Trojans: Inventing Cultural Identity in the Middle Ages," *Exemplaria: A Journal of Theory in Medieval and Renaissance Studies* 7.2 (1995), pp. 269–290; Barlow, "Gregory of Tours and the Myth of the Trojan Origins of the Franks," pp. 86–95; E. Ewig, "Trojamythos und fränkische Frühgeschichte" in *Die Franken und die Alemannen bis zur "Schlacht bei Zülpich" (496/97)*, ed. D. Geuenich (Berlin and New York, 1998), pp. 1–31; E. Ewig, "Troja und die Franken," *Rheinische Vierteljahrsblätter* 62 (1998), pp. 1–16. See also N.K. Yavuz, *Transmission and Adaptation of the Trojan Narrative in Frankish History between the Sixth and Tenth Centuries*, PhD dissertation (University of Leeds, 2015); Yavuz, "From Caesar to Charlemagne"; N.K. Yavuz, "Late Antique Accounts of the Trojan War: A Comparative Look at the Manuscript Evidence," *Pecia* 17 (2014), pp. 149–170; T. J. MacMaster, "The Origin of Origins: Trojans, Turks, and the Birth of the Myth of Trojan Origins in the Medieval World," *Atlantide* 2 (2014), pp. 1–12. On the usage in late medieval historiography, see C. Beaune, "L'utilisation politique du mythe des origines troyennes en France à la fin du Moyen Âge," in *Lectures médiévales de Virgile: Actes du colloque de Rome (25–28 octobre 1982)* (Rome: École Française de Rome, 1985), pp. 331–355. On Jewish usage, see R. Ben-Shalom, "The Myths of Troy and Hercules as Reflected in the Writings of Some Jewish Exiles from Spain," in *Jews, Muslims and Christians in and around the Crown of Aragon: Essays in Honour of Professor Elena Lurie*, ed. H.J. Hames (Leiden and Boston: Brill, 2004), pp. 229–254. For exhaustive literature on the Trojan myth, see Y. Hen, "Canvassing for Charles: A Context for London, BL Arundel 375," in *Zeit und Vergangenheit in fränkischen Europa*, eds. R. Coradini and H. Reimitz (Vienna: Verlag der österreichischen Akademie der Wissenchaften, 2010), pp. 121–28, at p. 125, n.31; M. Gosman, "Alain Chartier: le mythe romain et le pouvoir royal français," in *Entre fiction et histoire: Troie et Rome au Moyen Âge*, eds. E. Baumgartner and L. Harf-Lancer (Paris: Presses de la Sorbonne Nouvelle, 1997), pp. 161–182, esp. at p. 165; Niles, "Myths of the Eastern Origins of the Franks," pp. 395–399.

Additionally, the treatment of Frankish origins in *Fredegar* may have been styled to convey a message about *Fredegar*'s royal contemporaries. It was undoubtedly intended to evoke in the reader connotations of the Roman origin myth, appropriating it and thereby fielding the audacious claim that the Franks were just as much the inheritors of this myth as were the Romans. By inference, Frankish dominion over extensive swaths of the *orbis Romanus* was justified.[48]

In the *Excerpt from the Chronicle of Jerome* found in Book II, the Frankish origin story appears as an offshoot of the Trojan narrative. *Fredegar* follows Jerome in recounting that Priam, Helen's abductor, unwittingly caused the breakout of the ten-year Trojan war. He likewise reports on Memnon and the Amazons' rally to Priam's aid and on the fall of the city. But there he breaks off from Jerome to explore an alternative storyline: the origin of the Franks. *Fredegar* announces the new topic by declaring, "thereafter was the origin of the Franks," after which he identifies Priam as their first king.[49] Priam was succeeded by Friga, who led half of the escapees on a circuitous journey that ended in their settlement, under their new king Francio, between the Danube and the Rhine, where they came under Roman rule.[50] The Franks eventually rebelled against the Romans and freed themselves, never again to be yoked by foreign oppressors. Friga is inserted strategically into the next few chapters, but this is where the interpolation in Eusebius-Jerome ends.

Another version of the Troy story is included in the early chapters of the third book of the chronicle, the so-called *Excerpt from the Chronicle of Bishop Gregory of Tours*.[51] The Trojan narrative, which is absent from the *Histories*, is also *Fredegar*'s first departure from Gregory. The account repeats the tale of the destruction of the city and the fate of its survivors.

---

[48] E. Ewig, "Le mythe troyen et l'histoire de France," in *Clovis, histoire et mémoire: Baptême de Clovis, l'événement*, ed. M. Rouche (Paris: Presses de l'Université de Paris-Sorbonne, 1997), pp. 817–847, at p. 822; H.-W. Goetz, "Gens, Kings and Kingdoms: The Franks," in *Regna* and *Gentes: The Relationship between Late Antique and Early Medieval Peoples and Kingdoms in the Transformation of the Roman World*, eds. H.-W. Goetz, J. Jarnut, and W. Pohl (Leiden and Boston: Brill, 2003), pp. 307–344, at pp. 339–341; A. Fischer, "Reflecting Romanness in the Fredegar Chronicle," *Early Medieval Europe* 22, 4 (2014), pp. 433–445.

[49] *Fredegar* II.4, p. 45: "Exinde origo Francorum fuit." For the employment of Jerome by the Fredegar chronicler as a conscious refutation of Gregory, see Reimitz, "The Early History of Frankish Origin Legends," p. 161.

[50] He opens by stating that he received his information *per historiarum libros scriptum est*, which suggests that the chronicler was relying on a separate textual tradition, if not several. For a discussion of *Fredegar*'s sources, see Schwedler, "Lethe and 'Delete'," p. 74.

[51] *Fredegar*, preface to Book III, p. 89: "Incipit capetolares libri quarti, quod est scarpsum de cronica Gregorii episcopi Toronaci." Trans. in Reimitz, "Genre and Identity in Merovingian Historiography," p. 185.

Here, too, the refugees split into two groups. One made its way to Macedonia, while the other, under the leadership of Friga, eventually settled on the shore of the Danube. There, another division took place, from which two nations arose—the Turks, led by Torcoth, and the Franks, by Francio.[52] After this time, adds *Fredegar*, the Franks were led by *duces*.

Fredegar's interpolation in the second book and the opening to the third are primarily concerned with the Franks and their origins. Only later do they turn to discuss the question of Frankish kingship and, even then, in a way that leaves many questions unanswered. In both accounts, the chronicler interpolates into his source text material that was preoccupied with the division into recognizable *ethne*: the Macedonians, the Turks, and the Franks. It is true that the king-figures leading the Trojans on their journey into Frankishness have names and are thus an element of any subsequent lineage one could draw from this text. Yet they are figures that function only as templates for the ethnonyms adopted by the groups they helped constitute, not as active characters in a historical drama. The point of this name-giving process is, of course, to introduce Francio, after whom the Franks are called.

This theme ties into the discussion of Merovingian beginnings rather uneasily. Though the kinship between the semi-historical Frankish leaders, Ricimer, Theudemer, and Clodio, and their mythological forbears, Priam, Friga, and Francio, is eventually revealed, their link to the Merovingians is left unresolved. The Trojan story is therefore constructed in such a way that prioritizes the formation of the Franks in their various stages of development over the institution of kingship, and certainly over the emergence of the Merovingians. As the many twists in *Fredegar*'s treatment of the formation of Frankish kingship make clear, it is by no means obvious that *Fredegar* wished to endow the Merovingians with a Trojan ancestry. The only intent we can attribute to *Fredegar* with any certainty is that he claimed that the Franks more generally shared a Trojan history with other *gentes*, most crucially with the Romans whose traditions the text is clearly usurping, and that in the earliest stage of their history they were led by two sets of kings that had Trojan ancestries and long hair.[53]

The intervening period of Frankish history under the *duces* is equally important to our understanding of *Fredegar*'s origin narrative, as is the story of Clodio and Merovech. As we shall see, the chronicler's treatment of pre-Merovingian kings and *duces* does not promote the notion that the

---

[52] On the possible identity of these Turks, see Ewig, "Le mythe troyen," pp. 824–826; M. Wagner, "Die Torci bei Fredegar," *Beiträge zur Namenforschung* 19 (1984), pp. 402–410; Kim, *The Huns*, pp. 84–85.
[53] *Fredegar* III.9.

kings of his day had any preferential claim to Trojan origins. Rather, it functions as an important element in a storyline that was meant to delineate the emergence of a Frankish community and perhaps to propose a subtle view of the place of the Merovingian family within it.[54]

The section dealing with the Franks under the three *duces* is imported from Gregory, although their election in the place of kings is original to *Fredegar*.[55] As Woodruff has noted, the *Fredegar* chronicler may have misunderstood the account in the *Histories* on a number of points, namely the details surrounding the Frankish ambush of Roman legionaries in the Charbonnière and the shift the Franks had made from *duces* to kings after a respite from hostilities with the Romans.[56] *Fredegar* explains that, since the *duces* were dead, the Franks resumed the habit of electing kings from the same ancestral line as before, which wraps up this section of the narrative and provides a path to the subsequent narrative block— Ricimer, Theudemer, and Clodio.[57]

The chronicle contains no additional information about the *duces* after reporting on the incursions of Arbogast into Frankish territory, which were prompted by his hatred of Marcomer and Sunno.[58] Arbogast is said to have set the forest ablaze to avert possible traps, and to have depopulated the trans-Rhenish lands ruled by the Amai, most likely a misspelling of the Chamavi, one of the constituent tribes of the Frankish confederation.[59] Since *Fredegar* leaves open the question of how Arbogast's campaign concluded, one might assume that he meant for his readers to infer that these campaigns led to the deaths of Marcomer and Sunno, and that a change in the model of rulership was now required. Yet *Fredegar* is entirely dependent on Gregory here, who specified quite clearly that, while Arbogast's maneuvers across the Rhine were met with no Frankish opposition, the legionaries sighted a group of Amsivarii and Chatii, led by Marcomir. As far as Gregory was concerned, this is how the story ended, with at least one Frankish *dux* alive and well. This is also where Gregory

---

[54] On the *duces* as suggesting a perspective centered on the aristocracy, see Reimitz, "The Early History of Frankish Origin Legends," pp. 170–171.
[55] See I. Wood, "Defining the Franks: Frankish Origins in Early Medieval History," in *From Roman Provinces to Medieval Kingdoms*, ed. T.F.X. Noble (New York and London: Routledge, 2006), pp. 91–98, at p. 94; Plassmann, *Origo gentis*, pp. 154–155.
[56] Woodruff, J.E, "The *Historia Epitomata* (Third Book) of the *Chronicle of Fredegar*: An Annotated Translation and Historical Analysis of Interpolated Material," doctoral dissertation (University of Nebraska, 1987), p. 14, n.16.
[57] *Fredegar* III.5: "Dehinc, extinctis ducibus, in Francis dinuo regis creantur ex eadem stirpe, qua prius fuerant."
[58] Ibid. 4: "Arbogastis Marcomerem et Sonnonem ducibus odiis insectans, ..."
[59] On this, see James, *The Franks*, pp. 35–36; E. Taayke, "Some Introductory and Concluding Remarks," in *Essays on the Early Franks*, ed. E. Taayke et al., Groningen Archaeological Studies, vol. 1 (Eelde: Barkhuis, 2003), pp. ix–xvi, at p. x.

complains that Sulpicius Alexander abandoned his vague usage of *duces* and *regales* altogether and openly asserted that the Franks were led by a king, whose name he nevertheless failed to mention.[60] This moved Woodruff to propose that the *Fredegar* chronicler mistook Gregory's intent to mean that the *duces* were dead. While that is possible, *Fredegar*'s next move seems to suggest otherwise, as I argue on pp. 47–48. The narrative block which is concerned with the three *duces* stands uncomfortably between the first period of Trojan kingship and the second. The *Fredegar* chronicler had to come up with a workaround to connect the two periods coherently.

The author of the *Liber historiae Francorum* faced a similar problem. He—or she, the evidence seems inconclusive on this point[61]—also wanted to keep Marcomir and Sunno, who are called *principes*, so the solution was to make them out to be sons of Priam and Antenor, respectively.[62] The author of the *Liber historiae Francorum* did not entirely share *Fredegar*'s ambivalence toward the Merovingians' Trojan origins. The *LHF* allowed for a smoother transition between the progeny of Priam and the Merovingians proper, although it did leave room for uncertainty by claiming that Merovech was not Clodio's son, only his kinsman, "*de genere eius.*"[63] This imprecise terminology could have meant either that Merovech was Clodio's relative or his descendant. If the *LHF* was paraphrasing Gregory's "*de huius stirpe,*" we could be inclined to prefer the latter.[64] In the *LHF*, Sunno's death prompts Marcomir to nominate his son, Faramund, as the first king of the Franks.[65] Importantly, Faramund is the first to be described as *rex crinitus*, followed shortly thereafter by Clodio. The *LHF* author adds that from that time, the Franks began to have long-haired kings, which goes some way to assuaging any doubts attached to Merovech's paternity and his eligibility to claim Trojan origins, since he obviously met this criterion.[66]

---

[60] Gregory of Tours, *Histories* II.9, p. 55: "Iterum hic, relictis tam ducibus quam regalibus, aperte Francos regem habere designat, huiusque nomen praetermissum, ait: Dehinc Eugenius tyrannus, suscepto expeticionale procincto, Rheni limitem petit, ut, cum Alamannorum et Francorum regibus vetustis foederibus ex more initis, inmensum ea tempestate exercitum gentibus feris ostentaret."

[61] On this, see M. Hartmann, "Die Darstellung der Frauen im *Liber Historiae Francorum* und die Verfasserfrage," *Concilium medii aevi* 7 (2004), pp. 209–237.

[62] See Yavuz, "Transmission and Adaptation," pp. 166–169.

[63] *LHF*, ch. 5: "Chlodione rege defuncto, Merovechus de genere eius regnum eius accepi." The B recension contains no mention of this.

[64] Gregory of Tours, *Histories* II.9, p. 58.

[65] For Faramund as an eighth-century parable of proper rulership, see J. Kreiner, "About the Bishop: The Episcopal Entourage and the Economy of Government in Post-Roman Gaul," *Speculum* 86, 2 (2011), pp. 321–360, at p. 328.

[66] *LHF*, ch. 5: "Mortuo quippe Faramundo rege, Chlodionem, filium eius crinitum, in regnum patris sui elevaverunt. Id temporis crinitos reges habere coeperunt."

The *Chronicle of Fredegar*: The Ethics of an *origo* 47

Fredegar does not go that far. Although he ends up keeping Marcomir and Sunno, in order to return to a new cast of characters that boast Trojan origins he needs to kill off the *duces*. His solution is not altogether elegant, but it does allow him to reattach Ricimer, Theudemer, and Clodio to their Trojan roots. Priam, Friga, and Francio, we now learn, were themselves long-haired kings, so *Fredegar* might have intended long hair as a metonym for Trojan origins.[67] In this *Fredegar* differs from both the *Histories* and the *LHF*, which see the institution of long-haired kings as a constitutive break with the past, not a continuation of it.[68] The *Histories* never attempted to link Clodio to previous kings and remained on the fence on the question of his connection to Merovech. Yet, for Gregory, the connection between long-haired kings and Merovingians was unquestionable. *Fredegar*'s attitude towards the Merovingians is another matter entirely.[69] Any conclusions one wishes to draw are grounded in the story of Merovech's birth, for which the *Fredegar* chronicler presents a curious and by now well-known interpolation of the *Histories*:

> *It is said that when Clodio and his wife were living by the seaside in the summertime, the wife went to the sea to bathe at midday, and a beast of Neptune, not unlike a Quinotaur, sought her out. When later she became pregnant, either by the beast or the husband, she gave birth to a son named Meroveus, through whom the kings of the Franks were thereafter called Merovingians.*[70]

This is all that *Fredegar* has to say about Merovech. The next passage already turns to the debauchery of Childeric, Merovech's son, making it that much harder to decipher the chronicler's precise intent. The interpolation clearly means to convey a message about the formation of the royal family: Merovech came either from a line of Trojan kings or from an unnatural union with a sea-monster, a question *Fredegar* left intentionally open.

---

[67] *Fredegar* III.9: "Franci electum a se regi, sicut prius fuerat, crinitum, inquirentes diligenter, ex genere Priami, Frigi et Francionis super se creant nomen Theudemarem, filium Richemeris, qui in hoc prilio, co supra memini, a Romanis interfectus est."
[68] *LHF*, ch. 4: "Sunnone autem defuncto, acciperunt consilium, ut regem sibi unum constituerent, sicut ceterae gentes. Marchomiris quoque eis dedit hoc consilium, et elegerunt Faramundo, ipsius filio, et elevaverunt eum regem super se crinitum." It is surely meaningful that, in a passage taken from the *Pactus Legis Salicae*, the *LHF* reported that thereafter the Franks also submitted to the authority of laws.
[69] Gregory of Tours, *Histories* II.9: "Tradunt enim multi, eosdem de Pannonia fuisse degressus, et primum quidem litora Rheni amnes incoluisse, dehinc, transacto Rheno, Thoringiam transmeasse, ibique iuxta pagus vel civitates regis crinitos super se creavisse de prima et, ut ita dicam, nobiliore suorum familia."
[70] *Fredegar* III.9, p. 95: "Fertur, super litore maris aestatis tempore Chlodeo cum uxore resedens, meridiae uxor ad mare labandum vadens, bistea Neptuni Quinotauri similis eam adpetisset. Cumque in continuo aut a bistea aut a viro fuisset concepta, peperit filium nomem Meroveum, per co regis Francorum post vocantur Merohingii."

Alexander C. Murray and Ian Wood offer somewhat divergent readings of the episode, but on several points it seems possible to agree— firstly, that a version of this story could have circulated with the purpose of etymologizing the Merovingian dynasty, perhaps at a time when the name Merovech was making a comeback on Chilperic I's side of the family.[71] Secondly, that the overall orientation of this story is classical and should be understood in relation to the Trojan chapters.[72] The Trojan origin story was certainly meant to correspond to parallel stories recounted by different peoples, most notably the Romans. The version in the *Scarpsum de Cronica Hieronimi*, which contains a more fully developed rendering of the Frankish origin story, moves from Friga to Francio. In a corresponding plotline several chapters later, it suggests that Friga and Aeneas might have been brothers.[73] A short treatment of Latin ancestry and Roman republican history then follows. Jerome's *Chronicle* moves straight from the fall of Troy to the Latin kingship of Aeneas, so *Fredegar*'s decision to interpolate the story of Frankish origins here, of all places, seems aimed at creating a parallel between Franks and Romans. While Roman history is not expanded upon in any detail in Book III, the Trojan story does lead naturally into a Frankish encounter, under the three *duces*, with the Romans, whose own Trojan ancestry is acknowledged by *Fredegar* in Book II. In the third book, however, the Romans appear without any Trojan connotations as the ultimate losers in their encounter with the Franks, whose own Trojan bloodline frames the entire discussion.

For later chroniclers working from *Fredegar*, the Trojan narrative and the Quinotaur story were irreconcilable. In the end, the Trojan version prevailed. Using the story of Merovech's unusual birth would have meant taking on the challenging task of harmonizing it with the Trojan storyline, which was the more important part of the plot. The Quinotaur story seems also to have carried an unappealing pagan aftertaste. Regarding the source material, the intertextual relationship between the different works of Merovingian historiography has been overwhelmingly conservative. In the case of Marcomir and Sunno, for instance, both *Fredegar* and the *LHF* retain a narrative nucleus extracted from the *Histories*, even when they are forced to make concessions to accommodate it. The Quinotaur

---

[71] See A.C. Murray, "*Post vocantur Merohingii*: Fredegar, Merovech, and 'Sacral Kingship'," in *After Rome's Fall: Narrators and Sources of Early Medieval History*, ed. A.C. Murray (Toronto: University of Toronto Press, 1998), pp. 121–152; Wood, "Defining the Franks," pp. 93–96.

[72] Although, as noted by Wood, probably not extracted from classical texts but from diplomatic language. See Wood, "Defining the Franks," p. 94; Plassmann, *Origo gentis*, p. 157, highlights *Fredegar*'s usage of *bistea*, a term which for him carried negative connotations, and is connected to Basina's prophecy.

[73] *Fredegar* II.8, p. 47: "Aeneas et Frigas fertur germani fuissent."

story is different. It was probably lack of awareness of the story that kept the author of the *LHF* from relating to it, but later chroniclers largely deferred to the model proposed by the *LHF*, which on the question of Clodio's paternity of Merovech reflected the view expressed in the *Histories*.[74] *Fredegar* and the *LHF* are similar in that they maintain some distance between Clodio and Merovech, but neither rules out the possibility that Merovech, and subsequently the Merovingians, were heirs to the line of Priam.[75] Yet they go about doing this in different ways: The *LHF* takes a simpler approach, which rests on the supposition that Merovech was at the very least a relative but more likely a descendant of Clodio, and in any event shared his status as *rex crinitus*.

Fredegar's narrative contortions suggest that the chronicler had something else in mind, although the reasoning behind his inclusion of the Quinotaur subplot is lost to history. It may have caught an echo of a competing origin story, as suggested by Wood. The relative diversity found in all three major works of Merovingian historiography suggests that the Franks held on to several parallel traditions about the early days of Frankish kingship, and Merovech's birth could easily have been one of them. Indeed, the Trojan story may have derived from myths recounted by the Gallic segment of the population.[76] Moreover, the overall tone of the Quinotaur story was not a flattering one for the Merovingians.[77] This is true not only because an ancestry which issues from a random encounter with a sea-monster does little to advance royal prestige, certainly when compared to stories by competing royal lines.[78] The *Fredegar* chronicler ensured that his readers understood that Merovech's paternity was not attributable to either the Quinotaur or Clodio with any certainty. Taken against the backdrop of *Fredegar*'s thoroughly Christianized chronology, its pagan undertones make the Quinotaur element feel even more out of place.

While criticism of the Merovingians is a clear element of the story as related in *Fredegar*, it only really follows from one possible interpretative route of the Quinotaur story and should not be seen as its sole *raison d'être*. Two distinct possibilities, with a moral dimension attached to each, were

---

[74] Lake, "Aimoin of Fleury's *Gesta Francorum*," p. 502.
[75] Although in the *LHF*, it is Aeneas who is the progenitor of the Trojan line, with Priam appearing only later.
[76] Ewig, "Le mythe troyen," pp. 817–818; Barlow, "Gregory of Tours and the Myth of the Trojan Origins of the Franks," pp. 87–88.
[77] I. Wood, "Deconstructing the Merovingian Family," in *The Construction of Communities in the Early Middle Ages: Texts, Resources and Artefacts*, eds. R. Corradini, M. Diesenberger, and H. Reimitz (Leiden and Boston: Brill, 2003), pp. 149–171, at p. 152.
[78] See, for instance, H. Wolfram, "*Origo et religio*: Ethnic Tradition and Literature in Early Medieval Texts," *Early Medieval Europe* 3, 1 (1994), pp. 29–38.

envisaged by the chronicler. The content of these moral lessons is less easily determined, although we might suppose that they applied to the circumstances of the Merovingian kingdoms at the time of *Fredegar*'s composition in the early 660s. The Quinotaur story was concerned with problematic paternity and its unfortunate result, namely, that a Merovingian of dubious origins would occupy the royal throne. Denial of paternity was a useful weapon for delegitimizing royal candidates;[79] we might then ask to which candidates *Fredegar* is alluding here. The Grimoald affair that took place in the 650s seems to suggest itself as a possible point of reference. Wood has argued that the *Fredegar* chronicler was sympathetic to the Pippinids, and indeed his appraisal of Pippin I was impeccable. Yet he was not as decisively supportive of Grimoald.[80] If the story of Merovech's birth was a veiled reference to the coup, then Grimoald was its Quinotaur.

Thus, I suggest that we might read *Fredegar*'s interpolation as an expression of unease with the rule of Childebert "the Adopted," Grimoald's putative biological son.[81] The chronicler would surely have been aware of Grimoald's fate, and, depending on the exact date of the composition, could also have known of the death of Childebert, which could have taken place as late as 662. If *Fredegar* was composed in Childeric II's Austrasia or, indeed, in Chlothar III's Neustro-Burgundy, interpreting the story as a call to Merovingian loyalism seems quite plausible. For both *regna*, but especially Austrasia, the early 660s would have been a period of recuperation from the Grimoald affair, punctuated by the Neustrian takeover of the Austrasian throne with the implicit approval of Chimnechild, Sigibert III's widow, who wed her daughter Bilichild to Childeric II.[82] On a more pragmatic level, *Fredegar*'s Quinotaur story functioned, much like Gregory's Pannonia, as a point of narrative inflection, from which our reading of history might unfold in one of two ways. Now, this does not necessarily mean that the author wished for the identification of Grimoald

---

[79] E.T. Dailey, "Gregory of Tours, Fredegund, and the Paternity of Chlothar II: Strategies of Legitimation in the Merovingian Kingdoms," *Journal of Late Antiquity* 7, 1 (2014), pp. 3–27.

[80] R. Collins, *Fredegar*, Authors of the Middle Ages, vol. IV, no. 13 (Aldershot: Ashgate, 1996), pp. 107–111.

[81] For a recent interpretation of the Grimoald usurpation, see I. Wood, "'There Is a World Elsewhere': The World of Late Antiquity," in *Motions of Late Antiquity: Essays on Religion, Politics, and Society in Honour of Peter Brown*, eds. J. Kreiner and H. Reimitz (Turnhout: Brepols, 2016), pp. 17–43, at pp. 28–37.

[82] On this, see J. Hofman, "The Marriage of Childeric II and Bilichild in the Context of the Grimoald Coup," *Peritia* 17–18 (2003–2004), pp. 382–393; J. Nelson, "Queens as Jezebels: Brunhild and Balthild in Merovingian History," in *Medieval Women*, ed. D. Baker, Studies in Church History, Subsidia 1 (Oxford 1978), pp. 31–77, repr. in J. Nelson, ed., *Politics and Ritual in Early Medieval Europe* (London: Bloomsbury, 1986), pp. 1–48, at p. 20. See also Y. Hen, "Changing Places: Chrodobert, Boba, and the Wife of Grimoald," *Revue belge de philologie et d'histoire* 90, 2 (2012), pp. 225–243.

with the Quinotaur to be an obvious one. As the framing of the story suggests, other solutions were left on the table. It is only to be construed as an interpretive path that may or may not be followed, at the reader's discretion. If it is, the comparison with contemporary events on the political stage might suggest itself and, with it, the drawing of appropriate moral conclusions. The ethics of the *Fredegar* chronicler continued to play a role in his presentation of the story's next hero, Merovech's son, Childeric I.

As a character, Childeric is certainly amplified in *Fredegar*.[83] The general outline of the story's earlier events resembles the one found in the *Histories*, although the motives of Childeric and his supporting cast are explored in much greater depth. *Fredegar* follows Gregory in pointing to Childeric's licentiousness as the reason for his escape to Thuringia. Like his source, *Fredegar*'s Childeric is only able to return once his ally at court appeases the angry Franks, who have since invited Aegidius, the Roman *magister militum*, to rule over them. This ally, who remains unidentified in the *Histories*, is called Wiomad in both *Fredegar* and in the *LHF*. Yet here is where the similarities end. While for the most part the *LHF* sticks to Gregory's narrative, *Fredegar* introduces new details that take the plot in unexpected directions. Especially noteworthy is *Fredegar*'s evaluation of the courtly intrigues that went on when the king was in exile and the international networks that were activated to facilitate his return.

Wiomad appears at the very beginning of the story, where he is credited with having saved Childeric and his mother from Hunnic captivity.[84] If this indeed reflects a historical event, Wiomad would likely have been a generation older than Childeric, probably one of his father's men.[85] After Childeric departed for Thuringia, Wiomad won Aegidius's trust and was appointed *subregulus* over the Franks. Determined to bring about Childeric's return, he immediately began to undermine Aegidius's position with his leading men. First, he convinced Aegidius to impose increasingly steep levies on the Franks. Then, Wiomad insisted that the only way to prevent the Franks from rebelling was to carry out a mass execution, for which he selected 100 men described as being useless and unsuitable in times of need—"*inutiles et in necessitatibus incongruos.*"[86] Later, Wiomad riled up the indignant Franks against Aegidius, reminding

---

[83] *Fredegar* III.11, pp. 95–97.
[84] Ibid., p. 95: "Wiomadus Francus fidelissimus ceteris Childerico, qui eum, cum a Chunis cum matre captivus deceretur, fugaciter liberaverat [...]." At the very least this is consistent with the timeline of Attila's advances in Gaul and the position of the Franks as imperial allies in the early 450s.
[85] The most detailed discussion of this is in Kim, *The Huns*, pp. 80–83, although at times unnecessarily dismissive of earlier scholarship on Frankish-Hunnic associations.
[86] *Fredegar* III.11, p. 96.

them that those scheduled for execution were their *parentes*.[87] Having heard enough, the Franks were content to invite back Childeric. Wiomad then put into action the second part of his plan: Aegidius was lulled into thinking that his harsh measures were effective, and that now would be an opportune time to request from the emperor in the East financial support to put the neighboring peoples directly under imperial rule.[88] Wiomad then deceitfully inserted one of his men into the legation sent to Constantinople to procure the funds.

Wiomad's agent also had a secret task—to recall Childeric. The king was apparently ensconced not in Thuringia, his initial place of refuge, but in Constantinople, where he was a guest of the emperor. This is a surprising revelation, to which the *Fredegar* chronicler made no previous allusions. The Byzantine court is known to have regularly harbored foreign dissidents and refugees—Radegund's cousin Amalafrid who fled the Frankish conquest of Thuringia is one such example[89]—although in Childeric's case, the entire episode was an ahistorical narrative ploy. A dramatic scene at the imperial court follows, in which Childeric managed to prevail over Aegidius's emissaries, secure the emperor's support, and lay the ground for his return to Gaul. We next read that Wiomad and Childeric held a meeting in Gaul, where they hatched a plan for getting Childeric reinstated. The plan was adopted enthusiastically by the king's supporters, Childeric regained his throne, and went on to defeat Aegidius and his Romans on the battlefield.

Some of the details provided by *Fredegar* seem to have a basis in reality. The *LHF*, which is not dependent on *Fredegar*,[90] repeats the name Wiomad, likewise casting him in a leading role in Aegidius's court. And while he is not mentioned by name in the *Histories*, the character of Wiomad might nevertheless reflect some measure of historicity. His successful rescue of Childeric and his mother from the Huns is possibly another older, possibly oral, account of historical events. Yet, the

---

[87] Given their prior description, these may have been chosen from the elderly.
[88] *Fredegar* III.11, p. 96: "Dans idemque consilio, laegatus ad Mauricio imperatore dirigi, gentes qui vicinas erant possi adtrahi, ut vel quiquaginta milia soledorum ab imperatore dirigentur, quo pocius gentes accepto in munere se imperio subiecerint." See Plassmann, *Origo gentis*, p. 158.
[89] On the letters containing this information, see B. Brennan, "The Disputed Authorship of Fortunatus' Byzantine Poems," *Byzantion* 66, 2 (1996), pp. 335–345; A.M. Wasyl, "An Aggrieved Heroine in Merovingian Gaul: Venantius Fortunatus, Radegund's Lament on the Destruction of Thuringia, and Echoing Ovid's *Heroides*," *Bollettino di Studi Latini* 45, 1 (2015), pp. 64–75; I. Fielding, *Transformations of Ovid in Late Antiquity* (Cambridge: Cambridge University Press, 2017), pp. 182–207. Famously, Fortunatus's threnody employs Trojan motifs.
[90] Although this has recently been questioned, or at least nuanced somewhat. See Reimitz, "The Early History of Frankish Origin Legends," p. 174.

Wiomad story waves several red flags. For one, *subregulus*—Wiomad's office under Aegidius and probably also under Childeric—is an anachronism when applied to late fifth-century northern Gaul. More likely, it reflects the court hierarchy of *Fredegar*'s own day. It is not a word the chronicler uses again, so we have no way of comparing Wiomad's position to that of other characters. The long extract from Sulpicius Alexander in Book II of the *Histories* invokes the term to refer to the *duces* Marcomir and Sunno. Gregory frames these men as Frankish leaders who were not answerable to any king, although whether this was how Sulpicius Alexander wished the term to be understood is impossible to say.

Subregulus does appear in hagiographical compositions contemporary with the composition of *Fredegar*—the *Vita Romarici* and the *Vita Arnulfi*— where it is always used to refer to a mayor of the palace.[91] *Fredegar* shares other similarities with these hagiographies, not least of which is its close acquaintance with the *Vita Columbani*, so we might hazard a guess that *subregulus* was understood relatively uniformly by all three. As noted by Roger Collins, the *Fredegar* chronicler looked for particular virtues in his leading men, such as loyalty, patience, and, above all, good counsel.[92] With regard to these three traits, the wording of "Wiomad the Frank, more loyal to Childeric than all others" is reminiscent of the description of another *maior domus*, the seventh-century Aega. Fredegar described Aega as "outstanding amongst the other leading men of Neustria, acting with prudence and imbued with the fullness of patience."[93]

---

[91] *Vita Romarici abbatis Habendensis*, MGH SRM 4, ed. B. Krusch (Hanover: Hahnsche Buchhandlung, 1902), pp. 221–225, ch. 8, p. 224: " ... vir magnificus Grimoaldus subregulus ... "; *Vita Arnulfi episcopi Mettensis*, MGH SRM 2, ed. B. Krusch (Hanover: Hahnsche Buchhandlung, 1888), pp. 426–446, ch. 3, p. 433: "[Arnulfus] Gundolfo subregulo seu etiam rectori palatii vel consiliario regis exercitandus in bonis actibus traditur." On this, see Reimitz, *History*, p. 110; H. Grahn-Hoek, "*Gundulfus subregulus*—eine genealogische Brücke zwischen Merowingern und Karolingern?," *Deutsches Archiv* 59 (2003), pp. 1–47; G. Halsall, "Growing Up in Merovingian Gaul," in *Cemeteries and Society in Merovingian Gaul: Selected Studies in History and Archaeology, 1992–2009* (Leiden and Boston: Brill, 2010), pp. 383–412, at p. 387. For a discussion on the dating of the two Lives, see L. Cracco Ruggini, "The Crisis of the Noble Saint: The 'Vita Arnulfi'," in *The Seventh Century: Change and Continuity. Proceedings of a Joint French and British Colloquium Held at the Warburg Institute 8–9 July 1988*, eds. J. Fontaine and J.N. Hillgarth (London: Warburg Institute, 1992), pp. 116–153 (see p. 122, n.9 for Arnulf's duties at court); M.G. Nauroy, "La Vita anonyme de Saint Arnoul et ses modèles antiques: La figure de saint évêque entre vérité historique et motifs hagiographiques," *Mémoires de l'Académie nationale de Metz* (2002), pp. 293–321; C. M. Nason, "The Vita Sancti Arnulfi (BHL 689-692): Its Place in the Liturgical Veneration of a Local Saint," *Sacris Erudiri* 54 (2015), pp. 171–199, at pp. 174–176.
[92] Collins, *Die Fredegar-Chroniken*, pp. 23–24.
[93] *Fredegar* III.11, p. 95: "Wiomadus Francus fidelissimus ceteris Childerico ... "; *Fredegar* IV.80, p. 161: "Aega vero inter citiris primatebus Neustreci prudencius agens et plenitudinem paciencie inbutus, cumtis erat precellentior." Trans. in R. Collins, *The Fredegar Chronicles*, unpublished English version, p. 57.

The unstinting loyalty of Wiomad to Childeric may be helpfully compared to Aega's devotion to Dagobert I, and, more importantly, to his son, Clovis II. During the young prince's minority, Aega functioned as royal *nutritor* and staunch ally of Queen Nanthild, calling to mind Wiomad's Hunnic rescue of the underage Childeric and his mother. The years Wiomad spent in subterfuge under Aegidius are nothing if not evidence of his *paciencia*. And of course, had it not been for his sound advice, Childeric would never have been able to win back his kingdom. In fact, Wiomad's *consilium* is the main theme of chapter 11. He is a much more active character than Childeric, and his recommendations are the ones that dictate the fates of the episode's other protagonists. Similarly, Wiomad's kings can be juxtaposed with Aega's—Dagobert's debauchery reminds us of Childeric, and his avaricious behavior toward the nobles' property, of Aegidius. It seems likely, then, that *Fredegar* meant for the affair to function as a moral exploration of the power of loyalty and sound advice, and the king's reliance on both, and for this lesson to be applicable to a contemporary readership.

Now, let us consider the imperial angle of the story. Childeric's victory scene at the Constantinopolitan court is unique to *Fredegar*. It gained little traction in later historiography, primarily because it was rejected by Aimoin of Fleury's tenth-century *Gesta Francorum*, the main bottleneck such narrative blocks had to overcome were they to survive and reach medieval chronicles. Aimoin must have been aware of this scene because he made use of *Fredegar* in countless other instances, but here he decided to defer to the less detailed account found in the *LHF*.[94] More to the point, Aimoin would have had no reason to shine a light on the Constantinopolitan subplot, which would have been superfluous to his treatment.[95] It is likely that he considered the *LHF* as essentially a product of Gregory of Tours and relied on it and not on *Fredegar* where the two disagreed.[96]

What Aimoin lost by adhering to the *LHF*'s simplified plot, he made up for in the grandiloquence of his characters. Be that as it may, the story of Childeric in Constantinople did not withstand his scrutiny, nor, for that matter, should it withstand ours. As it is portrayed, the episode has several irregularities and here, again, we should read it not as an attempt at disinterested historical reportage; as is so often the case with *Fredegar*, Childeric's Byzantine adventure should probably be understood as a metaphor for contemporary events.

---

[94] Aimoin of Fleury, *Gesta Francorum*, 1.7., cols. 641–642.
[95] For some remarks on Aimoin's critical treatment of the Byzantines, see Lake, "Aimoin of Fleury's *Gesta Francorum*," p. 505.
[96] For some important exceptions to this, see pp. 67–68.

For Childeric to have had some relationship with the eastern court is not out of the question, of course. Coins from the reign of Marcian were found in his tomb, discovered in Tournai in 1653. The story of the tomb and its finds has a riveting history of its own and has been discussed by Bonnie Effros and others in detail.[97] On the more pragmatic level for our purposes, eastern artifacts recovered from the tomb might suggest some form of contact between Childeric and his *fideles* and the Roman court in Constantinople. As noted by Guy Halsall, however, the tomb and the message it was made to convey were not of Childeric's design, but of Clovis's.[98] The coins were obviously there to tell a story, but, as Fischer and Lind point out, any assembly of burial goods was "an independent ideological demonstration" that we should interpret separately from the question of its origin.[99] The contents of the hoard must have been curated to make a statement about legitimacy, and were probably assembled in a western context, but they teach us little about Childeric's relationship with the eastern court.

More likely, the story in *Fredegar* carried a different meaning. The misidentification of the emperor as Maurice (and not Marcian) could, of course, be a simple error; the names of the two emperors were similar.[100] But the *Fredegar* chronicler was well versed in international affairs, with a vista much broader than that of Gregory, who famously misplaced Antioch in Egypt.[101] The *Fredegar* chronicler's diplomatic horizons spanned across the Mediterranean, penetrating the Sasanian heartlands and beyond.[102] He is the first to mention the Göktürks, who dwelt to the

---

[97] B. Effros *Merovingian Mortuary Archeology and the Making of the Early Middle Ages* (Berkeley, CA: University of California Press, 2003), pp. 28–51; B. Effros, "Memories of the Early Medieval Past: Grave Artefacts in Nineteenth-Century France and Early Twentieth-Century America," in *Archaeologies of Remembrance: Death and Memory in Past Societies*, ed. H. Williams (New York: Springer, 2003), pp. 255–280, at p. 259; B. Effros, *Uncovering the Germanic Past: Merovingian Archaeology in France, 1830–1914* (Oxford: Oxford University Press, 2012), pp. 27–28 and *passim*; Lebecq, "The Two Faces of King Childeric," pp. 275–276; P. Fouracre, "Francia and the History of Medieval Europe," *The Haskins Society Journal* 23 (2011), pp. 1–22, esp. at pp. 5–6; P. Burke, "Images as Evidence in Seventeenth-Century Europe," *Journal of the History of Ideas* 64, 2 (2003), pp. 273–296, at pp. 284–286.
[98] Halsall, "Childeric's Grave," pp. 169–187. On the grave and the consequences of its discovery, see D. Quast, *Das Grab des fränkischen Königs Childerich in Tournai und die Anastasis Childerici von Jean-Jacques Chifflet aus dem Jahre 1655* (Mainz: Verlag des römisch-Germanischen Zentralmuseums, 2015).
[99] S. Fischer and L. Lind, "The Coins in the Grave of King Childeric," *Journal of Archaeology and Ancient History* 14 (2015), pp. 3–36.
[100] On Maurice's policies, see L. Sarti, "Byzantine History and Stories in the Frankish «Chronicle of Fredegar» (c. 613–662)", *Francia* 48 (2021), pp. 3–22. I thank Laury for sharing with me an unpublished version of this paper.
[101] Gregory of Tours, *Histories* IV.40.
[102] Information came, according to Sarti, through a delegation returning from Constantinople. See Sarti, "Byzantine History," pp. 3–6. For contacts between Franks and Byzantines in the run-up to this exchange, see P. Schreiner, "Eine

east of Iran, and is also the first among both western and eastern sources to mention Muslim advances against the Byzantines.[103] For him to have mistaken characters that were essential to his Frankish storyline was decidedly odd.

The gift of 50,000 *solidi* is evidence that the episode was written with a different message in mind. Memorably, Childebert II received an identical gift from the actual Maurice, given with the specific provision that the Franks invade Italy and dislodge the recently established Lombards.[104] Childeric's story was also about removing unwanted political authority, so the chronicler could have been alluding to a much more recent diplomatic exchange between the Franks and the Byzantines, one which took place in the 580s. It is also possible to see other layers in the story. We know of at least one other incident in which a Merovingian claimant—Gundovald—was laden with gifts and sent by the emperor to undermine the status quo in Gaul.[105] The chronology of Gundovald's departure from Constantinople is quite difficult to assess, although it was located close to Tiberius II's death and the ascent of Maurice in August 582. Whoever financed Gundovald—to the tune of 50,000 *solidi*, if what Walter Goffart suspected is correct—it is clear that Maurice had a stake in his royal aspirations, which unfolded completely within the emperor's first three years in office.[106]

However one chooses to read Childeric's story of exile and return, its components were invariably made to correspond to *Fredegar*'s understanding of the Byzantine policies of subsidy and intervention enacted under the emperor Maurice in the 580s. Yet this was about more than dressing up Childeric as a late sixth-century character. Contacts with the Byzantines were a developing story with contemporary significance for the *Fredegar* chronicler, evidenced by the detailed account of Heraclius's

merowingische Gesandtschaft in Konstantinopel," *Frühmittelalterliche Studien* 19, 1 (2015), pp. 195–200.
[103] See Esders, "Prophesied Rule," pp. 134–137.
[104] Gregory of Tours, *Histories* VI.42, p. 314. On this, see Y. Fox, "The Language of Sixth-Century Frankish Diplomacy," in *The Merovingian Kingdoms and the Mediterranean World: Revisiting the Sources*, eds. S. Esders, Y. Hen, P. Lucas, and T. Rotman (London and New York: Bloomsbury Press, 2019), pp. 63–75; A. Fischer, "Money for Nothing: Franks, Byzantines and Lombards in the Sixth and Seventh Centuries," in *East and West in the Early Middle Ages: The Merovingian Kingdoms in Mediterranean Perspective*, eds. S. Esders, Y. Fox, Y. Hen and L. Sarti (Cambridge: Cambridge University Press, 2019), pp. 108–126; A. Gillett, "Love and Grief in Post-Imperial Diplomacy: The Letters of Brunhild," in *Power and Emotions in the Roman World and Late Antiquity*, eds. Barbara Sidwell and Danijel Dzino (Piscataway, NJ: Gorgias Press, 2010), pp. 127–165.
[105] Gregory of Tours, *Histories* VI.24.
[106] W. Goffart, "Byzantine Policy in the West under Tiberius II and Maurice: The Pretenders Hermenegild and Gundovald, 579–58," *Traditio* 13 (1957), pp. 73–118, at pp. 100–101, 113.

career and his contacts with Dagobert I. As demonstrated by Stefan Esders, in the early 630s the Byzantines were once again interested in cajoling the Franks into a joint military adventure, this time against the Avars.[107] The *Fredegar* chronicler was not only well informed, he was also opinionated, if his later appraisal of Heraclius's demise and the unimaginable success of the Saracens is anything to go by. I would not go so far as to imply that Childeric's Byzantine episode was code for the events of the 580s, or that the attentive reader was meant, by making the correct inferences, to glean the chronicler's opinion about the policies of his own day. It seems safe, however, to read the treatment of Childeric in *Fredegar* as an astute meditation on the risks and benefits of playing along with Byzantine interventionism.

1.3 A Carolingian Interlude: The Trojan Comment in the *Gesta episcoporum Mettensium*

As the dynasty that displaced the Merovingians, the Carolingians would have had every reason to suspect *origo* stories that privileged their predecessors. The ambition of Carolingian historiography was primarily to broadcast a message of legitimacy. Dwelling on the accomplishments of the Merovingians was counterproductive, to say the least. It is no surprise, then, that the most iconic Carolingian work depicting Merovingians is one in which ridicule prevails. The first chapters of Einhard's *Vita Karoli* are a caricature of the late Merovingian kings, whose lethargy becomes their most defining feature. Einhard's vignette is partly true; while the actual career of Childeric III, the very last Merovingian, is almost entirely unknown, it is certain that he was firmly under the thumb of both Carloman and Pippin III.[108] Carloman and Pippin did not inherit Childeric from their father. Charles Martel had ruled without a king for the four final years of his life; the last Merovingian crowned in 743 was their own creation.[109] He was likely every bit as ineffectual as the sources make him out to have been. Still, Einhard does not limit his criticism solely to the final Merovingian. Fault lay equally with Childeric's predecessors. Einhard clearly says that: " ... this family

[107] Esders, "The Prophesied Rule," pp. 119–154.
[108] His only surviving charters, in *Diplomata* 96 and 97, ed. G.H. Pertz, MGH DD Mer. (Hanover: Hahnsche Buchhandlung, 1872), pp. 86–88, are confirmations of previously granted monastic privileges in Sithiu and Stablo-Malmédy, the last of which mentions Carloman prominently.
[109] I.N. Wood, *The Merovingian Kingdoms, 450–751* (London and New York: Routledge, 1993), pp. 290–292. See also C. Bouchard, "Childeric III and the Emperors Drogo Magnus and Pippin the Pious," *Medieval Prosopography* 28 (2013), pp. 1–16. For discussion of the death of Theuderic IV and the *Calculus of 737*, see Chapter 5.

(i.e., the *gens Meroingorum*), though it may be regarded as finishing with him, had long since lost all power, and no longer possessed anything of importance except the empty royal title."[110] Einhard, and Carolingian historiography more generally, was committed to a narrative of long decline. The sooner the Merovingians began to wane, the sooner Pippinid figures could be brought to the fore.

This is not to say the Merovingian-era chronicles did not have their place within the Carolingian historiographical project. The *Continuations of Fredegar* are perhaps the most conspicuous effort by the Carolingians to reframe Merovingian historiography to suit dynastic needs. They were compiled, together with the original chronicle, into what is essentially a new composition, the *Historia vel gesta Francorum*.[111] As shown by Helmut Reimitz, the *Fredegar Chronicle* was experimented upon widely in Carolingian *scriptoria*, with the earliest sections of the text arousing particular interest.[112] Carolingian authors also knew the *LHF* well and used it extensively, not least in their framing of the *Fredegar* continuations. In fact, most manuscripts containing the composition are Carolingian.[113] Although the initial purpose of the *LHF* was to legitimize Merovingian kingship and its cooperation with the Neustrian elites, the work could certainly lend itself to other interpretations.[114] It is not overtly hostile to the Carolingians and contains a quite favorable depiction of Pippin II and Charles Martel.[115] The details of the latter's career after 727 were of course unknown to the author of the *LHF*. One might assume that Martel's decisive dismantling of late Merovingian power might have changed the composition's tone.[116] Counterfactuals notwithstanding, the *LHF* was a valuable link in the Carolingians' historiographical chain. It was also the composition that

---

[110] Einhard, *Vita Karoli Magni*, MGH SRG 25, ed. O. Holder-Egger (Hanover and Leipzig: Hahnsche Buchhandlung, 1911), ch. 1: "Quae licet in illo finita possit videri, tamen iam dudum nullius vigoris erat, nec quicquam in se clarum praeter inane regis vocabulum praeferebat." Translation taken, with adjustments, from Eginhard, *The Life of Charlemagne*, ed. and trans. A.J. Grant (In parentheses Publications: Cambridge, Ontario, 1999).
[111] See Reimitz, *History*, p. 295; Collins, *Fredegar-Chroniken*, pp. 82–145; Yavuz, "From Caesar to Charlemagne," p. 260.
[112] Reimitz, *History*, pp. 236–239.
[113] See Krusch's introduction to the MGH edition, pp. 220–234. See also Yavuz, "Transmission and Adaptation," pp. 153–159. That it was understood as a component in the Carolingian framing of their ascent is suggested by the existence of manuscripts that contained the *LHF* as an introductory text to the *Annales regni Francorum* and the *Vita Karoli*. See R. McKitterick, *The Carolingians and the Written Word* (Cambridge: Cambridge University Press, 1989), pp. 65, 239.
[114] Reimitz, *History*, pp. 248–252.   [115] *LHF*, chs. 46–53, pp. 319–328.
[116] See R. Broome, "Approaches to Community and Otherness in the Late Merovingian and Early Carolingian Periods," doctoral dissertation (University of Leeds, 2014), pp. 22–23, 88–94.

took the Merovingians' association with Troy the farthest.[117] We must therefore assume that the *origines Francorum* presented in *Fredegar* and the *LHF* were on the minds of Carolingian authors and readers.

Of course, Trojan stories were in circulation long before they were ever put in writing, and oral versions probably survived well into the Carolingian period. Whether this corpus of written and oral material was understood to have foregrounded the Merovingians' place in the story or whether it was perceived as a shared myth of common origins applicable to all Franks is difficult to tell. Still, Carolingian authors were actively engaged in altering the stories they found in Merovingian-era chronicles and in oral tradition, such as it was. These authors also came up with fresh uses for the Trojan *origo*, such as the one we find in Paul the Deacon's *Gesta episcoporum Mettensium*. Composed in 784 in Francia at the behest of Angilram bishop of Metz, the *Gesta* took a novel approach to Trojan material, all the while consciously reflecting a vision of the Carolingians as they would have liked to be seen. The reworking and continuation of the *Chronicle of Fredegar* into the *Historia vel Gesta Francorum* was significant, as was the continued preoccupation with the Trojan theme in other early Carolingian works, such as the *Cosmographia* of Aethicus or the *Historia de origine Francorum* attributed to Dares of Phrygia.[118] Yet Paul the Deacon's surprising variation on Ansegisel-Anschisus, to which I shall turn shortly, is a new—and rare—use of the Trojan story by Carolingian historiography.[119]

In his history of the episcopacy of Metz, Paul would have been able to draw on comparable compositions, such as the *Liber Pontificalis*, which records the deeds of the bishops of Rome, ordered according to the sequence of their succession.[120] Scholarship has noted that, despite the

---

[117] Reimitz, "Genre and Identity in Merovingian Historiography," p. 190.
[118] See Aethicus Ister, *Cosmographia*, in M. Herren, ed. and trans., *The Cosmography of Aethicus Ister: Edition, Translation, and Commentary* (Turnhout: Brepols, 2011); D. Shanzer, "The *Cosmographia* Attributed to Aethicus Ister as *Philosophen-* or *Reiseroman*," in *Insignis Sophiae Arcator: Medieval Latin Studies in Honour of Michael Herren on His 65th Birthday*, eds. G.R. Wieland, C. Ruff, and R.G. Arthur (Turnhout: Brepols, 2006), pp. 57–86; I. Wood, "Aethicus Ister: An Exercise in Difference," in *Grenze und Differenz im frühen Mittelalter*, eds. W. Pohl and H. Reimitz (Vienna: Verlag der österreichischen Akademie der Wissenschaften, 2000), pp. 197–208; Yavuz, "From Caesar to Charlemagne," pp. 259–262. See also now J. Kreiner, *Legions of Pigs in the Early Medieval West* (New Haven, CT: Yale University Press, 2020), pp. 72–73.
[119] On the uncertain status of the *Historia de origine Francorum* as a product of the *Fredegar* continuators, see Yavuz, "Transmission and Adaptation," pp. 184–187; S. O'Sullivan, "From Troy to Aachen: Ancient Rome and the Carolingian Reception of Vergil," in *Inscribing Knowledge in the Medieval Book: The Power of Paratexts*, ed. R. Brown-Grant et al. (Berlin and Boston: De Gruyter, 2019), pp. 185–196.
[120] D. Kempf, "Paul the Deacon's *Liber de episcopis Mettensibus* and the Role of Metz in the Carolingian Realm," *Journal of Medieval History* 30, 3 (2004), pp. 279–299, at p. 283. On the so-called "Frankish redactions" of the *Liber Pontificalis*, see C. Vircillo Franklin, "Frankish Redaction or Roman Exemplar? Revisions and Interpolations in the Text of

Gesta's suggestive title, the composition is not so much preoccupied with the deeds of the bishops of Metz as it is with events on a regnal scale.[121] One indication of this is that a seemingly off-topic emphasis on the Carolingian lineage, or rather a heavily stylized version thereof, dominates large swaths of the *Gesta*. This becomes especially apparent in the passages dealing with Metz's twenty-ninth bishop, Arnulf, for whom Paul reserved the role of the Carolingian clan's *paterfamilias*. Paul reports that Arnulf's career, and the marvelous events that it occasioned, were based on stories he heard from the *praecelsus rex Karolus* himself. Charlemagne, adds Paul, was Arnulf's *trinepos*—his great-great-great-grandson, a noteworthy bit of information. It is also significant that this comes on the heels of the episcopacies of the senator Agiulf and his nephew, Arnoald, both of whom, according to Paul, were scions of none other than the daughter of Clovis, king of the Franks.[122] The qualifier *fertur* seems to introduce some skepticism about the veracity of the claim, though perhaps this reading should not be pushed too far. What is clear is that, for Paul, Merovingian roots were a historical dead end and that the future belonged to the progeny of Arnulf, whose own dynastic success he parades in subsequent passages. Arnulf's sons are presented in the next vignette, and it is here that we learn that his younger son Ansegisel, styled Anschisus, was named after Anschises, the father of Aeneas. Aeneas, so the story goes, went to Italy from Troy, the place where an "old tradition" claims the Franks had their beginning.[123] Paul's approach to the question of origins—the Merovingians, the Carolingians, and the Franks as a community—is meant to guide the reader toward certain conclusions about the desirable relationship between all three.

---

the *Liber pontificalis*," in *Inclusion and Exclusion in Mediterranean Christianities, 400–800*, eds. Y. Fox and E. Buchberger (Turnhout: Brepols, 2019), pp. 17–46.

[121] McKitterick, "Paul the Deacon and the Franks," pp. 319–339; G. Koziol, "The Future of History After Empire," in *Using and Not Using the Past After the Carolingian Empire, c. 900–c. 1050*, eds. S. Greer, A. Hicklin, and S. Esders (London and New York: Routledge, 2020), pp. 15–35, at pp. 23–24.

[122] Paul the Deacon, *GeM*, p. 70: "Vicesimus ac sextus Aigulfus, qui fertur, patre ex nobili senatorum familia orto, ex Clodovei regis Francorum filia procreatus. Post istum exstitit nepos ipsius, nomine Arnoaldus." For the factional tensions in the see of Metz at this time, see G. Halsall, *Settlement and Social Organization: The Merovingian Region of Metz* (Cambridge: Cambridge University Press, 1995), pp. 14–16. Given the years of their tenures (late sixth and early seventh centuries), this hypothetical ancestor can only be Clovis I.

[123] Paul the Deacon, *GeM*, p. 72: "Nam venerandus iste vir, ut ad superiora redeam, iuventutis sue tempore ex legitimi matrimonii copula duos filios procreavit, id est, Anschisum et Chlodulfum; cuius Anschisi nomen ab Anchise patre Aenee, qui a Troia in Italiam olim venerat, creditur esse deductum. Nam gens Francorum, sicut a veteribus est traditum, a Troiana prosapia trahit exordium."

Trojan Comment in the *Gesta episcoporum Mettensium* 61

First, the Merovingians. Although they were around for most of the period covered by the *Gesta*, Merovingian kings are nowhere mentioned.[124] As argued by Goffart, the Merovingian period lay silently in the interim between two important episcopacies, that of Bishop Auctor, who opposed the Huns, and that of Bishop Chrodegang, who enacted a series of ecclesiastical reforms.[125] The silence is only interrupted to report matters of special consequence, most notably the life of Arnulf.[126] The bishops who presided over the diocese of Metz in the days of Gregory of Tours are often no more than names in the *Gesta*, as are those that flourished after Arnulf's mid-seventh-century episcopacy.[127] Not only do the kings that preceded the Carolingians have no place in the account, even the bishops of Metz in their day amounted to little, apart from Arnulf, that is. This invisibility seems suggestive of Paul's understanding of the Merovingians' historical role.

Though he was an important element in Paul's structuring of the composition and merited several long paragraphs in the *Gesta*, not much of Arnulf as a person comes through. The *Vita Arnulfi* is only dimly reflected in the *Gesta*, which prefers to spotlight the contemporary Carolingian benefactors as opposed to the many unknowns of Arnulf's life. What perhaps does shine through Paul's depiction of Arnulf, if we accept Goffart's reading, is a thinly veiled portrait of Charlemagne. To his treatment, Paul appends an elaborate discussion of the progeny of Ansegisel and a set of four eulogies written for Charlemagne's wife and daughters, who were buried outside Metz, in St. Arnulf's oratory.[128] Since Arnulf was the progenitor of the *gens* that would supplant the Merovingians, it was as fitting a place as any to insert the Carolingian perspective on the Trojan story.

The *Gesta* offers a foundational story for a dynasty of kings, beginning with Arnulf and ending with the progeny of Charlemagne. With resolute strokes, Paul brushes away any ambiguity about the history of Carolingian succession.[129] According to him, it was a direct and untroubled affair,

---

[124] McKitterick, "Paul the Deacon," p. 333. Apart from the comment on Clovis, who is only used as a prop for Paul's discussion of Agiulf.
[125] Auctor: Paul the Deacon, *GeM*, pp. 62–70; Chrodegang: ibid., pp. 86–88.
[126] Arnulf: Paul the Deacon, *GeM*, pp. 70–78 is the lengthiest of the four more detailed treatments (Clemens, Auctor, Arnulf, and Chrodegang).
[127] See ibid., p. 70, where he admits to guessing certain bishops' origins based on their Greek-sounding names: "Successit huic quartus decimus Epletius. Deinde quintus decimus Urbicius. Sextus decimus Bonolus. Septimus decimusque Terentius. Octavus decimus Gonsolinus. Exinde Romanus. Vicesimus denique Fronimius. Post quem Grammatius. Deinde Agatimber. Tres itaque isti quos premisimus, sicut in eorum nominibus adtenditur, de origine credendi sunt emanare Grecorum."
[128] Ibid., p. 265.
[129] Bouchard, "Images of the Merovingians and Carolingians," p. 299.

from Arnulf to Anschisus and from him to his son, Pippin. Pippin left his position to his son, Charles (Martel), who was then succeeded by Pippin III, and finally by Charlemagne, whose many offspring by his wives were all accounted for in the text. No Grimoald, no Plectrude, and of course no Carloman, Grifo, or Drogo; this is a reductionist schema of Carolingian origins, and it was probably meant to be recognized as such, given that Paul ignores what other canonical Carolingian historiographies tacitly acknowledged, namely the numerous challenges faced by Charlemagne's ancestors in their quest for power.

The significance of Paul's mention of Troy becomes clearer when we consider it in relation to his intentions for the Carolingian *origo* model. Goffart has argued that Paul sought to link Arnulf to the Trojan past, and this is partly true. Going even further, Kempf has claimed that the Carolingians' appropriation of the Trojan *origo* was somehow meant to circumvent the Merovingian claim on this tradition.[130] Paul's framework, however, ties Troy to the entire *gens Francorum* rather than to any particular family. Not the Merovingians, surely, about whose near-contemporary scions Paul has little to say. But not the Carolingians either, whose progenitor flourished in the early seventh century. The suggestive exegesis of Ansegisel's name does not extend to a claim of exclusivity and is even qualified with a *creditur esse*. What it does is provide context for Paul's next statement about the Trojan origins of the Franks. Paul's Trojan comments and his version of the Carolingian family tree do not, in the end, cohere into a claim about the exclusivity of the Trojan story to any *genus* in particular. It is a tradition that applies to the people as a whole. These people, the Franks, are led by a family that embodies something of the Trojan spirit but whose ideological investment lies not so much in tales of mythological origins as in the Christian values personified by Anschisus.[131]

1.4 An Evolving Royalism: Dionysian Historiography and Its Influences

With the late thirteenth-century chronicle, the *Roman des rois*, we are on entirely new terrain. Primat, the author of this Old French work, addressed an audience that could not read Latin but still had a taste for historiography. This was an inquisitive and literate secular readership, dissatisfied with what was then available in the vernacular, namely, versified histories whose

---

[130] Kempf, "Paul the Deacon's *Liber de episcopis Mettensibus*," pp. 287–288.
[131] See Yavuz, "Transmission and Adaptation," p. 199, who claims that Paul links the Carolingians directly to the Trojan migrants.

emphasis was more on style than on historicity.[132] It wanted its history in prose, and the *Roman des rois* delivered. For generations, Saint-Denis's *scriptorium* housed authors working on Frankish history, and it is there that one finds the context and the source-base for Primat's work. Primat had expert guidance and unparalleled access to source material in Saint-Denis, and he used these resources fully in his *Roman des rois*. As expected, the monastery and its patron saint take center stage in the composition.[133]

In the prologue, Primat spells out the work's rationale: "Because many people doubt the genealogy of the kings of France, of what origin and of what line they are descended, he [Primat] set out to compose this work on the order of such a man that cannot be refused."[134] Whether this person whom one cannot refuse was King Louis IX, as Jules Viard believed, or the abbot of Saint-Denis, Matthew of Vendôme, as suggested by Bernard Guenée, Primat's work carries unmistakable royalist overtones.

It would nevertheless be unhelpful to view Primat's work as an expression of royal ideology as Louis IX or Philip III's courts would have understood it.[135] While the *Roman des rois* surely presents what it perceives to be the best framing of royal history, the articulation of this history echoes the perspective of a monk of Saint-Denis and his abbot, not the king's, inasmuch as the latter could even be expressed in narrativized form.[136] More to the point, Primat drew heavily on earlier sources. For example, his statement of doubt regarding the origins of the kings of

---

[132] B. Guenée, "The *Grandes chroniques de France*: The Roman of Kings (1274–1518)," in *Rethinking France: Les Lieux de Mémoire*, Volume 4: *Histories and Memories*, ed. P. Nora (Chicago: University of Chicago Press, 2010), pp. 205–230, at p. 208. See W.H. Sewell, Jr., "The Concept(s) of Culture," in *Beyond the Cultural Turn: New Directions in the Study of Society and Culture*, eds. V.E. Bonnell and L. Hunt (Berkeley and Los Angeles: University of California Press, 1999), pp. 35–61, at pp. 49–50 for comments on "coherence of culture" and Aurell's usage thereof for thirteenth-century historiography in Aurell, "From Genealogies to Chronicles," p. 252.

[133] On this, see I. Guyot-Bachy, "Les premiers Capétiens: de la protohistoire dionysienne au Roman des rois de Primat," in *La rigueur et la passion: Mélanges en l'honneur de Pascale Bourgain*, eds. C. Giraud and D. Poirel (Turnhout: Brepols, 2016), pp. 527–545.

[134] Viard, ed., *GCh*, p. 1: "Pour ce que pluseurs genz doutoient de la genealogie des rois de France, de quel origenal et de quel lignie ils ont descendu, enprist il ceste ouvre à fere par le commandement de tel homme que il ne pout ne de dut refuser." See G. Tyl-Labory, "Essai d'une histoire nationale au XIIIe siècle: la chronique de l'anonyme de Chantilly-Vatican," *Bibliothèque de l'école des chartes* 148, 2 (1990), pp. 301–354, at p. 304, and more generally for the links between Primat's work and the earlier anonymous vernacular composition known as the *Chronique des rois de France*. See also C. Buridant, "Connecteurs et articulations du récit en ancien et moyen français: le cas de la Chronique des rois de France," in *Texte et discours en moyen français: Actes du XIe colloque international sur le moyen français*, ed. A. Vanderheyden et al. (Turnhout: Brepols, 2007), pp. 73–94.

[135] For kings writing their own histories, see Aurell, "From Genealogies to Chronicles," pp. 235–264.

[136] See Ranum, *Artisans of Glory*, p. 6.

France, quoted above, is lifted almost verbatim from the early thirteenth-century *Gesta Philippi Augusti*, by the monk Rigord of Saint-Denis. Rigord helpfully alerts readers to his editorial process: "because many are wont to doubt the origins of the kingdom of France, how and in what manner the kings of the Franks are said to have descended from the Trojans themselves."[137] Since some of Primat's main sources offer an almost identical rationale to his, one hesitates to assign to the *Roman des rois* motives that are wholly subordinate to those of his royal patrons. Put differently, this was not merely a new spin on an old story, recycled here to express contemporary concerns. Primat was indeed tethered to previous traditions, in whose continued relevance Saint-Denis had an important stake.

In the end, Primat was able to produce a mature vision of royal history, one that included a meticulous treatment of the question of royal origins. It contains a historiographical mosaic that reflects distinct stages in the development of the origin story. In the following discussion I take as my main points of reference Aimoin of Fleury's *Gesta Francorum*, Rigord of Saint-Denis' *Gesta Philippi Augusti*, and William the Breton's reworking of the latter, in whose pages we will see a process that culminated with Primat.

The *Roman des rois* presents a fully developed Trojan story that serves as a central pillar of the composition's rationale.[138] The first order of business, states Primat in his prologue, is to cover "the noble line of the Trojans, from whom it [i.e., the French monarchy] is descended in long succession. Thus, it is certain that the kings of France, through whom the

---

[137] Rigord of Saint-Denis, *Gesta Philippi Augusti*, in *Œuvres de Rigord et de Guillaume le Breton, historiens de Philippe-Auguste*, ed. H.-F. Delaborde, 2 vols. (Paris: Société de l'histoire de France, 1882), 1, pp. 1–167, at ch. 37, p. 55: "Et quoniam multi solent dubitare de origine regni Francorum, quomodo et qualiter reges Francorum ab ipsis Trojanis descendisse dicantur." For an English translation and useful background material, see now *The Deeds of Philip Augustus, An English Translation of Rigord's* Gesta Philippi Augusti, trans. L.F. Field and eds. M.C. Gaposchkin and S.L. Field (Ithaca, NY and London: Cornell University Press, 2022). Also, see now M. Clarke, "The Legend of Trojan Origins in the Later Middle Ages: Texts and Tapestries," in *Origin Legends in Early Medieval Western Europe*, eds. L. Brady and P. Wadden (Leiden and Boston: Brill, 2022), pp. 187–212, esp. at pp. 193–196.

[138] When skepticism about Trojan origins began to mount in humanist scholarship in the fifteenth century, it was usually directed against the version of the story presented in the *Grandes Chroniques de France*, which remained largely unchanged once it was put down in writing in the *Roman des rois*. D. O'Sullivan, "Grandes chroniques de France," *Encyclopedia of the Medieval Chronicle*, eds. G. Dunphy and C. Bratu (Leiden: Brill, 2016). Consulted online on 07 May, 2019 ://dx.doi.org/10.1163/2213-2139_emc_SIM_01173 I make the distinction between Primat's composition—the *Roman des rois*—and the *Grandes Chroniques de France*, a later evolution of the text that underwent a lengthy process of revision, updating, and expansion in several different centers. On this process, see Guenée, "The Grandes chroniques de France," pp. 211–217. On Paolo Emilio and the response of humanist historiography, see pp. 100–101, in Chapter 2.

kingdom is glorious and renowned, descended from the noble line of Troy."[139]

These themes were central to the ideology of the French royalty. Just as their lineage was especially noble, so too were the kings glorious in victory, honorable in renown, and pious in belief. Christian kingship and Trojan origins are tightly intertwined in the prologue. For Primat, Troy was but one, albeit important, element in the glory associated with the kings of France, to whom "Our Lord has given [...] through His grace a prerogative and an advantage over all other lands and over all other nations, because never, since it converted and began to serve its creator, was faith more fervently and more righteously protected in any other land; through it was it multiplied, through it sustained, through it defended."[140] This faith owed its spread to the power of St. Denis, with whose cult Primat's monastery was so closely associated. As Primat explains toward the end of his prologue, the divine favor enjoyed by France was the product of an alliance between *clergie* and *chevalerie*. The two, he adds, are inseparable; one cannot survive without the other.[141] This *clergie* was embodied in the institution of Saint-Denis, whose links to the Frankish kings went back to Merovingian times.[142] Only once these essential elements are in place does Primat turn to narrate the story of Trojan descent.

The details of the story in the *Roman des rois* are familiar—Priam sends his son, Paris, to Greece to kidnap Helen. The enraged Greeks place Troy under a ten-year siege, leading to the deaths of Priam's sons and his wife, Hecuba, and the destruction and burning of the city along with its many inhabitants. More than a few managed to escape the flames, however, and among them were the three princes Helenus, Aeneas, and Antenor. Helenus and his 1,200 followers reached the kingdom of Pandrasius, whereas Aeneas and his 3,400 Trojans reached Dido's Carthage on their way to Italy. There, Aeneas was succeeded by his son, Ascanius, who married Lavinia, daughter of King Latinus. From this union would emerge Silvius, and from him Brutus, whose lineage came to rule Britain

---

[139] Viard, ed., *GCh*, p. 4: "Li commencemenz de ceste hystoire sera pris à la haute lignie de Troiens, dont ele est descendue par longue succession. Certaine chose est donques que li roi de France, par les quex li roiaumes est glorieus et renommez, descendirent de la noble lignie de Troie."

[140] Viard, ed., *GCh*, prologue, p. 5: "Si li a Nostre Sires doné par sa grace un prerogative et un avantage seur toutes autres terres et seur toutes autres nations, car onques puis que ele fu convertie et ele commença à servir à son creatour, ne fu que la foi n'i fust plus fervemment et plus droitment tenue que en nule autre terre; par lie est multipliée, par li est sustenue, par li est defendue."

[141] Viard, ed., *GCh*, prologue, pp. 5–6: "Si com aucun veulent dire, clergie et chevalerie sont touz jors si d'un acort, que l'un ne puet sanz l'autre; touz jors se sont ensemble tenues, et encore, Dieu merci, ne se departent eles mie."

[142] About Dagobert's patronage of Saint-Denis, see pp. 183–184, Chapter 4.

after evicting its indigenous giants, a theme adopted from Geoffrey of Monmouth's *Historia regum Brittaniae*.[143]

Primat's account becomes especially illuminating when he turns to discuss the royal cousins Francio and Turcus, the sons of Hector and Troilus, respectively. The two left Troy and proceeded to Thrace, where they crossed the Danube and dwelt for some time on its shores. Later they parted ways, with Turcus heading for Scythia Inferior to settle there with his people and Francio remaining on the Danube, where he founded the city of Sicambria. It was there that his people dwelt for 1,507 years. Eventually, four new peoples emerged from Turcus's Scythian Trojans: the Austrogoths, Hypogoths, Vandals, and Northmen (or Normans). This last element of the story is one of numerous borrowings from Rigord of Saint-Denis's *Gesta Philippi Augusti*, whose third and final version was produced by 1206.[144]

In Rigord's *Gesta*, the question of Frankish origins is introduced in a short diversion from the main storyline, the kingship of Philip Augustus. After a discussion of Philip's public works in Paris and its environs, Rigord makes an abrupt turn to the *origo* story in a way that quickly feeds back into the near-contemporary coverage of events. Brief though it is, the diversion is instructive. It begins with a family tree, in which the Trojan ancestry of the Franks and their relationships to the other branches formed by the Trojan exodus is put in order.[145] Priam, the king of Troy, sits at the top of the tree, succeeded by two sons, Hector and Troilus. Whereas the former enjoys a long succession of heirs terminating in Childeric,[146] Troilus receives but one successor, Turcus, from

---

[143] This element of the Trojan story is a simplified summary of Geoffrey's account. See p. 70 for relevant literature. Suger (d. 1151) quotes from Geoffrey of Monmouth's *Propheciae Merlini*, so may already have known his *Historia regum Brittaniae*, marking a relatively early point from which the composition was known and used in Saint-Denis. See E.A.R. Brown and M.W. Cothren, "The Twelfth-Century Crusading Window of the Abbey of Saint-Denis: *Praeteritorum Enim Recordatio Futurorum est Exhibitio*," *Journal of the Warburg and Courtauld Institutes* 49 (1986), pp. 1–40, at p. 11, n.49. See also E. Leschot, "The Abbey of Saint-Denis and the Coronation of the King of France," *Arts* 9, 111 (2020), pp. 1–15 [url: doi.org/10.3390/arts9040111, accessed April 13, 2022]. Rigord undoubtedly used extracts of Geoffrey's work. See H.-F. Delaborde, "Notice sur les ouvrages et sur la vie de Rigord, moine de Saint-Denis," *Bibliothèque de l'école des chartes* 45 (1884), pp. 585–614, at p. 594; F.-O. Touati, "Faut-Il En Rire? Le Médecin Rigord, Historien de Philippe Auguste," *Revue historique* 305, 2 (2003), pp. 243–265, at p. 253.

[144] Rigord of Saint-Denis, *Gesta Philippi Augusti*, 38, p. 56: "sed post paululum temporis, Turchus cum suis, a Francione consanguineo suo recedens, in Scythia inferiore se transtulit et ibi regnavit; a quo descenderunt Ostrogoti, Ypogoti, Wandali et Normanni."

[145] See the family tree at the bottom of Paris, BnF MS Lat. 5925, f. 259. See also the comments in *The Deeds of Philip Augustus*, trans. Field and eds. Gaposchkin and Field, p. 55.

[146] Interestingly, Rigord seems to acknowledge that Childeric was indeed a thematic endpoint, after which began a new epoch in Frankish history.

Dionysian Historiography and Its Influences 67

whom we later learn sprang forth those same four nations mentioned by Primat. Much of what Rigord had to say about Francio found its way into the *Roman des rois*. Unlike Rigord, however, who ignored the particulars of the Trojan war and skipped ahead to Francio, Primat gives Troy its due.

Despite its debt to Rigord, the narrative in the *Roman des rois* is mainly drawn from the *Gesta Francorum*. Primat borrows heavily from Aimoin, but we can detect a difference between the chroniclers' approaches even as early in the plot as the story of Trojan descent. While Aimoin generally followed the outline provided by the *LHF*,[147] Primat's Francio and Turcus are influenced by elements initially codified by *Fredegar*. Primat was not reading *Fredegar* directly; what reached him were refractions of *Fredegar* from his sources, among whom we find Aimoin again, but also Rigord and William the Breton. William's two works, an identically named reworking and continuation of Rigord's *Gesta Philippi Augusti* and an almost 10,000-line-long verse titled the *Philippide*,[148] are factually similar to Rigord's work, yet they narrativize Frankish origins differently. Instead of Rigord's thematic tangent wedged in the middle of the composition, William's *origo* assumes its natural place at the beginning of the composition, yielding a more coherent chronology, one that is at least partially embraced by Primat.[149] It thus seems plausible that the Francio material in the *Roman des rois* originated with Rigord, and that the overarching narrative structure was adopted from William's reworking.

Aimoin, Primat's preferred source, offered little on Francio. We may recall that the *LHF*, whose lead Aimoin seems to have been following, had no need for a Francio, since its royal lineage spanned directly from Aeneas to Merovech. Aimoin does mention Francio in the next chapter, titled *De Francorum appellatione altera opinio* ("A different opinion about the naming of the Franks"), alongside Torchotus, as one possible reason why the Franks were called by that name.[150] The travels of Friga and the associated details of Francio and Torchotus were probably drawn from *Fredegar*, but for Aimoin, Francio was no more than a sidenote to the real storyline.[151] The *Gesta Francorum*'s main narrative axis followed the *LHF*'s explanation for the meaning of the Franks' name: that the *Franci* were, in the

---

[147] Aimoin of Fleury, *Gesta Francorum*, 1, cols. 637–638.
[148] On the Philippide, see G. Spiegel, *Romancing the Past: The Rise of Vernacular Prose Historiography in Thirteenth-century France* (Berkeley and Los Angeles, CA: University of California Press, 1993), pp. 269–314.
[149] Spiegel, *Romancing the Past*, pp. 284–289.
[150] Aimoin of Fleury, *Gesta Francorum*, 2, col. 639.
[151] Aimoin would have been working with a manuscript from Krusch's "Group 3," which contained the relevant material, but not Book IV or the *Continuationes*. See Werner, "Die literarischen Vorbilder," pp. 202–203, and esp. n.33.

68   Trojans, Sea-monsters, and Long-haired Kings

Attic language, synonymous with the Latin *feroces*, given to the Trojans by the emperor Valentinian following their exploits in the Meotian Swamps. Aimoin thus knew of *Fredegar*'s Francio eponymic, but he bracketed it as an alternative explanation and returned quickly to the Swamps, signifying his clear preference for the *LHF* version.[152]

Yet preference did not mean absolute adherence, and on certain occasions Aimoin tempered the claims made by the *LHF*. Importantly, Aimoin ruled out the direct filiation of the Merovingians in particular, and the Frankish kings more generally, from the line of Trojan kings. In fact, he made no effort to link Marcomir (or his equals in command, Sunno and Genobaudes) to the Trojans. Kings, we gather from Aimoin, had no more of a claim to Trojan origins than did any other Frank. As noted by Justin Lake, Clovis's appeal to the Franks on the battlefield of Tolbiac emphatically insisted on this point.[153] If anything, in Clovis's address to his fighting men, Aimoin privileged the Christian faith over the ineffective pagan cults which he associated with Troy. What we see in the *Gesta Francorum* then is a political moment in which the Trojan narrative could be again ethnicized, especially as state fracture seemed the order of the day. None of the many claimants to royal power had any privileged stake in this story, although by Primat's day this changed with the crystallization of a particular rhetoric around the Capetians and their origins.

Primat's Trojan version thus had everything to do with the kings of France and, while much of his narrative was directly borrowed from Aimoin, for Marcomir he chose a different path to that of his source by adding that this Marcomir had been the son of King Priam of Austr(as)ia, who descended from the lineage of the great king Priam of Troy, in essence returning to the ancestry model provided by the *LHF*, though here mediated through the lens of Rigord's *Gesta Philippi Augusti* and William's reworking thereof.[154] Rigord elaborates on the *LHF*'s material, combining

---

[152] Lake, "Aimoin of Fleury's *Gesta Francorum*," p. 502.
[153] Aimoin of Fleury, *Gesta Francorum* 1.16, PL 139, cols 654C–655A: "Franci, inquit, Troiugenae (meminisse etenim vos nominis generisque vestri decet), quibus nunc usque servierimus diis ad memoriam reducere animos vestros virtutemque deposco." See Lake, "Aimoin of Fleury's *Gesta Francorum*," p. 513.
[154] Viard, ed., *GCh* ch. 4, p. 18: "En ce tens entra Marchomires en France. Cil Marchomires avoit esté fiuz au roi Priant d'Ostericke, qui estoit descenduz de la lignie le grant roi Priant de Troie." Rigord of Saint-Denis, *Gesta Philippi Augusti* 38, p. 56: "Egressi inde, Marcomiro [filio Priami regis Austrie], Sonnone [Antenoris filio], et Genebaudo ducibus ... "; William the Breton, *Gesta Philippi Augusti*, in *Œuvres de Rigord et de Guillaume le Breton, historiens de Philippe-Auguste*, ed. H.-F. Delaborde (Paris: Société de l'histoire de France, 1882), pp. 168–320, 4, p. 171: "Francio autem et qui ab illo descenderunt, regnaverunt apud Sicambriam et in partibus illis, mille quingentis septem annis, usque ad Priamum regem Austrie, cui, cum mortuus esset, successit Marcomirus filius eius. Cum autem iidem Franci negarent tributum iuxta morem ceterarum nationum solvere Romanis, Valentinianus imperator christianus,

Dionysian Historiography and Its Influences 69

it with an improved version of the crude genealogy employed by *Fredegar* to link the Trojans of myth and the Frankish *duces* of the late fourth century. In Rigord's account, the descendants of Francio's Trojans were expelled from Sicambria after refusing to pay tribute to Valentinian, causing them to resettle on the eastern banks of the Rhine, within the confines of Germany and Alamannia, in a place called Austria (i.e., Austrasia).[155] The leaders of the Sicambrian exiles at this time were Marcomir, Sunno, and Genobaudes. Tellingly, at this specific textual juncture, Paris, BnF MS Lat. 5925 contains an addition above the name Marcomir of *filio Priami regis Austrie*, and one line below, *Antenoris filio* for Sunno, written in a different hand.[156] The other extant medieval manuscript, a thirteenth-century composition possibly penned at Bourges, is Vatican City, BAV Reg. lat. 88. While at the same point in the text it does not contain a similar addition,[157] it includes an explanation of the Trojan lineage of the *duces* at other points.[158] Whether this suggests that the development of these elements of the plot was not entirely complete when Rigord was working is difficult to say. The superscript note in Paris, BnF MS Lat. 5925 could have been added to prevent confusion of the different Priams. However we choose to explain it, the simplified family tree had become part of the story by William's day.

Valentinian tried again to subdue the Trojans but eventually despaired, giving them the epithet *Franci* on account of their ferocity.[159] From that time, adds Rigord, the Franks were able to subjugate Germany and Gaul entirely, extending their power as far as the Pyrenees. Sunno and Genobaudes decided to remain in Austria, but Marcomir had different plans. For Rigord, relocating Marcomir to Gaul was a significant narrative choice, because it allowed him to focus exclusively on the kings of Gaul, which quickly become synonymous with the Neustrian branch of

---

anno ab incarnatione CCCLXXVI, eos inde expulit; qui inde egressi, predicto Marcomiro et Somnone filio Antenoris et Genebaudo ducibus, habitarunt iuxta ripam Rheni inter Germaniam et Alemanniam que regio vocatur Austria."

[155] Rigord of Saint-Denis, *Gesta Philippi Augusti*, p. 56: "Egressi inde, Marcomiro [filio Priami regis Austrie], Sonnone [Antenoris filio], et Genebaudo ducibus, venerunt et habitaverunt circa ripam Rheni in confinio Germanie et Alemannie, que terra Austria vocatur."

[156] Paris, BnF MS Lat. 5925, f. 259v, col. B.

[157] Vatican City, BAV Reg. lat. 88, f. 182v, col. A: "fuit Faramundus filius Marcomiri filii Priami regis Austrię."

[158] Vatican City, BAV Reg. lat. 88, f. 182v col. B.

[159] Which is attributed, in ms V, to the *lingua Arctica*, as opposed to the *LHF*'s *Attica lingua*. The etymological link was already made by Isidore of Seville in the seventh century. See Isidore of Seville, *Etymologies*, in *Isidori Hispalensis episcopi Etymologiarum sive originum libri XX*, ed. W.M. Lindsay, 2 vols. (Oxford: Oxford University Press, 1911), IX.ii.101, which also postulated the existence of a Francio.

the Merovingian family. By painting Sunno and Genobaudes out of the picture, Rigord in effect marginalized Austrasia and its contribution to this stage of Frankish history. The *Gesta Philippi Augusti* presents a streamlined chain of filiation that includes only Neustrian kings and plants its roots as far back in the past as Marcomir's departure from what they called Austria, or, in other words, trans-Rhenish Francia. By doing this, Rigord privileged the progeny of Marcomir as the only true heirs of the Trojan lineage. As we shall see, this motif resurfaces when the plot turns to the final Merovingians and the first Carolingians. We should consider how Rigord chose to present Marcomir's advent into Gaul: "But later, when Sunno and Genobaud remained *duces* in Austria, Marcomir, son of Priam, who descended from Francio, the descendant of Priam king of Troy, through numerous successive generations that it would here be slow to enumerate, came to Gaul with his followers."[160]

At this point, Rigord offers a synopsis of events recounted thus far—the fates of Helenus, Antenor, Aeneas, and Ascanius—and concludes with the story of Brutus, descendant of Antenor, and his takeover of Albion, henceforth called Britain in his honor. Some of this relied on Geoffrey of Monmouth, to be sure, and in this sense Rigord was engaging with the literary sources available to him as he worked. He was nevertheless more interested in Frankish origins, especially in what they might have meant in his day. Importantly, Rigord leaves out Sunno and Genobaudes's successors, providing instead a brief note on the kings that ruled Austrasia until the time of Childeric II (d. 675). "But," explains Rigord, "because they were deficient, the *duces* known as 'mayors of the palace' Pippin, Charles Martel and the others began to dominate."[161]

After dispensing with Austrasia, Rigord could finally turn to the adventures of Marcomir in Gaul, and adventures indeed they were. He opens with the exceptional story of Marcomir's alliance with the people of Gaul. This alliance was fated to occur, we learn, because the Gauls were the descendants of a group of 23,000 Trojans who had left Sicambria under the leadership of Duke Ibor, making Gaul their home. These Gallic Trojans founded Lutetia (later Paris), where they weathered the centuries of Roman domination until Marcomir came to their rescue. A mutual recognition of their shared ancestry is not long in the making: "When the

---

[160] Rigord of Saint-Denis, *Gesta Philippi Augusti*, pp. 56–57: "Sed postea, Sonnone et Genobaudo ducibus in Austria remanentibus, Marcomirus, filius Priami regis Austrie, qui a Francione, nepote Priami regis Troje, per multas successorum generationes quas hic longum esset enumerare, descenderat, in Galliam venit cum suis."
[161] Rigord of Saint-Denis, *Gesta Philippi Augusti*, pp. 57–58: "Sed tunc deficientibus regibus, duces dominari ceperunt qui maiores domus vocabantur ut Pipinus, Karolus Martellus et ceteri."

Parisians heard that he [i.e., Marcomir] was, like them, descended of the Trojans, they received him honorably. Because he instructed them in the use of arms and walled the cities against the frequent attacks of robbers, he was established by them as defender of all of Gaul."[162] This phrasing is almost identical to that used by Rigord in chapter 20 to depict the actions taken by Philip Augustus in the fourth year of his reign (1183) for the benefit of the people of Paris, demonstrating his desire to equate the two kings in greatness.[163]

Marcomir then moves off the stage to make room for his son. Faramund was the first to be crowned with the diadem of king of France, and under his rule Lutetia was renamed Paris, in honor of the son of Priam whose deeds brought about the Trojan exodus. In William's *Philippide*, the reunification of Gauls and Franks is developed further:

After this, however, the Franks learned that the Parisi were born of the same stock from which they themselves had descended, and the Frankish army made friends with them by means of a strong peace. They called them brothers of the Franks and by a perpetual treaty they became with the Parisi one people of Franks. And the city then first earned the name Paris, the very site to which they had previously given the name Lutetia.[164]

Primat adopts and adjusts William's (and thus, Rigord's) account in the *Gesta Philippi Augusti* of Ibor's Sicambrians and Marcomir's accomplishments in Gaul.[165] He must have been aware of the inconsistencies in the chronologies and storylines of his various sources, because he felt the need to offer an apology in the prelude to the next chapter: "We have heretofore reproduced the opinions of certain authors, but because we do not want anyone to take offense to this text, we shall take the material as it appears in the chronicles, which state thus, that after the Franks left Sicambria, and they conquered Germany and Alamannia, and defeated the Romans in

---

[162] Rigord of Saint-Denis, *Gesta Philippi Augusti*, p. 59: " . . . et audientes Parisii quod de Trojanis descenderat ab ipsis honorifice receptus est: quos quia ad exercitum armorum docuit et civitates, propter frequentes incursus latronum, murari fecit, ab ipsis defensor totius Gallie constitutus est."

[163] Rigord of Saint-Denis, *Gesta Philippi Augusti*, ch. 20, p. 34: " . . . in foro quod Campellis vocatur, ubi ob decorem et maximam institorum utilitatem, per ministeriorum predicti servientis qui in hujusmodi negotiis probatissimus erat, duas magnas domos quas vulgus halas vocat, edificari fecit, in quibus tempore pluviali omnes mercatores merces suas mundissime venderent, et in nocte ab incursu latronum tute custodirent."

[164] William the Breton, *Philippidos libri XII*, in *Œuvres de Rigord et de Guillaume le Breton, historiens de Philippe-Auguste*, ed. H.-F. Delaborde, 2 vols. (Paris: Société de l'histoire de France, 1882), 2, pp. 1–385; translation in G.P. Stringer, "Book 1 of William the Breton's 'Philippide': A Translation," MA thesis (University of New Hampshire, 2010), p. 81.

[165] The Sicambrian roots of the Franks were already acknowledged by Gregory during Clovis's baptism scene. See Gregory of Tours, *Histories* II.31, p. 77: "Mitis depone colla, Sigamber; adora quod incendisti. Incende quod adorasti."

72   Trojans, Sea-monsters, and Long-haired Kings

two battles, they crowned a king whose name was Faramund."[166] Primat's explanation comes just as he abandons Rigord, who did not continue to elaborate past this point. Instead of recounting the deeds of Clodio, Rigord provided an ancestral list, which simply stated: "Faramund begat Clodius, Clodius begat Meroveus, and from this good king the kings of the Franks were called Merovingians ... "[167] Rigord's list worked its way through the sequence of generations, taking a Neustrian trajectory through Childeric I, Clovis I, Chlothar I, Chilperic I, Chlothar II, Dagobert I, and Clovis II. Somewhat unexpectedly, he then went on to name Clovis's three sons by St. Balthild—Chlothar III, Theuderic III, and Childeric II. Why would Rigord make an exception to discuss all three sons of Clovis II, especially when Childeric II was primarily an Austrasian king?[168]

The answer probably lies at the tail end of the list, where we encounter three historically inaccurate kings after Childeric—Dagobert, Theuderic, and Chlothar. Rigord's understanding of later Merovingian history was obviously faulty, since Childeric's son Dagobert is not known to have sired any heirs, nor did he occupy the Frankish throne.[169] Rather, it was with the successors of Childebert III, Childeric II's nephew, that one could find a suitable Dagobert (III), a Theuderic (IV) and possibly also a Chlothar (IV). This confused sequence of kings could have been the result of a simple conflation of Childebert III with Childeric II. A more interesting option is that Rigord faulted the final Merovingians on the list with the degeneration of the Merovingian line, and that by implying that they were Austrasian kings, he was essentially shifting the blame.

Additional surprises lie in store. Historically, Charles Martel was perfectly happy to keep the throne vacant after Theuderic IV's death in 737. His sons, Carloman and Pippin III, found it necessary to appoint another Merovingian, Childeric III, who may have been related either to Theuderic IV or to Chilperic II. No trace of this remains in Rigord. Rather, the *Gesta Philippi* provides two unexpected names as the successors of the last Chlothar: Ansbert and Arnoald. That these two would be considered Merovingian kings is perhaps not as far-fetched as one would imagine, if we assume that, on this point, Rigord was not following the *LHF* but the

---

[166] Viard, ed., *GCh*, ch. V, pp. 20–21: "Jusques ci vous avons recites les oppinions d'aucuns actors, mais pour nous ne volons pas que nuls puisse trover contrarieté en ceste letter, nous prendrons la matiere si comme ele gist es chroniques, qui ensi dient que puis que li François se furent parti de Sicambre et il ourent Alemaigne et Germenie conquise et les Romains desconfit par II batailles, il coronerent un roi qui out non Pharamonz."
[167] Rigord of Saint-Denis, *Gesta Philippi Augusti*, p. 59: "Faramundus genuit Clodium: Clodius genuit Meroveum a quo rege utili reges Francorum Merovingi sunt appellati."
[168] Apart from a brief kingship over Neustro-Burgundy that ended with his murder in 675.
[169] Wood, *The Merovingian Kingdoms*, p. 349.

Gesta episcoporum Mettensium. Though in Paul the Deacon's account Ansbert was Arnoald's uncle (or grandfather, but certainly not father), this is replaced by direct filiation in Rigord's version. Nevertheless, in the *Gesta episcoporum Mettensium* both were members of the Merovingian family, and thus found their way into Rigord's list.

Ansbert and Arnoald also allowed Rigord to introduce Arnulf as both Arnoald's successor and the father of Ansegisel, identified here importantly as bearing two other names: Anschises and Ansedunus, obviously meant to evoke in the reader the memory of Troy.[170] Through Ansegisel, Arnulf becomes the forefather of another family with an ancestral list, the Carolingians. Their lineage is as follows: Pippin II, Charles Martel, Pippin III, Charlemagne, Louis the Pious, and terminating, in a manner befitting a monk of Saint-Denis, with Charles the Bald.[171] Rigord here leaves the question of the relationship between Chlothar and Ansbert unresolved. What remains is a continuous list of royal successions that lead smoothly from the Merovingian to the Carolingian era, without the need to elaborate on the co-existence of kings and mayors or, for that matter, to mention Childeric III, whose reign would have coincided with Pippin III's, described by Rigord solely as *rex*.[172] Rigord does call Pippin II a *maior domus*, but this in no way serves to diminish his stature—quite the contrary, in fact, given his place in the chain of succession. That this all comes as an introduction into the career of Philip Augustus is, of course, doubly significant, given the motif of *reditus regni ad stirpem Karoli Magni*, or the return of kingship to the seed of Charlemagne, as argued so convincingly by Werner and Spiegel.[173]

---

[170] Ansedunum is possibly another name for Cosa, mentioned in Virgil, *Aeneis*, ed. G. Biagio Conte (Berlin and New York: De Gruyter, 2009), x, 168, p. 300: "Massicus aerata princeps secat aequora Tigri: sub quo mille manus iuvenum, qui moenia Clusi quique urbem liquere Cosas, quis tela sagittae gorytique leves umeris et letifer arcus." For this identification, see H. Tamás, L. Van der Sypt, "Asceticism and Syneisaktism in Asterius' *Liber ad Renatum monachum*," *Zeitschrift für antikes Christentum* 17, 3 (2013), pp. 504–525, at pp. 509–512.

[171] For the Charles the Bald's special relationship with Saint-Denis, see J.L. Nelson, *Charles the Bald* (London and New York: Longman, 1996), pp. 4, 15–17, 62–63, 85, 95, 235; J. M. Wallace-Hadrill, *A Carolingian Renaissance Prince: The Emperor Charles the Bald* (London: British Academy, 1980), pp. 164–166. For his tomb, see B. de Montesquiou-Fézensac, "Le tombeau de Charles le Chauve à Saint-Denis," *Bulletin de la Société des Antiquaires de France* (1963), pp. 84–88; Suger, Gesta, in *Suger: Oeuvres*, ed. and trans. F. Gasparri, 2 vols. (Paris: Les Belle Lettres, 2008), 1, pp. 102, 130, 132, 150.

[172] Rigord of Saint-Denis, *Gesta Philippi Augusti*, p. 60: "Deinde regnavit Ansbertus qui genuit Arnoldum, qui sanctum Arnulfum postea Metensem episcopum; qui Anchisen vel Ansegisem vel Ansedunum, qui Pipinum maiorem domus, qui Karolum Martellum, qui Pipinum regem, qui Karolum Magnum imperatorem, qui Ludovicum pium imperatorem, qui Karolum Calvem imperatorem."

[173] K.F. Werner, "Die Legitimität der Kapetinger und die Entstehung der 'reditus regni Francorum ad stirpem Karoli'," *Die Welt als Geschichte* 12 (1952), pp. 203–225; Spiegel,

Rigord left us another composition, until now unedited, the *Courte chronique des rois de France*, or the *Brief Chronicle of the Kings of France*.[174] The work, as its name suggests, is a short chronicle focusing on French kings and royal succession. The *Brief Chronicle* offers a version like the one we encounter in the *Gesta Philippi Augusti*. It nevertheless differs from it in ways that are highly revealing:

> *On Childeric the Fool, king of the Austrasians:*
> *After Theuderic, Dagobert's younger son Childeric the Fool ruled for nine years. Pippin, son of Charles Martel, who was Childeric's mayor of the palace, sent word to Pope Zacharias, asking him whether it was proper that the kings of the Franks had almost no power and contented themselves solely with the royal name. The Roman pontiff responded that the person called king should be he who ruled the kingdom and put its interests before his own. Childeric was therefore tonsured and made a monk. Then, the Franks made Pippin their king. And with this Childeric, the last king of the Austrasian Franks, the royal line of Meroveus became defunct. And this transfer of the generations was accomplished through Blithild, daughter of Chlothar I, father of Sigibert, who was given in marriage to the senator Ansbert, by whom he begat Arnold. Arnold begat Arnulf, later the bishop of Metz. Arnulf begat Anchises who was also known as Ansegisus, Ansegisilus, and Ansedunus. Anchises begat Pippin the Short by his wife Begua. Pippin the Short begat Charles Martel. Charles Martel begat Pippin, the father of Emperor Charlemagne, [...] of Pippin, son of Charles Martel. After Childeric the Fool, the son of Charles Martel ruled with apostolic authority and by election of the Franks. He was anointed by Boniface, archbishop of Mainz, and consecrated king.*[175]

"The *Reditus Regni*," pp. 145–174. See also B. Schneidmüller, "Constructing the Past by Means of the Present: Historiographical Foundations of Medieval Institutions, Dynasties, Peoples, and Communities," in *Medieval Concepts of the Past: Ritual, Memory, Historiography*, eds. G. Althoff, J. Fried, and P.J. Geary (Washington, DC: German Historical Institute and Cambridge: Cambridge University Press, 2002), pp. 167–206, at pp. 168–175.

[174] On this, and the rest of Rigord's work, see Delaborde, "Notice sur les ouvrages," pp. 599–605. The composition was written before 1196, following a commission by John, the prior of Saint-Denis. See R. Reich, "Rigord," *Encyclopedia of the Medieval Chronicle*, 2 vols., ed. G. Dunphy (Leiden and Boston: Brill, 2010), vol. 2, pp. 1278–1279.

[175] *Brief Chronicle of the Kings of France*, ch. 53, in A.J. Stoclet, "À la recherche du ban perdu. Le trésor et les dépouilles de Waïfre, duc d'Aquitaine († 768), d'après Adémar de Chabannes, Rigord et quelques autres," *Cahiers de civilisation médiévale* 168 (1999), pp. 343–382, at pp. 353–354: "De Hilderico insensato rege Austrasiorum. Post Theudericum filium Dagoberti iunioris regem austrasiorum regnavit hildericus insensatus annis novem. Pippinus vero filius karoli martelli maior domus hilderici nuntios ad zachariam papam mittit interrgans eum si ita manere deberent reges francorum cum pene nullius potestatis essent, solo regie nomine contenti. Romanus pontifex illum debere vocari regem respondit qui rem publicam regeret et sue utilitati private publicam anteferret. detonso igitur hilderico et monaco facto. mox franci pippinum sibi regem statuunt. Et in isto hilderico rege austrasiorum francorum ultimo defecit genus regale merovei. Et huius generationis translatio facta est per blithildem filiam primi lotharii patris sigiberti qua data fuit in uxorem ansberto senatori ex qua genuit arnoldum. Arnoldus genuit arnulfum post metensem episcopum. Arnulfus genuit anchisem qui quandoque dictus fuit ansegisum vel ansegisilus vel ansedunus. Anchises genuit

With all its obvious faults, the chronology Rigord presents in the *Brief Chronicle* is much more in line with historical reality than the version in the *Gesta*. For one, he does not neglect to mention the kingship of Childeric III, whom he dubbed *insensatus*, "a fool." While the influence of Paul the Deacon is palpable, so is that of other Carolingian authors, most notably Einhard and the author of the *ARF* (*Annales Regni Francorum*).[176] Rigord's own understanding of the transfer of royal power nevertheless shines through, especially in his decision to edit out the royal vacancy of 737–743, portraying instead the succession as an uninterrupted process.

But, as Rigord makes clear, the actual dynastic transfer, the *translatio generationis*, occurred much earlier than that, during the time of Blithild, daughter of Chlothar I and sister of Sigibert I. Blithild fills a narrative role, but she was not an actual historical princess. She is a natural evolution of the daughter of Clovis from the *GeM*, only now she has a name and a slightly adjusted place in the Merovingian family tree. Casting her as sister to Sigibert I would have made sense, chronologically speaking, since she had an adult grandson at court in the 620s. Blithild, and Pippin's alleged claim to Merovingian ancestry through her, was an enduring myth; she even makes a surprise appearance in William Shakespeare's *Henry V*, where she is used to justify claims to inheritance based on the Salic Law.[177] As mentioned previously, she came into being as part of an extension of Paul the Deacon's genealogy in the *GeM*, but in her adjusted form she debuted in a text composed in the late eighth century at Metz and titled *Commemoratio de genealogia domni Arnulfi episcopi et confessoris*

pipinum brevem ex begua uxore sua. Pipinus brevis genuit karolum martellum. Karolus martellus genuit pipinum, patrem karoli magni imperatoris [...] de pipino filio karoli martelli. Post hildericum insensatum regnavit filius karoli martelli qui auctoritate apostolica et francorum electione a sancto bonefatio maguntivo archiepiscopo inungitur in regem consecratur."

[176] Compare *Annales Regni Francorum*, MGH SRG 6, ed. F. Kurze (Hanover: Hahnsche Buchhandlung, 1895), s.a. 750. See also R. Broome, "Pagans, Rebels and Merovingians: Otherness in the Early Carolingian World," in *The Resources of the Past in the Early Medieval World*, eds. C. Gantner, R. McKitterick, and S. Meeder (Cambridge: Cambridge University Press, 2015), pp. 155–171, at p. 167.

[177] W. Shakespeare, *Henry V*, in The *New Oxford Shakespeare: The Complete Works. Modern Critical Edition*, ed. G. Taylor et al. (Oxford: Oxford University Press, 2016), pp. 1529–1606, at p. 1538, act 1, scene 2, lines 97–91: "Besides, their writers say, King Pepin, which deposèd Childeric, did, as heir general, being descended of Blithild, which was daughter to King Clothair, make claim and title to the crown of France." The Blithild myth is likewise repeated in Paolo Emilio's *De rebus gestis Francorum*, p. 23. For Emilio and the *DRG*, see discussion in Chapter 2.

Christi.[178] We should, as Oexle pointed out, see her appearance in the context of the episcopal vacancy of Metz after the death of Angilram.[179] Restricting the kingship of the final Merovingians to Austrasia was likely meant to contextualize the ascent of the Pippinids, who were, after all, an Austrasian family. Rigord's intentions with this particular framing of the ancestral line can be traced to certain hints that he embeds in the text. Nonetheless, one might argue for alternative readings, given his insistence on the Neustrian line in the *Gesta* and the associated decision to lay the blame of the dynasty's decline at the feet of Austrasian kings. By using the genealogy of the *Commemoratio de genealogia domni Arnulfi*, Rigord might be insinuating that the progeny of the senator Ansbert and Blithild, daughter of Chlothar I, were the true heirs of the Austrasian line. It is perhaps in this context that we should understand the mention of the Austrasian king, Sigibert I. Yet it is also possible to read the text differently, as implying that the royal line of the Merovingians remained incorrupt until Blithild, who then transferred it intact to her Carolingian progeny. Regardless of which reading we adopt, Rigord insists on the Austrasian limits of early eighth-century royal power, disassociating the kingship of his day from the degeneration of the final Merovingians. It is worth recalling, at this point, his decision to marginalize the Austrasian *duces* and focus instead on Marcomir and his Gallic exploits.

---

[178] *Commemoratio genealogiae domni Karoli gloriosissimi imperatoris*, MGH SS 13, ed. G. Waitz (Hanover: Hahnsche Buchhandlung, 1881), ch. 2, p. 245: "Anspertus, qui fuit ex genere senatorum, praeclarus vir atque nobilis, in multis divitiis pollens, accepit filiam Hlotharii regis Francorum ad coniugem nomine Blîthilt et habuit ex ea filios tres et filiam unam. Primogenitus ipsius Arnoldus nominatus est, secundus Feriolus, tertius Modericus, et filia ipsius Tarsicia. [...] Arnoldus, primogenitus ipsius, genuit domnum Arnulfum [episcopum]. Domnus Arnulfus genuit Flodolfum et Anschisum. Flodolfus divina annuente gratia episcopus ordinatus est. Anschisus genuit Pipinum. Pipinus genuit Karolum. Karolus vero domnum regem Pipinum. Domnus Pipinus genuit Caesar gloriosum ac principem nobilissimum Karolum." Two other endings to the paragraph are extant in recensions B, D. See H. Reimitz, "Die Konkurrenz der Ursprünge in der fränkischen Historiographie," in *Die Suche nach den Ursprüngen. Von den Bedeutung des frühen Mittelalters*, ed. W. Pohl (Vienna: Verlag der Österreichischen Akademie der Wissenschaften, 2004), pp. 191–209, pp. 206–207; W. Pohl, "Genealogy: A Comparative Perspective from the Early Medieval West," in *Meanings of Community across Medieval Eurasia: Comparative Approaches*, eds. E. Hovden, C. Lutter, and W. Pohl (Leiden and Boston: Brill, 2016), pp. 232–269, at pp. 246–247. See also I. Wood, "Genealogy Defined by Women: The Case of the Pippinids," in *Gender in the Early Medieval World: East and West, 300–900*, eds. L. Brubaker and J.M.H. Smith (Cambridge: Cambridge University Press, 2004), pp. 235–256, at pp. 234–235.

[179] O.G. Oexle, "Die Karolinger und die Stadt des heiligen Arnulf," *Frühmittelalterliche Studien* 1, 1 (1967), pp. 250–364, at pp. 255–262.

Primat was apparently not satisfied with Rigord's terse remarks, and, for the earlier phases of the Merovingians' genealogy at least, relied mainly on Aimoin. Take, for example, the thorny issue of Merovech's paternity. As noted by Lake, Aimoin essentially decoupled Merovech from Clodio's Trojan ancestry.[180] Lake rightly argues that Aimoin's general adherence to the Trojan plot made him indispensable for Primat and the later editors and continuators of the *Grandes Chroniques*. His view that Aimoin and the *Fredegar* chronicler pull in opposite directions is less accurate. *Fredegar*'s treatment of Clodio and Merovech indicates that the chronicler had his doubts about the connection between the original Trojan émigrés to Pannonia and their Merovingian successors. Among the Merovingian-era chronicles, it is not *Fredegar*, but the *LHF* that comes closest to depicting a seamless link. Certainly, any ambiguity is eliminated in Rigord's *Gesta Philippi Augusti*, which laconically states *Clodius genuit Meroveum*, a sentiment followed obediently by William.[181]

Despite the *Roman des rois*'s strong royalist bent and clear acquaintance with Rigord and William, it embraces Aimoin's more cautious phrasing. In fact, it seems to go even further than its source in claiming that: "After Clodio had reigned for twenty years, he passed away. After him reigned Merovech. This Merovech was not his son but was from his lineage (*lignage*). From him issued the first generation of the kings of France; it persisted without fail from heir to heir until the generation of Pippin II, father of Charlemagne the Great."[182] Of course, how we read Primat on this point depends on our reading of *lignage* as either a claim of ancestry or more generally of kinship, much like the *LHF*'s *de genere eius*. It is closer to the *LHF* than it is to Aimoin's *eius affinis*, but still stops short of Rigord's decisive presentation. Viard has alerted us to the fact that the commentary on the Merovingian and Carolingian dynasties was a new addition, but this tells us only that Merovech was important as the eponymous ancestor of the royal line, not that he was Clodio's relation.

Clodio is anomalous in the *Roman des rois* in other respects, too. Primat uses the king's desire to "enlarge the honors of his kingdom" as a segue to a lengthy discussion of Gaul and its provinces, based largely on Aimoin's

---

[180] Lake, "Aimoin of Fleury's *Gesta Francorum*," p. 503.
[181] William the Breton, *Philippide* 1.171, p. 14: "at ille / Regia decendens Meroveo sceptra reliquit, / Patris jure sibi faciens succedere natum." In ms V, this sentence is preceded by "Clodius ipsius successit filius."
[182] Viard, ed., *GCh*, ch. IV, p. 26: "Quant li rois Clodio out regné XX ans, il paia le treü de nature. Après lui regna Merovées. Cil Merovées ne fu pas ses fiuz, mais il fu de son lignage. De cetui eissi la premiere generation des rois de France; si dura sans faillir d'oir en hoir jusques à la generation Pepin le secont, la pere le grant Challemaine." That Pippin III is known here as Pippin II is perhaps an indication that, like Rigord, Primat considered Arnulf, not Pippin I, as the Carolingian *paterfamilias*.

treatment in his *proemium*.[183] Aimoin's clear division between the institutions, religion, and geography of the Gallic past and the more recent Frankish episodes would have been out of place in the *Roman des rois*. Since Primat was not willing to jettison Aimoin's Gallic material entirely, he embedded it in the story of Clodio, a king for whose expansionistic designs he had solid evidence. It seems, then, that Primat regarded the *Gesta Francorum* as a more reliable source than the *Gesta Philippi Augusti*. He follows Aimoin even on this uncomfortable point, modifying only minimally the source's phrasing.

The question of Merovech's kingship is entirely subsumed within Aimoin's treatment of the Hunnic incursions of Gaul, and here Primat follows his source diligently. The miraculous deliverance of Orléans from the armies of Attila, present in both the *Gesta Francorum* and the *Roman des rois*, is a simplified version of the story told in Gregory of Tours's *Histories* II.7. In Gregory's account, Bishop Anianus instructed the terrified inhabitants of Orléans to make three visits to the city walls to seek signs of divine assistance, which eventually materialized with Aëtius and his Visigothic federates. The story was cut down in size by the author of the *LHF*, and from there it made its way to the *Gesta Francorum*.[184] Gregory did not tell the story in conjunction with the kingship of Merovech, but since it matched the chronology of his reign, it was inserted there by the *LHF* author, and continued to occupy this spot in the storyline thereafter.

Coverage of Childeric in the *Roman des rois* essentially echoes what we find in the *Gesta Francorum*. Aimoin drew on the *LHF* but also on *Fredegar* for thematic structure, dramatic elements, and dialogue. Wiomad (Winomad in the *Historia Francorum*, Guinemenz in the *Roman des rois*) is the main protagonist in both Aimoin's and Primat's accounts, but the focus of the story shifts in the *Roman des rois* to the attitude of the Frankish nobility—*les barons*—toward their rightful ruler, their foreign oppressor, and, more generally, the genealogical aspects of kingship. Childeric's *luxure* (lechery), and exile with Bissinus in Thuringia is dispensed with in two sentences. What follows is a flashback scene in which Wiomad counsels the king on the eve of his departure for exile. The barons, here, are driven by passion, their judgement clouded by anger, *l'ire des barons*. Remaining amidst the enraged Franks, Wiomad warns the king, would end in envy and hatred; departing would sway the heart toward

---

[183] Viard, ed., *GCh*, pp. 21–22: "Li rois Clodio, qui moult desiroit à eslargir les bonnes de son roiaume, envoia ses espies outre le Rin pour savoir quel defense li païs avoit," taken from Aimoin's "Rex autem Clodio angustos regni fines dilatare cupiens, exploratores a Disbargo trans Rhenum dirigit . . . ." For Aimoin's discussion of Gallic geography, see *Gesta Francorum*, proemia cap. IV, cols. 632–634 (*De Gallia secundum Caesarem*).
[184] *LHF*, ch. 5.

compassion.[185] After Childeric left for Thuringia, the barons, who did not wish to remain without a master, invited Giles/Gilon (Aegidius) to become their king. Primat follows Aimoin in condemning this choice, noting that "they did not remember the injuries and burdens that were done to them by Rome and by that same Gilon."[186]

Wiomad, being both wise and full of guile, befriended the new king and gained his confidence. Aegidius's escalating oppression of the Franks was another motif that Primat took from Aimoin, himself paraphrasing *Fredegar*. While *Fredegar* suggested that Wiomad, on orders of his master, condemned to death 100 *inutiles et in necessitatibus incongruos*, Aimoin's Winomad selected only those who were most vocally opposed to Childeric as a way of eroding the opposition's powerbase.[187] Primat further expands this structure, placing into Guinemenz's mouth the words: "You [i.e., Gilon] will not be able to crush the treachery nor the pride of the Franks, if you do not destroy some of their most noble and most powerful; in this way you will be able to easily bend the others to your will."[188] Gilon agrees, and Guinemenz, who is charged with carrying out the plan, selects those nobles who are Childeric's staunchest rivals. Ironically, those same nobles who are the most hostile to Childeric are tried before Gilon after having been charged with conspiracy and intent to harm the king.[189] Appalled by Gilon's cruelty, the other nobles confide in Guinemenz, who proceeds to rebuke them:

What madness came over you when you threw out of his realm your rightful lord, born of your people, and submitted to a proud person from a foreign nation? [...] You have despised and chased away your king, born and created by you yourselves, who was of good ancestry by nature and could yet be more beneficial and profitable to the realm if he were to give up the wantonness of his flesh, which he did not always control.[190]

---

[185] Viard, ed., *GCh* ch. 7, pp. 28–29: "Cil li loa que il donast lieu à l'ire des barons, car se il demoroit, il acroistroit plus leur malivolence que il ne l'apeticeroit, et la nature humaine si est tele que il portent envie et haine à celui que il voient en present, et quant il ne le voient noient, aucune foiz avient que il en ont compassion."

[186] Viard, ed., *GCh* ch. 7, p. 29: "Pas n'estoient remembrable des injures et des griés que il avoient fet à ciaus de Rome et à celi Gilon meismes."

[187] On the *inutilitas*, particularly of Childeric III, and its interplay with elite power, see E. Peters, *Shadow King: Rex Inutilis in Medieval Law and Literature, 751–1327* (New Haven, CT: Yale University Press, 1970), esp. pp. 40–44.

[188] Viard, ed., *GCh* ch. 8, p. 30: "Tu ne porras brisier la felonie ne l'orguel des François, se tu ne destruiz aucuns des plus nobles et des plus puissanz; par ce porras les autres legierement flechir à ta volenté."

[189] Viard, ed., *GCh* ch. 8, p. 31: "Guinemenz, [...], comença à ciaus qui avoient esté plus contraire au roi Childeric; de crime les reta et les prist, puis les envoia au roi Gilon pour fere joustice."

[190] Ibid.: "Quel forsenerie vous demenoit quant vous getastes fors de son regne vostre droit seigneur né de vostre gent, et vous souzmeistes à un orgueilleus d'alien nation. [...] Vous avez despit et chacié vostre roi, né et crié de vous meismes, qui estoit debonaires par nature et peust encor estre plus debonaires et profitable au roiaume s'il eust lessié la joliveté de son cors, que il ne maintenist pas touz jors."

The barons see the light and decide to orchestrate Childeric's return: "We greatly repent the indignity and the humiliations we have done to our rightful king, and, if we knew now where we could find him, we would send him messages and humbly beg him to agree to return to his realm."[191] Long story short: the golden half-*besant* is sent; Childeric is summoned, successfully engages Gilon in battle, and wins back his kingdom.

In the *Roman des rois*, the particulars of the Childeric story are not new. His exile, the atrocities of Aegidius's reign, and the dynamics between Wiomad and the leading Franks are all there, with a similar logic and narrative trajectory. But the subtle reframing of the details leaves one wondering whether this account can be taken as a commentary on more recent events. Childeric's liberties, his exile, and his relationship with the nobility were all potential *exempla* from which contemporary lessons might be drawn. Rebellious barons, a recurrent theme in the political narratives of Primat's day, are one such *exemplum*. To the readers of the *Roman des rois*, the scene presented here would have called to mind similar themes addressed in the *Song of Roland*, or, more concretely, the consequences of aristocratic rage epitomized in the murders of Thomas Becket and Charles the Good.[192] Nor was baronial recalcitrance and rebelliousness a foreign concept in the political world of Primat's royal patrons, Louis IX and Philip III. In fact, it was a problem that dogged the kingship of Philip Augustus, Louis's grandfather, whose struggles with the English over their continental holdings had made open enemies of many of his disgruntled barons. The expansion of Capetian power to the south from the 1220s resulted in mass expropriations of landed wealth from southern lords. In the 1240s, rebellions broke out, which soon spiraled into an attempt, backed by the English, to dislodge the Capetians. While Louis prevailed, the specter of future disturbance remained.[193]

---

[191] Viard, ed., *GCh* ch. 9, p. 32: "Nous nous repentons moult de la honte et des vilenies que nous avons fetes à nostre propre roi, et se nous saviens là où l'en le poust trover, nous envoissens à lui messages et li priissons humblement que il retornast à son regne."

[192] L. Sunderland, *Rebel Barons: Resisting Royal Power in Medieval Culture* (Oxford: Oxford University Press, 2016), esp. pp. 42–52; J. Deploige, "Political Assassination and Sanctification: Transforming Discursive Customs after the Murder of the Flemish Count Charles the Good (1127)," in *Mystifying the Monarch: Studies on Discourse, Power, and History*, eds. J. Deploige and G. Deneckere (Amsterdam: Amsterdam University Press, 2006), pp. 35–54; F. Barlow, *Thomas Becket* (Berkeley, CA: University of California Press, 1986), pp. 225–250; S. Gaunt and K. Pratt, "Introduction," in *The Song of Roland and Other Poems of Charlemagne*, ed. and trans. S. Gaunt and K. Pratt (Oxford: Oxford University Press, 2016), pp. xvi–xvii. On *Pseudo-Turpin* as a source for the *Chronique des rois de France*, see Buridant, "Connecteurs et articulations," p. 77.

[193] See W.C. Jordan, *Louis IX and the Challenge of Crusade: A Study in Rulership* (Princeton NJ: Princeton University Press, 1979), esp. pp. 14–34 and idem, *Men at the Center:*

Louis's barons could certainly be troublesome, and nowhere could this penchant for rebellion have been more devastating than when the king was away on crusade.[194] Well aware of the dangers his journey to Outremer could pose to his rule, Louis cajoled many of his nobles into joining him in his journey to the Holy Land. Count Raymond Berenger of Provence, whose dynastic ambitions were a constant concern for Louis, was a particularly worrisome nobleman. Had his plans come to fruition, they would have severely weakened the king's foothold in the south. Raymond wed his four daughters to leading figures in England and France. Margaret married Louis and Eleanor married Henry III, the king of England. Royal siblings were also part of this matrimonial mix. A third sister, Sanchia, was married off to Richard, Henry's brother.

Richard is an interesting figure whose career took many twists and turns. He was gifted Cornwall by his brother, making him a fortune he partly spent during the crusades when he rebuilt the fortifications of Ascalon.[195] But his more worrying claim, as far as the Capetians were concerned, was to Poitou, with whose governance Louis had charged his own brother, Alphonse. Louis eventually defused this challenge by arranging for Raymond Berenger's fourth daughter, Beatrice, to marry his brother, Charles I of Anjou. After briefly considering purchasing the kingship of Sicily, Richard ended up crowned at Aachen in 1257 as King of the Romans (*Romanorum rex*), a title whose first bearer was none other than Syagrius, thus styled in Gregory's *Histories*.[196] Naturally, in Primat, it is Gilon, father of Siagre, who first bears the title.

Richard would not have been a well-liked person in Dionysian circles, especially since he was responsible for the alienation of property owned by Saint-Denis in Deerhurst on the River Severn and the dispersal of the monks residing there.[197] His plans for transforming the Deerhurst estate into a castle eventually came to naught, although the disruption to the

---

Redemptive Governance Under Louis IX, Natalie Zemon Davis Annual Lectures, vol. 6 (Budapest and New York: Central European University Press, 2012).

[194] On Louis's nobility and Crusade, see X. Hélary, "French Nobility and the Military Requirements of the King (c. 1260–c. 1314)," in *The Capetian Century, 1214–1314*, eds. W.C. Jordan and J.R. Phillips (Turnhout: Brepols, 2017), pp. 115–142.

[195] D. Pringle, "King Richard I and the Walls of Ascalon," *Palestine Exploration Quarterly* 116.2 (1984), pp. 133–147.

[196] Gregory of Tours, *Histories* II. 27, p. 71: "Anno autem quinto regni eius (i.e., Chlodovechi) Siacrius Romanorum rex, Egidii filius, apud civitatem Sexonas, quam quondam supra memoratus Egidius tenuerat, sedem habebat." On Richard of Cornwall's German kingship, see B. Weiler, "Image and Reality in Richard of Cornwall's German Career," *English Historical Review* 113, 454 (1998), pp. 1111–1142.

[197] W.C. Jordan, *A Tale of Two Monasteries: Westminster and Saint-Denis in the Thirteenth Century* (Princeton, NJ, and Oxford: Princeton University Press, 2009), p. 30; G. Sivéry, *Philippe III le Hardi* (Paris: Fayard, 2003), p. 41.

dependencies of Saint-Denis was an obstacle on the path to a much-desired rapprochement between the English and French courts. While the affair was eventually resolved thanks to King Henry III's direct mediation, it caused Matthew of Vendôme much consternation.

Let us return for a moment to the question of royal absence. Baronial loyalty must have weighed heavily on Louis's mind, and likely on Primat's as well. Louis's time as a prisoner of the Egyptians following the Battle of al-Mansura in 1250 can even be considered an exile of sorts, although securing the king's return was, in this case, much costlier than half a *besant*—the symbolic value of which was obvious to a royal readership: Louis IX, accompanied by his son Philip, would frequent the monastery once a year to offer four *besants d'or* to the protector of the Capetian dynasty.[198] Royal patronage became an important facet of Saint-Denis's self-image. Not only was Louis's devotion to the saint a well-known and much-lauded motif in Dionysian historiography,[199] his institutional links to the monastic leadership were a cornerstone of his policy, culminating in the appointment of Matthew of Vendôme as regent in his absence during the ill-fated Seventh Crusade in 1270.[200] If Louis is to be the Childeric of this story, perhaps Matthew is its Wiomad/Guinemenz.

1.5 Conclusions

In this chapter, I have argued that the nucleus of most of the material presented in the chronicles surveyed can be traced to the *Histories* of Gregory of Tours and to interpolated material in the *Fredegar Chronicle* and the *LHF*. Coverage of the Trojan origins and the histories of the earliest Frankish kings was substantially augmented and recontextualized in later compositions, such as Aimoin of Fleury's *Gesta Francorum*, Rigord's (and William the Breton's) *Gesta Philippi Augusti*, and Primat's *Roman des rois*. Already contained in the nucleus narrative of the Merovingian-era historiographies are all of the themes that would later be developed in Aimoin, Rigord, William, and Primat. It would nevertheless be incorrect to view the evolution of the story as straightforwardly linear. Even when we feel confi-

---

[198] Jordan, *A Tale of Two Monasteries*, p. 30; G. Sivéry, *Philippe III le Hardi*, p. 41. For remarks about the history of this practice, see E.A.R. Brown, "Saint-Denis and the Turpin Legend," in *The* Codex Callixtinus *and the Shrine of St. James*, eds. J. Williams and A. Stones (Tübingen: Gunter Narr Verlag, 1992), pp. 51–88, at p. 62.
[199] Gaposchkin, *The Making of Saint Louis*, p. 148ff.
[200] As indeed his predecessor Suger had done for Louis VII. See A.D. Hedeman, *The Royal Image: Illustrations of the* Grandes Chroniques de France, *1274–1422* (Berkeley, CA: University of California Press, 1991), p. 10; F. Olivier-Martin, *Étude sur les régences: I. Les régences et le majorité des rois sous les Capétiens directs et les premiers Valois (1060–1375)* (Paris, 1931), pp. 94–108.

dent about the narrative aims of the authors in question, their authorial choices defy easy contextualization. Often, the power of conservatism seems equally decisive, pushing chroniclers to preserve, albeit in a modified form, material which does not coincide with our understanding of their overarching agendas.

Royal history was not meant to be read simply as a diversion. There would have been no point in delving into Merovingian history if the exercise brought no benefit to the reader, royal or otherwise. It is crucial to consider how contemporaneous audiences would have interpreted these texts. The Trojans, the *duces*, and the earliest Merovingians were thematic packages that, when applied correctly, could stand in for characters and circumstances of the present or the near past, and could offer a productive way of thinking about the future. While the analogies are never absolute, the universality and applicability of the lessons conveyed in these stories were intentional, and it is in this light that we must consider them.

2 *Capud victuriarum vestrarum Chlodovechus*[*]

Clovis occupies a special place in Frankish and French historiography. In Basina's prophetic vision, Clovis alone is the lion; his descendants are grouped collectively into creaturely categories of gradually decreasing prestige. When the *Fredegar* chronicler was writing, six generations after Clovis, the king was already established as the brightest jewel in the Merovingian crown. Of course, *Fredegar* and the *LHF* drew heavily on Gregory's *Histories*, in which the first Christian king played a pivotal role. While the two chronicles kept much of what they found in Gregory, they also incorporated additional material and reframed what was already there. Through subtle interpolation and omission, they ultimately produced a character with a new set of attributes and priorities.

One would be hard-pressed to depict the contours of a "Carolingian Clovis." Clovis is almost entirely absent from Carolingian historiography, if not from Carolingian hagiography, whose protagonists often flourished in the Merovingian period.[1] Frechulf of Lisieux, whose *Histories* are the first Carolingian work of historiography to attempt a new account of the relevant period, gives little attention to the Merovingians, and even less to Clovis.[2]

---

[*] Gregory of Tours, *Histories* v.praef., p. 193: "Recordamini, quid capud victuriarum vestrarum Chlodovechus fecerit, qui adversos reges interficet, noxias gentes elisit, patrias subiugavit, quarum regnum vobis integrum inlesumque reliquit!"

[1] He was famously mentioned in Hincmar's *Vita sancti Remigii*. See Hincmar of Reims, *Vita sancti Remigii archiepiscopi Remensis*, MGH SRM 3, ed. B. Krusch (Hanover: Hahnsche Buchhandlung, 1896), pp. 250–341. On this composition, see M.-C. Isaïa, "The Bishop and the Law, According to Hincmar's *Life of Saint Remigius*," in *Hincmar: Life and Works*, eds. R. Stone and C. West (Manchester: Manchester University Press, 2015), pp. 170–189. And in Hucbald of Saint-Amand's *Vita sanctae Rictrudis*, PL 132, ed. J.-P. Migne (Paris, 1853), cols. 829–848, at cols. 829–832, which, incidentally, also mentions the Trojan origin story and Arnulf of Metz. On this work, see J.M.H. Smith, "The Hagiography of Hucbald of St-Amand," *Studi Medievali* 35 (1994), pp. 517–542, esp. pp. 535–538. More generally, see A.K. Bosworth, "Learning from the Saints: Ninth-Century Hagiography and the Carolingian Renaissance", *History Compass* 8/9 (2010), pp. 1055–1066, url: https://onlineli brary.wiley.com/doi/epdf/10.1111/j.1478-0542.2010.00714.x?saml_referrer [accessed December 16, 2020].

[2] Frechulf of Lisieux discusses Clovis in the context of Theoderic's matrimonial policies but provides no additional information apart from citing his source, Jordanes. See Frechulf of

Still, Clovis was not uninteresting to Carolingian readers of history, who encountered him in the *LHF* and the *Historia vel gesta Francorum*. The narrative cores that formed these compositions may have been assembled during the Merovingian period, but to Carolingian readers they were part of a carefully curated body of texts that differed in aim and scope from the original works.[3] Placed in a narrative sequence that concluded with the rise of the Carolingians, Clovis was understood as part of a historical arc with an inevitable result. The fact remains, however, that he was not completely re-imagined as part of a broad Carolingian historiographical *réécriture*.

Clovis nevertheless made a forceful reappearance in post-Carolingian historiography. Aimoin's return to the Merovingians attests to an emerging historical understanding that could conceive of the Merovingian and Carolingian periods as discrete—and more importantly, bygone—stages of Frankish history. Balanced depictions of the Merovingians were no longer read as a challenge to royal authority, a development that opened seventh- and eighth-century chronicles to new interpretations. Of course, using and reframing Merovingian-era works was not a new practice; the final ten chapters of the *LHF* were imported into the *Historia vel Gesta* to supplement *Fredegar*. In his *Gesta Francorum*, Aimoin magnified Clovis's character considerably, with the result being quite different from the Clovis of *Fredegar* or the *LHF*, his two main sources for the subject at hand. Later, this perspective was enthusiastically adopted by Primat and his successors, who made much more of the alleged ancestral links between the early Pippinids and the Merovingians than Carolingian chroniclers ever had reason to. As we saw in the previous chapter, this was done in the service of an ideological program that promoted the notion of *reditus regni ad stirpem Karoli Magni*, an idea that built on the rehabilitation of the Merovingians in Aimoin.

As the generations passed and the sediment of detail accumulated, the treatment of Clovis came to reflect an evolving set of expectations that authors and readers, royal ones first and foremost, had of the office of

---

Lisieux, *Histories*, ed. M.I. Allen, CCSL 169A (Turnhout: Brepols, 2002), II.5.18, p. 710: "His ita prospere gestis gentem Francorum cupiens foederatam habere, missa legatione ad Lodouuic regem eorum filiam eius petens, impetratamque matrimonio suo copulauit, ut Iordanis historicus refert." The next we hear of the Merovingians is in the context of Chlodomer's invasion of the Burgundian kingdom and his death. See Frechulf of Lisieux, *Histories* II.5.20, p. 713: "Post cuius necem Chlodomeris rex Francorum contra Burgundiones dimicans, ut fuerunt, in proelio occiditur."

[3] Later sections of the *LHF* were reworked into Carolingian compilations in a way that emphasized Carolingian narrative aims. See *Annales Mettenses Priores*, MGH SRG 10, ed. B. von Simson (Hanover: Hahnsche Buchhandlung, 1905), s.a. 688–692; Broome, "Pagans, Rebels, and Merovingians," p. 170. For a detailed discussion of Frechulf's treatment of the Merovingians, see pp. 129–140, Chapter 3.

kingship.⁴ Clovis was not only the stuff of chronicles; his exploits were the subject of theatrical performances, artworks, and even saintly cult.⁵ It was the historiographical structuring of Clovis, however, that remained decisive for the development of his image in the Middle Ages. In 1484, Charles VI's entry into Reims was accompanied by a theatrical reenactment of Clovis receiving the holy balm of anointment.⁶ While initially a tradition restricted to the church of Reims, from the time of Louis IX it began to make its way into coronation ceremonies.⁷ Charles's coronation included another dramatization, this time of Faramund receiving the *Lex Salica* from four wise men —a connection first made by the *LHF*—so one would be correct in assuming that these symbols of royal authority were influenced by hagiography and historiography. In other words, the Clovis of royal ideology was very much a product of the Clovis of chronicle.⁸

As Colette Beaune has shown, the crystallization of the Clovis story was a selective process that amplified certain aspects of the king's "historical" career and drastically pruned others. Saint-Denis safeguarded the image of Clovis by presenting a canonical version of his life, but that does not mean that competing voices from outside its orbit were entirely stifled.⁹ The monastery responded to attempts to appropriate Clovis-related traditions with its own emendations. The monks argued, for instance, that the hermit of Jovenal who gave Clovis his lily shield was in fact Dionysius, a claim that had not really caught on in the popular imagination. Nevertheless, efforts by Dionysian historiography to control the narrative of Clovis prove its salience as a living tradition. Since the monks of Saint-Denis saw themselves as the guardians of this collective memory, they could not stray far from the agreed-upon narrative. Yet even other centers of composition that attempted to benefit from association with the king acquiesced to the power of narrative consensus, which was determined, in no small measure, by the storyline found in the *Grandes Chroniques*.

---

⁴ C. Beaune, *The Birth of an Ideology: Myths and Symbols of Nation in Late-Medieval France*, ed. F.L. Cheyette (Berkeley CA: University of California Press, 1991), p. 70.
⁵ See S. Olivier, "Clovis beyond Clovis: Individuality, Filiation, and Miraculous Intervention in the *Miracle de Clovis*," *European Medieval Drama* 22 (2018), pp. 127–148.
⁶ C. Taylor, "The Salic Law and the Valois Succession to the French Crown," *French History* 15, 4 (2001), pp. 358–377.
⁷ R.A. Jackson, *Vive le roi! A History of the French Coronation from Charles V to Charles X* (Chapel Hill, NC, and London: University of North Carolina Press, 1984), pp. 31–32.
⁸ The story's basic components were assiduously adhered to until the French Revolution. Jackson, *Vive le roi!*, pp. 177–178.
⁹ An additional layer of legend was incorporated into several late-medieval compositions, reflecting primarily local perspectives of proprietary or cultic nature. On this, see Beaune, *The Birth of an Ideology*, pp. 70–89.

This was not the end of Clovis's development as a character. The treatment he received at the hands of humanist historians is especially illuminating, not only because it sought to reimagine a Clovis whose virtues reflected their own worldview; that was true of every chronicle that dealt with this kind of material, humanist or otherwise. Rather, it is instructive because of the methodology that undergirded this new history. Humanist historians such as Flavio Biondo, Paolo Emilio, and many of their *cinquecento* successors rejected much of the material contained in the accumulated historiographical traditions of preceding centuries, preferring instead a more critical approach to the source material. At least in Emilio's case, the end-product was a body of historical writing that was much more dependent on Gregory of Tours and other sixth-century sources than it was on the medieval adaptations of Aimoin.[10] In this new approach, the miraculous and providential rationalizations so common to late-medieval compositions were downplayed to make room for the military and political explanations that interested humanist thinkers and satisfied their readership.

The discussion of Clovis in this chapter will begin with the emergence of a recognizable Clovis story in Gregory of Tours' *Histories*. Given the direct lines of influence between Gregory and early humanistic historiography produced in France, my investigation will then turn to Paolo Emilio's *De rebus gestis*, whose depiction of Merovingian history was complete by 1516.[11] Leapfrogging Carolingian and post-Carolingian historiography might appear unexpected. Certainly, there is much to be said about the development of the Clovis story from *Fredegar* to fourteenth-century chronicles.[12] For the purposes of the present discussion, however, I am primarily interested in the narrative links between Gregory and Emilio, and especially the ways in which the latter's decision to bypass the circuitous route through which medieval chroniclers arrived at their version of Clovis, resulted in a fresh treatment of a familiar character.

---

[10] Emilio used the *Grandes Chroniques* and other late medieval chronicles, but their effect on the depiction of Clovis was limited, as will be discussed, pp. 111–112, 119.

[11] For a discussion of Clovis in other humanist and Jewish historiographical compositions, see Y. Fox, "Chronicling the Merovingians in Hebrew: The Early Medieval Chapters of Yosef Ha-Kohen's *Divrei Hayamim*," Traditio 74 (2019), pp. 1–25.

[12] See, for instance, B. Guenée, "Primat, le fort roi Clovis et le bon roi Gontran," *Romania* 126 (2008), pp. 18–39; C. Carozzi and H. Taviani-Carozzi, "Clovis, de Grégoire de Tours aux Grandes Chroniques de France: Naissance d'un mémoire ambiguë," in *Faire mémoire: Souvenir et commémoration au Moyen Âge*, eds. C. Carozzi and H. Taviani-Carozzi (Aix-en-Provence: Publications de l'Université de Provence, 1999), pp. 41–61.

2.1 *Adora quod incendisti*: Gregory of Tours

Our earliest sources for Clovis predate the *Histories*: There is contemporary fifth- and sixth-century evidence, primarily of an epistolary nature.[13] The *Histories*, concluded some eighty years after Clovis's death, were the first to narrativize the king's life.[14] The passage of time gave Gregory ample perspective and enabled him to present the story of Clovis as a coherent plot. Gregory had very partial information about Clovis. Incomplete evidence was no doubt a hindrance, but it was also an opportunity. What he lacked in source material Gregory gladly made up for in ways that were conducive to his authorial aims.

The structure of the Clovis story in the *Histories* can be mapped, with partial success, onto the patchy chronology that emerges from other sources. Primarily through supporting epistolary and historiographical evidence, it is possible to match some of the episodes reported in the *Histories* to actual historical events—Clovis's ascent to power, his battle with the Alamanni, baptism, the Burgundian intervention, the war with the Visigoths, and death.[15] Evidence for other topics touched on by Gregory, such as the war with Syagrius, Clovis's marriage to Clothild, the birth of his children, and the internal assassinations he undertook later in life is almost entirely limited to the *Histories*.

---

[13] See, for instance, the letter by Remigius of Reims, *Epistulae Austrasicae* 2, found, with translation, in G. Barrett and G. Woudhuysen, "Remigius and the 'Important News' of Clovis Rewritten," *Antiquité Tardive* 24 (2016), pp. 471–500, at pp. 472–473. Or the letter by Avitus of Vienne, *Epistula* 46, MGH AA, ed. R. Peiper (Berlin: Weidmann, 1883), pp. 75–76, translated in Avitus of Vienne, *Letters and Selected Prose*, ed. and trans. D. Shanzer and I. Wood (Liverpool: Liverpool University Press, 2002), pp. 369–373.

[14] Although he used the *Vita Remigii* and the *Vita Maxentii* for supplementary information, unlike the *Histories*' earlier chapters, most of the details about Clovis were not drawn from written sources. See Gregory of Tours, *Histories*, II.31, 37; Wood, "Gregory of Tours and Clovis," p. 250; Wood, *The Merovingian Kingdoms*, pp. 41–42.

[15] Ascent to power in the *Epistulae Austrasicae* 2. See Barret and G. Woudhuysen, "Remigius and the 'Important News'," pp. 471–500; battle with the Alamanni, Cassiodorus, *Variae* II.41; baptism, Avitus of Vienne, *Letter 46*; the war of 500 is mentioned in Marius of Avenches, *Chronicle*, in *La Chronique de Marius d'Avenches (455–581)*, ed. and trans. J. Favrod (Lausanne: Université de Lausanne, 1991), p. 68, s.a. 500: "i. His consulibus pugna facta est Divione inter Francos et Burgundiones, Godegeselo hoc dolose contra fratrem suum Gundobaudum macenante. In eo proelio Godogeselus cum suis adversus fratrem suum cum Francis dimicavit et fugatum fratrem suum Gundobaudum regnum ipsius, paulisper obtinuit et Gundebaudus Avinione latebram dedit. ii. Eo anno Gundobaudus resumptis viribus Vienam cum exercitu circumdedit captaque civitate, fratrem suum interfecit pluresque seniores hac Burgundiones qui cum ipso senserant multis quaesitis tormentis morte damnavit regnumque quem perdiderat cum id quod Godegeselus habuerat receptum usque in diem mortis suae feliciter gubernavit." This is the first significant entry in over a generation.

Since the careers of the literary character and the historical king are not so easily reconciled,[16] attempts to reconstruct the latter, and primarily the timeline of his famous conversion, have been numerous.[17] All of them recognize the mixture of error and confabulation that makes up Gregory's account. Yet for all its flaws, the *Histories* still comes closest among extant works to a coherent rendering of Clovis's historical role, and our understanding of the man and his accomplishments would be severely hampered without it.

Equally important, certainly for our purposes, is Gregory's contribution to the legend of Clovis, which transformed a man who was, by all accounts, hardly a paragon of virtue, into a gauge for evaluating kingly performance and religious piety. This is not to say that Gregory's Clovis comes off as a saint; his strong-arming, wile, paranoia, and homicidal urges are given ample breadth. Ultimately, however, they too are harnessed to a narrative end from which emerges a character that is probably very different from the historical person it was designed to portray.

Gregory was working during the lifetime of Clovis's grandchildren and great-grandchildren, who were the prime beneficiaries of their great ancestor's success. Clovis's ruthless pruning of the Merovingian family tree meant that only his direct descendants had a justified claim to the Frankish throne. Until Pippin III usurped the kingship in 751, all the kings of the Franks traced their ancestry, rightly or not, to Clovis.[18] The kings of Gregory's day certainly looked back with admiration at Clovis, and for good reason. This is what qualified Clovis to become the mold with which Gregory could shape his own notions of kingship.

The *Histories* devote the second half of Book II to the life of Clovis, charting his progress from one of several regional leaders to the uncontested master of Gaul,[19] acclaimed *consul aut augustus* by the people and,

---

[16] Wood, "Gregory of Tours and Clovis," pp. 249–272.

[17] For a comprehensive introduction to the chronological problems, see W.M. Daly, "Clovis: How Barbaric, How Pagan?," *Speculum* 69 (1994), pp. 619–64; D. Shanzer, "Dating the Baptism of Clovis: the Bishop of Vienne vs the Bishop of Tours," *Early Medieval Europe* 7, 1 (1998), pp. 29–57.

[18] On this, see Wood, "Deconstructing the Merovingian Family," pp. 149–171; Dailey, "Gregory of Tours, Fredegund, and the Paternity of Chlothar II: Strategies of Legitimation in the Merovingian Kingdoms," *Journal of Late Antiquity* 7, 1 (2014), pp. 3–27. For the one possible exception, see M. Becher, "Der sogenannte Staatsreich Grimoalds: Versuch einer Neubewertung," *Francia* 37 (1994), pp. 119–147.

[19] Gregory of Tours, *Histories* II.42, III.prol. See H. Reimitz, "Transformations of Late Antiquity: The Writing and Re-Writing of Church History at the Monastery of Lorsch, c. 800," in *The Resources of the Past in Early Medieval Europe*, eds. C. Gantner, R. McKitterick, and S. Meeder (Cambridge: Cambridge University Press, 2015), pp. 262–282, at 273. For the effects of kingly discord on *Gallias totas*, see Gregory of Tours, *Histories* V.34.

implicitly, by imperial fiat.[20] Clovis's premature death at 45 left in its wake an unprepared kingdom, mostly in the form of underage heirs and no coherent model of inheritance.[21] But his life, as depicted by Gregory, was a completely fulfilled one, since it embodied all of the attributes the bishop wished to impart to his readership about Christian rulership, primarily with regard to its relations with the episcopate.

Clovis's long and bloody ascent to power did not escape Gregory. He notes, sarcastically, that when the king wryly remarked that he had no relatives left on which to rely, he wished merely to lure out any remaining ones and destroy them.[22] This incident follows the account of the duplicitous methods Clovis employed in his efforts to eliminate Sigibert and Chloderic in Cologne, Chararic and his son, Ragnachar of Cambrai and his brothers, as well as "many other kings and close relatives" who stood in his path.[23] Yet even here, Gregory saw fit to justify this behavior by pointing to the faults of Clovis's opponents—impatience, ambition, greed—as the reason for their undoing. The lesson from all of this is stated in the conclusion to the chapter on Sigibert "the Lame" and his son: "Daily, God placed his [i.e., Clovis's] enemies under his hand and enlarged his rule, because he walked with a righteous heart before him and did that which was pleasing in his eyes."[24]

The most conspicuous example of Gregory's rationalization of Clovis's violent nature is the tale of the Vase of Soissons, an episode that took place directly after Clovis's elimination of Syagrius, ca. 486.[25] In one of the *Histories* most recognizable scenes, the king attends the division of the loot taken by the Franks, at that point still pagan, from prominent Gallic churches. Clovis requests of his men that, apart from his fair share, a certain vase be given to him that was commandeered from a nearby church. Clovis wishes to return the vase to the bishop, who asked the king for it in person. All agree with this request except for one rowdy soldier, who throws his ax at the vase in defiance. The king is humiliated but recovers the vase and bears his insult with patience. Later that year, he

---

[20] Though this was undoubtedly a conscious misrepresentation, and one that is amended in Emilio. On this, see pp. 116–117.
[21] A good summary of the problem can be found in M. Widdowson, "Merovingian Partitions: A 'Genealogical Charter'?," *Early Medieval Europe* 17, 1 (2009), pp. 1–22.
[22] Gregory of Tours, *Histories* II.42. For Gregory's penchant for satire, see Goffart, *Narrators of Barbarian History*, pp. 197–203.
[23] Gregory of Tours, *Histories* II.42: "Interfectisque et aliis multis regibus vel parentibus suis primis . . . ."
[24] Ibid. 40: "Prosternebat enim cotidiae Deus hostes eius sub manu ipsius et augebat regnum eius, eo quod ambularet recto corde coram eo et facerit quae placita erant in oculis eius."
[25] For the various uses of this episode in French historiography, see Wood, *The Modern Origins*, pp. 25–28, 46, 49, 78, 183.

executes the soldier publicly as his troops gaze on in terror, after having inspected his battle readiness and found it wanting. Clovis's insistence on avenging the soldier's insult—to himself, surely, but also to the bishop—is the beginning of a relationship that becomes pivotal for Gregory's framing of the Christianization of the Franks.

Clovis's life in the *Histories* runs along two parallel and interlinked paths: consolidation of power and spiritual development. As a character, Clovis had to grow from a local pagan strongman into the Catholic king Gregory needed, which the author accomplished through a carefully thought-out sequence of vignettes, each encapsulating a challenge that was successfully overcome. To achieve this effect, Gregory made certain concessions to accuracy and cleverly streamlined the character's evolution. One technique he used often was delivery of the thematic blocks of Clovis's life in conjunction with other subplots, whose protagonists usually took opposite paths to the one taken by Clovis. When Clovis exhibited courage, they were beset by doubt; when they scorned the authority of the Church, he defended it, and so on. Examples of this narrative device abound.[26] By erecting a house of mirror images, Gregory was able to convey moral lessons about the kind of behavior he expected to see from his kings. Gregory also built up his characters as latter-day reflections of bygone heroes. This applied to Remigius, who embodied the traits of Sylvester, and to Clovis, who became *novus Constantinus*.[27] Evidence of the efficacy of such narrative devices and of Gregory's enduring influence surfaced in the works of Carolingian authors such as Hincmar of Reims, who wrote about his own relationship with Charles the Bald in ways that built on the imagery of Remigius and Clovis.[28]

For reasons that now seem almost self-explanatory, Gregory made Clovis the standard against which later Merovingians would be measured, and would invariably fail. The king was on the winning side of every military campaign of his career, uniting the Franks under a single leadership, and birthing the Frankish kingdom. Most importantly, he embraced a public persona of piety that made him, in the eyes of his episcopal contemporaries, an *ecclesiae catholicae filius*.[29] Clovis's choice of Nicene Christianity from all the available options earned him much

---

[26] On this see Fox, "Revisiting Gregory of Tours' Burgundian Narrative."
[27] M. Heinzelmann, *Gregory of Tours: History and Society in the Sixth Century* (Cambridge: Cambridge University Press, 2001), p. 133.
[28] See Nelson, *Charles the Bald*, pp. 146, 220; M.B. Gillis, *Heresy and Dissent in the Carolingian Empire: The Case of Gottschalk of Orbais* (Oxford: Oxford University Press, 2017), p. 218.
[29] *Concilium Aurelianense, 10 Iul. 511*, in *Les canons des conciles mérovingiens (VIe–VIIe siècles)*, eds. J. Gaudemet and B. Basdevant, Sources chrétiennes 353–354 (Paris: Éditions du CERF, 1989), I: 67–91, proemium, p. 70; Reimitz, *History*, p. 99.

ecclesiastical praise and, later, significant scholarly attention. The most obvious outcome of this decision, in both avenues of commentary, has been the enduring alliance between the Merovingians and the Gallic episcopate.[30] Nowhere is this development more keenly portrayed than in the *Histories*, which drew a direct line between Clovis's achievements and his embrace of the Gallic Church, represented primarily by its bishops.

The *Histories*' reader is led on a long journey before meeting Clovis. While news of his birth reaches the reader in chapter 12 of Book II, it is only in chapter 27 that we encounter him as an active figure. Gregory begins the book with the theme of persecution. The harsh measures enacted against Nicene Christians under Vandal and Visigothic rule prove the spiritual superiority of the victims over their persecutors. Clovis's career, discussed in Book II's final chapters, is presented as the culmination of centuries of struggle endured by the Catholic Church in Gaul. When the Gallic Church finally prevails, it is in no small measure thanks to Clovis. This is familiar scenery to readers of Eusebius-Jerome.

The *Histories* are silent about Clovis's childhood. We learn that he was born after Childeric recovered his rule of the Franks and returned to Gaul with Basina at his side.[31] Perhaps Gregory wished to highlight that Clovis came into a world in which Childeric's rule was well established. The reader is swiftly informed that Clovis would become "a great man and a distinguished warrior,"[32] after which we hear nothing of him, and very little about Childeric, until the latter is reported to have died and the former to have succeeded him. Subsequent chapters are concerned mostly with the bishopric of Clermont and the hardships it endured under the Goths, although some attention is also given to Tours. That Clovis, who would later deliver Clermont and Tours from the persecution of the Goths, seals this narrative block, is surely intentional.

Clovis assumed the kingship of the Franks *ca.* 481. While Gregory depicted the succession as a clean break—Childeric died and Clovis became king—there is every reason to think that Clovis played a role in

---

[30] See recently Y. Hen, "The Church in Sixth-Century Gaul," in *A Companion to Gregory of Tours*, ed. A.C. Murray (Leiden: Brill, 2016), pp. 232–255, at pp. 237–241; Barrett and Woudhuysen, "Remigius and the 'Important News' of Clovis Rewritten," pp. 471–500; P. Poveda Arias, "Clovis and Remigius of Reims in the Making of the Merovingian Kingdoms," *European Review of History: Revue européenne d'histoire* 26, 2 (2019), pp. 197–218.

[31] Considering the *Histories*' creative use of chronology, it would probably be unwise to rely on it too definitively to date the commencement of Childeric's second kingship to *ca.* 465–466, if indeed it reflects a historical event at all. See G. Halsall, "Childeric's Grave," p. 125.

[32] Gregory of Tours, *Histories* II.12: "Hic fuit magnus et pugnator egregius."

Adora quod incendisti: Gregory of Tours 93

his father's administration and military apparatus.[33] It was common practice for kings to send princes to fight and to rule on their behalf. Indeed, Theuderic, Clovis's eldest son, commanded troops at his father's behest, and so did several later Merovingian princes.[34] As king, Clovis's first order of business reflected the circumstances bequeathed him by his father, namely, to deal with the "kingdom of Soissons," Aegidius's enclave of Roman government situated to the west of Clovis's domain. Memorably, Aegidius played a formative role in the story of Childeric, whom he had temporarily replaced.[35] Clovis, who understood the challenge posed by the Soissons's Syagrii, immediately set out to neutralize it. Syagrius was vanquished, and, after escaping to Alaric, was surrendered to Clovis and killed. In his account, Gregory suggestively counterposes Childeric's exile to that of Syagrius. The reader is confronted with a detailed discussion about hospitality, sanctuary, and betrayal. Childeric receives sanctuary from Bissinus, but later betrays him by accepting his runaway wife as queen. Syagrius is granted sanctuary by Alaric but ends up being betrayed when the latter is pressed by Clovis, whom he fears. Aegidius's complacency and Alaric's cowardice feature in this chain of events, but it is Clovis, embodying the opposite traits, who serves as prime mover.

Gregory meant for the Vase of Soissons episode, which followed Clovis's victory over Syagrius, to function as the first step on the king's path of spiritual growth. The vase episode has been the topic of much scholarly and popular attention and is arguably one of the most famous scenes from Merovingian history.[36] The First World War memorial which stands at the Place Fernand Marquigny in Soissons features a bas relief by Raoul

---

[33] On Gregory's treatment of war, martial values, and heroism, see E. James, "Warlike and Heroic Virtues in the Post-Roman World," in *Early Medieval Militarisation*, ed. E. Bennett et al. (Manchester: Manchester University Press, 2021), pp. 253–265, esp. at p. 255.
[34] For the Burgundians, Sigismund played an equally active role under his father at Vouillé. On his role, see Y. Fox, "Anxiously Looking East: Burgundian Foreign Policy on the Eve of Reconquest," in *East and West in the Early Middle Ages: The Merovingian Kingdoms in Mediterranean Perspective*, eds. S. Esders, Y. Fox, Y. Hen, and L. Sarti (Cambridge: Cambridge University Press, 2019), pp. 32–44.
[35] For more on this, see pp. 38–40.
[36] H. Duranton, "Le vase de Soissons et les historiens du XVIIIe siècle," *Revue de synthèse* (1975), pp. 284–316, at p. 387; K.F. Werner, "De Childéric à Clovis: antécédents et conséquences de la bataille de Soissons en 486," Actes des VIIIe journées internationales d'archéologie mérovingienne de Soissons (19–22 Juin 1986), *Revue archéologique de Picardie* 3–4 (1988), pp. 3–7; E. James, "Childéric, Syagrius et la disparition du royaume de Soissons," Actes des VIIIe journées internationales d'archéologie mérovingienne de Soissons (19–22 Juin 1986), *Revue archéologique de Picardie* 3–4 (1988), pp. 9–12; M. Sot, "Le baptême de Clovis et l'entrée des Francs en romanité," *Bulletin de l'Association Guillaume Budé* 1 (1996), pp. 64–75; C. Grell, "Clovis du grand siècle aux lumières," *Bibliothèque de l'École des chartes* 154,1 (1996), pp. 173–218; M. D'Auria, *The Shaping of French National Identity: Narrating the Nation's Past, 1715–1830* (Cambridge: Cambridge

Lamourdedieu of the soldier shattering the vase as Clovis and Remigius look on. There are, of course, countless other cultural references to this incident, whose success is testament to Gregory's literary acumen. By emphasizing the king's attentiveness to the bishop's requests, while still pagan, Gregory signaled that Clovis was on the right path. Clearly this was not a path of contemplative pacifism, but that is not what Gregory wanted from his kings. Clovis was a warrior, and therein lay his utility to the Church.

Subsequent chapters prepare the ground for the narrative climax that was Clovis's conversion. Chapter 28 opens with a short description of the Burgundian royal family, whose named members were all descendants of the Gothic persecutor Athanaric. Gregory follows this with a report of Gundobad's fratricide, and the condition of his two orphaned nieces, Chroma and Clothild.[37] It closes with the Burgundian king agreeing to Clovis's marriage proposal to Clothild, all because he was too afraid to send the Frankish delegation back empty handed. The Gundobad that emerges from this chapter is the offspring of heretical persecutors, the murderer of his own brother, and a closet Catholic to boot. It was his cowardice and ineptitude that caused Gundobad to allow the marriage that ultimately proved the undoing of the Gibichung line. Indirectly, it was also responsible for persuading Clovis to choose Catholicism, lending the account an ironically pleasing sense of closure.

As a married woman, Clothild's first act was to attempt to bring her husband to the true faith. In the *Histories*, this takes the form of a long monologue accusing Clovis's gods of being nothing more than figments of human imagination. They are, importantly, the gods of the Roman pantheon—Saturn, Jupiter, Mars, and Mercury. It is doubtful that either Clothild or Clovis read the *Aeneid*, whose passages Gregory has the former recite to ridicule Jupiter, and it is difficult to determine to what degree Gregory's classicizing usage reflects the king's true cultic preferences.[38] If anything, this is another instance in which the *Aeneid* rears its head unexpectedly, before emerging in *Fredegar* to play a starring role. In any case, Gregory was not interested in Clovis's actual religious worldview, but in

University Press, 2020), pp. 215–217. For Clovis in the curriculum of French schools in the nineteenth century, see C. Faure, "L'image de Clovis et des Mérovingiens dans les manuels scolaires de la fin du XIXe siècle à nos jours: Reflet de l'évolution historiographique et des pratiques pédagogiques," *DIversité REcherches et Terrains* 10 (2018), pp. 41–60 [retrieved June 27, 2021, from url: www.unilim.fr/dire/935&file=1].

[37] On this, see M. Rouche, *Clovis* (Paris: Fayard, 1996), pp. 229–232.
[38] See Daly, "Clovis," pp. 619–664; J. Palmer, "Defining Paganism in the Carolingian World," *Early Medieval Europe* 15, 4 (2007), pp. 402–425, at p. 411. On Frankish paganism in Gregory, see Y. Hen, "Paganism and Superstitions in the time of Gregory of Tours: une question mal posée!," in *The World of Gregory of Tours*, eds. K. Mitchell and I.N. Wood (Leiden: Brill, 2002), pp. 229–40, at 232–234.

providing a pastiche of paganism to which Catholicism was a stark antithesis. Clovis's idolatry was introduced in the context of the birth of his first son, Ingomer, and Clothild's desire to have him baptized. Clothild brought her first child to the font, only to lose him soon thereafter. She persisted in her belief, baptizing her second son, Chlodomer, despite the protestations of her husband. The factual skeleton of this account is rather thin and serves mainly to accommodate Clothild's sermons, through which Gregory expresses his own views about divine action in the world. Of course, Clothild is apt to make such sermons in the *Histories* because she herself was set up as a model for royal women.[39] When Gregory deemed Clothild in the wrong—such as when she privileged her grandchildren's royal hair over their lives—he made excuses for her, much as he did for her husband.[40]

Clothild wishes for her husband to see the light, but he does not. It is only the war with the Alamanni that brings him to God. His army nearly overrun, Clovis recognizes Clothild was right about his gods being powerless. He calls out to Christ: "I wish to believe in you, provided I am delivered from my enemies." Miraculously, the tides turn and the Franks triumph. The Constantinian and biblical undertones of this story are hardly subtle ones. After his victory, Clovis comes home and tells his wife, who summons Remigius. The fulfillment of Clovis's vow begins in earnest. He studies under Remigius but is hesitant to make his convictions public because of the possibly hostile reaction of his soldiers. Nevertheless, he goes. The soldiers reassure him that they, too, wish to abandon idolatry and join him in the worship of God.

Clovis's conversion epitomized the kind of royal–ecclesiastical relationship Gregory envisaged for a Christian Gaul. By bringing the king into communion with his subjects, the baptism scene served as a narrative moment in which the Christian community was reconstituted to accommodate a Catholic king. Gregory employs the full force of his prose to create a vibrant image of Reims on the day of the ceremony, replete with the sensory language of sight and smell.[41] At the heart of it all was Remigius,

---

[39] Rouche perhaps makes too much of Clothild's belief in "la résurrection immédiate des enfants baptisés," more likely a point Gregory was anxious to make, as an indicator of her education. Rouche, *Clovis*, p. 246.
[40] Gregory of Tours, *Histories* III.18.
[41] See K. Robinson, "The Anchoress and the Heart's Nose: The Importance of Smell to Medieval Women Religious," *Magistra* 19, 2 (2013), pp. 41–64, at p. 56. On the sensory in Gregory of Tours's prose, see R. Penkett, "Perceiving the Other: Sensory Phenomena and Experience in the Early Medieval Other World," *Reading Medieval Studies* 25 (1999), pp. 91–106; J. Martínez Pizarro, "Images in Texts: The Shape of the Visible in Gregory of Tours," *The Journal of Medieval Latin* 9 (1999), pp. 91–101; N. Pancer, "Le silencement du monde: Paysages sonores au haut Moyen Âge et nouvelle culture aurale," *Annales HSS* 72-3 (2017) pp. 659–699; C.M. Woolgar, "Medieval Smellscapes," in *Smell and History: A Reader*, ed. M.M. Smith (Morgantown, WV: West Virginia University Press, 2019), pp.

who is seen presiding over a spectacle that included the king, the royal family, and the army.[42] From the font flowed a new understanding of the community of faith in Gaul.

The intervention in Burgundy in 500 develops into an exploration of Gundobad's religious quandaries and extolls the deeds and writings of the Burgundian kingdom's leading Catholic prelate, Avitus, bishop of Vienne. In Gundobad's case, fear of his men dictated that he keep his Catholicism secret, an episode that is to be read against Clovis's courage and candor when faced with an identical situation. Next comes the Visigothic War sequence. The Visigoths are not only Clovis's main opponents near the end of Book II; they are his opposites. Sensing the growing influence of the Franks, they turn on the Catholic bishops under their dominion, most notably Quintianus of Rodez, who was suspected of harboring Frankish sympathies. Realizing that his life was in danger, Quintianus escaped to Clermont, where he received sanctuary from Bishop Eufrasius.[43] He was well received by other bishops he encountered and even given control over some episcopal property.[44]

From this depiction in the *Histories*, and particularly its placement between the meeting of Clovis and Alaric and the former's decision to declare war, the reader is meant to infer what will soon be expressly said, namely, that Clovis's wish to see the end of Arian—meaning Visigothic—rule in Gaul was shared by the Catholic bishops under Gothic occupation. The episode goes on to describe the camaraderie between the bishops of Clermont and Lyon and the refugee Quintianus, with which Gregory hoped to accentuate the unity of the Church in Gaul and its natural alliance with the Catholic Merovingians. Since Gregory's uncle Gallus was Quintianus's protégé, and was beholden to the bishop for much of his advancement, the

---

50–75. Also, see the work of the Israel Institute for Advanced Studies research group "Sensing the Truth" for new directions for thinking of the premodern sensorium.

[42] On Gregory's usage of language for this scene and others, see D. Shanzer, "Gregory of Tours and Poetry: Prose into Verse and Verse into Prose," *Proceedings of the British Academy* 129 (2005), pp. 303–319, esp. p. 305.

[43] Gregory of Tours, *Histories* II.36.

[44] Gregory encourages his readers to supplement their knowledge with the treatment of Quintianus that he wrote for his *Vitae patrum*. At minimum, this suggests that his cult was able to generate some interest when Gregory was writing. See Gregory of Tours, *Liber vitae patrum*, MGH SRM 1.2, ed. B. Krusch (Hanover: Hahnsche Buchhandlung, 1885), pp. 211–283, at ch. 4, pp. 223–227. The details found in the *VP* and in the canons of Orléans differ on several points from the description in the *Histories*. Quintianus was present at the Council of Orléans, which means that his expulsion postdated the death of Clovis and did not occur in the run-up to the Battle of Vouillé. See *Concilium Aurelianense, a. 511*, *SC* 353, p. 88: "Quintianus episcopus Rotenus subscripsi." In the *Vitae patrum*, Quintianus becomes bishop of Clermont and plays an important role in saving the town from Theuderic's punitive campaign on the Auvergne, whose many horrors feature prominently in Gregory's hagiographical compilations.

story had added value.[45] As the inconsistencies in Gregory's portrayal of Quintianus—described by Ian Wood as "deliberately fraudulent"—show, Gregory was happy to distort the chronology to build up Clovis's image as the savior of the Gallic Church.[46] In light of this and other evidence, the *Histories'* linkage between the religious identity and the political loyalty of the episcopate seems like convenient fiction.

Ever the local patriot, Gregory slipped the cult of Martin into the mix. He did this first by portraying Verus and Volusianus, Tours' seventh and eighth bishops, as casualties of Visigothic persecution. The hostile Gothic attitude is contrasted with Clovis's fruitful cooperation with Remigius, and the severe Gothic treatment inflicted on Tours by the Visigoths is contrasted with Clovis's triumph in the city and his magnanimity toward its citizens. All these feats were achieved because the king gave due respect to Martin and the property belonging to the basilica in Tours. The encounter between the king and the saint occasioned an act of violence by Clovis—the execution of a soldier who ignored his orders to leave church property unmolested— which allows Gregory to direct attention to the king's developing piety.[47] Clovis's murders, if one may call them that, shine a light on important points along his developmental trajectory. When he kills, he either secures his hold on power or moves closer to fulfilling his role as *defensor ecclesiae*.[48]

According to the *Histories*, Clovis went to war against the Visigoths because he could not tolerate Arian rule in parts of Gaul.[49] That Martin and his teacher, Hilary of Poitiers, both champions of the struggle against the Arians, approved of this decision, is hardly coincidental. Messengers sent to Tours to request Martin's sanction of the war returned with a favorable response, and a column of smoke emanating from the basilica in Poitiers confirmed Hilary's support. In this respect, the recognition of Martin's authority and the saint's subsequent championing of Clovis's military push to overtake Gaul are where Gregory's two narrative arcs converge. When undertaking their own military campaigns, the kings of Gregory's day were meant to recall that Clovis emerged from his Visigothic war not only a military victor but also a client of St. Martin. Clovis's character in the *Histories* conforms to his description in the

---

[45] On Quintianus, see Heinzelmann, *Gregory of Tours*, p. 12; E. James, "Gregory of Tours, the Visigoths, and Spain," in *Cross, Crescent and Conversion Studies on Medieval Spain and Christendom in Memory of Richard Fletcher*, eds. S. Barton and P. Linehan (Leiden and Boston: Brill, 2008), pp. 43–64.
[46] Wood, "Gregory of Tours and Clovis," p. 257.
[47] On this see Y. Fox, "Saints and Their Spaces in Gregory of Tours" (forthcoming).
[48] For a less accommodating view of Clovis, see James, "Gregory of Tours, the Visigoths, and Spain," p. 50.
[49] Gregory of Tours, *Histories* II.37: "Igitur Chlodovechus rex ait suis: 'Valde molestum fero, quod hi Arriani partem teneant Galliarum'."

canons of the Council of Orléans as *son of the Catholic Church*.[50] Defender of Gaul's bishops, guardian of its property, and now beloved client of its major saints, the character in the *Histories* lives up to the title.

The penultimate section dedicated to Clovis has to do with the elimination of his internal rivals. Clovis's offer to the Franks of Cologne to become their master after the removal of Sigibert and Chloderic was not essentially different from the decision taken by Childeric's men to invite Aegidius to rule them, back in chapter 12. The symmetries are instructive, but so are the two stories' many differences. While Childeric and Aegidius are described as weak figures whose fates were ultimately decided by their followers, Clovis's strength sways the Franks of Cologne completely and permanently. Another instructive parallel can be found in the story of Ragnachar. Like Childeric, Ragnachar is undone by his wantonness, and like him he has a beloved advisor by his side.[51] However, here it was Clovis who took advantage of the situation, offering the Franks of Cambrai a bribe to betray their king. The tale is laden with moral significance—Clovis berates Ragnachar and Ricchar for allowing themselves to be bound, and the *leudes* for agreeing to take the armbands and sword belts to begin with. With the killing of the rulers of all three "petty" kingdoms, Clovis achieves complete dominion over the Franks.

In death, the king fulfills his spiritual destiny as well. Clovis's burial in the church of the Holy Apostles, which he and his wife had commissioned, cements the relationship between the royal family and the church. Holy Apostles would later be rededicated as Sainte-Geneviève, in honor of the woman whose close relationship with Childeric and Clovis helped reshape Paris as a Christian city.[52] After Clovis died, Clothild settled in the church of Saint-Martin at Tours, where she led a religious life.[53]

---

[50] *Conc. Aurel. a. 511*: "Domno suo catholicae ecclesiae filio Chlothovecho gloriosissimo regi omnes sacerdotes, quos ad concilium venire iussistis."

[51] The emendations to the story of Wiomad (who in the *Histories* remains unnamed) in *Fredegar* and the *LHF* invite further comparison.

[52] *Vita Genovefae virginis Parisiensis*, MGH SRM 3, ed. B. Krusch (Hanover: Hahnsche Buchhandlung, 1896), pp. 204–238, at ch. 26, p. 226 (Childeric) and ch. 56, pp. 237–238 (Clovis). See L.M. Bitel, *Landscape with Two Saints: How Genovefa of Paris and Brigit of Kildare Built Christianity in Barbarian Europe* (Oxford: Oxford University Press, 2009). Gregory makes very cursory mention of Genovefa, in *Histories* IV.1: "Quae Parisius cum magno psallentio deportata, in sacrario basilicae sancti Petri ad latus Chlodovechi regis sepulta est a filiis suis, Childeberthto atque Chlothachario regibus. Nam basilicam illam ipsa construxerat, in qua et Genuveifa beatissima est sepulta." On Gregory's attempt to downplay Genovefa's impact on Clothild and to promote Martin's, see J. McRobbie, "Gender and Violence in Gregory of Tours' *Decem libri historiarum*," doctoral dissertation (University of St. Andrews, 2012), p. 79.

[53] On Clothild as a model of royal widowhood, see Dailey, E.T., *Queens, Consorts, Concubines: Gregory of Tours and Women of the Merovingian Elite* (Leiden and Boston: Brill, 2015), pp. 39–44.

The memory of Clovis was famously invoked in Gregory's introductions to Books III and V. In the former, his triumphs were linked to his Catholicism, while Alaric's defeats were attributed to the Visigothic king's Arianism. In the latter, Clovis was celebrated as an invincible conqueror and recipient of God's favor, as opposed to his greedy and hot-headed descendants, *Fredegar*'s "bears and wolves." In these introductions Gregory's understanding of Clovis's role is laid out most clearly. The king's political fortunes and his treatment of the Church are inseparable. Importantly, this was not simply a call to respect ecclesiastical power; it was an invitation to adopt altogether more Christian perspectives on rulership. Clovis embodied Gregory's promise to the kings of his day that, were they to conduct themselves with restraint and wisdom, God's favor would surely follow.

We turn now to the composition *De rebus gestis Francorum* (*DRG*), written by Paolo Emilio. This early sixteenth-century work is not another elaborate rendition of characters as they were developed in *Fredegar*, Aimoin, and Dionysian historiography. The *De rebus gestis Francorum* went in a different direction. As I intend to show, Emilio was directly indebted to Gregory for much of his information about Clovis. Yet his authorial constraints were quite unlike those of his sixth-century source, resulting in a highly original reimagination of Clovis.

2.2 An Officer and a Gentleman: Paolo Emilio's *De rebus gestis Francorum*

Paolo Emilio was born in Verona around 1460, probably to a well-to-do family, and as a teenager travelled to Rome, to the curia of Pope Sixtus IV. By the early 1480s he was in Paris, having secured the patronage of Cardinal Charles of Bourbon, brother to Pierre de Beaujeu, who was regent for the minor king Charles VIII. The cardinal took the young Emilio as his secretary, in whose employ he remained until Charles of Bourbon's death in 1488. The following year, Emilio was put on the royal payroll, on which he remained throughout his life. Sometime before his own death in 1529 (possibly in 1511), he was given a canonicate in Notre Dame de Lyon on the orders of Louis XII, a position that came with a benefice on which he relied for income.[54] By the late 1480s, Emilio took

---

[54] The scope of his earnings, from this channel and others, is interesting insofar as it can shed some light on his intended readership and the degree to which we might call him a royal historiographer. On this and other aspects of his career, see K. Davies, "Late XVth Century French Historiography, As Exemplified in the *Compendium* of Robert Gaguin and the *De rebus gestis* of Paulus Aemilius," doctoral dissertation (University of Edinburgh, 1954). See also L. Rognoni and G.M. Varanini, "Da Verona a Parigi:

up with gusto a historiographical project that would produce numerous texts on Gallic and Frankish history, spanning a range of topics and periods. Through his works he was able to become a leading figure of French humanism, together with Jacques Lefèvre d'Étaples, Robert Gaguin, and others.

Emilio's oeuvre consists of compositions between which there is significant intertextuality. They often run parallel courses, borrowing freely from each other. Some can be regarded as drafts for later works, and some can be treated as expansions on previous storylines. His historiographical efforts cover Gaul, Francia, and France from early antiquity to the late fifteenth century. Emilio often visited the locations he mentioned in his work, and generally seems to have done his research in pursuit of historical facts. Although his work focuses on Gaul and the entities to which it gave rise, his interests were quite varied. In his appreciation of precision, he sometimes cast doubt on what had become, by his day, the hallowed conventions of French royal history.

Emilio exploited a rich range of sources. While he drew, as we shall see, on Gregory of Tours' *Histories*, he also relied on historical and legal works, in both Latin and Greek. Among these many texts we find Bede's *Ecclesiastical History* (*EH*) and Paul the Deacon's *History of the Lombards*, as well as later authors who based themselves on Gregory, Bede, and Paul, such as Aimoin of Fleury and Sigebert of Gembloux. Emilio consulted Tacitus, Jerome, and Orosius on origin stories, Ammianus Marcellinus and the Justinianic Code on legal questions, William of Tyre on the Crusades, and a slew of medieval sources on questions of royal and senior ecclesiastical succession. The works he read in preparation for his own writing came from all over Europe, from Britain in the west to Hungary in the east. Moreover, his usage was not strictly chronological, in the sense of relying exclusively on certain works to provide the factual backbone for specific periods. He excerpted relevant stories and details from his impressive corpus of sources and set them carefully in place within the large historiographical mosaic he was assembling. This is true also of his treatment of the Merovingian material.

While adamantly siding with the French monarchy, Paolo Emilio's Clovis strays quite far from the narrative put forward in the *Grandes Chroniques*, although he certainly knew and consulted the composition often.[55] For much of his discussion of Clovis, Emilio circumvented the *Grandes Chroniques* and its primary influence—Aimoin—turning instead

'Paulus Aemilius' autore del *De rebus gestis Francorum* e la sua famiglia," *Quaderni per la storia dell'università di Padova* 40 (2007), pp. 163–180; Maissen, *Von der Legende zum Modell*, pp. 176–210.
[55] Maissen, *Von der Legende zum Modell*, p. 186.

directly to Gregory of Tours so as to cleanse the narrative of elements he regarded as corrupt or extraneous.[56] Thus, Emilio was not tethered to the Clovis traditions and lore found in late medieval chronicles, which gazed distantly at Gregory through the lens of *Fredegar* and the *LHF*. It is this that makes his treatment so unique.

Of the many works Emilio composed in his productive career, we shall focus on one, *De rebus gestis Francorum libri X*, a composition that was highly regarded in its learned precision by such leading humanist figures as Erasmus.[57] The first printed editions of the *DRG* appeared in the 1510s, although Emilio continued to revise and rework the text, leaving it unfinished when he died.[58] At times, Emilio's close acquaintance with Gregory makes the *DRG* seem almost familiar to a reader of the *Histories*. Yet Emilio was aiming for something quite different from Gregory and the medieval chroniclers who followed him. Miraculous events and heraldic lore are completely sidelined in the *DRG*.[59] The return to the *Histories* is as to a factual anchor, not as a source of stylistic or philosophical inspiration. Concessions to traditional elements are made, though they, too, are qualified and reserved, as we shall see. Already in the opening remarks of the *DRG*, Emilio's incredulity prevails as he famously strays from a core tenet of royal ideology: "The Franks claim that they originate from Troy."[60] This skeptical eye to the evidence was applied consistently.[61]

Compared with its medieval antecedents, the *DRG* is highly character centric. Emilio delivers a flowing prose, interspersed with direct speech, delving into the mindsets of his characters. The chapter dedicated to Clovis is very long—it comprises thirteen pages in the 1520 Paris edition. While the author generally follows Gregory's narrative framework, he transposes some events to better suit Clovis's progression as a character and to recontextualize the acts and motivations of supporting figures such as Theoderic, Gundobad, and Clothild. The queen's plea to her husband to forgo his plans to destroy Gundobad, for example, came not from love of her uncle, according to Emilio, but out of concern for her *patria*.[62]

---

[56] M. Priesterjahn, "Back to the Roots: The Rediscovery of Gregory of Tours in French Historiography," *Mittelalter: Interdisziplinäre Forschung und Rezeptionsgeschichte* 4 (2016) [url: http://mittelalter.hypotheses.org/8158]. Retrieved June 26, 2019.
[57] Maissen, *Von der Legende zum Modell*, p. 183.   [58] Ibid., pp. 190–192.
[59] Davies, "Late XVth Century French Historiography," pp. 173, 264. Maissen, *Von der Legende zum Modell*, pp. 186, 198. On the lilies, see p.113.
[60] *DRG*, p. 3: "Franci se Troia oriundos esse contendunt."
[61] Maissen, *Von der Legende zum Modell*, p. 196.
[62] *DRG*, p. 9: "Intermissoque pauliesper, ac mox redintegrato bello, quod atrocius futurum videbatur, nihil non ausuro per desperationem Gundebaldo, Clotildis Regina, non hominis, sed nominis patriæque commiseratione [...]." Compare F. Biondo, *Historiarum ab*

Godegisel's rebellion of 500 was precipitated by an early act of brotherly betrayal. In short, characters always had motives, from which their actions flowed.

When we consider the attention the *DRG* devotes to Theoderic's diplomatic efforts, to the plight of the Alamanni, and to the various misadventures of Gundobad, it seems as though Emilio had in mind less of a "life of Clovis" than a treatment of Gaul in Clovis's day.[63] This is not to say that Emilio did not see Clovis as a unique figure, or that he did not consider Clovis's life as a distinct element of the *DRG* plotline. Clovis's baptism is of paramount importance to Emilio; the king is, after all, *conditor utique Francicae religionis*. Emilio builds on the *Histories'* baptism scene, with its white cloths and sticks of incense—a potent picture in its own right—to create an embarrassment of riches filled with gleaming priests, perfumed royal hairdos, intoxicating aromas, and worldly splendor. *Fredegar* disregarded Gregory's description of the decorations at Reims, as did Aimoin, whose only nod to the adornments was to preface the descent into the water with the words "the font was decorated."[64] Primat wanted to elaborate on Aimoin but was not aware of Gregory's scenic descriptions and thus did not include them. Emilio, by contrast, presented a fully developed scene thanks to his direct reliance on Gregory. Working 900 years after Gregory, Emilio was only once removed if we consider that, for this scene and many others, the *Histories* was the direct inspiration for what we encounter in the *DRG*.

Most striking of all in the *DRG* is its emphasis on continuity. Unlike previous treatments of Clovis's life, which were delivered as discrete vignettes, Emilio presents the king's life and the lives of those around him as a single, interconnected stream of events in which one episode leads naturally to the next. Indeed, the 1520 seven-book version of the *DRG* printed by Jodocus Badius has no chapter divisions. The books themselves break up the text according to significant dynastic developments: Book I from Faramund to the ascent of Charles Martel; Book II from Martel to the Spanish campaigns of Charlemagne; Book III from the imperial coronation to the inheritance arrangements of Robert of Normandy and his brother, William Rufus, and so on. The prose itself follows the reigns of kings, but it does not create caesurae in the text to introduce new rulers, nor does it attempt to advance the plot by providing

---

inclinatione Romanorum imperii decades (Venetiis: Octavianus Scotus Modoetiensis, 1483), I.3, p. 21: "Eo tamen bello interventu chrotchildis sedato."
[63] For his historical method, see Maissen, *Von der Legende zum Modell*, pp. 192–199.
[64] Aimoin, *Gesta Francorum* ch. 16, col. 655: "exornantur baptisterium," which could also simply mean "furnished" or "provided for." Note the significant Trojan overtones of Aimoin's baptism scene.

consistent regnal years or a dating system of significant events.[65] In the Badius edition, the reader does not even receive respite in the form of paragraphs. So, while the book is thematically partitioned, broadly speaking, the reading experience is of a single uninterrupted story.

The books of the *DRG* were produced and released gradually from 1516, when the first four were printed, to 1539, when the ten books were assembled by Michael Vascosanus.[66] The seven-book edition of 1520 jumps straight into the action, but later editions introduced certain assistive devices, facilitating navigation through Emilio's lengthy opus. The history of the *DRG* prints is somewhat obscure, although as many as four editions were published during Emilio's own lifetime, the earliest probably the four-book edition, which contained the Merovingian material in Book I. In the thirty years after it achieved its final form, the *DRG* was printed twice more by Vascosanus in Paris.[67]

The ten-book 1544 edition contained a convenient table of contents structured around the reign of kings (*Regum hisce Decem libris descriptorum Catalogus*), and so did the ten-book 1550 edition (*Series et ordo regum Francorum in Gallia*). Though it is an editorial addition introduced at a later point, the 1550 edition's table of contents captures much of Emilio's attitude with respect to Clovis:

Faramund the Sicamber, son of Marcomir, ruled 2 years;
Clodio the 'long-haired', his son, 18 years;
Merovech, his son, 10 years;[68]
Childeric, his son, 26 years;[69]
Clovis the Great, his son, first Christian king, protector of the faith, was chosen. Buried in the Paris church that he erected in honor of the apostles Peter and Paul, which is today called Sainte-Geneviève, 30 years.[70]

---

[65] There are exceptions. *DRG*: "Iam quintum decimum annum Clodoveus regnabat, cum arma Francorum in Alemannos mota . . . ."
[66] On the different stages of publication for the *DRG*, see Davies, "Late XVth Century French Historiography," pp. 159–177. The tenth book remained incomplete at the time of Emilio's death in 1529 and was put together with the help of his notes by his protégé, Daniel Zavarisi, also a native of Verona.
[67] Michael Vascosanus (Michel de Vascosan) overtook printing operations from Jodocus Badius in 1535 and was also married to Jodocus's daughter, Catharine. See S. Egerton Brydges, *Polyanthea librorum vetustiorum, italicorum, gallicorum, hispanicorum, anglicanorum et latinorum* (Geneva: G. Fick, 1822), pp. 393–395.
[68] Emilio himself had doubts about Clodio's paternity of Merovech, as indicated below.
[69] *DRG* 1548: "Faramundus Marcomiri filius Sicamber, regnavit annos II . . . ; Clodio comatus fil. an. 18 . . . ; Meroveus fil. an. 10 . . . Childericus filius an. 26 . . . ."
[70] Ibid.: "Clodoveus magnus fil. primus Rex Christianus, fidei protector electus. Lutetiae sepelitur in basilica quam apostolis Petro & Paulo erexerat: hodie templum Genovefes appellatur, an. 30 . . . ."

Brevity resumes when the table moves on to Clovis's sons, but a mention of burial place, now made relevant by the Merovingians' Christianity, is hereafter included:

{ Childebert over the people of Paris,   }   Buried in the Parisian Basilica of St-Ger-
{ Chlothar over the people of Soissons,   }   main, which he erected;[71]
{ Chlodomer over the people of Orléans,   }   his sons, 45 years ...[72]
{ Theuderic over the people of Metz   }

The tables of contents and partitions of the work introduced in the later editions were not integral to Emilio's vision, but they did reflect his attitude with regard to Clovis, whom he singled out for especial praise.[73] Even taken independently of Emilio, editors and publishers working in the mid-sixteenth century recognized that Clovis was a particularly interesting character. Providing such assistive devices at a time when an edition's commercial potential was a central concern would have assured that Clovis was easily located by anyone browsing through the work.

The observant reader immediately notices the mention of Faramund in the table of contents. Faramund, of course, was not an element of Gregory's prose but of the *LHF*'s. And indeed, Emilio seems somewhat uncomfortable with his inclusion, although apparently not enough to ignore him entirely. On Faramund and Clodio, Emilio has this to say:

Faramund, the son of Marcomir, was the very first to be called king of that nation, in the year of salvation 420. From him was begotten Clodio, nicknamed 'the long-haired', who entered Gaul, which is their [i.e., the Franks'] *homeland.*[74]

Clodio's account goes on for several more pages, although it very quickly becomes apparent that he is not the subject of these pages at all. In fact, it is rather a theoretical discussion of the Franks' reputation, gleaned, according to Emilio, from Cicero's letter to his friend Atticus and from the writings of Jerome. This is followed up by an excursus on imperial politics in the late

---

[71] i.e., Childebert I.
[72] *DRG* 1548: "Childebertus Parisiorum, Clotarius Suessionum, Clodamirus Aurelianensium, Theodoricus Mediomatricum, sepel. Lut. ad S. Germani quam erexit filii an. 45 ... ." Childebert I's reign, which Emilio dated at forty-five years, actually lasted from 511 to 558, forty-seven years. The error stems from Emilio's dating of Clovis's death to 514 and Childebert's to 559.
[73] See, for instance, *DRG*, p. 9 "Magnitudo vero tua caeteros supergressa, novam gloriam postulat. Defendisti Christianum nomen, ac potius orbem terrarum a Visigotthorum furore, qui et urbem Romam everterunt, & Imperiorum Regnorumque hostes erant. Tantique superis pietas tua visa est, ut tua unius manu, Dei hominumque hostem occidi volueris, inter tot tela hominum, tot caeli fulmina."
[74] *DRG*, p. 1: "Faramundum Marcomiri filium, primū omniū Regē gentis, anno salutis quadringentesimo uicesimo appellatum: Ab eo procreatū Clodionem cognomina Comatum, in Galliam transgressum: quæ illis patria est."

fourth and early fifth centuries, starring the Huns, Burgundians, Vandals, and Goths, but not the Franks. Only at the Battle of the Catalaunian Plains do the Franks reemerge, led by Merovech, which Emilio uses as an opportunity to discuss the perennial paternity problem:

> And in the vanguard the Franks were led and commanded by one Merovech, their king, who in the year of salvation 448 succeeded King Clodio—either because he was his son or not, the sources vary [on this point]—, who fought with the utmost exertion of the will.[75]

Humanist appetite for battle scenes dictated a detailed account of the battle, although Merovech plays a very ancillary role. Emilio once comments upon the Franks' martial acumen, and once more on the fact that Gaul came to be known as Francia because Merovech and his Franks had taken it, but that is all. Childeric's biography is limited to his Thuringian exile and territorial gains, all of which could have been extracted from Gregory, although the name of his advisor—Vidomar, an obvious corruption of Wiomad—was probably lifted from Aimoin, or directly from the *LHF*.

Emilio's account of Clovis's accession to the Frankish throne reveals his feelings about the king's special importance: "His [i.e., Childeric's] son Clovis succeeded him, assuredly the founder of religion in France."[76] The Franks, continues Emilio, had not yet received the sacraments, and had not had the benefit of hearing the words of holy men. The Gauls were Christians from the start and had sent many holy and educated men to preach to the Franks. First among them was St. Remigius of Reims, who brought the Franks to the sacred font. As we can see, Frankish Christianity is a prominent theme in the *DRG* even prior to the baptism of Clovis.

Next comes the war with Syagrius. Unlike Gregory, who held Clovis responsible for the hostilities, Emilio attributed culpability to Syagrius.[77] As always, the *DRG* characters were supplied with relatable context. In the process, Emilio rejected many of the attributes ascribed to Clovis by Gregory. Perhaps because Emilio's work with the sources was scrupulous, he was most critical of Gregory's simplistic usage of moral couplets.

---

[75] Ibid., p. 3: "& in primis Franci unius Merovei iam Regis ductu, imperioq;, qui anno salutis quadringētesimo duodequinquagesimo Clodioni Regi, sive filius, sive (quādo uariant authores) alienus successerat, summa cōtentione animi dimicatū est."

[76] *DRG*, p. 5: "Successit ei filius Chlodoveus, conditor utique Francicae religionis. Franci nondum nostra receperant sacra: necdum ad eos missus sanctos viros reperimus: credo, quod nullis certis sedibus permultas egissent aetates. Galli iam vulgo Christum agnoscebant: cum iam inde ab initio Christianae religionis et sanctissimi et doctissimi viri vita orationeque veram pietatem intulissent: nec postea aemulatio intermissa sanctorum est, ad divum usque Remigium Rhemorum Pontificem, iam inde ad iuventa sanctum. Ab hoc Franci sacro lavacro initiati sunt, ex bellicis rebus religionis spe exorta."

[77] Ibid.: "Syagrius Aegidii filius bellum Clodoveo movit." Markedly, these are a faithful reproduction of the names in the *Histories*, which are very different from the ones in the *Grandes Chroniques*.

Emilio's Clovis was written to embody a range of desired values, but under his pen many idiosyncrasies of Gregory's Clovis disappeared. Emilio's deletions are as important as his expansions. Syagrius, for example, receives much more limited treatment than he does in the *Histories*. We learn that Syagrius was situated in Soissons, where his father was once king. He was defeated and sought refuge with the Visigoths, but after Clovis threatened them, he was surrendered and killed. Here Emilio takes a detour through the marital connections that linked the various royal houses of the West:

At the same time the Visigoths, Franks, and Ostrogoths were linked by marriage. Theoderic the king of the Ostrogoths, meaning Italy, called to the kingdom of Italy from Spain (where in most regions the Visigoths lived) Eutharic, descendant of the royal family of the Balts, from whom he hoped to have heirs. He gave him his daughter Amalasuntha. He wed one of his two remaining daughters to Alaric, king of the Visigoths, and the other to Sigismund, son of Gundobad, king of the Burgundians. This same King Theoderic was married to Audofled, sister of King Clovis.[78]

This information could have been gleaned from Gregory, at least in part. *Histories* III.5 reports the marriage of Theoderic's daughter Areagni to Sigismund, and Audofled's to Theoderic is recounted in *Histories* III.39. Amalasuntha's marriage to Eutharic and Theodegotha's to Alaric II likely originated with Cassiodorus's letters.[79] Such data arrived in Emilio, as in so many other cases, through Biondo's *Historiarum ab inclinatione Romanorum imperii decades*.[80] Biondo was Emilio's first resource

---

[78] *DRG*, pp. 5–6: "Simul Visigotthi, Francique, ac Ostrogotthi affinitate iuncti sunt. Theodoricus Ostrogotthorum idem ac Italiae rex, ex Hispania (ubi maxima ex parte sedes Visigotthorum errant) Eutharicum Regia Balthorum familia ortum, ad se in ipsem haereditatis Regnique Italici accersivit: eique filiam Amalasiuntam despondit. Duae reliquiae eius filiae, altera Visigotthorum regi Alarico, altera Sigismundo Gundebaldi Burgundionis Regis filio nupserant. Ipsi vero Theodorico Regi Audefleda Clodovei Regis soror desponsa fuerat."

[79] Gregory's version includes Amalasuntha's fabled elopement with the slave Traguilla, which is absent from the *DRG*.

[80] See Cassiodorus, *Variae* I.46 (kinship between Theoderic and Gundobad), III.1 (kinship between Theoderic, Clovis, and Alaric II). Perhaps, it was also influenced by Jordanes's *Getica*, which contains similarly phrased comments on the relevant persons. See Theodegotha: Jordanes, *De origine actibusque Getarum*, in *Iordanis de origine actibusque Getarum*, eds. F. Giunta and A. Grillone (Rome: Istituto Storico Italiano per il Medio Evo, 1991), 58.297: "Antequam ergo de Audefledam subolem haberet, naturales ex concubina, quas genuisset adhuc in Moesia, filias, unam nomine Thiudigoto et aliam Ostrogotho. quas mox in Italiam venit, regibus vicinis in coniugio copulavit, id est unam Alarico Vesegotharum et aliam Sigismundo Burgundzonorum"; Eutharic: Jordanes, *Getica*, 14.81: "Vetericus item genuit Eutharicum, qui coniunctus Amalasuinthae genuit Athalaricum et Mathesuentam"; Balts: Jordanes, *Getica*, 5.42: "Tertia vero sede super mare Ponticum iam humaniores et, ut superius diximus, prudentiores effecti, divisi per familias populi, Vesegothae familiae Balthorum, Ostrogothae praeclaris Amalis serviebant." Compare Biondo, *Decades* I.3, p. 22, who makes direct mention of Cassiodorus as

beyond the confines of Gregory's prose. Emilio admired Biondo's reliability and approach, although remarkably left his influence unacknowledged in his own work.[81] Of course, the Franks were not the heroes of Biondo's plot; they were only one nation on a massive historical canvas. Thus, for Emilio the usefulness of the *Decades* was often limited. Emilio relied on the *Decades* to support and develop his themes, although, at least for the Merovingian material, this was done in the service of a narrative architecture put in place by the *Histories*.

After the exposition of marital alliances, Emilio moved on to the Vase of Soissons, for which he followed Gregory's version of the events quite closely. One interesting difference is in the motivation provided for the insubordinate soldier, who rejected the king's request to receive a vase plundered from a nearby church so that he could restore it to its rightful owner.[82] In Gregory's version, the soldier refused the king's plea because he was flippant, envious, and quick-tempered.[83] Emilio's explanation is different: The man was driven by contempt for a "foreign religion."[84] The killing of the insolent soldier a year later sowed the seeds of hope that Clovis would become Christian, something that is implied but never stated outright in Gregory.[85]

Like the *Histories*, the *DRG* next turns to Clothild and the Burgundians. In his opening, Gregory opted for a short description of the four sons of Gundioc, descendant of the persecutor Athanaric.[86] Emilio ignored this tradition altogether, omitting also the attendant anti-Arian angle that helped Gregory pigeonhole Gundobad as Clovis's evil *doppelganger*. The Burgundians were treated very differently in the *DRG*; instead of Gregory's moralizing soliloquy on the Burgundian kings, Emilio used Orosius, whom

---

a source. For Emilio's usage of Biondo, see Davies, "Late XVth Century French Historiography," pp. 196–197.

[81] On this, see Maissen, *Von der Legende zum Modell*, pp. 194–195.
[82] Identified in Emilio, but not in Gregory, as Remigius. The bishop was first identified in *Fredegar* III.16 and, subsequently, in Aimoin, *Gesta Francorum*, ch. 12, col. 650. *LHF*, ch. 10 echoes Gregory more closely.
[83] Gregory of Tours, *Histories*, II.27: " ... unus levis, invidius ac facilis ... ."
[84] *DRG*, p. 6: "Miles, sive vecordia ingenii, sive sacrilegii poenis agentibus, in medium progressus, ferociter negat religioni alienae restituendum videri bello virtuteque partum."
[85] Ibid.: "Et nostri sperare coepere Regem Christianum effici posse."
[86] Some doubt has been expressed concerning this assertion in modern scholarship. See I. N. Wood, "*Gentes*, Kings and Kingdoms – The Emergence of States. The Kingdom of the Gibichungs," in *Regna and Gentes: The Relationship between Late Antique and Early Medieval Peoples and Kingdoms in the Transformation of the Roman World*, eds. H.-W. Goetz, J. Jarnut, and W. Pohl (Leiden and Boston: Brill, 2003), pp. 243–270, at p. 268. On this reconstruction, see H. Wolfram, *History of the Goths* (Berkeley, CA: University of California Press, 1988), p. 33; A. Demandt, "The Osmosis of Late Roman and Germanic Aristocracies." in *Das Reich und die Barbaren*, eds. E.K. Chrysos, and A. Schwarcz (Vienna and Cologne: Veröffentlichungen des Instituts für Österreichische Geschichtsforschung, 1988), pp. 75–86, at p. 86.

he cited directly, to discuss the Burgundians' Christianity and the respectful reception they accorded the priests sent to proselytize them.[87]

The kings of the Burgundians, remarked Emilio, were not as tranquil as their subjects. Of the four sons born to Gundioc, Gundobad is reported to have been the eldest. He was followed by Godomar, Chilperic, and Godegisel, in that order. Emilio marched in relative lockstep with the *Histories* up to this point in the story, but here he launched into an entirely independent subplot about the Burgundian royal family's internal intrigues. The two middle brothers—Chilperic and Godomar—were, as it turns out, fierce youths bent on wresting control of the kingdom from their older sibling. With the help of their trans-Rhenish allies, they were able to defeat Gundobad, who was forced into hiding, aided by loyal supporters. Having been misled into thinking Gundobad was dead, the barbarian auxiliaries returned to their homes across the Rhine, allowing Gundobad to emerge from his hiding place and take Vienne by surprise. First he killed Chilperic, then Godomar, who was burned alive inside the tower into which he retreated in defense. This scene, influenced, of course, by Godegisel's rebellion of 500 story in the *Histories*, is here set in a separate, original subplot. Tellingly, Emilio makes no mention of the elimination of Chilperic's wife, so graphically described by Gregory.[88] The utility of this subplot might be in that it allowed Emilio to provide a justifiable context for the killing of Chilperic and to tie the loose end that was Godomar, who is mentioned once by Gregory and then never again.[89]

Emilio's depiction of the Gundobad character ensured that his readers encountered not Gregory's fratricidal heretic, but a reasonable sovereign acting to maintain his rule in the face of unwarranted aggression. He was,

---

[87] Compare Orosius, *Historiae adversus paganos*, ed. K. Zangemeister (Hildesheim Georg Olms, 1967), VII.32: "Burgundionum quoque nouorum hostium nouum nomen, qui plus quam octoginta milia, ut ferunt, armatorum ripae Rheni fluminis insederunt. hos quondam subacta interiore Germania a Druso et Tiberio, adoptiuis filiis Caesaris, per castra dispositos in magnam coaluisse gentem atque ita etiam nomen ex opere praesumpsisse, quia crebra per limitem habitacula constituta burgos uulgo uocant, eorumque esse praeualidam et perniciosam manum Galliae hodieque testes sunt, in quibus praesumpta possessione consistunt; quamuis prouidentia Dei Christiani omnes modo facti catholica fide nostrisque clericis, quibus oboedirent, receptis blande mansuete innocenterque uiuant, non quasi cum subiectis Gallis sed uere cum fratribus Christianis."

[88] A heavy stone was tied to her neck, and she was thrown into the river. Gregory of Tours, *Histories*, II.28. See Rouche, *Clovis*, pp. 230–231. For similarities with the execution of Sigismund and his family, see Wood, "Gregory of Tours and Clovis," p. 253.

[89] The inconsistencies of Gregory's depiction of the Burgundian royal family are discussed in an unpublished 2003 paper by Danuta Shanzer, titled "Kinship and Marriage among the Burgundians," as part of the "Studies in Historical Archaeoethnology," sponsored by The Center for Interdisciplinary Research on Social Stress in San Marino. My thanks to Professor Shanzer for allowing me to read and cite this paper.

moreover, a king with a chronic insubordination problem, something that will play an important role in his developing relationship with Clovis. It is worthwhile to stress the significance of these authorial decisions, namely, that Emilio was cognizant of Gregory's artifices, and that he was able to neutralize them with subtle (and less subtle) editorial choices of his own. The kind of storytelling that interested Emilio was one in which characters moved across the chessboard of history as rational actors.[90]

Rejoining the narrative pace dictated by Gregory, Emilio turns to discuss Chilperic's daughters, Mucutima (Chroma in the *Histories*) and Clothild. Here, too, the characters are moved by different concerns than they are in the *Histories* and end up taking different actions. Emilio's Clothild was not coy in stating her expectations of Clovis; she conditioned the marriage on his adoption of Christianity. Gundobad, conscious of the potential complications entailed by this condition, was at some loss for a response, but his desire to give his niece's hand in marriage to a Frankish king trumped this concern. He thus conveyed Clothild's demand. To the surprise of the Burgundians, the Frankish legates confirmed that Clovis was already considering baptism, and that he would consent to it if the marriage were favorably contracted. Hesitant to make any further demands on the Franks, Gundobad conceded and sent Clothild to Paris, accompanied by a lavishly equipped entourage.

The marriage arrangements were also covered by Biondo, and the differences between the two versions are instructive. Biondo recounts:

Not long afterwards [i.e., the establishment of Ravenna as the Ostrogothic *sedes regiae*], *King Clovis took Clothild as a wife. He went to war against Gundobad, his wife's uncle, and the Burgundians. In this war he annexed to his rule the cities and towns situated between the Loire and the Seine rivers. This war was brought to rest with Clothild's intervention.*[91]

There is no discussion of Christianity at this point at all, and certainly no promises made on its account. Only later, when Clovis's army begins

---

[90] Emilio outlines his agenda in his brief prologue. See *DRG*, prol.: "Cum genere humano bene ac praeclare ageretur, si summi Duces Regesque ac Imperatores quae gerunt, ea velut in omnium gentium theatro, ac posteritatis oculis se gerere arbitrarentur: & quae maxime excellunt, historicorum monumentis consecrata, caeteri vitutis studio accensi lectitarent." Davies, "Late XVth Century French Historiography," pp. 279, 309.

[91] Biondo, *Decades*, 1.3, p. 21: "Nam Clodoveus Rex non multo postquam Crotchildem acceperat uxorem: bellum gessit adversus gundobaldum uxoris patruum & burgundiones. Quo in bello civitates & oppida: ligerim inter & secanam amnes sita suo adiunxit imperio. Eo tamen bello interventu crotchildis sedato." Compare Aimoin, *Gesta Francorum* 1.15, col. 653: "Unde cum Clodoveus regnum suum usque Sequanam, atque postmodum usque Ligerim fluvios ampliasset." Here, as in *Fredegar*, Clothild does the opposite to bringing the war to rest.

to crumble under the Alamannic pressure on the battlefield of Tolbiac, does he recall a promise heretofore unmentioned:

When, in the battle, he saw his army turn in flight, he remembered having made a promise. He suspected that because he neglected to fulfill the requests made often by his wife, these adversities in battle had befallen him. Then he vowed with intent to the God of heaven and earth to which Clothild preached to acquiesce in his advice and appeal.[92]

We would certainly be right to suspect that Emilio borrowed Clothild's premarital stipulations from Biondo; Clothild's desire to bring the war to an end likewise originated with the *Decades*. But Emilio put these motifs to slightly different use. Since he wanted Clothild to function as a moral compass from the start, he inserted the condition to convert into the marriage deliberations. In his coverage of Clovis's Burgundian war, Emilio chose to include an emotional plea by Clothild to her husband, begging him to preserve her homeland. By doing so, Emilio was able to show the queen's commitment to bring about the cessation of hostilities.[93]

From the marriage, Gregory moved on to Clothild's sermons and the births of Ingomer and Chlodomer. Emilio, for his part, skipped ahead to the war with the Alamanni, ignoring these episodes altogether. Angrily insisting that his sons were to be dedicated in the name of his gods, Gregory's Clovis comes off as a belligerent pagan, contemptuous of Clothild's belief. Emilio could not accept such a regression in his main character. His Clovis gave his word that he would convert; the king's conduct in Soissons had raised hope that he would soon fulfill that promise. The baptism of Ingomer and Chlodomer was thus deemed redundant and was duly discarded.

Emilio's treatment of Clovis's baptism sequence can best be described as a loose dramatization of Gregory's rendition, though more elaborate in exposition and energetic in pace. The Alamanni were not mere casualties of Clovis's insatiable hunger for land and power, but aggressors in another conflict, which pit them against the Sicambri, the Franks' allies. Clovis, who had previously promised his friendship to the Sicambri, did not hesitate to make good on his promise: "The two armies, Franks and Sicambrians, together marched on Alemannia. They fought fiercely in the town of Tolbiac."[94]

---

[92] Biondo, *Decades* I.3, p. 21: "quo in praelio suos in fugam conversos videns memor est factus promissionis, quam multotiens requisites uxori servare neglexerat & ipsam praelii adversitatem, ob id solum sibi accidere suspiciatus est. Hinc deo caeli & terrae, quem Crotchildis uxor praedicaret, vovit illius consilio precibusque acquiescere." See Maissen, *Von der Legende zum Modell*, pp. 198–199.
[93] See Davies, "Late XVth Century French Historiography," p. 184.
[94] *DRG*, p. 6: "In Alemaniam egregiae copiae ductae, simul Francorum, Sicambrorumque. Pugnatum est acriter ad Tilbiacum oppidum."

This, says Emilio, was miraculous on two counts, the first, that the two nations, so warlike and well-trained, could be threatened by a single enemy;[95] the second, that, having been severely routed, they could regroup and achieve a seemingly impossible victory. From this comment, readers are meant to infer that the Franks were not only faithful to their allies but also tenacious in their pursuit of victory, even when the odds were stacked against them. A depiction of the battle ensues, complete with in-depth coverage of the movements of the Frankish cavalry, led by Clovis, and infantry, commanded by his close friend, Sigibert of Cologne.[96]

Not only is the drama that unfolds on the battlefield indicative of Emilio's historiographical horizons, it is also likely meant to be read as a lesson in leadership and martial spirit that would be of interest to any aspiring general.[97] Sigibert sustains injuries and is replaced by his son, whereas Clovis is unable to keep his mounted troops in formation. A crushing defeat seems eminent. When hope is nearly extinguished, Clovis remembers the promise he made to his wife when she agreed to his offer of marriage. He appeals to God, promising to become Christian if he makes it home.

We might pause here and consider that in the *Histories*, Sigibert "the Lame" was not mentioned in the chapter that dealt with the Battle of Tolbiac. We learn of his role and the injury he sustained fighting the Alamanni only later, when Gregory discusses the presence of Chloderic, his son, on the battlefield at Vouillé.[98] Emilio used this information to stage a more intricate battle scene, one in which his own inventiveness played a central role. Since Sigibert was based in Cologne, he was styled *Sicamber* by Emilio, who turned him and Clovis into close friends and their armies into allies on the battlefield. He could not have been influenced in this by any of the usual sources; in *Fredegar*, neither Sigibert nor Chloderic are mentioned prior to their elimination by Clovis,[99] and in the *LHF* they are not mentioned at all.[100] Aimoin and the *Grandes Chroniques*

---

[95] Compare *DRG*, pp. 6–7: "Miraculo utrunque extitit, primum, duas gentes instructissimas bellicosissimasque ab una vinci ... " and Biondo, *Decades* 1.3, p. 21: " ... viris fortibus armisque instructissima praelio decertavit."
[96] This division creates the impression that Clovis and Sigibert commanded two forces of the same army, with Clovis's command marking him as superior.
[97] See Emilio's preface to the *DRG*: "Cum genere humano bene ac praeclare ageretur, si summi Duces, Regesque, ac Imperatores, quae gerunt ea velut in omnium gentium theatro, ac posteritatis oculis se gerere arbitrarentur, et quae maxime excellunt, historicorum monumentis consecrata, caeteri virtutis studio accensi lectitarent."
[98] Gregory of Tours, *Histories*, II.37: "Habebat autem in adiuturium suum filium Sygiberthi Claudi nomen Chlodericum. Hic Sygiberthus pugnans contra Alamannos apud Tulbiacensim oppidum percussus in genuculum claudicabat."
[99] In the context of Sigibert's alliance with Clovis against the Goths. See *Fredegar* III.25.
[100] In *LHF*, ch. 18 the author makes do with this laconic observation: "Quibus mortuis vel peremptis, omnem regnum eorum et thesauros Chlodoveus accepit, interfectisque multis et magnis regibus vel parentibus suis."

follow the *LHF* in their silence, as does Biondo. Thus, Emilio must have pieced together this scene from bits he found in Gregory. He supplied the military movements and dramatic turns in the plot from his own imagination.

Emilio takes an interesting approach to the military miracle that occurs. In Gregory's account, Clovis focuses his appeal on the futility of the pagan gods. More importantly, Gregory attributes the panic that spread through the Alamannic army to divine intervention. In Emilio's version, Clovis turns to God in fulfillment of a prior obligation to Clothild. Having made his appeal, it is not God, but Clovis's newly found resolve that tips the scales in favor of the Franks. Revitalized, he selects a group of elite cavalrymen, sounds the trumpet, and rallies his battered troops. Seeing their king's steadfastness, the exhausted captains return to the battle refreshed, sowing confusion in the ranks of the enemy. The day is won. While Emilio did admit that it was Clovis's petition that changed the tide of battle,[101] it is notable that the king is the only character with agency in this entire episode. God lurks in the background, to be sure, along with Sigibert and all the rest, but, more than a call to faith, this remains a tale of Clovis's psychological strength.

Clovis returned home, intent on fulfilling his promise to Clothild. Emilio adds that since he was a man of dignity and now also of orthodoxy, he understood the danger of becoming contaminated with the Arian heresy, a condition to which his sister Lantechild had fallen victim. By introducing the Arian threat at such an early point in the plot, Emilio was laying the foundation for a prolonged deliberation about the reasons for the outbreak of war with the Visigoths and its consequences. The Visigothic war is the longest element of the *DRG*'s Clovis narrative, and its significance for the progression of the plot is revealed only gradually.

Remigius is summoned, and he prepares to baptize Clovis and 3,000 of his men. The gilded scene that follows and its implications for Emilio's approach has been remarked upon already. It is nevertheless important to return to it once more, if only to mention that, apart from showing Emilio's skill in creating such picturesque dramatizations, the scene advances a vision of its two main protagonists that well exceeded Gregory's narrative scope. Remigius stands in the middle of the ecclesiastical entourage, more august than we would imagine a mere mortal could be. Clovis, whose long hair, so emblematic of the Merovingian *stirps*, is washed and perfumed,

---

[101] *DRG*, p. 5: "Tunc vero velut caelesti nomine rem Francicam respiciente, mutata praelii fortuna, qui terga passim dederant, exhortantibus ducibus obliti vulnerum, laborisque, ad delendum dedecus in praelium restitutis ordinibus rediere." On Merovingian (and, more generally, dynastic) *fortuna*, see Maissen, *Von der Legende zum Modell*, pp. 201–204.

descends to the baptismal basin dressed in a white gown, transformed into a humble private person. From the waters emerges a new man, Ludovicus, the name Emilio uses instead of Clodoveus for the remainder of the section. The remark made at this point is worthy of our attention: "In this manner, he was sprinkled with holy water and, as though by celestial mandate, was anointed with the chrism. Then, in place of the three red crowns against a white field that were depicted until that day by the insignia of the gentiles, he accepted the sign of the lilies."[102]

The baptism of Clovis constitutes something of an outlier when we consider Emilio's overall use of the sources. After all, he was writing as a court historian, even if the particulars of his formal nomination are somewhat unclear. He would in any case have been remiss if he had ignored the narrative components of the baptism that had been added to Gregory's account in subsequent centuries, and which his prospective royal patrons would have considered sacrosanct and indispensable. Emilio's two observations, first that Clovis was anointed by a celestial chrism and then that he replaced his coat-of-arms, were no doubt a nod to the power of an established and cherished tradition.[103] Yet here his critical approach as a humanist becomes apparent, because the statements remain either qualified or incomplete, leaving ample room for interpretation. As opposed to previous traditions that first emerged in the eleventh century, and which explained the transformation of the previous coat-of-arms (incidentally, of three frogs) as a miracle, Emilio casually mentioned that Clovis was the one who replaced his old insignia. As for the dove that descended from heaven bearing the holy ampulla, another central component of the Clovis myth dramatically described in Hincmar's *Life of Remigius*, it is here only implied and even then, qualified with *velut*.

For her part, Clovis's sister Lantechild realizes the error of her ways, rejecting the teachings of her heretical masters and joining her brother in the one true faith. Clovis's soldiers and the rest of the Franks also accepted Catholicism that day, marking very clearly the moment the Gauls and the Franks became one in their faith, a united and resolute community. The Alamanni, who remained on the sidelines, began to worry that their tributary status would worsen because of the conversion. They appealed to Theoderic for protection, opening a long section dedicated to the king of the Ostrogoths. A quote from Cassiodorus's Letter II.41 follows, although the lengthy address that comes next is a pronounced departure from the

---

[102] *DRG*: "Ita sacra lustratus aqua, & velut coelestis muneris chrismate delibutus. Cumque tribus diadematibus rubris in alba parma depictis ad eam diem usus fuisset, pro gentilitiis insignibus Liliata signa accepit."
[103] See Priesterjahn, "Back to the Roots," pp. 7–8.

epistle's reserved tone. Letter II.41 was written to dissuade Clovis from pursuing another war against the Alamanni, and this is also the premise of Emilio's paraphrase. But what begins as an appeal to Clovis's clemency turns into an unabashed encomium, celebrating the Frankish king's piety, his glory, and the unique appreciation he has merited in Theoderic's eyes.[104] Emilio's use of Cassiodorus, mediated by Biondo, is circumspect, cleverly building an image of both protagonists in anticipation of a future clash.

Theoderic's missive was carried to Gaul by legates who were received by King Clovis in Orléans, just as he was preparing to convoke a Church Council there. As we know, the Council of Orléans was only held in 511, very close to Clovis's death. Here it is presented as having been convened before the Battle of Vouillé, which we know took place in 507. Clovis retorted with a letter of his own, which he hoped would allay the Ostrogoths' concerns; the Alamanni would receive the good peace and just laws they requested.

Meanwhile, an even more ominous storm was brewing on the horizon. The Franks, fueled by their hatred for the heretical Visigoths, were itching for war. It is possible that Emilio wanted to introduce an image of Clovis as the leader of his church and convoker of councils as the back story to the war with the Goths. Since Orléans 511 was not mentioned in the *Histories*, Emilio could have rearranged the timeline, pushing the council forward by four years. Moreover, since Emilio believed that Clovis died in 515, his chronology could have accommodated a council in the run-up to Vouillé, especially when this played well into the character's development. Another letter is quoted shortly thereafter, based loosely on *Variae* III.4, to which Clovis also responds, this time with an indictment of Alaric.[105] As previously remarked, this back-and-forth creates the effect of a protracted dialog, from which both Clovis and Theoderic emerge as temperate and calculated, in keeping with Emilio's efforts to present a nuanced back story.

In preparation for war, the Franks seek and receive the alliance of the Burgundians, but a rebellion, led by Godegisel, breaks out against Gundobad. Godegisel invites Clovis to intervene. If he is successful, argues Godegisel, Gundobad's share of the kingdom would be Clovis's to take. After all, he was the Burgundian king's kinsman by marriage. Clovis is persuaded and mobilizes his troops. It is Clothild, whose marriage to Clovis

---

[104] On the humanist use of such narrative artifices, see F. Gilbert, *Machiavelli and Guicciardini: Politics and History in Sixteenth-Century Florence* (Princeton, NJ: Princeton University Press, 1965), p. 211.

[105] Emilio's Clovis was apparently committed to the protocols of diplomacy, a point that was important enough for the *DRG* to make.

was at the crux of Godegisel's offer, that goes out of her way to soothe her husband to prevent all-out war between Franks and Burgundians. The details of the rebellion are quite like those outlined by the *Histories*, but the end is surprising, to say the least. The Franks take offense at Gundobad's elimination of Godegisel, and they encircle his stronghold in Vienne. Having given up hope of victory, Gundobad escapes to the Ostrogoths, and the *proceres* of Clovis and Clothild appoint Sigismund king in his stead.

Two major departures from Gregory's narrative are found in this account. The first is that Clovis in the *DRG* pursues his commitment to Godegisel to its natural end instead of aborting it when offered tribute. Again, the Franks are true to their word and tenacious in battle. The second difference is that, while Gundobad maintained his hold on the Burgundian kingdom for sixteen years after the events depicted here, and, if we believe Gregory, managed to wriggle his way out of the tribute agreement fairly quickly, in the *DRG* he is given a different end. The escape to Italy was lifted from a later episode of Burgundian history, the assaults of Clothild's children on Gundobad's son Godomar. Strikingly, it is the Frankish royal couple that determines the identity of Gundobad's heir, Sigismund.

Emilio's treatment of the Battle of Vouillé in the subsequent scene turns on its head the motif introduced in the Battle of Tolbiac, namely, royal perseverance in the face of adversity. We recall that in Tolbiac, Clovis was able to regroup and prevail, but in his account of Vouillé, Emilio tells the story from the perspective of Alaric, the loser of the engagement. When Alaric's troops break formation and retreat before the advancing Franks, he attempts to prevent the collapse of his army: "Alaric stood in the way of the retreating troops. He ordered them back into battle: 'Not by the feet and back of those unwilling to fight, but by the armed right hand is protection and safety to be found. In strength and courage is victory, booty, and glory obtained; in flight and cowardice is found servitude, disgrace, and destruction'."[106] These poignant words resound not so much with Alaric's men, but with the Frankish king, who, moved by the desire for plunder and glory, charges the Visigothic ranks. He is narrowly saved from the spears of Alaric's cavalrymen, but in the end prevails. The Visigoths are scattered and, while some seek refuge in Angoulême, they are quickly routed by the Franks, who also take hold of Bordeaux, Bazas, Cahors, Rodez, and, of course, Toulouse. Since

---

[106] *DRG*, p. 8: "Alaricus fugientibus obstare: in pugnam redire iubere: non a pedibus tergoque imbelli, sed ab armata dextra praesidium saluti quaerendum: in virtute audaciaque victoriam, praedam, gloriam positam: in fuga ignaviaque servitutem, dedecus, exitium collocatum."

that day, remarks Emilio, the place where the Visigoths were defeated was known as *Campus Arrianus*, "the Arian field."

During the final phase of Clovis's political life, Gregory has him pursue absolute power over the Franks through a premeditated spree of assassinations. This is another instance in which Emilio took liberty with the chronology presented in the *Histories*. In the *Histories*, this happened after he defeated the Visigoths, for which he received from the emperor the title of patrician. In Emilio's narrative, the elimination of Ragnachar (Cannacarius in the *DRG*), Sigibert, and Chararic precedes the imperial honors bestowed on Clovis by Anastasius, in what he describes as a domestic affair of a more modest scale.[107] Given his own sensibilities, Emilio may well have considered the bestowal of imperial titulature the apex of Clovis's career, and thus placed it toward the end. Hailing Clovis as consul and patrician when his own house was still in disarray would have been poor form. Titles were not the only gift Clovis received; the emperor sent a golden crown, which Clovis had encrusted with pearls and precious gems. This was done not for his own edification, but for the glory of the Church. Clovis sent the crown to Rome, where it was deposited in St. John Lateran.[108]

Ragnachar, the first of three domestic adversaries, is styled "petty king of Cambrai and Arras."[109] In a significant sidebar, Ragnachar is reported by Emilio to have challenged Clovis's ancestral claim to the Frankish throne by boasting that he was the scion of the oldest noble family: "He claimed to be the great-grandson of Clodio, king of the Franks, and said that according to the laws of the Franks the kingdom should go to him. It was not his strength, but his words that the king found unacceptable."[110]

The relationship of Merovech, Clovis's oldest verified ancestor, to Clodio was left hanging by both Gregory and Emilio. In the *DRG*, Clodio nevertheless appears as a source of legitimacy with which Ragnachar was able to provoke Clovis into action. In the *Histories*, the Ragnachar episode was never about royal blood. Rather, it was a story about Clovis's aptitude for taking advantage of opportunities when those came his way. In the *DRG*,

---

[107] *DRG*, p. 11: " ... regressus Rex ad minora etiam domi sananda tollendaque mala animum convertit."
[108] Compare this with the accounts of Clovis II's treatment of St. Denis's arm in Dionysian compositions. Emilio ignored it entirely in his account of Clovis II's reign.
[109] *DRG*, p. 11: "Cannacarius Cameracensium idem & Atrebatium Regulus, vetustissima generis nobilitate tumebat."
[110] Ibid.: "Clodionis Regis Franci abnepotem se praedicabat: ac ad se legibus Francorum Regnum perventurum fuisse dicebat. Non vires hominis, sed causa ingrata Regi erat." For a comparable episode, see the Munderic affair in Gregory of Tours, *Histories*, II.40–42; Reimitz, "The Early History of Frankish Origin Legends," pp. 168–169.

Clodio's role can be interpreted in one of two ways. Ragnachar might be saying that Merovech was not the rightful heir of Clodio, from which we are left to infer that Clovis was a usurper. Then again, Ragnachar might only have been claiming a stake in the kingship as the descendant of a recognized—and "long-haired"—king of the Franks, and we should not read more into this than that. Clovis's ire is perhaps an indication that Emilio meant for us to favor the former interpretation.

Clovis of course went on to eliminate Ragnachar and many others, including Sigibert "the Lame." The ruse devised by Clovis to rid himself of Sigibert and Chloderic presented some difficulty for Emilio. At least as it was presented in the *Histories*, this was a tale of cruel cunning. But if we recall that Clovis came to Sigibert's aid in Emilio's version of the battle at Tolbiac, Emilio's agenda would have been poorly served by embracing Gregory's narrative. Instead, Emilio reminds us that Sigibert—styled here as *ex proceribus Francis* as opposed to Clovis's *rex*—had shed his blood for the glory of the king. This, explains Emilio, is why Clovis decided to reward him by allowing his son to succeed him. At first, Chloderic also seemed worthy of this privilege; he lent crucial help to Clovis during the Battle of Vouillé.[111] Sadly, the impatient son interpreted Clovis's generosity as a signal that the king would look the other way if he murdered his father and thus wasted no time in seizing his prize. Straight away, the king had Chloderic killed, and we learn that "Clovis avenged the insult to the old man by killing his son."[112] Clovis's justice was swift and severe, allowing him complete control of his aristocracy and overwhelming dominance over other royal claimants.

The Byzantine legation that seals the penultimate section of the plot finds Clovis in Tours, where he was stationed after his victory over the Visigoths. The *oratores* Anastasius sent bore a message for Clovis, which Emilio delivers as direct speech: "The emperor greets you as consul and patrician, because he could devise no greater and more distinguished summit than the titles of majesty which adorned Caesar."[113]

Clovis had completed his transformation. It remained only to describe the circumstances of his death. The amity between Franks and Greeks, forged after Clovis sent the crown to Rome, alarmed Theoderic. He sent 80,000 troops, and, supported by his Gepid and Visigothic allies, was able

---

[111] *DRG*, p. 9: "Beneficio loricae, ac auxilio Clodorici iuvenum fortissimi aequato Marte, incruentus periculum evitavit." Compare Gregory of Tours, *Histories*, II.37.
[112] Ibid., p. 12: "Ludovicus supplicio filii necem senis est ultus."
[113] Ibid.: "Te Augustus Consulem Patriciumque salutat, qua tituli maiestate secundum Caesarum decus, nullum maius excelsiusque fastigium excogitare potuit." Note that Emilio uses Gregory's terminology—*augustus*—but attributes the titles to Anastasius as he addresses Clovis, thereby correcting the obvious titular blunder. A more fitting *patricius* is added for stylistic considerations.

to secure Provence for himself and Gascony for Amalaric. This, argues Emilio, is why sole domination of Gaul eluded Clovis in his lifetime. The Ostrogoths were content with the accomplishment and did not attempt to mount an invasion of Frankish territory. It seemed enough to them that Clovis was intimidated into forgoing additional expansion. Clovis wanted to avenge the insult, of course, but died before having had the chance to do so. He was buried in the Church of the Apostles in Paris, later known as Sainte-Geneviève.

Emilio's Clovis rested on the narrative basis established by Gregory's *Histories*, but the result was a character quite different in its disposition and motivations. The *DRG* insists on Clovis's trustworthiness, a trait concerning which Gregory's account finds him wanting. For Emilio, Clovis is a fierce enemy but also a staunch ally, again not something the *Histories* seems to emphasize. He is pious, but only insofar as his piety illuminates his dependability, self-reliance, and psychological fortitude. Unlike Gregory, Emilio makes clear that Clovis's piety is not an expression of submission to divine will. As we saw, it was the king's agency, not God's, that led him to triumph. Under Emilio's pen, Clovis emerges as a rational actor, moved by considerations that are clearly relatable to a humanist readership. In this he is not alone. The entire cast of characters in the Clovis sequence acts in accordance with Emilio's understanding of historiography, its methods, and its aims.

2.3 Conclusions

Like Gregory, Emilio sought to portray Clovis's life as a series of successfully overcome challenges, leading its protagonist along a path of personal evolution. Ultimately, both used Clovis as an exemplum of princes from which contemporary rulers were to draw inspiration. But while Gregory's Clovis was designed to inform these rulers about their responsibilities toward God's earthly representatives, Emilio was more interested in the secular obligations of the king to his army and to matters of state. In the *Histories*, Clovis's relationship with the Church, its saints, and its bishops was seen as a natural conclusion to a larger discussion about the spread of Catholic Christianity in Gaul in the face of significant hardship.

More concerned with Clovis the soldier and statesman, Emilio steered clear of Gregory's hero/villain binary. He provided Clothild, Theoderic, and Gundobad with the background necessary to justify their own actions and to shine a positive light on Clovis. For Clovis's virtues to become manifest, his supporting cast needed a richer background, which Emilio duly provided. Emilio's return to Gregory is also a comment on the inadequacy of the medieval Clovis narrative for Early Modern tastes.

Conclusions

The miraculous elements of the Clovis narrative strewn throughout the *Grandes Chroniques* and elsewhere in medieval prose give way in the *DRG* to a rational, calculated consideration of the traits that make an ideal king—martial prowess, diplomatic acumen, trustworthiness, and dogged determination. For these traits he was rewarded with the "titles of majesty which adorned Caesar." Gregory's misuse of "consul aut augustus" demonstrates clearly that his priorities as an author were elsewhere.

With Clovis's heirs we enter a new phase of the Merovingian story, one marked by stasis, division, and internal strife. While the *Histories* devote the better part of seven books to this "period," it will be reduced by the chroniclers and historians of the following centuries to a story of internecine conflict and, ultimately, of failure to rule. It is to this failure that we now turn.

Part II

Bears and Wolves

3 *Taedit me memorare*:[*] The Middle Merovingians

The intermediate chapter of the Merovingian storyline extends from the death of Clovis in 511 to the death of Dagobert I in 639. During this nearly 130-year period, Gaul had changed completely. Clovis no doubt succeeded in expanding Frankish rule over large swaths of Gaul and in checking internal challenges to his rule. He was a distinguished military commander whose accomplishments, at least as they are portrayed in sympathetic sources, seem to dwarf those of his successors.

Clovis, in his time, was continuing a Frankish expansionist thrust that began much earlier. The forces that brought the Franks into Gaul were already at play in the 440s, and, by the 480s, were defining the horizon of political possibilities that made Clovis's accomplishments feasible. To say that he stood, at the time of his death, at the head of a kingdom that was essentially identical to the political groupings described in the last five books of Gregory's *Histories*, much less in Book IV of *Fredegar*, would be a mistake.[1]

In 590, Gaul was divided between several centers of power. Each center was controlled by a descendant of Clovis, one grandson and two great-grandsons. Gregory documented the workings of the royal administration and its effect on urban and rural life. Counts, tax men, judges, diplomats, and royal financiers fill the pages of the *Histories*. They indicate an efficient mode of governance that allowed for the extraction of wealth, used in turn to develop infrastructure, raise armies, and maintain a foreign policy.[2]

---

[*] Gregory of Tours, *Histories*, V.1: "Taedit me bellorum civilium diversitatis, que Francorum gentem et regnum valde proterunt, memorare; in quo, quod peius est, tempore illud quod Dominus de dolorum praedixit initium iam videmus: 'Consurgit pater in filium, filius in patrem, frater in fratrem, proximus iam propinquus'."

[1] On the changing political visions between Gregory and *Fredegar*, expressed most clearly in the six-book version of the *Histories*, see H. Reimitz, "Social Networks and Identities in Frankish Historiography: New Aspects of the Textual History of Gregory of Tours' *Historiae*," in *The Construction of Communities in the Early Middle Ages: Texts, Resources and Artefacts*, eds. R. Corradini, M. Diesenberger and H. Reimitz (Leiden and Boston: Brill, 2003), pp. 229–268.

[2] See the contributions of Yitzhak Hen, Laury Sarti, Gregory Halfond, and Peregrine Horden in Effros and Moreira, eds., *The Oxford Handbook of the Merovingian World*, pp. 217–319.

There was also violence. The *Histories* describes numerous military engagements, assassinations, and other tools of "hard power" as integral features of middle Merovingian rule.[3] Yet Gregory's jeremiads about the havoc these conflicts wreaked should be read with his moral framework in mind.[4] Taken at face value, they appear to have been necessary, albeit deadly, results of royal power. Whether to prune the family tree of royal claimants or to ensure the ongoing loyalty of aristocratic circles on which kings relied so heavily, violence had rational motivations and was applied toward rational means.

The Church played a prominent role in the day-to-day tasks of government. Often working together with the civil authorities, it arbitrated legal disputes and diffused outbreaks of violence.[5] Additionally, the Church functioned as an alternative to the secular network in brokering back-channel diplomatic efforts. Bishops in the service of the court seem to have been a perennial feature of early medieval politics, and this is certainly apparent in Merovingian-era sources.[6]

Readers of the *Histories* hear a great deal about Gregory's royal service. Yet, his proximity to royal power was exceeded by some of his episcopal colleagues. The 610s saw Leudemund of Sion conspire in a plot to overthrow Chlothar II (in Burgundy, at least).[7] He was pardoned through the mediation of the Abbot of Luxeuil, another figure who, in those years, had the ear of the king. In the 650s, several decades after the *terminus ante quem* for this chapter, Bishop Dido of Poitiers was a co-conspirator in the Grimoald coup, entrusted with the task of spiriting away the young prince

---

[3] For a particularly bloody view, see B.W. Reynolds, "The Mind of Baddo: Assassination in Merovingian Politics," *Journal of Medieval History* 13 (1987), pp. 117–124; B. S. Bachrach, "The Imperial Roots of Merovingian Military Organization, in *Military Aspects of Scandinavian Society in a European Perspective, AD 1–1300: Papers from an International Research Seminar at the Danish National Museum, 2–4 May 1996*, eds. A. Nørgård Jørgensen and B.L. Clausen (Copenhagen: Danish National Museum, 1997), pp. 25–31.

[4] Especially as they pertain to the application of a "feuding society" model. On this, see G. Halsall, "Violence and Society in the Early Medieval West: An Introductory Survey," in *Violence and Society in the Early Medieval West*, ed. G. Halsall (Woodbridge: Boydell and Brewer, 1998), pp. 1–45; G. Halsall, "Reflections on Early Medieval Violence: The Example of the 'Bloodfeud'," *Memoria y Civilización* 2 (1999), pp. 7–29; I.N. Wood, "The Bloodfeud of the Franks: A Historiographical Legend," *Early Medieval Europe* 14, 4 (2006), pp. 489–504.

[5] Hen, "The Church in Sixth-Century Gaul," pp. 232–255. For the views of Enlightenment scholars on this period, see Wood, *The Modern Origins*, pp. 27, 38–39, 47.

[6] On this, see now G.I. Halfond, *Bishops and the Politics of Patronage in Merovingian Gaul* (Ithaca, NY: Cornell University Press, 2019); M.E. Moore, *A Sacred Kingdom: Bishops and the Rise of Frankish Kingship, 300–850* (Washington, DC: The Catholic University of America Press, 2011).

[7] *Fredegar* IV.44, pp. 142–143.

Dagobert II to Ireland.[8] We can imagine that Gregory would have been outraged by such conduct. Although he was not entirely above-board himself; as his uncanonical appointment and untoward involvement in the rebellion that broke out at the nunnery of the Holy Cross in Poitiers suggest,[9] he was never one to undermine royal rule.[10]

In *Fredegar*'s Gaul, the three spheres of royal power radiating from Paris, Orléans, and Metz had solidified into distinct territorial kingdoms.[11] Counties and cities continued to change hands through the designs of inheritance and the vagaries of war, but the contours of this division were maintained overall, even after periods of sole rule. Each kingdom had a court bureaucracy and an army, whose senior posts were mostly held by a wealthy landed elite with local holdings and ties to the king. The local interests of these men did not prohibit the formation of broader regional alliances. The *regna Francorum* were perceived by the Merovingians and their ruling class as a distinct cultural and political space, albeit one whose constituent parts were apt to violently disagree with one another.[12]

All the while, the Franks continued to push against their borders in an effort to subdue neighboring peoples and either directly conquer them or subject them to tribute. There were intermissions in this effort, to be sure—Clovis's early death dictated one such hiatus—but Chlodomer, the ex-king's oldest son by Clothild, invaded the Burgundian kingdom as soon as he was strong enough to do so. He was killed in 524, but the Burgundians were eventually overrun. Chlodomer's brothers and half-brother likewise pursued an expansionist campaign against the Thuringians at their earliest opportunity.

The next generation of monarchs, during whose reigns Gregory predominantly wrote, also did not hesitate to seek expansion. Most impressive in

---

[8] *LHF*, ch. 43. On this affair there is voluminous literature. For some initial reading, see Becher, "Der sogenannte Staatsstreich Grimoalds," pp. 119–147; Gerberding, *The Rise of the Carolingians and the Liber Historiae Francorum*; Hen, "Changing Places," pp. 225–244.

[9] Gregory describes his involvement in the rebellion, led by the royally born nuns Basina and Clothild against the abbess Leubovera, in *Histories* IX.39–43. See E.T. Dailey, "Misremembering Radegund's Foundation of Sainte-Croix," in *Erfahren, erzählen, erinnern: narrative Konstruktionen von Gedächtnis und Generation in Antike und Mittelalter*, ed. H. Brandt et al. (Bamberg: University of Bamberg Press, 2012), pp. 117–140; J.C. Edwards, *Superior Women: Medieval Female Authority in Poitiers' Abbey of Sainte-Croix* (Oxford: Oxford University Press, 2019), pp. 77–85; C.M.M. Casias, "Rebel Nuns and the Bishop Historian: The Competing Voices of Radegund and Gregory," *Studies in Late Antiquity* 6, 1 (2022), pp. 5–34.

[10] Although he was accused of maligning the queen, a serious, if not comparably grave, offense. Gregory of Tours, *Histories*, v.18, v.49. On this, see Dailey, *Queens, Consorts, Concubines*, pp. 152–156.

[11] See E. Ewig, *Die fränkischen Teilungen und Teilreiche (511–613)* (Wiesbaden: Franz Steiner Verlag, 1953).

[12] See now Y. Hen, "The Merovingian Polity: A Network of Courts and Courtiers," in Effros and Moreira, eds., *The Oxford Handbook of the Merovingian World*, pp. 217–237.

this regard were the interventions of Theudebert I in Pannonia and, importantly, in North Italy, which established a Frankish presence in the Apennine peninsula that lasted until the early 560s.[13] Among the other Merovingian kings then in power, Sigibert I, Theudebert's cousin, fought the Avars and the Saxons, and Guntram, Sigibert's brother, was active on the Spanish front against the Visigoths. It is true that considerable military energy was expended on internecine wars, which interfered with the Merovingians' ability to project their power outward. Nonetheless, among the post-Roman successor states in the West, the Franks emerged from this era as the strongest, most culturally and militarily vibrant society, shepherded confidently by capable, aggressive kings.

Expansion continued in the following generation. With Theuderic II and Theudebert II, the immediate reaches of Alamannia again came into view, playing a central role in the two brothers' deadly competition. And under Chlothar II, the Saxons were beaten and forced to pay tribute. This was but a prelude to what would ensue. Chlothar's son, Dagobert I, positioned himself as the most important man in western Europe. Under him, the Franks' reach was felt in Italy, Bavaria, Alamannia, Spain, Thuringia, Saxony, and Frisia. He also cooperated with the Eastern Empire.[14]

Gaul's Church was heavily involved in all of these matters. Already in Clovis's day if not before,[15] investment in religious institutions was seen as worthwhile. After Clovis's death, his widow and children gave even more ostentatiously to the Church. Most memorable were Childebert I's generosity toward the church of Paris and Chlothar I's patronage of Saint-Medard in Soissons.[16] Radegund went so far as to

---

[13] See A. Gillet, "Telling off Justinian: Theudebert I, the *Epistolae Austrasicae*, and Communication Strategies in Sixth-Century Merovingian-Byzantine Relations," *Early Medieval Europe* 27, 2 (2019), pp. 161–194; S.T. Loseby, "Gregory of Tours, Italy, and the Empire," in *A Companion to Gregory of Tours*, ed. A.C. Murray (Leiden: Brill, 2016), pp. 462–497; F. Beisel, *Theudebertus magnus rex Francorum: Persönlichkeit und Zeit* (Idstein: Schulz-Kirchner Verlag, 1993), pp. 65–109; J.J. Arnold, "The Merovingians and Italy: Ostrogoths and Early Lombards," in Effros and Moreira, eds., *The Oxford Handbook of the Merovingian World*, pp. 442–460, at pp. 451–454.

[14] See S. Esders, "Herakleios, Dagobert und die 'beschnittenen Völker': Die Umwälzungen des Mittelmeerraums im 7. Jahrhundert in der Chronik des sog. Fredegar," in *Jenseits der Grenzen. Beiträge zur spätantiken und frühmittelalterlichen Geschichtsschreibung*, eds. A. Goltz, H. Leppin, and H. Schlange-Schöningen (Berlin and New York: De Gruyter, 2009), pp. 239–311.

[15] On Childeric's relationship with St. Genovefa, see *Vita Genovefae*, ch. 26, p. 226; Halsall, "Childeric's Grave, Clovis' Succession," pp. 120, 127; Bitel, *Landscape with Two Saints*, pp. 70–77.

[16] Childebert, see Venantius Fortunatus, *De ecclesia Parisiaca*, MGH AA 4, ed. F. Leo (Berlin: Weidmann, 1881), pp. 39–40; J. Dérens and M. Fleury, "La construction de la cathédrale de Paris par Childebert Ier, d'après le *De ecclesia Parisiaca* de Fortunat," *Journal des savants* (1977), pp. 247–256. For Chlothar, see Gregory of Tours, *Histories*, IV.19.

take the veil,[17] and though she was perhaps the first member of the royal family to do so, she was certainly not the last. Even more important was royal patronage of monastic institutions. The contours of royal–aristocratic cooperation on the monastic front crystallized gradually, and reached maturity only in the 660s, but already in the generation of Guntram and Sigibert (the latter inspired, it seems, by his father Chlothar) the Merovingians pledged significant resources to monastic communities. A new model of elite rural monasticism, first tried with Columbanus's community in Annegray and then in Luxeuil, was implemented to varying degrees in monastic projects across Gaul. By Clovis II's time, prominent members of the elite, such as Bishop Audoin of Rouen, were perfecting this model and employing it to great effect.[18]

The Church, whose wealth grew in lockstep with the opulence of the Merovingians, used its association with royal power to augment its already immense portfolio of landed holdings and diversify its sources of income.[19] Kings likewise benefitted from this association, which might help explain their usually generous and respectful attitude toward the Church and its prelates. The proliferation of the cult of saints, the construction of royally supported monasteries, and the close involvement of bishops in matters of state were extensively covered by the *Histories* and, to a lesser extent, by *Fredegar* and the *LHF*. These were also prominent themes in the hagiographical and visionary literature emanating from Merovingian-era centers of learning. They attest to the deep cooperation between secular and ecclesiastical power in the late sixth and early seventh centuries.

It could thus be argued that this middle phase of Merovingian history represented a period of positive growth and consolidation for Gaul, which should have been lauded as an impressive achievement. For many reasons, it was not.[20] While cumulatively remarkable, this slow crawl to regional

---

[17] After the death of Clovis, Clothild lived a religious life in Tours, although she was still very much involved in royal affairs and continued to visit Paris. Gregory of Tours, *Histories* II.43: "Chrodechildis autem regina post mortem viri sui Toronus venit, ibique ad basilica Beati Martini deserviens, cum summa puditicia atque benignitate in hoc loco commorata est omnibus diebus vitae suae, raro Parisius visitans."

[18] On Audoin and his family, see Y. Fox, *Power and Religion in Merovingian Gaul: Columbanian Monasticism and the Frankish Elites* (Cambridge: Cambridge University Press, 2014), pp. 65–81.

[19] S. Wood, *The Proprietary Church in the Medieval West* (Oxford: Oxford University Press, 2006), pp. 66–79, 109–139; I.N. Wood, "Entrusting Western Europe to the Church, 400-750," *Transactions of the Royal Historical Society* 23 (2013), pp. 37–73. And see now his *The Christian Economy of the Early Medieval West: Towards a Temple Society* (Binghampton, NY: Gracchi Books, 2022).

[20] See, for instance, Bernard Guenée's pessimistic periodization in "Primat, le fort roi Clovis et le bon roi Gontran," *Romania* 126 (2008), pp. 37–38.

supremacy was interspersed with prolonged bouts of inner conflict and, naturally, also setbacks on the international front. When the system failed, the *Histories* and *Fredegar* were there to report it. But the incremental advances that transformed Clovis's military conquests into three effective and relatively cooperative political powerhouses were usually neglected. We therefore lack a dispassionate survey of the accomplishments of the Merovingian kings from Clovis to Dagobert. This is not to say that they had none.

For all its faults, middle Merovingian rule was more stable than that of adjacent kingdoms, which either did not survive the transfer of power, or were hampered by years of interregnal bloodshed. None in Gregory's nor *Fredegar*'s Gaul seriously entertained the possibility of replacing the Merovingians.[21] At least nominally, they remained the formal face of the Frankish kingdom even until the 740s, when Carloman and Pippin considered it necessary to appoint a Merovingian to make up for what they lacked in legitimacy.[22] In Gregory's day this was all still very much in the future, yet by the time the *LHF* was composed, the fissures that ran through Merovingian Gaul were apparent to anyone who bothered to look. The fact remains, however, that it was a conscious choice to depict the middle Merovingian period as a time of incessant internal strife, as numerous works of history indeed chose to do.

This chapter will consider the coverage of Frankish history from 511 to 639. It will not examine the story as it is depicted in Merovingian-age historiographical compositions, however. Rather, it will look at two later works, the first composed in the early ninth century by Bishop Frechulf of Lisieux and the second in the late ninth century by Archbishop Ado of Vienne. Since both authors knew how the Merovingian story ended and were at a historical remove from the events, they applied models of periodization that were unavailable to Merovingian-era authors, and which were central to their understanding of the period. It is this that makes their treatment of the middle Merovingians—or lack thereof—instructive.

Frechulf and Ado composed world chronicles. Accordingly, Frankish history occupied a relatively modest place in Ado's account and a minuscule role in that of Frechulf. Both works were products of, and intended for, a Carolingian literate elite, whose outlook on the earlier chapters of Frankish history was influenced by three main constraints. The first was the need to consider the events in Gaul in the context of a greater human

---

[21] On Alethius's attempt, see Y. Fox, "Image of Kings Past: The Gibichung Legacy in Post-Conquest Burgundy," *Francia* 42 (2015), pp. 1–27, at pp. 17–23.
[22] On the portrayal of Childeric III, see Barnwell, "Einhard, Louis the Pious, and Childeric III," pp. 129–139; Bouchard, "Childeric III and the Emperors Drogo Magnus and Pippin the Pious," pp. 1–16.

history rooted in the biblical past. The second was the changing role of Frankish history in a world dominated by imperial rhetoric, whose ambitions exceeded those of a single, albeit uniquely important, ethnically defined community. Finally, in these works we find a necessary distinction, given Carolingian dynastic sensibilities, between Merovingian history and Frankish history. Forging a workable heuristic that would harmonize these demands is at the heart of the two compositions examined in this chapter.

The first section of this chapter examines Frechulf's silence on Frankish history. His *Histories*, composed *ca.* 830, end rather surprisingly in the seventh century. The work had much to say about the ingress of various *gentes* into the Roman Empire and its resulting disintegration. Yet the Franks themselves were hardly mentioned, and when they were it was in rather ancillary roles. This is surprising given Frechulf's framing, which singled out the Franks and the Lombards as central to his narrative program. The establishment of the Franks in Gaul and their subsequent imperial aspirations had a decisive influence on the formation of Frechulf's world, which makes his silence all the more puzzling.

Though far more verbose that Frechulf's *Histories*, Ado's *Chronicle* still provides a shorthand version of Merovingian history, carefully constructed for ethical utility. As we shall see, Ado's editorial choices reflect a new understanding of the Merovingians' historical role. In this depiction, the less glamorous aspects of the Merovingians were highlighted, particularly their proclivity for violence. Both Frechulf and Ado attempted to harmonize the period in question with their larger historiographical project but ended up offering two very different historical visions.[23]

3.1 Frechulf of Lisieux's *argumentum ex silentio*

One might legitimately question the choice to include the *Histories* of the early ninth-century bishop Frechulf of Lisieux in the present consideration of the Merovingians in historiography, as the author has very little to say about them. Frechulf was bishop of Lisieux from 824/5 until his death in 850/852 and in this capacity was an active agent of the Carolingian state. He was educated at the monastery of Fulda under the renowned Hrabanus Maurus, from whom he requested spiritual guidance shortly after his installation at Lisieux, resulting in the composition of an exegesis on the Pentateuch.[24] Frechulf was sent by Louis the Pious to Rome at the

---

[23] See Koziol, "The Future of History After Empire," pp. 15–35.
[24] On his correspondence with Hrabanus and the subsequent compositions, see *Frechulfi Lexoviensis Episcopi Opera Omnia*, ed. M.I. Allen, CCCM, 169A (Turnhout: Brepols, 2002), pp. 5–7; Hrabanus Maurus, *Epistolae* 8–12, MGH Epp. 5, ed. E. Dümmler (Berlin: Weidmann, 1899), pp. 393–400.

very beginning of his episcopacy to present the Frankish position on image worship to the pope.[25] In 835, he was briefly entrusted with the care of the deposed archbishop Ebbo of Reims,[26] and is known to have participated in other councils convened in the 820s and 830s.[27]

Frechulf's most important work is a universal chronicle divided into two parts, numbering seven and five books respectively.[28] The first part was an account of history from the Creation to the Incarnation, dedicated to Louis the Pious's chancellor Helisachar; the second, dedicated to Queen Judith, picked up where the first one left off and ran until the seventh century. The concluding event in the *Histories* was the inauguration of the Pantheon as a church dedicated to the Virgin Mary under the emperor Phocas and Pope Boniface IV, *ca.* 609. The work then goes on to give a short survey of ecumenical councils, the last of which took place toward the end of the same century. The latter chapters of the fifth book of the second part chronologically correspond to the period under question in this chapter, although, as we shall see, Frechulf gives the Franks only brief, passing mention.

Compared with the other *gentes* vying for power in the late-Roman and post-Roman West, the Franks were clearly shorted on coverage in Frechulf's *Histories*. The Visigoths, Ostrogoths, and Vandals each received several dedicated chapters and were mentioned in other chapters that dealt with imperial and ecclesiastical affairs. The Lombards, relative newcomers into (previously) Roman space, also received more coverage than did the Franks.

---

[25] *Concilium Parisiense, a. 825*, MGH Conc. Aevi Karolini 2, 2, ed. A. Werminghoff (Hanover: Hahnsche Buchhandlung, 1908), p. 482. See also J.M. O'Brien, "Locating Authorities in Carolingian Debates on Image Veneration: The Case of Agobard of Lyon's *De picturis et imaginibus*," *Journal of Theological Studies* 69, 1 (2011), pp. 176–206.

[26] *Concilium Ingelheimense, a. 840 (Narratio clericorum Remensium)*, MGH Conc. Aevi Karolini 2, 2, ed. A. Werminghoff (Hanover: Hahnsche Buchhandlung, 1908), p. 808.

[27] See *Concilium Parisiense, a. 829* and *Acta spuria ad Concilium Cirisiacense spectantia, a. 838*, MGH Conc. Aevi Karolini 2, 2, ed. A. Werminghoff (Hanover: Hahnsche Buchhandlung, 1908), pp. 605–606 and 850, respectively.

[28] On Frechulf's life and work, see *Frechulfi Lexoviensis Episcopi Opera Omnia*, 169, pp. 11–18; M.I. Allen, "Frechulf of Lisieux," in *The Oxford Guide to the Historical Reception of Augustine*, eds. K. Pollmann and W. Otten (Oxford: Oxford University Press, 2013), vol. 2, p. 1010; W. Goez, "Zur Weltchronik des Bishofs Frechulf von Lisieux," in *Festgabe für Paul Kirn zum 70. Geburtstag, dargebracht von Freunden und Schülern*, ed. E. Kaufmann (Berlin: Erich Schmidt Verlag, 1961), pp. 93–110; R. Savigni, "Storia universale e storia ecclesiastica nel Chronicon di Frechulfo de Lisieux," *Studi Medievali* 28 (1987), pp. 155–192; G.A. Ward, *History, Scripture, and Authority in the Carolingian Empire: Frechulf of Lisieux* (Oxford: Oxford University Press, 2022). On structure and sources of the *Histories*, see C.F. Natunewicz, "Freculphus of Lisieux, His Chronicle, and a Mont St. Michel Manuscript," *Sacris Erudiri* 17 (1966), pp. 90–134; S. Ottewill-Soulsby, "'Hunting Diligently Through the Volumes of the Ancients': Frechulf of Lisieux on the First City and the End of Innocence," in *Remembering and Forgetting the Ancient City*, eds. J. Martinez Jiménez and S. Ottewill-Soulsby (Oxford: Oxbow Books, 2022), pp. 225–245.

Additionally, apart from one mention, Frechulf's Franks were relegated to secondary roles in plots whose main protagonists were Burgundians, Ostrogoths, Byzantines, and Visigoths. Even if Frechulf thought that ninth-century readers had easy access to Frankish history, one would still need to account for his readiness to incorporate episodes about other *gentes* and kingdoms, whose histories would have been equally accessible.

Why, then, bother with Frechulf when other works provide more Merovingian data? To answer this question, we should begin with Frechulf himself, and the explanation he offered at the end of the *Histories*: "With the expulsion of Roman judges and Goths from Italy and Gaul, and the succession of the Franks and the Lombards in those kingdoms, I have decided to set an end to my books."[29] By placing his chronological terminus in the seventh century, Frechulf signaled to his readership that this date constituted a watershed moment for world history that depended upon the establishment of Frankish power in Gaul and Lombard power in Italy. As noted by Michael Allen, these events demarcated the spatial contours of the Carolingian world.[30] It is therefore not coincidental that the Franks and the Lombards were chosen, especially given the formative effect of the Italian war of 774 in shaping this new space. The conquest of the Lombard kingdom not only redrew the boundaries of the Carolingians' political geography but also redefined Charlemagne's kingship, which remained centered on the Franks and the Lombards even after the imperial coronation of 800.[31]

This remains a curious periodization, at least from the perspective of the political events that underpinned it. After all, the *Histories* do not reach 774. They end abruptly, long before the formation of the Carolingian world was underway. Frechulf's framing was often seen as ensuing from his utilization of a six-age, four-kingdom model, informed primarily by Bede's treatment in *De temporum ratione*. Bede's model was itself the byproduct of centuries of historiographical experimentation.[32] The four kingdoms, an idea that had begun as a feature of Hellenistic writing and made its way to the book of Daniel, was later expanded to accommodate

---

[29] Frechulf, *Histories*, 11.5, 27, p. 724.
[30] M.I. Allen: "Universal History 300–1000: Origins and Western Developments," in *Historiography in the Middle Ages*, ed. D. Mauskopf Deliyannis (Leiden: Brill, 2003), pp. 17–42, at p. 40.
[31] M.I. Allen, "Fréculf de Lisieux: l'histoire de l'Antiquité comme témoignage de l'actualité," *Tabularia* 8 (2008), pp. 59–79, at p. 63.
[32] Bede, *De temporum ratione*, ed. C.W. Jones. CCSL 123b (Turnhout: Brepols, 1977); Natunewicz, "Freculphus of Lisieux," pp. 112–115; Savigni, "Storia universale," p. 157. On Frechulf's Augustinian influences and the idea of *Christiana tempora*, see N. Staubach, "*Christiana tempora*. Augustin und das Ende der alten Geschichte in der Weltchronik Frechulfs von Lisieux," *Frühmittelalteriche Studien* 29 (1995), pp. 167–206.

a fifth kingdom, that of the Romans. The six ages were a Christian development based not on empires but on events portrayed in the Bible, which meant that harmonizing it with the four-kingdom model required some effort. Articulated by Origen and embraced by Eusebius of Caesarea and Isidore of Seville, the six-age model's adoption by such luminaries essentially ensured its lasting impact on western historiographical tradition.[33] It is clear from Frechulf's dependence on this model that he saw the progression of history as the fulfillment of God's will, as does his division of the work according to the two cosmic events of biblical chronology—Creation and Incarnation. Yet this is not much of an explanation. Frechulf's narrative emphases were not incongruous with the topics that interest us here, namely, early Frankish history. Frechulf happily discussed dynastic developments and territorial advances elsewhere in his work. All things considered, his decision to end his *Histories* where he did was not an obvious one, given the requirements of the model he employed. More to the point, it does little to explain the secondary role awarded the Franks. Since the establishment of the Lombards and the Franks was clearly important to Frechulf, his cursory, seemingly random, discussion of the Merovingians is doubly puzzling, especially when we consider his relatively elaborate coverage of other post-Roman kingdoms.

The Franks first appear in the *Histories* as an epilogue to the Trojan narrative found in Part I. As we have seen, Frechulf was not alone in his willingness to entertain the Trojan myth. In the *Histories*, we find some equivocation on the Trojan question. While he was prepared to include the story, at least as it applied to the Franks as a group, Frechulf also offered an alternative origin, first devised by Jordanes, which saw them emerge from Scanza:

Wandering through many regions with their wives, they freely elected from their own a king named Francio, after whom they are called Franks. It is said that this Francio was strongest in war, and after fighting many nations, guided his followers to Europe and settled between the Rhine and the Danube. And when Francio died they had many battles, from which, by their hand, remained insignificant dregs. Then they appointed from among themselves duces, and always refused to accept any other yoke.

Some believe that in this manner the Franks had their origins. Others affirm that they originated from the island of Scanza, which is the womb of nations, and from which came the Goths and other Theodisc nations, as their language testifies.[34]

---

[33] G. Dunphy, "Six Ages of the World," in *The Encyclopedia of the Medieval Chronicle*, ed. G. Dunphy (Leiden: Brill, 2010), vol. 2, pp. 1367–1370.

[34] Frechulf, *Histories* I.2, 26, pp. 147–148: "quae per multas regiones vagando cum uxoribus et liberis eligentes regem ex se Francionem nomine, ex quo Franci vocantur, eo quod fortissimus ipse Francio in bello fuisse fertur, et dum gentibus cum plurimis pugnasset, in Europam iter suum dirigens inter Renum et Danubium consedit. Ibique mortuo

As noted by Matthew Innes, interest in linguistic similarities and their effect on common origins was a product of Frechulf's cultural setting.[35] Innes further pointed out that this was essentially a tangent of a much longer Trojan storyline reported in *Histories* I.2,26, and was not connected in any way to the Frankish narrative found in Part II. The *Histories*' interest in the Trojan elements of the Frankish *origo gentis* is nevertheless significant because it was the last great Carolingian work of historiography to show such an interest. Later authors, such as Ado of Vienne (discussed later in this chapter) and Regino of Prüm, did not feel the need to go down a similar path. Like Frechulf, they grounded their narratives, composed in 870 and 906 respectively,[36] in the biblical story. Unlike him, they ignored the Trojan myth altogether. The tale of Trojan origins eventually made a comeback with post-Carolingian authors such as Aimoin of Fleury, but from the *LHF* to Paul the Deacon's *GeM* to Frechulf's *Histories* there is a palpable decline in its importance, until it disappeared completely from the chronicles of later Carolingian authors. Frechulf's narrative gesture, coupled with the alternative Scandinavian *origo*, suggests that it sat rather uncomfortably in his worldview.

The *Histories*' fifth and final book, which contains all of the Frankish material, begins with a chapter titled: *On the promotion of Arcadius and Honorius to imperial rank after the death of their father, and the persecutions of John bishop of Constantinople who, unjustly accused, died in exile*.[37] It goes on to cover the events of the fifth and sixth centuries, alternating between secular and ecclesiastical history. For the purposes of the present discussion, Book V becomes especially relevant in its final chapters, which explore the advance of the various *gentes* into the empire, the Lombard invasion of Italy, Hermenigild's rebellion and "martyrdom," and Reccared's ascent to the kingship in Spain. It closes on a distinctly ecclesiastical note, with the deeds of popes Gregory I and Boniface IV, and a brief account of ecumenical conciliar activity from Nicaea I (325) to Constantinople III (680/681).

Francione proelia multa gesserunt, quibus adtriti parva ex ipsis manus remansit. Hinc duces ex se constituerunt, attamen iugum alterius semper negantes ferre. Haec quidam ita se habere de origine Francorum opinantur. Alii vero adfirmant eos de Scanza insula, quae vaginae gentium est, exordium habuisse, de qua Gotthi et ceterae nationes Theodistae exierunt, quod et idioma linguae eorum testatur."

[35] M. Innes, "Teutons or Trojans? The Carolingians and the Germanic Past," in *The Uses of the Past in the Early Middle Ages*, eds. Y. Hen and M. Innes (Cambridge: Cambridge University Press, 2000), pp. 227–249, at pp. 234–235.

[36] See S. Airlie, "'Sad Stories of the Death of Kings': Narrative Patterns and Structures of Authority in Regino of Prüm's *Chronicle*," in *Narrative and History in the Early Medieval West*, eds. E.M. Tyler and R. Balzaretti (Turnhout: Brepols, 2006), pp. 105–132.

[37] Frechulf, *Histories*, II.5, Capitula libri quinti 1, p. 670: "De provectione Archadii et Honorii post obitum patris ad imperium, et persecutionibus Iohannis episcopi Constantinopoleos qui iniuste dampnatus in exilio moritur."

134   *Taedit me memorare*: The Middle Merovingians

The treatment of these episodes is more thematic than chronological, although the progression in each of the "themes" (e.g., papal succession, imperial succession, deeds of kings, and other events of note) is more or less in line with conventional chronology.[38]

All told, Frechulf provides six snippets of Frankish history. These do not appear in correct chronological order, nor do they seem to capture the most conspicuous events from the period in question. Unmentioned are the most obvious episodes, such as the establishment of the dynasty under Merovech, the baptism of Clovis, the reunification of the *regna Francorum* under Chlothar II, and the reign of Dagobert. What we do find is the following, in order of appearance: the Franks' involvement in the Burgundian war of 500,[39] Clovis's marital connections to the Ostrogothic king Theoderic,[40] the downfall of Sigismund and the death of Chlodomer,[41] the battle of Vouillé,[42] Chramn's rebellion against his father and Chlothar's victories in Brittany and Saxony,[43] and finally the Frankish involvement in Italy, under Theudebert I's duke Buccelen.[44]

The events of 500 in the Burgundian kingdom appear in the latter part of chapter 17, which Frechulf titled: *On the quick succession of rulers, and how they lost the Western Roman empire*.[45] After discussing the ascent of Majorian to imperial honor in the West, the peace he negotiated with the Visigoths, and the preparations he made for war with the Vandals, Frechulf moved on to the situation in Gaul. But the events Frechulf depicted in the subsequent passage, taken from Marius of Avenches' *Chronicle*, transpired not in 458 with Majorian, but in 500.[46] Since he returns, in the next paragraph, to the affairs of the late 460s, Frechulf undoubtedly misplaced the Burgundian entry.

Why the forty-year jump into the future here? It is difficult to say. Majorian did, in fact, briefly recapture Lyon from the Burgundians in 458.[47] Frechulf's information for the earlier events covered in chapter 17 was also based on Marius of Avenches and supplemented by Book II of *Fredegar*.[48] Marius had nothing to say about Majorian's gains against the Burgundians, whom he mentions in 456 as having occupied a part of Gaul

---

[38] On Frechulf's system of chronology, see Natunewicz, "Freculphus of Lisieux," p. 120.
[39] Frechulf, *Histories*, II.5, 17, p. 704.   [40] Ibid., 18, p. 710.   [41] Ibid., 20, p. 713.
[42] Frechulf, *Histories*, II.5, 22, p. 717.   [43] Ibid., p. 718.   [44] Ibid., 23, p. 720.
[45] Ibid., Capitula libri quinti 17, p. 671: "De crebris mutationibus principum, et sic perdiderunt Occidentis imperium Romani."
[46] Marius of Avenches, *Chronicle*, a. 500.
[47] Sidonius Apollinaris, *Carmen* 5 (Panegyric for Majorian), in *Sidoine Apollinaire: poèmes et lettres*, ed. A. Loyen (Paris: Belles Lettres, 1960–1970), lines 565–580; I. Wood, "The Fall of the Western Empire and the End of Roman Britain," *Britannia* 18 (1987), pp. 251–262, at p. 258; H. Elton, *The Roman Empire in Late Antiquity: A Political and Military History* (Cambridge: Cambridge University Press, 2018), p. 212
[48] Allen, *Frechulfi opera*, vol. I, p. 291 (Fredegar), p. 317 (Marius).

and divided it with its senators,[49] and neither did *Fredegar*. If Frechulf had any knowledge of the conflict between Majorian and the Burgundians, it would have come from the only work covering these events—Sidonius Apollinaris's panegyric to Majorian[50]—although this is not identified by Allen as one of his sources. It is therefore unclear why Frechulf felt the need to expand the entry here to include information about the Burgundians. Assumedly, he knew of a Burgundian connection but lacked precise information. In an attempt to fill the gap, he simply went to the very next entry that mentioned Burgundians in Marius of Avenches' *Chronicle*, which was for the year 500, and inserted it there almost verbatim. In Marius's *Chronicle* the Franks were mentioned as combatants, but the fact that they were led by Clovis was not, so it probably would have been harder for Frechulf to recognize the timing discrepancy and correct his mistake.

The next mention of the Franks identified Clovis by name, but only as an aside to Theoderic's matrimonial policies. Here Frechulf named his source—Jordanes—when he reported that Theoderic wished to forge an alliance with the Franks.[51] The Ostrogothic king therefore sent an embassy, successfully securing the hand of Clovis's daughter in marriage. Frechulf followed Jordanes in relating all of the other ties of marriage woven by the Ostrogothic king with the Visigoths, Vandals, Burgundians, and Thuringians.[52] Jordanes's account was riddled with errors. The first was that Audofled was Clovis's sister, not his daughter,[53] and the second was his muddling of the names of Clovis's sons.[54] But the most misleading part of Jordanes's report was the reference to Clovis as *Lodoin*

---

[49] Marius of Avenches, *Chronicle*, a. 456: "Eo anno Burgundiones partem Galliae occupaverunt terrasque cum Galiis senatoribus diviserunt." See C.E. Stevens, *Sidonius Apollinaris and His Age* (Oxford: Clarendon, 1933), p. 42.
[50] Stevens, *Sidonius*, p. 43.
[51] Frechulf, *Histories*, II.5, 18, p. 710: "His ita prospere gestis gentem Francorum cupiens foederatam habere, missa legatione ad Ludovvic regem eorum filiam eius petens, imperatamque matrimonio suo copulavit, ut Iordanis historicus refert."
[52] Jordanes, *Getica*, LVII.295–296: "Cui et primum concedens Theodoricus postmodum ab hac luce privavit tertioque, ut diximus, anno ingressus sui in Italia Zenonemque imp. consultu privatum abitum suaeque gentis vestitum seponens insigne regio amictu, quasi iam Gothorum Romanorumque regnator, adsumit missaque legatione ad Lodoin Francorum regem filiam eius Audefledam sibi in matrimonio petit. Quam ille grate libenterque concessit suosque filios Celdebertum et Heldebertum et Thiudebertum credens hac societate cum gente Gothorum inito foedere sociari. Sed non adeo ad pacis concordiam profuit ista coniunctio, quia saepenumero propter Gallorum terras graviter inter se decertati sunt, numquamque Gothus Francis cessit, dum viveret Theodoricus."
[53] Gregory of Tours, *Histories*, III.31.
[54] Jordanes, *Getica* LVII.296: "Quam ille grate libenterque concessit suosque filios Celdebertum et Heldebertum et Thiudebertum credens hac societate cum gente Gothorum inito foedere sociari." While either the first or the second name could have been a reasonable approximation of Childebert I, who indeed was Clovis's son, it is

Francorum rex,⁵⁵ which Frechulf transcribed as *Ludovvic*. Since in subsequent reports, such as the Battle of Vouillé, Frechulf refers to Clovis by the more standardized *Chlodoveus*, it is at least possible that he did not make the connection between the two and assumed that they were different Frankish rulers which, after all, was not entirely far-fetched given the plurality of kings up until Clovis's last days.⁵⁶ Of course, Clovis was hardly an obscure figure, and we might thus be tempted to read intent into Frechulf's ignorance.

Frechulf's next foray into Frankish affairs came with the accounts of the deaths of Sigismund and Chlodomer, likewise inspired by Marius of Avenches.⁵⁷ This, again, was not a story that dealt directly with the Franks but with the Burgundian king, who was betrayed by his own men and handed over to the enemy.⁵⁸ The death of Chlodomer, which followed that of Sigismund, was an offshoot of this main narrative strand, not a story that stood on its own.

The title of the chapter that contained the Battle of Vouillé was the first to mention the Franks explicitly:

Under the imperium of Justinian, the Franks, having fought the Goths, deprived them of their kingdom in Gaul, and, having fought against the Saxons conquered them and subjugated the Bretons.

On the Franco-Visigothic war, Frechulf had this to say:

*At that time war stirred up in the region of Gaul between Alaric king of the Goths and Clovis king of the Franks. Although many previous disputes of varying outcomes broke out between them, at last on that occasion a meeting of forces took place on the field of Vouillé, ten miles from the city of Poitiers, in which Clovis king of the Franks killed Alaric king of the Goths and cut to pieces most of his army. And the kingdom which the Goths had long since held from the River Loire to the Rhône and from the Pyrenees to the Ocean was taken away and placed under Frankish rule.*⁵⁹

Vouillé preceded the Battle of Vézéronce by seventeen years, but in Frechulf's account it was the later of the two. This error seems to have

---

difficult to identify Chlodomer and Chlothar from this list. Theudebert was Theuderic's son, which would have made him Clovis's grandson.

⁵⁵ Reflecting the orthography used by Cassiodorus, *Variae*, II.41 and III.4.
⁵⁶ Frechulf did have access to *Fredegar*, the *LHF*, and possibly Gregory of Tours, each of which could have amended this mistake quite easily.
⁵⁷ Marius of Avenches, *Chronicon*, a. 523.
⁵⁸ Compare *Passio sancti Sigismundi regis*, MGH SRM 2, ed. B. Krusch (Hanover: Hahnsche Buchhandlung, 1888), pp. 329–340, at ch. 9, pp. 337–338.
⁵⁹ Frechulf, *Histories*, II.5, 22, p. 717: "Qua tempestate partibus Galliarum ortum est bellum inter Alaricum Gothorum regem et Chlodoveum regem Francorum. Quamvis prius inter eos vario eventu plurima existerent certamina, tunc demum in campania Voglavense decimo ab urbe Pictavensi miliario fit certaminis congressio ubi Chlodoveus Francorum rex Alaricum Gothorum regem interfecit et maximam partem illius exercitus trucidavit; regnumque quod Gothi diu tenuerunt a Ligere fluvio usque ad Rodanum, per montes Perineos usque ad Oceanum mare abstulit et ditioni Francorum subdidit."

been part of a larger rhetorical framework comparing the fates of Roman and Gothic power.[60] Here Frechulf went on to marvel at the bizarre similarity, brought about through divine intervention, between Roman dominion, which stretched between Augustus and Augustulus, and that of the Goths, which similarly stretched between the reigns of Alaric I and Alaric II. Be that as it may, this was, once again, a Gothic treatment. Frechulf had much more to say about Alaric and the Goths than he did about Clovis, who appeared fleetingly and then never again.

As promised by the title, the latter part of this chapter depicted the accomplishments of Chlothar I against the Saxons and Bretons.[61] Chlothar's military gains were preceded by a short mention of Chramn's rebellion, the only reference to an internal Frankish event in the entire composition:

At that time Chramn presumed to rebel against Chlothar, king of the Franks, that is, his father. While seized with recklessness he did not rest. He escaped to Brittany and armed its people and their king against his father. Chlothar pursued (the king of the Bretons) with his other sons and the Frankish army. Having killed the king of the Bretons and having captured his son, he [i.e., Chramn], *together with his wife and sons, was shut up in a certain house and burned alive. Chlothar defeated the Bretons and subjected their people to the Franks, making them tributaries. The rebellious Saxons he overpowered in the heaviest battles and subdued them, not without much bloodshed on their part.*[62]

This chapter in the *Histories* is followed by a chapter about the Lombards, entitled *On Narses the patrician, who obliterated the Goths in Italy only to provoke the Lombards, so they say, into seizing it*. This Lombard chapter contains the last mention of the Franks. They appear as an additional foe in the war against the Ostrogoths, during which Narses killed Teia, defeated the Gothic army, and liberated Italy. Once this task was accomplished,

---

[60] G. Ward, "The Sense of an Ending in the *Histories* of Frechulf of Lisieux," in *Historiographies of Identity, vol. III: Carolingian Convergence and Its Later Uses*, eds. H. Reimitz, R. Kramer, and G. Ward (Turnhout: Brepols, 2021), pp. 291–315.
[61] Since Frechulf saw the conquests of Chlothar as a continuation of Clovis's accomplishments, this suggests that indeed he did not perceive of Ludovvic and Chlodoveus as identical.
[62] Frechulf, *Histories*, II.5.22, p. 718: "Qua tempestate Chramnus contra Chlotharium Francorum regem, suum scilicet patrem, rebellare praesumpsit. Qui dum accepta temeritate non quiesceret, ad Brittaniam se contulit gentemque illam cum rege suo contra patrem armauit, quem Chlotharius insecutus cum reliquis suis filiis et Francorum exercitu. Interfecto Brittonum rege Chramnus est conprehensus, atque cum uxore et filiis quadam domo clausus uiuus est incensus. Chlotharius uero de manubiis Brittonum triumphans, gentemque illam Francis subiectam fecit tributrariam. Saxones uero rebellantes grauissimis proeliis prostrauit et non sine multo suorum sanguine deuicit." On this episode as a reflection of Louis the Pious's regnal dramas, see P. Depreux, "L'actualité de Fréculf de Lisieux: à propos de l'édition critique de son œuvre," *Tabularia* 4 (2004), pp. 53–60, at p. 55. On the language of rebellion in Carolingian historiography, see Broome, "Pagans, Rebels, and Merovingians," pp. 161–165.

Narses turned to engage the Franks, who were, at the time, conducting a campaign of their own in northern Italy under Theudebert's general, Buccelen: "From there, he [i.e., Narses] went into battle against Buccelen, who, they say, once they joined in battle was lost together with all of his army."[63]

This episode was described by Gregory of Tours, who spun it into a fantastical account of Frankish victory with territorial gains as far south as Sicily.[64] It was then interpolated and corrected in *Fredegar*, which described rather succinctly Narses's victory against Buccelen.[65] *Fredegar* was one of Frechulf's sources, as was Marius of Avenches, who provides a similar account.[66] In this instance, the Franks were brought up as part of the *Histories*' coverage of the Justinianic reconquest and as a preview to the eventual establishment of the Lombards on Italian soil. Since the Franks were decisively vanquished, they played no additional role in the events that follow. This chapter was supplemented by chapter 25, which brought the Lombard invasion of Italy to its natural conclusion and was titled by Frechulf *On the Lombard invasion of Italy, and the martyrdom of Hermenigild, son of the king of the Goths*.[67]

Thus, the final chapters set out to do what Frechulf expressly stated as his agenda, namely, to explain the establishment of Frankish and Lombard power in Gaul and Italy. The Frankish and the Lombard chapters are the last to discuss military and political developments in the West. The remaining chapters are dedicated to the deeds of Pope Gregory I, Pope Boniface IV, and the ecumenical councils. Bede's *Chronicle*, which was one of Frechulf's most important sources, made no mention of Frankish military conquests. Yet his other sources, namely *Fredegar*, Marius of Avenches, the *Lex Salica*, the *LHF*, and possibly Gregory of Tours all provided copious material on Frankish, and especially Merovingian, history. What then are we to make of Frechulf's treatment of the Franks, and particularly his silence on the Merovingians?

The early ninth century was a tense time in Frankish politics, rife with dynastic anxiety. It was also a time in which literary responses began to reflect a need to contend with the relatively recent past. Memorably, Einhard's *Vita Karoli Magni*, which was completed several years before work on the *Histories* was begun in earnest, caricatured the Merovingians and presented them as unfit to rule. Frechulf, whose scope was much

---

[63] Frechulf, *Histories*, II.5.23, p. 720: "Hinc contra Buccilinum Francorum ducem congressione facta pugnavit, quem, ut fertur, cum omni exercito suo interemit."
[64] Gregory of Tours, *Histories*, III.32. [65] *Fredegar* III.50.
[66] Marius of Avenches, *Chronicle*, a.555.
[67] Frechulf, *Histories*, II.5, Capitula libri quinti, p. 671: "De Longobardis Italiam invadentibus, et de martyrio Hermingyldi regis Gothorum filii."

more ambitious than Einhard's, chose a different path that altogether minimized the Merovingian contribution to the formation of his readers' world.

More to the point, it seems that Frechulf wished to defer the establishment of Frankish power in Gaul and, accordingly, Lombard power in Italy, to the late sixth and early seventh centuries. One might possibly make a case for this with the Lombards, but it was an absurd proposition when applied to the Franks. The seventh century indeed saw the Pippinids take their first steps onto the public stage, so it would be possible to view Frechulf's periodization as setting the stage for Carolingian ascendancy. Yet notably, the Pippinids are also absent in the *Histories*. Other works produced in the courts of Charlemagne and Louis the Pious were hard at work retracing—or, rather, creating *de novo*—the Carolingian family tree back to this time.[68] This was not a theme picked up by Frechulf.

With Frankish power becoming a reality only in the seventh century and understood as a constituent part of a political space defined, not through the conquests of the Merovingians, but through the campaigns of Charlemagne, Frechulf was subtly alluding to an alternative history of the Frankish kingdom, one whose roots were intertwined with the story of the Carolingian Empire. Even more importantly, with the preponderance of Roman imperial symbolism in the *Histories*, Frechulf wished to make the Carolingians of his day heirs, not of their Merovingian predecessors, but of their Roman ones.

The *Histories* was composed for the sake of *utilitas*.[69] Frechulf stated explicitly that it was meant as a didactic tool for Charles the Bald, to whose mother, Judith, he dedicated the second part of the composition.[70] The *Histories*, Frechulf explained, were written to present the young prince with examples about the past deeds of emperors and the acts of churchmen. With the help of these two narrative strands—secular and ecclesiastical—Charles was encouraged to choose models on which to base his future rulership.[71] These were models rooted in Roman and

---

[68] Of which the *Annales Mettenses priores* is a good example. See *Annales Mettenses Priores*, a. 688; Y. Hen, "The Annals of Metz and the Merovingian Past," in *The Uses of the Past in the Early Middle Ages*, eds. Y. Hen and M. Innes (Cambridge: Cambridge University Press, 2000), pp. 175–190.
[69] Frechulf, *Histories*, II.1, 1, p. 440.   [70] Ibid., prologue, p. 437.
[71] M.I. Allen, "Bede and Frechulf at St. Gallen," in *Beda Venerabilis: Historian, Monk, and Northumbrian*, eds. L.A.J.R. Howen and A.A. MacDonald (Groningen: Egbert Forsten, 1996), pp. 61–80, at p. 69; R. McKitterick, "Charles the Bald (823–877) and His Library: The Patronage of Learning," *The English Historical Review*, 95, 374 (1980), pp. 28–47, at pp. 30–31; G. Ward, "Lessons in Leadership: Constantine and Theodosius in Frechulf of Lisieux's *Histories*," in *The Resources of the Past in Early Medieval Europe*, eds. C. Gantner, R. McKitterick, and S. Meeder (Cambridge: Cambridge University Press, 2015), pp. 68–83, at p. 71.

ecclesiastical history, both of which Frechulf deemed appropriate topics on which to educate a prince who might one day lead a Christian empire. It is therefore possible that Frechulf concluded his opus with the establishment of Frankish and Lombard power not so much because it circumscribed the political space of Carolingian imperial hegemony, although this was probably part of the reason. It is that Frankish and Lombard dominion over Gaul and Italy spelled the end of the world from whose exempla Charles the Bald was meant to learn. The earlier chapters of Frankish history were interesting insofar as they illuminated the undoing of the Christian Roman Empire, but otherwise they were a redundant and counterproductive interlude.[72] It is this process of undoing and the Vandal and Gothic role therein that justified Frechulf's outsized attention to these particular *gentes*. This narrative schema left very little room for the Merovingians and their accomplishments or, indeed, for the familial origins of the Carolingians, to which Frechulf seems altogether indifferent. If we take him at his word, he was primarily interested in the analogical bridge between the two Christian empires. While the *Histories* come to an end too early for some questions to be definitively answered, it is this abrupt end that might hold a clue as to how Frechulf conceived of his own time in relation to previous centuries.

3.2   *Pro multis sceleribus*: Ado of Vienne's Tales of Woe

After years of monastic training in such prestigious centers of Carolingian learning as Ferrières and Prüm, Ado arrived in Vienne,[73] where he was consecrated archbishop in 859 or 860, a post he held until his death in 875.[74] Ado came highly recommended; the letter sent by his old teacher, Lupus of Ferrières, to the regional ruler, Duke Gerhard of

---

[72] On Frechulf's reluctance to employ biblical models in depicting the Merovingians, see Savigni, "Storia universale," p. 188, although his depiction of Gregory of Tours' approach to the kings of his day has not stood the test of time: "La stilizzazione della regalità merovingia operata da un Gregorio di Tours – che evidenziava l'intrinseca sacralità della figura carismatica del *rex*, proiettandola al di fuori di precisi limiti istituzionali – non trova riscontro nel *Chronicon* [...]."

[73] Ado of Vienne, *Chronicon sive Breviarium de sex mundi aetatibus ab Adamo usque ad annum 869*, PL 123, ed. J.P. Migne (Paris: Petit-Montrouge, 1852), pp. 23–143 [hereafter: Ado of Vienne, *Chronicle*], at col.112A: "Brunichildis regina pro multis sceleribus suis in praesentia Chlotharii regis judicantibus Francis, indomitis equis, religata brachiis et cruribus divaricatis, membratim discinditur, ac igni ossa illius cremata."

[74] On Ado, see W. Kremers, "Ado von Vienne: sein Leben und seine Schriften," doctoral dissertation (Friedrich-Wilhelms-Universität Bonn, 1911); R. McKitterick, *Perceptions of the Past in the Early Middle Ages* (Notre Dame, IN: University of Notre Dame Press, 2006), pp. 29–30; E. Mégier, "Karolingische Weltchronistik zwischen Historiographie und Exegese: Frechulf von Lisieux und Ado von Vienne," in *Diligens scrutator sacri eloquii: Beiträge zur Exegese- und Theologiegeschichte des Mittelalters: Festgabe für Rainer Berndt SJ*

Provence,[75] brims with the usual accolades regarding Ado's illustrious ancestry and erudition. Importantly, it also names some of Ado's ecclesiastical supporters, men such as Abbot Marcward of Prüm, Archbishop Remigius of Lyon, Bishop Hebbo of Grenoble, and Archbishop Guenilo of Sens. Ado had patrons in the highest echelons of church and court.

Reports of his intellectual capabilities were apparently not exaggerated, since as archbishop he composed a number of notable works, the most famous of which was his *Martyrology*.[76] Ado's great historiographical oeuvre, which he completed *ca.* 870, was the *Chronicon sive Breviarium de sex mundi aetatibus ab Adamo usque ad annum 869*. As its name suggests, this was a world chronicle divided into six books, corresponding to the six ages, set according to important events in biblical history, such as Creation, the Deluge, the birth of Abraham, and so on.[77] The *Chronicle*, and its presentation of Merovingian history confined entirely to the sixth book, will be the focus of this section. Notably, Ado was also a capable hagiographer, writing at least two *Lives*, one of Abbot Theudarius and another of Bishop Desiderius of Vienne.[78] The narrative horizons of these hagiographies, both of which are situated in Merovingian Gaul, reflect Ado's thinking about the period and are thus worth discussing in tandem with his *Chronicle*. Let us set the stage with the unassuming *Life of Abbot*

---

zum 65. Geburtstag, eds. H.P. Neuheuser, R.M.W. Stammberger, and M.M. Tischler (Munster: Aschendorff Verlag, 2016), pp. 37–52; N. Nimmegeers, *Évêques entre Bourgogne et Provence: La province ecclésiastique de Vienne au haut Moyen Âge (V*[e]*–XI*[e] *siècle)* (Rennes: Presses universitaires de Rennes, 2014), pp. 15–18, 20–22, 140–142; S. Raisharma, "Much Ado about Vienne? A Localizing Universal *Chronicon*," in *Historiographies of Identity, Volume 3: Carolingian Convergence and Its Later Uses*, eds. R. Kramer, H. Reimitz, and G. Ward (Turnhout: Brepols, 2021), pp. 271–290; M.-C. Isaïa, "La Chronique d'Adon de Vienne (†875): méthode, projet et public," *Revue d'histoire de l'Eglise de France* 108 (2022), pp. 225–254.

[75] Lupus of Ferrières, *Epistola* 110, in *Loup de Ferrières: Correspondance II (847–62)*, ed. L. Levillain (Paris: Librarie ancienne Honoré Champion, 1935), pp. 150–153; trans. G. W. Regenos, *The Letters of Lupus of Ferrières* (The Hague: Martinus Nijhoff, 1966), pp. 127–128. He is alternatively known as Count Gerhard of Vienne. He later inspired the character of Gerard of Rousillon.

[76] Ado of Vienne, *Martyrology*, in *Le martyrologe d'Adon, ses deux familles, ses trois recensions: texte et commentaire*, ed. and trans. J. Dubois and G. Renaud (Paris: Éditions du Centre National de la Recherche Scientifique, 1984). The most elaborate treatment is still H. Quentin, *Les martyrologes historiques du moyen age* (Paris: J. Gabalda, 1908), pp. 466–681. See also M. Maskarinec, *City of Saints: Rebuilding Rome in the Early Middle Ages* (Philadelphia: University of Pennsylvania Press, 2018), pp. 282–306.

[77] See H.-W. Goetz, "Historiographisches Zeitbewußtsein im frühen Mittelalter: Zum Umgang mit der Zeit in der karolingischen Geschichtsschreibung," in *Historiographie im frühen Mittelalter*, eds. A. Scharer and G. Scheibelreiter (Vienna: Böhlau, 1994), pp. 158–178, at p. 168; Raisharma, "Much Ado," p. 275.

[78] It is not certain but likely that he also wrote the *Vita sancti Severi Viennensis* (BHL 7692), published in *Analecta Bollandiana* 5 (1886), pp. 416–424.

Theudarius of Vienne,[79] after which we will turn to Ado's *Chronicle* and second hagiography.

Theudarius, the hero of the *Vita Theudarii abbatis Viennensis*, was a native of Vienne. As a young man, he considered joining the renowned monastic community in Lérins but ended up training under Bishop Caesarius of Arles instead.[80] With its resplendent past,[81] Lérins had become something of a hagiographical *topos* for youthful, aspiring monastic saints. One example of this, which Ado doubtless would have known given his connections to the royal family, appeared in the *Life of Arnulf of Metz*, the putative ancestor of the Carolingians. Here it was Romaric, Arnulf's friend and monastic inspiration, who considered joining the community, only to settle in Luxeuil.[82] Another example was John of Réomé, whose hagiography came from the pen of Jonas of Bobbio, hagiographer to Luxeuil's founder and first abbot.[83]

Initially Theudarius went to Arles thinking that with the help of its bishop, Caesarius, he would gain entry into the monastery. In the end, he stayed with Caesarius, who was sufficiently impressed with Theudarius to elevate him to the diaconate. After having spent some time in Arles, Theudarius went home to visit his family, and in Vienne he became a hermit and eventually a monastic founder. By describing Theudarius's meanderings through the Viennois, Ado was able to provide a panorama of the sanctoral topography of the *civitas*.[84] The chapters of the *Life* concerned

---

[79] Ado of Vienne, *Vita Theudarii abbatis Viennensis*, MGH SRM 3, ed. B. Krusch (Hanover: Hahnsche Buchhandlung, 1896), pp. 525–530.

[80] On the meeting of the two saints, see M.C. Isaïa, "La prophétie dans l'hagiographie latine du haut Moyen Âge (VIe–IXe siècle). L'histoire comme destin, prédestination et providence," in *Hagiographie et prophétie (VIe–XIIIe siècles)*, eds. P. Henriet, K. Herbers, and H.-C. Lehner (Florence: Sismel, Edizioni del Galluzo, 2017), pp. 15–50.

[81] Even Gregory of Tours associated miracles with Lérins. See *Liber in gloria confessorum*, MGH SRM 1.2, ed. B. Krusch (Hanover: Hahnsche Buchhandlung, 1885), pp. 284–370, at ch. 95, p. 359.

[82] *Vita Arnulfi episcopi Mettensis*, MGH SRM 2, ed. B. Krusch (Hanover: Hahnsche Buchhandlung, 1888), pp. 426–446, at ch. 6, p. 433: "Cum hoc igitur, consilio inito, secundum praeceptum Domini, qui dixit: 'Vade, vende omnia quae habes et da pauperibus, et habebis tesaurum in caelo, et veni, sequere me', relictis omnibus, Lerinum usque monasterium ad peregrinandum propter Christum iterare disposuit." Compare *Vita Theudarii*, chs. 2, 3, p. 526: "Sarcina igitur temporali exhoneratus ac saeculi veste ad plenum nudatus, ut perfectius domino Iesu Christi serviret, Lyrinense coenobium expetere cogitavit." On this, see Fox, *Power and Religion*, p. 91. For Luxovian influences on Ado's hagiography, see pp. 145–146, 162–165.

[83] Jonas of Bobbio, *Vita Iohannis abbatis Reomaensis*, MGH SRM 3, ed. B. Krusch (Hanover: Hahnsche Buchhandlung, 1896), pp. 502–517, at ch. 4, p. 508. Trans. in A. O'Hara, and I. N. Wood, Jonas of Bobbio, *Life of Columbanus, Life of John of Réomé, and Life of Vedast*, Translated Texts for Historians, vol. 64 (Liverpool: Liverpool University Press, 2017).

[84] I. Wood, "Topographies of Holy Power in Sixth-Century Gaul," in *Topographies of Power in the Early Middle Ages*, eds. M. de Jong and F. Theuws (Leiden, Boston, Cologne: Brill, 2001), pp. 137–154, at p. 150. For Ado's emphasis on Vienne's topography, see Raisharma, "Much Ado," pp. 279–280, and comments in Isaïa, "La *Chronique*," p. 227.

Pro multis sceleribus: Ado of Vienne's Tales of Woe   143

with this intermediate phase of Theudarius's career contain not only scenic depictions of the *castra* adjoined by Vienne's walls and the surrounding countryside through which Theudarius travelled, but also of the saints to whose cults he was dedicated. The first of those, to whom Theudarius dedicated a *domuncula*, was Bishop Eusebius of Vercelli.[85] Eusebius was something of an ecclesiastical celebrity in the fourth century, as is evident from his appearance in Jerome-Gennadius's *de viris illustribus*, a crucial source for Ado's *Chronicle*.[86] Among Gallic authors he was known to Sulpicius Severus,[87] and to Gregory of Tours, appearing in both the *Histories* and the *Liber in gloria confessorum*.[88] Eusebius is mentioned in the month of August in Ado's *Martyrology*,[89] and in that of Bede,[90] whose martyrological and historiographical work had an immense influence on Ado.[91] Another saint is Symphorian, whose cultic

---

[85] Ado of Vienne, *Vita Theudarii*, ch. 8, p. 528: "Cum igitur vir Dei locum sessionis suae requireret, pervenit tandem ad locum solitudini suae aptum, non nimis procul ab urbe, ibique in honori domini nostri Iesu Christi sub veneratione beati Eusebii Vercellensis episcopi et martyris domunculam aedificare coepit."

[86] Jerome-Gennadius, *De viris illustribus*, ed. A. Ceresa-Gastaldo (Florence: Nardini, 1988), XCVI: "Eusebius, natione Sardus, et ex Lectore urbis Romanae, Vercellensis episcopus, ob confessionem fidei a Constantio principe Scythopolim et inde Cappadociam relegatus, sub Juliano imperatore ad Ecclesiam reversus, edidit in psalmos commentarios Eusebii Caesariensis, quos de Graeco in Latinum verterat. Mortuus est Valentiniano et Valente regnantibus." See McKitterick, *Perceptions*, p. 29.

[87] Sulpicius Severus, *Chronica*, ed. P. Parroni, CCSL 63 (Turnhout: Brepols, 2017), II.39: "Tum Eusebius Vercellensium et Lucifer a Carali Sardiniae episcopi relegati. ceterum Dionysius, Mediolanensium sacerdos, in Athanasii damnationem se consentire subscripsit, dummodo de fide inter episcopos quaereretur." Sulpicius Severus's *Vita Martini* could have been the inspiration for an episode in the *Vita sancti Severi*, although, of course, Ado's authorship is uncertain. Compare *Vita sancti Severi*, chs. 2–3 and *Vita sancti Martini*, ed. and trans. P. Burton (Oxford: Oxford University Press, 2017), chs. 13–14.

[88] Gregory of Tours, *Histories* v.44 mentions Eusebius in the context of Chilperic's ill-fated theological decree, wherein he advocated something akin to modalistic Monarchianism. In his rebuttal of Chilperic, Gregory implores the king to back down: "Hac credulitate relicta, pie rex, hoc te oportit sequi, quod nobis post apostolus alii doctores eclesiae reliquerunt, quod Elarius Eusebiusque docuerunt, quod in baptismo es confessus," to which the king angrily responds: "Manifestum est mihi in hac causa Elarium Eusebiumque validos inimicos habere." See also *Liber in gloria confessorum* 3, which probably locates the saint's cult in Chalon-sur-Saône, not far from Vienne.

[89] Ado of Vienne, *Martyrology*, I kal. Augusti, p. 242: "Apud Italiam, civitate Vercellis, beati Eusebii episcopi et confessoris, qui ob confessionem fidei a Constantio principe Scythopolim, et inde Cappadociam relegatus, sub Iuliano imperatore ad ecclesiam suam reversus est. Novissime persequentibus Arianis martyrium passus."

[90] Bede, *Martyrology*, in *Édition pratique des martyrologes de Bède, de l'anonyme lyonnais et de Florus*, eds. J. DuBois and G. Renaud (Paris: Éditions du Centre National de la Recherche Scientifique, 1976), I kal. Augusti: "Et in Vercellis Eusebii episcopi, qui moventibus persecutionem Arianis, sub Constantio principe martyrium passus est."

[91] Savigni, "Storia universale," p. 169; for Eusebius of Vercelli, see N. Everett, "Narrating the Life of Eusebius of Vercelli," in *Narrative and History in the Early Medieval West*, eds. E.M. Tyler and R. Balzaretti (Turnhout: Brepols, 2006), pp. 133–165.

center was based in Autun.[92] In the *Vita*, he appeared in a vision to urge Theudarius to construct a monastic cell in his honor on the banks of the Gère, one of the tributaries of the Rhône that runs through Vienne. The third saint was another regional hero, St. Maurice, to whom a relative of Theudarius dedicated an oratory.

After some time in seclusion in a nearby forest, Theudarius's asceticism earned him a nocturnal vision: an angel revealed to him a secret place where he could construct a monastery. Theudarius obeyed, dedicating the small monastery to the Virgin Mary. It was endowed by his relatives and populated by monks living "according to the rule of the saintly fathers" (*iuxta regulam sanctorum patrum*).[93] Theudarius's establishments were not of the kind that required vast investments of land and other material resources such as those that feature in the *Vita Columbani* and the other hagiographies it inspired. Nor were they foundations that would upend power relations or threaten the bishop's authority in any way. They were, however, important enough to merit Ado's attention.

It should come as no surprise that the saints' shrines dotting the Viennois in the *Vita Theudarii* reflect ninth-century proprietary concerns. The church dedicated to St. Maurice and the *cellula sancti Symphoriani* both appear in an immunity diploma (BM² 570), issued in 815 by Louis the Pious at the request of Ado's predecessor Bernard, and interpolated at a later stage to expand its proprietary scope.[94] The cult of St. Maurice, a perennial favorite of Ado's, seems to have become a feature of Vienne's religious scene no earlier than the eighth century, although the *Vita Theudarii* conveniently retro-projected it on the sixth.[95]

---

[92] See Y. Labaune, "Quelques observations récentes sur des sites de l'Antiquité tardive à Autun (2001–2008)," in *L'Antiquité tardive dans l'Est de la Gaule I. La vallée du Rhin supérieur et les provinces gauloise limitrophes: actualité de la recherche, Actes de la table-ronde de Strasbourg, 20–21 novembre 2008*, eds. M. Kasprzyk and G. Kuhnle (Dijon: Société Archéologique de l'Est, 2011), pp. 41–68.

[93] For a similarly vague phrasing, see Krusch's discussion of the rule of Stablo-Malmédy in his introduction to the *Vita Remacli episcopi et abbatis*, MGH SRM 5, ed. B. Krusch (Hanover: Hahnsche Buchhandlung, 1910), p. 89: "*iuxta patrum traditionem.*" This phrasing has been taken to imply Lerinian or Caesarian regular influences. The latter would stand to reason given Caesarius of Arles's role in Theudarius's education. On this, see L. Dupraz, *Contribution à l'histoire du Regnum Francorum pendant le troisième quart du VIIe siècle, 656–680* (Fribourg-en-Suisse, 1948), p. 304; F. Prinz, *Frühes Mönchtum im Frankenreich: Kultur und Gesellschaft in Gallien, den Rheinlanden und Bayern am Beispiel der monastischen Entwicklung dargestellt* (Munich: R. Oldenbourg Verlag, 1965), pp. 75–76.

[94] B. Schilling, "Zu einem interpolierten Diplom Ludwigs des Frommen für die Kirche von Vienne (BM² 570)," *Archiv für Diplomatik* 57 (2011), pp. 63–104. Ado may have been the author of the miracles of Bernard. See *Translatio seu elevatio S. Bernardi*, PL 123, cols. 451–452.

[95] Preceded probably by a cult of the Maccabees, also mentioned by Ado. See Ado of Vienne, *Passio sancti Desiderii*, PL 123, cols. 435–442, at cols. 440D–441A: "Erat tunc temporis ager Fasianus, iam ut proprius delegatus pauperibus sanctorum martyrum in

As a hagiographical protagonist, Theudarius offers us little more than clichés of monastic piety. He cannot be connected to concrete historical events from his day, particularly those transpiring on a level that interested historiographers. Nor is he endowed with the depth of character that would make him an especially appealing protagonist, limiting his appeal to audiences outside the Viennois. Yet Ado's hagiography is more than a narrative attempt to reassert legal rights on alienated ecclesiastical property, although this was certainly one of its goals.[96] Like all other hagiographical heroes, Ado's *dramatis personae* were meant to convey a model of sanctity fitted to specific social contexts—an unassuming hermit and founder of rural *cellulae* in Theudarius's case, a spiritual leader of the flock and a guardian of moral righteousness in Desiderius's. To better understand Ado's intentions regarding these characters, we should ask whether he was influenced in his hagiographical work by earlier *Lives*.

One expression Ado uses to describe Theudarius is suggestive: "the fame of the man of God grew and was spread far and wide," a phrase reminiscent of Jonas of Bobbio's *Vita Columbani*.[97] Other textual borrowings are perhaps not as direct, such as Theudarius's portrayal as *feris ac serpentibus amicus* (friend of wild beasts and serpents), a motif that is quite common in the *Vita Columbani*.[98] Theudarius sought the approval of Bishop Philipp of Vienne before embarking on his monastic projects, so in many ways he was unlike the historical Columbanus, who was much more inclined to confront meddlesome bishops than submit to their

quorum honore Viennensis Ecclesia fundata consistit; nam ante sicut idem martyr in testamento suo quod fecit sanctis martyribus Machabaeis, et sancto Mauricio, ac sex millibus sexcentis sexaginta, commemorat, ex maternis et paternis eadem villa, sorte beato Desiderio obvenerat." On this, see R. McKitterick, "The Scripts of the Bobbio Missal," in *The Bobbio Missal: Liturgy and Religious Culture in Merovingian Gaul*, eds. Y. Hen and R. Meens (Cambridge: Cambridge University Press, 2004), pp. 19–52, at pp. 41–42; Raisharma, "Much Ado," p. 281.

[96] Especially since Ado was involved in asserting Vienne's proprietary rights through creative "reinvention." On this, see B. Schilling, "*Ansemundus dux*, das Ende des Burgunderreichs und der Senat von Vienne: Zur gefälschten Gründungsurkunde des Andreasklosters (Vienne)," *Archiv für Diplomatik* 46, 1 (2000), pp. 1–47 for his activity on Saint-André.

[97] Ado of Vienne, *Vita Theudarii*, ch. 9, p. 528: "Crescebat autem fama viri Dei ac longe lateque spargebatur...." Compare Jonas of Bobbio, *Vita Columbani discipulorumque eius libri II*, MGH SRG 37, ed. B. Krusch (Hanover: Hahnsche Buchhandlung, 1905), II.18: "Creverat iam passim fama sancti viri in universas Galliae vel Germaniae provincias..." This similarity was recognized by Krusch, ibid., n.3.

[98] *Vita Columbani* I.27, 30. But compare also Seneca the Younger, *De beneficiis*, ed. C. Hosius (Leipzig: Teubner, 1900), IV.22: "Sed illud intuere, an ad istam virtutem, quae saepe tuta ac facili aditur via, etiam per saxa et rupes et feris ac serpentibus obsessum iter fueris iturus" and Lactantius, *Divinae Institutiones*, ed. C. Ingremeau, Sources Chrétiennes 509 (Paris: Éditions du CERF, 2007), VI.18.22: "Nam et pecudes si lacessas, aut calce aut cornu repugnant, et serpentes ac ferae, nisi persequare ut occidas, negotium non exhibent..."

authority.[99] It is true that in Jonas's treatment, the man of God's rough edges were smoothed out, especially his free-spirited attitude toward bishops. It is thus possible at least to entertain the influence of the *Vita Columbani* on the *Vita Theudarii*, although such an influence would have been very selective. In the end, Theudarius, the well-behaved hermit who embodied both a love of ascetic solitude and a reverence for episcopal authority, was nothing like Columbanus, a man who threatened kings and spent his life evading their wrath.[100] Ado's *Vita Theudarii* sets out to elaborate—and put into proper historical context—the beginnings of the monastic traditions in the archdiocese of Vienne, traditions that were commonly known during Ado's episcopacy. In so doing, Ado drew upon hagiographical models that later served him in the *Chronicle* and the *Passio Desiderii*, both compositions in which Vienne's ecclesiastical history played a prominent role.

Ado's interest in his seventh-century episcopal predecessor Desiderius of Vienne brings us back to the *Vita Columbani (VC)*, especially to its account of the persecutions suffered by Desiderius at the hands of Brunhild and Theuderic.[101] Of course, Ado need not have looked far for alternative sources of inspiration on which to base his hagiographical *réécriture*. His *Passio sancti Desiderii* was influenced by two previous works, King Sisebut's *Vita Desiderii* and an anonymous *Passio sancti Desiderii* composed in Vienne in the seventh century.[102] The textual influences present in Ado's *Passio sancti Desiderii* go beyond the hagiographical; this is a composition steeped in historiography. In his attempt to provide the *Passio* with historical context, it is thus only natural that Ado made extensive use of his *Chronicle*, to which we now turn.

---

[99] C. Stancliffe, "Columbanus and the Gallic Bishops," in *Auctoritas: Mélanges offerts au Olivier Guillot*, eds. G. Constable and M. Rouche, Cultures et Civilisation Médieval 33 (Paris: Sorbonne PUPS, 2006), pp. 205–215.

[100] Schilling, "Zu einem interpolierten," pp. 72–73.

[101] *VC* I.27, p. 214: "Eo itaque in tempore Theodoricus atque Brunichildis non solum adversum Columbanum insaniebant, verum etiam et contra sanctissimum Desiderium Viennensis urbis episcopum adversabantur. Quem primo exilio damnatum multis iniuriis adfligere nitebantur, ad postremum vero glorioso martyrio coronarunt; cuius gesta scripta habentur, quibus et quantis adversitatibus gloriosus apud Dominum meruit habere triumphos." See Y. Fox, "The Bishop and the Monk: Desiderius of Vienne and the Columbanian Movement," *Early Medieval Europe* 20, 2 (2012), pp. 176–194, and now J.F. Dobschenzki, *Von Opfern und Tätern: Gewalt im Spiegel der merowingischen Hagiographie des 7. Jahrhunderts* (Stuttgart: Kohlhammer 2015), esp. pp. 102–103.

[102] J.C. Martín, "Une nouvelle édition critique de la 'Vita Desiderii' de Sisebut, accompagnée de quelques réflexions concernant la date des 'Sententiae' et du 'De viris illustribus' d'Isidore de Séville," *Hagiographica* 7 (2000), pp. 127–180, at pp. 147–163; *Passio sancti Desiderii episcopi Viennensis*, ed. C. De Smedt et al., *Analecta Bollandiana* 9 (Brussels, 1892), pp. 250–262. See Krusch's introduction to Ado's *Passio Desiderii*, p. 628.

At first sight, Ado's *Chronicle* corresponds closely to its sources and conveys its history in a rather conservative manner.[103] While nothing here is entirely new, Ado achieves a novel result by accentuating specific stories.[104] In this universal chronicle, he sought to provide a wide perspective on international affairs, both secular and ecclesiastical. He used the six-age model to great effect, incorporating into each a moral lesson applicable to his contemporary audience.[105] Ado's local considerations dictated that he emphasize the episcopal history of his hometown, and indeed Vienne received much of his attention.[106]

Although Merovingian history is a necessary background for understanding the affairs of the church of Vienne from the sixth to the eighth centuries, it is not a topic that is discussed in great detail. This is understandable since most of the *Chronicle* is concerned with biblical events. Even the final sixth book (*aetas sexta: a Christo ad mundi finem*), which is longer than all previous five combined, devotes relatively little space to the centuries in which the Merovingians were active, and even less to actual Merovingian history. What Ado does mention was lifted entirely from the *LHF*, although this does not mean that the material did not undergo careful selection. As we shall see, in this process of selection, the accomplishments of the Merovingians were either belittled or presented in a way that highlighted their barbarity. Ado broke his narration of Merovingian history into short textual bursts, usually no more than a few sentences long, interposed with sections that dealt with other kingdoms or, more importantly, with ecclesiastical affairs. The constant shifts from episcopal acts of piety, devotion, and self-sacrifice to the earthly, often bloody, power struggles of the Merovingians make the Frankish narrative appear by turns banal and horrifying.

---

[103] On Ado's sources, see Kremers, "Ado von Vienne," pp. 78–81. Also see the remark in G. Scheibelreiter, "Fredegar – Chronist einer Epoche," in *The Medieval Chronicle: Proceedings of the 1st International Conference on the Medieval Chronicle Driebergen/Utrecht 13–16 July 1996*, ed. E. Kooper (Amsterdam and Atlanta, GA: Rodopi, 1999), pp. 251–259, at p. 251.

[104] This is especially true of his account of the Saracens. On this, see N. Bade, "Muslims in the Christian World Order: Comprehension and Knowledge of the Saracens in Two Universal Histories of the Carolingian Empire," *Millennium: Jahrbuch zu Kultur und Geschichte des ersten Jahrtausends nach Chr.* 10, 1 (2013), pp. 293–310. For a discussion of compilation and editing, and their influence on medieval historiography, see R. Corradini, R. Meens, C. Pössel, and P. Shaw, eds., *Texts and Identities in the Early Middle Ages*, Forschungen zur Geschichte des Mittelalters 12, Denkschriften der Österreichischen Akademie der Wissenschaften, Philosophische Klasse 344 (Vienna: Austrian Academy of Sciences Press, 2006).

[105] McKitterick, *Perceptions*, p. 29.

[106] On Vienne as the city to which Herod Archelaus, Herod Antipas, and Pontius Pilate were exiled, see Ado of Vienne, *Chronicle*, cols. 75, 77; McKitterick, *Perceptions*, p. 29.

148   *Taedit me memorare*: The Middle Merovingians

In the *Chronicle*, as in the *LHF*, the Franks came to Valentinian's aid in the Maeotian swamps, earning them the name Franci, which in the Attic language signified ferocity, toughness, and daring. Later, when they refused to pay tribute to the Romans, they retreated to Sicambria, located on the farthest shores of the Rhine in Germany. There, they lived under the rule of the *principes* Marcomir and Sunno.[107] Ado goes on to note that: "This (i.e., Sicambria) is where they later installed over themselves their first king Faramund and placed themselves under the laws that their leading men Wisovast, Wisogast, Artogast, and Salegast formulated."[108]

All of this was obviously taken from the *LHF* (and, gazing further into the past, from the prologue to the *Pactus legis Salicae*), but some differences do stand out. The first is one of omission. Ado made no mention of the Trojan storyline so integral to the *LHF* author's framing of the story. Without their Trojan mythology, the Franks become simply one people among many. Secondly, in Ado's *Chronicle*, Faramund was not the son of Marcomir. He was appointed by popular consensus and provided no pedigree. The exclusion of the Trojan background material and the ancestral caesura that Ado introduced between the Franks' *principes* and their *reges* pulls the rug out from under the *LHF*'s vision of the Franks and their kings. For an archbishop with close ties to the Carolingian court of Charles the Bald, writing in a period of heightened political uncertainty, Ado's reluctance to rehearse Merovingian ancestral mythologies is perhaps understandable. Unlike Paul the Deacon, however, he deprives the Franks as a whole of their claim to a Trojan pedigree. His decision to do so merits some consideration.

Any interpretation of Paul's and Ado's approaches to the Trojan myth should take into account the differences in the authors' historical circumstances. The scope and perspective of the *Chronicle* forced Ado to consider Carolingian history against the wider stage of empire.[109] The Carolingian kings of Ado's day were no mere Franks; they were emperors and potential emperors—albeit Frankish ones—fighting over the vestiges of a great empire, which included many peoples and regions. At least nominally,

---

[107] In the *LHF*, the establishment of Sicambria is part of the Trojan storyline, and the city is said to have been located in Pannonia, near the swamps: "Ingressi Meotidas paludes navigantes, pervenerunt intra terminos Pannoniarum, iuxta Meotidas paludes et coeperunt aedificare civitatem ob memoriale eorum appellaveruntque eam Sicambriam."
[108] Ado of Vienne, *Chronicle*, col. 95C: "Ubi primum regem Pharamundum sibi postmodum statuunt, legibusque se subdunt, quas priores eorum Wisovastus et Wisogastus, Artogastus, Salegastus invenerunt."
[109] As he indeed makes clear in the prologue, col. 23A: "Horum nos temporum summam, ab exordio mundi usque ad imperatoris Lotharii ac Ludovici fratris ejus, ac Ludovici et Caroli regum principatum, quanta potuimus brevitate notavimus." See also Raisharma, "Much Ado," pp. 274–275.

the Carolingians harbored pretensions to act as the leaders of Latin Christendom. To attempt an exclusively Frankish history at this point would have subverted the Carolingians' understanding of their place on the world stage. While the *LHF* provided crucial data on the Frankish side of the story and Ado relied on it heavily, not all of it was useful. Ado not only pruned his source, but also expunged elements that did not conform to his historical vision.

Ado completed his *Chronicle* almost a century after Paul the Deacon wrote his *Gesta episcoporum Mettensium* (*GeM*) in ca. 784.[110] These were different worlds; in the 780s, the crystallization of a Carolingian imperial ideology was still several decades in the future. The *GeM* had a more localized setting—the city and church of Metz, set against the background of Charlemagne's family, both past and present. Building up Carolingian legitimacy would have been Paul's most pressing priority.[111] He appropriately denied the Merovingians' privileged association with the Trojan past but stopped short of jettisoning the Trojan plot entirely; it was deftly applied to the Franks as a whole, because the Franks, and particularly one Frankish family, were uniquely important for the *GeM*.

Ado's circumstances were quite different. Carolingian legitimacy was hardly in question since all of the relevant actors had the right ancestry. The partition of Lothar II's patrimony between his two uncles, Charles the Bald and Louis the German, was the defining political event of the years in which the *Chronicle* was written.[112] It certainly had broad implications for anyone with an eye on the imperial title.[113] Importantly for Ado, its effects were also felt immediately in Vienne. The Treaty of Meersen (870) placed Vienne and the entire Rhône-Saône basin under Charles's control, but it left out most of Lotharingia, with the symbolically significant cities of

---

[110] The latest events covered in the *Chronicle* took place in 869, and Ado himself died in 875, which allows for a relatively precise dating of the composition. For a discussion of dating, see Kremers, "Ado von Vienne," pp. 58, 77.
[111] See "Introduction," in Paul the Deacon, *GeM*, pp. 13–14.
[112] For Ado's support for Charles's appropriation of Lothar's domains, see Nelson, *Charles the Bald*, p. 223. For his involvement in Lothar's divorce, K. Heidecker, *The Divorce of Lothar II: Christian Marriage and Political Power in the Carolingian World* (Ithaca, NY, and London: Cornell University Press, 2010), pp. 157, 183. On Lothar I and the context for Lothar II's marriage and inheritance issues, see E. Screen, "Remembering and Forgetting Lothar I," in *Writing the Early Medieval West*, eds. E. Screen and C. West (Cambridge: Cambridge University Press, 2018), pp. 248–260; E. Screen, "Lothar I in Italy," in *Problems and Possibilities of Early Medieval Charters*, eds. J. Jarrett and A.S. McKinley (Turnhout: Brepols, 2013), pp. 231–252.
[113] Charles's move on his nephew's land, which Ado duly supported, was depicted by John Scotus Eriugena, using very imperial-sounding language. See Nelson, *Charles the Bald*, pp. 223–224. On Louis the German's parallel aspirations, see E.J. Goldberg, *Struggle for Empire: Kingship and Conflict under Louis the German, 817–876* (Ithaca, NY: Cornell University Press, 2006).

Aachen and Metz, which Charles initially held but was later forced to relinquish to Louis.[114]

If we are inclined to read intent into Ado's errors, we might speculate that the territorial exchanges built into the Treaty of Meersen could explain why Ado replaced the *LHF*'s Alani with the more evocative Alamanni as the ones subdued by Frankish ferocity in the Maeotian swamps.[115] Be that as it may, Meersen had an immediate effect on the power structures in Vienne. Gerard, who opposed the treaty, was confronted by Ado and Remigius of Lyon, whom we met in Lupus's letter of recommendation. Charles took Vienne, Gerard was removed, and Boso, Charles's relative, was put in his place.

As Ado was composing the *Chronicle*, his candidate was already making preparations to seize the imperial title, for which he managed to obtain papal support in 872. The grander scheme of Ado's oeuvre is therefore not confined to Frankish history. Rather, it aimed to provide a comprehensive view of world affairs, as befitting an imperially minded piece of historiography. Let us now look at Ado's treatment of the Merovingians, particularly his innovative retelling of the period 511–638.

Although Ado briefly mentioned Clodio's capture of the city of Cambrai, he quickly moved on to more important matters such as the ecclesiastical history of Vienne and other cities of note. When we meet the Franks again, it is after Clodio's death: "When King Clodio died, having reigned twenty years, Merovech succeeded, after whom the kings of the Franks are called Merovingians."[116] Unlike the *LHF*, Ado did not linger on the relationship between the two kings. Merovech was the first Merovingian and not the scion of an older royal *gens*. Of his accomplishments we learn only that he took Metz, Trier, and Orléans. Childeric, relatively well-covered by the *LHF*, was given even less consideration than his father; all that is said is that he ruled for twenty-four years. Then, Ado turned to Clovis.

---

[114] P. Riché, *The Carolingians: A Family Who Forged Europe* (Philadelphia, PA: University of Pennsylvania Press, 1993), p. 199; M. Gaillard, "La place des abbayes dans la politique territorial des souverains francs et germaniques en Lotharingie, de 869 à 925," *Revue du Nord* 351, 3 (2003), pp. 655–666.

[115] *LHF*, ch. 2: "Eo itidem tempore gens Alanorum prava ac pessima rebellaverunt contra Valentinianum imperatorem Romanorum ac gentium"; Ado of Vienne, *Chronicle*, col. 95C: "Valentiniani, et Valentis tempore rebellantes Alamannos, Franci inter Danubium et Maeotides paludes juncti Romanis, superaverunt." On rebellion and its terminology, see P. Fouracre, "The Incidence of Rebellion in the Early Medieval West," in *Making Early Medieval Societies: Conflict and Belonging in the Latin West, 300–1200*, eds. K. Cooper and C. Leyser (Cambridge: Cambridge University Press, 2016), pp. 104–124.

[116] Ado, *Chronicle*, col. 97D: "Clodione rege defuncto, qui viginti annis Francis regnavit, Meroveus successit, a quo Francorum reges Merovingi sunt appellati."

The rhythm and brevity of Ado's account dictated a more restricted account that could not compete with the wealth of details regarding Clovis which one finds in Gregory, *Fredegar*, or the *LHF*. Yet even with this limitation in mind, Clovis cuts a rather lackluster figure in Ado's *Chronicle*. We learn of him in the context of the Frankish advance on Gaul, in which Cologne was taken from Aegidius. After his death and the death of Childeric, their sons Syagrius and Clovis enter the stage. The two immediately go to war, Clovis prevails, and Syagrius escapes to the Goths. He is later extradited and killed. In his account of the event, Ado remarks: "Thus the power of the Romans in Gaul collapsed."[117] He cryptically continues: "In his place, Aëtius, who waged great battles with the Vandals and other nations, was later appointed *patricius*."[118] Ado could not have meant anyone other than Valentinian III's maverick general, although in reality, Aëtius seems to have made every effort to avoid the Vandals and the African theater more generally.[119] More to the point, Aëtius was active a generation before Syagrius, so he could not have been his successor.

The reason for this chronological inconsistency could be that Ado was attempting to downplay the extent of Clovis's dominion over northern Gaul, although here he seems to contradict his earlier statement about the collapse of Roman power there. Or, it could have been just a simple mistake. Bede's *Chronicle* sums up Aëtius's life with the remark: "with him fell the Western realm, and to this day it has not had the strength to be revived," which may have provided the thematic connection to Roman collapse.[120] Regardless, the Frankish king did not emerge from this account favorably. Clovis, in Ado's telling of the story, was then made king of the Franks— what had he been until now? —and married Clothild.[121] The baptism scene that came next was dispensed with in one sentence: "Clovis, after the victory over the Alamanni in the fifteenth year of his reign, believed and was baptized."[122] In his depiction of the royal baptism, Ado was perhaps

---

[117] Ado of Vienne, *Chronicle*: "Sic Romanorum vires intra Gallias ceciderunt."
[118] Ibid.: "In cujus loco postea Aetius patricius constitutus est, qui maxima praelia cum Wandalis aliisque nationibus gessit."
[119] See J.W.P. Wijnendele, "The Early Career of Aëtius and the Murder of Felix (c. 425– 430 CE)," *Historia* 66, 4 (2017), pp. 468–482; A. Merrills and R. Miles, *The Vandals* (Malden, MA, and Oxford: Wiley-Blackwell, 2010), pp. 111–119; R.W. Mathisen, "Sigisvult the Patrician, Maximinus the Arian, and Political Stratagems in the Western Roman Empire c. 425–40," *Early Medieval Europe* 8, 2 (1999), pp. 173–196.
[120] Bede, *Chronicle*, a.4410, trans. F. Wallis, Bede, *The Reckoning of Time* (Liverpool: Liverpool University Press, 2004), p. 22.
[121] Interestingly, when Ado introduces the Burgundian royal family, he changes the *LHF*'s *ex genere Athanarici regis* to *ex genere fertur Alarici*, perhaps with the intent of distancing the Burgundians from Athanaric's legacy of persecution.
[122] Ado of Vienne, *Chronicle*: "Chlodoveus rex post victoriam Alamannorum quindecimo anno regni sui, credens baptizatur."

inspired by Bede's condensed narrative tempo in chapter 66 of *De temporum ratione*.[123] Yet it still reads like an intentionally underwhelming depiction, especially given the bishop's insistence on covering less flattering aspects of the king's career, as we shall see.

Ado proceeded to report on the Frankish involvement in the Burgundian kingdom in 500, followed by the Battle of Vouillé, which he curiously summed up with these words: "Clovis the Burgundian king subjugated Toulouse, Saintes, and the remaining cities and all the lands of Aquitaine, expelling from them the Arian Goths; he established there the Catholic Franks."[124] Since the Burgundians did, in fact, fight alongside the Franks in Vouillé, the text was probably meant to have read *Chlodoveus Burgundiorumque rex*.[125] No mention was made of the assistance afforded to the Franks by St. Martin, although, as we shall see, the connection between Martin and Clovis was made shortly thereafter.

As in the *LHF*, the *Chronicle* makes Clovis's final act his disposal of his Frankish competitors. It is telling that, while Ado was usually tightfisted with details, he chose to elaborate on Clovis's gilded armband ruse, which concluded with the death of Ragnachar and Ricchar (the latter is here unnamed) at Clovis's hands and the submission of their treacherous men. Ado spotlighted Clovis's duplicity and belligerence, a strategy he repeated with all of Clovis's successors.

Notably, Ado disconnected Clovis's victory at Vouillé from the imperial honors he received from Anastasius. These appeared later, as a preamble to the discussion of the king's death, dated by Ado to the thirtieth year of his reign, 112 years after the death of Martin of Tours.[126] Martin was then used to date the episcopacies of two important bishops of Vienne, Martin and Mamertus: "From the death of St. Martin, the third bishop of Vienne (the first was Crescens, followed by the martyr Zacharias) to the death of Martin the bishop of Tours 290 years, and to

---

[123] Which does not mention Clovis at all.
[124] Ado of Vienne, *Chronicle*, col. 104B: "Chlodoveus Burgundiorum rex Tolosam, Sanctonas, et reliquas civitates omnemque terram Aquitanicam subjugavit, Gothos Arianos inde expellens; Francos ibi catholicos habitare constituens." An alternative translation could see *Burgundiorum* as referring to *civitates*, and while this would solve Clovis's title problem, it would create a new one since the cities in question were undoubtedly Visigothic, not Burgundian.
[125] Manuscripts I have had occasion to examine contain the abbreviation Clodouec' burgundiorū rex, which might explain the error in Migne's edition. See, for instance, Cambridge, Corpus Christi College, MS 290, f. 158v or Bern, Burgerbibliothek Cod. 120.1, f. 40r. Alternatively, it is omitted in favor of a shorter phrasing in Paris, BnF MS lat. 5512 f. 96v: "Chlodoveus rex Francorum cum Alarico rege Gothorum pugnavit." A marginal note adds: "miliario decimo ab urbe Pictavi."
[126] Ado of Vienne, *Chronicle*, col. 106B: "Regnavit a Francis triginta annos. Fuerunt autem a transitu sancti Martini, usque ad transitum Chlodovei regis annis centum duodecim."

the death of St. Mamertus, bishop of the church of Vienne all counted passed 328 years."[127]

This would place Martin of Vienne's death in the year 107 (calculated according to our current dating of Martin of Tours's death to 397) or in 149 (calculated according to Mamertus's in 477) and is evidence of the inaccuracy with which Vienne's earlier episcopacies were dated by Ado.[128] Mamertus's episcopacy, about which Ado certainly had some concrete historical knowledge,[129] was placed in the *Chronicle* after the baptism of Clovis and Godegisel's attempt to overthrow Gundobad, so more than two decades after our current dating, but still in line with the *LHF*.[130]

The usage of Martin of Tours as a chronological anchor with which to date Clovis's kingship was likely inspired by the connection made between the saint and the king, first by Gregory of Tours and then by the author of the *LHF*.[131] For obvious reasons, Martin constituted a point of special importance on Gregory's timeline, but this does not explain why Ado adopted him, seemingly uncritically so.

Ado used Martin of Tours to date his own, earlier Martin, who was his city's third bishop. His martyrology had little to say about Martin of Vienne other than his place in the order of episcopal succession, and the *Chronicle* added very little to that.[132] Martin of Tours, on the other hand,

---

[127] Ado of Vienne, *Chronicle*, cols. 106B, C: "A transitu sancti Martini Viennensis tertii episcopi (nam primus Crescens, sequens Zacharias martyr) usque ad transitum Martini Turonorum episcopi ducenti nonaginta anni, et usque ad transitum sancti Mamerti Viennensis ecclesiae episcopi, colliguntur anni trecenti viginti octo."
[128] Raisharma, "Much Ado," p. 282. On Ado's approach to episcopal succession, see S. Patzold, *Episcopus: Wissen über Bischöfe im Frankenreich des späten 8. bis frühen 10. Jahrhunderts* (Sigmaringen: Jan Thorbecke Verlag, 2008), pp. 430–434.
[129] L. Duchesne, *Fastes épiscopaux de l'ancienne Gaule*, 4 vols. (Paris: Thorin et fils, 1907), I, p. 153.
[130] Which likewise places it after Clovis's Burgundian intervention in 500. See *LHF*, ch. 16. Mamertus's establishment of rogations following the catastrophes visited on Vienne (probably ca. 472) is very similar to the account in the *LHF*. On the development of Rogationtide, see N. Ristuccia, *Christianization and Commonwealth in Early Medieval Europe: A Ritual Interpretation* (Oxford: Oxford University Press, 2018), pp. 1–63; J. Hill, "The *Litaniae maiores* and *minores* in Rome, Francia and Anglo-Saxon England: Terminology, Texts and Traditions," *Early Medieval Europe* 9, 2 (2000), pp. 1–13.
[131] Gregory of Tours, *Histories*, II.37, 38; *LHF*, ch. 17. For Frechulf's treatment of Martin see Allen, "Bede and Frechulf," p. 67.
[132] Bede, *Martyrology*, I kal. Iulii: "Viennae, B. Martini, tertii eiusdem urbis episcopi, ab apostolis ab praefatam urbem missi"; Ado of Vienne, *Martyrology*, I kal. Iulii, p. 211: "Viennae, sancti episcopi Martini, ab apostolis ad praefatam urbem missi, in pace gloriose quiescentis. Hic tertius a Crescente fuit." This entry is found in the "third recension." Ado of Vienne, *Chronicle*, col. 81D: "Nam primus Crescens discipulus apostolum Viennae aliquot annos resedit; quo ad Galatiam reverso, tertius Martinus episcopus et discipulus apostolorum Viennae resedit."

received several mentions that expanded upon his wonder-working abilities, his death, and his chronological relationship to Clovis.[133] We might agree, then, that Martin of Tours was an important reference point, but thematically his relationship to Clovis's death is hardly self-evident.

Ado did not explain why he interrupted the narrative continuum to insert the short passage on dating, but reliance on Gregory might go some way toward explaining it. The deaths of Martin and Clovis seal two of Gregory's books and, as such, function as secure timepoints around which he structured his narrative. Ado relied on a different system of delivery, attached to the tenures of emperors, which he had to reconcile with his sources' very different methodology and overall sense of historical time. The *LHF*, which was one of these sources, did not use the death of Clovis, let alone Martin, to create special partitions in the text.[134] This is perhaps a small hint that Ado relied directly on Gregory's *Histories*; as we shall see, it is not the only one.

In almost all other works of historiography surveyed thus far, Clovis's death constituted an end of an era and the opening of a new thematic block. Dating it, as Ado did in this instance, would thus signify to the readers that they were entering a new period of history. Since Ado opened each of his chronicle's six *aetates*, which were clearly meant to signify new chronological periods, with similar dating references, this is a plausible interpretation.[135] Something might even be said about the broader Carolingian approach to legitimacy and its perception of time through its usage of sanctoral history. The importance of Martin to the Carolingians, and of the institution that represented him—Saint-Martin at Tours—is unquestionable. Charlemagne and Louis the Pious were preoccupied with Saint-Martin, as suggested by the nomination of such a lofty figure as Alcuin to the abbacy and its transformation in 815 into a house of canons. Symbolically, Martin's cape continued to function as a legitimating artifact for royal oath-taking, while the ceremonies undertaken at the saint's tomb were attended by the king at Easter. More to the point, Martin was consciously being made into a figure

---

[133] Ado of Vienne, *Chronicle*, col. 96C (miracles), 97C (death).

[134] *LHF*, ch. 19 ("De morte Chlodovechi, et quia quattuor filii eius in regnum succedunt, et de Danis, qui in Gallias inruunt") discusses Clovis's death as well as other events, like the Danish invasion.

[135] See, for instance, the opening to the *Aetas sexta*, col. 75: "Igitur eo tempore, anno scilicet Caesaris Augusti quadragesimo secundo, a morte vero Cleopatrae et Antonii, quando et Ægyptus in provinciam versa est, anno vigesimo septimo, olympiadis centesimae tertiae anno tertio, ab Urbe condita septingentesimo quinquagesimo secundo, id est eo anno quo compressis cunctarum orbis terrae gentium motibus firmissimam verissimamque pacem ordinatione Dei Caesar composuit, Jesus Christus Filius Dei, sextam mundi aetatem suo consecravit adventu."

of national importance.[136] For the next generation of Carolingians, and especially in Charles the Bald's embattled Neustria, Saint-Martin functioned as a node of political and cultural power, a process that gathered steam under the abbacy of Hugh the Abbot, who stepped in to fill the role of Robert the Strong and to institute a centralizing policy of governance.[137] It is in this context that the legitimating function of Martin *vis-à-vis* the institution of kingship needs to be appraised in Ado's day, and it is perhaps also possible to read it as a silent recognition of Clovis's formative role. Clovis's importance for the *Chronicle*'s thematic division might even tell us something about late-Carolingian attitudes to dynastic time. Yet this point should not be pushed too far. Even though Ado seems to have chosen to tie the Merovingian king to Martin, his Clovis hardly measured up to the one found in the *LHF*, much less in Gregory or *Fredegar*.

As one of the most prominent bishops of his day in Gaul, Avitus of Vienne's episcopacy received ample attention from Ado, his thirty-first successor to the see.[138] Ado not only extolled the bishop's erudition and provided a short list of his works, which he seems to have read, but even cited several lines from his epitaph. Avitus is said to have instructed Sigismund in the faith, after which the Burgundian prince founded Saint-Maurice d'Agaune.[139] Ado's Sigismund was depicted as a martyr, having suffered terribly and then been killed by the Franks.[140] Unlike the *LHF*, which simply states that Sigismund was executed with his wife and children by Chlodomer and thrown down a well,[141] Ado says that he was later exhumed and his body placed in Saint-Maurice, where he went on to perform miracles.[142] Given Saint-Maurice's regional status, the unambiguous acceptance of Sigismund as a martyr and miracle worker

---

[136] S. Farmer, *Communities of Saint Martin: Legend and Ritual in Medieval Tours* (Ithaca, NY: Cornell University Press, 2019), pp. 124–125.

[137] See F. McNair, "Governance, Locality and Legal Culture: The Rise and Fall of the Carolingian Advocates of Saint-Martin of Tours," *Early Medieval Europe* 29, 2 (2021), pp. 201–224, at p. 207.

[138] This according to Duchesne's reconstruction in *Fastes épiscopaux*, 1, p. 148, based primarily on evidence provided by Ado himself. As noted by Duchesne, confidence in this list, especially its earlier components and their "apostolic" lineage, should not be exaggerated.

[139] Whose number of martyrs increases from the *LHF*'s 6600 to 6666 in Ado.

[140] Ado, *Chronicle*: "Quem [Sigismundum] postmodum captum, et a Francis occisum, vehementissime doluit."

[141] Although the *LHF* repeats Gregory of Tours' petition by the abbot Avitus to spare the king's life, which Ado does not.

[142] Ado, *Chronicle*, col. 106D: "Sed per revelationem postea inde ab abbate sanctorum martyrum levatus non longe ab ecclesia eorum in monasterio, quod ipse construxit, ubi eorum corpora, scilicet Mauritii, sociorumque eius sex millium sexcentorum sexaginta sex posita sunt honorifice sepultus est: ubi virtutibus postmodum et ipse claruit."

is not unexpected.[143] The discovery of the body through the vision of the abbot and the description of the translation both point to the *Passio sancti Sigismundi regis* as the most likely source.[144] Ado was naturally silent on the murder of Sigistrix, which could be the fault of his sources, since neither the *LHF* nor the *Passio sancti Sigismundi regis* made mention of it.[145] It is nevertheless likely that he knew the story. He was certainly more than willing to relate comparable crimes committed by the Merovingians and, as discussed on p.154, there is some evidence that he was influenced by Gregory's *Histories*, which would make his silence on the matter intentional. As in other instances, the Merovingians are here the masterminds of misery, only this time their aggression concluded with a royal martyrdom and the creation of a regionally important saint. The short narrative block on Burgundian history ends with Chlodomer's death at Vézeronce, and the eventual Frankish conquest.

[143] For the cult of Sigismund at Saint-Maurice, see J.-M. Theurillat, "L'abbaye de St-Maurice d'Agaune: des origines à la réforme canoniale, 515–830 environ," *Vallesia* 9 (1954), pp. 30–84; F. Masai, "La *Vita patrum iurensium* et les débuts du monachisme à Saint-Maurice d'Agaune," in *Festschrift Bernhard Bischoff zu seinem 65. Geburtstag*, eds. J. Autenrieth and F. Brunhölzl (Stuttgart: A. Hiersemann, 1971), pp. 43–69; B.H. Rosenwein, "One Site, Many Meanings: St-Maurice d'Agaune as a Place of Power," in *Topographies of Power in the Early Middle Ages*, eds. M. de Jong, F. Theuws, and C. van Rhijn (Leiden, Boston, Cologne: Brill, 2001), pp. 271–290; A. Diem, "Who is Allowed to Pray for the King? St-Maurice d'Agaune and the Creation of a Burgundian Identity," in *Strategies of Identification: Ethnicity and Religion in Early Medieval Europe*, eds. W. Pohl and G. Heydemann (Turnhout: Brepols, 2013), pp. 47–88; F. Paxton, "Power and the Power to Heal: The Cult of St Sigismund of Burgundy," *Early Medieval Europe* 2, 2 (1993), pp. 95–110; F. Paxton, "Liturgy and Healing in an Early Medieval Saint's Cult: The Mass *in honore sancti Sigismundi* for the Cure of Fevers," *Traditio* 49 (1994), pp. 23–43.

[144] *Passio sancti Sigismundi regis*, ch. 10: "Transactum triennium, sanctus ac venerabilis Venerandus monasterii sanctorum Augaunensium abba per angelum in visu admonitus est, ut sacra corpora, sicut animae eorum in caelestibus sanctae legioni erant coniunctae, ita et in eo loco sepulturae sociarentur"; ch. 11: "Tunc cum magna admiratione sancta corpora de puteo abstracta, cum psallentium choris Agauni monasterio in ecclesia quae est in honore beatissimi Iohannis apostoli et evangelistae dignissimae sepulturae tradiderunt. In quo loco tantas virtutes Domini misericordia praestare dignatur..." Another option is Gregory of Tours, *Liber in gloria martyrum* 74, although Gregory does not mention the well but does open with Sigismund's murder of his son, an element that is missing from Ado's *Chronicle*. See also the comments in Schilling, "*Ansemundus dux*," p. 37.

[145] Although it is perhaps indirectly hinted at in *Passio sancti Sigismundi regis*, ch. 5: "Et dum haec vir Deo plenus in corde suo die noctuque incessanter pertractaret, non aliter nisi a domino nostro Iesu Christo, qui dixit: 'qui recipit prophetam in nomine prophetae, mercedem prophetae accipiet,' ita se ipsum circa martirum limina inpendere conatus est, ut mercedem martirum accipere mereretur." While Saint-Maurice d'Agaune was established in 515 and Sigistrix was murdered in the early 520s, *Fredegar* III.33 claims that it was constructed as penance for the murder, again much like the depiction found in Gregory of Tours, *Liber in gloria martyrum*, MGH SRM 1.2, ed. B. Krusch (Hanover: Hahnsche Buchhandlung, 1885), ch. 74.

Pro multis sceleribus: Ado of Vienne's Tales of Woe   157

When we next encounter the Merovingians, they are invading Thuringia. For this and the several sections that follow, Ado tracked the *LHF* closely, but only insofar as it served his emphasis on the bloodier aspects of the story. Theuderic, Childebert, and Chlothar move against Hermenfrid, who escapes, is lured by Theudebert into a trap, and killed alongside his young children.[146] Childebert declares war on Amalaric to avenge the injuries the Spanish king had visited on his wife, Childebert's sister. The Goths are defeated, Amalaric is killed trying to escape, and Childebert returns home with bountiful treasure, but without his sister, who died en route. Chlothar and Childebert then murder two of Chlodomer's sons, while the third, Chlodoald, becomes a cleric.[147] Next, Theuderic I dies and is succeeded by his son, Theudebert I, and Childebert and Chlothar return to Spain, placing a siege on Saragossa that is only lifted when its inhabitants surrender the tunic of Saint Vincent to Childebert.

Notably, Ado here skipped the *LHF*'s report about the pact Childebert made with his nephew Theudebert to attack Chlothar.[148] While this episode starts out with the kind of internecine violence that would have appealed to Ado, we learn that it was resolved by divine intervention brought about through Clothild's prayers at the tomb of St. Martin. Not only does this episode fail to deliver on its potential for violence, it attributes intercessory abilities to a member of the Merovingian family, and with Martin no less. As Ado found both narrative components disagreeable, the episode was omitted.

Instead, we are presented with an unbroken sequence of deaths. Theudebert subjugates the Lombards, then dies, followed shortly by his grandmother, Clothild, who is buried alongside her husband in the Church of St. Geneviève in Paris. Chramn then revolts against his father and is captured and killed with his wife and child. Next to die is St. Medard,

---

[146] For the obvious parallels between the Burgundian and Thuringian storylines, see Fox, "Revisiting Gregory of Tours' Burgundian Narrative."

[147] After his death, Chlodoald attained sainthood, meriting a hagiography, dated by Krusch to the ninth century, which expands on material found in the *Histories* and the *LHF* and attribute to him the foundation of the monastery of Nogent-le-Roy. There was apparently a cult by the seventh century, mentioned in *Fredegar* III.38: "Chlodoaldus ad clerecatum tundetur, dignamque vitam gerens; ad cuius sepulcrum Dominus virtutes dignatur ostendere." He is also mentioned in Ado's and in Usuard's *Martyrology*. See *Vita sancti Chlodovaldi*, MGH SRM 2, ed. B. Krusch (Hanover: Hahnsche Buchhandlung, 1888), pp. 349–357. Ado of Vienne, *Martyrology*, VII idus Septembris, p. 302: "Parisius, vico Novegente, natale sancti Clodoaldi, presbyteri et confessoris. Hic regali cum esset ortus prosapia, divino cultu se mancipavit atque terrenum despiciens, caeleste consecutus, multis usque hodie miraculis fulget"; Usuard, *Martyrology*, PL 124, VII idus Septembris: "Item in territorio Parisiacensi, sancti Chlodoaldi presbyteri, tam generis quam mentis nobilitate conspicui." See also Dailey, *Queens, Consorts, Concubines*, pp. 41–42.

[148] *LHF*, ch. 25.

buried *gloriose* by Chlothar, who soon follows the bishop to a grave in the same church. This, so far, is the *Chronicle*'s longest stretch of uninterrupted Frankish history, and it does not stray from its central themes.

In his subsequent depiction of Chlothar's sons and their deeds, Ado does not depart from his condensed narrative style, which continues to focus almost exclusively on warfare, betrayal, and death. The two most prominent figures in this section of the narrative are Fredegund and Brunhild, whose machinations are surveyed in much more depth than that afforded to any of the other characters. But even when other Merovingians are discussed, the picture that emerges is one of ruthless elimination of competitors, at home and abroad.

Once Chlothar's kingdom was partitioned, Sigibert went off to fight the Huns (i.e., the Avars), then his own brother Chilperic. Charibert died and Sigibert decided to take Brunhild, daughter of the Visigothic king Athanagild, as his wife. Chilperic soon followed suit, marrying Brunhild's sister, Galswinth. It is here that Fredegund's scheming is introduced as a leitmotif, first in relation to Galswinth, then to Chilperic's other wife and mother of his three children, Audovera. As previously noted, Fredegund captured much more of Ado's attention than did the kings of her day, even ones about whom Ado had relatively positive things to say, such as Sigibert and Guntram. St. Germanus of Paris attempted to pacify Sigibert and Chilperic, but Fredegund undermined his efforts by ordering Sigibert's assassination. Brunhild reciprocated with an objectionable move of her own, taking as her husband Chilperic's son, Merovech, who was then captured, tonsured, and relegated to a monastery.

Ado reported, incorrectly, that Chilperic and Fredegund's daughter Ri(n)child was taken as a wife by Liuvigild.[149] First, Chilperic and Fredegund's daughter was not named Richild, but Rigunth. Second, Rigunth was not intended for Liuvigild, but for his son, Reccared. Finally, the betrothal never came to fruition, since Rigunth's treasure was stolen by the aristocratic retinue that accompanied her to Spain and she was returned, humiliated, to her mother. Richild, as Ado certainly would have known, was the niece of Teutberga and the wife of Charles the Bald, whose marriage to the future emperor took place as the finishing touches were being put on the *Chronicle*.[150] Richild was the key to Boso's

---

[149] Ado of Vienne, *Chronicle*, col.110B: "Leubigildus rex filiam Chilperici et Fredegundis nomine Rinchildem, duxit uxorem."
[150] Another Richild, whose identity is all but unknown, appears alongside Radegund as the addressee of a letter from Caesaria II, abbatial successor to the sister of Bishop Caesarius of Arles. For her, see *Ep. 11*, MGH Epp. 3, ed. W. Gundlach (Berlin: Weidmann, 1892), pp. 450–451: "Dominabus sanctis Richildae et Radegundi Caesaria exigua."

promised abbacy at Saint-Maurice d'Agaune, held by his uncle Hubert under Lothar II, and to his appointment to the countship of Vienne, previously held by Gerald, who was ousted in late 870.[151] She was also Charles's ticket to a strategically crucial Lotharingia. All of these developments were of great consequence to Ado, but if replacing Rigunth with Richild was an intentional attempt on his part to convey some sub-textual message, it is unfortunately lost on us, since he provides no additional information. In fact, he does not mention Charles's second wife at all.[152]

Fredegund's affair with Landeric and the subsequent killing of her husband soon follow, as does the retelling of the ruse Fredegund devised in her war against the Austrasians—having her army carry sticks with bells on them, misleading the enemy into thinking they were hearing cattle bells. Significantly, this single act of deception received more coverage than the entirety of Guntram's career, which spanned thirty-one eventful years.[153] It is the last of several such ruses on which Ado reported, making Fredegund perhaps the best-covered figure since Clovis. Not far behind, in terms of the treatment she received, we find Fredegund's arch-nemesis, Brunhild.

The subsequent episode takes us directly from Fredegund's underhandedness to Brunhild's. The aged queen convinced her grandson Theuderic to declare war on his brother Theudebert. Theuderic proceeded to defeat Theudebert and entered Cologne, where his brother was hiding. He killed Theudebert, carried off his severed head, and then killed his children. All but one, that is. In a twisted turn of events, Theudebert's daughter caught the eye of her fratricidal uncle, who decided to make her his wife. Brunhild prohibited it, but lest we mistakenly think that she too was appalled by the idea, we soon learn from Ado that she was worried about the effect of such a union on her standing at court. In a phrase more befitting hagiography than the generally reserved tone of chronicle, Brunhild *spewed forth her*

---

[151] Nelson, *Charles the Bald*, pp. 221–228. For some context on Boso, see S. MacLean, "The Carolingian Response to the Revolt of Boso, 879–887," *Early Medieval Europe* 10, 1 (2001), pp. 21–48.

[152] On Ado's handling of Charles the Younger's injury and subsequent death, see E. J. Goldberg, "'A Man of Notable Good Looks Disfigured by a Cruel Wound': The Forest Misadventure of Charles the Young of Aquitaine (864) in History and Legend," in *Historiography and Identity III: Carolingian Approaches*, eds. R. Kramer, H. Reimitz, and G. Ward (Turnhout: Brepols, 2021), pp. 355–386. On Richild and her political entanglements, all of which postdate Ado's *Chronicle*, see S. MacLean, "Queenship, Nunneries and Royal Widowhood in Carolingian Europe," *Past & Present* 178 (2003), pp. 3–38. Also see G. Kornbluth, "Richildis and her Seal: Carolingian Self-Reference and the Imagery of Power," in *Saints, Sinners, and Sisters: Gender and Northern Art in Medieval and Early Modern Europe*, eds. J.L. Carroll and A.G. Stewart (London and New York: Routledge, 2016), pp. 161–181.

[153] In fairness, neither did his main source, the *LHF*. See *LHF*, ch. 35.

venom (venenum porrexit), convincing Theuderic to put the girl to death. Ado then reports that: *The Burgundians and the Austrasians made peace with the rest of the Franks and raised Chlothar as king on all three realms.*[154] This, we know, only took place in 613, after Brunhild was defeated and put to death, but not in Ado's *Chronicle*, which returned to discuss Brunhild's mistreatment of the bishop Desiderius of Vienne:

At that time Desiderius, whose family came from Autun, was serving in the order of the diaconate in the church of Vienne. Gregory shone in excellence as bishop and doctor of the Roman church. St. Desiderius then succeeded Bishop Verus. This most holy man made manifest Queen Brunhild's impieties, so she ordered her dukes to kill him in the territory of Lyon on the River Chalaronne, and the glorious martyr entered the heavenly kingdom.[155]

Here we should pause to recognize the debt Ado's hagiography owed to his historiographical work. Ado made extensive use of the *Chronicle* when he wrote the *Passio sancti Desiderii*, evident not only in the character-building of the protagonist, but also in his use of Merovingian dynastic history to chronologically place the career of the martyred bishop of Vienne. Take, for example, the introduction to the *Passio*:

Desiderius, the most brilliant bishop of the church of Vienne, was indeed, since he was a child, imbued with sanctity, pure of life, educated like none other in the knowledge of Scripture, and accomplished in the service of the bosom of holy mother Church. Having then advanced to the pontifical summit, he revealed the extent of his grace through the honor of martyrdom.[156]
This same man lived in the time of Chlothar, Clovis's son,[157] *and the sons of this same Chlothar, namely Charibert, who had his seat in Paris; Chilperic, who had his seat in Soissons; Guntram, who had his seat in Orléans; Sigibert, who had his seat in the city of Rheims, and who took as a wife Brunhild, the daughter of Athanagild the king of Spain, who was initially an Arian but was later joined to the sacrament of the Catholic faith and disjoined from it by shameful deeds. By her Sigibert begat Childebert. Chilperic first had her sister Galswinth, who later, thanks to the contrivance of Fredegund, was strangled. At that time the emperors of the Roman republic were Justinian the elder and then Justinian the younger, in whose day the body of St. Antony the monk, discovered through divine revelation, was buried in the Church of St. John the Baptist near*

---

[154] Ado of Vienne, *Chronicle*, col. 111A: "Burgundiones et Austrasii cum reliquis Francis pace facta Chlotharium in tribus totis regnis super se regem levaverunt."
[155] Ado of Vienne, *Chronicle*, col. 111D: "Hujus tempore Desiderius Augustodunensis genere, in ordine diaconi Ecclesiae Viennensi serviebat. Gregorius Romanae Ecclesiae praesul et doctor eximius claruit. Post Verum episcopum sanctus Desiderius succedit. Hic beatissimus Brunichildem reginam ex impietatibus suis arguens a comitibus eius ipsa iubente in territorio Lugdunensi super fluvium Calaronam perimitur, martyrque gloriosus caeleste regnum ingreditur."
[156] Ado is mimicking Sisebut here.
[157] The *majoris* here seems to refer to Clovis being the elder Clovis (i.e., Clovis I) and not to Chlothar being the eldest of Clovis's sons, which he was not.

Pro multis sceleribus: Ado of Vienne's Tales of Woe   161

Alexandria and the atrocious nation of the Vandals was expelled from Africa.[158] *He was succeeded by Justin, under whom the Lombard people invaded Italy. Then reigned Tiberius, and after him Maurice.*[159]

This opening was extraordinary for a hagiography, which is generally not known for its detailed historical expositions. Moreover, we do not need most of this information to understand subsequent events. It is also a very close rendition of the text found in the *Chronicle*, which probably served as the basis for the *Passio*.[160]

The story of the *Passio* is concerned primarily with the conflict between Desiderius of Vienne and Brunhild.[161] The remaining Merovingians, not to mention the Vandals, Lombards, Byzantines, and eastern saints featured in the composition, are entirely superfluous. More than a mere comment on Ado's methodology, however, such instances of borrowing indicate that for him, historical framing was necessary, even if the information it contained was not imperative. Indeed, this is not the only historical tangent incorporated into the *Passio*. We need only read on for one more paragraph to encounter another digression:

Then, after Sigibert was killed by Fredegund's partisans, Queen Brunhild, together with Theuderic, King Childebert's son, at that point still a child, obtained Burgundy.

---

[158] Ado is confusing the chronology here—Justinian was preceded by Justin I and succeeded by Justin II.

[159] Ado of Vienne, *Passio sancti Desiderii*, cols. 435C–437A: "Desiderius, Viennensis Ecclesiae clarissimus pontifex, fuit a puero quidem sanctissime imbutus, vita purus, scientia Scripturarum non parum eruditus, in gremio sanctae matris Ecclesia exercitate profecit. Inde ad culmen pontificale provectus, quantae gratiae fuerit, honor martyris patefecit.
    Fuit idem vir temporibus Chlotarii regis Chlodovei majoris filii, ac filiorum ipsiis Chlotarii, Hereberti, qui sedit Parisiis; Chilperici, qui sedit Suessionis; Gunthramni, qui sedit Aurelianis; Sigiberti, qui sedit Rhemensium urbe, qui accepit Brunnehildem Anagildi regis Hispanorum filiam, quae primum Ariana, postmodum sacramento fidei catholicis juncta, operibus flagiotissimis disjuncta; de qua Childebertum Sigibertus genuit. Hujus sororem Gansildam Chilpericus primum habuit, quae postmodum, dolo Fredegundis strangulata est. Imperatores autem tunc temporis in Republica Romana Justinianus fuit major. Post quem Justinianus minor. Cujus tempore corpus B. Antonii monachi, revelatione divina repertum, in Ecclesia B. Joannis Baptistae apud Alexandriam sepultum est; et ab Africa atrocissima gens Wandalorum expulsa. Cui imperatori Justinus succedit, sub quo gens Langobardorum Italiam invasit. Deinde imperavit Tiberius, post quem Mauricius."

[160] Ado of Vienne, *Chronicle*, col. 109B: "Quatuor fratres filii Chlotarii regnum inter se dividunt. Charibertus accepit regnum Childeberti, sedemque constituit Parisiis; Gunthchramnus regnum Chlodomiri, constituitque sedem Aurelianis; Chilpericus, regnum Chlotarii patris sui, Suessionisque civitate sedem sibi statuit; Sygibertus accepit regnum Theoderici, sedemque sibi constituit Rhemis. [...] Sygibertus rex Brunichildem Athanaildi regis filiam uxorem accepit, eamque sub Arianis baptizatam in nomine individuae Trinitatis rebaptizare praecepit. Ejus sororem Chilpericus rex ad patrem in Hispaniam mittens, Chilsuintam expetiit; et cum alias uxores haberet, ipsum superduxit; quam tamen postea consilio usus Fredegundis, per noctem in lecto suo strangulavit."

[161] Theuderic II plays a very minor role in Ado's composition, unlike Sisebut's *Vita Desiderii*.

Obviously an exceptionally libidinous woman, she was not afraid to incestuously involve herself with Merovech, Chilperic's son, her husband's nephew. And after he was tonsured and made a priest – for only by such means could the father barely restrain him – [162] *she grew hot with passion for various young men and exposed herself in her most filthy whorehouse to filthy young men.* [163]

Brunhild's licentious reputation has left numerous textual traces,[164] but the phrasing leaves little doubt that in this instance Ado was again relying on the *Vita Columbani*.[165] Nonetheless, the remark about Sigibert's death, Brunhild's move to Burgundy, and her marriage to Merovech were inspired by the historiographical sources at Ado's disposal. Sigibert was murdered in 575, and Brunhild's short-lived marriage to Merovech took place perhaps one year after that.[166] Her move to Burgundy occurred much later, occasioned by the hostility of Theudebert II's aristocrats once he reached majority, so probably around 599.[167] Ado shuffled these events around to better serve his narrative needs. Brunhild was probably 60 years old when Desiderius was martyred,[168] and by 613, her great-grandson Sigibert II was old enough to be present on the battlefield, which means that she might have been even older than that. The purpose of this intervention in the chronology was to demonstrate that Brunhild's sexual

---

[162] This is in reference to Merovech's escape attempts. See Gregory of Tours, *Histories*, v.14, 18.
[163] Ado of Vienne, *Passio sancti Desiderii*, col. 437B: "Igitur, interfecto Sigiberto rege factione Fredegundis reginae, Brunnehildis regina cum Theoderico admodum parvulo, Childeberti regis filio, Burgundiam obtinuit. Femina incomparabilis libidinis, quippe quae non timuerit incestuosissime Merovaeo Chilperici filio, mariti sui nepoti, se misceri. Illoque tonsurato presbyteroque facto, tali namque ordine pater vix eum potuit coercere, per diversorum juvenum libidines excanduit, turpissimum lupanar ipsa semetipsam turpissimis juvenibus exponens'." On Brunhild as a whore and heretic in Ado and Notker Balbulus, see M.-L. Weber, "Die Merovingerkönigin Brunichilde in den Quellen des lateinischen Mittelalters," in *Nova de veteribus: Mittel- und neulateinsiche Studien für Paul Gerhard Schmidt*, eds. A. Bihrer and E. Stein (Munich and Leipzig: K.G. Saur, 2004), pp. 45–70, at pp. 68–70.
[164] Though, tellingly, all posthumous. See, for instance, *Fredegar* IV.24. For an analysis of the Latin, see B. Combettes, "La subordination dans la Chronique de Frédégaire: les propositions non régies', in *Latin tardif, français ancien: Continuités et ruptures*, eds. A. Carlier and C. Guillot-Barbance (Berlin and Boston: De Gruyter, 2018), pp. 373–412, at p. 380. On Merovingian queens and accusations of a sexual nature, see Nelson, "Queens as Jezebels," pp. 31–77; E.J. Thomas, "The Second Jezebel: Representations of the Sixth-Century Queen Brunhild," doctoral dissertation (University of Glasgow, 2012).
[165] Jonas of Bobbio, *Vita Columbani*, I.19: "Cui Brunichildis ait: 'Regis sunt filii; tu eos tua benedictione robora.' At ille: 'Nequaquam,' inquid, 'istos regalia sceptra suscepturus scias, quia de lupanaribus emerserunt'."
[166] Gregory of Tours, *Histories*, v.2. [167] *Fredegar* IV.19.
[168] Her marriage to Sigibert took place after Charibert's death in 567, which would make her birth in 550 a reasonable assumption. Desiderius's martyrdom would have taken place in 607 at the earliest, but probably slightly later, which would make Brunhild close to 60 during the events depicted in the *Passio*.

appetites were not sated even at her advanced age, thus providing an even more damning evaluation of her character.

The incorporation of seemingly unnecessary historical detail could also have served to pad the *Passio sancti Desiderii*, which is much thinner in detail than both hagiographies on which it was based. Yet it is also indicative of Ado's perception of the interplay between historiography and hagiography, which in his works appears much closer than current genre divisions allow. In fact, even the space allotted to the hagiographical protagonist is meager. The bishop's efforts to correct the queen's ways earn him a stint at island exile. On the island, he ministers to the diseased inhabitants and performs various miracles.[169] After four years, he is recalled and reinstated to his see. Shortly thereafter, Desiderius is summoned to the royal palace by Brunhild, who asks his opinion about her marrying or, instead, carrying on with various young men. When the bishop opts for the former, the enraged Brunhild conspires against him, and he is declared a rebel. Here again, Ado makes use of angelic visions, granting Desiderius foreknowledge of his impending martyrdom.[170] He is captured by three of the queen's counts and led to the outskirts of Lyon, where he is publicly stoned and buried in a makeshift grave. From the earlier hagiographies of Desiderius and Columbanus we get a sense that the conflict was not about Brunhild's matrimonial prospects, but Theuderic's. In the *Vita Columbani*, the holy man was asked by Brunhild to bless Theuderic's children, hardly an inappropriate request after the generosity she had previously showed. Columbanus adamantly refused, throwing in an insult for good measure, which, after all, is where Ado's brothel comment originated. The king's marital status was indeed serious business, and both Desiderius and Columbanus disapproved of the court's conduct. But for Ado this was just a story about Brunhild's unbridled sexual appetites and their catastrophic consequences.

After eulogizing Desiderius, Ado describes the divine vengeance visited on Brunhild. Under the order of King Chlothar II, she is sentenced to be bound to wild horses by her arms and dragged to her death. The death sentence, while described in both *Fredegar* and the *LHF*, was likely

---

[169] On leprosy in Carolingian thought, see M. Rouche, "Miracles, maladies et psychologie de la foi à l'époque carolingienne en France," in *Hagiographie, cultures et sociétés IVe–XIIe siècles: Actes du Colloque organisé à Nanterre et à Paris (2–5 mai 1979)* (Paris: Études Augustiniennes, 1981), pp. 139–160; A.K. Bosworth, "Criminals, Cures, and Castigation: Heiric of Auxerre's *Miracula Sancti Germani* and Ninth-Century Carolingian Hagiography," Doctoral dissertation (Purdue University, 2008), pp. 25, 144–145.

[170] Following the anonymous Vienne *Passio Desiderii*, ch. 7: "Tunc vir sanctus et nimia humilitate colenda animo in Domino intrepidus accedit excipere quod sibi angelo evangelizante olim cognoverat esse promissum."

inspired by either Sisebut's *Vita Desiderii* or the anonymous Vienne *Passio*. Both *Lives* would have been available to Ado when he wrote, and, unlike the *Chronicle*, make explicit the connection between her death and the persecution of Desiderius. The phrasing of the queen's punishment in Ado's *Passio* was taken verbatim from the *Chronicle*, although the overt connection with Brunhild's persecution of the bishop was unique to the *Passio*. In the *Chronicle*, Ado made do with the following: "On account of her many wicked deeds, Queen Brunhild was judged by the Franks in the presence of King Chlothar, was tied by her arms and legs to unbroken horses, her body stretched and torn apart, and her bones burned in a fire."[171]

The next chapter of Ado's *Passio* is devoted to the competition for Desiderius's remains, which were claimed by both Lyon and Vienne. Tensions between the parties escalated, each claiming their right to the body of the deceased bishop, with the Viennois arguing that he was their priest and the Lyonnais that he was martyred in their diocese. The citizens of Vienne, who had the stronger case, hatched a scheme to obtain the body. They secretively dug up the grave and loaded the body onto a fishing vessel docked on the Saône and then returned by foot to Lyon bearing an empty bier. While the Lyonnais mistook this for victory, assuming that the body was now theirs, the ship was already making its way down the Rhône to Vienne.

Gregory of Tours tells an almost identical story about the relics of St. Martin, only there it was the people of Poitiers and Tours who fought for ownership of the saint's remains.[172] Both parties made claims similar to those provided in the *Passio*. In the end the body was again achieved through theft and carried off by a boat, which made its way to Tours on two rivers, the Vienne and the Loire. As we have seen in the *Chronicle*, Ado was interested in Martin of Tours and his miracles. It is therefore quite possible that Gregory's *Histories* served as the inspiration for the story in the *Passio*.

---

[171] Ado of Vienne, *Chronicle*, col. 112A: "Brunichildis regina pro multis sceleribus suis in praesentia Chlotharii regis judicantibus Francis, indomitis equis, religata brachiis et cruribus divaricatis, membratim discinditur, ac igni ossa illius cremata." The notion of the Franks' (i.e., the Neustrian elites') counsel, so central to the *LHF*'s worldview, was conserved by Ado. Compare Ado of Vienne, *Passio Desiderii*, col. 439C: "Quae autem ultio in praesenti impiam illam perculerit, ut ne impune quis credat se peccare, breviter attingam: Chlothario rege iudicantibus Francis, indomitis equis religata brachiis, et cruribus divaricates, membratim discinditur, Deo illi pro voluptatibus suis dignam poenam retribuente."

[172] Gregory of Tours, *Histories*, 1.48. Krusch makes the same observation in the *Vita Theudarii*, p. 646, n.1.

The *Passio Desiderii* relies on a whole body of hagiographical work, from previous *vitae* and *passiones* dedicated to Desiderius to the *Vita Columbani*. The same may be said of Ado's other hagiography, the *Vita Theudarii*, in which we again find echoes of the *Vita Columbani* and, perhaps more distantly, of the *Vita Arnulfi* or the *Vita Iohannis Reomaensis*. But more importantly, the *Passio Desiderii* relied on historiographical material gleaned not only from the *Chronicle* but, possibly, from Gregory of Tours's *Histories*. Gregory's impact on the *Chronicle* is less direct, although the repeated mentions of Martin of Tours suggest it as a source. Ado's works thus built on a corpus that provided a distinctly multifaceted picture of the Merovingians, which was not preserved in the *Passio Desiderii*. This work contains only royal villains or hurried, casual mentions, but no positive portrayals.

Brunhild, the main villain of the *Passio*, was moved by two hungers: lust and power. Ado followed the anonymous Vienne *Passio*'s lead in making her solely responsible for Desiderius's persecution. Her grandson Theuderic II, who in Sisebut's *Vita Desiderii* and Jonas of Bobbio's *Vita Columbani* took equal share in the blame, was left out entirely. The only other member of the Merovingian family whom Ado endowed with a modicum of agency was Fredegund, whose evil deeds were briefly alluded to in the introduction. Although Chlothar II made two appearances in the *Passio*, his treatment was entirely superficial. As the judge presiding over Brunhild's execution, he was simply referred to as *Chlotharius rex*, and when he decided to organize Desiderius's translation, he received the epithet *pius*.[173] This stands in clear opposition to his role in the *Vita Columbani*.

Given the seemingly derivative nature of the *Passio*, its value for our discussion requires some explanation. Firstly, it is through the *Passio* that we learn of Gregory's possible influence on Ado. But even more importantly, examining the hagiography for traces of historiographical methodology and framing highlights the permeability of generic boundaries, especially when we are dealing with a single author. The *Passio* demonstrates that Ado considered the background work he undertook for the *Chronicle* as an essential component in the framing of his hagiographical hero, a fact that again highlights the limits of genre taxonomy for understanding narrative development.

Let us then return to the *Chronicle*. Of the historiographical Chlothar we learn only that he devastated Saxon land, leaving no man alive. Shortly thereafter he died, and his rule went to his son, Dagobert,

---

[173] Compared with the anonymous *Passio*'s *rectus iudex et iustus princeps*. See *Passio Desiderii*, ch. 12, p. 260.

described by Ado, perhaps surprisingly, thus: "Dagobert his son, a vigorous man and severe in judgement, succeeded him. He had two sons, Sigibert and Clovis, of which one, Sigibert, he sent to Austrasia with Duke Pippin; Clovis the younger he kept at his side. The mayor of the palace, Gundolandus, died, and in his place Dagobert appointed Erchinoald."[174] This, however, is not all. After a discussion about events that took place forty years later—Queen Æthelthrith's virginity and the incorrupt nature of her remains—Ado suddenly returns to Dagobert, in the rarest of positive appraisals for a Merovingian king: "King Dagobert enriched the churches of the saints and with many gifts ruled the kingdom of the Franks peacefully and quietly."[175]

This unprecedented praise is also the last we hear of the Merovingians for quite a while. The *Chronicle* goes on to discuss the Byzantine–Persian war and other events from Africa, Asia Minor, even Britain. When we again hear of the Franks, it is with the death of Dagobert, which was cause for great grief.[176] As the unexpected praise of Dagobert shows, Ado was aware that with his death, a new period had begun. He expresses this explicitly in his assessment of Clovis II's catastrophic reign: "From this time as the Franks held power, their rule began to crumble, after various grievous troubles."[177]

* * *

The Merovingian family plays only a peripheral role in Ado of Vienne's historiographical and hagiographical corpus. The scope of the *Chronicle* is expansive, taking up human history from its very beginnings to Ado's own time, while the *Passio sancti Desiderii* is more focused on the saint and his posthumous cult. But neither of the works imparts even a tempered favorable impression of the Merovingians. Working on the *Passio*, Ado had access to sources from which he could have, had he wished, crafted a nuanced portrait of the Merovingian kings and queens of Desiderius's day. But he chose not to. Even when using the Merovingians for historical context in the

---

[174] Ado of Vienne, *Chronicle*, col. 113A: " ... successitque ei [i.e., Chlothario] Dagobertus filius eius vir strenuus et in iudiciis severus. Habuit autem duos filios, Sygibertum et Chlodoveum quorum unum, Sygibertum, in Austriam cum Pipino duce direxit; Chlodoveum iuniorem secum retinuit. Gundolandus maior domus moritur, cuius loco Herthenoldus a Dagoberto constituitur." Gundoland was taken from *LHF*, ch. 40 and also appears in *Fredegar* IV.45. He seems to have been the Neustrian mayor during Chlothar's final years. Erchinoald actually replaced Aega as the Neustrian mayor.
[175] Ado of Vienne, *Chronicle*, col. 115C: "Dagobertus rex ecclesias sanctorum ditavit, eisque multa largitus pacifice et quiete regnum tenuit Francorum."
[176] Ibid., col. 115D: "luxeruntque eum Franci diebus multis." Again, echoing the *LHF*.
[177] Ibid., col. 116A: "Ab eo tempore sicut Franci tenuerunt, regnum ipsum cadere coepit, variis casibus molestatum."

introduction to the *Passio sancti Desiderii*, Ado cannot resist including comments about Fredegund's complicity in the murders of Galswinth and Sigibert.

Likewise, the *Chronicle* used its historiographical sources, which in the case of the Merovingian material consisted primarily of the *LHF*, to accentuate the Merovingians' cruelty and to downplay their accomplishments. The *LHF* was composed during a time in which the weaknesses of Merovingian rule were becoming apparent, but it was not a fatalistic composition. To be sure, the author argued for the necessity of closer cooperation between the Neustrian elite and the Merovingians, but he did not see the royal family as a lost cause. For the Merovingian section of his plot, Ado's reliance on the *LHF* was near absolute, yet his Merovingians were mere shadows of their *LHF* selves.

Merovingian kings and queens who left a positive imprint on posterity received scant attention in the *Chronicle*. When reporting on their deaths, Ado depicted Clothild as *plena bonis operibus* and Guntram as *bonae satis memoriae*, but these were the only positive portrayals in more than a century and a half of history.[178] Episodes that highlighted Merovingian piety, such as the visions of Clovis or the intercession of Clothild, were entirely omitted. The only outlier, as noted, was Dagobert, the exception that proves the rule. On the other hand, accounts of bloody battles, betrayals, assassinations, infanticide, and outright cruelty abound. Nowhere is this clearer than in the case of Fredegund and Brunhild, whom Ado excoriates. As for the *Vita Theudarii*, it does not contain any mention of the Merovingians, even though it takes place in the second half of the sixth century. One could be forgiven for wondering whether this was due to Ado's inability to somehow work Merovingian wickedness into the plot.

Ado is not the first member of the Carolingian elite to expound a version of history that disparages the previous dynasty. Previous chroniclers usually leveraged the inefficacy of late Merovingian rule to justify Carolingian ascent. Ado's treatment, by contrast, provides a pessimistic appraisal of the dynasty's complete tenure, not only its so-called *rois fainéants*. Ado distilled Merovingian history down to an ideologically charged barebones account, showing the kings and queens of this period at their worst. Since the *LHF*'s usefulness ran out for events that took place after 727, Ado was forced to make use of alternative sources in his portrayal of the Carolingians' rise. These sources, it seems, were received altogether differently than the Merovingian material. The air of pessimism so prevalent in his depictions of the Merovingians was abandoned when Ado reached Charles Martel, who appeared in the *Chronicle* as the hero of the Battle of Poitiers. As part

[178] Both phrases were lifted from the *LHF*, chs. 18 (Clothild), 35 (Guntram).

of his overarching approach to the Merovingian centuries, Ado adopted the narrative framework that saw the period 511–639 as essentially defined by its *bella civilia*. Dagobert's death sealed this chapter of Merovingian history, ushering in a time of final decline.

3.3 Conclusions

Frechulf and Ado both wrote the Franks into a composite vision of world history informed primarily by ecclesiastical models of periodization. It is thus not surprising to find Frankish history as a secondary strand of a much larger historiographical project. Still, the history of the Franks needed to be harmonized with this larger project, and to a degree also with the ideology of its patrons, the Carolingians. To delineate the contours of the world they inhabited, both Frechulf and Ado were forced to contend with the earlier stages of the Frankish past, but they took very different approaches to this task.

Frechulf explained that he chose to end his *Histories* with the establishment of Franks and Lombards on territories previously occupied by the Romans and the Goths. At the very least, this suggests that he considered these political realities as central to the order that emerged with the conclusion of his opus. Whether this order can be mapped onto the boundaries of Carolingian hegemony is uncertain. Regardless of our interpretation of Frechulf's choice, his reluctance to incorporate more episodes of Frankish history into his account may attest to the unease with which he handled his source material. Frechulf would have had little difficulty accessing compositions that contained all of the information he needed. For his sporadic mentions of Gaul, he clearly did just that, especially with the help of the *Chronicle of Marius of Avenches* and *Fredegar*. The details that Frechulf selected for inclusion do not seem to cohere into a well-formulated claim about the Merovingians. If anything, his selections appear quite arbitrary. Taken together with the many loud silences, the overall performance of Merovingian kings in the *Histories* is underwhelming. Their significant ties to the Church, such as the baptism of Clovis, subsequent monarchs' generous patronage of ecclesiastical institutions, and the ubiquity of bishops in royal service are left entirely out of the picture. In the end, Merovingian history was probably uninteresting to Frechulf because it happened after the West was lost, and the Roman judges from whose histories the reader was meant to draw inspiration were but a memory.

Ado's response was penned more than a generation later, under very different circumstances. Unsurprisingly, it also differed in its approach to that past. Unlike Frechulf, Ado did not obscure pre-Carolingian history.

Conclusions 169

Clovis and his descendants were covered, however briefly. Their unflattering image in Ado's *Chronicle* was not something he inherited from the *LHF*, his only source on the topic, apart from the possible indirect influence of Gregory's *Histories*. Ado was unimpressed by the Merovingian past and reworked his source material to reflect this. His decision to portray the Merovingians as especially violent and divisive surely served to accentuate the accomplishments of their early Carolingian successors, which Ado covers glowingly. While the Merovingians are often preoccupied with internal squabbles, Charles Martel and his descendants work to conquer and subdue foreign foes. Ado's language is entirely legitimist, referring to the opposition to Carolingian power as rebellion and perfidy and rehearsing fully the Carolingian version of Pippin's ascent through Frankish election and papal sanction.[179] Like Frechulf, Ado was not writing a history of the Franks, yet in his treatment he is much more willing to engage with the pre-Carolingian chapters of the history he was writing. The result is highly charged, ideologically, and not in the Merovingians' favor. Yet even here, Ado can recognize the positive contribution of some royal figures, such as Clothild and Guntram. He is also open about the flourishing of religious institutions during the period in question, although, as the story of Desiderius and Brunhild demonstrates, the Church sometimes flourished despite the Merovingians' best efforts. This overall image of violence and wanton cruelty is contrasted with the reign of Dagobert, whose magnanimity toward the Church garnered rare praise from Ado.

It is to Dagobert that we now turn.

[179] See Ado's references to Aistulf and Waifar of Aquitaine, *Chronicle*, col. 123.

4 *Omni ecclesiastica dignitate nobilitavit*: "Good King Dagobert"

Of all the Merovingian kings who came after Clovis, none has been held in higher regard than Dagobert I.[1] For a very long time, he was considered to have been the last effective Merovingian, followed by increasingly less capable kings until the inevitable demise of the dynasty. We find this view expressed in chronicles and other works, as well as in much of the scholarship on the Frankish kingship, up until the mid-twentieth century. While this depiction no longer holds, Dagobert was without doubt a successful king. His reign was not especially long, but for the last eight years of it he ruled alone, positioning himself as the most formidable sovereign in western Europe.

According to the sources, Dagobert had expansive international interests. Frankish influence under him was felt in Bavaria, the Slavic lands, Visigothic Spain, Lombard Italy, the Avar kingdom, Thuringia, Saxony, the Basque country, the British Isles, and Brittany. Moreover, he maintained an active line of communication with the Byzantine emperor on matters of regional importance. Rich endowments to religious institutions, particularly to Saint-Denis, and involvement in monastic foundation, "church reform," and possibly even proselytization efforts won him the praise of secular and ecclesiastical writers alike.[2] He therefore stands as a singularly impressive figure among his arguably mediocre predecessors and successors.

---

[1] Regino of Prüm, *Chronicon*, MGH SRG 50, ed. F. Kurze (Hanover: Hahnsche Buchhandlung, 1890) [hereafter, Regino, *Chronicle*], at p. 33, a.612–631: "Qui quamvis omnia loca sancta excoluisset, tamen prae caeteris monasteria sanctorum Dionysii, Martini, atque Mauritii excoluit, et omni ecclesiastica dignitate nobilitavit."

[2] For Dagobert's involvement in possible attempts at (forcible) conversion, see *Vita Amandi episcopi I*, MGH SRM 5, ed. B. Krusch (Hanover: Hahnsche Buchhandlung, 1910), pp. 428–449, chs. 15, 16, and 20, pp. 439–440 and 443–444, respectively. See also Y. Fox, "*Ego bar-iona:* Jews and the Language of Forced Conversion in Columbanian Circles," in *Barbarian and Jews: Jews and Judaism in the Early Medieval West*, eds. Y. Hen and T.F.X. Noble (Turnhout: Brepols, 2019), pp. 155–181. For Dagobert as lawgiver, see the *Lex Baiwariorum*, MGH LL Nat. Germ., ed. E. von Schwind (Hanover: Hahnsche Buchhandlung, 1926), praef., pp. 202–203: "Haec omnia Dagobertus rex gloriosissimus per viros inlustros Claudio, Chadoindo, Magno et Agilulfo renovavit et omnia vetera legum in melius transtulit et unicuique genti scriptam tradidit, quae usque hodie perseverant." This tradition is unsurprisingly reminiscent of the preface to the *Lex Salica*. On this passage and its applications beyond

As a literary construct, however, Dagobert requires reconsideration. His appearance in the *LHF*, though brief, captures his image as a fair judge, a fearsome warrior, and a magnanimous patron of the Church:

And this Dagobert was a most powerful king, a nourisher of the Franks, very severe in judgement, a patron of the churches. He was first to order that treasure from the palace fisc be generously distributed to the churches of the saints. He established peace in all of his kingdom. His fame resounded with many peoples. He struck fear and terror in all of the surrounding kingdoms. He was a peacemaker, like Solomon, and kept tranquil the kingdom of the Franks.[3]

The narrativization of Dagobert, which began with chronicles and hagiographies, soon expanded to other genres, where the character of the king received various inflections. His relationship with Saint-Denis gave rise to a rich literary and artistic tradition that sought, rather successfully, to fuse his memory with the cult of the monastery's patron saint.[4] Additionally, Dagobert captured the popular imagination. He was famously memorialized in an eighteenth-century French children's song, whose catchy opening phrase—*Le bon roi Dagobert*—provided the title for two cinematic treatments in the late twentieth century.[5]

It is in hagiography, however, that we find Dagobert's deepest footprint. He makes appearances in such compositions as the *Lives* of Columbanus, Wandregisel of Fontenelle, Arnulf of Metz, Desiderius of Cahors, Eligius

---

the narrow confines of the *Lex Baiwariorum*, see Esders and Reimitz, "Legalizing Ethnicity," pp. 307–309.

[3] *LHF*, ch. 42: "Fuitque ipse Dagobertus rex fortissimus, enutritor Francorum, severissimus in iudiciis, ecclesiarum largitor. Ipse enim elimosinarum copia de fisco palacii per ecclesias sanctorum primus distribuere censum iussit. Pacem in cuncto regno suo statuit. In multis gentibus rumor eius personuit. Timorem et metum in universis regnis per circuitum incussit. Ipse pacificus, velut Salomon, quietus regnum obtenuit Francorum." This is a slightly altered version of B.S. Bachrach, trans., *Liber historiae Francorum* (Lawrence, KA: Coronado Press, 1973), p. 100.

[4] For the memorialization of Dagobert in Saint-Denis, see Y. Hen, "'Flirtant' avec la liturgie: Rois et liturgie en Gaule franque," *Cahiers de civilisation médiévale* 50 (2007), pp. 33–42.

[5] These were the 1963 film directed by Pierre Chevalier and the 1984 French-Italian production directed by Dino Risi, both comedies. The two films were preceded by adaptations for television. On the crystallization of Dagobert in French memory, see L. Theis, *Dagobert: Un roi pour un peuple* (Paris: Fayard, 1982); For thirteenth- and fourteenth-century developments of the character of Dagobert, see R. Bossuat, "Le roi Dagobert, héros de romans du Moyen Age," *Comptes rendus des séances de l'Académie des Inscriptions et Belles-Lettres*, 108, 2 (1964), pp. 361–368. For monastic foundation legends incorporating the memory of Dagobert, see G. Bischoff, "Le bon roi Dagobert entre Vosges et Rhin: une mémoire militante," in *Le pouvoir au Moyen Âge: Idéologies, pratiques, représentations*, eds. C. Carozzi, H. Taviani-Carozzi (Aix-en-Provence: Presses de L'Université de Provence, 2005), pp. 51–67.

of Noyon, Gertrude of Nivelles, and Audoin of Rouen, to name but a few.[6] In most of these works, Dagobert is painted in a distinctly flattering light, unlike in *Fredegar*, where he receives a fair share of critique.[7] Still, the *Fredegar* chronicler always stopped short of questioning Dagobert's (and his successors') rightful hold on power.[8] Dagobert's character in the historiographical tradition was based on his representation in *Fredegar*, although for most of the later chronicles, this information was mediated through a composition written in the Carolingian period and known as the *Gesta Dagoberti I regis Francorum*, whose image of the king was entirely positive.[9] Consequently, in these later works not much of *Fredegar*'s ambivalence survived.

The *Gesta Dagoberti*, of unknown authorship, drew on the Dagobert narrative in *Fredegar* and the *LHF* to construct an alternative, more personalized and syntactic, dramatic character. Additionally, the *Gesta Dagoberti* made explicit use of hagiographical sources, some of which were mentioned in the previous paragraph. Others, such as the *Life of Geneviève*, the *Life of Gall*, and the *Life of Eligius of Noyon*, were alluded to indirectly.[10] The Dagobert of the *Gesta Dagoberti* was placed in scenes that roughly corresponded to those found in the *Fredegar* storyline, but they were delivered within a wider story about idealized Christian kingship, as understood by a highly literate ninth-century ecclesiastical elite. Dagobert is transformed into a triumphant, beneficent king whose most pressing concern is to endow the Church with his riches. Some scholars have suggested that the composition was an effort by the monks of

---

[6] *Vita Columbani* I.26, pp. 209–210; *Vita Wandregiseli abbatis Fontanellensis*, MGH SRM 5, ed. B. Krusch (Hanover: Hahnsche Buchhandlung, 1910), pp. 1–24, at ch. 7, p. 16; *Vita Desiderii Cadurcae urbis episcopi*, MGH SRM 4, ed. B. Krusch (Hanover: Hahnsche Buchhandlung, 1902), pp. 547–602, at ch. 13, p. 571; *Vita Eligii episcopi Noviomagensis*, MGH SRM 4, ed. B. Krusch (Hanover: Hahnsche Buchhandlung, 1902), pp. 663–741, at II.1, p. 694; *Vita Arnulfi*, chs. 11–12, pp. 436–437; *Vita sanctae Geretrudis*, MGH SRM 2, ed. B. Krusch (Hanover: Hahnsche Buchhandlung, 1888), pp. 447–464, at ch. 1, p. 454; *Vita Audoini episcopi Rotomagensis*, MGH SRM 5, ed. W. Levison (Hanover: Hahnsche Buchhandlung, 1910), pp. 536–567, at ch. 2, p. 555. This list is far from complete.

[7] For a notable exception in the *Vita Arnulfi*, see pp. 213–214.

[8] J.M. Wallace-Hadrill, "Fredegar and the History of France," *Bulletin of the John Rylands Library* 40, 2 (1958), pp. 527–550, at p. 541.

[9] *Gesta Dagoberti I regis Francorum*, MGH SRM 2, ed. B. Krusch (Hanover: Hahnsche Buchhandlung, 1888), pp. 396–425. For additional comments, see *Gesta Dagoberti I regis Francorum*, MGH SRM 7, Appendix: Tomus II, ed. B. Krusch (Hanover: Hahnsche Buchhandlung, 1920), pp. 778–782; S. Olivier, "La mémoire mérovingienne à travers ses réécritures. Dagobert et Saint-Denis: élaboration, circulation et instrumentalisation d'une association (IXe–XVIe siècle)," doctoral dissertation (University of Geneva, 2022), pp. 129–138.

[10] J.M. Wallace-Hadrill, *The Long-Haired Kings and Other Studies in Frankish History* (London: Methuen, 1962), p. 97.

Saint-Denis to petition Louis the Pious to relieve the community of episcopal supervision. It has even been proposed that the composition was commissioned by the same Carolingian emperor.[11]
Several scholars have attempted to dispel the anonymity of the *Gesta Dagoberti*'s author. Léon Levillain argued forcefully for Hincmar as the author of the composition. This identification was accepted by Wallace-Hadrill, partly because the two oldest extant manuscripts originated from Rheims and Saint-Bertin, both centers associated with Hincmar, but also because of the stylistic similarities between the *Gesta Dagoberti* and the *Vita Remigii*, whose Hincmarian authorship is certain.[12] As pointed out by Jean Devisse, however, those stylistic similarities are hardly as compelling as Levillain made them out to be. Devisse adopts the compromise offered by Max Buchner, namely, that the *Gesta Dagoberti* might have been composed by Hincmar while he was still a monk in Saint-Denis, but under the supervision of his then abbot, Hilduin.[13] Michael Lapidge does not object to the identification of Hincmar or Hilduin as authors, although he does cast doubt on the link proposed by Levillain between the *Gesta Dagoberti* and another composition, the *Inventio et translatio S. Dionysii tempore Dagoberti*, which Levillain believed was meant to preface a third composition, the *Miracula S. Dionysii*.[14] The *Miracula* was composed at Saint-Denis around 835 or 836, and Levillain argued that the *Inventio*, which he also attributed to Hincmar, served as a model for the *Gesta Dagoberti*, which was composed later.[15] Lapidge conceded that the *Gesta Dagoberti* and the *Inventio* displayed mutual influence, but cautioned that the direction of the relationship was poorly understood, leaving the identity of the author unresolved. John Contreni seemed to have preferred Hilduin

---

[11] L. Levillain, "Études sur l' abbaye de Saint-Denis à l' époque mérovingienne," *Bibliothèque de l'École des chartes* I: 82 (1921), pp. 5–116; II: 86 (1925), pp. 5–99; III: 87 (1926), pp. 20–97, 245–346; IV: 91 (1930), pp. 5–65, 264–300, at 82 (1921), p. 22. For a reference to the composition by Louis, see *Epistolae variorum*, MGH Epp. 5, ed. E. Dümmler (Berlin: Weidmann, 1899), ep. 19, p. 326: "Ut videlicet unus ex priscis Francorum regibus Dagoberthus, qui eundem pretiosissimum Christi martirem veneratus non mediocriter fuerat, et vita inmortali est sublimatus, et per eius adiutorium, sicut divina ac celebris ostensio perhibet, a poenis est liberatus inque vita perenni desiderabiliter constitutus." On Louis, Hilduin, and St. Denis, see C. Booker, "The Dionysian Mirror of Louis the Pious," *Quaestiones Medii Aevii Novae* 19 (2014), pp. 241–264; A.L. Taylor, "Poetry, Patronage, and Politics: Epic Saints' Lives in Western Francia, 800–1000," doctoral dissertation (University of Texas at Austin, 2006), pp. 38–122.
[12] A point that Levillain makes in "Études," p. 92. See Wallace-Hadrill, *The Long-Haired Kings*, pp. 97–105. On the *Vita Remigii*, see Isaïa, "The Bishop and the Law," pp. 170–189.
[13] M. Buchner, "Zur Entstehung und zur Tendenz der Gesta Dagoberti," *Historisches Jahrbuch* 47 (1927), pp. 252–274; J. Devisse, *Hincmar, archevêque de Reims, 845–882*, 3 vols. (Geneva: Librarie Droz, 1975–1976), II, p. 1092, n.174.
[14] M. Lapidge, *Hilduin of Saint-Denis: The Passio S. Dionysii in Prose and Verse* (Leiden and Boston: Brill, 2017), pp. 105–106 and 456, n.22.
[15] Levillain, "Études sur l' abbaye de Saint-Denis," I, pp. 111–116.

174 *Omni ecclesiastica dignitate nobilitavit*

as a single author.[16] No consensus has thus been reached on this question, although a new doctoral dissertation by Sarah Olivier has done much to dispel uncertainty about the *Gesta Dagoberti* and its relationship with other Dionysian literature, as well as to chart the composition's effect on later medieval works.[17] From what we know so far, it is clear that the *Gesta Dagoberti* was composed at Saint-Denis, probably in 835 or shortly thereafter. It is likely that Hilduin, Hincmar, or both, were involved in its production, although not in any verifiable way. While this is hardly an ideal starting position, it does provide several clues with which to contextualize the composition, as I hope to do in what follows. In the early tenth century, Regino of Prüm used the *Gesta Dagoberti* as the sole source for narrating the life of King Dagobert in his *Chronicle*. The character Regino extracted from the *Gesta Dagoberti* was remolded to serve a different set of authorial aims, although it did so, as we shall see, by building on narrative models already present in the source.

This chapter is divided into two parts. The first will follow the story as it was related in *Fredegar* and the changes it underwent when it was revised for use in the *Gesta Dagoberti*, itself not a work of historiography so much as a biography with hagiographical and visionary overtones.[18] The second part will turn to the adaptation and incorporation of the hagiographically inflected Dagobert narrative back into historiography in the tenth-century *Chronicle* of Regino of Prüm.

4.1   *Fredegar* and the *Gesta Dagoberti*

The historical Dagobert owed his success to the exceptional conditions of his childhood. The events of the early 610s resulted in the elimination of the successors of Childebert II, who several years earlier enjoyed overwhelming superiority over their beleaguered cousin. Chlothar II's takeover in 613 created a unique set of circumstances in the *regna Francorum*, which meant that Dagobert was spared the kind of dynastic struggles with which all previous generations were forced to contend. His earlier years were touched upon briefly by the *LHF*, and not at all by *Fredegar*. The

---

[16] J.J. Contreni, "The Carolingian Renaissance: Education and Literary Culture," in *The New Cambridge Medieval History, Volume II: c.700–c.900*, ed. R. McKitterick (Cambridge: Cambridge University Press, 1995), pp. 709–757, at p. 751.
[17] Olivier, "La mémoire mérovingienne." For a discussion of the *Inventio vis-à-vis* the *Gesta Dagoberti*, see pp. 41–86, 96–103. For date and authorship, pp. 125–128. Olivier takes a traditional view on these questions.
[18] H. Stegeman, "The Growth of an Austrasian Identity: Processes of Identification and Legend Construction in the Northeast of the *Regnum Francorum*, 600–800," doctoral dissertation (University of Groningen, 2014), p. 40.

LHF contains the story of Dagobert's fight against the Saxons, and his deliverance from defeat after a lock of his hair was presented to Chlothar, who came rushing to his aid.[19] The story was covered entirely in the introduction to the *Gesta Dagoberti*.[20] Both the *LHF* and the *Gesta Dagoberti* speak of Chlothar killing every Saxon who was taller than his sword, a unique detail not found in *Fredegar*.[21]

The *Gesta Dagoberti* devoted its first few chapters to a story that took place when Dagobert was still a young man, before the earliest events covered by *Fredegar*:

He (i.e., Chlothar) had a son named Dagobert, whom he fathered by Queen Bertrude, who (i.e., Dagobert) deservedly succeeded his father with zeal and strength. Then, when he was in his childhood years, he was given by his father to the venerable and most saintly Arnulf, bishop of the city of Metz, to raise him according to his own wisdom, and to show him the path of the Christian religion, and to be his defender and his support. When he (i.e., Dagobert) was young, as was the custom of the Frankish people, he led a hunting expedition, and on a certain day decided to follow a deer. Quickly discovered, and with the swiftness that this animal is said to possess, it tried to escape the zeal of the dogs, barking and in hot pursuit, to the woods and mountains, crossing streams as it ran. Finally defeated, it brought itself to a village named Catulliacus.[22] This place was around five miles from the city of Lutetia, also called Paris. In that city, the kings of the Franks had the custom of holding their scepter.[23]

---

[19] *LHF*, ch. 41.   [20] *Gesta Dagoberti*, ch. 14.

[21] *LHF*, ch. 41: "Rex vero, tota terra Saxonorum vastata, populo illo interfecto, non ibi maiorem hominem viventem reliquit, nisi ut gladius suus, quod spata vocant, per longum habebat." *Gesta Dagoberti*, ch. 1: "Qui elaborata a maioribus dignitate potitus, cum et plurima strenue gesserit, tum praecipue illud memorabile suae potentiae posteris reliquit indicium, quod rebellantibus adversum se Saxonibus, ita eos armis perdomuit, ut omnes virilis sexus eiusdem terrae incolas, qui gladii, quod tum forte gerebat, longitudinem excessissent, peremerit, quippe ut iunioribus tumoris ausum recordatio illius vitalis seu mortiferi gladii amputaret." For the biblical dimensions of this episode, see Reimitz, "Genre and Identity in Merovingian Historiography," pp. 192–193. This is mediated by the A version of the *Inventio*. See Olivier, "La mémoire mérovingienne," pp. 50–51.

[22] The noblewoman Catulla, after whom the villa was named, is first identified in the Dionysian hagiography known as the *Post beatam et gloriosam*. On this and the transmission to the *Inventio* and the *Gesta Dagoberti*, see Olivier, "La mémoire mérovingienne," pp. 51–54.

[23] *Gesta Dagoberti*, ch. 2: "Huic fuit filius nomine Dagobertus, quem ex Bertedrude regina susceperat, qui patri succederet et industria dignus et viribus. Hic denique in annis puerilibus positus, traditus est a genitore venerabili ac sanctissimo Arnulfo Mettensium urbis episcopo, et eum secundum suam sapientiam enutriret, eique tramitem christianae religionis ostenderet atque eius custos et baiulus esset. Cum autem adolescentiae aetatem, ut genti Francorum moris est, venationibus exerceret, agere cervum quadam die instituit. Qui facile repertus, oblatrantibus atque certatim insequentibus canum agminibus, ea pernicitate qua illud animal fertur silvas montesque et, si qua occurrere, flumina transcurrens, canum industriam effugere conabatur. Tandem ergo victus ad vicum qui Catulliacus dicitur se contulit. Hic ab urbe quae Lutecia sive Parisius vocatur quinque ferme milibus abest. Siquidem in ea urbe reges Francorum maxime sceptra tractare consueverant."

Dagobert's dogs tracked the deer to a dilapidated chapel, built more than a century earlier by St. Geneviève. However hard they tried, the dogs could not enter; it was as if they were being repulsed by a supernatural power. This miracle greatly astounded Dagobert, who thereafter kept the place dear to his heart. Time passed, and Dagobert was again placed under the tutelage of a *nutritor*. This time around it was Sadregisel, who was supposed to be an ideal influence for the ambitious young prince. The esteemed Aquitanian aristocrat possessed all the qualities that Chlothar sought in someone to whom he could entrust his heir, or so he thought. Gradually, Sadregisel's contempt for Dagobert was revealed. At first, the prince tolerated his *nutritor*'s indignance, but eventually decided to punish Sadregisel by ordering him to be flogged and shorn of his beard. The similarities to the ceremony of *barbatoria*—a symbolic shaving of a boy's first beard, meant to signify his coming of age—are striking. When done amicably by consenting parties and with Church approval, it created a spiritual bond of kinship between the participants. Here, it was an insult that sought to infantilize Sadregisel and put him in his place.[24]

This episode was an entirely new, ninth-century addition, written independently of the historiographical sources.[25] Stripped to the bone, it provided the narrative basis for Dagobert's special attachment to St. Dionysius and the generosity with which he later endowed the monastery. It did not hesitate to describe these gifts in detail—church ornaments, agricultural plots, and tax revenues of entire estates, all listed and accounted for throughout the composition. The emphasis on proprietary and legal precedents from the distant past suggests that the author was arguing for the right of the monastic community to enjoy immunity from episcopal jurisdiction, and that this claim was based on a rich, although not always entirely authentic, archival record. Scholarship has provided exhaustive and convincing argumentation on this point.[26]

---

[24] On the cultural significance of *barbatoria*, see Hen, *Culture and Religion in Merovingian Gaul*, pp. 137–143; Y. Hen, "The Early Medieval *barbatoria*," in *Medieval Christianity in Practice*, ed. M. Rubin (Princeton: Princeton University Press, 2009), pp. 21–24.

[25] Although the donation lists so common to this storyline were based on Dionysian charters. See pp. 183–184, 197.

[26] M. Diesenberger, "Hair, Sacrality and Symbolic Capital in the Frankish Kingdoms," in *The Construction of Communities in the Early Middle Ages: Texts, Resources and Artefacts*, eds. Corradini, R., M. Diesenberger, and H. Reimitz (Leiden and Boston: Brill, 2003), pp. 173–212, at pp. 202–203. See also Y. Hen, *Roman Barbarians: The Royal Court and Culture in the Early Medieval West* (Basingstoke and New York, 2007), at pp. 112–116; Spiegel, "The *Reditus Regni ad Stirpem Karoli Magni*," pp. 144–145 (which identifies the author as Hincmar); Wood, *The Merovingian Kingdoms*, pp. 156–157; P. Fouracre, "Eternal Lights and Earthly Needs: Practical Aspects of the Development of Frankish Immunities," in *Property and Power in the Early Middle Ages*, eds. W. Davies and P. Fouracre (Cambridge: Cambridge University Press, 1995), pp. 53–81, at p. 57, n.7; C. Wickham, *Framing the Early Middle Ages: Europe and the Mediterranean, 400–800*

Jurisdiction and ownership were no doubt important elements in the *Gesta Dagoberti*.[27] However, there was more to the composition than that. The author built a storyline that was effective on several levels. It not only introduced Dagobert as an energetic, very "Frankish," and very pious prince; it also explored his relationship with his father, with the saints, and with two nobles, Arnulf of Metz and Sadregisel. We know that the author used the *Life of Arnulf* as a source,[28] and it is obvious that, for him, the bishop of Metz was more than stylistic flourish. Of course, the bishop's Carolingian credentials did not hurt, but he was ultimately meant to fill a purpose as one part of a narrative diptych, playing the foil of true *nutritor* to Sadregisel's false one.

The Sadregisel storyline has been, perhaps correctly, read as designed to evoke certain images in the minds of ninth-century readers. Buchner and Levillain offered possible identifications for the characters portrayed. In Buchner's case, these were Louis the Pious (Chlothar), his son Pippin (Dagobert), and Bernard of Septimania (Sadregisel); in Levillain's, a looser reflection of Louis's relationship with his sons— particularly Lothar—between 830 and 833.[29] Each of these interpretations has merit, in the sense that imagery from the *Gesta Dagoberti* would have prompted certain readers to make such connections.

However, it is possible that a ninth-century reader would have struggled to correctly decipher the story, just as modern historians have done. We know that the prospect of an unfavorable reading was a constant concern, and that authors were worried that their works would be intentionally misunderstood and turned against them.[30] Most likely, such pressures would have restrained any desire to embed too close a historical parallel in the text. It seems more helpful to assume that the stories were simplified, idealized literary exercises. In other words, it is possible to view the *Gesta Dagoberti* as a kind of "Mirror of Princes," in which the hero is placed in fictitious, but ultimately conceivable, situations, from which readers could

---

(Oxford: Oxford University Press, 2007), p. 109, n.134; S. Saito, "The Merovingian Accounting Documents of Tours: Form and Function," *Early Medieval Europe* 9, 2 (2000), pp. 143–161, at p. 159.

[27] On the proprietary interests of Saint-Denis and the legal infrastructure that underpinned them, see B.H. Rosenwein, *Negotiating Space: Power, Restraint, and Privileges of Immunity in Early Medieval Europe* (Ithaca, NY: Cornell University Press, 1999), pp. 74–118.

[28] See Krusch's introduction to the *Gesta Dagoberti*, p. 396; Olivier, "La mémoire mérovingienne," pp. 109–110.

[29] Buchner, "Zur Entstehung," pp. 271–273; Levillain, "Études sur l'abbaye de Saint-Denis à l'époque mérovingienne," pp. 104–106.

[30] See Regino, *Chronicle*, p. 40; C. West, "Knowledge of the Past and the Judgement of History in Tenth-Century Trier: Regino of Prüm and the Lost Manuscript of Bishop Adventius of Metz," *Early Medieval Europe* 24, 2 (2016), pp. 137–159, p. 139, n.7; MacLean, *History and Politics*, p. 8.

draw lessons about rulership.[31] As Rachel Stone has noted, in Carolingian mirrors only good kings are worthy of the title king, and Dagobert's character is about as close to perfection as we might hope to find. The fact that Hincmar tried his hand at royal mirrors later on in his career might support his identification as a possible author of the *Gesta Dagoberti*.[32] Indeed, the ideology espoused in the *De regis persona et regio ministerio* seems to align with the need to humble and punish offenders such as Sadregisel.[33] Yet, as far as we can parse the text for hidden critiques of historical characters, the author of the *Gesta Dagoberti* required his readers to glean lessons and come up with appropriate conclusions on their own.

The *Gesta Dagoberti* was not the first composition to play on the theme of the public flogging of an aristocrat. The *LHF*, one of its sources, tells the story of the unjustified flogging of a prominent Frank (read: Neustrian) named Bodilo by a brash Childeric II.[34] Bodilo's maltreatment so enraged the Franks that they rose in rebellion against their king. Bodilo and his friends ambushed Childeric, killing him and his pregnant wife. The themes are similar enough to have perhaps inspired some elements of the Sadregisel story. The order of actions is, in any event, reversed; in the *LHF* the flogging leads to defiance, while in the *Gesta Dagoberti* it is the other way around. While the *LHF*'s treatment was an indictment of Childeric II, the *Gesta Dagoberti*'s was a vindication of Dagobert. Whatever influences lay at the foundation of the Sadregisel story, it seems unwise to view it as a thin political parable in which the allegorical alter-egos could be transparently and uniformly decoded by contemporaries.[35] Rather, it is a meditation on royal authority in which

---

[31] R. Stone, "Kings Are Different: Carolingian Mirrors for Princes and Lay Morality," in *Le prince au miroir de la littérature politique de l'Antiquité aux Lumières*, eds. F. Lachaud and L. Scordia (Mont-Saint-Aignan: Publications des Universités de Rouen et du Havre, 2007), pp. 69–86; Y. Hen, "Specula principum carolingi e l'immagine di Costantino," in *Constantini I – Enciclopedia Constantiniana sulla figura e l'immagine dell'imperatore del cosiddetto editto di Milano*, 313–2013 (Rome, 2013), II, pp. 515–522; A. Dubreucq, "Le prince et le peuple dans les miroirs des princes carolingiens," in *Le Prince, son peuple et le bien commun. De l'Antiquité tardive à la fin du Moyen Âge*, eds. H. Oudart, J.-M. Picard, and J. Quaghebeur (Rennes: Presses universitaires de Rennes, 2013), pp. 97–114.

[32] Hincmar of Reims, *De regis persona et regio ministerio*, PL 125, cols. 833–856.

[33] R. Meens, "Politics, Mirrors of Princes and the Bible: Sins, Kings and the Well-Being of the Realm," *Early Medieval Europe* 7, 3 (1998), pp. 345–357, at p. 355.

[34] *LHF*, ch. 45. On the narrative aims of this episode, see J. Kreiner, *The Social Life of Hagiography in the Merovingian Kingdom* (Cambridge: Cambridge University Press, 2014), pp. 77–79. See also S. Zale, "The French Kill Their King: The Assassination of Childeric II in Late-Medieval French Historiography," *Fifteenth-Century Studies* 27 (2002), pp. 273–294, for uses of Bodilo to dismiss French regicide in medieval historiography.

[35] On parable, proximity, and other forms of encoding information in Carolingian texts, see J. Contreni, "'By Lions, Bishops Are Meant; By Wolves, Priests': History, Exegesis, and the Carolingian Church in Haimo of Auxerre's *Commentary on Ezechiel*," *Francia* 29, 1 (2002), pp. 29–56.

royal–aristocratic and familial relations are explored through the character of the young prince.

* * *

Several observations about the mention of the scepter, back at Dagobert's early hunt, are in order. It is perhaps surprising that the author decided to inform this politically savvy readership that Paris was once the seat of royal power. It seems that he wished to highlight the alliance between the earliest kings of the Franks and the embryonic Parisian church. The mention of Geneviève is a step in that direction, especially given her ties to the cult of St. Denis.[36] But along the way, the author made a surprising remark: *In that city, the kings of the Franks had the custom of holding their scepter.* Since the plot hardly hinged on the previous dynasty's power and its attendant symbolism, the scepter reference is best understood as a deliberate narrative tangent. We encounter it again in the chapter that discusses Dagobert's ascent to the throne: "He governed well with the royal scepter, showing similar kindness to the pious, and like a fiery lion he bent the necks of rebels. Armed with fortitude of spirit, he most cleverly triumphed over the ferocity of foreign peoples."[37] The scepter was not a particularly Merovingian piece of regalia,[38] but it certainly would have resonated with a Carolingian readership, especially given its Old Testament and Roman imperial connotations. A miniature of

---

[36] Bitel, *Landscape with Two Saints*, pp. 58–60. See also M. Sluhovsky, *Patroness of Paris: Rituals of Devotion in Early Modern France* (New York, Cologne: Brill, 1998), esp. pp. 11–16.

[37] *Gesta Dagoberti*, ch. 23: "Qui optime regalia sceptra gubernans et piis semet ipsum benignissimum exhibens, ut leo tamen fervidus rebellium colla deprimens, exterarum gentium feritatem, vallante fortitudine animi, sepissime triumphabat."

[38] There are, however, mentions of the scepter in Merovingian hagiographies. One such mention relating to Dagobert is *Vita Sadalbergae abbatissae Laudunensis*, MGH SRM 5, ed. B. Krusch (Hanover: Hahnsche Buchhandlung, 1910), pp. 40–66, at ch. 10, p. 55: "Per idem tempus Francorum sceptra regnique gubernacula Dagobertus regebat, vir inprimis acer ingenio et principatu clarus et non solum ob fidei iura sibi subiectis, verum etiam exterorum vicinarumque gentium fama metuendus," which is reminiscent of the depiction in the *LHF*. For a late seventh-century dating of the *Life of Sadalberga*, pace Krusch, see H. Hummer, "Die merowingische Herkunft der Vita Sadalbergae," *Deutsches Archiv für Erforschung des Mittelalters* 59, 1 (2003), pp. 459–494. Other instances are of Merovingian saints, but mostly composed in Carolingian contexts, such as the *Life of Nivard of Reims*, which was composed by the monk Almann of Hautevillers in Hincmar's day. See Almann of Hautevillers, *Vita Nivardi episcopi Remensis*, MGH SRM 5, ed. W. Levison (Hanover: Hahnsche Buchhandlung, 1910), pp. 157–171, at p. 158 (dating) and ch. 1, p. 160: "Nam tempore, quo Childericus fortis rex Francorum honeste sceptra gubernabat, extitisse cognoscitur." Or, the early ninth-century *Life of Lantbert*, abbot of Saint-Wandrille and bishop of Lyon. See *Vita Lantberti abbatis Fontanellensis et episcopi Lugdunensis*, MGH SRM 5, ed. W. Levison (Hanover: Hahnsche Buchhandlung, 1910), pp. 606–612, at p. 607 (dating) and ch. 2, p. 610: "Perseveravit autem in eodem coenobio annos XIII et menses octo sub tribus fratribus regibus sceptra regni Francorum per ordinem vicissim tenentibus, id est Hlothario, Hilderico atque Theodorico."

Lothar I in a mid-ninth-century psalter (London, British Library add. MS 37768) depicts him with a scepter, as does the Martyrology of Wandalbert of Prüm (Vatican City, BAV Reg. lat. 438).[39]

Recognition of the Merovingian dynasty was not limited to this brief remark. A similar overture was made already in the first chapter of the composition: "Fourth from Clovis, who was the first of the kings of the Franks to have converted, led by the blessed Remigius bishop of Reims to the cult of God, Chlothar, son of Chilperic, was made king."[40] This was not the feigned forgetfulness or open derision universal chroniclers and royal biographers had been known to employ when it came to the Merovingians. Quite the opposite.

The question of the memory of the Merovingians in the *Gesta Dagoberti* is an especially interesting one because this is a Carolingian-era composition dedicated to the heroic exploits of a Merovingian king. One might think to compare the *Gesta Dagoberti* to the *Passio Sigismundi*, since both discuss kings from earlier dynasties, although the latter ultimately wanted to tell a story about martyrdom and saintly cult.[41] The *Gesta Dagoberti*, by contrast, was concerned with the person of Dagobert and his evolving relationship with the Church and its saints. In search of a more wellrounded portrayal, the author gave Dagobert parents, grandparents, and offspring, and placed him in a direct line of succession to his ancestor, Clovis, the first king to become Christian.

Yet the Merovingian invocation probably goes beyond mere backdrop. Whether we consider the *Gesta Dagoberti* a proprietary manifesto or a mirror of princes, the decision to deploy the memory of Dagobert would have been central to its success. The author and his superiors were operating in a specific political setting and, judging by the composition's reception, they read the room well.[42] Favorable depictions of the

---

[39] I. Garipzanov, *The Symbolic Language of Authority in the Carolingian World (c. 751–877)* (Leiden and Boston: Brill, 2008), pp. 243–244; M.E. Moore, "The King's New Clothes: Royal and Episcopal Regalia in the Frankish Empire," in *Robes and Honor: The Medieval World of Investiture*, ed. S. Gordon (New York: St. Martin's and Palgrave, 2000), pp. 95–135. For some remarks on the *sceptra Francorum* and other royal regalia, as well as the scepter as indicative of other regions over which the Frankish king exercised power, see E. A.R. Brown, "'Franks, Burgundians, and Aquitanians' and the Royal Coronation Ceremony in France," *Transactions of the American Philosophical Society* 82, 7 (1992), pp. i–xii and 1–189, at pp. 41, 52, 67, 72, 86.

[40] *Gesta Dagoberti*, ch. 1: "Quartus ab Chlodoveo, qui primus regum Francorum ad cultum Dei, docente beato Remigio Remensi episcopo, conversus est, Chlotharius, filius Chilperici, regnum sortitus est." The mention of the bishop of Reims in this context is perhaps indicative of authorship.

[41] *Passio sancti Sigismundi*, pp. 329–340.

[42] See H. Reimitz, "The Social Logic of Historiographical Compendia in the Carolingian Period," in *Herméneutique du texte d'histoire*, ed. O. Kano (Nagoya: Nagoya University Press, 2012) pp. 17–28, at p. 23; Stegeman, "The Growth of an Austrasian Identity,"

Merovingians could, in some cases, be mobilized to reach a Carolingian readership. It was all in the framing, and to this end a pious and philanthropic Merovingian monarch would have been tolerated.

As we shall see, Dagobert, and the Merovingian dynasty more generally, were still valuable memes in the ninth century. Their usage in the *Gesta Dagoberti* attests to a historical vision that did not see the need to suppress the memory of the Merovingians, unlike most of the historiography emanating from Carolingian centers of production at the time.[43] From the author's standpoint, the relations of the Merovingian dynasty with Saint-Denis were not an expendable aspect of the plot. Saint-Denis was already a royal necropolis half a century before Dagobert was buried there,[44] a practice that continued, alongside the bestowing of lavish royal gifts and donations, well into the Carolingian period. The *Gesta Dagoberti* makes this connection explicit:

[...] *it is nonetheless believed, that with a distribution of such charity and prayer to the saints, whose shrines he incessantly committed to decorate and basilicas to enrich for the redemption of his soul above all previous kings, he could very easily procure, from the most merciful Lord, his clement forgiveness.*[45]

Saint-Denis's prestige, then, was fully entwined with royal patronage, which was showcased by dynastic continuity. Gifts to the monastery were offered by kings dedicated to the well-being of the church and confident that its intercessory abilities would deliver them safely into the hereafter. It was not a responsibility Saint-Denis was willing to relinquish, even if the reputations of some of these kings were tarnished in certain literary traditions.

Let us return to Dagobert: "When Chlothar heard what his son had done to Sadregisel, he grew furious, summoning Dagobert to appear before him immediately. The prince instead decided to seek asylum with

---

p. 126. On Aimoin of Fleury's usage, see Werner, "Die literarische Vorbilder," p. 80. On reading the *Gesta Dagoberti* in the twelfth century and beyond, see R. Grosse, *Saint-Denis zwischen Adel und König: Die Zeit vor Suger (1053–1122)* (Stuttgart: Thorbecke Verlag, 2002), pp. 131–133; E. Inglis, "Técnicas perdidas y halladas: la concepción medieval de la historia de las técnicas artísticas', *Quintana* 16 (2017), pp. 15–50.

[43] The Carolingian family itself oversaw the cult and eventual translation of Clovis II's wife, Balthild. See *Translatio sanctae Baltechildis*, MGH SS 15, ed. O. Holder-Egger (Hanover: Hahnsche Buchhandlung, 1887), pp. 284–285. J.L. Nelson, "Gender and Genre in Women Historians of the Early Middle Ages," in *L'historiographie médiévale en Europe*, ed. J.-P. Genet (Paris: CNRS, 1991), pp. 149–163, at p. 157; MacLean, "Queenship, Nunneries and Royal Widowhood," p. 18.

[44] Lapidge, *Hilduin*, p. 13; Hen, "'Flirtant' avec la liturgie," pp. 34–35.

[45] *Gesta Dagoberti*, ch. 23: "[...] credendum est tamen, quod tantarum erogatio elemosinarum atque sanctorum oratio, quorum memorias ornare et basilicas ditare ob redemptionem suae animae supra omnes anteriores reges incessanter studebat, apud misericordissimum Dominum, ut hoc ei clementer indulgeret, facillime impetrari posse." For more on this paragraph, see p. 191.

the saints and made his way to the small chapel in Catulliacum."[46] Once again, the saints of the chapel provided refuge; all the king's troops could not drag the prince outside. Here, the author neatly transposed the roles in the earlier hunting story; with Dagobert as the proverbial deer, the predator is transformed into prey. The deer is a familiar hagiographical trope. St. Eustachius (aka Placidas), a second-century Roman martyr, was converted upon seeing a crucifix wedged in the antlers of a deer he was hunting. Christ spoke to Eustachius through the deer, ordering him to seek out the nearest city and there to approach a bishop and be baptized.[47] Deer had also become associated with the cult of St. Hubert, the early eighth-century founder and patron of Liège.[48] The cruciferous stag motif, however, appeared only in the eleventh-century *vita quarta*, and would not have been linked by the Carolingians to Hubert.[49] In fact, the third installment of Hubert's Life, the so-called *vita tertia*, was composed by Jonas of Orléans, whose own *De institutione laicali* had criticized aristocratic hunting.[50]

Be that as it may, hunting was symbolically significant to Carolingians. As Eric Goldberg has noted, portrayals of the hunt in compositions from the time of Louis the Pious were used to justify Louis's succession to his father.[51] That the *Gesta Dagoberti* employs the hunt to explore its protagonist's relationship with his father is thus striking.[52] Stylistically, the "bent

---

[46] *Gesta Dagoberti*, chs. 7–11.
[47] *De SS. Eustathio, Uxore ejus et Filiis*, AASS Sept. VI (Antwerp: B.A. van der Plassche, 1757), cols. 123–137, at col. 125A. On this composition, see S. Batalova, "The Tradition of St. Eustathius Placidas in Latin," *Scripta & e-Scripta* 2 (2004), pp. 325–354.
[48] Hubert's career was marked by the rise of Pippinid fortunes in the Ardenne, and indeed Grimoald "the Younger" was murdered while praying at the shrine of St. Lambert in Liège, erected by Hubert. See *LHF*, ch. 50.
[49] On the development of Hubert's hagiographical portrayal, see C. Saucier, *A Paradise of Priests: Singing the Civic and Episcopal Hagiography of Medieval Liège* (Rochester, NY: University of Rochester Press, 2014), pp. 94–136. See also Olivier, "La mémoire mérovingienne," pp. 55–59.
[50] Jonas of Orléans, *De institutione laicali*, PL 106, chs. 22–23, cols. 213–218. On early medieval hunting, see L. Sarti, *Perceiving War and the Military in Early Christian Gaul (ca. 400–700 A.D.)* (Leiden, Boston: Brill, 2013), pp. 166–171; C. Loveluck, *Northwest Europe in the Early Middle Ages, c. AD 600–1150: A Comparative Archaeology* (Cambridge: Cambridge University Press, 2013), pp. 124–149; J. Kreiner, "Pigs in the Flesh and Fisc: An Early Medieval Ecology," *Past & Present* 236 (2017), pp. 3–42. See P. Godman, "The Poetic Hunt: From St Martin to Charlemagne's Heir," in *Charlemagne's Heir: New Perspectives on the Reign of Louis the Pious (814–840)*, eds. P. Godman and R. Collins (Oxford: Oxford University Press, 1990), pp. 565–589. Incidentally, the *Vita Amandi*, *Gesta Dagoberti*, and Jonas's *De institutione laicali* were all sources for Hucbald of Saint-Amand's *Vita sanctae Rictrudis*. See Smith, "Hucbald," pp. 535–538.
[51] E.J. Goldberg, "Louis the Pious and the Hunt," *Speculum* 88, 3 (2013), pp. 613–643. See also M. de Jong, *In Samuel's Image: Child Oblation in the Early Medieval West* (Leiden, New York, Cologne: Brill, 1996), p. 202.
[52] The father-son motifs were emphasized by Levillain, pp. 104–106.

necks" of *Gesta Dagoberti* ch. 23 are reminiscent of similar elements in Theodulf of Orléans' poem in praise of Louis and, later, Walahfrid Strabo's *De imagine Tetrici*, both of which invoke hunting prowess to predict military proficiency.[53] The mention of the hunt as a "custom of the Franks" may echo Einhard's *Vita Karoli Magni* ch. 19, although, if the *Gesta Dagoberti* was indeed composed under the auspices of Hilduin, it would have probably avoided consciously mimicking Einhard.[54]

As the story goes, Chlothar eventually came in person and witnessed firsthand the power of the saints. Meanwhile, his son received a visionary dream from the inhabitants of the tombs in the chapel, the saints Dionysius, Rusticus, and Eleutherius, a bishop, a priest, and a deacon who had suffered their martyrdom "in the time of Domitian, who was second to Nero in persecuting the Christians [...]."[55]

These martyrs were unhappy with their burial arrangements and offered the beleaguered prince a favorable resolution to his predicament in exchange for a promise to make their tomb a worthy monument to their sanctity. Dagobert gladly complied. With the intercession of the saints, father and son made peace, and the relationship between Dagobert and the shrine of St. Denis was established. Of course, this relationship was based on historical fact, grounded in Dagobert's personal devotion to Dionysius and his companions. There is independent evidence not only of Dagobert's munificence toward Saint-Denis, but also of Chlothar's, who likewise received good press in the composition.[56] The *Gesta Dagoberti*'s image of Dagobert as benefactor was doubtless pieced together using the archives of Saint-Denis. The scope of Dagobert's patronage was extensive, although

---

[53] Theodulf of Orléans, *Carmina* 39.7–12, MGH Poetae 1, ed. E. Dümmler (Berlin: Weidmann, 1881), p. 531; Walahfrid, *De imagine Tetrici*, lines 250–255 in M.W. Herren, "The *De imagine Tetrici* of Walahfrid Strabo: Edition and Translation," *Journal of Medieval Latin* 1 (1991), pp. 118–139; Goldberg, "Louis the Pious and the Hunt," pp. 623–624, 633.

[54] On the two's enmity, see Einhard's portrayal of Hilduin in the second book of his *Translation and Miracles*. See Einhard, *Translatio et miracula sanctorum Marcellini et Petri. Translation und Wunder der Heiligen Marcellinus und Petrus*, ed. and trans. D. Kries, Acta Einhardi 2 (Seligenstadt: Einhard Gesellschaft, 2015), pp. 44–140, at I.2, II.1–6, pp. 48–50, 68–74, respectively; P.E. Dutton, *Charlemagne's Courtier: The Complete Einhard* (Peterborough and Ormskirk: University of Toronto Press, 1998), pp. xxv–xxvii.

[55] *Gesta Dagoberti*, ch. 3, p. 401: "In eo sane vico, temporibus Domiciani, qui secundus ab Nerone in christianos arma corripuit, primum memoratae urbis episcopum beatissimum Dyonisium cumque eo Rusticum et Eleutherium, quorum alter presbiter, alter diaconus erat, pro Christi nomine in prospectu ipsius civitatis interemptos quaedam materfamilias vocabulo Catulla, a qua et vico deductum nomen dicunt, quia palam non audebat, clam sepulturae mandavit."

[56] *Die Urkunden der Merowinger*, DD Merov., ed. T. Kölzer, 2 vols. (Hanover: Hahnsche Buchhandlung, 2001), 1, nos. 22, 28, pp. 63–64 and 75–77; Hen, *Roman Barbarians*, pp. 107–108.

just how extensive it is impossible to say with any accuracy. As mentioned by Wallace-Hadrill and others, the authenticity of some of the charter evidence is suspect.[57] Such questions notwithstanding, the author of the *Gesta Dagoberti* relied on Saint-Denis's archival records, from which emerged an image of a prolonged relationship between Dagobert and the monastery of Saint-Denis, which *Fredegar* fully corroborated.[58]

We learn from *Fredegar*'s first mention of Dagobert that in 622, he received a subkingship, something that was a novelty in his day but thereafter became a fixture of Merovingian politics.[59] As ruler of Austrasia, the young prince had the luxury of a royal period of "apprenticeship," as well as an opportunity to build connections with the Austrasian elites, a theme copiously commented on by the *Fredegar* chronicler. Entries for those years yield a complicated picture. Dagobert was actively cultivating ties with certain aristocratic groups (e.g., Arnulf of Metz, Pippin I) at the expense of others (e.g., Chrodoald). His dealings with his father, which are the topic of chapters 52–54, were at times explosive. Disgraced magnates from Chlothar's kingdom found asylum in Dagobert's and vice versa, which would seem to indicate strained relations between father and son.

While the depiction of the historical circumstances is generally realistic in the *Chronicle of Fredegar*, it delivers a carefully curated picture on Dagobert's failings, as its narrative choices demonstrate. The first example is the uncanonical marriage to his stepmother's sister Gomatrude. *Fredegar* does not broadcast his disapproval, but the account of Godinus's marriage to his father's widow, recorded immediately afterwards, can be read as a mocking mirror-image of Dagobert's marriage to Gomatrude. Unlike his royal *doppelgänger*, Godinus received the full brunt of *Fredegar*'s—and Chlothar's—opprobrium. Unsurprisingly perhaps, it was Dagobert, embroiled in a similarly uncanonical mess, who sought to have Godinus pardoned. This subtextual irony is the first hint of a critical leitmotif about Dagobert's performance as king interwoven into *Fredegar*'s portrayal. As always, the marriage had political dimensions. Gomatrude was Sichild's

---

[57] Wallace-Hadrill, *The Long-Haired Kings*, p. 224. For creative usage of Dagobert in the eleventh century, see Grosse, *Saint-Denis zwischen Adel und König*, pp. 110–112.

[58] *Fredegar* IV.79; *LHF*, ch. 43. See A.J. Stoclet, *Fils de Martel: l'éducation et la jeunesse de Pépin, dit "Le Bref" (v. 714–v. 741)* (Turnhout: Brepols, 2013), p. 113, n.69.

[59] In fact, in keeping with his father's practice, Dagobert gave his eldest son Sigibert III the Austrasian subkingship. See *Fredegar* IV.76. On Carolingian subkingship and royal fathers and sons, see M. Costambeys, M. Innes, and S. MacLean, *The Carolingian World* (Cambridge: Cambridge University Press, 2011), pp. 208–213; E. Screen, "Carolingian Fathers and Sons in Italy: Lothar I and Louis II's Successful Partnership," in *After Charlemagne: Carolingian Italy and Its Rulers*, eds. C. Gantner and W. Pohl (Cambridge: Cambridge University Press, 2021), pp. 148–163.

sister and was therefore related to Brodulf,[60] who would later enjoy decisive influence over Dagobert's younger half-brother, Charibert II. The marriage could have been meant as another check on Dagobert's attempts to dominate his brother. As we shall see, the storyline developed quite differently in the *Gesta Dagoberti*, which imposed a much stricter black-and-white framework on the plot. Portraying the ongoing factional tensions would have cast Dagobert in a less glamorous light. It is quite likely that the author recognized the disapproving note embedded in the Godinus story and chose to skip over it.

In *Fredegar*, open discord between Chlothar and Dagobert erupted after the wedding at Clichy. Father and son disagreed heatedly about the division of the realm, a division whose contours continued to spark disagreement in the 650s, when the *Fredegar* chronicler was working.[61] The argument involved more than territory; the two were at odds about questions of final authority in the lands Dagobert controlled on behalf of his father. Sovereignty is a throughline in the chapters that dealt with Dagobert's Austrasian subkingship. One wonders whether the Grimoald coup, whose effects loomed heavily over the *Fredegar* chronicler's writing, played any role in this portrayal, since its fate was decided by the intervention of the Neustrian king in Austrasia. Dispensing with Grimoald would have required a cooperative Austrasian elite, to whose critically needed mediation *Fredegar* was perhaps alluding when it spoke of the trusty advisors cleverly defusing the situation a generation earlier. With the counsel of twelve of the kings' closest men, first among whom was Arnulf of Metz, father and son eventually came to an agreement. Dagobert would receive sovereignty over Austrasia, although what would later become the nucleus of Charibert's kingdom remained in Chlothar's hands, probably with the intent of securing some inheritance for his younger son.

This episode resurfaces in the *Gesta Dagoberti*, with the author following *Fredegar*'s political explanation down to its territorial contours. It is perhaps noteworthy that Sadregisel, who did not appear in this chapter, was named *dux Aquitaniae*.[62] If his character contains any semblance of historicity, it is only because under Clothar II there would likely have

---

[60] According to the *Gesta Dagoberti*, she would have been his sister. See *Gesta Dagoberti*, ch. 16: "Brunulfus quoque, qui frater fuerat Sichildis reginae ... "
[61] On *Fredegar* and the Grimoald affair, see Collins, *Fredegar*, pp. 107–111.
[62] The first *Passio sancti Dionysii*, later reworked by the same Hilduin of Saint-Denis who likely oversaw the composition of the *Gesta Dagoberti*, was probably composed in Aquitaine *ca.* 750, although by Hilduin's day it was known in Paris. See *Passio sancti Dionysii*, in M. Lapidge, The 'Ancient Passio' of St Dionysius (BHL 2171)," *Analecta Bollandiana* 132 (2014), pp. 241–285; Lapidge, *Hilduin of Saint-Denis*, p. 83. The composition itself can be found in pp. 229–303.

been an official charged with maintaining Charibert's future realm, which was at the core of the conflict at Clichy.[63] Even before the death of their father, then, Dagobert was challenged by his younger half-brother. Charibert II was already a semi-independent player in 628, and apparently had a sizable elite following in the royal assembly that was convoked in parallel with the Council of Clichy in 626/7. During this assembly, one of his men, a certain Erm(en)arius, was killed by the followers of a Saxon partisan of Dagobert.[64] Interestingly, *Fredegar* refers to Ermarius as a *gubernator palatii*, which implies that Charibert had a *palatium*, although, of course, this could be anachronistic terminology applied in hindsight to the 620s.

The *Gesta Dagoberti* is mum on Dagobert's troubles with his brother prior to Chlothar's death. Charibert is only introduced later, upon receiving his share of the kingdom, based on the borders described earlier in *Fredegar*. Both accounts agree that the decision to concede to Charibert the kingdom of Toulouse was motivated by *misericordia* and good counsel, but this was, in fact, a deliberately skewed perspective. After 628 Charibert's uncle Brodulf, who was already influential at Clichy, took an increasingly dominant role in controlling Charibert's affairs. The *Fredegar* chronicler reports that, with Brodulf at his side, Charibert made a bid for the entire kingdom, which was unsuccessful because of his *simplicitas*. Nevertheless, he received a kingdom centered on Toulouse, which he managed to hold until his death. *Fredegar* does not mention a *divisio regni* made by Chlothar during his final years, but from everything the account does tell us it seems that Charibert was meant to receive a kingdom in Aquitaine, and that Chlothar's forces were instrumental in making this a reality.

As suggested by the strikingly similar arrangements Dagobert put in place when he was preparing to die, Charibert's claim to rule was not as preposterous as is made out in the chronicle. Like his father, Dagobert appointed his eldest to the subkingship of Austrasia and kept his youngest at his side, building his support base and shielding him from an aggressive sibling with a significant advantage. Thus, it appears that what *Fredegar* had Dagobert relinquish out of pity was in reality a reluctant recognition

---

[63] *Gesta Dagoberti*, ch. 6, p. 402: "Itaque Dagobertus sic probitate ut aetate in dies crescebat spemque future regis optimam subinde indiciis operum ingerebat. Et pater Clotharius quondam, ut putabat, spectate fidei Sadregisilum rebus sub se tractandis praefecerat, Aquitaniae ducatu specialiter ei commisso." See G. Krutzler, "Fremdwahrnehmungen in der frühmittelalterlichen Ethnographie," doctoral dissertation (Universität Wien, 2009), p. 65.

[64] On him, see H. Ebling, *Prosopographie der Amtsträger des Merowingerreiches, von Chlothar II. (613) bis Karl Martell (741)*, Beihefte der Francia 2 (Munich: Wilhelm Fink, 1974), CLXI, p. 140.

that Chlothar's designs had materialized. As for Charibert wresting control of the entire kingdom, this seems a little far-fetched, unless our understanding of the situation is entirely off.[65] Since Dagobert eventually exacted his revenge on Brodulf and, apparently, also on Charibert's infant son, the chronicler may have sought an "original sin" to justify the severity of Dagobert's later actions.[66] The *Gesta Dagoberti*'s account is not as informative. Among the few takeaways of the story there is that Aquitaine was a constant headache for Frankish kings.[67] Given the Carolingians' history in the region, which was anything but serene, this depiction seems right on target. But in terms of the realities of Charibert's rule, the *Gesta Dagoberti* offers little of value.

Fredegar reports that Charibert was able to expand his kingdom through conquest, after having subdued the Wascones. Dagobert, in the meantime, took a tour of Burgundy.[68] Although it caused a panic among the lay and ecclesiastical elites, the alarm turned out to be a false one; Dagobert was there to give justice to the poor, not settle scores. There was, however, one exception. After a royal visit to Langres and Dijon, Dagobert arrived in Saint-Jean-de-Losne, where he ordered the assassination of Brodulf. This was carried out quickly, and Dagobert was soon on the move again, traveling to Chalon-sur-Saône, Autun, Auxerre, Sens, and finally Paris, dispensing justice as he went.

A fitting end to Dagobert's *tour de force* was the termination of his marriage to Gomatrude, a logical move now that Brodulf was out of the way. *Fredegar* mentions, with noticeable glee, that the king left her in the same villa where he married her and took instead a servant girl named Nanthechild. Dagobert's resounding success was neatly explicated: "From the beginning of his reign until that day he would take counsel from the blessed Arnulf, bishop of the city of Metz and Pippin, mayor of the palace, and he ruled with such prosperity in Austrasia that he won the joint praise of an immense number of peoples."[69] The troublesome Avars and Slavs on the frontier were subdued, and Dagobert's power was generally accepted in

---

[65] *Fredegar* IV.56.   [66] Ibid. 58, 67.
[67] See Fouracre, *The Age of Charles Martel*, pp. 81–89; R. Collins, "Deception and Misrepresentation in Early Eighth-Century Frankish Historiography: Two Case Studies," in *Karl Martell in seiner Zeit*, eds. J. Jarnut, U. Nonn, and M. Richter (Sigmaringen: Jan Thorbecke Verlag, 1994), pp. 227–247, at pp. 235–246; B.S. Bachrach, *Charlemagne's Early Campaigns (768–777): A Diplomatic and Military Analysis* (Leiden and Boston: Brill, 2013), pp. 108–138; J.F. Boyer, *Pouvoirs et territoires en Aquitaine du VIIe au Xe siècle: enquête sur l'administration locale* (Stuttgart: Franz Steiner Verlag, 2018), pp. 217–274.
[68] Geary, *Before France and Germany*, p. 155; Kreiner, "About the Bishop," p. 325.
[69] *Fredegar* IV.58: "usque eodem tempore ad inicio quo regnare ciperat consilio primetus beatissime Arnulfi Mettensis urbis pontefice et Pippino maiorem domus usus, tante prosperetatis regale regimen in Auster regebat ut a cunctis gentibus inmenso ordine laudem haberit."

Francia and beyond. The connection between success and appropriate counsel resurfaced toward the end of the chapter, when Arnulf withdrew from royal service and Chunibert of Cologne stepped in.

The *Fredegar* chronicler's views on the role of the Austrasian aristocracy in ensuring the success of the king are known, although it is worthwhile to devote some more attention to the trip to Burgundy. Since Dagobert's success and failure were constructs put in place by the chronicler, one wonders what role the Burgundian tour was really meant to serve, as opposed to the presentation in *Fredegar*. The concern of the secular and ecclesiastical elites might suggest that the region was only tenuously held, and that Dagobert was conducting a public show of force. Burgundy was a cause for concern after Chlothar II assumed power there in 613. At that time, it was a patrician named Alethius who attempted to stage a coup by enticing the queen to switch sides.[70] The plan backfired, and Chlothar had the patrician killed. After justice was served, the king summoned the Burgundian leadership, both secular and ecclesiastical, to an audience in which their concerns were aired and answered. Dagobert's Burgundian story has overlaps with that of his father. Both take place in a newly acquired Burgundy whose elite were still on the fence about the ruler. And both feature the elimination of a threat to power: in Chlothar's case, a usurper, in Dagobert's, a dangerous puppet master. The language of *iustitia*, which peppers the Dagobert story, shows up in Chlothar's as well: "And there he considered their just petitions and confirmed the previous concessions."[71]

Any theories about the historicity of Burgundian challenges to the new branch of Merovingian rulers must remain just that. Yet in terms of the story's narrative aim, namely, to portray Dagobert as coming into his own, the argument seems to be on much surer footing. By releasing him from any residue of his father's designs, particularly Brodulf and Gomatrude, *Fredegar* was offering his commentary on the correct handling of such moments in a king's life. A worthy ruler should unshackle himself from the cumbersome arrangements he inherited, but he should do so with care, and with good counselors at hand. Tellingly, this chapter is also the turning point in *Fredegar*'s coverage of Dagobert. After fathering a son from a new woman in the subsequent chapter, Dagobert moved to Paris, where he allowed himself to sink into the depths of decadence. He despoiled the church, took many more wives and concubines, and, worst of all, angered his Austrasian following.

---

[70] On this, see Y. Fox, "New *honores* for a Region Transformed: The Patriciate in Post-Roman Gaul," *Revue Belge de Philologie et d'Histoire* 93 (2015), pp. 1–38, at pp. 25–30.

[71] *Fredegar* IV.44: "Ibique cunctis illorum iustis peticionibus annuens preceptionebus roboravit."

Through his own negligence, he drove a wedge between them and his closest *fidelis*, Pippin.[72]

The *Gesta Dagoberti* rejected *Fredegar*'s narrative volte-face. From beginning to end, the king remained an exemplary figure. On Charibert, the *Gesta Dagoberti* diverged slightly from its source, such as when it introduced him explicitly as the son of Sichild, a fact to which *Fredegar* only alluded. This was related just prior to the Sadregisel story, after which we hear nothing of Charibert until the death of Chlothar and the meeting with the Neustrian, Burgundian, and Austrasian elites in Rheims, where Dagobert's claim was recognized.[73] The interim is filled with marvelous adventures, such as the vision of Dionysius and his associates and Chlothar's duel with Bertoald the Saxon chieftain, the latter lifted entirely from *LHF*, ch. 41.[74] Dagobert's ascent to power and the divisions that took place thereafter closely mimic *Fredegar*, again attributing Charibert's inability to make a successful claim to a kingdom to his *simplicitas*.[75] Dagobert was moved by pity to allow Charibert a kingdom in Aquitaine, a description which sat well with the overall vision expounded in the *Gesta Dagoberti*, which is probably why it was left intact. Once more the author turned to other things, such as the translation of the saints Dionysius, Eleutherius, and Rusticus in fulfillment of Dagobert's previous commitment or the generosity he showed to the churches of Marseilles, Valence, Fos, and Lyon. Saint-Denis was second to none, receiving on that same occasion a jewel-encrusted golden cross made by the renowned royal goldsmith Eligius.[76] The cross was one of many lavish gifts Dagobert gave to Saint-Denis, which included landed and mobile riches beyond measure.

Only then does the author return to the topic of Charibert's kingdom, with the killing of Brunulf, the *Gesta Dagoberti*'s rendition of *Fredegar*'s Brodulf. Gomatrude is briskly cut loose, although here two features stand out. The first is the term "with the council of the Franks" (*cum consilio Francorum*), which is missing from *Fredegar*.[77] This small addition might then have been inspired by the author's desire to illuminate points that were of special interest for a ninth-century reader, namely, the theme of

---

[72] *Fredegar* IV.60.   [73] *Gesta Dagoberti*, ch. 13.   [74] Ibid. ch. 14.
[75] Ibid. ch. 16: "Hairbertus autem, frater eius, nitebatur, si potuisset, regnum assumere; sed illius voluntas pro simplicitate parum sortitur effectum."
[76] For Eligius as a hagiographical character, see Y. Fox, "The Clergy between Town and Country in Late Merovingian Hagiography," *Journal of Medieval History* 49,2 (2023), pp. 135–158.
[77] It is a turn of phrase we would expect from the *LHF*, which was after all important in informing the *Gesta Dagoberti*'s point of view. In truth, however, the *LHF* is remarkably thin when it comes to Dagobert, limiting its discussion to a single chapter. See Diesenberger, "Hair, Sacrality, and Symbolic Capital," pp. 202–203; P. Dörler, "The *Liber historiae Francorum*—A Model for a New Frankish Self-Confidence," *Networks and Neighbours* 1.1 (2013), pp. 23–43, at pp. 38–43.

dissolving royal marriages. The most infamous Carolingian divorce case took place a generation after the composition of the *Gesta Dagoberti*, but there were enough examples of queenly dismissal from which to draw inspiration, such as the repudiation of Desiderius's daughter in 771 by Charlemagne. The Frankish king wanted to untangle himself from familial checks on his freedom, put in place, again, to protect a younger brother. The theme was a common one and worthy of commentary.

The second salient feature is that here a reason is given for Dagobert's decision to leave Gomatrude: her sterility. Rejecting a royal wife was hard to reconcile with the *Gesta Dagoberti*'s pious buildup of Dagobert. Justification was required, and the invocation of sterility was necessary to reach an audience used to conceiving of royal marriages as potent and binding acts.[78] However one wishes to interpret the dismissal of Gomatrude, Dagobert emerges from it none the worse for wear, and wastes no time taking the young and beautiful Nanthechild in marriage.

The author of the *Gesta Dagoberti* follows *Fredegar* in discussing Dagobert's dependence on the Austrasian magnates Pippin I and Arnulf of Metz, and later also Chunibert of Paris. Dagobert's exemplary performance while relying on these men is repeated almost verbatim, but here the plots diverge once more. For *Fredegar*, the move to Paris was the beginning of Dagobert's moral downfall, but for the author of the *Gesta Dagoberti* it was nothing of the sort. In fact, it brought the king closer to Saint-Denis and was therefore cause for celebration. *Fredegar* IV.59 is dedicated to Dagobert's womanizing, which resulted in the birth of his firstborn son, Sigibert III. The whole chapter has something of a lurid feel to it, especially when we consider that Dagobert had just dismissed Gomatrude in favor of Nanthechild and was now admitting Ragnetrudis into his bedchamber. *Fredegar*'s criticism sharpens in the subsequent chapter, which scathingly reports on Dagobert's sexual corruption. The author of the *Gesta Dagoberti* was forced to acknowledge Dagobert's depravity, but he did so with delicacy. Mention of Ragnetrudis, Dagobert's third partner, was deferred

---

[78] On the contemporary understanding of royal marriage, see S.F. Wemple, *Women in Frankish Society: Marriage and the Cloister, 500 to 900* (Philadelphia, PA: University of Pennsylvania Press, 1989), pp. 75–123; K. Heene, *The Legacy of Paradise: Marriage, Motherhood, and Woman in Carolingian Edifying Literature* (Frankfurt-am-Main: Peter Lang, 1997), pp. 142–145; Heidecker, *The Divorce of Lothar II*, pp. 78, 108–110; R. Stone, "'Bound from Either Side': The Limits of Power in Carolingian Marriage Disputes, 840–870," *Gender & History* 19, 3 (2007), pp. 467–482; J.M.H. Smith, "Did Women Have a Transformation of the Roman World', *Gender & History* 12, 3 (2000), pp. 552–571; J. Brundage, *Law, Sex and Society in Medieval Europe* (Chicago: University of Chicago Press, 1987), pp. 169–175; S. Joye, *La femme ravie: Le mariage par rapt dans les sociétés occidentales du haut Moyen Âge* (Turnhout: Brepols, 2012), pp. 357–370; R. Le Jan, *Famille et pouvoir dans le monde franc (viie–xe siècle)* (Paris: Éditions de la Sorbonne, 1995), pp. 263–327.

until the author completed a prefatory exoneration of Dagobert, written as a response to the debauchery portrayed in *Fredegar* IV.60 and its consequences for the loyal Pippin in IV.61. The author of the *Gesta Dagoberti* opened by reminding the readers of the king's piety, his judiciousness, and his military prowess, motifs likely inspired by the depiction found in the *LHF*. His agility, physical strength, and proclivity for the hunt as redeeming traits came second. Then came the bitter pill, but even this admission was qualified and rationalized:

Of course, he committed certain reprehensible acts according to religion, burdened by the weight of governing and lured by the rashness of youth, that were less cautious than otherwise behooves one to commit, because no one can be perfect in everything ...[79]

The reader is not left hanging, however:

... it is nonetheless believed, that with a distribution of such charity and prayer to the saints, whose shrines he incessantly committed to decorate and basilicas to enrich for the redemption of his soul above all previous kings, he could most easily procure, from the most merciful Lord, his clement forgiveness.[80]

The Dionysian undertones emerge most clearly here, and it is apparent that, while the author was forced to acknowledge certain inconvenient details about the past, he did not adopt his source's critical approach to Dagobert. Of course, the king's misdeeds could have been expunged entirely, so why did they remain? It is true that the author of the *Gesta Dagoberti* stayed faithful to his source throughout most of the composition, conserving as much historical detail as possible. It is also true that, when it suited him, he was more than willing to break loose. We must assume that he had something to gain by mentioning the king's indiscretions. This editorial choice becomes clearer when we consider the stake that Saint-Denis had in Dagobert's redemption. As we shall see, the saint played a formative role in Dagobert's eventual salvation. For Dagobert to have been saved, he first needed to be damned, and it is this that made the mention of his transgressions necessary.

We should bear this in mind as we interpret the *Gesta Dagoberti*'s approach to Sigibert's birth. The relationship with Ragnetrudis is framed

---

[79] *Gesta Dagoberti*, ch. 23, p. 409: "Nempe etsi aliqua more humano reprehensibilia circa religionem gravatus regni pondere ac iuvenilis inlectus aetatis mobilitate minus caute secus quam oportebat exegit, quia nemo in omnibus perfectus esse potest."
[80] *Gesta Dagoberti*, ch. 23: "[...] credendum est tamen, quod tantarum erogatio elemosinarum atque sanctorum oratio, quorum memorias ornare et basilicas ditare ob redemptionem suae animae supra omnes anteriores reges incessanter studebat, apud misericordissimum Dominum, ut hoc ei clementer indulgeret, facillime impetrari posse." See here also remarks by Olivier, "La mémoire mérovingienne," pp. 118–124.

so as to explain the dismissal of Gomatrudis, from which we gather that Nanthechild had still not produced any offspring:

Then, in the eighth year of his reign, when he was travelling around Austrasia on state business,[81] *and being despondent beyond measure because he could not even have a son who would succeed him, he took a certain girl named Ragnetrudis to his bed, from whom that year, by the grace of God, he had a son, obtained through many prayers and the granting of alms.*[82]

This is a far cry from the description in *Fredegar*, and, indeed, even from the one found in the *Life of Amandus*, dedicated to the saint's role in the baptism of the infant Sigibert. In the *Life*, as in *Fredegar*, the story began with Dagobert's lasciviousness, which was quickly replaced by contrition for want of a son:

Meanwhile King Dagobert, who was given to excessive love of women and burned with every filth of desire, had no offspring whatsoever, but nevertheless took refuge in God's help, pleading sedulously that he would deign to give him a son, who would wield the scepters of his reign after him.[83]

Krusch argued that both *Fredegar* and the *Life of Amandus* informed the account in the *Gesta Dagoberti*, a convincing assertion in light of the role that Amandus played in blessing Sigibert and baptizing him.[84] The accounts diverge on several minor details. In the *Gesta Dagoberti* it is Charibert who received Sigibert from the baptismal font in Orléans and Amandus officiated at the ceremony, while in the *Life of Amandus* Charibert was not mentioned and the affair took place at the royal villa in Clichy. But both recounted the same miracle toward the end: after Amandus was finished with his prayer, and when none of the attendees responded with the required "Amen," God opened the mouth of the infant—according to the *Gesta Dagoberti* Sigibert was then only forty days old—who answered "Amen" in their stead. Amandus's hagiographer obviously wanted to highlight the role of the saint in Dagobert's transformation, but for the author of the *Gesta Dagoberti* any discussion of the

---

[81] The phrasing until this point is entirely *Fredegar*'s.
[82] *Gesta Dagoberti*, ch. 24: "Denique anno octavo regni sui, cum Austriam regio cultu circumiret mestusque esset nimium, eo quod filium, qui post eum regnaret, minime habere posset, quandam puellam nomine Ragnetrudem stratu suo adscivit, de qua eo anno, largiente Domino, habuit filium, multis precibus atque elemosinarum largitionibus adquisitum."
[83] *Vita Amandi*, ch. 17, p. 440: "Interea Dagobertus rex, amore mulierum plus quam opportet deditus omnique spurcitia libidinis inflammatus, sobolem minime videbatur habere, sed tamen ad Domini confugit auxilium depraecabaturque sedule, ut ei filium dare dignaretur, qui post eum regni sui gubernaret sceptra."
[84] *Gesta Dagoberti*, ch. 24, p. 409.

king's wantonness would have been incongruent with the image he was attempting to build and was subsequently left out.

* * *

At this point in the plot, the *Fredegar* chronicler turned to the triumphs and tragedies of Heraclius. A short version of this rather lengthy treatment remained in the *Gesta Dagoberti*, including the emperor's misguided request to have the Jews of Gaul baptized.[85] While it mostly adhered to its source, the *Gesta Dagoberti* again used this opportunity to incorporate the motif of *consilium*, which it incorporated with the king's zeal to create something slightly different than *Fredegar*'s original account:

> King Dagobert, seizing the opportunity and driven by divine zeal, with the counsel of bishops and wise men, ordered all the Jews who refused to submit to the regeneration of sacred baptism to be banished from the boundaries of his kingdom.[86]

Certainly, the theme of episcopal and lay *consilium* would have been central to any political commentary put forward during the 830s. If we entertain the notion that Hilduin of Saint-Denis or Hincmar of Rheims (while still a monk at Saint-Denis) exerted some influence on the text or even composed it, this preoccupation with *consilium* is better understood. If, and this is again sheer speculation, Hincmar had the opportunity to revisit the composition as he was preparing to write the *Life of Remigius*, other interpretative horizons open up. Of course, we cannot say with any certainty that Hincmar was the author or that such reediting indeed took place. This is also the point at which to note that the narrative devices used in the *Life of Remigius* bear testimony to a more developed hortatory tone. Hincmar's handling of the plot, which involves alternating between parable and moral lesson, is much more heavy-handed than what one finds in the *Gesta Dagoberti*, which does not wear its moral objectives on its sleeve. Whether this is a case of an author's style maturing or an entirely different author remains unanswerable.

In his retelling of Charibert's death, in the ninth year of Dagobert's reign, the author again reveals his narrative leanings. Charibert left a son—Chilperic in *Fredegar*, Childeric in most manuscripts of the *Gesta Dagoberti*—who did not long outlive him.[87] *Fredegar*'s candor about Dagobert's hand in Chilperic's death was not shared by the author of the *Gesta Dagoberti*, who preferred to bypass his source's

---

[85] On this passage and its historiographical permutations, see Fox, "Chronicling the Merovingians in Hebrew" and in Chapter 5.
[86] *Gesta Dagoberti*, ch. 24: "Rex vero Dagobertus hac occasione nactus et Dei zelo ductus, cum consilio pontificum atque sapientium virorum omnes Iudaeos, qui regenerationem sacri baptismatis suscipere noluerunt, protinus a finibus regni sui pellere iussit."
[87] *Gesta Dagoberti*, ch. 25, p. 410.

insinuation. One is almost tempted to wonder whether the misnaming of the prince was deliberate, considering that the last Merovingian, deposed by a Carolingian ancestor of the intended reader of the composition, was also named Childeric.[88]

The next episode in *Fredegar* involved Samo and the Slavs, and was used to deliver a direct critique of Dagobert:

This victory that the Wends won against the Franks was obtained not so much because of Slavic courage as by the desertion of the Austrasians, who believed that they incurred Dagobert's hatred and were routinely despoiled by him.[89]

The author of the *Gesta Dagoberti*, by contrast, sealed his depiction of the campaign with a laconic statement of victory: "The king, after having laid waste to their lands, returned to his own kingdom."[90] He then skipped the chapters in *Fredegar* devoted to the Lombards, although he did include a story not taken from *Fredegar*—the death and burial of Nanthechild's brother, Landegisel.[91] The inclusion was clearly meant to highlight the burial in Saint-Denis, arranged by Dagobert, which positioned the monastery as a final resting place for the extended royal family. The *Gesta Dagoberti* rejoined its source with the Avar episode, to which it appended the Samo narrative, presented separately in *Fredegar*.

As *Fredegar* relates it, this was a quarrel over power in Pannonia between Avars and Bulgars. The matter was decided in battle, in which the Avars defeated the Bulgars, chasing them out of Pannonia and into Frankish-dominated Bavaria. The 9,000 Bulgarian warriors pleaded with Dagobert for sanctuary for them and their families. Dagobert agreed to allow them to winter in Bavaria, pending the outcome of deliberation among the Franks about their final status. Eventually, the Franks decided that it would be better to eliminate the Bulgars, and this was swiftly carried out. Only a small contingent of Bulgars were able to flee with their families, taking refuge with the Wends.[92] The *Gesta Dagoberti* tweaks

---

[88] See the offhanded remark (*ignavissimus Francorum rex*) in Notker, *Gesta Karoli Magni*, MGH SRG n.s. 12, ed. H.F. Haefele (Berlin: Weidmann, 1959), p. 13, ch. 10.

[89] *Fredegar* IV.68: "Estaque victuria qua Winidi contra Francos meruerunt, non tantum Sclavinorum fortitudo optenuit quantum dementacio Austrasiorum, dum se cernebant cum Dagoberto odium incurisse et adsiduae expoliarintur."

[90] *Gesta Dagoberti*, ch. 27, p. 410: "Rex vero terram illam vastans, ad proprium regnum reversus est."

[91] Ibid., ch. 26. Possibly to be identified with Boso-Landegisilus of *Vita Lupi episcopi Senonici*, MGH SRM 4, ed. B. Krusch (Hanover: Hahnsche Buchhandlung, 1902), pp. 176–187, at ch. 11, p. 182. See Ebling, *Prosopographie*, no. 91, pp. 91–92.

[92] On this, see W. Pohl, *Die Awaren: Ein Steppenvolk in Mitteleuropa, 567 – 822 n. Chr.* (Munich: Beck, 1988), pp. 269–270, now translated into English in W. Pohl, *The Avars: A Steppe Empire in Central Europe, 567–822* (Ithaca, NY: Cornell University Press, 2018); W. Goffart, "The Fredegar Problem Reconsidered," *Speculum* 38, 2 (1963), pp. 206–241, at p. 238, who argues that the episode took place after Dagobert died.

this story in the mildest of manners; *consilium Francorum* (counsel of the Franks) becomes *sapienti consilio Francorum* (wise counsel of the Franks), while the carnage leaves no survivors.[93]

The retention of this story is interesting, as it does not shed particularly favorable light on Dagobert. Clearly, the author did not view the act critically, although admittedly not much more can be said. The *Gesta Dagoberti* continued to adhere to *Fredegar* for the remainder of the thematic block concerned with the king's international sphere of influence, charting a course between Spain, Thuringia, Saxony, and the Wendish territories. The author did use the Spanish episode to again highlight Dagobert's openhandedness toward Saint-Denis and the various construction projects it included.[94]

* * *

A new turn in the plot commences with the appointment of Sigibert III to the Austrasian kingship. This was an important event for the *Fredegar* chronicler, who viewed with approval the installation of a Merovingian on the Austrasian throne, aided by the local magnates Chunibert of Metz and Adalgisel, and the provision of treasure. Austrasian military performance improved as a result, as we soon discover, confirming the veracity of *Fredegar*'s earlier assertion.[95] Next we learn of the birth of Clovis II and the *divisio* put in place by Dagobert, in which Sigibert retained a slightly reduced Austrasia and Clovis received Neustria-Burgundy, an arrangement that was to hold until the composition of the chronicle.

To this the *Gesta Dagoberti* had nothing new to add, except for what has now become the convention accompanying regnal changes, namely, the subsequent generosity shown to Saint-Denis.[96] But then it departed completely from its source, offering an entry for Dagobert's thirteenth year. In *Fredegar* there is no thirteenth year; it skips directly to year fourteen. The author uses this digression to revisit an old storyline, that of Sadregisel:

In the thirteenth year of his (i.e., Dagobert's) *reign, Sadregisel, duke of the Aquitanians, was killed by certain men. We mentioned him previously, on account of his contempt, for which Dagobert, in his youth, ordered him to be whipped and his beard shaven; and because for fear of his father, he* (i.e., Dagobert) *sought out the protection of the holy martyrs. And since this Sadregisel had sons that were educated in the palace and could*

---

[93] *Gesta Dagoberti*, ch. 28, p. 411: "Quod protinus a Baiuvariis impletum est, nec quisquam ex illis remansit."
[94] Ibid., ch. 29.   [95] *Fredegar* IV.75.
[96] Which mentions a forged diploma antedating the royal privilege of holding a market at Saint-Denis from Clovis's day to Dagobert's. See *Gesta Dagoberti*, p. 413, n.3.

easily have avenged the death of their father but were unwilling to, they were accused by the great men of the realm according to Roman law and lost all of their paternal possessions.[97]

The tale of Sadregisel's death seems irrelevant to the propulsion of Dagobert's story. Of the king, we learn only what we already know. The story leads up to the loss of the *paternas possessiones*: Sadregisel was killed, and the sons were expected to avenge him; their inability to do so put them in breach of Roman law; the magnates rightly seized their lands. This is a very odd claim. Vendettas occurred in Rome,[98] but Roman law did not know a duty to avenge one's father in this way.[99] The state, which kept punitive power firmly in hand, did not give legal standing to private vendettas.[100] Retributive violence was likewise a familiar feature of Merovingian society, but the law and the courts overwhelmingly preferred a compensatory approach to conflict resolution.[101] Frankish law conceded that violent conflicts were a reality, but it certainly did not conceive of them as a legal duty. The attempts to link the seizure of Sadregisel's lands to his children's legal negligence indicates not only that the author was not versed in Roman murder legislation, but also that the point of the story was elsewhere, namely, in Sadregisel's bequest.

The landed holdings of the duke of Aquitaine were both significant in scope and spread out geographically, comprising one villa in Angers and nine in Poitiers, as well as salt pans, too numerous to mention, and several other unnamed properties. As it happens, the confiscated lands

---

[97] *Gesta Dagoberti*, ch. 35: "Anno itaque 13 regni sui cum Sadregisilus dux Aquitaniorum a quibusdam hominibus interfectus esset, de quo supra mentionem fecimus, quod propter contemptum sui eum flagellis adfici et barbae rasione deturpari in sua infantia Dagobertus iusserit, et ob hoc patrem metuens, tutelam sanctorum martyrum expetierit, et cum haberet ipse Sadregiselus filios in palatio educatos, qui cum facillime possent, mortem patris evindicare noluerunt, propterea postea secundum legem Romanam a regni proceribus redarguti, omnes paternas possessiones perdiderunt."

[98] See, for instance, Appian, *Bella civilia*, in *Appiani Historia Romana I*, eds. P. Viereck, A. G. Roos, E. Gabba (Leipzig: Teubner, 1962), 1.20; J.P. Hallett, *Fathers and Daughters in Roman Society: Women and the Elite Family* (Princeton, NJ: Princeton University Press, 2014), p. 45, n.14.

[99] Unless the author means that by enlisting the judiciary resources available to the sons because of their position in court, they would be better positioned to exact revenge on their father's assailants, which is a possible, albeit hardly literal, reading.

[100] R.A. Bauman, *Crime and Punishment in Ancient Rome* (London and New York: Routledge, 1996), p. 1; O.F. Robinson, *Penal Practice and Penal Policy in Ancient Rome* (London and New York: Routledge, 2007), p. 4; J.-W. Krause, *Kriminalgeschichte der Antike* (Munich: C.H. Beck, 2004), pp. 203–205, which gives a somewhat antiquated notion of bloodfeud in Gaul; C.A. Barton, *The Sorrows of the Ancient Romans: The Gladiator and the Monster* (Princeton, NJ: Princeton University Press, 1995), p. 182. See, for instance, the attitude of the *Codex Theodosianus*, eds., T. Mommsen and P. Meyer (Berlin, 1905), 16.8.21 on vengeance against Jews.

[101] Esders and Reimitz, "Legalizing Ethnicity," pp. 298–299.

went directly to the royal fisc, and then were disbursed by "the most excellent King Dagobert" almost entirely to Saint-Denis. The remainder went toward the institution of *turmae* in Saint-Denis, Saint-Maurice d'Agaune, and Saint-Martin in Tours, and toward reparations made to their respective monastic populations for their liturgical services.[102] As we shall see, those same three holy men would repay the debt to their royal benefactor. The parameters of the entire gift were recorded by a donation charter, which, the author assures us, is available to the inquisitive reader:

He (i.e., Dagobert) recorded one by one the donation of these same villas under one charter, signed with his own name and sealed with the impression of the ring. If some diligent person wishes to inquire, he should request the same donation charter from the archive of the same church and, I believe, he will find the names of twenty-seven villas inserted there.[103]

This stylistic model, which incorporates entries from *Fredegar* with original additions on the donation of property to Saint-Denis, continues for several more chapters. Chapter 39 introduces something new, and it is one of the few instances where Dagobert breaks the fourth wall, speaking directly to his audience and, through it, to the reader. It begins with the designation of the two princes as kings in a general assembly attended by the Frankish elite:

Then, as was the custom of the kings of the Franks, seated on the throne and wearing a golden crown, to everyone standing in his presence, he began thus: "Hear me, oh you kings and sweetest of sons, all you magnates and most powerful dukes of our realm! Before the call of death suddenly comes, it is fitting to be vigilant for the health of the soul, lest perchance one is found unprepared, and, without a second glance, he will be taken away from the present light and delivered to perpetual darkness and eternal torment."[104]

---

[102] On the liturgical regimen of Saint-Maurice d'Agaune, see B.H. Rosenwein, "Perennial Prayer at Agaune," in *Monks and Nuns, Saints and Outcasts: Religion in Medieval Society. Essays in Honor of Lester K. Little*, eds. S. Farmer and B.H. Rosenwein (Ithaca, NY, and London: Cornell University Press, 2000), pp. 37–56.

[103] *Gesta Dagoberti*, ch. 35, p. 414: "Easdem autem villas infra unius praecepti conclusionem nominatim inserens, proprii nominis subscriptione atque anuli inpressione firmavit. Quarum nomina si aliquis diligentius perquirere voluerit, ipsam praeceptionis cartam in archivo ipsius ecclesiae requirat et, ut reor, viginti et septem villarum nomina inibi inserta inveniet."

[104] *Gesta Dagoberti*, ch. 39: "Cumque, ut Francorum regibus moris erat, super solium aureum coronatus resideret, omnibus coram positis, ita exorsus est: 'Audite me, o vos reges et dulcissimi filii omnesque proceres atque fortissimi duces regni nostri. Priusquam subitanea transpositio mortis eveniat, oportet pro salute animae vigilare, ne forte inveniat aliquem imparatum eique sine aliquo respectu praesentem lucem auferat atque perpetuis tenebris et aeternis tormentis tradat.'"

Dagobert then delivers a long sermon, mapping out the paths to eternal life in the company of the saints. Chief among them, no surprise, was patronage of religious institutions. After extolling the virtues of such patronage, Dagobert provides a list of donations and the mechanisms by which they are to be carried out and recorded. He continues with an appeal to Sigibert and Clovis to maintain and protect the tenets of his testament, and then enlists all present as witnesses and guarantors. One more extract from *Fredegar* follows, after which the *Gesta Dagoberti* turns to the king's death.

A eulogy of Dagobert preceded the actual report of his death:

It would be too long to narrate how farsighted this same king Dagobert was in counsel, how cautious in judgement, how vigorous in military training, how generous in alms and zealous in ensuring the peace of the churches, and in particular how devoted to enriching the monasteries of the saints. It is less important to declare the present deeds than it is to spare tedium from the fastidious reader, especially since there is evidence of the brighter light of their effects that no amount of time can erase.[105]

Finally, the author turns to the death itself. After sixteen years of rule, Dagobert sensed that his end was near. He was carried from Épinay to Saint-Denis, where he had his mayor Aega, his wife Nanthechild, and his son Clovis II join him. After placing Nanthechild and Clovis under the protection of Aega, he convoked the leading men of the realm, to whom he also commended the care of his wife and child. The author then provides the details of another generous grant of property to Saint-Denis, after which Dagobert addressed his audience, repeating some of the same messages he delivered in his previous sermon. In the king's parting address, moral teachings are interspersed with references to donations of property.[106] The *Gesta Dagoberti* did not fail to report that Clovis II, Bishop Audoin of Rouen, and the rest of the men in attendance signed Dagobert's testament, no doubt to ensure that the king's wishes were carried out. Then the king died. Afterward, according to the author: "An intolerable pain immediately filled all of the palace, and the entire realm was overcome with lament because of that most bitter death."[107]

---

[105] *Gesta Dagoberti*, ch. 42, p. 419: "Longum est enarrare, quam providus idem rex Dagobertus in consilio fuerit, cautus iudicio, strenuus militari disciplina, quam largus elemosinis quamque studiosus in compenda pace ecclesiarum, precipueque, quam devotus exstiterit in ditandis sanctorum cenobiis, praesenti opere declarare, minusque necessarium et maxime ob fastidientium lectorum vitandum tedium, praesertim cum nullis abolenda temporibus luce clariora earum rerum extent indicia."

[106] See L. Morelle, "Une somme d'érudition dédiée aux actes royaux mérovingiens," *Bibliothèque de l'École des chartes* 161, 2 (2003), pp. 653–675, at p. 664.

[107] *Gesta Dagoberti*, ch. 42, p. 421: "Intolerabilis autem luctus subito totum replevit palatium, universumque regnum ob ipsius mortem acerbissima occupavit lamentatio."

This portrayal of a king at the end of life putting his affairs in order is far from unique to the *Gesta Dagoberti*. Einhard's *Vita Karoli Magni*, for example, discusses many of the same topics, employing similar imagery. Chapter 30, which depicts Charlemagne's coronation of his son, Louis the Pious, shares elements with the *Gesta Dagoberti*'s deathbed scene. Most notably, the transfer of royal power is a public performance by a dying king and his heirs, to which the assembly of nobles stands as witness and guarantor. Einhard's usage of pietistic language was naturally more reserved than that of the *Gesta Dagoberti*, although even he conceded that the move gained wide approval with the assembly, because it seemed to have been divinely inspired.[108]

A marvelous funeral ensued, during which the body of the deceased king, decorated and perfumed, was deposited in a lavish tomb in Saint-Denis. His many accomplishments were again recounted, especially his role in instituting an *ordo psallentium*—this should probably be taken to mean the *laus perennis* liturgical regimen—in Saint-Denis, Saint-Maurice, and Saint-Martin.[109] The laxity of Abbot Haigulf, which spelled the end of this liturgy in Saint-Denis, was duly noted.[110]

* * *

Although he was dead and buried, Dagobert was not quite finished. What follows is another original storyline that depicts his soul in its travels between heaven and hell. The episode is framed as a vision, which would have been an appropriate stylistic choice given the abundance of visionary writing in the years immediately before and after the composition of the *Gesta Dagoberti*.[111] We come to know of the fate of Dagobert in the afterlife thanks to Bishop Ansoald of Poitiers, whose mission to Sicily led him to a wise old man named John, who lived on a nearby island:

As it so happens, at that time Ansoald, the illustrious defender of the church of Poitiers, led a delegation to the region of Sicily. With this accomplished, and having returned to

---

[108] Einhard, *Vita Karoli Magni*, ch. 30, p. 34: "Susceptum est hoc eius consilium ab omnibus qui aderant magno cum favore; nam divinitus ei propter regni utilitatem videbatur inspiratum."
[109] See Hen, *Roman Barbarians*, pp. 114–115.
[110] This was taken from *Fredegar* IV.79. See G.I. Halfond, "The Endorsement of Royal-Episcopal Collaboration in the Fredegar 'Chronica'," *Traditio* 70 (2015), pp. 1–28, at pp. 25–27.
[111] See D. Ganz, "Charlemagne in Hell," *Florilegium* 17 (2000), pp. 175–194; P. Dutton, *The Politics of Dreaming in the Carolingian Empire* (Lincoln, NE, and London: University of Nebraska Press, 1994), esp. pp. 23–49; J. Keskiaho, *Dreams and Visions in the Early Middle Ages: The Reception and Use of Patristic Ideas, 400–900* (Cambridge: Cambridge University Press, 2015), pp. 66–71ff; M. van der Lugt, "Tradition and Revision. The Textual Tradition of Hincmar of Reims' *Visio Bernoldi* with A New Critical Edition," *Bulletin Du Cange* 52 (1994), pp. 109–149.

the ship, he landed on a certain small island where a most reverent old man, whose name was John, led a solitary life; many seafarers sought the support and consolation of his prayer. In this island, Ansoald was driven by divine wish to seek the many merits of this man. While conversing with him about celestial joys, the old man then asked him whence and why he came. When informed that he was sent on a mission from Gaul, the old man asked to be told about the habits and character of Dagobert, king of the Franks. This having been done diligently, the old man added that the other day, because he was naturally broken with old age and tired by vigils, he allowed himself briefly to rest, when a certain white-haired man approached him and thereafter began to eagerly admonish him to quickly get up and pray for divine clemency for the soul of Dagobert king of the Franks, who had died that very day.

When he agreed to do this, there appeared to him not too far from shore foul spirits, who were dragging King Dagobert on a boat through the sea, whipping him from above and pushing him to the underworld, while the saints Dionysius and Maurice the martyrs and the most holy confessor Martin were demanding the release of Dagobert with joined voices. Without delay the heavens thundered, lightning exploded through the storm, and in the midst suddenly appeared the most excellent men dressed in white clothes, whom he (i.e., Dagobert) *asked, trembling, who they were. They answered that Dagobert called them, meaning Dionysius and Maurice and Martin, to carry him away to the Bosom of Abraham. Then, with the enemies of mankind quickly pursuing the spirit, which they were tormenting with whips and threats, it was plucked into the air and lifted itself up, singing: Blessed is the one You choose and bring near, o Lord; he will dwell in Your courts. We are filled with the goodness of Your house, Your temple is holy, wondrous in justice.*[112]

There in the abovementioned charter, among other things mentioned, which can seem, I believe, as unlikely despite being entirely accurate, [it says that] this same king, who, like others, enriched the churches far and wide, at that time in particular endowed copiously those [churches] before others in which he was admiringly remembered, and from which after death he pleaded for help.[113]

---

[112] Psalms 65, 4.

[113] *Gesta Dagoberti*, ch. 44, pp. 421–422: "Legationem tum forte illustris Defensor Pictavensis ecclesiae Ansoaldus in partes Siciliae agebat. Ea peracta, cum navali reverteretur subsidio, applicuit ad quandam brevem insulam, in qua reverentissimus quidam senex, cui erat nomen Iohannes, solitarium ducebat vitam, ad quem mare commeantium, ut orationis eius fulcirentur solatio, plurimi ventitabant. In hanc ergo insulam tanti viri meritis redimitam appulsus divino nutu Ansoaldus, dum de caelestibus gaudiis cum eo sermocinaretur, interrogat senex, unde vel cur venisset. Igitur cognito, de Galliis qua de causa missus fuisset, rogat senex, ut Dagoberti regis Francorum sibi mores studiumque exponat. Quod cum ille dilligenter fecisset, senex addidit, quod dum quadam die, utpote iam fractus aetate et fatigatus vigiliis, quieti paululum indulsisset, accessisse ad se virum quendam canicie venerandum seque expergefactum admonuisse, quatinus propere surgeret et pro Dagoberti regis Francorum anima divinam clementiam exoraret, eo quod ipse die spiritum exalasset. Quod dum facere maturaret, apparuisse sibi haud procul in pelago teterrimos spiritus, vinctum regem Dagobertum in lembo per spatium maris agitantes atque ad Vulcania loca, inflictis insuper verberibus, trahentes, ipsumque Dagobertum beatos Dyonisium et Mauricium martyres et sanctissimum Martinum confessorem ad sui liberationem continuis vocibus flagitantem. Nec mora intonuisse caelum, fulminaque per procellas disiecta, interque ea repente apparuisse praecellentissimos viros niveis comptos vestibus, seque tremefactum ex eis quaesisse, quinam essent, illosque respondisse, quos Dagobertus in adiutorium vocaverat, Dyonisium scilicet et

The message of the tale seems clear enough: The king—and any future reader, for that matter—who gave lavishly throughout his life, could expect help in the afterlife from the patron saints of his preferred institutional beneficiaries.[114] It is not out of place for the *Gesta Dagoberti* to explain the spiritual returns on religious patronage, especially considering the attention it lavishes on religious donation throughout the work. Ansoald of Poitiers is nevertheless an interesting addition. Ansoald was bishop of Poitiers between 673/7 and 696/7, so could not have been conducting missions on behalf of the diocese or the kingdom in 638–639.[115] His anachronistic appearance may have been related to dramatic effect or to other ends entirely. He is known to us as the dedicatee of the B version of the *Passio Leudegarii* and as a character in the work, competing for the martyr's relics.[116] He was witness, in some of the manuscripts at least, to a miracle performed by St. Eligius, and also played host to Filibert when the latter was expelled from Jumièges, helping him found Noirmoutier.[117] There is also verified evidence that Ansoald owned land in the region of Chalon-sur-Saône. All of this is in keeping with what we would expect of a late Merovingian bishop of a high-profile see.

Mauricium ac Martinum esse, ut eum ereptum in sinu Abrahae collocarent. Itaque hostes humani generis velociter insequentes, animam, quam verberibus minique vexabant, ereptam ad ethera secum levasse, canentes: Beatus quem elegisti et assumsisti, Domine; inhabitabit in atriis tuis. Replebimur in bonis domus tuae, sanctum est templum tuum, mirabile in equitate. Haec in memorata carta, inter alia ferebantur, quae non tam veri similia quam verissima, ut arbitror, videri possunt, quoniam idem rex, cum et alias longe lateque ecclesias ditasset, tum praecipue horum copiosissime locupletavit. Unde et eorum post mortem flagitabat auxilium, quos prae ceteris se dilexisse meminerat."

[114] See Y. Hen, "Visions of the Afterlife in the Early Medieval West," in *The Cambridge Companion to Visionary Literature*, ed. R. Pollard (Cambridge: Cambridge University Press, 2021), pp. 25–39, esp. at pp. 33–36.

[115] See C. Mériaux, "Parochiæ barbaricæ? Quelques remarques sur la perception des diocèses septentrionaux de la Gaule pendant le haut Moyen Âge," *Revue du Nord* 360–361 (2005), pp. 293–303, at pp. 296–297. For his connection to Ursinus, see Y. Hen, "Defensor of Ligugé's Liber Scintillarum and the Migration of Knowledge," in *East and West in the Early Middle Ages: The Merovingian Kingdoms in Mediterranean Perspective*, eds. S. Esders, Y. Fox, Y. Hen, and L. Sarti (Cambridge: Cambridge University Press, 2019), pp. 218–229, at p. 220.

[116] P. Fouracre and R.A. Gerberding, ed. and trans., *Late Merovingian France: History and Hagiography 640–720* (Manchester and New York: Manchester University Press, 1996), pp. 197, 207.

[117] *Vita Eligii* II.20, p. 712; *Vita Filiberti abbatis Gemeticensis et Heriensis*, MGH SRM 5, ed. W. Levison (Hanover: Hahnsche Buchhandlung, 1910), pp. 568–604, at ch. 25; Wood, *The Merovingian Kingdoms*, pp. 230–231; C. Mériaux, *Gallia Irradiata: saints et sanctuaires dans le nord de la Gaule du haute Moyen Âge* (Stuttgart: Franz Steiner Verlag, 2006), pp. 70–71.

It has also been suggested that, like his predecessor Dido of Poitiers, Ansoald had connections in Ireland.[118] Whether we infer this from the putative links to the Columbanian nexus through Filibert, or from the Irish exile of Dagobert II facilitated by Ansoald's predecessor Dido of Poitiers, the delegation to Sicily recounted in the *Gesta Dagoberti* stands apart from this evidence and can do little to substantiate Ansoald's international portfolio.[119] Simon Loseby used this voyage to argue for the survival of trade and international movement along the Provençal coast,[120] but this claim presents some difficulties. If we accept the story as essentially historical, Ansoald's Sicilian mission could either be made to suggest contacts during a period later in the century or to argue for a mission led by someone other than Ansoald and undertaken around the time of Dagobert's death. As an additional thought experiment, we might posit a Sicilian mission to the court of Constans II, which indeed resided in Syracuse.[121] Ebroin's opposition to the networks crystallizing between England and Byzantium and Ansoald's opposition to Ebroin—based primarily on hagiographical evidence that connects the bishop of Poitiers to Leudegar and Filibert—could contextualize the delegation. Yet our willingness to indulge in these conjectures should be restrained by the ninth-century date of composition for the *Gesta Dagoberti* and, most importantly, by the fact that this section of it was not influenced by *Fredegar* nor any other Merovingian-era source we know of. Since it was most likely an original addition, it should be considered no more accurate than the stories of Dagobert's vision and Sadregisel's downfall.

Taking into account the chronological inconsistencies and the creative nature of the source, Ansoald's mission should probably be deemed to bear little relation to historical fact. The visionary symbolism is relatively familiar, although it has the advantage of taking place in a foreign topography, removed by time and space from any historical circumstances an *aliquis diligentius* might otherwise attempt to verify. This may explain the

---

[118] Famously, Dido appears in another visionary composition—the *Visio Baronti*. See *Visio Baronti monachi Longoretensis*, MGH SRM 5, ed. W. Levison (Hanover: Hahnsche Buchhandlung, 1910), pp. 368–394; Y. Hen, "The Structure and Aims of the Visio Baronti," *Journal of Theological Studies* 47 (1996), pp. 477–497.

[119] See E. James, "Ireland and Western Gaul in the Merovingian Period," in *Ireland in Early Medieval Europe: Studies in Memory of Kathleen Hughes*, eds. D. Whitelock, R. McKitterick, and D. Dumville (Cambridge: Cambridge University Press, 1982), pp. 362–386, at pp. 377–379.

[120] S.T. Loseby, "Marseilles and the Pirenne Thesis II: 'Une ville morte'," in *The Long Eighth Century: Production, Distribution and Demand*, eds. I.L. Hansen and C. Wickham (Leiden, Boston, and Cologne: Brill, 2000), pp. 167–194, at p. 179.

[121] Although Constans's death date (668) fits neither Dagobert's rule nor Ansoald's episcopacy. On his death in a Syracuse bath, see D. Woods, "Theophilus of Edessa on the Death of Constans II," *Byzantine and Modern Greek Studies* 44, 2 (2020), pp. 212–219.

author's remark that while the events of the episode seem unlikely, they can be corroborated by the charter.

* * *

Some of the subsequent chapters are again a return to *Fredegar*; they are concerned with the political realities that followed the death of Dagobert, and then with the passing of the generation of Aega and Pippin, Neustrian and Austrasian mayors respectively, and the appointment of their successors, namely, Erchinoald in Neustria and Floachad in Burgundy. The focus on Clovis's Neustro-Burgundian realm is understandable, given that Saint-Denis was situated there, and not in Sigibert's Austrasia. We therefore hear nothing more of Sigibert.

The closing passages are concerned with the relationship of the king and the monastery in the post-Dagobertian era. Chapter 51 quotes in its entirety a diploma given by Clovis II to Saint-Denis. This diploma provided Saint-Denis with the king's protection and granted it immunity from royal intervention. In so doing, it redefined the monastery's relationship with its royal and episcopal partners, whose own monastic exemptions soon solidified the new arrangement. The significance of this move for the status and freedom Saint-Denis now enjoyed, but also for the benefits earned and costs borne by the king and the bishop, have been meticulously analyzed by Barbara Rosenwein.[122] As she has shown, the monastery was moving out of episcopal jurisdiction and into a new model that leaned more heavily on self-government, but which accorded a privileged place to the relationship with the king. The reinstitution of the *laus perennis* as part of this thrust has been understood by some to have made Saint-Denis into a "royal monastery." Rosenwein does not entirely adopt this perspective, although she does concede that " ... the initiative for this drive was clearly royal."[123] In this she is likely correct.

The monastic landscape underwent dramatic changes under Dagobert and Clovis II. The sixth-century model described by Gregory of Tours would have felt increasingly ineffectual when applied to the rural, elite-dominated monasticism of the late seventh century. That new provisions were being made to mitigate the system's shortcomings was to be expected. The legal infrastructure that underwrote the new *klosterpolitik* put in place by Dagobert and then by Clovis and his queen have been exhaustively discussed elsewhere, although the narrative aims of this chapter in the context of the *Gesta Dagoberti* have not.[124]

---

[122] Rosenwein, *Negotiating Space*, pp. 74–77.   [123] Ibid., p. 77.
[124] See E. Ewig, "Das Privileg des Bischofs Berthefrid von Amiens für Corbie von 664 und die Klosterpolitik der Königin Balthild," in E. Ewig, *Spätantikes und Fränkisches Gallien: Gesammelte Schriften (1952–1973)*, Beihefte der Francia 3/2 (Munich: Artemis Verlag,

The chapter envisioned a model for monastic–royal relations that liberated Saint-Denis from the threat of intervening external forces, royal or episcopal, which could compromise the integrity of the community's holdings and revenue streams. Trouble could come in numerous guises, even clothed as exaggerated piety. By letting the king have a say in determining the routines of monastic life, Saint-Denis gave him a foothold in the monastery, a step whose unfortunate consequences become apparent in the next chapter. The author of the *Gesta Dagoberti* built on the *LHF* to tell the story of Clovis's appropriation of the arm of St. Denis, a highly charged, symbolic event in the institutional memory of the monastery:

> *The days of King Clovis's reign were altogether without wars and peaceful, but, as fate would have it, he once came in his final years to the bodies of the above-mentioned martyrs, as though with the purpose of praying, and since he wished to have their relics with him, ordered that the grave be opened. When he saw the body of the holy and most excellent martyr and bishop Dionysius, less religiously than greedily, he broke off and took away the bone of his arm. Immediately stunned, he lapsed into madness. Such terror, dread, and darkness filled that place, that all present were most terrified, and sought safety in escape.*[125] *After this happened, when he returned to his senses, he gave certain villas to that place; the bone that he took from the holy body he decked in gold and precious stones and returned it there. But he only regained a small part of his faculties, never completely, and two years later he ended his life and his kingship.*[126]

It is quite possible that Saint-Denis and the king held very different understandings of what transpired.[127] Obviously the former saw the actions of the latter as being grave, as this account surely indicates. However critical it might seem, the portrayal of Clovis severing the arm of Dionysius in the *Gesta Dagoberti* is mild compared with the one found in *LHF*. The *LHF* contains no mention of Clovis's insanity, although it does openly attribute to the king such traits as drunkenness and licentiousness and blames him for

---

1979), pp. 538–583, at pp. 576–83; Rosenwein, *Negotiating Space*, pp. 78–81; Y. Hen, *Culture and Religion in Merovingian Gaul, 481–751* (Leiden, New York, and Cologne: Brill, 1995), pp. 54–58.

[125] Compare with the announcement of Dagobert's death in *Gesta Dagoberti*, ch. 42.

[126] *Gesta Dagoberti*, ch. 52: "Hlodowius itaque rex cunctis diebus absque bellis in regno pacem habuit, sed, fortuna impellente, quondam in extremis vitae suae annis ad supradictorum martyrum corpora quasi causa orationis venit, volensque eorum pignora secum habere, discoperiri sepulchrum iussit. Corpus autem beati et excellentissimi martyris atque pontificis Dyonisii intuens, minus religiose, licet cupide, os brachii eius fregit et rapuit, confestimque stupefactus, in amentiam decidit. Tantusque terror et metus ac tenebre locum ipsum repleverunt, ut omnes qui aderant timore maximo consternati, fuge praesidium peterent. Post haec vero, ut sensum recuperaret, villas quasdam ad ipsum locum tradidit; os quoque, quod de sancto corpore tullerat, auro ac gemmis miro opera vestivit ibique reposuit. Sed sensum ex aliquantula parte recuperans, non autem integre recipiens, post duos annos vitam cum regno finivit."

[127] Wood, *The Merovingian Kingdoms*, pp. 156–157.

the kingdom's ruin. Unlike the *Gesta Dagoberti*'s version, which gives some weight to Clovis's efforts to remedy the situation, the king recovers none of his reputation in the *LHF*. But while the *Gesta Dagoberti*'s version is measured, is it still highly critical, and builds on the tradition of criticizing Clovis for his crimes against monastic autonomy and property.[128]

The *Gesta Dagoberti* promoted the view that Clovis II's reign was catastrophic because he was the one who violated the remains of its patron saint, a view obviously based on the portrayal found in the *LHF*, and, one would assume, oral monastic traditions. The Dionysian origins of the *LHF* have been called into question by Richard Gerberding and others,[129] and while no conclusive evidence has been put forward to rule out Saint-Denis as the place of the *LHF*'s composition,[130] let us assume that the work was indeed penned at Soissons. The story may still have originated at Saint-Denis, since the author indicated that he or she knew of additional sources about Clovis II, which contained similarly critical reports of the king.[131] Even though the author of the *Gesta Dagoberti* made it a point to note that Clovis acted as he had because he wanted the relics with him always, the king emerged from this episode badly. The agency of Dionysius was expanded considerably when compared with the *LHF*'s rendition, which would have aligned well with the composition's attempt to highlight the saint's powers, as both punisher and intercessor. This tradition of animosity against Clovis II was amplified by the outsized influence of Dionysian compositions on the historiographical tradition. In many ways, it contributed to the emergence of a periodization model that saw the years after Dagobert's death as a sharp downward turn, heralding the decline of the Merovingians. This approach will become especially conspicuous in the Merovingian account found in the *Chronicle* of Regino of Prüm, to which we now turn.

---

[128] For an entirely different vision of Clovis's reign, see *Actus pontificum Cenomanensis in urbe degentium*, in *Geschichte des Bistums Le Mans von der Spätantike bis zur Karolingerzeit: Actus pontificum Cenomanensis in urbe degentium und Gesta Aldrici*, ed. M. Weidemann, 3 vols. (Mainz: Verlag des Römisch-Germanischen Zentralmuseums in Kommision bei Habelt, 2002), 1, XII, p. 71; W. Goffart, "Le Mans, St. Scholastica, and the Literary Tradition of the Translation of St. Benedict'," *Revue Bénédictine* 77 (1987), pp. 107–141, esp. at p. 130.

[129] Gerberding, *The Rise of the Carolingians*, p. 152, suggested Saint-Médard. For alternative suggestions, see Nelson, "Gender and Genre," pp. 160–161; Hartmann, "Die Darstellung der Frauen," p. 213.

[130] Which was the view expressed by Monod, Kurth, and eventually also Krusch. See G. Monod, "Les origines de l'historiographie à Paris," *Mémoires de la société de l'histoire de Paris et de l'Ile-de-France* 3 (1876), pp. 219–240; G. Kurth, "Études critiques sur les Gesta regum Francorum," *Bulletin de l'Académie royale de Belgique* 2, 18 (1889), pp. 261–291; B. Krusch, "Die neueste Wendung im Genovefa-Streit II," *Neues Archiv* 40 (1915), pp. 265–327, at pp. 276 and 310.

[131] *LHF*, ch. 44, p. 316: "Multa enim scriptores eius finem condempnant; nescientes finem nequitiae eius, in incertum de eo alia pro aliis referunt." See also Hartmann, "Die Darstellung der Frauen," p. 211, n.16.

4.2 Regino and the Rehistoricized Dagobert

Like many of the sources surveyed thus far, Regino of Prüm's *Chronicle* devotes little space to Dagobert.[132] This is to be expected, since events in early seventh-century Francia were but one modest facet of a wide and ambitious historiographical oeuvre, covering nine centuries, from the birth of Christ until 906.[133] This ambitious historiographical work was, as Simon MacLean has observed, a gloomy rumination on the fate of Carolingian power that was doubtless punctuated by the setbacks suffered by Regino himself.[134] Once abbot of the monastic powerhouse of Prüm, Regino was ejected from his post in 899 as part of a larger power struggle over the kingdom of Lotharingia. Having found shelter at Trier, he was given the abbacy of Saint-Martin by the archbishop Ratbod, and in this capacity he composed the *Chronicle*, as well as several other important works on music and liturgy. We know very little about Regino's career before he became abbot of Prüm in 892, although the web of connections he was attempting to weave through the dedications of his literary works is a good indication of where power was centered in East Francia during the first years of the tenth century, and of how he conceived of a possible path

---

[132] The literature on Regino of Prüm, especially in German, is extensive. From the later twentieth century and on, see H. Löwe, "Regino von Prüm und das historische Weltbild der Karolingerzeit," *Rheinische Vierteljahrsblätter* 17 (1952), pp. 151–179; A.-D. von den Brincken, *Studien zur lateinischen Weltchronistik bis in das Zeitalter Ottos von Freising* (Düsseldorf: Triltsch, 1957), pp. 128–133; K. F. Werner, "Zur Arbeitsweise des Regino von Prüm," *Die Welt als Geschichte* 19 (1959), pp. 96–116; O. Prinz, "Die Überarbeitung der Chronik Reginos aus sprachlicher Sicht," in *Literatur und Sprache im europäischen Mittelalte: Festschrift für Karl Langosch zum 70. Geburtstag*, ed. A. Önnerfors (Darmstadt: Wissenschaftliche Buchgesellschaft, 1973), pp. 122–141; H.-W. Goetz, "Historiographisches Zeitbewußtsein im frühen Mittelalter. Zum Umgang mit der Zeit in der karolingischen Geschichtsschreibung," in *Historiographie im frühen Mittelalter*, eds. A. Scharer and G. Scheibelreiter (Vienna: Oldenbourg, 1994), pp. 158–178; H.-H. Kortüm, "Weltgeschichte am Ausgang der Karolingerzeit: Regino von Prüm," in *Historiographie im frühen Mittelalter*, eds. A. Scharer and G. Scheibelreiter (Vienna: Oldenbourg, 1994), pp. 499–513. See MacLean's *History and Politics in Late Carolingian and Ottonian Europe: The Chronicle of Regino of Prüm and Adalbert of Magdeburg* (Manchester: Manchester University Press, 2009) for translation and commentary. See also, R. Meens, "Opkomst en ondergang van de Karolingers. De kroniek van Regino van Prüm," *Millennium* 24 (2010), pp. 3–18; Airlie, "Sad Stories of the Death of Kings"; McKitterick, *Perceptions of the Past*, pp. 30–32; S. MacLean, "Insinuation, Censorship and the Struggle for Late Carolingian Lotharingia in Regino of Prüm's Chronicle," *The English Historical Review* 124 (2009), pp. 1–28; E. Goosmann and R. Meens, "A Mirror of Princes who Opted Out: Regino of Prüm and Royal Monastic Conversion," in *Religious Franks: Religion and Power in the Frankish Kingdoms: Studies in Honour of Mayke De Jong*, ed. R. Meens et al. (Manchester: Manchester University Press, 2016), pp. 296–313; R. Meens, "The Rise and Fall of the Carolingians: Regino of Prüm and His Conception of the Carolingian Empire," in *Faire lien. Aristocratie, réseaux et échanges compétitifs: Mélanges en l'honneur de Régine Le Jan*, ed. L. Jégou et al. (Paris: Sorbonne, 2015), pp. 315–323.
[133] Although he intended to bring it up to 908. See Airlie, "Sad Stories," p. 118.
[134] MacLean, *History and Politics*, p. 3.

back into royal favor under Louis "the Child." Ultimately, this was not to be; Regino remained in Saint-Martin until his death in 915. As it relates to the interests of this chapter, however, Regino's sensitivity to the waxing and waning of political power, and the finiteness of kingdoms more generally, was certainly expressed in his narrative treatment of the Merovingians, whose zenith and swift downturn was elegantly encapsulated in the transition of power from Dagobert I to Clovis II.

Among the sources Regino used in the first book of his *Chronicle*, Friedrich Kurze noted in his preface to the 1890 MGH edition the following historiographical compositions: Bede's *World Chronicle*, the *Liber historiae Francorum*, Paul the Deacon's *History of the Lombards*, the *Liber pontificalis*, and the *Annals of Saint-Amand*.[135] Other works also played a role in Regino's presentation of Book I. These were quite varied, and included the Bible, Ado of Vienne's *Martyrology*, a Spanish canon collection of local and papal decretals, and a whole slew of hagiographies, such as the *Lives* of Severinus of Cologne, Martin of Tours, Columbanus, Vedast, Arnulf of Metz, and Eligius of Noyon.

Dagobert's coverage in the *Chronicle* benefitted immensely from the existence of the *Gesta Dagoberti*, which enabled Regino to provide more details about him than any other Merovingian king. While the *Gesta Dagoberti* is not strictly speaking a historiographical composition, it so comprehensively relied on *Fredegar*'s chronological progression of the king's life that one might consider *Fredegar* to have been an important—if indirect—source for Regino. The *Gesta Dagoberti*'s historiographical skeleton, imported wholesale from *Fredegar*, was especially important for Regino, who made much greater use of it than he did the miraculous, visionary, and donative components of the *Gesta Dagoberti*. If indeed Hilduin is to be seen as the author of the *Gesta Dagoberti*, his close contacts with the monastery of Prüm, where he possibly also ended his life, could explain Regino's dependence on this text.[136]

Regino's *Chronicle*, and especially several key entries in Book II, have been used to great effect to contextualize the abbot's tumultuous career, especially his connections with the courts of Arnulf of Carinthia and Zwentibald and his attempts to reclaim the abbacy of Prüm.[137] The parts of Regino's work that have received the most attention from scholars are naturally the ones in which Regino reported from memory and

---

[135] F. Kurze, "Praefatio," in Regino, *Chronicle*, pp. vii–viii. For Regino's use of Bede and his overall pessimism, see Koziol, "The Future of History," pp. 16–25. For the possibility that Regino knew Ado's *Chronicle*, see L. Boschen, *Die Annales Prumienses. Ihre nähere und ihre weitere Verwandschaft* (Düsseldorf: Schwann, 1972), p. 218. MacLean, *History and Politics*, p. 12, n.42 is skeptical.
[136] McKitterick, *History and Memory in the Carolingian World*, pp. 214–215; MacLean, *History and Politics*, p. 19.
[137] MacLean, "Insinuation," p. 4.

personal knowledge on events that took place in his recent past.[138] Certainly, those entries that could illuminate unknown details about the author's life should be especially prized. Yet Simon MacLean, Stuart Airlie, and others who have worked on the *Chronicle* have recognized that it deserves to be understood as a unitary whole, and that Book I played an important role in Regino's overall agenda.[139] In this section I shall heed their advice, following Regino of Prüm's use of his sources in the construction of a Merovingian storyline, paying special attention to his treatment of the *Gesta Dagoberti*.

It would be worthwhile to pause and consider why Regino needed a "Merovingian storyline" to begin with. As Regino himself reports, it was his intent to provide a history of the Franks comparable to that of the Hebrews, Greeks, and Romans.[140] No doubt, the structure of the composition bears witness to the continued salience of Carolingian dynastic succession for Regino. This is amply illustrated throughout, but perhaps most conspicuously by two features of the *Chronicle*. The first was Regino's choice to end Book I with the death of Charles Martel, "most warlike and most victorious prince of the Franks."[141] The second was his complete reliance on the *ARF* not only as a source of information but also as a conceptual model that informed his outlook on the Carolingians.[142] Without delving into the question of Regino's authorial agenda and his attendant political affiliation, both of which have garnered a range of scholarly answers, one can affirm that Carolingian ascent and decline, transfer of power, and royal performance were of utmost interest to him. Since, according to the *Chronicle*, Carolingian power was on the decline

---

[138] After 813 Regino became increasingly short of sources. His solutions are outlined in West, "Knowledge of the Past." It was only around 870 that he began to rely significantly on personal knowledge.

[139] MacLean, *History and Politics*, pp. 16–17 and p. 120, n. 420; West, "Knowledge of the Past," p. 150; Airlie, "Sad Stories," pp. 119–120, on the *Chronicle*'s "thematic unity."

[140] Regino, *Chronicle*, p. 1: "Indignum etenim mihi visum est, ut, cum Hebreorum, Grecorum et Romanorum aliarumque gentium historiographi res in diebus suis gestas scriptis usque ad nostrum notitiam transmiserint, de nostris quamquam longe inferioribus temporibus ita perpetuum silentium sit, ut quasi in diebus nostris aut hominum actio cessaverit aut fortassis nil dignum, quod memoriae fuerit commendandum, egerint aut, si res dignae memoratu gestae sunt, nullus ad haec litteris mandanda idoneus inventus fuerit, notariis per incuriam otio torpentibus"; McKitterick, *Perceptions of the Past*, pp. 30–32.

[141] Regino, *Chronicle*, a.655–718, p. 37: "Anno XXVI regni sui Carolus bellicosissimus et victoriossimus princeps Francorum moritur." For Regino's appraisal of the Carolingian past, see West, "Knowledge of the Past."

[142] Regino, *Chronicle*, a.813, p. 73; C.M. Booker, *Past Convictions: The Penance of Louis the Pious and the Decline of the Carolingians* (Philadelphia, PA: University of Pennsylvania Press, 2009), pp. 69–73; F.C.W. Goosman, "Memorable Crises: Carolingian historiography and the making of Pippin's reign, 750–900," doctoral dissertation (University of Amsterdam, 2013), pp. 63, 73; MacLean, *History and Politics*, p. 16.

since the death of Charlemagne, Regino's attention was naturally drawn to the vacuum that was left after great kings departed. Regino was known to "retro-project" his late ninth-century sensibilities onto his sixth- and seventh-century subjects, so we would be right to suspect that the way he chose to tell the Merovingian story reveals something about his perceptions of power and its vicissitudes.

The construction of Dagobert in Regino's *Chronicle* is therefore especially telling. Dagobert became a Merovingian Charlemagne of sorts, in the limited sense that his death was the point of dynastic decline, although this was not nearly as drawn-out a process as was its Carolingian parallel. In order to evaluate the role of Dagobert and the Merovingians in Regino's *Chronicle*, as I intend to do in the following pages, it is necessary to consider the way the author used his two main sources for this particular theme and timeframe—the *LHF* and the *Gesta Dagoberti*—and what this usage reveals about his own conceptual approaches to Frankish history. In addition, one must consider how these sources were worked into the greater tapestry that was the *Chronicle*, and how the placement of certain entries in specific points along the narrative arc served to modify their original meaning.

* * *

The coverage of the first centuries after Christ was dominated in Regino's *Chronicle* by Bede's *World Chronicle*, which Regino used to report on eastern affairs, such as the deaths and appointments of emperors, wars, and notable ecclesiastical events. Regino also followed Bede in recording the history of papal Rome, Britain, and other western provinces.[143] As noted by Geoffrey Koziol, this was not blatant borrowing. Regino heavily abbreviated and ideologically modified the information found in his source.[144] Gradually, additional sources began to appear, first Ado's *Martyrology* and then the *Liber pontificalis*, although they continued to be structured around details gleaned from Bede. The *Martyrology* and the *Liber pontificalis* are texts concerned with the memorialization of saints and with papal power, two themes that were of interest to Regino.[145] Most importantly, by incorporating them, he was able to hollow out Bede's emphasis on the accomplishments of emperors, transforming them into narrative prefaces to the histories of martyrs and popes.[146] In his portrayal of the fifth century, Regino began to incorporate hagiographical sources and decretals, again used to supplement yearly entries built primarily around Bede, while for

---

[143] See, for instance, Bede, *World Chronicle*, a.4557 and Regino, *Chronicle*, a.517–537, p. 25, reporting on Hermenegild's rebellion, Reccared's ascent to the Gothic kingship, and the adoption of Catholicism alongside Pope Gregory's English mission.
[144] Koziol, "The Future of History"; Burgess and Kulikowski, *Mosaics of Time*, p. 267.
[145] MacLean, *History and Politics*, pp. 24–25; Airlie, "Sad Stories," p. 116.
[146] Koziol, "The Future of History," pp. 17–20.

events in Italy, Paul the Deacon's *History of the Lombards* came into common use.

It is interesting to note that in Regino's account, the Franks arrived on the scene only with Clovis. Despite his reliance on the *LHF*, Regino omitted all of the events that preceded Clovis, which in the *LHF* and other compositions provided not only the overall rationale for the Franks' arrival in Gaul, but also a wealth of mythological and historical material. This is what Regino had to say about Clovis:

Clovis, king of the Franks, ruled for thirty years in Gaul, killed the patrician Syagrius, and drove out Gundobad king of Burgundy. He made the Alamanni his tributaries, and in the fifteenth year of his reign was baptized with the Franks by Remigius bishop of Rheims. Vedast was appointed bishop of Arras by St. Remigius.[147] *Mamertus, bishop of Vienne, instituted three-day litanies before the Ascension of the Lord.*

Clovis fought Alaric, king of the Goths, in Aquitaine near Poitiers and took both his reign and his life. Amalaric, son of Alaric, obtained his father's rule in Spain. Emperor Anastasius sent Clovis royal gifts.

Clovis killed his kinsman and co-ruler Reginarius.[148] *From the death of St. Martin to that of Clovis passed 112 years. His four children, Theuderic, Chlodomer, Childebert, and Chlothar divided between them their father's kingdom.*[149]

Regino chose to begin his treatment of the Franks no earlier than Clovis.[150] It is possible to see how the Trojan storyline would indeed have collided with Regino's chronological framing, anchored as it was in

---

[147] This sentence was probably taken from the *Vita Vedastis*. See Jonas of Bobbio, *Vita Vedastis episcopi Atrebatensis*, MGH SRG 37, ed. B. Krusch (Hanover and Leipzig: Hahnsche Buchhandlung, 1905), pp. 295–320, at ch. 5, p. 313.

[148] On the usage of the term *consors regni*, primarily as it related to royal spouses, see P. Delogu, "Consors regni: un problema carolingio?," *Bulletino dell'Istituto storico italiano per il medio evo* 76 (1964), pp. 47–98; F.-R. Erkens, "'Sicut Esther regina': Die westfränkische Königin als *consors regni*', *Francia* 20, 1 (1993), pp. 15–38; C. La Rocca, "Consors regni: A Problem of Gender? The Consortium between Amalasuntha and Theodahad in 534," in *Gender and Historiography: Studies in the Earlier Middle Ages in Honour of Pauline Stafford*, eds. J. Nelson, S. Reynolds, and S.M. Johns (London: Institute of Historical Research, 2012), pp. 127–144; A. Fößel, "Gender and Rulership in the Medieval German Empire," *History Compass* 7, 1 (2009), pp. 55–65; S. MacLean, *Ottonian Queenship* (Oxford: Oxford University Press, 2017), pp. 33–44, 119–152, and elsewhere.

[149] Regino, *Chronicle*, a.421–449, pp. 19–20: "Glodoveus rex Francorum in Gallias regnat XXX annos, Siagrium patricium interficit, Gumbadum regem de Burgundia expulit, Alamannos tributarios fecit, anno XV regni sui a sancto Remigio Remorum episcopo una cum Francis baptizatur. Atrabatus Vedastus episcopus ordinatur a sancto Remigio. Mamertus episcopus Viennensis ecclesiae triduanas letanias instituit ante ascensionem Domini. Clodoveus cum Alarico, rege Gothorum, in Aquitaniam iuxta Pictavis confligit eumque regno et vita privat. Amalricus filius Alarici in Hispaniam regnum paternum obtinuit. Anastasius imperator Clodoveo dona regia mittit. Clodoveus Reginarium propinquum atque consortem regni interficit. A transitu sancti Martini usque ad mortem Clodovei sunt anni CXII. Quatuor filii eius Theodoricus, Clodomerus, Childebertus et Chlotharius regnum patris inter se diviserunt."

[150] On this, see MacLean, *History and Politics*, p. 86, n.213.

the Incarnation. Regino did not provide *origines gentium* for any of the other nations, and while the Franks were meant to function as the centerpiece of the composition, theirs was by no means a solo act. Clovis was thus a natural point of departure, and yet even his career was treated with relative brevity. Main points in the king's life were mentioned, but while they were delivered chronologically, no attempt was made to weave them into a coherent narrative. Subsequent generations of Merovingians were similarly dispensed with. The period spanning 511 to *ca.* 620 holds eight pages in the MGH edition, most of which are concerned with events outside Francia and reliant on sources other than the *LHF*.

Since Regino made extensive use of Paul the Deacon, in his *Chronicle* we are privy to information about the Franks that is absent from the *LHF*, such as Childebert II's Italian and Spanish involvement, his appointment of Tassilo as duke of Bavaria, and his various Byzantine entanglements.[151] Other, primarily hagiographical, sources complete the picture in Gaul throughout this time. The result is a thematic block of Frankish history dependent mainly on the *LHF*, with supplementary information taken from Paul the Deacon and hagiography. Frankish kings were not simply placeholders for martyrs and important bishops, however. Their actions were recounted for their own sakes, and together they made up a coherent section that began with Clovis, the first Christian king, and ran until Dagobert, for whom a new source, the *Gesta Dagoberti*, was introduced:

At that time Arnulf was mayor of King Chlothar's palace, a man beloved by God, who would later distinguish himself and, after achieving worldly glory, placed himself in Christ's admirable service and rose to the episcopacy. When Dagobert, son of Chlothar, was a young boy, he was entrusted to him (i.e., Arnulf) by his father, so that he would rear him according to his wisdom and show him the path of the Christian religion.[152] *Then, when he reached adulthood, he had Sa(n)dregisel, duke of Aquitaine and his father's beloved counselor, whose obstinacy he despised, whipped and his beard shaven. When his father learned of this, he summoned him to be punished. Fearing the fury of his father, he escaped to the basilica of St. Dionysius and his associates and implored humbly for their protection. Because of the merits of these helpers, he could not be pulled out until such a time as the father forgave him. After that he cherished this place above all others and thereafter endowed it with many gifts and with numerous rewards. Later, he would be sent by his father to reign with Duke Pippin in Austrasia and to commend himself to the counsel of Arnulf, bishop of Metz.*[153]

---

[151] Regino, *Chronicle*, a.517–537, p. 25. Regino refers to Tassilo as "super Baiovariam ... dux," and not, as Paul reports, "His diebus Tassilo a Childeperto rege Francorum aput Baioariam rex ordinatus est." See Paul the Deacon, *HL* (*Historia Langobardorum*), IV.7.

[152] This is not the first mention Regino makes of Dagobert. Earlier, he used a phrase from the *LHF* to introduce him. See *LHF*, ch. 35; Regino, *Chronicle*, a.510–516, p. 24.

[153] Regino of Prüm, *Chronicle*, a.546–571, p. 28: "Per idem tempus fuit maior domus in palatio Chlotharii regis Arnulfus, vir, ut postmodum claruit, Deo amabilis, qui post gloriam seculi Christi se servitio subdens mirabilis in episcopatu extitit. Huic Dagobertus filius

212 *Omni ecclesiastica dignitate nobilitavit*

From what was one of the *Gesta Dagoberti*'s most dramatic and memorable scenes remained a barebones version, the relationship with Sadregisel was flattened, and the miraculous intercession of Dionysius and his associates was almost entirely deflated.[154] Dagobert continued to surface in the plot as events in his life synchronized with Regino's general chronological progression. The next reference to Dagobert is to his role in the Saxon wars fought under his father. Although the story originated with the *LHF*, this was clearly not the direct source, since the location of the episode in the Dagobert storyline mirrored its placement in the *Gesta Dagoberti*, after the appointment to the Austrasian subkingship. Next, we learn of Chlothar's death and of Dagobert's ascent to the Frankish throne, followed by the elimination of Charibert's uncle Brunulf (i.e., Brodulf).

As quickly becomes apparent, Regino selectively quarried the *Gesta Dagoberti* for historical facts about Dagobert's life. The *LHF* covered Dagobert with no more than a paragraph, so it was less than adequate for Regino's needs. The *Gesta Dagoberti* primarily built on *Fredegar*'s elaborate treatment, and so had much more to offer Regino than the *LHF*. The vast sections of the work devoted to religious patronage were gone, however, and with them much of the *Gesta Dagoberti*'s authorial agenda. What remained was a historical précis, which, in fact, bears considerable similarity to *Fredegar* in terms of narrative content and progression.

Be that as it may, Regino delivered a very favorable account of Dagobert's reign:

After St. Arnulf's departure Dagobert still took counsel from Pippin the mayor of the palace and Cuni(ch)bert, bishop of the city of Cologne, was strongly admonished by them, embracing the love of prosperity and justice, and was held in high regard by all the people who were subject to him. He had a son by a certain girl named Regintrude, whom his brother Charibert came to Orléans to receive from the holy font. For when Bishop Amandus blessed this boy and admitted him to the catechumenate, and, at the end of the service none responded Amen, the Lord opened the mouth of the boy, who was no older

---

Chlotharii in annis puerilibus positus traditus est a genitore, ut eum secundum suam sapientiam enutriret eique tramitem christianae religionis ostenderet. Hic, postquam ad virilem aetatem pervenit, Sandragisilum ducem Aquitaniae et percarum consiliarium patris, eo quod se quadam contumatia despiceret, verberibus affecit et barbae rasione deturpavit. Quod cum pater cognovisset, eum ad supplicia requirit. Ille furorem patris timens in basilicam sanctorum Dionisii et sociorum eius confugit eorumque tutelam supplex exposcit. Quorum suffragantibus meritis a nullo potuit inde extrahi, quousque commissum facinus pater indulgeret. Unde et illum potissimum pre ceteris dilexit locum, ubi postmodum ingentia dona contulit et numerosa predia dedit. Post haec Dagobertus cum Pippino duce in Austria regnaturus a patre dirigitur et sancti Arnulfi Metensis episcopi consiliis commendatur."

[154] See MacLean, *History and Politics*, p. 102, n.315.

than forty days, and with everyone listening responded Amen. This boy was called Sigibert.
[Bishop Arnulf and Abbot Romaric were important].

In that year, the legates of King Dagobert Servatus and Paternus returned from Constantinople, and the emperor requested from Dagobert that he order all the Jews of his kingdom baptized according to the Catholic faith or that he expel them from the kingdom, since indeed he learned from the signs of the stars that, by God's will, his empire would be devastated by circumcised peoples. The king certainly carried this out with utmost care, yet this was to be demonstrated to the emperor not by the Jews, but by the circumcised Saracens.

After this Charibert died, having left a small son by the name of Chilperic,[155] who also died a short while later. The kingdom that he had went to Dagobert.

Grimoald, king of the Lombards, entered into a most enduring peace treaty with Dagobert.[156]

This particular sequence is a composite of several texts, most importantly the *Gesta Dagoberti*, but also the *Vita Arnulfi* and Paul's *History of the Lombards*, all of which coalesce to produce a very complimentary image of the king. The *Vita Arnulfi* was not as unremittingly laudatory as the *Gesta Dagoberti* had been. In fact, it contained a scene that portrayed Dagobert as a murderous obstacle to Arnulf's ascetic aspirations:

But when an unbreakable desire urged him [i.e., Arnulf] *to hasten to the desert, King Dagobert, who wanted and deemed it wise to intimidate him with threats because he did not wish to go without his counsel and solace, said to him: "Your lovely sons are doomed, unless you remain with us, because I will behead them." To this he responded: "The life of*

---

[155] Extant manuscripts of the *Gesta Dagoberti* which include the relevant chapter contain variations on the name Childeric. See *Gesta Dagoberti*, p. 410, n.c. (cap. 25); for examples of this, see Paris, BnF Reg. lat. 5569, f.37v and Vatican, BAV Reg. lat. 571, f.103v. Consequently, Regino may have been consulting another composition or a different, now lost, recension of the *Gesta Dagoberti*.

[156] Regino, *Chronicle*, a.605–611, p. 31: "Post discessum igitur beati Arnulfi adhuc consilio Pippini maioris domus et Cunichberti ponitificis urbis Coloniae Dagobertus utens, ob ipsis fortiter admonitus, prosperitatis et iustitiae amorem complexus, universarum sibi gentium subditarum favoribus extollebatur. Habuit filium ex quadam puella nomine Regintruda, quem frater eius Heribertus Aurelianis veniens de sacro fonte suscepit. Namque dum eundem puerum Amandus episcopus benediceret eumque caticuminum faceret, finita oratione cum nemo respondisset Amen, aperuit Dominus os pueri, qui non amplius quam XL dies habebat, et cunctis audientibus respondit Amen. Vocatus est idem puer Sigibertus. [Arnulfus episcopus et Romaricus abba clari habentur]. Eo anno legati regis Dagoberti Servatus et Paternus a Constantinopoli regressi sunt, petiitque imperator Dagobertum, ut omnes Iudeos regni sui secundum fidem catholicam baptizare preciperet aut de regno expelleret, siquidem in siderum signis cognoverat, quod a circumcisis gentibus divino nutu eius imperium esset vastandum. Et rex quidem hoc summo peregit studio, sed imperatori non de Iudeis, sed de Sarracenis circumcisis fuerat demonstrandum. Post haec Heribertus moritur reliquens filium parvulum nomine Helpricum, qui etiam paulo post moritur. Regnum, quod tenuerat, ad Dagobertum transiit. Grimaldus rex Langobardorum cum Dagoberto pacis firmissimae foedus iniit." On the delegation, see P.S. Barnwell, "War and Peace: Historiography and Seventh-Century Embassies," *Early Medieval Europe* 6, 2 (1997), pp. 127–139, at p. 130.

my sons is in God's hand; you forfeit control of your own life when you wish to take the life of innocents." The king grew angry at him and drew his blade. Then the blessed Arnulf, who thought nothing of dying by the king's wrath, firmly said: *"What are you doing, you wretch? You wish to repay my good with evil? Look, I am ready now! Wield your weapon to shed my blood, if your soul so desires. I do not hesitate to die for his commands, he who gave me life and who died for me."* Then one of the nobles said: *"Do not do this to yourself, o good king; do you not see that the holy man is destined for martyrdom and desires it, so why are you not fearful of hurting the servant of the Lord Christ?"* And with this said, by God's command, his anger was quickly soothed.[157]

Dagobert came around, and Arnulf went on to have a brief but illustrious career as a hermit under the supervision of Romaric, abbot of Habendum (later, Remiremont).[158] In Regino's adaptation, details about Arnulf gleaned from the *Vita Arnulfi* were worked into appropriate timepoints in the narrative. He appeared as the Austrasian mayor of the palace for Theudebert II, a claim that was borrowed from a passage in the hagiography that dealt with Arnulf's official duties, including the administration of six provinces.[159] Regino took some liberty with the text but remained roughly loyal to the timeline of Arnulf's career. We meet Arnulf again only as the *nutritor* of Dagobert, and then, finally, upon his departure from court, and his and Romaric's renown.[160] Since Regino had already broached themes of conflict between royal and saintly power, he could have included the collision between Dagobert and Arnulf in his account. But he did not do so. Both Arnulf and Dagobert remained above

---

[157] *Vita Arnulfi*, ch. 17, p. 439: "Sed cum insolubile desiderio ad heremum properare disponeret, voluit et suspicatus est prudens rex Dagobertus eum minis terrere, scilicet ut ab ipsius consilio vel solacio non discederet, dicens ad eum: 'Dilectissimi filii tui quia ita amissum habent, nisi nobiscum consistas, capita amputabo.' Ad haec ille respondes, dixit: 'Filiis meis vita in manu Dei est; iam tu tuam non possides vitam, quando ab insontibus vitam auferre dispones.' Tunc rex iratus adversus eum, dependentem ex publite mucronem manu arripuit. Tunc beatus Arnulfus regis morituri parvi pendens iram, constanter dixit: 'Quid agis, o miserrime? Mala pro bonis mihi rependere vis? Nunc autem hecce me paratum! Exerce arma in sanguinem meum, ut tuis libet animis. Ego pro illius mandatis mori non dubito, qui mihi et vitam dedit et pro me mortuus est.' Tunc unus procerum ait: 'Noli impie contra temet ipsum agere, o bone rex; annon vides virum sanctum destinatum et cupidum esse ad martyrium, aut quur non pertimescis Christi domini servum lacescere?' Et his dictis, iubente Deo, ira eius irritata paulisper contiguit."

[158] Fox, *Power and Religion in Merovingian Gaul*, pp. 90–99.

[159] Regino, *Chronicle*, a.517–537, p. 26: "Post idem Childebertus moritur; habebat autem duos filios, unum ex concubina, nomine Theudobertum, qui maior natu erat, alterum ex regina, nomine Theodoricum. [Huius regis maior domus fuit sanctus Arnolfus]." See also *Vita Arnulfi*, chs. 3–4, p. 433. Regino's phrasing makes it seem as though he was Theuderic's mayor, not Theudebert's.

[160] Nutritorship would have been a familiar concept for Regino from contemporary sources. For Louis IV's depiction of Adalbero as his *nutritor*, see MGH DD LdK, ed. T. Schieffer (Berlin: Weidmannsche Verlagsbuchhandlung, 1960), 4, 9, 65, pp. 100–101, 102–103, 195–196, respectively. MacLean, *History and Politics*, p. 7.

contention. The *Vita Arnulfi* was used here only insofar as it allowed Regino to date its protagonist's hermitage, not to complicate the favorable depiction of Dagobert with unnecessary conflict. Of course, Arnulf of Metz had another function, revealed much later in the text, which was to serve as the ancestor of the Carolingian family:

Year 880 of the Lord's incarnation
[...]
No offspring were born of the legitimate matrimony because of the infertility of the wife, but from a certain noblewoman he [i.e., Carloman of Bavaria] *received a son of the most elegant appearance, whom he decreed would be called Arnulf, in memory of the most reverent Arnulf, bishop of the church of Metz, of whose holy seed and that of others descended the family of the kings of the Franks.*[161]

Just as Arnulf of Metz signified the birth of the Carolingian dynasty, his eponymous descendant, Arnulf of Carinthia, spelled its demise. Arnulf was thus an important figure in Regino's construction of dynastic change from the Merovingians to the Carolingians, and, with his latter-day namesake, would usher in a post-Carolingian future.

Regino's treatment of saints in this period continues the approach found in the earlier sections of the *Chronicle*, although here, saints and kings serve to contextualize each other. In Columbanus's case, for example, this meant that his mention appeared after the battle between Theuderic II and Chlothar II, and before the ascent of Agilulf to the Lombard throne and Phocas's to the imperial throne, in 591 and 602, respectively. If we identify the battle depicted in *LHF*, ch. 37 as the same encounter covered in *Fredegar* IV.20, then we would be inclined to date it *ca.* 600, nine years later than a subsequent entry. The battle at the river Orvanne was taken from the *LHF*, Agilulf and Phocas from Paul, and while the chronology Regino pieced together from these two sources contained some inconsistencies, he obviously meant to place the emphasis on Columbanus's activities in the last decade of the sixth century, and within the context of Brunhild's queenship.[162] Since Regino based his chronology on an AD model, of which no equivalent existed in his sources, it was up to him to think of solutions for reconciling his timeline with works that operated

---

[161] Regino, *Chronicle*, a.880, p. 116: "Anno dominicae incarnationis DCCCLXXX. [...] Huic ex legitimo matrimonio non est nata soboles propter infecunditatem coniugis, sed ex quadam nobili femina filium elegantissimae speciei suscepit, quem Arnolfum nominari iussit, ob recordationem reverentissimi Arnolfi, Metensis ecclesiae episcopi, de cuius sancto germine sua aliorumque regum Francorum prosapia pullulaverat." See also Booker, *Past Convictions*, pp. 70–71. On Carloman and Arnulf, see J. Fried, "The Frankish Kingdoms, 817–911: The East and Middle Kingdoms," in *The New Cambridge Medieval History, Vol. II: c.700–c.900*, ed. R. McKitterick (Cambridge: Cambridge University Press, 1995), pp. 142–168.

[162] On Regino's approach to chronology, see MacLean, *History and Politics*, pp. 20–23.

under very different premises. For this to work, he was forced to make some compromises, which meant that the natural narrative rhythm of the sources was condensed, dilated, or reordered.

* * *

Dagobert's penultimate mention addressed his wars with the Slavs and the Bulgars, and his dealings with Sisenand. Regino then bid him farewell with an account of the king's *divisio regni*, his death, burial, and eulogy:

> *King Dagobert came to Metz and with the counsel of the bishops and magnates placed his son Sigibert on the Austrasian throne and commended him to Chuni(ch)bert bishop of Cologne and to Duke Pippin.*
>
> *The following year he had a son by Queen Nanthechild, whom he named Clovis; he ordered that the kingdom of Neustria and Burgundy be given to him* (i.e., to Clovis) *after his own death.*
>
> *After this Dagobert died and was buried in the basilica of Saint-Denis; he was farsighted in counsel, cautious in judgement, vigorous in military training, generous in alms and zealous in ensuring the peace of the churches, and in particular devoted to enriching the monasteries of the saints. However much he cultivated all holy places, still he endowed above all others the monasteries of Sts Dionysius, Martin, and Maurice and ennobled them with every ecclesiastical dignity. His realm, just as he divided it when he was alive, was ruled by his sons. Aega the mayor of the palace and Queen Nanthechild governed Clovis's realm.*[163]

King Clovis II is only mentioned once, very briefly. It comes as no surprise to discover which of his deeds made it into the *Chronicle*:

> *King Clovis uncovered the body of the blessed Dionysius and, less religiously than desirously, broke off and carried away the bone of his arm: immediately stunned, he lapsed into insanity and after two years ended his life and his reign.*[164]

It is with this episode that Regino chose to end his account of the Merovingians; Dagobert was to be their swansong. His successor, Clovis, was remembered solely for his transgression against the saint

---

[163] Regino, *Chronicle*, a.612–631, p. 33: "Dagobertus rex Mettis veniens cum consilio pontificum et procerum filium suum Sigibertum in regno Austriae sublimat eumque Cuni(ch)berto episcopo Coloniensis ecclesiae et Pippino duci commendat. Sequenti anno ei filius natus est ex Nantilde regina, quem Ludowicum appellavit; cui regnum Neptricum atque Burgundiae dandum post suum discessum denominavit. Post haec idem Dagobertus moritur et in basilica sancti Dionisii sepelitur; fuit autem providus in consilio, cautus in iudicio, strenuus in militari disciplina, largus in elemosinis, studiosus in componenda pace ecclesiarum et precipue devotus in ditandis sanctorum coenobiis. Qui quamvis omnia loca sancta excoluisset, tamen pre ceteris monasteria sanctorum Dionisii, Martini atque Mauricii excoluit et omni ecclesiastica dignitate nobilitavit. Regnum eius, sicut ipse vivens diviserat, filii eius tenuerunt. Ega maior domus cum Nantilda regina regnum Ludowici administrat."

[164] Regino, *Chronicle*, a.635–641, p. 34: "Ludowicus rex corpus beati Dionisii discooperiens minus religiose, licet cupide, os brachii eius fregit et rapuit: confestimque stupefactus in amentiam incidit et post duos annos vitam cum regno finivit."

and after him, the dynasty was relegated to oblivion. Regino depended on Dionysian compositions as his main sources. The *Gesta Dagoberti* was a distinct product and a vocal proponent of Saint-Denis's interests; the same may have been true of the *LHF*, or at least it may have been influenced by such traditions. Thus, it is not entirely unexpected that Dagobert was portrayed so favorably and Clovis so poorly. Yet Regino was also attempting something new, because in his *Chronicle* the Merovingians do not simply decline, they fail immediately once Dagobert is dead.[165]

Coverage of the Merovingians effectively ended in Regino with Clovis II's removal of St. Dionysius's arm and his subsequent descent into madness. The *Gesta Dagoberti* carried Regino this far, although the *LHF* could have carried him much farther, had he so wished, since it contained an account until the year 727. But Regino did not return to the *LHF*. Instead, he went to Paul the Deacon for information about Pippin II and Charles Martel. Given what has already been said about Paul's framing of early Carolingian history in the *GeM*, it is not surprising to see Regino use Paul to diminish the role of the later Merovingians and to provide an outsized one for the earliest Carolingians. Yet even Paul was aware that the Merovingians did not vanish after Clovis II.[166]

The *Gesta Dagoberti*'s alarmist conclusion undoubtedly informed Regino's account, as did Paul the Deacon's overall approach to the later Merovingians. But the decision to end the Merovingian story with Clovis II, when evidence of its endurance was available to Regino in the *LHF* and Paul, was a conscious one, based on his ideas of Carolingian ascent that were likely informed by the *ARF*. When Regino did return to Paul, it was to report the following:

Among the Franks, Pippin died, and his son Charles succeeded him as ruler, who through many battles and struggles took it from Reginfrid's hand. Because when he (i.e., Reginfrid) *held him* (i.e., Charles) *in custody, by God's wishes he escaped, and within two or three days went into battle against Reginfrid with few followers. In the end he* (i.e., Charles) *defeated him in a great struggle at Vichy. He gave him, so they say, one city— Angers—in which to reside, and he himself took governance over all of the Franks.*[167]

---

[165] Although similar motifs can be seen in Erchanbert's *Breviarium regum Francorum*, ed. Ussermann, *Germaniae sacrae prodomus* 2 vols. (St. Blasian, 1790), 1, pp. xli–lii, at p. xlv: "Post non multum rex (i.e., Chlothar) praefatum Pippinum in Austris cum filio suo iam adulto Dagoberto misit, ibidem eum regem constituendum, ipsumque ei in Maiorem domus ac paedagogum constituens." See Goosman, "Memorable Crises," pp. 190–191.

[166] See, for instance, a reference to Dagobert II in Paul the Deacon, *Historia Langobardorum*, MGH SRL, eds. L. Bethmann and G. Waitz (Hanover: Hahnsche Buchhandlung, 1878), pp. 12–187, at p.32. Whether Paul was indeed naming the correct king here is questionable, although he was certainly aware of him.

[167] Regino, *Chronicle*, a.642–647, p. 35: "Apud Francorum quoque gentem Pippino vita exempto eius filius Karolus in principatu successit, licet per multa bella et certamina de

Reginfrid (i.e., Ragamfred) was, of course, not working alone, as the author of the *LHF* knew very well.[168] But Regino drew a veil over the involvement of Chilperic II in Charles Martel's ascent to power.[169] This was a fight between two nobles, in which Charles prevailed and came to rule the entirety of the Frankish kingdom. From then on, while he is often termed *princeps* in the *Chronicle*, Martel is described as the sole power in every regard. The *Chronicle* provides his regnal years (*Anno V° regni sui* [. . .]), and does not refer, even indirectly, to the existence of kings under whose nominal authority he was acting.

Had the paragraph devoted to Martel's ascent been influenced by a source that obscured the late Merovingian period, one might draw the conclusion that Regino was merely following its lead. Since it was inspired by Paul, it would be correct to say that Regino chose to regard the *History of the Lombards*' account of the late Merovingians, however cursory it might have been, as an expendable, indeed an undesirable, part of the plot. The period between the death of Clovis II (658) and the death of Pippin II (714) spanned fifty-six years, which were covered in a brief section taken mostly from Paul that concerned imperial affairs and Ansbrand the Bavarian's unsuccessful invasion of Italy. Quite obviously, Regino meant for the late Merovingians to languish in obscurity, with Clovis II's impiousness as the dynasty's enduring monument. The Carolingians in Regino did not so much replace the Merovingians as emerge to fill a regnal vacancy. This was decided upon through contest between prominent magnates, a reality that would have been all too familiar to Regino.

We catch a final glimpse of the Merovingians in the entry for the year 749:

In the 749th year of the Incarnation, Burchard, bishop of the church of Würzburg, and Fulrad the capellanus were sent to Rome to Pope Zacharias, to ask him whether it is right that the kings of Francia, who at the time had no royal power, should be called kings or not. And the aforementioned pope answered Pippin that it seems preferable to him that he who has the power be called king rather than the one who has no royal power; and so that Christianity is not thrown into disorder, by the apostolic authority he decreed that Pippin be created king and anointed with the oil of unction.[170]

---

manu Reginfridi eundem principatum sustulerit. Nam cum in custodia teneretur, divino nutu ereptus aufugit ac primum contra Regimfridum cum paucis bis terque certamen iniit, ad extremum eum apud Vinciacum magno certamine superavit. Cui tamen unam, ut ferunt, hoc est Andegavensem civitatem ad habitandum concessit, cunctam vero Francorum gentem ipse gubernandam suscepit."

[168] For a discussion of the *LHF*'s treatment of Charles Martel and Ragamfred, see Fouracre, *The Age of Charles Martel*, pp. 64–65.

[169] Unlike the *Annales Mettenses Priores* (*AMP*), which features Chilperic II extensively from 716 to 720. See *AMP*, pp. 21–26.

[170] Regino, *Chronicle*, a.749, p. 43: "Anno dominicae incarnationis DCCXLVIIII Burchardus Wirziburgensis ecclesiae episcopus et Folradus capellanus missi sunt Romae ad Zachariam

As noted by Stuart Airlie and Charles West, Regino's account framed the ninth century as a prelude to the ensuing disintegration of Carolingian power in the early tenth, a model that would impact generations of later historians.[171] It clearly had much to say about the Carolingians' climb to power, in which the Merovingians played their part *in absentia*. While Regino did not entirely expunge the Merovingians from the historical record, he skirted the need to mention them directly in his coverage of the last century of their rule. It is difficult to tease out any concrete lessons from this treatment, since there is so little to go on. Even the reasoning that underlay the decline of the Merovingians was extracted from the sources at Regino's disposal and cannot be considered his own. If anything, his approach bears an imprint of the *ARF*, yet his argument ended up very far from that profoundly influential chronicle. Regino recognized that the Carolingian project and its underlying ideologies, expressed so forcefully in previous historiographies, were as ephemeral as any other, a point remarked upon by Airlie and Koziol.[172] We might wish to interpret his willingness to forget the late Merovingians in this same vein. *Fortuna* would dispense of the Carolingians much as it had done their unsung predecessors.

With regard to the question of how Regino perceived the Merovingians, we might be able to agree that he restricted their historical role to the period that spanned one King Clovis to another (481–658). Perhaps the symmetry with the Carolingian Arnulf, who played a similar role for the Carolingians, was meant to harbor some meaning. Regino's treatment of the Merovingians could also have been intended as a brief lesson in how quickly the impressive achievements of the past evaporate under poor leadership. Yet, more than anything, the choice to conclude with Dagobert and Clovis II is an indication of the pervasiveness of Saint-Denis's influence on the historiographical treatment of the Merovingians, and its effects on models of periodization we encounter in works composed outside Saint-Denis.

---

papam, ut interrogarent de regibus in Francia, qui illis temporibus non habentes regiam potestatem reges tamen vocabantur, si bene esset an non? Et prefatus papa mandavit Pippino, melius sibi videri, illum regem vocari, qui potestatem haberet, quam illum, qui sine regali potestatem manebat; et ne perturbaretur christianitatis ordo, per auctoritatem apostolicam iussit Pippinum regem creari et sanctae unctionis oleo inungi." Compare *ARF* a.749, p. 8. On Regino's treatment of Carloman, see Goosman, "Memorable Crises," pp. 151–158. On this passage and the events it depicted, see R. McKitterick, "The Illusion of Royal Power in Carolingian Annals," *English Historical Review* 115, 460 (2000), pp. 1–20.
[171] West, "Knowledge of the Past," p. 158.
[172] Airlie, "Sad Stories," p. 108; Koziol, "The Future of History," pp. 16–17.

The character of Dagobert Regino found in his source was undoubtedly trimmed down to fit the restricted boundaries of genre. After all, Regino was writing a chronicle, and simply could not devote any more attention to Dagobert than he already did. His authorial approach made much of the information he found in his sources, such as Dagobert's donations to Saint-Denis, redundant anyway. As a result, most of the material about the king's interaction with the saints and his generosity toward their shrines was removed. But Saint-Denis's framing endured. In the end, Regino went farther than the monks of Saint-Denis ever had reason to go, using their construction of Dagobert and Clovis II to mark the dynasty's zenith and its ensuing collapse, in preparation for the vision presented by his next main source, the *ARF*.

4.3   Conclusions

The route that the character of Dagobert took from *Fredegar* to the *Gesta Dagoberti* and then to Regino's *Chronicle* is interesting for many reasons, chief among them the fact that it twice traversed generic boundaries while remaining essentially intact. If anything, this is evidence of the inability of generic taxonomy to map on to the intricacies of the transmission process. Despite the similarities between the ways the Dagobert story unfolded in these three compositions, the character itself was employed to serve altogether different aims. For the *Fredegar* chronicler, Dagobert was a vivid memory. The chronicle was completed *ca*. 660, a generation after Dagobert died, in a world whose geopolitical contours were not much different than the ones the late king left behind. Austrasia and Neustria-Burgundy were the main political entities that defined the world of *Fredegar*, and many of the same factional dynamics that the chronicler described persisted from the time of Dagobert. The king's career could be used to impart lessons about good kingship, counsel, and delegation of authority that were applicable to the chronicler's own audience. In particular, *Fredegar* spoke to the anxiety felt in Austrasian circles about royal authority or absence thereof. Ever since 613, the choice to rule from Paris was a strain on the relationship between the royal court and the Austrasian elites, among whose effects *Fredegar* mentioned military demoralization, factional enmity, and moral depravity. The solutions that were adopted were often imperfect, although an Austrasian subkingship, meant as a period of apprenticeship, and delegated to the older royal heir, seems to have gained overall acceptance. The 660s, during which Austrasia was reeling from the effects of the Grimoald coup, were a perfect time in which to revisit the successes and failures of Dagobert, lessons that would surely have made sense to contemporary and, indeed, later readers.

The *Gesta Dagoberti* constructed its plot around the report found in the *Fredegar* chronicle, but the character that emerged was unique. Royal misconduct and its consequences were not the lessons the author of the *Gesta Dagoberti* wished to impart. The composition was clearly concerned with the proprietary aspects of Saint-Denis's relationship with centers of ecclesiastical and royal power, and its employment of the Dagobert character voiced this concern forcefully. The *Gesta Dagoberti* eliminated controversial aspects of the king's career and made his relationship with the saints the axis around which the plot revolved. The composition is also important for its decision to identify the change in Merovingian tides with the death of Dagobert, a model of periodization that was adopted and adapted in subsequent compositions. That Clovis II was chosen as the one responsible for this decline had to do, in Dionysian writing at least, with his transgression against the relics of the saint. While Dagobert's generous patronage of monasteries brought him political and military success, Clovis's mismanagement of his monastic responsibilities had the opposite results. This was a necessary conclusion to the *Gesta Dagoberti*'s rationale, but it is doubtful that the monks of Saint-Denis experienced the period after Clovis II as one of sustained collapse.[173]

Much of the donative and pietistic elements of the *Gesta Dagoberti* were ill-suited for the type of work Regino was doing. Some of the storylines particular to the *Gesta Dagoberti*, such as Sadregisel's downfall, were kept, although they were stripped of ethical baggage and treated as any other event in Dagobert's life. Importantly, Regino managed to discard much of the ninth-century additions without damaging Dagobert's coherence as a character.

In Regino's work, the coverage devoted to the Merovingians was limited. We should not examine Dagobert in isolation from the rest of the Merovingian storyline, or indeed from the entire plot, which was obviously more ambitious in scope. Dagobert remained beyond reproach in Regino, although we know that this was done using sources that offered competing portrayals, primarily the *Vita Arnulfi*. It is thus apparent that Dagobert had a role to play in Regino's schema. By casting him as the last effective Merovingian and his son Clovis as the ruin of the Frankish kingdom and the last pre-Carolingian ruler whose existence he

---

[173] This point is obviously strengthened if we choose to regard the *LHF* as a Dionysian composition. For Clovis II as a Carolingian, see Spiegel, "*Reditus regni*," p. 152; G. Sommers, "A Royal Tomb Program in the Reign of St. Louis," *The Art Bulletin* 56, 2 (1974), pp. 224–243, at pp. 238–241. This is discussed in the subsequent chapter.

acknowledged, Regino introduced a *caesura*, both chronological and narratological, between the period of Merovingian decline and that of Pippinid ascent. His choice to do this was naturally connected to the portrayal he found in the *ARF*, but it went further than either the *ARF* or Dionysian sources in eliminating the late Merovingians altogether. While in Regino's *Chronicle* the final Merovingian kings were anonymous and entirely ineffectual, other sources, such as the ones we shall meet in the next chapter, took a rather different approach.

Part III

Dogs and Lesser Beasts

5 *Regibus solo nomine regnantibus*: The Late Merovingians

The story of Merovingian decline is inextricably linked to that of Carolingian ascent.[1] This coupling is reflected in the historiographical record, which, as we have seen, has adopted various tactics in recounting the demise of the first royal dynasty. Some chroniclers, such as Ado of Vienne, attempted to push back the timeline of Merovingian degeneration to the period after Clovis I, while others, such as Frechulf of Lisieux and Regino of Prüm, ended the story 100 years too early, essentially omitting the final chapter of Merovingian history. Whether this revision was due to the sources they had at hand, contemporary political realities that precluded the possibility of presenting effective late Merovingian kings as part of the narrative, or some combination of the two, what we receive is a fundamentally Carolingian take on the period from 650 to 750.

As we have also seen, other voices have not entirely been silenced. The *Gesta Dagoberti* sang the praises of a Merovingian king in the 830s, a period both of unquestionable regional Carolingian dominance and dangerous internal instability, making the composition a unique feature in the literary landscape. All in all, however, it is difficult to escape the conclusion that Carolingian historiography's tendency to either malign or ignore the Merovingians had a decisive effect on the way that their later years would be remembered. In this chapter, I would like to move away from Carolingian compositions in order to evaluate to what extent this dire view of the last Merovingian century persisted in later historiographical works.

It would perhaps be redundant to tell early twenty-first-century readers that the view of the late Merovingians as nothing more than puppets has held up poorly under recent scholarly scrutiny. If we take the *LHF* at its word, the Merovingians were still a realistic source of political legitimacy, around which Neustrian aristocrats could rally well into the 710s. The

[1] Sigebert of Gembloux, *Chronica*, MGH SS 6, ed. D.L.C. Bethmann (Hanover: Hahnsche Buchhandlung, 1844), pp. 300–375, at p. 325: "Abhinc Francorum regibus a solita fortitudine et scientia degenerantibus, regni potentia disponebantur per maiores domus, regibus solo nomine regnantibus."

LHF's laudatory depiction of the reign of Childebert III (694–711) is corroborated by a long list of *placita*, evidence of a functioning system of governance able to exert its influence throughout the kingdom.[2]

Naturally, the *AMP* and the compositions it directly influenced offer a very different view.[3] Even though we have every reason to doubt the trustworthiness of an account from the early ninth century, especially on a topic like this, we have still essentially adopted its underlying assumption that Merovingian and Carolingian power were mutually exclusive.[4] This was quickly becoming the reality under Chilperic II; after his death in 721, it became truer still. Yet it would be fair to say that the Merovingian kingdom trudged along rather efficiently under Theuderic III and Childebert III, so that the Grimoald coup, the crisis of 675, and the short and unremarkable reigns of Clovis III and Dagobert III should be regarded more as ephemeral periods of instability than as evidence that the machinery of state was coming apart, or, alternatively, that the Pippinids were now firmly at its helm. This is not to say that Pippin II and Charles Martel were insignificant players on the political scene. It is, however, possible to imagine, as did the *LHF*, a working political system built around Merovingian kingship well into the eighth century. It naturally follows that the early Pippinids strove for power without assuming, as did those with the benefit of hindsight, that their quest would only end with the displacement of the incumbent dynasty. Pippin III's decision to rid himself of his Merovingian fig leaf only became feasible when conditions ripened in the late 740s. For understandable reasons, it was retrojected onto earlier decades by Carolingian historiographers and propagandists.

Even in the depths of their *fainéance*, the Merovingians remained potent symbols. Theuderic IV and Childeric III were only elevated to the kingship to endow the early Carolingians with the semblance of legitimacy, and the fact that they were deemed necessary is telling in and of itself. Taciturn about the late Merovingians though they might

---

[2] *LHF*, ch. 49; *Fredegar*, cont. 6. See Gerberding, *The Rise of the Carolingians*, pp. 158–162; Fouracre and Gerberding, ed. and trans., *Late Merovingian France*, pp. 25–26; D. Sonzogni "Un acte de vente inédit du chartrier de Saint-Denis (11 avril 702?)," *Bibliothèque de l'école des chartes* 159, 2 (2001), pp. 609–613. Clovis's and Childebert's diplomas for Saint-Denis are found in *Diplomata*, MGH DD Merov., ed. G.H. Pertz (Hanover: Hahnsche Buchhandlung, 1872), 61 and 77, pp. 54–55, 68–69. Hen, *Culture and Religion in Merovingian Gaul*, pp. 232–233. See also Wood, *The Merovingian Kingdoms*, pp. 256, 257, 261. For a somewhat less enthusiastic appraisal of the situation under Childebert III, see B. Dumézil, *Servir l'État barbare dans la Gaule franque: IVe–IXe siècle* (Paris: Tallandier, 2013), p. 261.

[3] Wood, *The Merovingian Kingdoms*, pp. 257–258.

[4] Y. Hen, "The Annals of Metz and the Merovingian Past," in *The Uses of the Past in the Early Middle Ages*, eds. Y. Hen and M. Innes (Cambridge: Cambridge University Press, 2000), pp. 175–190.

have been, Carolingian sources betray a lingering preoccupation with questions of legitimacy. By the ninth century, this was probably not prompted by the specter of the Merovingians' return; however, it was certainly true that the Carolingians saw the need to explain and justify what they were trying to accomplish.

The success of Carolingian propaganda is evident in the adoption of its perspective in later works of historiography and hagiography. While it is now widely agreed that the death of Dagobert I did not herald the collapse of the Merovingian kingdoms, this view certainly gained traction in post-Carolingian compositions. It appears in the two sources I will present in the following chapter, the twelfth-century *Chronica* of Sigebert of Gembloux and the sixteenth-century *Sefer Divrei Hayamim leMalkei Tzarfat uVeit Otoman Hatogar* [The Book of the Histories of the Kings of France and the Turkish House of Ottoman]. Both were composed at considerable remove from the Carolingian period, yet they bear the traces of its historiography's far-reaching influence. This is especially noticeable in their periodization of the Merovingian era.

The *Chronica* of Sigebert of Gembloux is an intricate composition, threading a very large number of sources into a coherent historical vision of enormous scope, both chronologically and geographically.[5] Sigebert's return, *mutatis mutandis*, to the Eusebius-Jerome model made the *Chronica* hugely successful, warranting numerous continuations and allowing it to become the basis upon which a panoply of high and late-medieval chroniclers constructed their own narratives. It contains a relatively detailed account of the late Merovingian period, for which it relied on such works as Gregory of Tours' *Histories*, *Fredegar* and its continuations, the *LHF*, and a wide range of hagiographies dedicated to the lives of Merovingian-era saints. Bede's *Ecclesiastical History*, Paul the Deacon's *History of the Lombards*, Flodoard's *History of the Church of Reims*, and Aimoin of Fleury's *Gesta Francorum* provide additional information, giving Sigebert's Frankish account an eclectic, albeit coherent, style. The scope and depth of this work and the attention it affords the period that interests us here make it a natural candidate for investigation. Sigebert is not often portrayed by scholarship as a trailblazer, yet under his traditionalist adherence to form – primarily Eusebius-Jerome's – there is much to regard as new.[6] For instance, if Michel de Waha's arguments are to be accepted, Sigebert (or

---

[5] See Bethmann's introduction to Sigebert's *Chronica*, pp. 275–276; M. Chazan, *L'Empire et l'histoire universelle de Sigebert de Gembloux à Jean de Saint-Victor (XIIe–XIVe siècle)* (Paris: Champion, 1999), pp. 121–147, esp. pp. 129–131.

[6] For a treatment of Sigebert's historical philosophy, see J. Beumann, *Sigebert von Gembloux und der Traktat de investitura episcoporum* (Sigmaringen: Jan Thorbecke Verlag, 1976), pp. 39–44, 50–57.

a member of his entourage) forged key diplomas, in essence distorting the circumstances pertaining to the foundation of Gembloux that are depicted in his *Vita Wigberti abbatum conditoris* and *Gesta abbatum Gemblacensium*.[7] As far as the *Chronica* is concerned, Sigebert was not only prone to use past precedent to justify contemporary claims, but in so doing was responding to the ideologues of the papal camp, who were busy doing the same.[8] Determining the point wherein the transfer of power from the Merovingian kings to the Carolingian mayors took place becomes pivotal for ascertaining the role of Pope Zacharias in legitimizing Frankish kingship, which Sigebert obviously wished to minimize. The historiography of Sigebert is thus to be regarded as a creative endeavor that used the sources at its disposal, early medieval ones included, to fashion a manifesto that argued for a specific vision of the present and future. It is this that makes him interesting as a narrator of Merovingian history.

Interestingly, earlier in his career Sigebert composed a *Life* dedicated to King Sigibert III at the behest of the monks of St. Martin's in Metz, probably to mark the translation of the royal remains in 1063 and the beginning of a cult dedicated to the king.[9] The image of the king portrayed in the *Life of Sigibert* was, as one would expect of a hagiographical protagonist, spotless. The *Life* drew on the sources Sigebert was able to cobble together, and, while it is remarkably forthcoming in historical detail, it is nevertheless quite thin in the other dimensions one would expect to see in a hagiography. Because of its peculiarities, it is able to shed some light on Sigebert's earlier notions of late Merovingian history, notions that would later be developed and more fully fleshed out in the *Chronica*.

Sefer Divrei Hayamim is something of an outlier. Unlike most of the compositions surveyed in this book (with the exception of the *Grandes Chroniques de France*), it was not composed in Latin. Additionally, it was written by a Jewish physician in *cinquecento* Genoa for a Jewish readership, making it the only account authored by a non-Christian discussed in this book. Yosef Ha-Kohen's narrative program regarded the two grand forces at play in his day – the Christian West (represented primarily by the French and Habsburg states) and the Muslim Ottoman East – as sides in an epic historical struggle, in which the Jews had a pivotal role. Since Ha-Kohen focused most of his attention on contemporary and near-contemporary

---

[7] M. de Waha, "Sigebert de Gembloux faussaire? Le chroniqueur et les 'sources anciennes' de son abbaye," *Revue belge de philologie et d'histoire* 55, 4 (1977), pp. 989–1036.

[8] Beumann, *Sigebert von Gembloux*, pp. 55–57.

[9] *Historia translationis miraculorum s. Sigiberti*, AASS Feb. 1, pp. 236–237; R. Folz, *Les saints rois du Moyen Âge en Occident (VIe–XIIIe)* (Brussels: Société des Bollandistes, 1984), p. 75; M. Chazan, "Sigebert de Gembloux, un historien engagé," in *Sigebert de Gembloux*, ed. J.-P. Straus (Barcelona and Madrid: Fédération Internationale des Instituts d'Études Médiévales, 2015), pp. 1–50, at pp. 14–15.

history, the late Merovingian period received only minor coverage; the Merovingians interested Ha-Kohen only insofar as they were able to illuminate the origins of the French monarchy. Still, the later members of the dynasty are sufficiently present in Ha-Kohen's account to warrant a discussion of the reception and periodization of late Merovingian history in *Sefer Divrei Hayamim*. While his work was at times influenced by the *Grandes Chroniques*, his main source of information on the Merovingians was a history penned by an Italian humanist named Vittorio Sabino, who worked for the French court of Francis I. To be sure, these were very different sources, yet both owed much, albeit indirectly, to *Fredegar* and the *LHF*.

5.1 Eighty-eight years of *fainéance*: Sigebert of Gembloux's Late Merovingians

Sigebert of Gembloux opened his historiographical opus, the *Chronica*, thus:

With God's help, we shall say something about the contemporaneity of kingdoms, but first we shall say a little about the origins of each of the peoples; so that we are able to follow the traces of the elders, we shall keep to the paths of history. We have placed in the first line the kingdom of the Romans, in the second that of the Persians, in the third that of the Franks, in the fourth that of the Vandals, in the fifth that of the English, in the sixth that of the Lombards, in the seventh that of the Visigoths, in the eighth that of the Ostrogoths, in the ninth that of the Huns.[10]

True to his promise, Sigebert went on to recount the *origines* of each of the *gentes* he mentioned in the introductory passage. First came the Romans, whom he placed in Daniel's four-kingdom schema. Sigebert allotted very little space to imperial glories before diving into Rome's failures, against the Persians under Julian "the Apostate" and then against its own subject peoples. Those same peoples turned on Rome and dismembered it, carving kingdoms for themselves from its enormous cadaver. The fall of Rome loomed heavily over the *Chronica*, setting the stage for everything that was to follow. It was an image of decline that one would expect of a work framed as a continuation of the chronicle of Eusebius-Jerome.[11] However, Sigebert's world was very different than

---

[10] Sigebert of Gembloux, *Chronica*, p. 300: "Dicturi aliquid iuvante Deo de contemporalitate regnorum, primum pauca dicamus de origine singularium gentium; quatenus sequi poterimus vestigia maiorum, directi per semitas historiarum. Poemus in prima linea regnum Romanorum, in secunda Persarum, in tertia Francorum, in quarta Wandalorum, in quinta Anglorum, in sexta Langobardorum, in septima Visigotharum, in octava Ostrogotharum, in nona Hunorum."

[11] On Jerome's interpretation of Daniel, see M.A. Travassos Valdez, *Historical Interpretations of the "Fifth Empire": The Dynamics of Periodization from Daniel to António Vieira, S.J.* (Leiden and Boston: Brill, 2019), pp. 157–173; Chazan, *L'Empire et l'histoire*

Jerome's. While it took its structure and historiographical philosophy from Eusebius-Jerome, Sigebert's work was adapted to suit a changed reality. Still, the concept of empire played an equally central role,[12] and it guided the *Chronica*'s treatment of the Merovingians and Carolingians, as we shall see.

To the Persians, Sigebert devoted even fewer lines than he did the Romans, since, as he pointed out, the Persians were an ancient people whose histories were amply recorded in the writings of antique historians, which any reader could access.[13] He did make a point of mentioning the Persians' role in oppressing Rome and the Christians, especially under their king, Shapur. Then, Sigebert moved on to the Franks, faithfully replicating the Trojan narrative presented in the *LHF*, his main source for Merovingian history.[14] Frankish history differed from that of other nations, however, since it was a history "of our people" – *gentis nostrae*. We should not overstate this identification; Sigebert also referred to himself as a *gallus*,[15] resulting in a fusion that, for Mireille Chazan, captures an echo of his Lotharingian origins.[16] It is likely that Sigebert was a native of Hesbaye or its environs, and that his career at Gembloux would not have taken him far from home. Be that as it may, the self-identification as *francus* would have been significant to Sigebert on more than the restricted geographical level outlined by Chazan. It would have carried the full weight of Frankish history and its attendant *Geschichtsbewusstsein*. More importantly, it was the only narrative strand, other than the Roman one, that persisted throughout the composition. Other *gentes* appeared and dropped out of the *Chronica* as their fortunes waxed and waned; only Romans and Franks were covered throughout. The order in which Sigebert presented the textual blocks that divided his *Chronica* – columns in some manuscripts, paragraphs in others – is evidence of their importance.[17] After the imperial

---

universelle, pp. 15–17. For Sigebert's Eusebian and Hieronymian influences, see Sigebert of Gembloux, *Libellus de viris illustribus*, PL 160, cols. 547–588, at col. 588: "Imitatus Eusebium Pamphili, qui primus apud Graecos Chronica tempore Abrahae digessit, ipse quoque a loco intermissionis eius usque ad annum 1111 omnem consequentiam temporum, et regum gestarum, quanta potui styli temperantia, ordinavi."

[12] M. Chazan, "La nécessité de l'Empire de Sigebert de Gembloux à Jean de Saint-Victor," *Le Moyen Age: Revue d'histoire et philologie* 106 (2000), pp. 9–13.

[13] Sigebert of Gembloux, *Chronica*, p. 300: "Porro regni Persarum originem altius repetere modo non videtur utile, quia quae huius regni fuerit antiquitas, quanta et quam potens huius antiquitatis nobilitas, satis recolet lector per antiquorum historias."

[14] For the Trojan narrative in the *Vita brevior*, see p. 239.

[15] Sigebert of Gembloux, *Libellus de viris illustribus*, ch. 84, cols. 566–567.

[16] Chazan, *L'Empire et l'histoire universelle*, p. 34.

[17] A. Goderniaux, "*Eique victoria provenit in omnibus*. De Charlemagne à Henri IV: appropriations des exploits militaires des Pippinides et des Carolingiens par Sigebert de Gembloux durant la Querelle des Investitures," *Revue belge de philologie et d'histoire* 93, 3–4 (2015), pp. 753–769, at pp. 755–756.

coronation of 800, the Franks assumed first place in this hierarchy. Sigebert's demotion of the Romans, by now Byzantines, to second place demonstrates that, to his mind, the process of *translatio imperii* was well and truly underway.[18] It would culminate with the Ottonians-Salians, whose own authority was being challenged as he wrote. The papacy, which occupied a central role in the Carolingian propaganda campaign, was the main adversary of Sigebert's emperor, Henry IV. It is therefore understandable that he chose to adapt his sources' terminology, aligning it with his desire to downplay papal centrality.

Sigebert's use of the Carolingians and the lessons he hoped his readership would glean from their history were closely attached to the events that defined his own time, central among them the Investiture Controversy. As a staunch ally of the empire, Sigebert saw the crystallization of imperial power and authority as central to his greater argument. His approach to the Carolingian question, with its obvious papal dimensions, was doubtless informed by his argumentation of Henry IV's position *vis-à-vis* that of Pope Gregory VII.[19] Echoes of Carolingian grandeur resound clearly in the *Chronica*. One might even say that the efforts of Carolingian chroniclers to attribute the rise of the dynasty to divine intervention were not wasted on Sigebert.

Sigebert was working with a specific model of periodization in mind, one that spoke of Merovingian decline and Carolingian ascent in familiar tones. Again, this does not mean that he uncritically adopted the simplistic narrative he found in his Carolingian sources. The *Chronica* was perfectly capable of delivering a layered and even critical argument of its favored protagonists, as it did with Henry IV and many others. For the purposes of the present chapter, this approach is most clearly evident in his treatment of Grimoald, Pippin II, and Charles Martel.

Since Sigebert conceived of the *Chronica* as the continuation of Eusebius-Jerome, biblical chronology would not have been far from his mind as he wrote. In many of the manuscripts described by Bethmann, Sigebert's *Chronica* was bound up with other chronicles. Most common among those was Eusebius-Jerome and its continuations, evidence that Sigebert's framing was accepted by the compilers of these manuscripts.[20]

---

[18] Beumann, *Sigebert von Gembloux*, p. 42.
[19] On the applicability of remote historical episodes as subjects of comparison, see H.-W. Goetz, "The Concept of Time in the Historiography of the Eleventh and Twelfth Centuries," in *Medieval Concepts of the Past: Ritual, Memory, Historiography*, eds. G. Althoff, J. Fried, and P.J. Geary (Washington DC: German Historical Institute and Cambridge: Cambridge University Press, 2002), pp. 139–166.
[20] See Bethmann's introduction to the *Chronica*, pp. 284–297; M. Verweij, "Les manuscrits des œuvres de Sigebert de Gembloux à la Bibliothèque royale de Belgique" in *Sigebert de Gembloux*, ed. J.-P. Straus (Turnhout: Brepols, 2015), pp. 91–116, at pp. 108–111.

Still, the Christocentric structure so characteristic of Carolingian works was absent. What we find instead is an *origo* that amplified the Franks' heroic lineage and portrayed them, first and foremost, as a nation of divinely inspired conquerors. The nature of this divine inspiration was also different than what we find in Carolingian works. In the *Chronica*, God's favor was direct, not mediated by the pope.[21] This relationship came to the fore most clearly when Sigebert discussed Frankish emperorship.[22] As for the origin story, it was a natural point of entry into the topic of Frankish settlement, expansion, and eventual *imperium*. Sigebert further simplified the *LHF* narrative, accentuating the Merovingians' direct link to Troy, a link that earlier compositions, even ones generally sympathetic to the Merovingians, attempted to obscure or problematize.[23]

Another element of Sigebert's prose that should be mentioned is his preoccupation with time and particularly contemporaneity, which is acknowledged in the *Chronica*'s opening sentence as its entire *raison d'être*. Sigebert's treatment of time, presented in parallel chronological strands in the *Chronica*, was nothing if not conscious.[24] In fact, it stood at the very heart of his historiographical methodology. His attacks on the calculus of Dionysius Exiguus, which pepper his *Chronica* and *Liber Decennalis*, certainly betrayed a technical interest in the correct order of time and historical events. Yet Sigebert was interested in time for more than just accuracy's sake. Lunisolar cycles, or "Great Years," were not merely arbitrary rules imposed on history. By correcting Dionysius and setting events in their proper place, Sigebert was able to uncover symbolic meanings previously obscured by corrupt chronologies. Yet, while he took great care to place historical events in the correct sequence in his grand historical opus, he could just as easily collapse his meticulous chronologies. Using comparisons between remote historical stages, Sigebert reordered and juxtaposed events in order to imbue them with symbolic significance. This historiographical approach, so prevalent in the *Chronica*, was the culmination of a methodology already visible in the hagiographical projects he undertook at the earliest stages of his career.

After the end of the exposition, which included the origin stories of the other *gentes*, Sigebert began his historical account. The first year of this

---

[21] Goderniaux, "*Eique victoria provenit in omnibus*," pp. 757–758.

[22] On Sigebert's approach as a rebuttal of papal ideology, see Beumann, *Sigebert von Gembloux*, pp. 57–60.

[23] Sigebert of Gembloux, *Chronica*, a.448, p. 309: "Merovecus filius Clodii super Francos regnat annis 10, a quo nimis utili rege Franci cognominati sunt Merovingi"; Compare *LHF*, ch. 5, or another of Sigebert's sources, Aimoin's *Gesta Francorum*, ch. 6, col. 640, which follows the *LHF*.

[24] Sigebert of Gembloux, *Libellus de viris illustribus*, ed. R. Witte (Bern and Frankfurt am Main: Lang, 1974), 172, p. 105; Goetz, "The Concept of Time," pp. 144–145.

account – 381 – was designated in the *Chronica*'s Frankish column as the first year of Priam "the younger," after whom royal kingship – with a thirty-six-year ducal *interregnum* by Marcomer and Sunno – proceeded according to the timeline set forth by the *LHF*. Sigebert charted Frankish history primarily with the help of the *LHF*, although he availed himself of a large corpus of supplementary material, such as Gregory's *Histories*, *Fredegar*, and a slew of hagiographical works, such as the *Life of Geneviève*, the *Life of Germanus of Auxerre*, the *Life of Remigius of Reims*, and Gregory's hagiographical compilations.[25] Sigebert was cognizant of his sources' limitations and used them judiciously, even occasionally recording when an important source's coverage came to an end.[26]

By the time he reached Dagobert, Sigebert was relying more heavily on *Fredegar*, and many of the episodes he incorporated are therefore familiar. So, too, was the king's death scene, although it did not echo *Fredegar*, but rather the *Gesta Dagoberti*:

Dagobert king of the Franks died, about whom a certain person had a vision revealed to him, in which his [i.e., Dagobert's] *soul was taken to God's judgement, and many saints protested against it on account of the spoliation of their churches, and with them were evil angels who wanted to take it to the punishments of the inferno, [but] with the intervention of the holy martyr Dionysius of Paris, to whom he was devoted, it was released from punishment. Clovis, Dagobert's son, reigned after him for 17 years. Sigibert, his brother, was already reigning in Austrasia. [Erchinoald was this Clovis's mayor of the palace].*[27]

The *Gesta Dagoberti* was not one of Sigebert's direct sources, and the origin of this passage is quickly revealed to have been Aimoin of Fleury's *Gesta Francorum*.[28] All in all, Dagobert received a detailed and well-rounded treatment based primarily on *Fredegar*, with additions from Bede, the *LHF*, Flodoard's *History of the Church of Reims*, Aimoin of Fleury, and a number of hagiographical works. The role of the hagiography

---

[25] This is, of course, a very partial list. Sigebert used dozens of hagiographical compositions, and their usage was not confined to the Frankish strand.
[26] Sigebert of Gembloux, *Chronica*, a.593, p. 320: "Hucusque Gregorius Turonensis historiam Francorum digessit."
[27] Ibid., a.645, p. 324: "Dagobertus rex Francorum moritur; de quo visionem cuidam revelatum est, quod anima eius ad iudicium Dei rapta sit, et multis sanctis contra eam pro expoliatione suarum aecclesiarum reclamantibus, cum eam iam mali angeli vellent ad poenas inferni rapere, interventu sancti martyris Dionisii Parisiensis, cui ipse devotus fuerat, a poenis liberata est. Clodoveus filius Dagoberti regnavit post eum annis 17. Sigiberto fratre eius iam regnante in Austria. [Huius Clodovei maior domus fuit Erchanoaldus]." The brackets indicate elements found only in the A recensions of the *Chronica*, to which Brussels, KBR 18239–18240 was the direct forbear (ms. 1 in Bethmann's stemma). It will be the one most referred to in what follows. See Bethmann's introduction, *Sigeberti Chronica*, pp. 284–285.
[28] Aimoin of Fleury, *Gesta Francorum*, ch. 34; Werner, "Die literarischen Vorbilder."

was, as one would expect, to highlight the activities of saints who lived and worked during Dagobert's day. This it certainly did, although it also set the stage for Sigebert's discussion of the Pippinid family, whose role grew ever more pronounced as the family inched its way to royal power. One example of this kind of usage is the tenth-century *Life of Chlodulf*, which served as the inspiration for the following passage:[29]

St. Arnulf, who went from being mayor of the palace to bishop of Metz, and from bishop to hermit, slept in Christ. His son Chlodulf, afterwards also bishop of Metz, imitated his father's sanctity. Doda, mother of that same Chlodulf, secluded herself in Trier and served Christ.[30]

Sigebert quickly appended this sentence from the *LHF*: *King Dagobert sent his son to be king of Austrasia, under the tutelage of Pippin and Bishop Chunibert.*[31]

This style of threading hagiographical notices into a historiographical account was, of course, not new. We encountered it with Ado of Vienne and with Regino of Prüm. Sigebert used this technique throughout, inserting Gregory of Tours' saints as well as other hagiographical protagonists into the appropriate chronological rubrics well before he reached the Pippinids. We should again recall that Frankish history was only one part of a grander historical narrative, which featured other western *gentes*, as well as events taken from the Persian, Byzantine, and Saracen spheres of influence, and, of course, from papal Rome.[32] Hagiography was employed in these narrative strands with equal frequency. In the Frankish case, it was skillfully used to ingrain the Pippinids into the plot so as to illuminate their rise to power. Sigebert deployed this device in several instances such as this example: *Modoald, the brother of Itta and uncle of St. Gertrude, shone in his teachings and sanctity as archbishop of Trier. His sister Severa, an abbess in that same city, matched her brother in sanctity.*[33]

---

[29] For a discussion of the *Life*, see H.E. Bonnell, "Excurs I: Die Biographie des Bischofs Chlodulf von Metz," in *Die Anfänge des karolingischen Hauses* (Berlin: Duncker und Humblot, 1866), pp. 137–139. Any hagiography of Chlodulf's would certainly have been available to Sigebert during the time he spent in Metz.

[30] Sigebert of Gembloux, *Chronica*, a.640, p. 324: "Sanctus Arnulfus ex maiore domus Mettensium episcopus, et ex episcopo solitarius, dormit in Christo. Clodulfus filius eius, post Mettensem episcopus, sanctitatem patris imitatur. Doda mater ipsius Clodulfi, Treveris reclusa, Christo ancillatur."

[31] Sigebert of Gembloux, *Chronica*, a.640, p. 324: "Dagobertus rex Sigibertum filium suum Austrasiis regem mittit, sub tutela Pippini et Chuniberti episcopi."

[32] On Sigebert's use of the *ARF* and the *Liber Pontificalis* to portray the events of the 750s, see Beumann, *Sigebert von Gembloux*, pp. 59–60.

[33] Sigebert of Gembloux, *Chronica*, a.646, p. 324: "Modoaldus frater Ittae et avunculus sanctae Gertrudis, archiepiscopatum Trevirensem doctrina et sanctitate sua illustrat. Soror quoque eius Severa abbatissa in eadem urbe a fratris sanctitate non degenerat."

Again, Sigebert followed this description with an excerpt from the *LHF*: *Pippin mayor of the palace died; his son Grimoald mightily ruled the court of King Sigibert.*[34]
Sigebert continues to zigzag between secular and ecclesiastical history for some time. All the while Sigibert III was still king of Austrasia, but his role was to hold the plot together chronologically, not to serve as its narrative focal point. So, for instance, we learn with Bede's help of Gertrude's role in the patronage of Fosses; then, through *Fredegar*, of Sigibert's Thuringian war; then, again, of Ansegisus's marriage to Begga, sister of Grimoald, probably with the help of the *Life of Gertrude* and the *Life of Chlodulf*. The *Life of Gertrude* was mined repeatedly throughout the relevant timeframe: to discuss the foundation of Nivelles through the persuasive efforts of Amandus and the agency of Itta, and to note the deaths of both Itta and Gertrude. But the Pippinid-Arnulfing political subplot is always present, hemmed into a narrative superstructure. Sigebert's approach becomes especially interesting when we consider its treatment of the Grimoald affair, whose details he extracted from the *LHF*. The tension builds slowly:

King Sigibert adopted Childebert, son of the mayor of the palace Grimoald, as a son and heir.[35]

This was already a charged claim, as it suggested that the Merovingian king intended to bequeath his kingship to Childebert "the Adopted," having begotten no children of his own. We soon learn the whole story, but not before encountering Sigebert's report on Grimoald's involvement in the establishment of Stablo-Malmédy, erected by King Sigibert and St. Remaclus:

King Sigibert was desperate for the posterity of children, so he built here and there twelve monasteries for God, the most eminent of which were Stablo and Malmédy, in whose establishment he cooperated with the mayor of the palace Grimoald and Remaclus, bishop of Utrecht.[36]

This reasoning smacks of the claim made about Dagobert I in the *Life of Amandus* and adopted later by Aimoin's *Gesta Francorum* – two sources at

---

[34] Ibid., a.647, p. 324: "Pippinus maior domus moritur; Grimoaldus filius eius in aula Sigeberti regis potenter principatur."
[35] Sigebert of Gembloux, *Chronica*, a.652, p. 325: "Sigibertus rex Hildebertum filium Grimoaldi maioris domus adoptat in filium et in regnum."
[36] Sigebert of Gembloux, *Chronica*, a.651, p. 324: "Rex Sigibertus de posteritate prolis desperans, duodecim monasteria hinc inde Deo construxit, in quibus Stabulaus et Malmundarium eminebant, cooperante sibi in his maiore domus Grimoaldo et Traiectensium episcopo Remaclo."

Sigebert's disposal – that he contributed to the Church, hoping he would be rewarded with an heir. We know that Sigibert III turned out to be this successor.[37] Of course, in the *Chronica* this motif was not used to discuss Dagobert's efforts to secure an heir, but rather his son's. The *Life of Remaclus*, the main source for Sigibert's and Grimoald's patronage of Stablo-Malmédy, had nothing to say about the king's childlessness. If anything, it seems to suggest that Sigibert already had sons, for whose health the monks were meant to pray:

Meanwhile, while (he was) engaged in this purpose, girded with faith, fortified with hope, and founded on charity, it happened, by God's favor, that the pious leaders of the kingdom of the Franks King Sigibert and Duke Grimoald, by the will of God and the counsel of their nobles, commanded that monasteries be constructed within the forest in the region called Ardenne, known as Malmédy and Stablot, wherein religious monks will reside together, serving Christ spiritually in that place and will pray to the almighty Lord for the health of the king and his sons, and those who oversaw the care of the kingdom.[38]

Sigebert's decision to embed this narrative element at this particular point in the plot becomes understandable when we consider his next mention of Grimoald:

Sigibert king of the Austrasians died and his son Dagobert, who was still young, was entrusted to Grimoald, so that he would help him rule.[39]
[...]
The mayor of the palace Grimoald, having had his lord Dagobert, son of Sigibert, tonsured and sent to Ireland by Dido, bishop of Poitiers, made his own son Childebert king of the Austrasians. The Franks, pained by Grimoald's betrayal of Sigibert's son, captured him and presented him in Paris to Clovis for judgement. Clovis had him

---

[37] *Vita Amandi* I, ch.17, p. 440; Aimoin of Fleury, *Gesta Francorum*, ch. 20, col. 781. Compare also *Gesta Dagoberti*, ch. 24. See discussion in Chapter 4.

[38] *Vita Remacli*, ch. 4, p. 106: "Interim dum in hoc tenore propositi accinctus fide, spe munitus, caritate fundatus perseverat, contigit, Deo favente, iubere piis principibus regni Francorum Sigiberto regi et Grimoaldo duci ex voluntate Dei et consilio optimatum suorum, ut construerentur infra forestem monasteria sita in pago qui Ardoinna dicitur, cognominata Malmundarium seu Stabulaus, in quibus commanerent religiosi monachi, qui spiritaliter inibi Christo famularentur et pro statu totius regni et regis salute vel filiorum sive curam regni exercentium omnipotentem dominum exorarent." Given that the foundation of Stablo-Malmédy took place in 648, Dagobert II would have either been a small baby or *in utero* and no other sons are known to have existed. The *LHF* in any event provides no insight into Dagobert's birth year. See *LHF*, ch. 43; P. Fouracre, "Forgetting and Remembering Dagobert II: The English Connection," in *Frankland: The Franks and the World of the Early Middle Ages*, eds. P. Fouracre and D. Ganz (Manchester: Manchester University Press, 2008), pp. 70–89, pp. 70–73.

[39] Sigebert of Gembloux, *Chronica*, a.656, p. 325: "Sigibertus rex Austrasiorum moritur, Dagoberto filio suo admodum parvulo fidei Grimoaldi commendato, ut in regnum eius auxilio promoveatur." For a discussion of Sigebert of Gembloux's dating of this event, see M. Weidemann, "Zur Chronologie der Merowinger im 7. Und 8. Jahrhundert," *Francia* 25, 1 (1998), pp. 177–230, at p. 199.

painfully chained in prison and put to death. He made his own son Childeric king of the Austrasians. Itta, mother of St. Gertrude, died.[40]

One might read the passage about the royal adoption as partially mitigating the severity of Grimoald's actions, although, on the whole, Sigebert did not pull his punches. Given his commitment to Carolingian exceptionalism, it seems odd that he chose to relate the Grimoald *coup d'état* in all its unpleasantness. While the affair lurked in the background and provided the context for much of its dramatic action, the *Life of Gertrude*, one of Sigebert's sources for the period in question, was able to skirt the matter with relative success. Although it was undoubtedly the reason for many of Gertrude's travails at Nivelles and perhaps also for Foillan's murder – related in the hagiographical appendix known as the *Additamentum Nivialense de Fuillano* –[41] it nevertheless remained unmentioned.

Sigebert rejected this solution in favor of an honest discussion of the coup. His reliance on the *Life of Gertrude*, the *Life of Chlodulf*, and the *Life of Remaclus* ensured that Itta, Gertrude, Chlodulf, and other early Pippinid and Arnulfing figures appeared in the *Chronica* in a way that faithfully replicated their portrayal in the hagiography. In other words, saints continued to function as saints. Sigebert processed the material for brevity but did not attempt to read it against the grain. This can perhaps be read as an attempt to shift the focus from Grimoald and his treachery, yet even with this alternating usage of hagiographical and historiographical voices, we are left with a straightforward account of the Grimoald affair, indicating Sigebert's relative independence from his Carolingian sources and his multifaceted approach. More importantly, it demonstrates that Sigebert regarded secular and holy histories as distinct narrative strands.

Considering his overall adherence to the *LHF* and his candor with regard to the Grimoald affair, it appears that Sigebert judged the Merovingians to have been generally successful rulers, up to a point. He recognized that they inevitably began to weaken, and, as we shall see, made a point of noting, periodizing, and explaining this process. But Sigebert did

---

[40] Sigebert of Gembloux, *Chronica*, a.657–658, p. 325: "Grimoaldus maior domus, domino suo Dagoberto Sigiberti filio attonso et per Didonem Pictavensem episcopum in Scottiam directo, Hildebertum filium suum facit Austrasiorum regem. Franci dolentes super infidelitate Grimoaldi contra filium Sigiberti, captum eum presentant Parisius iudicio Chlodovei; quem Chlodoveus vinculatum amara in carcere fecit morte consumi; filiumque suum Hildricum regem fecit Austrasiorum. Obiit Itta mater sanctae Gerdrudis."
[41] For a discussion of the *Life*, the *Additamentum*, and their political meaning, see Fouracre and Gerberding, ed. and trans., *Late Merovingian France*, pp. 302–326; Fox, *Power and Religion in Merovingian Gaul*, pp. 172–184.

not manipulate Merovingian decline so as to push Carolingian ascendancy much further into the past or to endow the family with characteristics that would have made its hold on power more justifiable. Rather, he treated the Merovingians neutrally for most of their history, which he was happy to present using a range of Merovingian-era sources. Nevertheless, Sigibert III emerges as an unremarkable figure in the *Chronica*. We learn of his birth, the few battles he conducted, his monastic patronage, and his death, which precipitated a political crisis in which the Pippinids played a central role. The bulk of the material used by Sigebert actually had nothing to do with the king; it was concerned with saintly activity, primarily of personages connected to the Pippinid orbit. The scarcity of source material that produced the *Chronica*'s lackluster account had posed an even more acute problem several years earlier, when Sigebert was tapped to compose a hagiography for the king.

The *Life of Sigibert* poses some difficulty, since there are two compositions that bear the name. The so-called *Vita brevior*, which appears in vol. 160 of the *Patrologia Latina*, is quite different in content and style from the *Vita altera*, which appears in vol. 87. Historically, both have been attributed to the pen of Sigebert of Gembloux, alongside an account of the king's posthumous miracles, although the *Vita brevior*'s origins have recently come into question. Prevailing scholarly opinion now leans toward regarding the *Vita brevior* as a composition presented to Sigebert for *réécriture*, an assertion with which I agree.[42] In fact, the *Vita brevior* does not much resemble a hagiography, and, while it gives King Sigibert pride of place in its pages, most of the composition has very little to do with him. The authorship of the *Vita altera* seems to be on surer footing, but the process whereby the *Vitae Sigiberti* assumed their final forms is by no means clear, and the manuscript evidence does little to alleviate the confusion.[43]

The *Vita altera* was penned around 1063 or shortly thereafter, when Sigebert was a schoolmaster at Saint-Vincent of Metz. It was likely designed to support a nascent cult of the king, whose remains had recently been deposited in Saint-Martin of Metz's high altar.[44] Images of kings as

---

[42] It may have been given to him by the party commissioning what would become the *Vita altera*, although this naturally depends on our confidence in identifying this party. More on this on p. 244.

[43] On this, see J. Meyers, "*Vitarum scriptor*: une analyse critique et litteraire de la methode hagiographique de Sigebert de Gembloux," in *Sigebert de Gembloux*, ed. J.-P. Straus (Barcelona and Madrid: Fédération Internationale des Instituts d'Études Médiévales, 2015), pp. 51–76, at p. 54. T. Licht, *Untersuchungen zum hagiographischen Werk Sigiberts von Gembloux* (Heidelberg: Mattes Verlag, 2005), p. 77. See also M.L. Demaison, "Étude critique sur la Vie de Saint Sigibert III roi d'Austrasie par Sigebert de Gembloux," *Travaux de l'Académie Nationale de Reims* 3, 4 (1887–8), pp. 1–30.

[44] On Sigibert's patronage of the ecclesiastical institutions in Metz, see Y. Fox, "From Metz to Überlingen: Columbanus and Gallus in Alamannia," in *Columbanus and the Peoples of*

Sigebert of Gembloux's Late Merovingians 239

heroes of a saintly cult were constructed to present paragons of Christian kingship. The account of Sigibert III was no different. Because of a dearth of sources, however, inventiveness was necessary, as it was in other instances. In Sigebert's case, this was accomplished with the help of the supporting evidence found in historiographical and other hagiographical sources.

As hagiographies go, the *Vita altera* is not particularly long. It holds eleven columns in Migne's *Patrologia Latina* edition and takes up less than four pages of the 1863 *Acta Sanctorum*.[45] Sigebert was not inclined to introduce elements of his own invention into this work, nor, as far as we can tell, did he have access to any oral or hitherto unidentified written traditions. This, unsurprisingly, resulted in a narrative patchwork sewn together from a familiar coterie of sources. The lion's share of the details found in the *Life* were drawn from *Fredegar*, the *LHF*, and Aimoin of Fleury's *Gesta Francorum*, although there are also echoes of the *Annales Mettenses Priores*, monastic charters, and, of course, other hagiographies.

Of the five chapters that make up the *Life*, the first was dedicated to the king's ancestors, with special emphasis on Dagobert. Actual information about the composition's protagonist was in short supply, so it is perhaps not surprising that historiographical material only loosely relevant to the topic at hand was used. Indeed, the *Vita brevior* took this to the extreme, resulting in a very strange piece of literature. Not only did the *Vita brevior* begin its account with the Trojan origin story, but it went on to produce what can best be called a complete summary of the *LHF*, rehearsing an account of all the kings until Sigibert and their respective histories. The first section of Duchesne's 1636 edition, later reproduced by Migne, ran from Troy until the fifth year of Merovech's reign.[46] Since it was based on Vatican City, BAV Reg. lat. 980, a twelfth-century manuscript with missing intervening folio(s),[47] it leapt from Merovech directly to Dagobert. Indeed, it is this significant lacuna that warranted the adjective *brevior*. But Brussels KBR 19598–19599, a fifteenth-century fragment from Stablo, contained the lengthy *LHF*-based account in its entirety.

Post-Roman Europe, ed. A. O'Hara (Oxford: Oxford University Press, 2018), pp. 205–224.
[45] Sigebert of Gembloux, *Vita sancti Sigiberti regis*, *AASS* Feb. I (Paris, 1863), pp. 228–232, repr. in *PL* 87, ed. J.P. Migne (Paris, 1841–1867), cols. 303–314.
[46] This roughly corresponds to a section covered by *LHF*, chs. 1–5. Notably, the fragment of the *Vita brevior* in BAV Reg. lat. 980 does away with this introduction, beginning its account with: "Nam quamvis Dagobertus rex...."
[47] After "... Merovechi anno quinto," found in f. 18v, Reg. Lat. 980 picks up with "Nam quamvis Dagobertus," found in 15r and runs until the end. Duchesne saw the manuscript in the library of Alexandre Petau ("Ex Cod. Ms. Bibliothecae Alexandri Petavii Senatoris Parisiensis"), later sold to the Vatican.

Ironically, then, in its full form the so-called *Vita brevior* was longer than the *Vita altera*. For obvious reasons, the *Vita altera* did not venture as far into the Frankish past as its hagiographical precursor. Yet it did provide some historical context, beginning with Sigibert's grandfather:

> *In the five hundred and eighty sixth year of the Incarnation of our Lord, Chlothar II, son of King Chilperic and Fredegund, began to rule in Francia to the limits befitting a young boy. When he later reached the age of reason, he began to strive to attain honorable conduct. Exalted by God, he thus proceeded, so that he may merit to accept sole rule over the kingdom of the Franks. In the thirty-ninth year of his reign, he took his son Dagobert as co-ruler; and so that he [i.e., Dagobert] would not deviate from the righteous life because of the liberties of royal power and the intemperance of youth, he [i.e., Chlothar] placed him under the power and sanctity of the noble men St. Arnulf, former mayor of the palace and bishop of Metz, and the mayor of the palace Pippin, who at that time were both preeminent courtiers in power and wisdom.*[48]

There are several chronological blunders here, such as the year in which Chlothar II assumed power or the year he associated Dagobert with him as *consors regni*.[49] There are also some analytical mistakes. Firstly, Chlothar only became sole ruler in 613, after having eliminated Sigibert II and his family, events that were not mentioned here. Secondly, Arnulf of Metz was never mayor of either Chlothar's or Dagobert's palace. The latter is perhaps a forgivable error that originated with Sigebert's sources.[50] The decision to depict Chlothar as sole ruler from the start and to ignore his early struggles possibly speaks to Sigebert's desire to introduce the motif of puerile subkingship, which he later applied to the *Life*'s hero.

Sigebert used the historiographical literature to build a chronological and thematic skeleton and the hagiographical corpus to flesh out his

---

[48] Sigebert of Gembloux, *Vita Sigiberti*, 1.1, col. 303: "Anno dominicae Incarnationis quingentesimo octogesimo sexto Lotharius Secundus, Chilperici regis et Fredegundis filius, in Francia admodum puer regnare coepit. Qui postquam ad intelligibilem aetatem venit, honestati morum studere coepit. Unde a Deo exaltatus, eo usque processit, ut monarchiam regni Francorum mereretur accipere solus. Hic anno regni sui tricesimo nono Dagobertum filium suum in consortium regni ascivit; et ne regiae potestatis licentia, et juvenilis aetatis intemperantia exorbitaret a via rectitudinis, ei viros potentia et sanctitate claros substituit, sanctum, scilicet, Arnulphum, ex majore domus metensem episcopum, et Pipinum majorem domus, tunc temporis cunctis aulicis praeeminentem potentia et prudentia."

[49] Chlothar became king in 584 with the murder of Chilperic (albeit under the regency of his mother Fredegund), and Dagobert became subking in 622, in the thirty-eighth year of Chlothar's reign.

[50] This misinterpretation of the *Vita Arnulfi*, chs. 3–4, p. 433 was also made by Regino of Prüm, *Chronicle*, a.546–571, p. 28: "Per idem tempus fuit maior domus in palatio Chlotharii regis Arnulfus ... ." For Sigebert's use of Regino with regard to Arnulf, see Chazan, *L'Empire et l'histoire universelle*, p. 136.

characters.[51] His treatment of Sigibert's birth and miraculous baptism is one example of a style that, in the *Chronica*, was later honed to perfection. An identical paragraph depicting Dagobert's womanizing is present in both the *Vita brevior* and the *Vita altera*:

For, however much King Dagobert was a skilled warrior, a pious lover of God's priests and churches, a generous supporter of Christ's poor and performer of many good deeds, still he indulged excessively in the disease of carnal incontinence, until the fame of his name contracted the mark of loathsome infamy and (what is worse) he inflamed the wrath of the king of kings against him. He repudiated his queens for other ones on false charges, and those he replaced with the love of concubines. And because he was so given to carnal intercourse, he had no hope for the propagation of posterity, having received a son from none of his wives.[52]

The footprints of the *Life of Amandus* are conspicuous in this passage. While the *Vita brevior* does not make this identification explicit, resolving the issue of Dagobert's childlessness with a rather laconic appeal to divine clemency, the subsequent chapter in the *Vita altera* focuses entirely on Amandus and his relationship with the Merovingians.[53] Here, Amandus took on the same role that he had in his own *Life*, that of a fearless missionary priest who had fallen out with the king on account of his staunch criticism of Dagobert's capital crimes. Both the *Life of Amandus* and the *Vita altera* mentioned Amandus's expulsion to the farthest reaches of the Frankish kingdom, where he took up the mantle of mission, preaching to and proselytizing the inhabitants of this remote region.

Amandus was later recalled, and when he came face to face with Dagobert at the latter's villa in Clichy, the king remorsefully prostrated himself at the saint's feet, begging the man of God to forgive him. As part of his apology, Dagobert beseeched Amandus to baptize his newly born son Sigibert and to serve as the boy's *nutritor*. The saint of course refused, recalling the words of 2 Timothy about the duty of the man of God to abstain from involving himself in secular affairs.[54] Amandus removed himself from the palace, opting for quiet solitude away from the king's

---

[51] Ibid., pp. 132–133.
[52] *Vita Sigiberti*, cols. 727–728 (*brevior*) and ch. I.2, col. 305 (*altera*): "Nam, quamvis Dagobertus Rex esset egregius bellator, sacerdotum Dei et Ecclesiarum pius amator, pauperum Christi largus sublevator et multarum bonarum artium exsecutor; tamen carnalis incontinentiae morbo nimis laborabat, unde et claritudinis nominis sui foedam infamiae notam contraxerat, et (quod gravius erat) Regis regum iram contra se accenderat. Reginas enim suas fictis ex causis alias pro aliis repudiabat, ipsis quoque desponsatis pellicum amores superducebat. Et quamvis adeo deditus esset carnali commercio, nullam tamen spem propagandae posteritatis habebat, ex nulla tot uxorum filio suscepto."
[53] *Vita brevior*, col. 728: "Justus et pius Dominus, qui hominum erratibus ad iram attrahitur, precibus etiam humilium ad misericordiam reducitur."
[54] 2 Timothy II.4.

gaze. Later, Dagobert dispatched Eligius of Noyon and Audoin of Rouen to convince the saint to change his mind.[55] Only after extracting from the king the promise of free rein in his missionary endeavors, did Amandus eventually come around.[56] This narrative was lifted almost verbatim from the *Life of Amandus*.[57] The miraculous response given by the infant Sigibert, missing entirely from the *Vita brevior*, was also recorded. Here, though, Sigebert made sure to name both Amandus and Dagobert's brother Charibert II as having participated in the ceremony, which he placed in Orléans, not Clichy. Sigebert was thus simultaneously using an account found in the *Life of Amandus* and in *Fredegar*, taking care to supplement his composition with details that were omitted from his main sources and correct those details he deemed corrupt.[58]

Sigebert then returned to his historiographical source material, with whose help he was able to comment on the mayoralty of Pippin I and the prince's ascent to the Austrasian throne in 632. He likewise mentioned Samo's rebellion, the birth of Clovis II, the partition of the *regnum Francorum* upon Dagobert's death, and the redivision of Dagobert's treasure between Sigibert and Clovis.[59] The death of Pippin I signaled a thematic turning point.[60] The plot of the chapter, while held together by Sigibert's kingship, was dominated by the Pippinids/Carolingians, from Grimoald all the way to Charlemagne:

> *The following year the greatest grief descended on Sigibert and his kingdom when Pippin the mayor of the palace was taken from this light. Pippin cared for Sigibert's father since he was a boy, and with the help of his strong arm sustained him through the weakness of childhood and adolescence. Useful in all things of government and notable over all others in ancestry, power, prudence, and fortitude, he made his son Grimoald heir to his affairs. He was survived, to the praise and glory of his line, by two daughters, Gertrude and Begga. One of whom, Gertrude, preferred Christ to a carnal spouse, and decided to serve the holy religion in the monastery of Nivelles, founded by her mother, unceasingly bearing spiritual offspring to God. Her sister Begga married the son of Bishop Arnulf of Metz Ansigisus, who was adorned with kingly honors and who died because of the unheard-of idleness of the kings of the Franks, which was rectified by her offspring. She later gave birth to Pippin, and Pippin to Charles, who was called Martel, meaning hammer. Charles begat King Pippin, and Pippin Charles, known as the Great, king of the*

---

[55] On Sigebert's knowledge of these two men, see his *Libellus de viris illustribus*, LVIII, col. 560.
[56] Sigebert of Gembloux, *Vita sancti Sigiberti*, ch. 2, cols. 305–308.
[57] *Vita Amandi*, ch. 17, pp. 440–442.
[58] The baptism in the *Life of Amandus* was placed in a scene that began in Dagobert's villa in Clichy but was not expressly identified. Nevertheless, Orléans was not mentioned, and neither was Charibert.
[59] Discussed in Sigebert of Gembloux, *Vita sancti Sigiberti*, chs. II–III.
[60] It was relegated to a new chapter in Duchesne's edition, although not in Vatican City, BAV Reg. lat. 980.

Franks and emperor of the Romans, who proceeded with such honor and power, that none of the kings of the Franks, either before or after him, could compare to him.[61]

The text above appears in both recensions of the *Life of Sigibert*. It obviously provides a straightforward account of Carolingian ascendancy, culminating as it does with Charlemagne's unrivaled greatness. Importantly, it repeats the Carolingian talking point about Ansegisel's death having been caused by Merovingian *desidia*, or, in other words, *fainéance*. The *Annales Mettenses Priores* mention Ansegisel's *principatum* and his demise at the hands of Gundoin, whose own mayoralty, we assume, was the result of the Pippinids' withdrawal from public life after the Grimoald affair.[62] More to the point, the *AMP* present Pippinid power as a corrective measure working to counteract Merovingian weakness and mayoral corruption. This image was faithfully replicated here, with the *AMP* as its possible source.[63] The theme will return in the *Chronica*. It is therefore quite jarring to find, alongside this stellar evaluation of the Carolingian family present in both *Lives*, such an explicitly critical account of Grimoald's betrayal as the one contained in the *Vita brevior*:

Oh, how often ambition misleads many men! Oh, how often divine vengeance brings low many traitors! After King Sigibert died, Grimoald the mayor of the palace tonsured his [i.e., Sigibert's] son Dagobert, who was commended to him so that he might obtain

---

[61] Sigebert of Gembloux, *Vita sancti Sigiberti*, IV.10, cols. 309–310: "Sequens annus luctum maximum intulit regi Sigeberto ejusque regno, Pipino majore domus ex hac luce subtracto, qui ipsum Sigebertum paterne nutrierat a puero, et imbecillitatem pueritiae et adolescentiae ejus validi sui auxilii sustentaverat brachio. Hic omnimodis regno utilis, genere, potentia, prudentia et fortitudine super omnes nominabilis, Grimoaldum filium suum rerum suarum haeredem fecit: duas quoque filias, Gertrudem et Beggham, ad laudem et gloriam generis sui post se reliquit. Quarum una, Gertrudis, Christo, quam sponso carnali, malens nubere, sanctae religionis proposito inserviens in Nivellensi coenobio, a sua fundato matre, spiritualem prolem adhuc non desinit Deo gignere. Soror ejus Beggha nupta Ansigiso sancti Arnulphi Metensis episcopi filio, regiae dignitatis decus, quod penitus deperierat per regum Francorum inauditam desidiam, per suam reparavit prosapiam. Ipsa siquidem genuit Pipinum, Pipinus Carolum, qui Tudetes, id est Martellus est agnominatus: Carolus Pippinum regem, Pipinus Carolum, cognomento Magnum, Francorum regem et imperatorem Romanorum; qui eo honoris et potentiae processit, ut nullus de regibus Francorum, vel ante eum, vel post eum, ei comparare potuerit."

[62] *AMP*, ch. 1; Paul the Deacon, *HL* VI.37, pp. 177–178. See P. Fouracre, "The Long Shadow of the Merovingians," in *Charlemagne: Empire and Society*, ed. J. Story (Manchester: Manchester University Press, 2005), pp. 5–21, at pp. 5–7. On *princeps* as a Carolingian trope adapted by Sigebert, see pp. 250–251.

[63] The *AMP* was used in the *Chronica*, although this paragraph was inherited from the *Vita brevior*, whose authorship is in question. In the *Chronica*, the three main sources that served Sigebert for the Carolingian period were the *ARF*, the *Continuations of Fredegar*, and the *Annales Lobienses*. Of those, the *Continuations* were certainly at hand when he was composing the *Vita altera*. Since the *AMP* relied on the *ARF*, the intertextual dimensions of Sigebert's borrowings are difficult to uncover. On the Carolingian sources of the *Chronica*, see Goderniaux, "Eique victoria provenit," pp. 758–759.

kingship of the Austrasians. Through the counsel of Dido bishop of Poitiers, who was the uncle of the holy martyr Leodegar, and by the hands of that same bishop Dido, he sent the innocent boy to permanent exile in Ireland. He constituted his own son Childebert as king over the kingdom of the Austrasians.[64]

Apart from reporting that he died, this passage does not provide any information that can be regarded as relevant to King Sigibert or, for that matter, to his posthumous cult. It goes on to elaborate on Grimoald's capture and execution, as well as the nomination of Childeric II to the Austrasian throne. The report then ends abruptly with a flourish on St. Lambert, bishop of Maastricht, bringing the entire composition to a surprising halt.

Whatever the actual origins of the *Vita brevior*, some of its structural irregularities suggest that it was not the work of Sigebert of Gembloux. The fact that it tracked the *LHF* so closely, relating not only a vast amount of irrelevant information about Merovingian kings that predated its own protagonist by centuries, but also material that can be deemed damaging to its hagiographical cause, is, at the very least, suspect. Its sudden conclusion with St. Lambert was not, syntactically or narratively speaking, a natural place to end a *Life* dedicated to Sigibert III. In f. 15v, the text ends mid-column, followed by what appear to be erasure marks and a bar separating it from the next piece of text—a collection of letters from Pope Eugene III (d. 1153) to various recipients, such as Bishop Stephen of Metz (d. 1163) and Count Henry I of Salm, regarding the latter's unlawful appropriation of a monastic cell belonging to Saint-Mihiel. Since the text of the *Vita brevior* in Vatican City Reg. lat. 980 is so fragmentary, it is likely that the comment on St. Lambert was not intended to serve as its conclusion. Brussels KBR 19598–19599 is even less helpful here; it breaks off before the second part of Vatican City Reg. lat. 980 resumes, so that the original ending to the *Vita brevior* remains irrecoverable.

Since all of this seems superfluous in the context of Sigibert's hagiography,[65] it was discarded in the *Vita altera* in favor of a more organic

---

[64] *Vita brevior sancti Sigeberti*, PL 160, cols. 725–730, at col. 730: "O quam multos saepe ambitio decepit! O quam multos perfidos divina ultio saepe pessum dedit! Mortuo Sigiberto rege, Grimoaldus maior domus Dagobertum filium eius suae fidei commendatum, ut Austrasiorum potiretur regno, tonsoravit in clericum, consilio Didonis Pictaviensis episcopi, qui fuit avunculus sancti martyris Leodegarii, et per manum ipsius Didonis insontem puerulum in Scotiam direxit exilio inrevocabili. Filium vero suum Childebertum Austrasiorum regno constituit regem."

[65] Lambert was not the only bishop to have been martyred in his diocese. His predecessor, Theodoard, suffered a similar fate, and even Amandus is known to have felt the sting of the locals' hostility. See F. Theuws, "Maastricht as a Centre of Power in the Early Middle Ages," in *Topographies of Power in the Early Middle Ages*, eds. M. de Jong and F. Theuws (Leiden, Boston and Cologne: Brill, 2001), pp. 155–216, at pp. 179–180. Sigebert was acquainted not only with the career of Amandus but also with that of Theodoard, whose

Sigebert of Gembloux's Late Merovingians 245

and thematically justifiable conclusion. For obvious reasons, having mostly to do with his sources, Sigebert would have been hard-pressed to edit Grimoald out of the work entirely. His solution was to present the mayor in a positive light, thereby harmonizing him with the image of Carolingian excellence presented earlier in the composition. Grimoald was therefore depicted as a powerful and efficient mayor, whose performance stirred up the jealousy of other Austrasian nobles and especially of Otto, son of Uro.[66] Otto was not a fictitious hagiographical villain like Sadregisel. He was mentioned by *Fredegar* and was possibly related to the faction from which Ansegisel's assassin would later emerge.[67] Sigebert followed *Fredegar*'s account, citing the elimination of Otto by the Alamann duke Leuthar at Grimoald's instigation, but he did so in a way that left no doubt as to who was in the right. Along the way, Sigebert reported on Radulf's rebellion, but here he departed from *Fredegar* by transforming what was a devastating Frankish defeat into an impressive victory. The king's age, which *Fredegar* offered as the reason for the Franks' collapse, was transformed in the *Life* into the reason for the king's impressive triumph.[68]

Grimoald appeared again as Sigibert's right hand in the establishment of Stablo-Malmédy, alongside such figures as Remaclus and Chunibert of Cologne. His final mention in the *Life* was no less impressive:

Because he ascertained Grimoald the mayor of the palace thus far to be loyal, compliant, and cooperative to him in all things, he made his [i.e., Grimoald's] son Childebert his heir to the kingship of the Austrasians; this, however, on the condition that he himself would die without children. Indeed the king, since he was naturally ignorant of what was to come, made this agreement at the time. Later on he had a son, to whom he gave his father's name, Dagobert. And having annulled his previous testament, he gave him to the mayor of the palace Grimoald for the purpose of his upbringing, so that by his power he would be raised, protected against all, to the kingship of the Austrasians.[69]

---

hagiography he composed – or rather, reworked – in the 1090s. On this, see Meyers, "Vitarum scriptor," pp. 65–68.

[66] Sigebert of Gembloux, *Vita Sigiberti*, IV.11, col. 310.
[67] *Fredegar* IV.86–88; Fox, *Power and Religion*, p. 167.
[68] Sigebert of Gembloux, *Vita sancti Sigiberti*, IV.12, col. 310: "Sed quia cum aetate ei rubor et industria accrevit, non antea ab inimicorum insecutione destitit, quam superbiam eorum domuit, et Thuringos, qui instinctu Radulphi rebelles erant, sub jugo dominii sui victos et confusos reflexit."
[69] Sigebert of Gembloux, *Vita Sigiberti*, IV.15, col. 312: "Quia vero Grimoaldum majorem domus sibi in omnibus fidelem, morigerum et cooperatorem eatenus expertus erat, filium ejus Childebertum regni Austrasiorum haeredem delegat; hoc tamen proposito conditionis tenore, si ipsum contingeret sine liberis obire. Rex quidem, ut pote futurorum nescius, quod tunc sibi videbatur, ex temporis convenientia fecit: postea vero filium genuit, quem nomine patris sui Dagobertum vocavit: et priori testamento ad irritum redacto, hunc nutriendum commisit majori domus Grimoaldo, ut ejus potentia contra omnes tutus sublimaretur in Austrasiorum regno."

After such accolades, the *Vita altera* could only gloss in silence over Grimoald's *coup d'état*, any mention of which would have made a mockery of the image of the mayor that Sigebert was working so hard to build. The closing chapter of the *Vita altera* depicted, with great fanfare,[70] King Sigibert as a latter-day King Solomon of unparalleled wisdom, political acumen, and pious generosity. Sigebert's rendition of the *Life* not only provided his protagonist with the desired hagiographical credentials; it also streamlined Carolingian ascendancy by eliminating some of its most problematic features. From Pippin I and Arnulf, through Grimoald and his sisters, and eventually to Charlemagne, the chain of notable family members was kept unbroken. Some of these figures were mighty princes of the realm, others were saints, and still others kings and emperors, but all were above reproach. If indeed the *Vita altera* alone was the product of Sigebert's efforts and was actually a reworking of an earlier composition (known to us as the *Vita brevior*),[71] this streamlining would serve as proof of the author's astuteness and sensitivity as a hagiographer. Given the absolute trust which Grimoald enjoyed at Sigibert's court, revealing his betrayal would have painted the king not as a Solomon but as a dupe, hardly an image conducive to the aims of his hagiographer.

Grimoald's role in the events that transpired after Sigibert's death was not forgotten, and indeed found its way into the *Chronica*. But even here Sigebert attempted to whitewash the Carolingians of Grimoald's crimes by following the account of his downfall with the statement, "Itta, mother of St. Gertrude, died,"[72] refocusing the reader on the family's true claim to fame. When we next hear of the Merovingians it is in the year 662, with this remarkable passage:

Clovis king of the Franks died, and his son Chlothar succeeded him and reigned 4 years. His mayor of the palace after Erchinoald was Ebroin. Queen Balthildis, mother of Chlothar, constructed in God's honor the monasteries Corbie and Chelles. Since that time, having degenerated in intelligence and strength, the kings of the Franks were accustomed to hand over royal power to the mayors of the palace, ruling as kings in name only. It was their custom to rule according to descent, and to conduct and to distribute nothing but rather to eat and drink unreasonably, and to linger at home, and during the Kalends of May to preside over the general assembly, to greet and be greeted, accept and repay services and gifts, and so it was with them right on to the following May.[73]

---

[70] Of which Sigebert possibly knew through sources supplied by the monks of Stablo-Malmédy, as a possible party commissioning the piece.
[71] Chazan, *L'Empire et l'histoire universelle*, pp. 57–58.
[72] Sigebert of Gembloux, *Chronica*, a.658, p. 325: "Obiit Itta mater sanctae Geredrudis."
[73] Sigebert of Gembloux, *Chronica*, a.662, p. 325: "Chlodoveus rex Francorum obiit, et Lotharius filius eius succedit et 4 annis regnat. Huius maior domus post Erchanoaldum fuit Ebroinus. Balthildis regina, mater Lotharii, Corbeiam et Chalam monasteria Deo

This image of the final Merovingians is immediately familiar to readers of the *Vita Karoli*. It not only repeats the latter work's narrative in full, but goes even further, giving Einhard's dim assessment of Merovingian decrepitude a specific starting point – the death of Clovis II. Bethmann identified this passage as having originated with Paul the Deacon, by which he doubtless meant chapter VI.16 of the *History of the Lombards*.[74] There are indeed clear influences – the first sentence is almost entirely Paul's – but the *Vita Karoli*'s impact was even more decisive, with its treatment of the Merovingians' immoderation and their façade of power. Moreover, Paul set this passage between the kingship of Cædwalla in England and that of Cunincpert in Italy, which would place it between 685 and 688, markedly later than Sigebert had done. Paul topped off his description with an anachronistic account of the miracles of Arnulf of Metz, something that was entirely missing from Sigebert's account and would again point us in the direction of Einhard.

The *Chronica* then reported Chlothar's death in the year 666 and the ascent of his younger brother, Theuderic III. The use of the passive voice to describe royal action conveyed an ideological commitment to the transfer of royal power to the mayors of the palace: *Chlothar king of the Franks died. His brother Theuderic was raised to the kingship by Ebroin the mayor of the palace.*[75] This was a linguistic choice to which Sigebert almost always adhered.

The following year, as described in the *Chronica*, brought with it more calamities and the continued unraveling of Merovingian power:

Because of Ebroin's insolence, the Franks repudiated King Theuderic and jointly called his brother Childeric, who reigned in Austrasia, to rule them. Then Theuderic and Ebroin were tonsured, and Theuderic was sent to Paris to the monastery of Saint-Denis and Ebroin was sent to Luxeuil. Childeric's mayor of the palace was Wulfoald. He founded a monastery dedicated to St. Michael the Archangel in the diocese of Verdun on the Meuse.[76]

---

construxit. Abhinc Francorum regibus a solita fortitudine et scientia degenerantibus, regni potentia disponebatur per maiores domus, regibus solo nomine regnantibus; quibus moris erat principari quidem secundum genus, et nil agere vel disponere, quam irrationabiliter edere et bibere, domique morari, et Kalendis Maii presidere coram toto gente, et salutare et salutari, obsequia et dona accipere et rependere, et sic secum usque ad alium Maium habitare."

[74] Paul the Deacon, *HL*, VI.16: "Hoc tempore aput Gallias Francorum regibus a solita fortitudine et scientia degenerantibus, hi qui maiores domui regalis esse videbantur administrare regi potentiam et quicquid regibus agere mos est coeperunt; quippe cum caelitus esset dispositum, ad horum progeniem Francorum transvehi regnum."

[75] Sigebert of Gembloux, *Chronica*, a.666, p. 326: "Lotharius rex Francorum moritur. Theodericus frater eius ab Ebroino maiore domus in regnum sublimatur."

[76] Sigebert of Gembloux, *Chronica*, a.667, p. 326: "Theodericus rex propter insolentias Ebroini a Francis repudiatur, et frater eius Hildricus, qui in Austria regnabat, cunctis ad regnandum evocatur. Porro Theodericus et Ebroinus tonsorantur, et Theodericus Parisius in coenobio sancti Dionysii, Ebroinus in Luxovio relegantur. Hildrici maior

Gaul's saints were also affected by this grim state of affairs. Three *Lives* were used to recount the martyrdoms and persecutions of prominent churchmen, in which kings Childeric II and Theuderic III were involved, usually as culprits. So, for instance, Sigebert provided the following for the year 670:

> At this time shone St. Praejectus, citizen and bishop of the Auvergne, who was martyred by nobles of that same city as revenge for Hector, the patrician of Marseilles, who was slain by King Childeric because of the injustices he committed against the church of the Auvergne.[77]

For the year 672, he added this statement: "Amatus bishop of Sens was subjected to a hard and irrevocable exile by King Theuderic."[78] Finally, he opened his account of the year 676 with these words: "Because of the frivolousness of his ways, King Childeric ignited the hatred of the Franks against him. St. Leodegar bishop of Autun was imprisoned by him in Luxeuil."[79]

The consequences of this misconduct, certain to follow, were also recorded:

> Bodilo the Frank, whom Childeric ordered that he be tied to a pole and whipped, killed Childeric who had gone out hunting along with his pregnant wife Bilichild. Theuderic was reinstated as king. Following the advice of Leodegar, who was recalled from Luxeuil, and other nobles, Leudesius son of Erchinoald was appointed mayor of the palace.[80]
>
> [...]
>
> Ebroin came out of Luxeuil, resumed his powers, rallied his supporters, and rushed to King Theuderic, snatching his treasure and that of the church, and killing Leudesius the mayor of the palace. Pretending that a certain Clovis was the son of King Chlothar, he made him king, and forced all those whom he was able with punishments, threats, and blandishments to swear an oath of loyalty to him.[81]

---

domus erat Vulfoaldus. Hic in parochia Virdunensi supra Mosam coenobium sancti Michaelis archangeli fundavit."

[77] Ibid., a.670, p. 326: "Hoc tempore claruit sanctus Preiectus Arvernensis civis et episcopus, qui etiam martyrizatus est ab ipsius urbis primoribus in ultionem Hectoris Massiliensium patricii, ab Hildrico Francorum rege perempti propter iniustitias Arvernensi aecclesiae ab eo illatas."

[78] Ibid., a.672, p. 326: "Amatus episcopus Senonensis a rege Theoderico gravi et inrevocabili exilio diu tribulatur."

[79] Sigebert of Gembloux, *Chronica*, a.676, p. 326: "Hildricus rex levitate morum accendit in se odia Francorum. Sanctus Leodegarius Augustidunensis episcopus ab eo in Luxovio retruditur."

[80] Ibid., a.679, p. 326: "Bodilo Francus, quem Hildricus ligatum ad stipitem caedi precepit, Hildricum in venatione exceptum, cum Blithilde uxore eius pregnante interficit. Theodericus regno restituitur. Leudesius filius Erchonoaldi, consilio Leodegarii episcopi a Luxuvio revocati aliorumque principum, maior domus constituitur."

[81] Ibid., a.680, p. 326: "Ebroinus a Luxovio egressus, vires resumit, insidiatores suos premit, super Theodoricum regem irruit, thesaurus eius et aecclesiae deripit, Leudesium maiorem

Sigebert of Gembloux's Late Merovingians 249

In order to build his Ebroin narrative, Sigebert used not only the *LHF* but also the *Continuations of Fredegar* and the *Suffering of Leodegar*, the only source to name Ebroin's short-lived puppet king, Clovis.[82] Sigebert continued to alternate between the *LHF* and the *Continuations*, supplementing the narrative with hagiographical material where he saw fit. Throughout his coverage of the civil war of the 670s, which included the Austrasian defeat at Lucofao, the murder of Martin, the murder of Ebroin, and Pippin's victory at Tertry, Sigebert described the Merovingian kings in the passive voice, never portraying them as active characters.[83] The mayors, and especially Pippin, increasingly took the initiative:

Having met Pippin in battle, King Theuderic was defeated with Berthar; Berthar was killed by his own men; King Theuderic was captured by Pippin. Pippin subjugated Neustria and, reigning alone under Theuderic over all the kingdom, improved the state of affairs.[84]

We may recall that the reference to Pippin's beneficial effect on Frankish politics was already present in the *Life of Sigebert*, but here its true significance becomes clearer. It is thus quite telling that, despite Sigebert's profound dependence on the *LHF*, he chose to forgo its praise of Childebert III. Other than the brief notice of his ascent in 697, Childebert only appeared in the background, first during Grimoald the Younger's appointment as mayor:

Drogo the son of Pippin, duke of the Champagne, died. His brother Grimoald was set up by his father Pippin as mayor of the palace in the court of King Childebert, and was wed to the daughter of Radbod, duke of the Frisians.[85]

And then together with Autbert of Avranches' vision of the archangel:

When Childebert held the monarchy of the kingdom of the Franks, the archangel Michael appeared to Autbert bishop of Avranches, admonishing him once and twice to found a church in his memory in a place on the seaside that, because of its conspicuousness, is

---

domus perimit, Chlodoveum quendam fingens esse filium Lotharii regis regem sibi facit, ad eius sacramentum quos potest poenis, minis et blanditiis impellit."

[82] Compare *Passio Leodegarii* 1, MGH SRM 5, ed. B. Krusch (Hanover: Hahnsche Buchhandlung, 1910), pp. 282–322, at ch. 23, p. 305.

[83] With very few exceptions. See Sigebert of Gembloux, *Chronica*, a.693, p. 328: "Chlodoveus filius eius [i.e., Theodorici] regnat post annis 4"; a.697: "Mortuo Clodoveo, Hildebertus frater eius regnat post eum annis 16." The active voice is overwhelmingly confined to the verb *regnare*.

[84] Ibid., a.691, p. 328: "Theodericus rex cum Bertario, Pippino congressus, vincitur; Bertarius a suis perimitur; Theodericus rex a Pippino capitur. Pippinus Neustriam sibi subiugat, et sub Theoderico solus toti regno principando statum rerum meliorat."

[85] Sigebert of Gembloux, *Chronica*, a.699, p. 328: "Drogo filius Pipini, dux Campanensium, moritur. Grimoaldus frater eius a patre Pipino in aula Hildeberti regis maior domus statuitur, eique filia Rabbodi Fresonum ducis in uxorem desponditur."

called *Tumba* (burial mound), *wishing that such veneration be shown to him in the sea as that shown in Monte Gargano.*[86]

The plot, meanwhile, became increasingly focused on the Carolingians. The year 713 brought with it the murder of Grimoald and the installation of Theodoald, son of Drogo, as mayor of the palace. In the following year came the death of Pippin:

> Pippin the princeps died, leaving his son from Alpaida, Charles "the Hammer," also known as Martel, as his heir. Plectrude, Pippin's remaining wife, having captured her stepson Charles, held him in custody in Cologne and with her grandson the mayor of the palace Theodoald usurped the principate of the kingdom.[87]

The use of the term *princeps* in Carolingian historiography has often been noted.[88] As argued by Goderniaux, it allowed the Carolingian chroniclers to obscure the fact that Pippin II and Charles Martel were never kings. By invoking imperial terminology, it created a conscious link with the Roman imperial past, and, by extension, with the Frankish imperial future. For Sigebert, the added layer of Salian *imperium* made the terminology all the more appealing.[89] Since the principate became the semantic stand-in for royal power, building up Ansegisel as a holder of the office was necessary to avoid an embarrassing *lacuna* between the (supposed) mayoralty of Arnulf and the principate of Pippin II. And since the principate ran through Pippin to Charles Martel, Plectrude and Theodoald were to become usurpers,

---

[86] Sigebert of Gembloux, *Chronica*, a.709, p. 329: "Childeberto monarchiam regni Francorum tenente, archangelus Michael apparens Autberto Abrincatensi episcopo, monuit semel et iterum, ut in loco maris, qui propter eminentiam sui Tumba vocatur, fundaret aecclesiam in memoriam sui, volens talem venerationem exiberi sibi in pelago, qualis exibetur in monte Gargano." Monte Gargano in Apulia is the oldest shrine dedicated to Michael and its foundation was also prompted by an apparition. See G. N. Gandy, "*Revelatio* on the Origins of Mont Saint-Michel (Fifth–Ninth Centuries)," *Speculum* 95, 1 (2020), pp. 132–166. On the development of Autbert's and Michael's shared cult, see K.A. Smith, "An Angel's Power in a Bishop's Body: The Making of the Cult of Aubert of Avranches at Mont-Saint-Michel," *Journal of Medieval History* 29, 4 (2003), pp. 347–360.

[87] Sigebert of Gembloux, *Chronica*, a.714, p. 329: "Pipinus princeps obiit, et filium suum ex Alpaide Karolum, Tudetem sive Martellum cognomento, principatus sui heredem reliquit. Plictrudis relicta Pipini Karolum privignum suum captum in Colonia urbe custodiae mancipat; et cum nepote suo Theodoaldo maiore domus principatum regni usurpat."

[88] I. Heidrich, "Titulatur und Urkunden der arnulfingischen Hausmeier," *Archiv für Diplomatik, Schriftgeschichte, Siegel- und Wappenkunde* 11–12 (1965-6), pp. 78–86; Dutton, *The Politics of Dreaming*, pp. 65–69; K. Leyser, *Communications and Power in Medieval Europe: The Carolingian and Ottonian Centuries* (London: Hambeldon Press, 1994), p. 9. For the *princeps* in the masses for times of war and the benefit of the king, see M. Garrison, "The *Missa pro principe* in the Bobbio Missal," *The Bobbio Missal: Liturgy and Religious Culture in Merovingian Gaul*, eds. Y. Hen and R. Meens (Cambridge: Cambridge University Press, 2004), pp. 187–205.

[89] Goderniaux, "*Eique victoria provenit in omnibus*," p. 761.

especially since Sigebert's Pippin explicitly bequeathed his title to the son of Alpaida. But here as in Grimoald's case, Sigebert did not present an entirely convenient history from the Carolingian standpoint. Already in the entry for 698, quoting his own *Life of St. Lambert*, Sigebert lambasted Pippin's polygamy:

> *St. Lambert dared to rebuke the princeps Pippin for taking as a concubine Alpaida in addition to his legitimate wife Plectrude. He was martyred in Liège by Dodo, the brother of that same Alpaida, and buried in Maastricht, and was replaced as bishop by St. Hucbert.*[90]

The *Life of St. Lambert*, which Sigebert composed sometime after 1090 at the request of Henry of Montaigu, canon and deacon of the church of St. Lambert in Liège, was a mature and articulate hagiography.[91] Unlike the works undertaken in Metz, the *Life of St. Lambert* suffered no shortage of sources. In fact, Sigebert's efforts would produce the fourth and fifth renditions in the hagiographical corpus dedicated to the martyred bishop. A first attempt to write the saint's *Life* was made in the second quarter of the eighth century and resulted in the *Vita vetustissima*. It was followed in the early tenth century by a prose *Life* penned by Bishop Stephen of Liège, who also commissioned a hagiography in verse, initially attributed to Hucbald of Saint-Amand. Sigebert's additions are known as the *Vita prior* and the *Vita altera*, the latter an expanded and corrected version undertaken at Henry of Montaigu's request. In the *Life of St. Lambert*, Sigebert took special pains to distance Pippin II from the martyrdom of Lambert, an effort that carried over into the *Chronica*. In the *Life of St. Lambert*, Pippin was the "distinguished ruler above all other *principes* of the Franks, whose glory was enhanced by the numerous victories of his title."[92]

Under Sigebert's pen, the entire saintly clan was paraded for the reader: St. Gertrude, St. Arnulf, St. Chlodulf, and St. Begga were all there to endow Pippin with impeccable origins. But, as it turned out, the triumphs of war could not inoculate Pippin against the temptations of the flesh, embodied in the person of Alpaida. The final chapters of the *Life of Lambert* revolved around the bishop's reproaches of Pippin for his misconduct and the subsequent worsening of relations between Alpaida's kin

---

[90] Sigebert of Gembloux, *Chronica*, a.698, p. 328: "Sanctus Lambertus Pipinum principem increpare ausus, quod pelicem Alpaidem suae legitimae uxori Plictrudi superduxerit, a Dodone fratre ipsius Alpaidis Leodii martyrizatur, et Traiecti tumulatur, eique sanctus Hucbertus episcopus subrogatur."
[91] See Meyers, "Vitarum scriptor," pp. 68–74.
[92] Sigebert of Gembloux, *Vita prior sancti Lamberti*, PL 160, cols. 759–782, at ch. 16, cols. 771–772: "Pippinus, ut praediximus, principabatur egregie super omnes principes Francorum; cujus gloriam augebant crebri victuriarum tituli."

and Lambert's. Two relatives of Alpaida's brother Dodo attacked the church and were killed by Lambert's nephews. This, in turn, stirred the vengeance of Dodo against them and their episcopal uncle. The development of Lambert's cult after his death was indebted to Pippinid attention and patronage. Indeed, it was at Lambert's shrine that Grimoald the Younger met his end, an episode also recorded in the *Life of Lambert*.

However, Sigebert was determined to make the best of his character's unfortunate lapse in judgement:

Obviously, of this illicit marriage of Pippin and Alpaida was born Charles Martel; of Charles Pippin III, who was promoted from princeps to king of the Franks; of Pippin Charlemagne, who none of the kings of the Franks, either before or after him, was greater, and—who could doubt this? —was stronger or more fortunate, more powerful in public affairs or more religious in ecclesiastical discipline.

St. Lambert died on the 15th to the Kalends of October, in his fortieth episcopal year, under the king of the Franks Childebert, son of King Theuderic. After this Theuderic the kings of the Franks ruled in name only, and the royal power was handed over to the mayors of the palace until Pippin III.[93]

The *Life of Lambert* was Sigebert's retort to the *LHF*'s claim of a Merovingian resurgence under Childebert. His decision to include this passage seems to have been rooted in his desire to announce that mayoral power had now superseded royal authority. Since these events in the *Life* took place in the late 690s, neither Sigibert III nor Clovis II would have been around to take the blame. The date of Merovingian decline was thus pinned to the death of Theuderic in 693, with Lambert's martyrdom still comfortably accommodated within this timeframe.

In the *Chronica*, Childebert's death was reported unceremoniously:

King Childebert died, and Clovis, his son, reigned for 4 years.[94] *The Franks clashed together in a destructive war against Theodoald, and, with him defeated, appointed Ragamfred as mayor of the palace and Chilperic as king. Charles broke out, with divine approval, of his stepmother's custody, and immediately pressed upon Ragamfred to wrench his principate away from him.*[95]

---

[93] Sigebert of Gembloux, *Vita prior sancti Lamberti*, PL 160, cols. 759–782, at ch. 28, cols. 780–782: "Ex illicito quippe Pippini et Alpaidis conjugio, natus est Carolus Martellus; de Carolo Pippinus tertius, qui ex principe, in regem Francorum promotus est; de Pippino Carolus Magnus, quo nemo ante eum, vel post eum, inter Francorum reges, fuit maior, de quo dubitari potest fortior an felicior esset, potentior in republica, an religiosior in ecclesiastica disciplina.

Passus est S. Lambertus xv Kalend. Octobris, anno episcopatus sui quadragesimo, sub rege Francorum Hildeberto, Theodorici regis filio, a quo Theodorico reges Francorum solo nomine regnabant, penes maiores domus potentia regni constituta usque ad Pippinum tertium."

[94] This was corrected to Dagobertus by a later hand in Brussels, KBR 18239–18240.

[95] Sigebert of Gembloux, *Chronica*, a.715, p. 329: "Mortuo Hildeberto Francorum rege, Clodoveus, filius eius, regnat annis 4. Franci contra Theodoaldum damnoso utrimque

That Childebert failed to impress Sigebert is perhaps most apparent from his misnaming of Childebert's son as Clovis when it should have been Dagobert III. But even more damningly, Sigebert chose to name the mayor before naming the king. Chilperic was probably quite effective in opposing Charles Martel, at least for a time, and yet he cut a very lackluster figure in the *Chronica*. He quickly became the pawn of Ragamfred, then Eudo, and finally Charles Martel in their fight for hegemony. He was finally brought in to replace another unremarkable king, Chlothar IV, whom Charles Martel dominated for two years from the death of Dagobert III until Chlothar's own death two years later. Nothing of Chlothar's actions survived in the *Chronica*, which is to be expected given the paucity of evidence concerning him. In a break from his usual style, Sigebert depicted Martel's breakout of Cologne as having taken place *divino nutu* (with divine approval), which supported the framing of the principate as rightfully belonging to him.

When Chilperic died in 726, he merited no more than a brief mention, followed by an account of Martel's appointment of Theuderic IV, who reigned for fifteen years. During this period, many crucial events unfolded. The Battle of Poitiers, placed in the *Chronica* in 730, faithfully repeated the account of the *Fredegar Continuations*.[96] Martel's subjugation of Burgundy came next, followed by Gascony and Aquitaine. Then it was Frisia's turn, followed by another successful engagement against the Saracens. In all this time, Theuderic IV was left in the shadows. In 741, Sigebert only had this to say: *After Theuderic king of the Franks, Childeric reigned for 10 years*. According to a literal reading of this statement, Theuderic did not even die, like his predecessors; rather, he quietly evaporated to make room for another anemic puppet-king. This was, in fact, chronologically wrong, since Theuderic IV died in early 737, after which Charles Martel ruled without a king until his death.[97] Since Sigebert was loath to introduce into his chronology such irregularities, he postponed Theuderic's death to coincide with Martel's in 741. This also had the effect of pushing forward Childeric's appointment, which historically took place not under Martel but under his children— Carloman and Pippin III – in 743.[98]

In Sigebert's defense, it would have been quite impossible to calculate the beginning of the mayoral interregnum without the *Computus of 737*, which provides the date of Theuderic IV's death, or the diplomas issued

---

bello confligunt, eoque victo Raginfredum maiorem domus et Chilpericum regem statuunt. Karolus de custodia novercae divino nutu eripitur, moxque principatum suum de manu Raginfredi extorquere nititur."
[96] On this see Goderniaux, "*Eique victoria provenit in omnibus*," pp. 760–761.
[97] Weidemann, "Zur Chronologie," pp. 208–209.   [98] Ibid., p. 210.

under Martel after the king had died.[99] Sigebert is not known to have had access to these documents, although one might assume that even if he had, he would have found the *Computus*'s adherence to Dionysius Exiguus somewhat unappealing.[100] It is nevertheless not inconceivable for him to have known of the donation charter issued by Count Robert of Hesbaye to the nearby monastery Saint-Trond in 741, which is dated to the fifth year after the death of Theuderic IV.[101] All of this does little to explain the decision to jointly date the death of Martel and the accession to the throne of Childeric III to 741, so an intentional choice on Sigebert's part to create seamless continuity seems the most logical choice.

Childeric III, of course, fared no better than Theuderic. His only other mention, again in the passive voice, was concerned with his tonsure and placement in a monastery:

Childeric king of the Franks was tonsured as a monk; Pippin the princeps, by apostolic authority and election of the Franks, was anointed and consecrated king by St. Boniface, archbishop of Mainz, and reigned for 18 years [after about 88 years from when the mayors of the palace began to rule over the kings of the Franks].[102]

This small, eighty-eight-year calculation at the end of the passage is present in Brussels, KBR 18239–18240 and in a number of additional manuscripts, such as London, BL Harley MS 651 [ff. 99v-100 r], but absent from others, such as London, BL Add MS 24145 [f. 38v]. Whether we consider Brussels, KBR 18239–18240 to have been Sigebert's autograph or not, the bracketed entry is still a component of the earliest recension and many of its descendants. The entry seems to have been made at a later point and, while the script is very similar to that

---

[99] *Das Neustrische Streitgespräch von 737*, MGH QQ zur Geistesgesch. 21, 1, ed. A. Borst (Hanover: Hahnsche Buchhandlung, 2006), pp. 375–423, at ch. 30, p. 421: "A nativitate autem Domini usque ad praesentem annum, in quo Teudericus rex Francorum defunctus est, septingenti triginta septem." For Theuderic's diplomas, see MGH DD Merov., ed. H. Pertz (Hanover: Hahnsche Buchhandlung, 1872), 91–95, pp. 80–86. Theuderic's last diploma comes from 727, while Childeric's first dates from 743. Martel's gift in 741 of a villa in Clichy to the monastery of Saint-Denis, MGH DD Arnulf., ed. I. Heidrich (Hanover: Hahnsche Buchhandlung, 2011), 14, pp. 32–33 concludes with: "Actum Careciaco villa, in palatio, quod fecit mense Septembri die septimo decimo, anno quinto post defunctum Theodericum regem."

[100] On the Calculus and Dionysius Exiguus, see Borst's introduction to the *Computus of 737*, pp. 376–378.

[101] J.-M. Pardessus, ed., *Diplomata, Chartae, Epistolae, Leges ad res Gallo-Francicas spectantia*, 2 vols. (Paris: ex Typographio regio, 1843–9), II.542, pp. 379–380: " ... anno quinto post obitum Theoderici regis ...."

[102] Sigebert of Gembloux, *Chronica*, a.750, p. 332: "Hildricus rex Francorum in monachum tonsuratur; Pipinus vero princeps auctoritate apostolica et Francorum electione a sancto Bonefacio Moguntiae archiepiscopo in regem unguitur et consecratur, et regnavit annis 18 [post annos circiter octoginta octo, postquam maiores domus ceperunt principari super reges Francorum]."

found throughout the rest of the passage, the stroke is thinner and begins slightly higher on the ruled line than the text preceding it. As noted by Michiel Verweij, the manuscript saw numerous additions and was transformed into something of a working draft, so this should come as no surprise.[103] Subtracting 88 years from 750, we end up with 662, the very same year in which Sigebert first reported the transfer of power to the mayors of the palace.

* * *

At no point in his composition did Sigebert explain why he thought Merovingian royal power dissipated in 662. We should therefore look for clues to his reasoning in the preceding years. Obviously, Grimoald's *coup d'état* played a significant role in convincing Sigebert, although even here the monk of Gembloux took pains to ensure that the line of kings remained unbroken, first by insisting on the formal adoption of Childebert, then by crowning Childeric king immediately after the bloody resolution of the affair.[104] A second reason for Merovingian decline was to be found in Neustria, where Clovis's removal of the arm of St. Denis relegated the king to a state of *amentia perpetua* (perpetual madness), at least for the remaining two years of his life. Clovis's death notice was the narrative element that occasioned Sigebert's appraisal of Merovingian decline, so this was probably the more important of the two reasons for his dire assessment of the royal dynasty's condition. Sigebert was inclined to look for a place to insert the starting point of the process of Carolingian takeover, thanks, no doubt, to the influence of his Carolingian sources, primarily (but not exclusively) Paul the Deacon and Einhard. But it was the *LHF* that provided the perfect chronological window, since it was the only source that reported on everything that had gone awry in the *regna Francorum* before and after the deaths of Sigibert III and Clovis II.

The *Chronica* provides a well-thought-out buildup of the Pippinid family, alternating between historiography and hagiography to produce an image of sanctity, used not only to bolster the family's overall prestige, but also to mitigate its failings. The move to the *princeps* terminology was consonant with Carolingian sources; in the *Chronica*, however, it served not only to contextualize Carolingian *imperium*, but also that of the German emperors, bringing its program of *translatio imperii* to its desired destination. Sigebert's usage of Pippinid ascent and Merovingian decline demonstrated just how weak the papacy's ability had been to affect

---

[103] Verweij, "Les manuscrits des œvres de Sigebert de Gembloux," p. 111.
[104] Since Sigebert did not know the *Vita Wilfridi*, Dagobert II was not worked into his chronology.

dynastic transition, a critical question considering the clash between the papal and imperial parties felt so forcefully in his neck of the woods.[105]

Yet Sigebert's insistence on tight and orderly – if not always accurate – regnal chronologies meant that he included almost all the Merovingians in his narrative. And while they became far less imposing figures after 662, they were not forgotten. Rather, they were presented in a way that conceived of the transfer of royal power as a regular feature of Frankish history. For Sigebert it was important that this process remain free from *lacunae*, even when it was bereft of substance.

5.2 Yosef Ha-Kohen's Late Merovingians

Yosef Ha-Kohen, the son of Spanish exiles (Cuenca and, after 1412, Huete), was born in Avignon, where his parents had settled briefly after 1492.[106] Most of his adult life was spent in the environs of Genoa, where he became a leader of the Italian Jewish community and a prolific author whose oeuvre spanned a range of genres. His keen interest in writing and especially in historiography stemmed in part from the erudite environment of his parental home; he was born into a distinguished family that provided excellent resources for a budding physician and intellectual. However, it was also the result of a grander current sweeping Europe in his day, namely that of humanism. A reawakened interest in historiography, primarily in Italian and French circles, and the advent of print were two forces that did not leave Jewish scholarship unaffected.[107] This was especially true for Ha-Kohen, who relied on humanist histories, made accessible through the propagation of printed editions, as sources for his

---

[105] See Beumann, *Sigebert von Gembloux*, pp. 59–60.
[106] See the introduction in D. Gross, ed., *Sefer Divrei Hayamim lemalkei Tzarfat ulemalkei Beit Otoman haTogar* (Jerusalem: The Bialik Institute, 1955) [Hebrew]; M.A. Shulvass, 'To Which of Rabbi Joseph Hacohen's Works Had the Proof-Reader Written his 'Continuation'?," *Zion* 10 (1945), pp. 78–79 [Hebrew]; S. Simonsohn, "Joseph HaCohen in Genoa," *Italia: Studi e ricerche sulla cultura e sulla letteratura degli Ebrei d'Italia* 13–15 (2001), pp. 119–30; R. Bonfil, "Introduction," in Yosef Ha-Kohen, *Chronicle of the French and Ottoman Kings*, ed. R. Bonfil, 3 vols. (Jerusalem: Magnes Press, 2020) [Hebrew], 1, pp. 1–30 [hereafter, Ha-Kohen, *Divrei Hayamim*]. For a historically inspired dramatization of Ha-Kohen's life, see R. Bonfil, *The Life of Joseph* (Jerusalem: Magnes Press, 2020) [Hebrew].
[107] On Jewish historiography and humanism, see R. Bonfil, "Esiste una storiografia ebraica medioevale?," *Associazione Italiana per lo Studio del Giudaismo: Atti del Congresso* IV (1987), pp. 227–247; R. Bonfil, "How Golden Was the Age of the Renaissance in Jewish Historiography?," *History and Theory* 27 (1988), pp. 78–102; R. Bonfil, "Jewish Attitudes toward History and Historical Writing in Pre-Modern Times," *Jewish History* 11 (1997), pp. 7–40; Y.H. Yerushalmi, "Clio and the Jews: Reflections on Jewish Historiography in the Sixteenth Century," *Proceedings of the American Academy for Jewish Research* 46–47 (1979–80), pp. 607–638.

literary work.[108] The French occupation of northern Italy in the late fifteenth and early sixteenth century ensured that texts chronicling the first Frankish centuries were among those circulated when Ha-Kohen was researching his chronicle.[109]

Ha-Kohen produced two major chronicles. The first and most ambitious of these was *Sefer Divrei Hayamim lemalkei Tzarfat uVeit Otoman haTogar*, or *The Book of the Histories of the Kings of France and of the Kings of Ottoman Turkey*, a universal history completed shortly before 1554. Several years later he composed another work, *Sefer Emeq Habakha* or *The Book of the Vale of Tears*, which concentrated on the bitter history of the Jews from the destruction of the Second Temple to his own time.[110] Ha-Kohen's literary interests were not limited to historiography. Among his many translations are such works as *Sefer Metsiv Gevulot 'Amim* (*Book of the Setter of the Boundaries of Peoples*), a reworking of Joannes Boemus's *Omnium gentium mores, leges, et ritus*; *Sefer India* (*Book of India*) and *Sefer Fernando Cortez*, a revision of Gomara's *La historia general de las Indias*, both indicative of Ha-Kohen's avid interest in the news coming in from the New World at the height of the Age of Discoveries; and *Sefer Mekits Nirdamim* (*Book of the Waker of the Sleeping*), a translation of a medical treatise by Meir Alguades, physician to the kings of Castile and a preeminent Jewish leader in fourteenth-century Spain.[111] We also know of numerous letters sent and received by Ha-Kohen, as well as a number of smaller works on Hebrew grammar, epistolary protocol, and poetry.[112] From this body of work, we can surmise that Ha-Kohen spoke at least five languages with impressive proficiency.

---

[108] For Ha-Kohen's cultural influences, see M. Jacobs, "Joseph ha-Kohen, Paolo Giovio, and Sixteenth-Century Historiography," in *Cultural Intermediaries: Jewish Intellectuals in Early-Modern Italy*, eds. D.B. Ruderman and G. Veltri (Philadelphia: University of Pennsylvania Press, 2004), pp. 67–85; M. Jacobs, "Sephardic Migration and Cultural Transfer: The Ottoman and Spanish Expansion through a Cinquecento Jewish Lens," *Journal of Early Modern History* 21 (2017), pp. 516–42.

[109] See D. Abulafia, ed., *The French Descent into Renaissance Italy, 1494–95: Antecedents and Effects* (London: Routledge, 1995).

[110] Yosef Ha-Kohen, *Sefer 'Emek Ha-Bakha (The Vale of Tears) with the Chronicle of the Anonymous Corrector*, ed. K. Almbadh (Uppsala: Almqvist & Wiksell, 1981); Yosef Ha-Kohen, *Sefer 'Emek Ha-Bakha (The Vale of Tears)*, ed. R. Bonfil (Jerusalem: Magnes Press, 2020) [Hebrew].

[111] On Ha-Kohen's geographical interests, see L. Mintz-Manor, "The Discourse on the New World in Early Modern Jewish Culture," doctoral dissertation (Jerusalem: Hebrew University of Jerusalem, 2011) [in Hebrew]. On Alguades – and Ha-Kohen's mention thereof – see S.L. Einbinder, "Meir Alguades: History, Empathy, and Martyrdom," *Religion & Literature*, 42, 1/2 (2010), pp. 185–209.

[112] D. Avraham, *Irascible Historian: New Light on the Personality of the Sixteenth-Century Chronicler Joseph ha-Kohen from His Personal Correspondence* (Jerusalem: Beit David, 2004) [Hebrew]; D. Avraham, "The Joseph ha-Cohen Epistolary," *Italia* 5, 1–2 (1985), pp. 7–98 [Hebrew].

Of all these compositions, *Divrei Hayamim* is certainly the most expansive. Its chronology spans from Creation to the papally mandated burning of the Talmud in 1553. Calling it a world chronicle or a universal history is not entirely adequate, for several reasons. The first is that, while it began its narrative with Adam, from whom ensued a biblically inspired *Liber generationis*, humanity's earliest history takes up no more than a single paragraph, after which the authorial lens turns abruptly to the Franks.[113] In this sense, *Divrei Hayamim* resembles the *LHF* more than it does *Fredegar* or Sigebert's *Chronica*. Other *gentes* were certainly discussed; the Persians, Saracens, and Turks appeared early on, and were joined by other European and Middle Eastern nations as the plot progressed. But Ha-Kohen had no intention of providing a continuous commentary on world events, focusing only on those nations and regions that were conducive to his narrative aims, all of which were tightly connected to the histories of the French and the Turks.

Secondly, *Divrei Hayamim* consciously privileged the Jews' decisive role in the unfolding of history. We see this particularly in the choice to disrupt the rhythm of the plot and go into much more detail whenever Jews were involved. While Ha-Kohen was preoccupied with the chronological progression of history, he was perfectly capable, like Sigebert of Gembloux before him, of collapsing the chronology in order to emphasize elements that were of special importance. So, for instance, the conquest of the Holy Land by 'Umar ibn al-Khattab in 637–638 and the subsequent construction of the Dome of the Rock, with its attendant significance from the Jewish perspective, merited the following treatment, which looked both to the distant past and the distant future:[114]

In that time 'Umar ibn al-Khattab, who was the third generation to Muhammad, came with a very, very large army and they captured the land of Aramea and the land of the Philistines and their fame echoed throughout the land. They laid siege to Gaza and captured it. No city remained beyond their reach. They also forcefully

---

[113] On this passage, taken from Josippon, see *The Josippon (Josephus Gorionides)*, ed. and trans. D. Flusser, 2 vols. (Jerusalem, 2009) [Hebrew], 3–4; D. Flusser, "Josippon, a Medieval Hebrew Version of Josephus," in *Josephus, Judaism, and Christianity*, eds. L.H. Feldman and G. Hata (Leiden and Detroit: Brill, 1987), 386–397; S. Dönitz, "Historiography among Byzantine Jews – the Case of Sefer Yosippon," in *Jews in Byzantium: Dialectics of Minority and Majority Cultures*, ed. R. Bonfil et al. (Leiden: Brill, 2012), pp. 953–970; S. Dönitz, "Sefer Yosippon (Josippon)," in *A Companion to Yosefus*, eds. H. Howell Chapman and Z. Rodgers (Oxford and Malden, MA: Wiley-Blackwell, 2016), pp. 382–389.

[114] For a discussion of Muslim construction on the Temple Mount and its relationship to the Jewish temple, see P. Berger, *The Crescent on the Temple: The Dome of the Rock as Image of the Ancient Jewish Sanctuary* (Leiden and Boston: Brill, 2012), esp. pp. 31–74. See also L. Nees, *Perspectives on Early Islamic Art in Jerusalem* (Leiden and Boston: Brill, 2016).

took Damascus at that time. Heraclius heard and grew sad at heart because he was no match for them, and he returned to his land. Then the Arabs took all of the land of Israel and the land of Egypt. And they chose to dwell in those desolate cities and increased (their) families like flocks.[115] They also retook desolate Jerusalem and made a pact with the uncircumcised that dwelt within it and with the tomb of their messiah. And they had them pay tax which they placed on them as law.

'Umar ibn al-Khattab asked where the house was that Titus had destroyed, in which the name of God was recited. They showed him the ruined temple of God. He spent much silver and gold to build the house and to renew it as it once was. He fell to the ground and prayed to God, and they made haste to rebuild the house as 'Umar had decreed, and he provided the temple with income and an estate to carry out the daily worship of the Lord.

Jerusalem and all of the land of Israel and the land of Aramea were ruled by the Arabs for four hundred and ninety years, until the kings of the west went there in the year 4856. When Godfrey and his nobles went there, they captured it and dwelt there for 88 years, until God stirred Saladin, king of Egypt, who took it from them, and he cast them out to another land on that day.[116]

Divrei Hayamim was intended for a Jewish readership fluent in Hebrew, so Ha-Kohen used a linguistic register rich in biblical allusions and antiquated turns of phrase. He was nevertheless able to produce a narrative surprisingly flowing in style. His adaptations were not solely linguistic; Ha-Kohen expanded on historical episodes that pertained to the Jews and reduced drastically the favorable depictions of Christian piety he found in his sources. For the Rhineland massacres of 1096, to give one example, Ha-Kohen broke off from the main account of the First Crusade to provide a detailed depiction of the violence visited on the Jews of Speier, Mainz, Cologne, and several other cities. The conquest of Constantinople, to provide another, was depicted as the realization of a statement from Lamentations.[117] Historical persons in *Divrei Hayamim* were generally depicted favorably or critically based on their treatment of

---

[115] This is meant to connote Psalm 107:41, which is interpreted to mean that they grew plentiful like flocks.
[116] Ha-Kohen, *Divrei Hayamim*, 1, chs. 12–14, pp. 65–66: "בימים ההם בא עמר בן קטף והוא הדור׳ השלישי למחומד ועמו חיל גדול מאד מאד וילכדו את ארץ ארם וארץ פלשתים ויהי שמעם בכל הארץ. ויחנו על עזה וילכדוה. לא היתה קריה אשר שגבה מהם. וגם את דמשק לקחו ביד חזקה בעת ההיא. וישמע איראקליאו ויתעצב אל־ לבו מאד כי לא יכול להם. וישוב אל ארצו. אז לקחו הערביים את כל ארץ ישראל ואת ארץ מצרים. ובחרו לשבת בערים השוממות ההם. וישימו כצאן משפחות. וגם את ירושלים השוממה לקחו שנית. ויכרתו ברית את הערלים אשר בתוכה ואת קבר משיחם. ויתנו להם המס אשר שמו עליהם לחוק. וישאל עמר בן קטף ויאה הבית אשר הרס טיטוש אשר נקרא שם האלהים שם. ויראו לו את מקדש ה' ההרוס. ויוציא כסף וזהב לרוב ויצו לבנות את הבית ולהשיבה על תילה כבראשונה. וישתחו ארצה ויתפלל אל ה'. וימהרו לבנות את הבית כאשר צוה עומר ויתן אל המקדש הכנסות ושדה אחוזה להוציא לעבודת האלהים דבר יום ביומו. ותהי ירושלם וכל ארץ ישראל וארץ ארם ביד הערביים ארבע מאות ותשעים שנה עד אשר הלכו מלכי המערב בשנת שש וחמישים ושמנה מאות שנה וארבעת אלפים. בלכת שם גוטיפרידו והשרים אשר אתו וילכדוה וישבו בה שמונים ושמנה שנה. עד אשר הקים האלקים את שאלאדינו מלך מצרים ויקחנה מידם. וישליכם אל ארץ אחרת כיום הזה."
[117] Lamentations 4:21.

the Jews. 'Umar was thus a pious restorer of the Temple Mount, Queen Isabella of Spain a devil, who God repaid in kind, killing off her children and cursing her with malignant tumors.[118] While the Jews were not the stated protagonists of *Divrei Hayamim* – a role they would assume in the *Vale of Tears* – the book evaluated events through the prism of Jewish history.

Jews were not entirely absent from Ha-Kohen's account of the Merovingian period, although their appearances were confined to the reign of Dagobert.[119] For this reason, Ha-Kohen was content to use a tightly limited selection of sources in his coverage of the Merovingian centuries. In fact, the source he used almost exclusively was a little-known sixteenth-century Italian composition – no more than a pamphlet, really – titled *Le vite de tutti gli Re di Francia e degli duca di Milano* by Vittorio Sabino.[120] Having produced the first printed history of French kings in Italian, Sabino was a Francophile who wrote to justify French rule over northern Italy.[121] He admitted as much in the opening to his composition, where he explained why he had undertaken the assignment:

Wishing to write how and under what kings the great and richest Kingdom of France gained such repute, so it is first necessary to relate where they had their origins, for which I shall refer to what is said by the great part of ancient writers.[122]

It took Sabino all of two pages in the Minizio Calvo 1525 edition to rush through the entirety of Merovingian history. Granted, the section dedicated to the kings of France numbered twenty pages from start to finish, so Merovingian history occupied about as much space as one

---

[118] Ha-Kohen, *Divrei Hayamim*, 1, ch. 403, pp. 341–342: "ויקנא ה' לעמו ויתן למלכים האלה גמול במעשה ידיהם. וימות הבן הבכר אשר לפירדינאנדו במגפה ולא נשאר להם בן זכר יורש עצר. ואישאבילה אשתו קצתה בחייה ותאכל חצי בשרה מהנגע אשר יקראו סרטן ותמות. צדיק הוא ה'."

[119] For a detailed discussion of Ha-Kohen and the Merovingians, see Fox, "Chronicling the Merovingians in Hebrew."

[120] Vittorio Sabino, *Le vite di tutti gli Re di Francia fino alla presa del Re Francesco primo & le ragioni quali sua Maiestà pretendeva in Milano, Napoli, & Sicilia* (Rome: Minizio Calvo, 1525).

[121] E.W. Cochrane, *Historians and Historiography in the Italian Renaissance* (Chicago: University of Chicago Press, 1981), p. 342; R. Bonfil, "Riflessioni sulla storiografia ebraica in Italia nel cinquecento," *Italia Judaica* 2 (1986), pp. 56–66, at 58. For a dire appraisal of Sabino's capabilities as a historian, see G. Tiraboschi, *Storia della letteratura italiana* (Modena: Presso la Società Tipografica, 1792), vol. 7, p. 1019. Not much has been written about him since, although Maissen, *Von der Legende zum Modell*, pp. 171–172 provides some context for his work.

[122] Sabino, *Vite*, p. 1: "Volendo scrivere come & sotto quali Re sia venuto in tanta riputatione el grande & richissimo Regno di Francia, par quasi necessario prima raccontare, donde havessi origine, della quale ne referiro quello che dicono per la magior parte gli antichi scrittori." See Maissen, *Von der Legende zum Modell*, pp. 171–172.

would expect. Frankish origins were presented using the familiar story found originally in the *LHF*:

At the time when the Romans wanted to subdue the Gallic nation, France was ruled by diverse princes, much like Germany, in which today there are many lords, or as many republics as there are cities. But being a divided force, Caesar made war on this most rich and in other ways desirable nation to subjugate it to the Roman Empire. In this time, certain fierce peoples called the Franks were cast out of Sicambria for denying Caesar tribute.[123]

Other elements of the plot came not from the *LHF* but from *Fredegar*, such as the mention of the governor Lucius.[124] Of course, this use of sources was not the result of meticulous research that Sabino had conducted into early Frankish sources. Rather, it emerged from his complete reliance on a slightly more elaborate source, *De regibus Francorum libri* III, composed by Michele Riccio (d. 1508/1515), a Neapolitan lawyer with strong ties to the French courts of Charles VIII and Louis XII. His political service included such highlights as the presidency of the Provençal parliament and memberships in the Parisian parliament, the French parliament, and the *Conseil du roi*.[125]

De regibus Francorum was first published in 1505 and was itself indebted to the well-known apologist of French interventionism in Italy, Robert Gaguin (d. 1501).[126] Gaguin was a minister general for the Order of Trinitarians, a canon law professor at the University of Paris, a diplomat, and, most importantly for us, a renowned humanist historian. In his 1495 history, *Compendium de origine et gestis Francorum*, Gaguin based his work mainly on prints produced in the late fifteenth century of the *Grandes Chroniques de France* and several other Dionysian works, which exhibit

---

[123] Ibid.: "Al tempo che li Romani volsero domare la natione Gallica, la Francia era signoregiata da diversi principi, che quasi era simile alla Alamagnia, nella quale hoggidi vi sono tanti signori, o Republice quante vi sono citta. Pero essendo le forze divise, Cesare constrinse quella natione richissima & oltra modo desiderosa di guerre, a ubidire allo Imperio Romano. In questo tempo certi feroci populi, che si chiamavono Franci, furono scacciati di Sicambria, per che negavono a Cesare il tributo." See Maissen, *Von der Legende zum Modell*, p. 347.
[124] See *Fredegar* III.7. [125] Maissen, *Von der Legende zum Modell*, pp. 165–171.
[126] M. Riccio, *De regibus Francorum libri* III (Basle: Joannes Froben, 1517), p. 3v: "In Gallia primum potiti sunt urbe Treuerorum, Lucio Romano præfecto dedente." For the date of publication, see A. Schoysman, "Jean Lemaire de Belges et Josse Bade," *Le Moyen Age* 112, 3 (2006), pp. 575–584, at p. 577. Maissen, *Von der Legende zum Modell*, p. 171 refers to Sabino's dependence on Riccio's work as plagiarism. For Italian, particularly Milanese, usage of the Gaulish past to legitimize the present, see O. Margolis, "The Gaulish Past of Milan and the French Invasion of Italy," in *Local Antiquities, Local Identities: Art, Literature and Antiquarianism in Europe, c. 1400–1700*, eds. K. Christian and B. de Divitiis (Manchester: Manchester University Press, 2019), pp. 102–120.

certain irregularities in the Merovingian chapters.[127] In his treatment of the period, Ha-Kohen essentially mimicked Sabino, providing a literal Hebrew translation of the Italian.[128] Mistakes introduced in Gaguin were thus compounded and exacerbated in the subsequent reworkings and abridgements made to his work by Riccio, Sabino, and Ha-Kohen, resulting in a series of distortions of the Merovingian storyline, as we shall see.

Dagobert's Byzantine entanglements received additional attention from Ha-Kohen but, as already noted, this was because the Jews were involved. Other digressions from the source came when Sabino employed pietistic language, which Ha-Kohen found distasteful. We see this in Clovis's baptism, Dagobert's patronage of Saint-Denis, and, for the purposes of the present chapter, the monastic vocations of late Merovingian kings, such as Chilperic II and Theuderic IV.

In both Sabino and in Ha-Kohen, therefore, coverage of the late Merovingians was brief and unassuming. It took Ha-Kohen one and a half pages in the rather large font of the 1758 Propps edition to relate Frankish history from the death of Dagobert to the coup of 751, leaving little room for nuance. This skeletal report nevertheless points to certain inherited perceptions about the framing of Merovingian kingship and Carolingian ascent, as the following discussion will endeavor to demonstrate.

Immediately after the digression on 'Umar, Ha-Kohen turned to report on the death of Dagobert. Ha-Kohen's treatment of Dagobert provides a break from the usual rhythm of events, so it is worth pausing here to consider its role in the framing of Merovingian decline. *Divrei Hayamim* replicates some of Sabino's reporting, such as the fact that Dagobert "built up the temple of St. Dionysius, where the first king of the Franks was buried."[129] Ha-Kohen also inherited Sabino's unfortunate confusion of Charibert I with Charibert II, thereby leapfrogging sixty-five years of

---

[127] R. Gaguin, *Compendium de origine et gestis Francorum* (Lyon: Johann Trechsel, 1497), which is the second print that contains expansions and corrections of the first, undertaken in 1495 in Paris by Pierre le Dru, with which Gaguin was extremely unhappy. On these episodes, see Davies, "Late XVth Century French Historiography," p. 76 and, for the Merovingian errors, pp. 99–106.

[128] On Lucius, see *GCh*, ed. Viard, 1.3, pp. 17–18. On Ha-Kohen's sources, see J. Kessous, "La 'Chronique' de Joseph Ha-Cohen," *Archives Juives* 13 (1977), pp. 45–53; Bonfil, "Riflessioni," p. 58; M. Jacobs, *Islamische Geschichte in jüdischen Chroniken: Hebräische Historiographie des 16. und 17. Jahrhunderts*, Texts and Studies in Medieval and Early Modern Judaism 18 (Tübingen: Mohr Siebeck, 2004), p. 99.

[129] Sabino, *Vite*, 3: "Successegli [Chariberto] Dagoberto fratello da parte di madre, el quale edificio il tempoi di Santo Dionysio, dove il primo Re di Francia fu sepulto." Compare Ha-Kohen, *Divrei Hayamim*, 1, ch. 4, p. 58: "וישכב אריבירטו עם אבותיו בטולושה וימלוך דאגובירטו
בן אמו תחתיו. והוא בנה את במת הבעל דיאונישיו שמה נקבר המלך הראשון אשר מלך בצרפת."

Merovingian history (567–632).¹³⁰ Importantly, he also made some significant departures from his source. Dagobert was interesting to Ha-Kohen because he had attempted to forcefully baptize the Jews, following a request from the emperor Heraclius. Since Sabino was unhelpful in this regard, Ha-Kohen was forced to look elsewhere for information, and indeed his account follows that of the *Grandes Chroniques* quite closely. The *Grandes Chroniques* contains this account:

> *And because he was a great scholar and had a profound literary knowledge, at last he became an astrologer. He understood from the signs of the stars that his empire would be destroyed by a circumcised people, and because he thought that it would be the Jews, he requested through messengers that Dagobert, the king of France, have the Jews of all the provinces of his kingdom baptized, and that all those who would refuse should be condemned to exile. And this King Dagobert did, and thus all those who did not want to receive baptism were exiled and chased out of the kingdom of France.*¹³¹

In *Divrei Hayamim*, the episode is depicted thus:

> *Heraclius grew very wise in astrology, and in his wisdom, he saw the rule of Rome fall in his own day under the feet of the circumcised; and the scoundrel said in his heart: God will not deign to grant this honor to none but the Jews, because they are circumcised. And he raged against them and ordered that in all the cities of his rule those Jews that refuse to convert and turn away from God be killed. He sent messengers to Dagobert king of France so that he would do the same evil deed and Dagobert obeyed him and many converted. Many were put to the sword in France in those days.*¹³²

This passage went through several stages before trickling down to Yosef Ha-Kohen. I have already mentioned the story of Dagobert and the Jews in the introduction, as an example of historical "shards." Throughout this process, it retained most of its details and indeed was made to serve

---

¹³⁰ On this, see Fox, "Chronicling the Merovingians in Hebrew," pp. 438–439. This error stemmed from his fusing of Chlothar I and Chlothar II, both of whom had sons named Charibert who died early. While Riccio recognized the existence of two Chlothars, he had no knowledge of Charibert I, which might account for Sabino's – and Ha-Kohen's – mistake.

¹³¹ *Grandes Chroniques*, ed. Viard, 2, ch. 12, p. 145: "Et pour ce que il estoit granz clercs et de parfonde lettreure, devint-il au derannier astronomiens. Bien cognut par les signes des estoiles que ses empire devoit estre essilliez par un pople circoncis, et pour ce que il cuida que ce deust estre par les Juis, proia-il par ses messages Dagobert, le roi de France, que il feist baptizier les Juis de touts les provinces de son royaume, et que tuit cil qui ce refuseroient fussent dampné par essil. Ensi le fist li roi Dagoberz, car tuit cil qui baptesme ne vorent recevoir furent essillié et chacié dou roiyaume de France."

¹³² Ha-Kohen, *Divrei Hayamim*, ch. 11, p. 64: "ויתחכם איראקליאו בחכמת המזלות מאד. וירא בחכמתו ויפול ממלכות רומי בימיו תחת כפות רגלי הנמולים. ויאמר הבליעל בלבו, לא יחפוץ האלהים לעשות היקר הזה כי אם אל היהודים, כי מולים הם. ויחר אפו עליהם ויצו בכל ערי מלכותו להמית את היהודים אשר ימאנו להמיר את כבודם לשוב מאחרי ה'. ומלאכים שלח אל דאגובירטו מלך צרפת לעשות גם הוא כדבר הרע הזה וישמע אליו דאגובירטו ורבים המירו את כבודם ורבים הוכו לפי חרב בצרפת בימים ההם. ה'! ינקום דם עבדיו השפוך ונקם ישיב לצריו אמן ואמן."

different agendas. As in several other instances we have already discussed, the channel through which these stories flowed began with *Fredegar*, from which it proceeded to Aimoin of Fleury, and from there to the *Grandes Chroniques*. Taking one step back in the chain of evidence, we find this account in Aimoin of Fleury's *Gesta Francorum*:

> Because he was thoroughly educated in the study of letters, he eventually became an astrologer. He therefore recognized in the signs of the stars that his empire would be devastated by a circumcised people, and having affirmed it to refer to the Jews, sent messages to Dagobert, king of the Franks, and asked him that he order all those of Jewish descent who are subjects in his provinces to become Christian; and that those who refused would be punished by exile or death, which Dagobert willingly carried out, having driven away from the boundaries of Francia all of those who would not submit to baptism.[133]

And, finally, the original account found in *Fredegar*:

> Being very learned in letters, he became an astrologer. With God's help he discerned that his empire would be devastated by circumcised peoples. So he sent a delegation to the Frankish king Dagobert, requesting him to order all the Jews of his kingdom baptized to the Catholic faith; this Dagobert fulfilled promptly. Heraclius decreed that the same should be done in all the imperial provinces.[134]

There are important differences between the four versions of the Dagobert story. In Ha-Kohen's version, for example, Heraclius insists on denying the Jews victory, and decrees that any of them who refuses baptism be put to death. In this, Ha-Kohen differed from *Fredegar* and the *Grandes Chroniques*, both of which talk about exile as the favored form of punishment. Even Aimoin, who mentioned the death penalty, conceded that defiant Jews were exiled rather than killed. Ha-Kohen did not mince words in his depiction of the persecutions' severity, stating outright that many lost their lives as a result. As if to emphasize the gravity of the events, he concluded his account with a quote from Deuteronomy 32:43: "For he will avenge the blood of his servants, and will render vengeance to his adversaries."[135]

---

[133] Aimoin, *Gesta Francorum* IV.22, col. 783: "Cumque litteraris abunde esset instructus, ad ultimum astrologus efficitur. Agnoscens itaque in signis siderum, imperium suum a circumcisa gente vastandum, et autumans id de Judaeis fuisse praemonstratum, per inter nuntios Dagobertum rogavit regem Francorum, et cunctos Judaiae stirpis, qui in provinciis illi subjectis manebant, Christianos fieri praeciperet; eos vero qui nollent aut exsilio aut morte damnari. Quod Dagobertus volens effecit, omnes qui noluerunt baptisma suscipere procul a finibus eliminans Franciae."

[134] *Fredegar* IV.65, p. 153: "Cum esset litteris nimius aeruditus, astralogus effecetur; per quod cernens a circumcisis gentibus divino noto emperium esse vastandum, legationem ad Dagobertum regem Francorum dirigens, petens ut omnes Iudeos regni sui ad fidem catolecam baptizandum preciperit. Quod protenus Dagobertus emplevit. Aeraglius per omnes provincias emperiae talem idemque facere decrevit ... "

[135] Also in Nahum 1:2 and in prayer. See Ha-Kohen, *Divrei Hayamim*, p. 64, n.7.

The *Vale of Tears* contains an exact copy of the account found in *Divrei Hayamim*, with one important difference: The biblical quotation is missing. Considering the *Vale*'s overall consolatory tone, it is rather a surprising absence. Yet in *Divrei Hayamim*, the quotation serves to signal the end of one narrative strand (the Persian–Byzantine wars) and the beginning of another (the conquests of the Muslims), while at the same time underscoring the eschatological aims of the composition.[136] More importantly for us, this lengthy account also serves to set the stage for the Merovingians' final phase. It is impossible to say for certain whether Ha-Kohen saw Dagobert as the last successful Merovingian. Dagobert was certainly significant to Ha-Kohen as a persecutor of the Jews, although this contributes little to our understanding of the periodization model with which Ha-Kohen was working. Ha-Kohen's switch to a more laconic style, in which the final Merovingians fare poorly, is perhaps evidence of their diminished stature in his eyes, although this is hardly conclusive evidence. Since Ha-Kohen has very little to say on the matter, we must turn to Sabino, who provided a clearer statement of disapproval for Clovis II:

Clovis followed the aforementioned [i.e., Dagobert] *in rule, having died after 16 years of reigning without doing anything memorable, leaving after himself three children—Chlothar, Childeric, and Theuderic.*[137]

Ha-Kohen left out Sabino's snide remark about Clovis's performance, but otherwise echoed the *Vite de gli re* faithfully. He nevertheless indulged in some dramatic flair when depicting events that took place after Chlothar's untimely death:

The French made his youngest brother Theuderic king and abhorred Childeric, whom they banished, and he went to Austrasia and dwelt there for some days.[138]

---

[136] See Y.H. Yerushalmi, "Messianic Impulses in Joseph Ha-Kohen," in *Jewish Thought in the Sixteenth Century*, ed. B.D. Cooperman (Cambridge, MA: Harvard University Press, 1983), pp. 460–487.

[137] Sabino, *Vite*, p. 3: "Successegli [Chariberto] Dagoberto fratello da parte di madre, el quale edificio il tempoi di Santo Dionysio, dove il primo Re di Francia fu sepulto. Segui nel regno Ludovico figliuolo del sopradetto el quale in xvi anno che regno senza fare cosa alchuna memorabile mori lasciando di se tre figliuoli Clotario, Childerico, & Theodorico." Gaguin's *Compendium* contains a detailed account of Clovis's removal of the arm of St. Denis, although Riccio does not. See Riccio, *De regibus Francorum*, p. 6v: "Ludouicus autem nulla re memorabili gesta per annos sexdecim quibus imperauit, inglorius ab humanis excessit, ex Batilde uxore natione Saxonia Clotario, Childerico, & Theodorico superstitibus liberis, Clotarius qui ætatis priuilegio."

[138] Ha-Kohen, *Divrei Hayamim*, 1, ch. 20, p. 70: "וימליכו הצרפתים את טיאודריקו אחיו והוא הקטן ובקילדריקו געלה נפשם ויגרשוהו וילך לאאושטיריאה וישב שם ימים אחדים." The usage here probably connoted Leviticus 26:43.

As is evident here, Ha-Kohen also repeated Sabino's inaccuracies. Childeric was appointed to the kingship of Austrasia, not expelled there because of the disapproval of the Franks, as both authors contended. Later, the Franks deposed Theuderic and recalled Childeric from Austrasia, elevating him to the kingship. He was then killed on his return from the hunt together with his wife, after having ordered the flogging of a certain noble. Theuderic returned from his monastic exile – he was, Ha-Kohen says, "a priest unto his god at that time"[139] – and placed again on the throne. Two sons were born, whom he "appointed as commanders of his armies at the head of his people."[140] The Hebrew leaves ambiguous whether Theuderic appointed his sons or whether he provided generals for each of them. If the latter, this could point to Ha-Kohen's awareness of the growing influence of the mayors of the palace during Theuderic's second tenure. Otherwise, there are no references to mayors, whether Ebroin, Pippin II, or anyone else.[141] Competition over power came only with Charles Martel, who appeared out of the blue as Chilperic II's rival in both Sabino and Ha-Kohen, the latter of whom is quoted here:

Theuderic died and his eldest son Clovis succeeded him. Three years Clovis ruled and had no sons and died. Childebert his brother ruled for some days. Childebert died in the beginning of his kingship and Dagobert his son succeeded him, having been a young boy at the time. That boy died without issue. He left after himself no heir in the land. And because the seed of royalty was exhausted, the nobles chose Daniel, at that time a priest unto his God. They made him their king and called him by the name of Chilperic (by which he is known) until this day. Chilperic fought Martel son of Pippin and the day came when they met in battle. Chilperic was defeated by Martel and many a man was lost. Chilperic escaped to Eudo, head of the Gascons, and stayed with him there. Eudo discussed the matter of the king with Martel, and they struck an alliance. He [i.e., Martel] returned to him [i.e., to Chilperic] the cities of his kingdom, apart from the cities of his choosing, and returned the king to his throne and Chilperic made Martel constable in France at that time. Then he died, having also left no heir. The nobles of France and Martel the constable chose Theuderic, who was to them like a saint, and Theuderic ruled France for many days.

King Theuderic was simple and honest and was king in name only, while everything else was given to Martel. Whoever had any affairs to conduct was to come to him. And Martel fought the Suevi and they fell before his feet.[142]

---

[139] Ibid., ch. 20, p. 70: "... והוא כומר לאלוהיו בעת ההיא"
[140] Ibid., ch. 21, p. 71: "... ויתנם שרי צבאות בראש העם".
[141] Riccio, *De regibus Francorum*, pp. 6v–7r contains a relatively detailed account of Ebroin, Pippin II, Theodoald, and Ragamfred, all of whom are missing from Sabino's account.
[142] Ha-Kohen, *Divrei Hayamim*, 1, chs. 21–23, pp. 71–72: "וישכב טיאודוריקו עם אבותיו וימלוך קלודוביאו בנו הבכור תחתיו. ושלש שנים מלך קלודוביאו ובנים לא היו לו וישכב עם אבותיו. וימלוך תחתיו אחיו קידילברטו ימים אחדים. וישכב קידילברטו בראשית מלכותו עם אבותיו וימלוך דגוברטו בנו תחתיו והוא נער קטן בעת ההיא. וימות הנער הזה מבלי חפץ. ולא הניח אחריו מכלים בארץ יורש עצר. ויהי כי אפס זרע המלוכה

Several points stand out in the coverage of the period after the death of Theuderic III: firstly, the mistaken assertion regarding the brevity of Childebert III's rule, another error Ha-Kohen inherited from Sabino;[143] secondly, the matter of Chilperic II's lineage, which neither Sabino nor Ha-Kohen attempted to sugarcoat with a claim that he was the offspring of a previous Merovingian. The same applies to Theuderic IV. Why would Sabino and Ha-Kohen have omitted this information?

Since many of the modern reconstructions of the late Merovingians' paternities are admittedly tentative, it is perhaps not entirely surprising that the sources themselves do not always agree.[144] Riccio, Sabino's only source for these events, offers a somewhat fanciful depiction of Chilperic II's move from the priesthood to the throne:

And so, the root of the royal stock had failed. The nobles thus nominated a certain priest named Daniel, who was regarded by them as great, as first of the praetorians, and placed him at the head of the palace, after having waited for his hair and beard to grow in the common manner. Because when priests were ordained, following either Egyptian or Jewish custom, they gave up their hair at that time and, by the grace of God, did not nurture a half-shaved beard, contrary to common custom. With his haircut and clothes thus changed, he was promoted from the mayoralty to the royal summit and was called Chilperic instead of Daniel.[145]

Riccio therefore made Daniel a temporary mayor of the palace before crowning him king, an element he took from Gaguin. Both Gaguin and Riccio at least considered mayors to have been influential players and

ויבחרו השרים בדניאל והוא כמר לאלוהיו בעת ההיא. וימליכוהו עליהם למלך ויקראו שמו קילפיריקו עד היום הזה. וילחם קילפיריקו עם מארטילו בן פיפינו ויהי היום ויערכו מלחמה. וינגף קילפיריקו לפני מארטילו ויפלו אנשים חללים ארצה. ויברח קילפיריקו מפניו וילך אל איאודוני שר הגאשקוניה וישב עמו שם. וידבר איאודוני עם מארטילו על דבר המלך ויכרתו ברית ביניהם. וישב לו את ערי מלכותו לבד מהערים אשר בחר בהן. וישוב המלך על כיסא מלכותו ויעש קילפיריקו המלך את מארטילו קונדשטאבלי בצרפת בעת ההיא. וישכב עם אבותיו. ולא הניח גם הוא אחריו יורש עצר. ויבחרו שרי צרפת הקונדשטאבלי בטיאודוריקו אשר היה בעיניהם כקדש וימליכוהו עליהם למלך וימלוך טיאודוריקו בצרפת ימים רבים. ויהי טיאודוריקו המלך תם וישר רק שם המלוכה נקרא עליו וכל שאר הדברים היו למארטילו שר צבאו; מי בעל דברים יגש אליו. וילחום מארטילו עם האישביבי ויפלו תחת רגליו."

[143] And Sabino from Riccio, *De regibus Francorum*, p. 7r: "Childebertus huius nominis tertius, & in regia decimus quintus, in rebus humanis haud diu fuit."
[144] See Wood, "Deconstructing the Merovingian Family." The *Grandes Chroniques* speculate that Chilperic II's brother was Dagobert and that he was the son of Childeric II.
[145] Riccio, *De regibus Francorum*, p. 7v: "Et iam regium genus a stirpe defecerat. Igitur optimates sacerdotem quendam nomine Danielem, cuius ingens apud eos erat opinio, primum praetorianis imponunt, & palatio praeficiunt, expectato quo ad profanum in modum capilluum, barbamque promitteret. Quum iam tum sacris inaugurati, tradito uel ab Aegyptiis, uel a Iudaeis more caput haberent, ut hac etiam aetate, semirasum barbamque diuini libi gratia non nutrirent, contrario profanorum more. Quare tonsu, habituque mutato, e praefectura ad Regale fastigium prouectus, pro Daniele Chilpericus appellatur." Riccio refers to Pippin II's and Martel's position as *praefectura* in p. 7v. The term was adopted from Gaguin.

potential candidates for the throne.[146] Unlike Gaguin, however, who reported on Chlothar IV, Theuderic IV, and Childeric III, Riccio fused Theuderic and Childeric into one and ignored Chlothar altogether, but importantly included Theuderic's putative father, Dagobert III. Whatever nuance was left in his abridged treatment did not survive Sabino, let alone Ha-Kohen.

Information about Chilperic II's and Theuderic IV's hypothetical parentage was available to readers of the *Grandes Chroniques*, and indeed of Gaguin's *Compendium*, although neither were consulted by Sabino, who further abbreviated what little ancestral information was supplied by Riccio.[147] Sabino and Ha-Kohen's accounts provide an image of royal power as unproblematically transferred and exercised in and around Paris, which they demonstrated with the help of a simplified succession sequence: Dagobert-Clovis II-Chlothar III-Theuderic III-Clovis III-Childebert III-Dagobert III-Chilperic II-Theuderic IV. While Austrasian kings are infrequently mentioned, it is always in peripheral roles. As we have seen in previous chapters, the focus on Neustrian kings is a feature of all post-Carolingian historiography, although it becomes more conspicuous in the regnal shorthand of Sabino and Ha-Kohen. Neither historian understood the complexities of late-Merovingian power, nor did they have a personal stake in its consequences. Yet both clearly relied on a mental topography that excluded areas outside the heartlands of the French crown. Sabino and Ha-Kohen spoke of Childeric II's "banishment" to Austrasia, as though he were a refugee and not a king.[148] Most telling is the fatherlessness of Chilperic II and Theuderic IV,[149] which can be read as evidence that it was the recognized exercise of power from Paris that made a king, not his blood. It also explains the complete disregard, from Riccio on, for Chlothar IV, whom Martel probably only meant to install in Austrasia, and whose father – perhaps

---

[146] On Childeric III, who is merged with Theuderic IV, see Riccio, *De regibus Francorum*, p. 7v: "Nouus inde Rex principum suffragio creatur, adnitente Martello prætorii præfecto, quidam Childericus (ut ab aliis appellatur repperi) Theodoricus, Dagoberti filius eius nominis ultimi, quam speciose iactabant apud sacras uirgines oppidi Calensis educatum."

[147] *Grandes Chroniques*, ed. Viard, 2, ch. 25, p. 218 (Chilperic II): "Lors eslurent li François 1 clerc qui avoit non Daniel; mais aucunes hystoires dient que il fu freres ce roi Dagobert qui devant ot regné, ses cheveus li lessierent croistre et puis le coronerent; son non li changierent et l'apelerent Chilperic," and p. 221 (Theuderic IV): "Theoderis avoit non, droiz hoirs estoit, car il avoit esté fiuz le secont Dagobert et norriz en l'abbaïe de Chiel."

[148] On Childeric II's *nachleben*, see S. Zale, "The French Kill Their King," pp. 273–294.

[149] Whether Chilperic II was indeed the son of Childeric II is a matter for speculation, but the *LHF* is specific on Dagobert III's paternity of Theuderic IV. See *LHF*, ch. 53; *Fredegar*, Cont. 10.

Theuderic III or Childebert III – remained unnamed in the earlier sources.[150]

Ha-Kohen continued to mirror the account in the *Vite de gli re* in this and other matters, such as Chilperic's flight to Eudo. But while Sabino used this as a pretext for setting the stage for the events that led up to the Battle of Poitiers, Eudo's pact with Martel remained hanging in *Divrei Hayamim*, with the triumph against the Saracens deferred to a later passage. The Merovingian part of the narrative essentially ended here, although two final bits of information divulged what had become of the royal line. The first was a description of Martel's authority during his time as constable:

Martel became the sole authority in France for twenty-five years. He was renowned throughout the land. He divided his kingdom between his sons while the king still lived. And the king denied none of the things he set out to do.[151]

A second and final mention came after Martel's death and Carloman's departure for Mt. Soracte, where, we learn, he went to "worship his idol for many days":[152]

He [i.e., Carloman] *placed Pippin under Theuderic while the king still lived,*[153] *and his kingdom prospered immensely. Theuderic's laziness made him loathsome in the eyes of the peoples. Pope Zacharias anointed Pippin king and Theuderic returned to worship his idol as he once did. Pippin accomplished great and wondrous things in France that will never be forgotten.*[154]

It is therefore evident that neither Sabino nor Ha-Kohen recognized the reign of Childeric III, whose unremarkable career was subsumed by Theuderic's equally unimpressive rule.[155] Here, it is perhaps possible to detect a reticence found already in the *Grandes Chroniques*, which

---

[150] Wood, *The Merovingian Kingdoms*, p. 349.
[151] Ha-Kohen, *Divrei Hayamim*, 1, ch. 24, p. 72: "ויהי מארטילו המוציא והמביא בצרפת חמש ועשרים שנה, ויהי שומעו בכל הארץ. ויחלק את המלכות לבניו אחריו בחיי המלך, ולא מנע המלך ממנו מאומה מכל אשר יזם לעשות."
[152] Ibid., ch. 24, p. 73: "...ויעבוד פסלו שם ימים רבים."
[153] Mirroring the merger of Theuderic IV and Childeric III found in Riccio and adopted by Sabino.
[154] Ha-Kohen, *Divrei Hayamim*, 1, ch. 24, p. 73: "וישם את פיפינו אחיו בחיי טיאודוריקו המלך תחתיו ותכון מלכותו מאד. ויהי טיאודוריקו לעצלותו לנבזה בעיני העמים. וימשח האפיפיור זאקאריאה את פיפינו למלך וישוב טיאודוריקו לעבוד פסלו כאשר בהיותו שם. ויעש פיפינו בצרפת דברים גדולים ועצומים לא יסוף זכרם לעולם."
[155] Sabino, *Vite*, p. 4: "In questi tempi essendo il re Theoderico venuto quasi in contempto per la ignavia sua, Pipino fu creato re da Zacharia Papa, in modo che Theoderico fu necessitato ritornare a farsi monacho & Pipino non solo fece opera degne di memoria nel regno suo, ma anche passando le Alpi in aiuto di Italia, quale era predata da gli Longobardi...."

disregarded Childeric III almost entirely, stating only that: *Childeric, who was called king, was tonsured and sent to an abbey.*[156]

5.3 Conclusions

It is difficult to extract from the writings of Sabino and Ha-Kohen a well-formulated perspective of the Merovingians. For reasons of concision, both narratives simplified the serpentine tale of Merovingian decline, eliminating any opportunity for nuance along the way. Within its limitations, Sabino's text suggests that he saw power as emanating from Paris, not from Metz or Reims. It was this fact, more than a king's familial background, that, according to Sabino, determined his legitimacy.

Sabino was, at least nominally, a humanist.[157] It is true that his French allegiances dampened the desire to critically engage with the crown's foundational myths in any meaningful way. His was still a narrative governed by a rational causality of politics and war, and his terse and disillusioned account of the transfer of power is perhaps an indication of his humanist sensibilities. He was not an especially free-thinking author and is interesting only insofar as he was an influence on Yosef Ha-Kohen, who had the more challenging task of making the history resonate with a Jewish readership.

Ha-Kohen's tendency to regard any positive reference to Christian kingship as a problem in need of correction is evidence of this challenge. Given the state of the Jews in Europe when Ha-Kohen wrote, one would imagine that his readership had little appetite for the accomplishments of pious Christian kings. *Divrei Hayamim* was dotted with subtle expressions of displeasure with Christian kingship, parodying the monastic stints of Merovingians and Carolingians as idol worship and referring to the monastery as a temple to the Canaanite deity, Ba'al.[158] The fact that *Divrei Hayamim* was written at all is an indication of a Jewish curiosity about gentile history and about humanist historiographical methodology, so one might rightly consider Ha-Kohen's work to have been innovative, perhaps even subversive. But its authorial voice remained conservative. It found in the *Vite de gli re* a narrative that moved away from a model of divinely controlled history and toward a much more secular understanding of human affairs and turned it on its head.

---

[156] *GCh*, ed. Viard, t.2, p. 243: "Childeris, qui rois estoit apelez, fu tonduz et mis en une abbaïe."
[157] See his comments on Charles V in *Vite*, p. 21; Maissen, *Von der Legende zum Modell*, p. 172.
[158] Fox, "Chronicling the Merovingians," p. 439.

Conclusions 271

All of this, however, applied to the entirety of the composition, and therefore means little in terms of Ha-Kohen's perspective of the Merovingians. On this question, it is perhaps still possible to make several observations. If we attempt to draw from the works surveyed above a model of periodization, we might say that Sabino's and Ha-Kohen's interest in conquest and military success informed their appraisals of the Merovingians.[159] Kings who conquered were acting as they should. Accomplishments in battle were an essential part of the short royal biographies that made up the early chapters of *Divrei Hayamim*. From Clodio to Clovis I, all of these biographies included an account of gained territories. This stopped after the death of Clovis and was not picked up again until the conquests of Charles Martel, who was perceived as the progenitor of the Carolingian dynasty.

Sabino had already noted that Clovis II had accomplished nothing of importance but was willing to concede that the Merovingians were truly a spent force only under Martel's final puppet, Theuderic IV. This, we should note, is in line with contemporary thinking on the question. It is also important to remember that Charles Martel was not presented as the heir of an important family with impressive achievements of its own, only as a rival to Chilperic II. So, while one would be able to see, however dimly, the idea of a drawn-out process of Merovingian decline in the *Vite de gli re* and in *Divrei Hayamim*, any remnants of Carolingian propaganda had vanished. Gone were the early seventh-century mayors of the palace and saints that were so vital to the Carolingians' explanatory effort. Their takeover in 751 was seen for what it was: a grab for power that succeeded until they themselves became its victims. *Divrei Hayamim*'s report on the Carolingians' demise in 987 made this patently clear:

The war raged powerfully in France, and they rose up against each other.[160] *For there were many who wished to rule this great kingdom. And the progeny of Martel held no more power. Hugh, son of Hugh the Great and nephew of Emperor Otto, became king.*[161]

---

[159] On this see I. Sherer, "Joseph ha-Kohen, Humanist Historiography and Military History," *Journal of Jewish Studies* 69 (2018), pp. 86–108.
[160] Isaiah 3:5.
[161] Ha-Kohen, *Divrei Hayamim*, p. 3b: "ותהי המלחמה חזקה בצרפת. וירהבו איש ברעהו. כי רבים היו המבקשים למלוך במלכות הגדול הזה. ולא עצרו עוד כוח יוצאי חלצי מארטילו. וימלוך אוגו בן אגון הגדול ובן אחות אוטוני הקיסר."

Conclusions

The Merovingian period as we know it was as much a narrative creation as it was a historical epoch. As such, it came into being through a prolonged process of transmission and adaptation. The period was used to justify and discredit, praise and malign. This was as true of Gregory of Tours as it was of the nineteenth-century editors of his work. The telltale signs of the story's evolution are strewn everywhere in the historiographical record.

In the various compositions surveyed in this book, the Merovingian period was conceived of as a discrete period of history. Its beginning was murky, emerging from a mythological past presented through the use of origin stories. Two narrative traditions – biblical and Trojan – represent the historiographical efforts to frame the period's onset and the preference for one or the other depended, to a great extent, on the objective of the composition. Chronicles and histories with universal ambitions naturally gravitated toward the biblical framework that offered the authors a rich background story, into which they could inject their own subject matter. Of the authors we have discussed, Gregory of Tours, Frechulf of Lisieux, Ado of Vienne, Regino of Prüm, Sigebert of Gembloux, and Yosef Ha-Kohen employed a biblical narrative architecture of one form or another. As we have seen, each wrote for a different reason, but all agreed on the usefulness of the biblical material. Naturally, there was notable diversity in how authors understood and engaged with this tradition. Some chose Creation as a starting point, others built on the Abrahamic timeframe set down by Eusebius-Jerome, while still others began with the Incarnation. They also differed in style, which is why Gregory used the Bible as a proper thematic preamble to the events that took place in Gaul, but Sigebert incorporated it piecemeal into his column-based style of reportage.

The Trojan story, on the other hand, was employed by authors for whom Frankish history was an especially important historical reference point, albeit not necessarily the only one. Putting aside for a moment the problem of distinguishing royal from Frankish history, it would have been impossible to write a history of the former without offering an origin story for the latter. Even works such as the *Grandes Chroniques*, which leaned heavily in the direction of royal history, recognized the need to account for the origin of the *gens*, not just its leaders. Since it drew so profoundly on works dedicated to Frankish history, such as Aimoin of Fleury's *Gesta Francorum* and, more distantly, the *LHF*, the Franks' past, as opposed to royal history proper, remained an indispensable component of the *Grandes Chroniques'* storyline.

The two traditions need not have been mutually exclusive, as demonstrated by *Fredegar*, although for obvious reasons they usually were. Setting a chronicle in the biblical framework left little room for the classically oriented constructs of the Trojan origin story. *Fredegar* was in many respects an experimental composition, and this is evident also in the multiplicity of origin stories it contains. More to the point, it resided in a liminal space between the vision of the community posited by Gregory of Tours and that of the author of the *LHF*. As we have seen, the *Fredegar* chronicler supplemented the chapters of ancient history found in the *scarpsa* of Eusebius-Jerome and the six-book version of the *Histories* with information about Frankish origins. It is nevertheless in Book IV that his overarching intent is clearly revealed. *Fredegar*'s Book IV was not an ecclesiastical history of Gaul, nor was it a dedicated history of the Franks, although it exhibits features of both perspectives. If we consider it apart from the *scarpsa* that preceded it, we find ourselves in a world defined by the political superstructures of the Merovingian realm but not limited by its geographical, and certainly not its ethnic, contours. In other words, the *Fredegar* chronicler was happy to discuss events that transpired in other corners of the world and did not see himself as narrating the history of an ethnic community but rather that of a particular political space, set against the wider canvas of Christendom.

In other compositions, and especially Carolingian-era world chronicles, the Franks were part of a salvific Christian view of human history. Their Trojan origin story was thus incongruous with the historical vision proposed by the biblical schema. The Carolingians were also the masters of a multiethnic imperial state. Considerations of scope and style would have made the *origines gentium* of the now plentiful denizens of the empire too cumbersome to recount. Singling out the Franks as the only ones with an origin would have clashed with these works' intended purpose, which privileged other narrative traditions, and primarily those centered on papal and imperial Rome as well as local ecclesiastical history. Thus, Carolingian-era historiographies usually preferred the Bible to Troy.

It is difficult to determine to what degree the Merovingians were seen as the true heirs to the heritage of Troy. In Rigord's work, this link is made explicit, although this seems to be the exception that proves the rule. In some of the works, such as the *LHF*, the narrative lens expands and contracts, at times treating the Franks as the descendants of the Trojans, and on other occasions privileging kings and successions, making the author's stance difficult to ascertain. It is true that most works depict an ancestral model of inheritance which began in Troy and concluded with the Merovingians. Most of the time, this model was also patrilineal. Yet, even in works that are decidedly "royalist" in nature, such as the *Grandes Chroniques*, the link between the kings of Troy and the first royal dynasty was problematized. Primat had a lot riding on Trojan ancestry, on whose veracity rested the success of *reditus regni*. Still, he cared enough about precision to rephrase Aimoin:

> *After Clodio had reined for twenty years, he passed away. After him reigned Merovech. This Merovech was not his son but was from his lineage (lignage). From him issued the first generation of the kings of France; it persisted without fail from heir to heir until the generation of Pippin II, father of Charlemagne the Great.*[1]

Memorably, the *LHF*, which arguably provided the smoothest transition from Trojan to Frankish kings, resisted the urge to identify Clodio as the father of Merovech, doubtless an inheritance from Gregory of Tours. This ambivalence is likewise present in *Fredegar*, a work that was unknown to the *LHF* author but also had Gregory as a source. The Merovingians were central to the *LHF*'s argumentation, but to call the composition royalist would be anachronistic. It was at most "loyalist," in the sense that it expressed the worldview of the Neustrian ruling class, which depended on the revitalization of Merovingian kingship. It thus had little reason to exclude the political elite from such a prestigious origin story.

By the time the *LHF*'s *origo* made its way – with the help of Aimoin – to the *Grandes Chroniques*, it had become enshrined in tradition and was left unchallenged. Paul the Deacon considered the story of Trojan origins to apply to all Franks, not just their kings, although he generally seemed to lend it little credence. Doubt was also a feature of Emilio's *DRG*, for reasons that had more to do with his general incredulity as a humanist historian. In most of the works we have examined, the dawn of the Merovingians was inextricably linked to the formation of the Franks, and the two developments were hardly, if ever, discussed separately. All

---

[1] Viard, ed., *GCh*, ch. IV, p. 26: "Quant li rois Clodio out regné XX anz, il paia le treü de nature. Après lui regna Merovées. Cil Merovées ne fu pas ses fiuz, mais il fu de son lignage. De cetui eissi la premiere generation es rois de France; si dura sanz faillir d'oir en hoir jusques à la generation Pepin le secont, la pere le grant Challemaine." That Pippin III is known here as Pippin II is perhaps an indication that, like Rigord, Primat considered Arnulf, not Pippin I, as the Carolingian *paterfamilias*. See Chapter 1 for discussion.

Conclusions 275

in all, the privileged claim of the Merovingian family to Trojan origins seems to have been tenuous at best.

Numerous authors remarked on the internal division of the Merovingian period. While we can only really speak of the treatment of the Merovingians' final decline in works composed after 751, the parable of Basina, a product of the seventh century, is a convenient heuristic with which to think about this process. I have highlighted it and its tripartite schematization as a useful metaphor for the common historiographical habit to view the Merovingian centuries as characterized by three phases: meteoric ascent, internecine conflict, and ultimate degeneration and collapse. It is not difficult to assume that such a well-known story provided the correct mindset for authors who were preoccupied with related questions. More importantly, we repeatedly see authors choosing the same events to signal the conclusion of one phase and the transition to another.

For many of the compositions I have examined, the transfer of power from Dagobert I to Clovis II was precisely such an event. Dagobert's reign was the summit from which one could see the unraveling of Merovingian power. The fact that Clovis was chosen as the scapegoat for the dynasty's failure was indeed tied to his father's unusual success, but also to his personal trespasses, particularly against the relics of Dionysius. The *LHF*, which contains the earliest mention of the story, was not an unquestioned product of Saint-Denis, yet the tidbit about the seizure of the saint's arm recorded in its pages probably was. Importantly, the *Gesta Dagoberti* and the *Grandes Chroniques* were created in Saint-Denis, and they openly adopted the *LHF*'s position. If we assume that Hilduin made it to Prüm, this might suggest the path through which Dionysian influence reached Regino. Regardless of how it happened, Regino was clearly working with the *Gesta Dagoberti* and considered its treatment fitting for his own periodization, in which Clovis II starred as the final Merovingian. Even Sigebert of Gembloux saw the death of Clovis II as an important turning point. It was followed by an aphoristic remark about the duration of Chlothar III's reign and summed up with this tepid assessment: "The kings of the Franks were accustomed to hand over royal power to the mayors of the palace, ruling as kings in name only." The influence of Saint-Denis ensured the success of the image of Dagobert as the last effective Merovingian and, aptly, of Clovis as the first in a line of "do-nothing kings."

Each of the works examined in the book offered a somewhat different explanation of the final chapter of the story, which saw power transferred from the Merovingians to the Carolingians. Some chose the path of least resistance by ignoring this process altogether. Frechulf of Lisieux used Merovingian history, not as a narrative element in its own right, but rather as a way of setting an endpoint to the power of previous regimes, most notably that of the Romans. As a result, in his *Chronicle*, Frankish history shrinks into insignificance. It is likewise absent in the *GeM*, which regarded the sanctoral careers of the early Pippinids and Arnulfings, not the failings of the last Merovingians, as the appropriate setup for the accomplishments of Charlemagne and the Carolingian family that so preoccupied Paul the Deacon.

For authors who wished to continue the account up to their own day, this was not an option, so they came up with alternative solutions. Regino of Prüm pruned Merovingian history so that it concluded on a discordant note with the failure of Clovis II. Ado of Vienne focused on the bloodier aspects of pre-Carolingian Frankish history, painting it as a period of barbarity contrasted with the deeds of the saints, the popes, and his contemporary Carolingians. Whatever the approach, the Merovingian period fared poorly in the works of Carolingian-era authors. The *Gesta Dagoberti* was the only such composition that contained a positive image of a Merovingian king, and even here the author acknowledged that Dagobert's death meant that the dynasty's glory days were over.

Once the Carolingians were safely in the rearview mirror, more positive evaluations of the Merovingian period could emerge. This is evident in the compositions of Aimoin of Fleury, Sigebert of Gembloux, and the *Grandes Chroniques*, all of which engage head on with the history in question, sometimes admiringly. This is not to say that the Carolingian influence on historiographical work undertaken in subsequent centuries had all but vanished. Since the last available Merovingian-era work of historiography was the *LHF*, anyone who wished to discuss events that took place after 727 was forced to rely on the *ARF*, Einhard's *Vita Karoli*, and other comparable compositions, whose views on late Merovingian power were anything but favorable.

We also witness a return to the Trojan narrative in the works of Aimoin, Sigebert, Primat, and Ha-Kohen. While the willingness to reengage with this tradition can be attributed to a sense of autonomy from Carolingian historical philosophy, it is also the result of a particular focus on the Franks present in all three works. The fact that the Trojan origin story was picked up so naturally suggests that it never really disappeared, despite its unpopularity in Carolingian world chronicles. Here, too, we can witness the influence of Saint-Denis, which may have done more than most to keep the tradition alive.

An important idea explored in this book is that some narrative episodes were meant to function as parables, with morals applicable to the time of composition. There can be no doubt that medieval and early modern authors meant for their stories to be read with an eye to the present or the recent past. They tell us so on numerous occasions. We should nevertheless be wary of imposing too close a reading on the material. Take, for example, Chramn's rebellion against his father Chlothar. The episode is found not only in Frechulf, who, certain scholars suggested, fashioned it to function as an allegory for specific early ninth-century events.[2] It is also found in Gregory of Tours,[3] the *LHF*,[4] Ado of Vienne,[5] Aimoin of Fleury,[6] the *Grandes Chroniques*,[7] and Emilio's *DRG*.[8] Each considered the episode an important element for the progression of the plot, but none used it to allude to specific historical personages from the time of composition, and this is true also of Frechulf. Predicting how a work would be received was tricky, and the political ground was prone to shift without warning. Thus, it would have been prudent to keep such stories relatively ambiguous. For us, a more productive way to think of the interactions between historical figures is as narrative exercises that could help the audience make sense of common dynamics, ones that played out time and again throughout history, such as sibling rivalry or princely ambition. In this sense, the author could depict models of desirable and undesirable conduct without drawing parallels that had the potential of landing him in hot water, while the universality of the themes discussed guaranteed their relevance.

Reading through the historiographical corpus, we encounter the same people, reprising the same roles in the same historical dramas. Adherence to the sources' narrative architecture is evidence that authors exhibited strong conservatist tendencies. While the effect of local – possibly, oral – traditions that could have taken the plot in new directions was at times decisive, the storyline generally retained its structure. This is not unexpected, given historians' and chroniclers' overwhelming reliance on written historiographical sources, which they frequently identified by name. Conservatism was critical for the success of the text, given the expectations of a readership familiar with the historical *dramatis personae* and their exploits, and therefore also capable of critically evaluating the author's trustworthiness. On a less instrumental level, it was a show of respect for past authors, whose works sometimes provided the only window into bygone eras. Of course, conservatism does not mean complete adherence. Adjustments that were made were often suggestive of the author's desire to counteract his source's artifices and agendas. Emilio

---

[2] On this, see Chapter 3. [3] Gregory of Tours, *Histories*, IV.20. [4] *LHF*, ch. 28.
[5] Ado of Vienne, *Chronicle*, col. 108D.
[6] Aimoin of Fleury, *Gesta Francorum*, chs. 28, 30, cols. 685–687.
[7] *Grandes Chroniques*, ch. 29, pp. 174–177, which draws the requisite parallels with David and Absalom.
[8] Paulo Emilio, *DRG*, 1550 ed., p. 12.

effectively neutralized Gregory of Tours' simplistic moral couplets, substituting them with narrative devices of his own. Yosef Ha-Kohen removed any source phrase that smacked of Christian piety, replacing it with a more appropriate expression of opprobrium.

The story thus endured a delicate but continuous process of adjustment under different pens. It nevertheless resisted dramatic rewrites that would have offered an altogether different narrative trajectory. Even when the sources seemed to stand in the way of the agenda a new author was promoting, much of their material was kept. Sigebert of Gembloux was aware of the damage that mention of the Grimoald coup could inflict on his construction of the saintly image of King Sigibert III, so he expunged it from the *Life*. This awareness did not carry over into the *Chronicle*, which remained faithful to the account found in the *LHF*. For the purposes of Sigebert's historiographical project, accuracy and deference to his source mattered more. Whatever message the author wished to impart, changes necessarily remained subtle, so that the overarching structure of the plot was not compromised.

Sigebert's divergent approaches to the *Life* and the *Chronicle* indicate that he set separate aims and scope for each of his projects. This is perhaps as close as we can come to a generic taxonomy at work. Here, also, it would be prudent to consider how salient generic categories were for authors who penned such different works. We should not discount their usefulness or be tempted to argue that medieval authors saw biography, hagiography, and historiography as indiscernible. Clearly, they did not. That does not make the borders separating these categories any less porous. Sigebert and the author of the *Gesta Dagoberti* needed the historical framework of *Fredegar* and the *LHF* to flesh out their characters. Historiography provided the backbone for both, just like it had for Ado's *Suffering of Desiderius*, which built on his *Chronicle*. Generic categorization tends to obscure the multivalent connections that linked families of texts that were themselves in a constant state of rearticulation and experimentation.

* * *

In his 1957 novel, *The Short Reign of Pippin IV, A Fabrication*, John Steinbeck paints a surreal caricature of early twentieth-century French politics through the various misadventures of Monsieur Pippin Arnulf Héristal, an astronomy aficionado from Paris's Eighth Arrondissement and the sole surviving member of the Carolingian house. After a parliamentary crisis that toppled the French government brings about the unexpected reconstitution of the monarchy, representatives from the

Conclusions 279

various dynasties begin to quarrel about which of them should provide the king:

For a day and a night the battle raged while noble voices grew hoarse and noble hearts pounded. Of all the aristocratic partisans, only the Merovingians sat back quiet, listless, content, and faint.

It is their representative, the evocatively named Childéric de Saône, who finally comes up with a solution to the impasse:

My kings, it is recorded, disappeared through lassitude. We Merovingians do not want the crown.
[...]
I am content to live as my latter kings lived and to solve the problem as they did. I suggest for the throne of France the holy blood of Charlemagne.[9]

And so, Monsieur Héristal, Childéric's "mayor of the palace," is crowned king; through their reluctance to rule, the *rois fainéants* again hand over royal power to the Carolingians. While Steinbeck's vision of French politics is clearly meant as absurd, the foundational myth of Merovingian passivity persists, and is so effectively satirical exactly because is it such an easily recognizable element of the national mythology.

The purpose of the present book has not been to determine whether the Merovingians earned their questionable reputation as do-nothings but to understand how the various components of this reputation came about. As I have attempted to show, the story of the first royal dynasty of the Franks was told and retold for more than a millennium after they concluded their historical role. It continues to be reinterpreted even today. In that they have held such an enduring fascination throughout the ages, the Merovingians have overcome the troubled legacy of their historiography.

---

[9] J. Steinbeck, *The Short Reign of Pippin IV, A Fabrication* (New York: The Viking Press, 1957), pp. 28–30.

Bibliography

Manuscripts cited

Bern, Burgerbibliothek, Cod. 120.I
Brussels, KBR, 18239–18240
Brussels, KBR, 19598–19599
Cambridge, Corpus Christi College, MS 290
London, British Library, add. MS 24145
London, British Library, add. MS 37768
London, British Library, Harley MS 651
Paris, BnF MS lat. 5512
Paris, BnF MS lat. 5569
Paris, BnF MS lat. 5925
Vatican City, BAV Reg. lat. 88
Vatican City, BAV Reg. lat. 438
Vatican City, BAV Reg. lat. 571
Vatican City, BAV Reg. lat. 980

Primary sources

Acta spuria ad Concilium Cirisiacense spectantia, a. 838, MGH Conc. Aevi Karolini 2, 2, ed. A. Werminghoff (Hanover: Hahnsche Buchhandlung, 1908), pp. 835–853.

Actus pontificum Cenomanensis in urbe degentium, in *Geschichte des Bistums Le Mans von der Spätantike bis zur Karolingerzeit: Actus pontificum Cenomanensis in urbe degentium und Gesta Aldrici*, ed. M. Weidemann, 3 vols. (Mainz: Verlag des Römisch-Germanischen Zentralmuseums in Kommision bei Habelt, 2002).

Ado of Vienne, *Chronicon sive Breviarium de sex mundi aetatibus ab Adamo usque ad annum 869*, PL 123, cols. 23–143.

Martyrology, in *Le martyrologe d'Adon, ses deux familles, ses trois recensions: texte et commentaire*, ed. and trans. J. Dubois and G. Renaud (Paris: Éditions du Centre National de la Recherche Scientifique, 1984).

Passio sancti Desiderii episcopi Viennensis, PL 123, cols. 435–442.

Vita Theudarii abbatis Viennensis, MGH SRM 3, ed. B. Krusch (Hanover: Hahnsche Buchhandlung, 1896), pp. 525–530.

Bibliography   281

Aethicus Ister, *Cosmographia*, in *The Cosmography of Aethicus Ister: Edition, Translation, and Commentary*, M. Herren ed. and trans. (Turnhout: Brepols, 2011).
Aimoin of Fleury, *Historia Francorum libri quattuor*, PL 139, cols. 627–802.
Vita sancti Abbonis, in *L'Abbaye de Fleury en l'an mil*, ed. and trans. R.-H. Bautier and G. Labory (Paris: Centre National de la Recherche Scientifique, 2004), ch. 20, pp. 118–126.
Almann of Hautevillers, *Vita Nivardi episcopi Remensis*, MGH SRM 5, ed. W. Levison (Hanover: Hahnsche Buchhandlung, 1910), pp. 157–171.
Annales Mettenses Priores, MGH SRG 10, ed. B. von Simson (Hanover: Hahnsche Buchhandlung, 1905).
Annales Regni Francorum, MGH SRG 6, ed. F. Kurze (Hanover: Hahnsche Buchhandlung, 1895).
Ammianus Marcellinus, *Res gestae*, ed. and trans., J.C. Rolfe, 3 vols. (Cambridge, MA: Harvard University Press, 1935–1939).
Appian, *Bella civilia*, in *Appiani Historia Romana I*, eds. P. Viereck, A. G. Roos, E. Gabba (Leipzig: Teubner, 1962).
Avitus of Vienne, *Epistula* 46, MGH AA, ed. R. Peiper (Berlin: Weidmann, 1883), pp. 75–76.
Letters and Selected Prose, ed. and trans. D. Shanzer and I. Wood (Liverpool: Liverpool University Press, 2002).
Bede, *De temporum ratione*, ed. C.W. Jones. CCSL 123b (Turnhout: Brepols, 1977).
Ecclesiastical History of the English People, eds. B. Colgrave and R. A. B. Mynors (Oxford: Clarendon Press, 1969).
Martyrology, in *Édition pratique des martyrologes de Bède, de l'anonyme lyonnais et de Florus*, eds. J. DuBois and G. Renaud (Paris: Éditions du Centre national de la recherche scientifique, 1976).
The Reckoning of Time, trans. F. Wallis (Liverpool: Liverpool University Press, 2004).
Biondo, F., *Historiarum ab inclinatione Romanorum imperii decades* (Venice: Octavianus Scotus Modoetiensis, 1483).
Brief Chronicle of the Kings of France, in Stoclet, A.J., "À la recherche du ban perdu. Le trésor et les dépouilles de Waïfre, duc d'Aquitaine (f 768), d'après Adémar de Chabannes, Rigord et quelques autres," *Cahiers de civilisation médiévale* 168 (1999), pp. 343–382.
Caesarius of Arles, *Epistola 11*, MGH Epp. 3, ed. W. Gundlach (Berlin: Weidmann, 1892), pp. 450–451.
Cassiodorus, *Variae*, MGH AA 12, ed. T. Mommsen (Berlin: Weidmann, 1894); trans. M.S. Bjornlie, *The Variae: The Complete Translation* (Oakland, CA: University of California Press, 2019).
Codex Theodosianus, eds., T. Mommsen and P. Meyer (Berlin, 1905); trans. in C. Pharr, *The Theodosian Code* (Princeton, NJ, 1952).
Commemoratio genealogiae domni Karoli gloriosissimi imperatoris, MGH SS 13, ed. G. Waitz (Hanover: Hahnsche Buchhandlung, 1881).
Concilium Aurelianense, 10 Iul. 511, in *Les canons des conciles mérovingiens (VIe–VIIe siècles)*, ed. J. Gaudemet and B. Basdevant, Sources chrétiennes 353–354 (Paris: Éditions du CERF, 1989), I: 67–91.

Bibliography

Concilium Ingelheimense, a. 840 (Narratio clericorum Remensium), MGH Conc. Aevi Karolini 2, 2, ed. A. Werminghoff (Hanover: Hahnsche Buchhandlung, 1908), pp. 806–814.

Concilium Parisiense, a. 829, MGH Conc. Aevi Karolini 2, 2, ed. A. Werminghoff (Hanover: Hahnsche Buchhandlung, 1908), pp. 605–680.

Claudian, *De consulatu Stilichonis libri IV*, in *Carmina*, ed. J.B. Hall, Bibliotheca scriptorum Graecorum et Romanorum Teubneriana (Leipzig: Teubner, 1985), pp. 190–238.

Das Neustrische Streitgespräch von 737, MGH QQ zur Geistesgesch. 21, 1, ed. A. Borst (Hanover: Hahnsche Buchhandlung, 2006), pp. 375–423.

De SS. Eustathio, Uxore ejus et Filiis, AASS Sept. VI (Antwerp: B.A. van der Plassche, 1757), cols. 123–137.

Der inluster vir Hausmeier Karl (Martell), sohn des verstorbenen Pippin, schenkt dem Kloster St. Denis die villa Clichy im Gau von Paris mit allem Zubehör, worunter auch Weinberge, MGH DD Arnulf., ed. I. Heidrich (Hanover: Hahnsche Buchhandlung, 2011), 14, pp. 32–33.

Die Urkunden der Merowinger, MGH DD Merov. 1–2, ed. T. Kölzer (Hanover: Hahnsche Buchhandlung, 2001).

Diplomata, MGH DD Merov., ed. G.H. Pertz (Hanover: Hahnsche Buchhandlung, 1872).

Einhard, *Translatio et miracula sanctorum Marcellini et Petri. Translation und Wunder der Heiligen Marcellinus und Petrus*, ed. and trans. D. Kries, Acta Einhardi 2 (Seligenstadt: Einhard Gesellschaft, 2015), pp. 44–140.

Vita Karoli Magni, MGH SRG 25, ed. O. Holder-Egger (Hanover and Leipzig: Hahnsche Buchhandlung, 1911); trans. A.J. Grant, *The Life of Charlemagne* (Cambridge, Ont.: In Parentheses Publications, 1999).

Emilio, P., *De rebus gestis Francorum ad christianissimum Galliarum regem Franciscum Valesium, eius nominis primum, libri decem, ex postrema authoris recognitione. Additum est de regibus item Francorum Chronicon, ad hæc usque tempora studiosissime deductum, cum rerum maxime insignium indice copiosissimo* (Paris: M. Vasconsanus, 1550).

Erchanbert, *Breviarium regum Francorum*, ed. A. Ussermann, *Germaniae sacrae prodomus*, 2 vols. (St. Blasian, 1790), i, pp. xxxix–lii.

Eusebius-Jerome, *Chronicon*, eds. R. Helm and T. Mommsen, *Eusebius Werke*, vol. vii.1: *Die Chronik des Hieronymus* (Leipzig: Teubner, 1913).

Frechulf of Lisieux, *Opera Omnia*, ed. M.I. Allen, CCCM 169 (Turnhout: Brepols, 2002).

Fredegar, *Chronicarum quae dicuntur Fredegarii scholastici libri IV cum continuationibus*, MGH SRM 2, ed. B. Krusch (Hanover: Hahnsche Buchhandlung, 1888).

Gaguin, R., *Compendium de origine et gestis Francorum* (Lyon: Johann Trechsel, 1497).

Grandes Chroniques de France, ed. J. Viard, 3 vols. (Paris: Société de l'histoire de France, 1920).

Gesta Dagoberti I regis Francorum, MGH SRM 2, ed. B. Krusch (Hanover: Hahnsche Buchhandlung, 1888), pp. 396–425 and MGH SRM 7, Appendix: Tomus II, ed. B. Krusch (Hanover: Hahnsche Buchhandlung, 1920), pp. 778–782.

Gregory of Tours, *Liber in gloria confessorum*, MGH SRM 1.2, ed. B. Krusch (Hanover: Hahnsche Buchhandlung, 1885), pp. 284–370.
Liber in gloria martyrum, MGH SRM 1.2, ed. B. Krusch (Hanover: Hahnsche Buchhandlung, 1885), pp. 34–111.
Liber vitae patrum, MGH SRM 1.2, ed. B. Krusch (Hanover: Hahnsche Buchhandlung, 1885), pp. 211–283.
Libri Historiarum X, MGH SRM 1.1, ed. B. Krusch and W. Levison (Hanover: Hahnsche Buchhandlung, 1951).
Ha-Kohen, Y., *Chronicle of the French and Ottoman Kings*, ed. R. Bonfil, 3 vols. (Jerusalem: Magnes Press, 2020) [Hebrew].
Sefer 'Emek Ha-Bakha (The Vale of Tears) with the Chronicle of the Anonymous Corrector, ed. K. Almbadh (Uppsala: Almqvist & Wiksell, 1981); *Yosef Ha-Kohen, Sefer 'Emek Ha-Bakha (The Vale of Tears)*, ed. R. Bonfil (Jerusalem: Magnes Press, 2020) [Hebrew].
Hilduin of Saint-Denis, *Passio sancti Dionysii*, in *Hilduin of Saint-Denis: The Passio S. Dionysii in Prose and Verse* ed. M. Lapidge (Leiden: Brill, 2017), pp. 229–303.
Hincmar of Reims, *De regis persona et regio ministerio*, PL 125, cols. 833–856.
Vita sancti Remigii archiepiscopi Remensis, MGH SRM 3, ed. B. Krusch (Hanover: Hahnsche Buchhandlung, 1896), pp. 250–341.
Historia Brittonum, in *British History and the Welsh Annals*, ed. and trans. J. Morris (London: Philimore, 1980).
Historia translationis miraculorum s. Sigiberti, AASS Feb. 1, pp. 236–237.
Hrabanus Maurus, *Epistolae 8–12*, MGH Epp. 5, ed. E. Dümmler (Berlin: Weidmann, 1899), pp. 393–400.
Hucbald of Saint-Amand, *Vita sanctae Rictrudis*, PL 132, cols. 829–848.
Isidore of Seville, *Etymologies*, in *Isidori Hispalensis episcopi Etymologiarum sive originum libri XX*, ed. W.M. Lindsay, 2 vols. (Oxford: Oxford University Press, 1911).
Jerome-Gennadius, *De viris illustribus* ed. A. Ceresa-Gastaldo (Florence, 1988).
Jonas of Bobbio, *Vita Columbani discipulorumque eius libri II*, MGH SRG 37, ed. B. Krusch (Hanover: Hahnsche Buchhandlung, 1905), pp. 1–294; trans. in O'Hara, A., and I.N. Wood, Jonas of Bobbio, *Life of Columbanus, Life of John of Réomé, and Life of Vedast*, Translated Texts for Historians, vol. 64 (Liverpool: Liverpool University Press, 2017).
Vita Iohannis abbatis Reomaensis, MGH SRM 3, ed. B. Krusch (Hanover: Hahnsche Buchhandlung, 1896).
Vita Vedastis episcopi Atrebatensis, MGH SRG 37, ed. B. Krusch (Hanover and Leipzig: Hahnsche Buchhandlung, 1905), pp. 295–320.
Jonas of Orléans, *De institutione laicali*, PL 106, cols. 121–278.
Jordanes, *De origine actibusque Getarum*, in *Iordanis de origine actibusque Getarum*, eds. F. Giunta and A. Grillone (Rome: Istituto Storico Italiano per il Medio Evo, 1991).
Josippon (Josephus Gorionides), ed. and trans. D. Flusser, 2 vols. (Jerusalem: The Bialik Institute, 2009) [Hebrew].
Lactantius, *Divinae Institutiones*, ed. C. Ingremeau, Sources Chrétiennes 509 (Paris: Éditions du CERF, 2007).
Lex Baiwariorum, MGH LL Nat. Germ., ed. E. von Schwind (Hanover: Hahnsche Buchhandlung, 1926).

Liber historiae Francorum, MGH SRM 2, ed. B. Krusch (Hanover: Hahnsche Buchhandlung, 1888), pp. 215–328; trans. in B.S. Bachrach, *Liber historiae Francorum* (Lawrence, KA: Coronado Press, 1973).

Louis IV, *Epistulae,* MGH DD LdK, ed. T. Schieffer (Berlin: Weidmannsche Verlagsbuchhandlung, 1960).

Louis the Pious, *Epistola 19,* in *Epistolae variorum,* MGH Epp. 5.VII, ed. E. Dümmler (Berlin: Weidmann, 1899), pp. 326–327.

Lupus of Ferrières, *Epistola* 110, in *Loup de Ferrières: Correspondance II (847–62),* ed. L. Levillain (Paris: Librarie ancienne Honoré Champion, 1935), pp. 150–153; trans. Regenos, G.W., *The Letters of Lupus of Ferrières* (The Hague: Martinus Nijhoff, 1966).

Marius of Avenches, *Chronicle,* in *La Chronique de Marius d'Avenches (455–581),* ed. and trans. J. Favrod (Lausanne: Université de Lausanne, 1991).

Mozarabic Chronicle of 754, in *Corpus scriptorium muzarabicarum,* ed. J. Gil, 2 vols. (Madrid: Instituto Antonio de Nebrija, 1973).

Notker, *Gesta Karoli Magni,* MGH SRG n.s. 12, ed. H.F. Haefele (Berlin: Weidmann, 1959).

Orosius, *Historiae adversum paganos,* ed. K. Zangemeister (Hildesheim, 1967).

Pardessus, J.-M., ed., *Diplomata, Chartae, Epistolae, Leges ad res Gallo-Francicas spectantia,* 2 vols. (Paris: ex Typographio regio, 1843–1849).

Passio Leodegarii I MGH SRM 5, ed. B. Krusch (Hanover: Hahnsche Buchhandlung, 1910), pp. 282–322.

Passio Quirini, ed. and trans. P. Chiesa, in *Le passioni dei martiri aquileiesi e istriani,* vol. 2, ed. E. Colombi (Rome: Istituto storico Italiano per il medio evo, 2013), pp. 499–583.

Passio sancti Desiderii episcopi Viennensis, ed. C. De Smedt et al., *Analecta Bollandiana* 9 (1892), pp. 250–262.

Passio sancti Dionysii, in M. Lapidge, "The 'Ancient Passio' of St. Dionysius (BHL 2171)," *Analecta Bollandiana* 132 (2014), pp. 241–285.

Passio sancti Sigismundi regis, MGH SRM 2, ed. B. Krusch (Hanover: Hahnsche Buchhandlung, 1888), pp. 329–340.

Paul the Deacon, *Historia Langobardorum,* MGH SRL, eds. L. Bethmann and G. Waitz (Hanover: Hahnsche Buchhandlung, 1878), pp. 12–187.

Liber de episcopis Mettensibus, ed. and trans. D. Kempf, *Dallas Medieval Texts and Translations* 19 (Paris, Leuven, and Walpole, MA: Peeters, 2013).

Pertz, G.H., ed., *Diplomata regum Francorum e stirpe Merowingica,* MGH DD 1 [Merov] (Hanover: Hahnsche Buchhandlung, 1872).

Regino of Prüm, *Chronicon,* MGH SRG 50, ed. F. Kurze (Hanover: Hahnsche Buchhandlung, 1890).

Riccio, M., *De regibus Francorum libri III* (Basle: Joannes Froben, 1517).

Rigord of Saint-Denis, *Gesta Philippi Augusti,* in *Œuvres de Rigord et de Guillaume le Breton, historiens de Philippe-Auguste,* ed. H.-F. Delaborde, 2 vols. (Paris: Société de l'histoire de France, 1882), 1, pp. 1–167; trans. in *The Deeds of Philip Augustus, An English Translation of Rigord's Gesta Philippi Augusti,* trans. L.F. Field, eds. M.C. Gaposchkin and S.L. Field (Ithaca, NY, and London: Cornell University Press, 2022).

Bibliography 285

Sabino, V., *Le vite di tutti gli Re di Francia fino alla presa del Re Francesco primo & le ragioni quali sua Maiestà pretendeva in Milano, Napoli, & Sicilia* (Rome: Minizio Calvo, 1525).
Seneca the Younger, *De beneficiis*, ed. C. Hosius (Leipzig: Teubner, 1900).
Shakespeare, W., *Henry V*, in *The New Oxford Shakespeare: The Complete Works. Modern Critical Edition*, ed. G. Taylor et al. (Oxford: Oxford University Press, 2016), pp. 1529–1606.
Sidonius Apollinaris, *Epistulae*, ed. W.B. Anderson (Cambridge, MA, and London: Harvard University Press, 1936).
Sidoine Apollinaire: poèmes et lettres, ed. A. Loyen (Paris: Belles Lettres, 1960–1970).
Sigebert of Gembloux, *Chronica*, MGH SS 6, ed. G.H. Pertz (Hanover: Hahnsche Buchhandlung, 1844), pp. 300–375.
Libellus de viris illustribus, PL 160, cols. 547–588.
Libellus de viris illustribus, ed. R. Witte (Bern and Frankfurt am Main: Lang, 1974).
Vita prior sancti Lamberti, PL 160, cols. 759–782.
Vita sancti Sigiberti regis, AASS Feb. i (Paris, 1863), pp. 228–232, repr. in PL 87, cols. 303–314.
Sisebut, *Vita Desiderii episcopi Viennensis*, in J.C. Martín, ed., "Une nouvelle édition critique de la 'Vita Desiderii' de Sisebut, accompagnée de quelques réflexions concernant la date des 'Sententiae' et du 'De viris illustribus' d'Isidore de Séville," *Hagiographica* 7 (2000), pp. 127–180, at pp. 147–163.
Suger, *Oeuvres*, ed. and trans. F. Gasparri, 2 vols. (Paris: Les Belle Lettres, 2008).
Sulpicius Severus, *Chronica*, ed. P. Parroni, CCSL 63 (Turnhout: Brepols, 2017).
Vita sancti Martini episcopi, ed. and trans. P. Burton (Oxford: Oxford University Press, 2017).
The Song of Roland and Other Poems of Charlemagne, ed. and trans. S. Gaunt and K. Pratt (Oxford: Oxford University Press, 2016).
Theodulf of Orléans, *Carmina*, MGH Poetae 1, ed. E. Dümmler (Berlin: Weidmann, 1881).
Translatio sanctae Baltechildis, MGH SS 15, ed. O. Holder-Egger (Hanover: Hahnsche Buchhandlung, 1887), pp. 284–285.
Translatio seu elevatio S. Bernardi, PL 123, cols. 451–452.
Usuard, *Martyrologium*, Patrologia Latina 124, ed. J.-P. Migne (Paris, 1852), cols. 459–992.
Venantius Fortunatus, *Carmina*, MGH AA 4,1, ed. F. Leo (Berlin: Weidmann, 1881).
De ecclesia Parisiaca, MGH AA 4, ed. F. Leo (Berlin: Weidmann, 1881), pp. 39–40.
Virgil, *Aeneis*, ed. G. Biagio Conte (Berlin and New York: De Gruyter, 2009).
Visio Baronti monachi Longoretensis, MGH SRM 5, ed. W. Levison (Hanover: Hahnsche Buchhandlung, 1910), pp. 368–394.
Vita Amandi episcopi I MGH SRM 5, ed. B. Krusch (Hanover: Hahnsche Buchhandlung, 1910), pp. 428–449.
Vita Arnulfi episcopi Mettensis, MGH SRM 2, ed. B. Krusch (Hanover: Hahnsche Buchhandlung, 1888), pp. 426–446.

Vita Audoini episcopi Rotomagensis, MGH SRM 5, ed. W. Levison (Hanover: Hahnsche Buchhandlung, 1910), pp. 536–567.
Vita brevior sancti Sigeberti, PL 160, cols. 725–730.
Vita Desiderii Cadurcae urbis episcopi, MGH SRM 4, ed. B. Krusch (Hanover: Hahnsche Buchhandlung, 1902), pp. 547–602.
Vita Eligii episcopi Noviomagensis, MGH SRM 4, ed. B. Krusch (Hanover: Hahnsche Buchhandlung, 1902), pp. 663–741.
Vita Filiberti abbatis Gemeticensis et Heriensis, MGH SRM 5, ed. W. Levison (Hanover: Hahnsche Buchhandlung, 1910), pp. 568–604.
Vita Genovefae virginis Parisiensis, MGH SRM 3, ed. B. Krusch (Hanover: Hahnsche Buchhandlung, 1896), pp. 204–238.
Vita Lantberti abbatis Fontanellensis et episcopi Lugdunensis, MGH SRM 5, ed. W. Levison (Hanover: Hahnsche Buchhandlung, 1910), pp. 606–612.
Vita Lupi episcopi Senonici, MGH SRM 4, ed. B. Krusch (Hanover: Hahnsche Buchhandlung, 1902), pp. 176–187.
Vita Remacli episcopi et abbatis, MGH SRM 5, ed. B. Krusch (Hanover: Hahnsche Buchhandlung, 1910), pp. 104–108.
Vita Romarici abbatis Habendensis, MGH SRM 4, ed. B. Krusch (Hanover: Hahnsche Buchhandlung, 1902), pp. 221–225.
Vita Sadalbergae abbatissae Laudunensis, MGH SRM 5, ed. B. Krusch (Hanover: Hahnsche Buchhandlung, 1910), pp. 40–66.
Vita sanctae Geretrudis, MGH SRM 2, ed. B. Krusch (Hanover: Hahnsche Buchhandlung, 1888), pp. 447–464.
Vita sancti Chlodovaldi, MGH SRM 2, ed. B. Krusch (Hanover: Hahnsche Buchhandlung, 1888), pp. 349–357.
Vita sancti Severi Viennensis (BHL 7692), *Analecta Bollandiana* 5 (1886), pp. 416–424.
Vita Wandregiseli abbatis Fontanellensis, MGH SRM 5, ed. B. Krusch (Hanover: Hahnsche Buchhandlung, 1910), pp. 1–24.
Walahfrid, *De imagine Tetrici*, in M.W. Herren, "The *De imagine Tetrici* of Walahfrid Strabo: Edition and Translation," *Journal of Medieval Latin* 1 (1991), pp. 118–139.
William the Breton, *Gesta Philippi Augusti*, in *Œuvres de Rigord et de Guillaume le Breton, historiens de Philippe-Auguste*, ed. H.-F. Delaborde (Paris: Société de l'histoire de France, 1882), pp. 168–320.
Philippidos libri XII, in *Œuvres de Rigord et de Guillaume le Breton, historiens de Philippe-Auguste*, ed. H.-F. Delaborde, 2 vols. (Paris: Société de l'histoire de France, 1882), 2, pp. 1–385.

Literature

Abulafia, D., ed., *The French Descent into Renaissance Italy, 1494–95: Antecedents and Effects* (London and New York: Routledge, 1995).
Africa, T., "Worms and the Death of Kings: A Cautionary Note on Disease and History," *Classical Antiquity* 1, 1 (1982), pp. 1–17.
Airlie, S., "'Sad Stories of the Death of Kings': Narrative Patterns and Structures of Authority in Regino of Prüm's Chronicle," in *Narrative and History in the*

Bibliography 287

Early Medieval West, eds. E.M. Tyler and R. Balzaretti (Turnhout: Brepols, 2006), pp. 105–131.

Allen, M.I., "Bede and Frechulf at St. Gallen," in *Beda Venerabilis: Historian, Monk, and Northumbrian*, eds. L.A.J.R. Howen and A.A. MacDonald (Groningen: Egbert Forsten, 1996), pp. 61–80.

"Fréculf de Lisieux: L'histoire de l'Antiquité comme témoignage de l'actualité," *Tabularia* 8 (2008), pp. 59–79.

"Frechulf of Lisieux," in *The Oxford Guide to the Historical Reception of Augustine*, eds. K. Pollmann and W. Otten (Oxford: Oxford University Press, 2013), vol. 2, p. 1010.

"Universal History 300–1000: Origins and Western Developments," in *Historiography in the Middle Ages*, ed. D. Mauskopf Deliyannis (Leiden: Brill, 2003), pp. 17–42.

Anton, H.-H., "Troja-Herkunft, origo gentis und frühe Verfasstheit der Franken in der gallisch-fränkischen Tradition des 5. und 8. Jhs," *Mitteilungen des Instituts für österreichische Geschichtsforschung* 108 (2000), pp. 1–30.

Arnold, J.J., "The Merovingians and Italy: Ostrogoths and Early Lombards," in *The Oxford Handbook of the Merovingian World*, eds. B. Effros and I. Moreira (Oxford: Oxford University Press, 2020), pp. 442–460.

Aurell, J. "From Genealogies to Chronicles: The Power of the Form in Medieval Catalan Historiography," *Viator* 36, pp. 235–264.

Avraham, D., *Irascible Historian: New Light on the Personality of the Sixteenth-Century Chronicler Joseph ha-Kohen from His Personal Correspondence* (Jerusalem: Beit David, 2004) [Hebrew].

"The Joseph ha-Cohen Epistolary," *Italia* 5, 1–2 (1985), pp. 7–98 [Hebrew].

Bachrach, B.S., *Charlemagne's Early Campaigns (768–777): A Diplomatic and Military Analysis* (Leiden and Boston: Brill, 2013).

"The Imperial Roots of Merovingian Military Organization," in *Military Aspects of Scandinavian Society in a European Perspective, AD 1–1300: Papers from an International Research Seminar at the Danish National Museum, 2–4 May 1996*, eds. A. Nørgård Jørgensen and B.L. Clausen (Copenhagen: Danish National Museum, 1997), pp. 25–31.

Bade, N., "Muslims in the Christian World Order: Comprehension and Knowledge of the Saracens in Two Universal Histories of the Carolingian Empire," *Millennium: Jahrbuch zu Kultur und Geschichte des erste Jahrtausends nach Chr.* 10, 1 (2013), pp. 293–310.

Baldwin, J.W., *The Government of Philip Augustus: Foundations of French Royal Power in the Middle Ages* (Berkeley, CA: University of California Press, 1991).

Barlow, F., *Thomas Becket* (Berkeley, CA: University of California Press, 1990).

Barlow, J., "Gregory of Tours and the Myth of the Trojan Origins of the Franks," *Frühmittelalterliche Studien* 29 (1995), pp. 86–95.

Barnwell, P.S., "Einhard, Louis the Pious, and Childeric III," *Historical Research* 78, 200 (2005), pp. 129–139.

"War and Peace: Historiography and Seventh-Century Embassies," *Early Medieval Europe* 6, 2 (1997), pp. 127–139.

Barrett, G., and G. Woudhuysen. "Remigius and the 'Important News' of Clovis Rewritten," *Antiquité tardive* 24 (2016), pp. 471–500.

Barton, C.A., *The Sorrows of the Ancient Romans: The Gladiator and the Monster* (Princeton, NJ: Princeton University Press, 1995).
Batalova, S., "The Tradition of St. Eustathius Placidas in Latin," *Scripta & e-Scripta* 2 (2004), pp. 325–354.
Bauman, R.A., *Crime and Punishment in Ancient Rome* (London and New York: Routledge, 1996).
Bautier, R.H. ed., *La France de Philippe-Auguste: Le temps des mutations* (Paris: Centre National de la Recherche Scientifique, 1982).
"La place de l'abbaye de Fleury-sur-Loire dans l'historiographie française du IXe au XIIe siècle," in *Études ligériennes d'histoire et d'archéologie médiévales: mémoires et exposés présentés à la Semaine d'etudes médiévales de Saint-Benoit-sur-Loire du 3 au 10 Juillet 1969*, ed. R. Louis (Paris: Publications de la Société des Fouilles Archéologiques et des Monuments Historiques de l'Yonne, 1975), pp. 25–33.
Beaune, C., "L'utilisation politique du mythe des origines troyennes en France à la fin du Moyen Âge," in *Lectures médiévales de Virgile: Actes du colloque de Rome (25–28 octobre 1982)* (Rome: École Française de Rome, 1985), pp. 331–355.
The Birth of an Ideology: Myths and Symbols of Nation in Late-Medieval France, ed. F.L. Cheyette (Berkeley, CA: University of California Press, 1991).
Becher, M., "Der sogenannte Staatsstreich Grimoalds: Versuch einer Neubewertung," in *Karl Martell in seiner Zeit*, eds. J. Jarnut, U. Nonn, and M. Richter (Sigmaringen: Jan Thorbecke Verlag, 1994), pp. 119–147.
Beisel, F., *Theudebertus magnus rex Francorum: Persönlichkeit und Zeit* (Idstein: Schulz-Kirchner Verlag, 1993).
Ben-Shalom, R., "The Myths of Troy and Hercules as Reflected in the Writings of Some Jewish Exiles from Spain," in *Jews, Muslims and Christians in and around the Crown of Aragon: Essays in Honour of Professor Elena Lurie*, ed. H. J. Hames (Leiden and Boston: Brill, 2004), pp. 229–254.
Berger, P., *The Crescent on the Temple: The Dome of the Rock as Image of the Ancient Jewish Sanctuary* (Leiden and Boston: Brill, 2012).
Beumann, J., *Sigebert von Gembloux und der Traktat de investitura episcoporum* (Sigmaringen: Jan Thorbecke Verlag, 1976).
Bischoff, G., "Le bon roi Dagobert entre Vosges et Rhin: une mémoire militante," in *Le pouvoir au Moyen Âge: Idéologies, pratiques, représentations*, eds. C. Carozzi and H. Taviani-Carozzi (Aix-en-Provence: Presses de L'Université de Provence, 2005), pp. 51–67.
Bitel, L.M., *Landscape with Two Saints: How Genovefa of Paris and Brigit of Kildare Built Christianity in Barbarian Europe* (Oxford: Oxford University Press, 2009).
Bjornlie, M.S., ed., "Constantine in the Sixth Century: From Constantinople to Tours," in *The Life and Legacy of Constantine: Traditions Through the Ages* (London and New York: Routledge, 2017), pp. 92–114.
Bonfil, R., "Esiste una storiografia ebraica medioevale?," *Associazione Italiana per lo Studio del Giudaismo: Atti del Congresso* IV (1987), pp. 227–247.
"How Golden Was the Age of the Renaissance in Jewish Historiography?," *History and Theory* 27 (1988), pp. 78–102.
"Jewish Attitudes toward History and Historical Writing in Pre-Modern Times," *Jewish History* 11 (1997), pp. 7–40.

"Riflessioni sulla storiografia ebraica in Italia nel cinquecento," *Italia Judaica* 2 (1986), pp. 56–66.
The Life of Joseph (Jerusalem: Magnes Press, 2020) [Hebrew].
Bonnell, H.E., "Excurs I: Die Biographie des Bischofs Chlodulf von Metz," in *Die Anfänge des karolingischen Hauses* (Berlin: Dunder und Humblot, 1866), pp. 137–139.
Booker, C.M., *Past Convictions: The Penance of Louis the Pious and the Decline of the Carolingians* (Philadelphia, PA: University of Pennsylvania Press, 2009).
"The Dionysian Mirror of Louis the Pious," *Quaestiones Medii Aevii Novae* 19 (2014), pp. 241–264.
Boschen, L., *Die Annales Prumienses. Ihre nähere und ihre weitere Verwandschaft* (Düsseldorf: Schwann, 1972).
Bossuat, R., "Le roi Dagobert, héros de romans du Moyen Age," *Comptes rendus des séances de l'Académie des Inscriptions et Belles-Lettres*, 108, 2 (1964), pp. 361–368.
Bosworth, A.K., "Criminals, Cures, and Castigation: Heiric of Auxerre's *Miracula Sancti Germani* and Ninth-Century Carolingian Hagiography," Doctoral dissertation (Purdue University, 2008).
"Learning from the Saints: Ninth-Century Hagiography and the Carolingian Renaissance," *History Compass* 8, 9 (2010), pp. 1055–1066.
Bouchard, C.B., "Childeric III and the Emperors Drogo Magnus and Pippin the Pious," *Medieval Prosopography* 28 (2013), pp. 1–16.
"Images of the Merovingians and Carolingians," *History Compass* 4, 2 (2006), 293–307.
Remembering Saints and Ancestors: Memory and Forgetting in France, 500–1200 (Philadelphia, PA: Pennsylvania University Press, 2014).
"The Carolingian Creation of a Model of Patrilineage," in *Paradigms and Methods in Early Medieval Studies*, eds. C. Chazelle and F. Lifshitz (New York: Palgrave Macmillan, 2007), pp. 135–152.
Bourdieu, P. "Rethinking the State: Genesis and Structure of the Bureaucratic Field," in *State/Culture: State Formation after the Cultural Turn*, ed. G. Steinmetz (Ithaca and London: Cornell University Press, 1999), pp. 53–75.
Boyer, J.F., *Pouvoirs et territoires en Aquitaine du VIIe au Xe siècle: enquête sur l'administration locale* (Stuttgart: Franz Steiner Verlag, 2018).
Bradbury, J., *Philip Augustus: King of France, 1180–1223* (London and New York: Routledge, 1998), pp. 226–234.
Breisach, E., *Historiography: Ancient, Medieval, & Modern*, 3rd edition (Chicago and London: University of Chicago Press, 2007).
Brennan, B. "The Disputed Authorship of Fortunatus' Byzantine Poems," *Byzantion* 66, 2 (1996), pp. 335–345.
Brincken, A.-D. von den, *Studien zur lateinischen Weltchronistik bis in das Zeitalter Ottos von Freising* (Düsseldorf: Triltsch, 1957).
Broome, R., "Approaches to Community and Otherness in the Late Merovingian and Early Carolingian Periods," Doctoral dissertation (University of Leeds, 2014).
"Pagans, Rebels and Merovingians: Otherness in the Early Carolingian World," in *The Resources of the Past in the Early Medieval World*, eds. C. Gantner,

R. McKitterick, and S. Meeder (Cambridge: Cambridge University Press, 2015), pp. 155–171.

Brown, E.A.R., "'Franks, Burgundians, and Aquitanians' and the Royal Coronation Ceremony in France," *Transactions of the American Philosophical Society* 82, 7 (1992), pp. i–xii and 1–189.

"Saint-Denis and the Turpin Legend," in *The Codex Callixtinus and the Shrine of St. James*, eds. J. Williams and A. Stones (Tübingen: Gunter Narr Verlag, 1992), pp. 51–88.

and Cothren, M.W., "The Twelfth-Century Crusading Window of the Abbey of Saint-Denis: Praeteritorum Enim Recordatio Futurorum est Exhibitio," *Journal of the Warburg and Courtauld Institutes* 49 (1986), pp. 1–40.

Bruce, S., "The Dark Age of Herodotus: Shards of a Fugitive History in Early Medieval Europe," *Speculum* 94, 1 (2019), pp. 47–67.

Brundage, J., *Law, Sex and Society in Medieval Europe* (Chicago: University of Chicago Press, 1987).

Buchner, M., "Zur Entstehung und zur Tendenz der Gesta Dagoberti," *Historisches Jahrbuch* 47 (1927), pp. 252–274.

Burgess, R.W., and M. Kulikowski, *Mosaics of Time: The Latin Chronicle Traditions from the First Century BC to the Sixth Century AD, Volume I: A Historical Introduction to the Chronicle Genre from Its Origins to the High Middle Ages* (Turnhout: Brepols, 2013).

Buridant, C., "Connecteurs et articulations du récit en ancien et moyen français: le cas de la Chronique des rois de France," in *Texte et discours en moyen français: Actes du XIe colloque international sur le moyen français*, ed. A. Vanderheyden et al. (Turnhout: Brepols, 2007), pp. 73–94.

Burke, P. "Images as Evidence in Seventeenth-Century Europe," *Journal of the History of Ideas* 64, 2 (2003), pp. 273–296.

Cain, A., "Miracles, Martyrs, and Arians: Gregory of Tours' Sources for His Account of the Vandal Kingdom," *Vigiliae Christianae* 59, 4 (2005), pp. 412–437.

Carozzi, C., "Clovis, de Grégoire de Tours aux Grandes Chroniques de France: Naissance d'un mémoire ambiguë," in *Faire mémoire: Souvenir et commémoration au Moyen Âge*, eds. C. Carozzi and H. Taviani Carozzi (Aix-en-Provence: Publications de l'Université de Provence, 1999), pp. 41–61.

Casias, C.M.M., "Rebel Nuns and the Bishop Historian: The Competing Voices of Radegund and Gregory," *Studies in Late Antiquity* 6, 1 (2022), pp. 5–34.

Castelli, E.A., *Martyrdom and Memory: Early Christian Culture Making* (New York: Columbia University Press, 2004).

Certain, E. de, *Les miracles de Saint Benoît écrits par Adrevald, Aimoin, André, Raoul Tortaire et Hugues de Sainte Marie, moines de Fleury* (Paris: Mme. Ve. Jules Renouard, 1858).

Chazan, M., "La nécessité de l'Empire de Sigebert de Gembloux à Jean de Saint-Victor," *Le Moyen Age: Revue d'histoire et philologie* 106 (2000), pp. 9–13.

L'Empire et l'histoire universelle de Sigebert de Gembloux à Jean de Saint-Victor (XIIe-XIVe siècle) (Paris: Champion, 1999).

Bibliography 291

"Sigebert de Gembloux, un historien engagé," in *Sigebert de Gembloux*, ed. J.-P. Straus (Barcelona and Madrid: Féderation Internationale des Instituts d'Études Médiévales, 2015), pp. 1–50.
Clarke, M., "The Legend of Trojan Origins in the Later Middle Ages: Texts and Tapestries," in *Origin Legends in Early Medieval Western Europe*, eds. L. Brady and P. Wadden (Leiden and Boston: Brill, 2022), pp. 187–212.
Cochrane, E.W., *Historians and Historiography in the Italian Renaissance* (Chicago: University of Chicago Press, 1981).
Collins, R., "Deception and Misrepresentation in Early Eighth-Century Frankish Historiography: Two Case Studies," in *Karl Martell in seiner Zeit*, eds. J. Jarnut, U. Nonn, and M. Richter (Sigmaringen: Jan Thorbecke Verlag, 1994), pp. 227–247.
Die Fredegar-Chroniken, MGH Studien und Texte 44 (Hanover: Hahnsche Buchhandlung, 2007), pp. 8–81.
"Frankish Past and Carolingian Present in the Age of Charlemagne," in *Am Vorabend der Kaiserkrönung: Das Epos "Karolus Magnus et Leo Papa" und der Papstbesuch in Paderborn 799*, eds. P. Godman, J. Jarnut, and P. Johanek (Berlin: Akademie Verlag, 2011), pp. 301–322.
Fredegar, Authors of the Middle Ages, vol. IV, no. 13 (Aldershot: Ashgate, 1996).
The Fredegar Chronicles, unpublished English version.
Combettes, B., "La subordination dans la Chronique de Frédégaire: les propositions non régies," in *Latin tardif, français ancien: Continuités et ruptures*, eds. A. Carlier and C. Guillot-Barbance (Berlin and Boston: De Gruyter, 2018), pp. 373–412.
Contreni, J.J., "'By Lions, Bishops Are Meant; By Wolves, Priests': History, Exegesis, and the Carolingian Church in Haimo of Auxerre's *Commentary on Ezechiel*," *Francia* 29, 1 (2002), pp. 29–56.
"The Carolingian Renaissance: Education and Literary Culture," in *The New Cambridge Medieval History, Volume II: c.700–c.900*, ed. R. McKitterick (Cambridge: Cambridge University Press, 1995), pp. 709–757.
Corradini, R., R. Meens, C. Pössel, and P. Shaw, eds., *Texts and Identities in the Early Middle Ages*, Forschungen zur Geschichte des Mittelalters 12, Denkschriften der Österreichischen Akademie der Wissenschaften, Philosophische Klasse 344 (Vienna, 2006).
Costambeys, M., M. Innes, and S. MacLean, *The Carolingian World* (Cambridge: Cambridge University Press, 2011).
Coumert, M. "La mémoire de Troie en Occident, d'Orose à Benoît de Sainte-Maure," *Actes des congrès de la Société des historiens médiévistes de l'enseignement supérieur public, 36e congrès: Les villes capitales au Moyen Age* (2005), pp. 327–347.
Cracco Ruggini, L., "The Crisis of the Noble Saint: The 'Vita Arnulfi'," in *The Seventh Century: Change and Continuity. Proceedings of a Joint French and British Colloquium held at the Warburg Institute 8–9 July 1988*, eds. J. Fontaine and J.N. Hillgarth (London, 1992), pp. 116–153.
Dachowski, E., *First Among Abbots: The Career of Abbo of Fleury* (Washington, DC: The Catholic University of America Press, 2008).
D'Auria, M., *The Shaping of French National Identity: Narrating the Nation's Past, 1715–1830* (Cambridge: Cambridge University Press, 2020).

Dailey, E.T., "Gregory of Tours, Fredegund, and the Paternity of Chlothar II: Strategies of Legitimation in the Merovingian Kingdoms," *Journal of Late Antiquity* 7, 1 (2014), pp. 3–27.
"Misremembering Radegund's Foundation of Sainte-Croix," in *Erfahren, erzählen, erinnern: narrative Konstruktionen von Gedächtnis und Generation in Antike und Mittelalter*, ed. H. Brandt et al. (Bamberg: University of Bamberg Press, 2012), pp. 117–140.
Queens, Consorts, Concubines: Gregory of Tours and Women of the Merovingian Elite (Leiden and Boston: Brill, 2015).
Daly, W.M., "Clovis: How Barbaric, How Pagan?," *Speculum* 69 (1994), pp. 619–664.
Davies, K., "Late XVth Century French Historiography, As Exemplified in the *Compendium* of Robert Gaguin and the *De rebus gestis* of Paulus Aemilius," doctoral dissertation (University of Edinburgh, 1954).
Delaborde, H.-F., "Notice sur les ouvrages et sur la vie de Rigord, moine de Saint-Denis," *Bibliothèque de l'école des chartes* 45 (1884), pp. 585–614.
Delayae, H., *Oeuvre des Bollandistes 1615 à 1915* (Brussels: Bureaux de la Société des Bollandistes, 1920).
Delogu, P., "Consors regni: un problema carolingio?," *Bulletino dell'Istituto storico italiano per il medio evo* 76 (1964), pp. 47–98.
Demaison, M.L., "Étude critique sur la Vie de Saint Sigibert III roi d'Austrasie par Sigebert de Gembloux," *Travaux de l'Académie Nationale de Reims* 3, 4 (1887–1888), pp. 1–30.
Demandt, A., "The Osmosis of Late Roman and Germanic Aristocracies," in *Das Reich und die Barbaren*, eds. E.K. Chrysos, and A. Schwarcz (Vienna and Cologne: Veröffentlichungen des Instituts für Österreichische Geschichtsforschung, 1988), pp. 75–86.
Deploige, J., "Political Assassination and Sanctification: Transforming Discursive Customs after the Murder of the Flemish Count Charles the Good (1127)," in *Mystifying the Monarch: Studies on Discourse, Power, and History*, eds. J. Deploige and G. Deneckere (Amsterdam: Amsterdam University Press, 2006), pp. 35–54.
Depreux, P., "L'actualité de Fréculf de Lisieux: à propos de l'édition critique de son œuvre," *Tabularia* 4 (2004), pp. 53–60.
Dérens, J., and M. Fleury, "La construction de la cathédrale de Paris par Childebert Ier, d'après le *De ecclesia Parisiaca* de Fortunat," *Journal des savants* (1977), pp. 247–256.
Devisse, J., *Hincmar, archevêque de Reims, 845–882*, 3 vols. (Geneva: Librarie Droz, 1975–1976).
Diem, A., "Vita vel regula: Multifunctional Hagiography in the Early Middle Ages," in *Hagiography and the History of Latin Christendom, 500–1500*, ed. S. Kahn Herrick (Leiden: Brill, 2019), pp. 123–142.
"Who is Allowed to Pray for the King? St-Maurice d'Agaune and the Creation of a Burgundian Identity," in *Strategies of Identification: Ethnicity and Religion in Early Medieval Europe*, eds. W. Pohl and G. Heydemann (Turnhout: Brepols, 2013), pp. 47–88.

Bibliography 293

Diesenberger, M., "Hair, Sacrality and Symbolic Capital in the Frankish Kingdoms," in *The Construction of Communities in the Early Middle Ages: Texts, Resources and Artefacts*, eds. Corradini, R., M. Diesenberger, and H. Reimitz (Leiden and Boston: Brill, 2003), pp. 173–212.

Dobschenzki, J.F., *Von Opfern und Tätern: Gewalt im Spiegel der merowingischen Hagiographie des 7. Jahrhunderts* (Stuttgart: Kohlhammer 2015).

Dönitz, S., "Historiography among Byzantine Jews – the Case of Sefer Yosippon," in *Jews in Byzantium: Dialectics of Minority and Majority Cultures*, ed. R. Bonfil et al. (Leiden: Brill, 2012), pp. 953–970.

"Sefer Yosippon (Josippon)," in *A Companion to Yosefus*, eds. H. Howell Chapman and Z. Rodgers (Oxford and Malden, MA: Wiley-Blackwell, 2016), pp. 382–389.

Dörler, P., "The *Liber historiae Francorum*—A Model for a New Frankish Self-Confidence," *Networks and Neighbours* 1, 1 (2013), pp. 23–43.

Dubois, E., "The Benedictine Congregation of Maurists in Seventeenth-Century France and Their Scholarly Activities," *Seventeenth-Century French Studies* 14, 1 (1992), pp. 219–233.

Dubreucq, A., "Le prince et le peuple dans les miroirs des princes carolingiens," in *Le Prince, son peuple et le bien commun. De l'Antiquité tardive à la fin du Moyen Âge*, eds. H. Oudart, J.-M. Picard, and J. Quaghebeur (Rennes: Presses universitaires de Rennes, 2013), pp. 97–114.

Duchesne, L., *Fastes épiscopaux de l'ancienne Gaule*, 4 vols. (Paris: Thorin et fils, 1907).

Dumézil, B., *Servir l'État barbare dans la Gaule franque: IVe–IXe siècle* (Paris: Tallandier, 2013).

Dumville, D., "What Is a Chronicle?," *The Medieval Chronicle* 2 (2002), pp. 1–27.

Dunphy, G., "Chronicles (terminology)," in *Encyclopedia of the Medieval Chronicle* eds. G. Dunphy, C. Bratu 2 vols. (Leiden, Boston: Brill, 2010), vol. 1, pp. 274–282.

"Six Ages of the World," in *The Encyclopedia of the Medieval Chronicle*, eds. G. Dunphy, C. Bratu (Leiden: Brill, 2010), vol. 2, pp. 1367–1370.

Dupraz, L., *Contribution à l'histoire du Regnum Francorum pendant le troisième quart du VIIe siècle, 656–680* (Fribourg-en-Suisse: Impr. St.-Paul, 1948).

Duranton, H., "Le vase de Soissons et les historiens du XVIIIe siècle," *Revue de synthèse* (1975), pp. 284–316.

Dutton, P.E., *Charlemagne's Courtier: The Complete Einhard* (Peterborough, Ont. and Ormskirk: University of Toronto Press, 1998).

The Politics of Dreaming in the Carolingian Empire (Lincoln, NE, and London: University of Nebraska Press, 1994).

Ebling, H., *Prosopographie der Amtsträger des Merowingerreiches, von Chlothar II. (613) bis Karl Martell (741)*, Beihefte der Francia 2 (Munich: Wilhelm Fink, 1974).

Edwards, J.C., *Superior Women: Medieval Female Authority in Poitiers' Abbey of Sainte-Croix* (Oxford: Oxford University Press, 2019).

Effros, B., "Memories of the Early Medieval Past: Grave Artefacts in Nineteenth-Century France and Early Twentieth-Century America," in *Archeologies of*

Remembrance: Death and Memory in Past Societies, ed. H. Williams (New York: Springer, 2003), pp. 255–280.
Merovingian Mortuary Archeology and the Making of the Early Middle Ages (Berkeley, CA: University of California Press, 2003).
Uncovering the Germanic Past: Merovingian Archaeology in France, 1830–1914 (Oxford: Oxford University Press, 2012).
Effros, B., and I. Moreira, eds., *The Oxford Handbook of the Merovingian World* (Oxford: Oxford University Press, 2020).
Egerton Brydges, S., *Polyanthea librorum vetustiorum, italicorum, gallicorum, hispanicorum, anglicanorum et latinorum* (Geneva: G. Fick, 1822).
Einbinder, S.L., "Meir Alguades: History, Empathy, and Martyrdom," *Religion & Literature* 42, 1/2 (2010), pp. 185–209.
Elton, H., *The Roman Empire in Late Antiquity: A Political and Military History* (Cambridge: Cambridge University Press, 2018).
Erkens, F.-R., "'Sicut Esther regina': Die westfränkische Königin als *consors regni*," *Francia* 20, 1 (1993), pp. 15–38.
Esders, S., et al, eds., *East and West in the Early Middle Ages: The Merovingian Kingdoms in Mediterranean Perspective* (Cambridge: Cambridge University Press, 2019).
"Herakleios, Dagobert und die 'beschnittenen Völker': Die Umwälzungen des Mittelmeerraums im 7. Jahrhundert in der Chronik des sog. Fredegar," in *Jenseits der Grenzen. Beiträge zur spätantiken und frühmittelalterlichen Geschichtsschreibung*, eds. A. Goltz, H. Leppin, and H. Schlange-Schöningen (Berlin and New York: De Gruyter, 2009), pp. 239–311.
"The Prophesied Rule of a 'Circumcised People': A Travelling Tradition from the Seventh-Century Mediterranean," in *Barbarians and Jews: Jews and Judaism in the Early Medieval West*, eds. Y. Hen and T.F.X. Noble (Turnhout: Brepols, 2018), pp. 119–154.
and H. Reimitz, "Legalizing Ethnicity: The Remaking of Citizenship in Post-Roman Gaul (Sixth–Seventh Centuries)," in *Civic Identity and Civic Participation in Late Antiquity and the Early Middle Ages*, eds. C. Brélaz and E. Rose (Turnhout: Brepols, 2021), pp. 295–329.
Everett, N., "Narrating the Life of Eusebius of Vercelli," in *Narrative and History in the Early Medieval West*, eds. E.M. Tyler and R. Balzaretti (Turnhout: Brepols, 2006), pp. 133–165.
Ewig, E., "Das Privileg des Bischofs Berthefrid von Amiens für Corbie von 664 und die Klosterpolitik der Königin Balthild, in E. Ewig, *Spätantikes und Fränkisches Gallien: Gesammelte Schriften (1952–1973)*, Beihefte der *Francia* 3, 2 (Munich: Artemis Verlag, 1979), pp. 538–583.
"Der Bild Constantins des Grossen in den ersten Jahrhunderten des abendländischen Mittelalters," *Historisches Jahrbuch* 75 (1956), pp. 1–46.
Die frankischen Teilungen und Teilreiche (511–613) (Wiesbaden: Franz Steiner Verlag, 1953).
"Le mythe troyen et l'histoire de France," in *Clovis, histoire et mémoire: Baptême de Clovis, l'événement*, ed. M. Rouche (Paris: Presses de l'Universite de Paris-Sorbonne, 1997), pp. 817–847.
"Troja und die Franken," *Rheinische Vierteljahrsblätter* 62 (1998), pp. 1–16.

Bibliography 295

"Trojamythos und fränkische Frühgeschichte" in *Die Franken und die Alemannen bis zur "Schlacht bei Zülpich" (496/97)*, ed. D. Geuenich (Berlin and New York: De Gruyter, 1998), pp. 1–31.
Fabbro, E., "'Capitur urbs quae totum cepit orbem': The Fates of the Sack of Rome (410) in Early Medieval Historiography," *The Medieval Chronicle* 10 (2015), pp. 49–67.
Farmer, S., *Communities of Saint Martin: Legend and Ritual in Medieval Tours* (Ithaca, NY: Cornell University Press, 2019).
Faure, C., "L'image de Clovis et des Mérovingiens dans les manuels scolaires de la fin du XIXe siècle à nos jours: Reflet de l'évolution historiographique et des pratiques pédagogiques," *DIversité REcherches et Terrains* 10 (2018), pp. 41–60.
Fielding, I., *Transformations of Ovid in Late Antiquity* (Cambridge: Cambridge University Press, 2017).
Fischer, A., "Money for Nothing: Franks, Byzantines and Lombards in the Sixth and Seventh Centuries," in *East and West in the Early Middle Ages: The Merovingian Kingdoms in Mediterranean Perspective*, ed. S. Esders et al. (Cambridge: Cambridge University Press, 2019), pp. 108–126.
"Reflecting Romanness in the Fredegar Chronicle," *Early Medieval Europe* 22, 4 (2014), pp. 433–445.
Fischer, S., and L. Lind, "The Coins in the Grave of King Childeric," *Journal of Archaeology and Ancient History* 14 (2015), pp. 3–36.
Flusser, D., "Josippon, a Medieval Hebrew Version of Josephus," in *Josephus, Judaism, and Christianity*, eds. L.H. Feldman and G. Hata (Leiden and Detroit: Brill, 1987), pp. 386–397.
Folz, R., *Les saints rois du Moyen Âge en Occident (VIe–XIIIe)* (Brussels: Société des Bollandistes, 1984).
Fößel, A., "Gender and Rulership in the Medieval German Empire," *History Compass* 7, 1 (2009), pp. 55–65.
Fouracre, P., "Eternal Lights and Earthly Needs: Practical Aspects of the Development of Frankish Immunities," in *Property and Power in the Early Middle Ages*, eds. W. Davies and P. Fouracre (Cambridge: Cambridge University Press, 1995), pp. 53–81.
"Forgetting and Remembering Dagobert II: The English Connection," in *Frankland: The Franks and the World of the Early Middle Ages*, eds. P. Fouracre and D. Ganz (Manchester: Manchester University Press, 2008), pp. 70–89.
"Francia and the History of Medieval Europe," *The Haskins Society Journal* 23 (2011), pp. 1–22.
The Age of Charles Martel (New York: Routledge, 2000).
"The Incidence of Rebellion in the Early Medieval West," in *Making Early Medieval Societies: Conflict and Belonging in the Latin West, 300–1200*, eds. K. Cooper and C. Leyser (Cambridge: Cambridge University Press, 2016), pp. 104–124.
"The Long Shadow of the Merovingians," in *Charlemagne: Empire and Society*, ed. J. Story (Manchester: Manchester University Press, 2005), pp. 5–21.
Fouracre, P., and R.A. Gerberding, ed. and trans., *Late Merovingian France: History and Hagiography 640–720* (Manchester and New York: Manchester University Press, 1996).

Fox, Y., "Anxiously Looking East: Burgundian Foreign Policy on the Eve of Reconquest," in *East and West in the Early Middle Ages: The Merovingian Kingdoms in Mediterranean Perspective*, ed. S. Esders et al. (Cambridge: Cambridge University Press, 2019), pp. 32–44.

"Chronicling the Merovingians in Hebrew: The Early Medieval Chapters of Yosef Ha-Kohen's *Divrei Hayamim*," *Traditio* 74 (2019), pp. 423–447.

"*Ego bar-iona*: Jews and the Language of Forced Conversion in Columbanian Circles," in *Barbarian and Jews: Jews and Judaism in the Early Medieval West*, eds. Y. Hen and T.F.X. Noble (Turnhout: Brepols, 2019), pp. 155–181.

"From Metz to Überlingen: Columbanus and Gallus in Alamannia," in *Columbanus and the Peoples of Post-Roman Europe*, ed. A. O'Hara (Oxford: Oxford University Press, 2018), pp. 205–224.

"Image of Kings Past: The Gibichung Legacy in Post-Conquest Burgundy," *Francia* 42 (2015), pp. 1–27.

"New *honores* for a Region Transformed: The Patriciate in Post-Roman Gaul," *Revue Belge de Philologie et d'Histoire* 93 (2015), pp. 1–38.

Power and Religion in Merovingian Gaul: Columbanian Monasticism and the Frankish Elites (Cambridge: Cambridge University Press, 2014).

"Revisiting Gregory of Tours' Burgundian Narrative," in *Les royaumes de Bourgogne jusque 1032 à travers la culture et la religion*, eds. A. Wagner and N. Brocard, Culture et sociétés médiévales 30 (Brepols: Turnhout, 2018), pp. 227–238.

"Saints and Their Spaces in Gregory of Tours" (forthcoming).

"The Bishop and the Monk: Desiderius of Vienne and the Columbanian Movement," *Early Medieval Europe* 20, 2 (2012), pp. 176–194.

"The Language of Sixth-Century Frankish Diplomacy," in *The Merovingian Kingdoms and the Mediterranean World: Revisiting the Sources*, eds. S. Esders, Y. Hen, P. Lucas, and T. Rotman (London and New York: Bloomsbury Press, 2019), pp. 63–75.

Fried, J., "The Frankish Kingdoms, 817–911: The East and Middle Kingdoms," in *The New Cambridge Medieval History, Vol. II: c.700–c.900*, ed. R. McKitterick (Cambridge: Cambridge University Press, 1995), pp. 142–168.

Frye, D., "Aegidius, Childeric, Odovacer and Paul," *Nottingham Medieval Studies* 36 (1992), pp. 1–14.

Gaillard, M., "La place des abbayes dans la politique territorial des souverains francs et germaniques en Lotharingie, de 869 à 925," *Revue du Nord* 351, 3 (2003), pp. 655–666.

Gandy, G.N., "*Revelatio* on the Origins of Mont Saint-Michel (Fifth–Ninth Centuries)," *Speculum* 95, 1 (2020), pp. 132–166.

Ganz, D., "Charlemagne in Hell," *Florilegium* 17 (2000), pp. 175–194.

Gaposchkin, M.C., *The Making of Saint Louis: Kingship, Sanctity, and Crusade in the Later Middle Ages* (Ithaca, NY, and London: Cornell University Press, 2008).

Garipzanov, I., *The Symbolic Language of Authority in the Carolingian World (c.751–877)* (Leiden and Boston: Brill, 2008).

Bibliography 297

Garrison, M., "The *Missa pro principe* in the Bobbio Missal," in *The Bobbio Missal: Liturgy and Religious Culture in Merovingian Gaul*, eds. Y. Hen and R. Meens (Cambridge: Cambridge University Press, 2004), pp. 187–205.

Gaunt, S. and K. Pratt, ed. and trans., "Introduction," in *The Song of Roland and Other Poems of Charlemagne* (Oxford: Oxford University Press, 2016), pp. vii–xxv.

Geary, P.J., *Before France and Germany: The Creation and Transformation of the Merovingian World* (Oxford and New York: Oxford University Press, 1988).

Furta Sacra: Thefts of Relics in the Central Middle Ages (Princeton, NJ: Princeton University Press, 1978), pp. 120–122.

Phantoms of Remembrance: Memory and Oblivion at the End of the First Millennium (Princeton, NJ: Princeton University Press, 1994).

Gerberding, R., *The Rise of the Carolingians and the* Liber Historiae Francorum (Oxford: Clarendon Press, 1987).

Gilbert, F., *Machiavelli and Guicciardini: Politics and History in Sixteenth-Century Florence* (Princeton, NJ: Princeton University Press, 1965).

Gillet, A., "Love and Grief in Post-Imperial Diplomacy: The Letters of Brunhild," in *Power and Emotions in the Roman World and Late Antiquity*, eds. B. Sidwell and D. Dzino (Piscataway, NJ: Gorgias Press, 2010), pp. 127–165.

"Telling off Justinian: Theudebert I, the *Epistolae Austrasicae*, and Communication Strategies in Sixth-Century Merovingian-Byzantine Relations," *Early Medieval Europe* 27, 2 (2019), pp. 161–194.

Gillis, M.B., *Heresy and Dissent in the Carolingian Empire: The Case of Gottschalk of Orbais* (Oxford: Oxford University Press, 2017).

Glatthaar, M., "Boniface and the Reform Councils," in *A Companion to Boniface*, eds. M. Aaij and S. Godlove (Leiden: Brill, 2020), pp. 219–246.

Goderniaux, A., "*Eique victoria provenit in omnibus*. De Charlemagne à Henri IV: appropriations des exploits militaires des Pippinides et des Carolingiens par Sigebert de Gembloux durant la Querelle des Investitures," *Revue belge de philologie et d'histoire* 93, 3–4 (2015), pp. 753–769.

Godman, P., "The Poetic Hunt: From St. Martin to Charlemagne's Heir," in *Charlemagne's Heir: New Perspectives on the Reign of Louis the Pious (814–840)*, eds. P. Godman and R. Collins (Oxford: Oxford University Press, 1990), pp. 565–589.

Goetz, H.-W., "Gens, Kings and Kingdoms: The Franks," in *Regna and Gentes: The Relationship between Late Antique and Early Medieval Peoples and Kingdoms in the Transformation of the Roman World*, eds. H.-W. Goetz, J. Jarnut, and W. Pohl (Leiden and Boston: Brill, 2003), pp. 307–344.

"Historiographisches Zeitbewußtsein im frühen Mittelalter. Zum Umgang mit der Zeit in der karolingischen Geschichtsschreibung," *in Historiographie im frühen Mittelalter*, eds. A. Scharer and G. Scheibelreiter (Vienna: Oldenbourg, 1994), pp. 158–178.

"The Concept of Time in the Historiography of the Eleventh and Twelfth Centuries," in *Medieval Concepts of the Past: Ritual, Memory, Historiography*, eds. G. Althoff, J. Fried, and P.J. Geary (Washington, DC: German Historical Institute and Cambridge: Cambridge University Press, 2002), pp. 139–166.

Goez, W., "Zur Weltchronik des Bishofs Frechulf von Lisieux," in *Festgabe für Paul Kirn zum 70. Geburtstag, dargebracht von Freunden und Schülern*, ed. E. Kaufmann (Berlin: Erich Schmidt Verlag, 1961), pp. 93–110.

Goffart, W., "Byzantine Policy in the West under Tiberius II and Maurice: The Pretenders Hermenegild and Gundovald, 579–585," *Traditio* 13 (1957), pp. 73–118.

"Le Mans, St. Scholastica, and the Literary Tradition of the Translation of St. Benedict," *Revue Bénédictine* 77 (1987), pp. 107–141.

"The Fredegar Problem Reconsidered," *Speculum* 38, 2 (1963), pp. 206–241.

The Narrators of Barbarian History (A.D. 550–800): Jordanes, Gregory of Tours, Bede, and Paul the Deacon (Princeton, NJ: Princeton University Press, 1988).

Goldberg, E.J, "'A Man of Notable Good Looks Disfigured by a Cruel Wound': The Forest Misadventure of Charles the Young of Aquitaine (864) in History and Legend," in *Historiography and Identity III: Carolingian Approaches*, eds. R. Kramer, H. Reimitz, and G. Ward (Turnhout: Brepols, 2021), pp. 355–386.

"Louis the Pious and the Hunt," *Speculum* 88, 3 (2013), pp. 613–643.

Struggle for Empire: Kingship and Conflict under Louis the German, 817–876 (Ithaca, NY: Cornell University Press, 2006).

Goosman, F.C.W., "Memorable Crises: Carolingian Historiography and the Making of Pippin's Reign, 750–900," doctoral dissertation (University of Amsterdam, 2013).

Goosmann, E., and R. Meens, "A Mirror of Princes who Opted Out: Regino of Prüm and Royal Monastic Conversion," in *Religious Franks: Religion and Power in the Frankish Kingdoms: Studies in Honour of Mayke De Jong*, ed. R. Meens et al. (Manchester, Manchester University Press, 2016), pp. 296–313.

Gosman, M., "Alain Chartier: le mythe romain et le pouvoir royal français," in *Entre fiction et histoire: Troie et Rome au Moyen Âge*, eds. E. Baumgartner and L. Harf-Lancer (Paris: Presses de la Sorbonne Nouvelle, 1997), pp. 161–182.

Grahn-Hoek, H., "*Gundulfus subregulus*—eine genealogische Brücke zwischen Merowingern und Karolingern?," *Deutsches Archiv* 59 (2003), pp. 1–47.

Graus, F., "Troja und trojanische Herkunftssage im Mittelalter" in *Kontinuität und Transformation der Antike im Mittelalter: Veröffentlichung der Kongreßakten zum Freiburger Symposium des Mediävistenverbandes*, ed. W. Erzgräber (Sigmaringen: Thorbecke Verlag, 1989), pp. 25–43.

Grell, C., "Clovis du grand siècle aux lumières," *Bibliothèque de l'École des chartes* 154, 1 (1996), pp. 173–218.

Gross, D., 'Introduction', in Yosef Ha-Kohen, *Sefer Divrei Hayamim Lemalkei Tzarfat uLemalkei Beit Otoman haTogar*, ed. D. Gross (Jerusalem: The Bialik Institute, 1955), pp. 3–26 [Hebrew].

Grosse, R., *Saint-Denis zwischen Adel und König: Die Zeit vor Suger (1053–1122)* (Stuttgart: Thorbecke Verlag, 2002).

Guenée, B., "Chanceries and Monasteries," in *Rethinking France: Les Lieux de mémoire, vol. 4: Histories and Memories*, ed. P. Nora (Chicago and London: University of Chicago Press, 2001), pp. 1–26.

"Histoires, annales, chroniques: Essai sur les genres historiques au Moyen Âge," *Annales, Économies, Sociétés, Civilisations* 28 (1973), pp. 997–1016.
"Primat, le fort roi Clovis et le bon roi Gontran," *Romania* 126 (2008), pp. 18–39.
"The *Grandes chroniques de France*: The Roman of Kings (1274–1518)," in *Rethinking France: Les Lieux de Mémoire, Volume 4: Histories and Memories*, ed. P. Nora (Chicago: University of Chicago Press, 2010), pp. 205–230.
Guyot-Bachy, I., "Les premiers Capétiens: de la protohistoire dionysienne au Roman des rois de Primat," in *La rigueur et la passion: Mélanges en l'honneur de Pascale Bourgain*, eds. C. Giraud and D. Poirel (Turnhout: Brepols, 2016), pp. 527–545.
Haillan, Bernard de Girard du, *Histoire générale de des Roys de France* (Paris: Sebastien Cramoisy, 1615), pp. 283–286.
Halfond, G.I., *Bishops and the Politics of Patronage in Merovingian Gaul* (Ithaca, NY: Cornell University Press, 2019).
"The Endorsement of Royal-Episcopal Collaboration in the Fredegar 'Chronica'," *Traditio* 70 (2015), pp. 1–28.
Hallett, J.P., *Fathers and Daughters in Roman Society: Women and the Elite Family* (Princeton, NJ: Princeton University Press, 2014).
Halsall, G., "Childeric's Grave, Clovis' Succession, and the Origins of the Merovingian Kingdom," in *Cemeteries and Society in Merovingian Gaul: Selected Studies in History and Archaeology, 1992–2009* (Leiden: Brill, 2010), pp. 169–187.
"Growing Up in Merovingian Gaul," in *Cemeteries and Society in Merovingian Gaul: Selected Studies in History and Archaeology, 1992–2009* (Leiden and Boston: Brill, 2010), pp. 383–412.
"Nero and Herod? The Death of Chilperic and Gregory's Writings of History," in *The World of Gregory of Tours*, eds. K. Mitchell and I. Wood (Leiden and Cologne: Brill, 2002), pp. 337–50.
"Reflections on Early Medieval Violence: The Example of the 'Bloodfeud'," *Memoria y Civilización* 2 (1999), pp. 7–29.
Settlement and Social Organization: The Merovingian Region of Metz (Cambridge: Cambridge University Press, 1995).
"Transformations of Romanness: The Northern Gallic Case," in *Transformations of Romanness: Early Medieval Regions and Identities*, ed. W. Pohl et al. (Berlin: De Gruyter, 2019), pp. 41–58.
"Violence and Society in the Early Medieval West: An Introductory Survey," in *Violence and Society in the Early Medieval West*, ed. G. Halsall (Woodbridge: Boydell and Brewer, 1998), pp. 1–45.
Hartmann, M., "Die Darstellung der Frauen im *Liber Historiae Francorum* und die Verfasserfrage," *Concilium medii aevi* 7 (2004), pp. 209–237.
Hedeman, A.D., *The Royal Image: Illustrations of the Grandes Chroniques de France, 1274–1422* (Berkeley, CA: University of California Press, 1991).
Heene, K., *The Legacy of Paradise: Marriage, Motherhood, and Woman in Carolingian Edifying Literature* (Frankfurt-am-Main: Peter Lang, 1997).
Heidecker, K., *The Divorce of Lothar II: Christian Marriage and Political Power in the Carolingian World* (Ithaca, NY, and London: Cornell University Press, 2010).

Heidrich, I., "Titulatur und Urkunden der arnulfingischen Hausmeier," *Archiv für Diplomatik, Schriftgeschichte, Siegel- und Wappenkunde* 11–12 (1965–1966), pp. 78–86.

Heinzelmann, M., *Gregory of Tours: History and Society in the Sixth Century* (Cambridge: Cambridge University Press, 2001).

"Gregory of Tours: The Elements of a Biography," in *A Companion to Gregory of Tours*, ed. A.C. Murray (Leiden and Boston: Brill, 2016), pp. 7–34.

"The Works of Gregory of Tours and Patristic Tradition," in *A Companion to Gregory of Tours*, ed. A.C. Murray (Leiden and Boston: Brill, 2016), pp. 281–336.

Hélary, X., "French Nobility and the Military Requirements of the King (c. 1260–c. 1314)," in *The Capetian Century, 1214–1314*, eds. W.C. Jordan and J.R. Phillips (Turnhout: Brepols, 2017), pp. 115–142.

Hempfer, K.W., "Some Aspects of a Theory of Genre," in *Linguistics and Literary Studies*, eds. M. Fludernik and D. Jacob (Berlin: De Gruyter, 2014), pp. 405–422.

Hen, Y., "Canvassing for Charles: A Context for London, BL Arundel 375," in *Zeit und Vergangenheit in fränkischen Europa*, eds. R. Coradini and H. Reimitz (Vienna: Verlag der Österreichischen Akademie der Wissenchaften, 2010), pp. 121–128.

"Changing Places: Chrodobert, Boba, and the Wife of Grimoald," *Revue belge de philologie et d'histoire* 90, 2 (2012), pp. 225–243.

"Clovis, Gregory of Tours, and Pro-Merovingian Propaganda," *Revue belge de philologie et d'histoire*, 71, 2 (1993), pp. 271–276.

"Compelling and Intense: The Christian Transformation of Romanness," in *Transformations of Romanness: Early Medieval Regions and Identities*, ed. W. Pohl et al. (Berlin and Boston: De Gruyter, 2018), pp. 59–69.

Culture and Religion in Merovingian Gaul, 481–751 (Leiden, New York, and Cologne: Brill, 1995).

"Defensor of Ligugé's Liber Scintillarum and the Migration of Knowledge," in *East and West in the Early Middle Ages: The Merovingian Kingdoms in Mediterranean Perspective*, ed. S. Esders et al. (Cambridge: Cambridge University Press, 2018), pp. 218–229.

"'Flirtant' avec la liturgie: Rois et liturgie en Gaule franque," *Cahiers de civilisation médiévale* 50 (2007), pp. 33–42.

"Paganism and Superstitions in the time of Gregory of Tours: une question mal posée!," in *The World of Gregory of Tours*, eds. K. Mitchell and I.N. Wood (Leiden: Brill, 2002), pp. 229–40.

Roman Barbarians: The Royal Court and Culture in the Early Medieval West (Basingstoke and New York: Palgrave Macmillan, 2007).

"Specula principum carolingi e l'immagine di Costantino," in *Costantino I – Enciclopedia Constantiniana sulla figura e l'immagine dell'imperatore del cosiddetto editto di Milano, 313–2013*, 3 vols. (Rome: Istituto della Enciclopedia italiana fondata da Giovanni Treccani, 2013), II, pp. 515–522.

"The Annals of Metz and the Merovingian Past," in *The Uses of the Past in the Early Middle Ages*, eds. Y. Hen and M. Innes (Cambridge: Cambridge University Press, 2000), pp. 175–190.
"The Church in Sixth-Century Gaul," in *A Companion to Gregory of Tours*, ed. A.C. Murray (Leiden: Brill, 2016), pp. 232–255.
"The Early Medieval *barbatoria*," in *Medieval Christianity in Practice*, ed. M. Rubin (Princeton: Princeton University Press, 2009), pp. 21–24.
"The Merovingian Polity: A Network of Courts and Courtiers," in *The Oxford Handbook of the Merovingian World*, eds. B. Effros and I. Moreira (Oxford: Oxford University Press, 2020), pp. 217–237.
"The Structure and Aims of the Visio Baronti," *Journal of Theological Studies* 47 (1996), pp. 477–497.
"Visions of the Afterlife in the Early Medieval West," in *The Cambridge Companion to Visionary Literature*, ed. R. Pollard (Cambridge: Cambridge University Press, 2021), pp. 25–39.
Hen, Y., and M. Innes, eds., *The Uses of the Past in the Early Middle Ages* (Cambridge: Cambridge University Press, 2000).
Hill, J., "The *Litaniae maiores* and *minores* in Rome, Francia and Anglo-Saxon England: Terminology, Texts and Traditions," *Early Medieval Europe* 9, 2 (2000), pp. 1–13.
Hofman, J., "The Marriage of Childeric II and Bilichild in the Context of the Grimoald Coup," *Peritia* 17–18 (2003–2004), pp. 382–393.
Hommel, H., "Die trojanische Herkunft der Franken," *Rheinisches Museum für Philologie* 99, 4 (1956), pp. 323–341.
Hummer, H., "Die merowingische Herkunft der Vita Sadalbergae," *Deutsches Archiv für Erforschung des Mittelalters* 59, 1 (2003), pp. 459–494.
Inglis, E., "Técnicas perdidas y halladas: la concepción medieval de la historia de las técnicas artísticas," *Quintana* 16 (2017), pp. 15–50.
Innes, M., "Teutons or Trojans? The Carolingians and the Germanic Past," in *The Uses of the Past in the Early Middle Ages*, eds. Y. Hen and M. Innes (Cambridge: Cambridge University Press, 2000), pp. 227–249.
Isaïa, M.-C., "La Chronique d'Adon de Vienne (†875): méthode, projet et public," *Revue d'histoire de l'Eglise de France* 108 (2022), pp. 225–254.
"La prophétie dans l'hagiographie latine du haut Moyen Âge (VIe–IXe siècle). L'histoire comme destin, prédestination et providence', in *Hagiographie et prophétie (VIe–XIIIe siècles)*, eds. P. Henriet, K. Herbers, and H.-C. Lehner (Florence: Sismel, Edizioni del Galluzo, 2017), pp. 15–50.
"The Bishop and the Law, According to Hincmar's Life of Saint Remigius," in *Hincmar: Life and Works*, eds. R. Stone and C. West (Manchester: Manchester University Press, 2015), pp. 170–189.
Jackson, R.A., *Vive le roi! A History of the French Coronation from Charles V to Charles X* (Chapel Hill, NC, and London: University of North Carolina Press, 1984).
Jacobs, M., *Islamische Geschichte in jüdischen Chroniken: Hebräische Historiographie des 16. und 17. Jahrhunderts*, Texts and Studies in Medieval and Early Modern Judaism 18 (Tübingen: Mohr Siebeck, 2004).
"Joseph ha-Kohen, Paolo Giovio, and Sixteenth-Century Historiography," in *Cultural Intermediaries: Jewish Intellectuals in Early-Modern Italy*, eds. D.

B. Ruderman and G. Veltri (Philadelphia: University of Pennsylvania Press, 2004), pp. 67–85.

"Sephardic Migration and Cultural Transfer: The Ottoman and Spanish Expansion through a Cinquecento Jewish Lens," *Journal of Early Modern History* 21 (2017), pp. 516–42.

James, E., "Childéric, Syagrius et la disparition du royaume de Soissons," Actes des VIIIe journées internationales d'archéologie mérovingienne de Soissons (19–22 Juin 1986), *Revue archéologique de Picardie* 3–4 (1988), pp. 9–12.

"Gregory of Tours, the Visigoths, and Spain," in *Cross, Crescent and Conversion Studies on Medieval Spain and Christendom in Memory of Richard Fletcher*, eds. S. Barton and P. Linehan (Leiden and Boston: Brill, 2008), pp. 43–64.

"Ireland and Western Gaul in the Merovingian Period," in *Ireland in Early Medieval Europe: Studies in Memory of Kathleen Hughes*, eds. D. Whitelock, R. McKitterick, and D. Dumville (Cambridge: Cambridge University Press, 1982), pp. 362–386.

The Franks (Oxford and Cambridge, MA: Blackwell, 1988).

"Warlike and Heroic Virtues in the Post-Roman World," in *Early Medieval Militarisation*, ed. E. Bennett et al. (Manchester: Manchester University Press, 2021), pp. 253–265.

Jong, M. de, *In Samuel's Image: Child Oblation in the Early Medieval West* (Leiden, New York, Cologne: Brill, 1996).

Jordan, W.C., *A Tale of Two Monasteries: Westminster and Saint-Denis in the Thirteenth Century* (Princeton, NJ, and Oxford: Princeton University Press, 2009).

Louis IX and the Challenge of Crusade: A Study in Rulership (Princeton, NJ: Princeton University Press, 1979).

Men at the Center: Redemptive Governance Under Louis IX, Natalie Zemon Davis Annual Lectures, vol. 6 (Budapest and New York: Central European University Press, 2012).

Joye, S., *La femme ravie: Le mariage par rapt dans les sociétés occidentales du haut Moyen Âge* (Turnhout: Brepols, 2012).

Kempf, D., "Paul the Deacon's Liber de episcopis Mettensibus and the Role of Metz in the Carolingian Realm," *Journal of Medieval History* 30, 3 (2004), pp. 279–299.

Keskiaho, J., *Dreams and Visions in the Early Middle Ages: The Reception and Use of Patristic Ideas, 400–900* (Cambridge: Cambridge University Press, 2015).

Kessous, J., "La 'Chronique' de Joseph Ha-Cohen," *Archives Juives* 13 (1977), pp. 45–53.

Kim, H.J., *The Huns, Rome and the Birth of Europe* (Cambridge: Cambridge University Press, 2013).

Kitchen, J., *Saints' Lives and the Rhetoric of Gender: Male and Female in Merovingian Hagiography* (Oxford and New York: Oxford University Press, 1998).

Kölzer, T., "Die letzten Merowingerkönige: rois fainéants?," in *Der Dynastiewechsel von 751: Vorgeschichte, Legitimationsstrategien und Erinnerung*, eds. M. Becher and J. Jarnut (Münster: Scriptorium, 2004), pp. 33–60.

Kornbluth, G., "Richildis and her Seal: Carolingian Self-Reference and the Imagery of Power," in *Saints, Sinners, and Sisters: Gender and Northern Art in*

Medieval and Early Modern Europe, eds. J.L. Carroll and A.G. Stewart (London and New York: Routledge, 2016), pp. 161–181.

Kortüm, H.-H., "Weltgeschichte am Ausgang der Karolingerzeit: Regino von Prüm," in *Historiographie im frühen Mittelalter*, eds. A. Scharer and G. Scheibelreiter (Vienna: Oldenbourg, 1994), pp. 499–513.

Koziol, G., "The Future of History After Empire," in *Using and Not Using the Past After the Carolingian Empire, c. 900–c. 1050*, eds. S. Greer, A. Hicklin, and S. Esders (London and New York: Routledge, 2020), pp. 15–35.

Krause, J.-W., *Kriminalgeschichte der Antike* (Munich: C.H. Beck, 2004).

Kreiner, J. "About the Bishop: The Episcopal Entourage and the Economy of Government in Post-Roman Gaul," *Speculum* 86, 2 (2011), pp. 321–360.

Legions of Pigs in the Early Medieval West (New Haven, CT: Yale University Press, 2020).

"Pigs in the Flesh and Fisc: An Early Medieval Ecology," *Past & Present* 236 (2017), pp. 3–42.

The Social Life of Hagiography in the Merovingian Kingdom (Cambridge: Cambridge University Press, 2014).

Kremers, W., "Ado von Vienne: sein Leben und seine Schriften," doctoral dissertation (Friedrich-Wilhelms-Universität Bonn, 1911).

Krusch, B., "Die neueste Wendung im Genovefa-Streit II," *Neues Archiv* 40 (1915), pp. 265–327.

Krutzler, G., "Fremdwahrnehmungen in der frühmittelalterlichen Ethnographie," doctoral dissertation (Universität Wien, 2009).

Kurth, G., "Études critiques sur les Gesta regum Francorum," *Bulletin de l'Académie royale de Belgique* 2, 18 (1889), pp. 261–291.

La Rocca, C., "Consors regni: A Problem of Gender? The Consortium between Amalasuntha and Theodahad in 534," in *Gender and Historiography: Studies in the Earlier Middle Ages in Honour of Pauline Stafford*, eds. J. Nelson, S. Reynolds, and S.M. Johns (London: Institute of Historical Research, 2012), pp. 127–144.

Labaune, Y., "Quelques observations récentes sur des sites de l'Antiquité tardive à Autun (2001–2008)," in *L'Antiquité tardive dans l'Est de la Gaule I. La vallée du Rhin supérieur et les provinces gauloise limitrophes: actualité de la recherche, Actes de la table-ronde de Strasbourg, 20–21 novembre 2008*, eds. M. Kasprzyk and G. Kuhnle (Dijon: Société Archéologique de l'Est, 2011), pp. 41–68.

Lake, J.," Authorial Intention in Medieval Historiography," *History Compass* 12, 4 (2014), pp. 344–360.

"Rewriting Merovingian History in the Tenth Century: Aimoin of Fleury's Gesta Francorum," *Early Medieval Europe* 25 (2017), pp. 489–525.

Lapidge, M., *Hilduin of Saint-Denis: The Passio S. Dionysii in Prose and Verse* (Leiden and Boston: Brill, 2017).

"The 'Ancient Passio' of St Dionysius (BHL 2171)," *Analecta Bollandiana* 132 (2014), pp. 241–285.

Lebecq, S. "The Two Faces of King Childeric: History, Archeology, Historiography," in *From Roman Provinces to Medieval Kingdoms*, ed. T.F. X. Noble (London and New York: Routledge, 2006), pp. 272–288.

Leffler, P.K. "French Historians and the Challenge to Louis XIV's Absolutism," *French Historical Studies* 14, 1 (1985), pp. 1–22.

"From Humanist to Enlightenment Historiography: A Case Study of François Eudes de Mézeray," *French Historical Studies* 10, 3 (1978), pp. 416–438.

Le Goff, J. "Au Moyen Âge: temps de l'Église et temps du marchand," *Annales* 15, 3 (1960), pp. 417–433.

Time, Work and Culture in the Middle Ages trans. A. Goldhammer (Chicago and London: The University of Chicago Press, 1980).

"Le temps du travail dans la crise du XIVe siècle: du temps médiéval au temps moderne," *Le Moyen Âge* 69 (1963), pp. 597–613.

Le Jan, R., *Famille et pouvoir dans le monde franc (VIIe–Xe siècle)* (Paris: Publications de la Sorbonne, 1995).

Levillain, L., 'Études sur l'abbaye de Saint-Denis à l' époque mérovingienne', *Bibliothèque de l'École des chartes* 82, I: (1921), pp. 5–116; II: 86 (1925), pp. 5–99; III: 87 (1926), pp. 20–97, 245–346; IV: 91 (1930), pp. 5–65, 264–300.

Leyser, K., *Communications and Power in Medieval Europe: The Carolingian and Ottonian Centuries* (London: Hambeldon Press, 1994).

Licht, T., *Untersuchungen zum hagiographischen Werk Sigiberts von Gembloux* (Heidelberg: Mattes Verlag, 2005).

Liebeschuetz, W., "Warlords and Landlords," in *A Companion to the Roman Army*, ed. P. Erdkamp (Malden, MA, and Oxford: Blackwell, 2007), pp. 479–494.

Lifshitz, F., "Beyond Positivism and Genre: 'Hagiographical' Texts as Historical Narrative," *Viator* 25 (1994), pp. 95–114.

Loseby, S.T., "Gregory of Tours, Italy, and the Empire," in *A Companion to Gregory of Tours*, ed. A.C. Murray (Leiden: Brill, 2016), pp. 462–497.

"Marseilles and the Pirenne Thesis II: 'Une ville morte'," in *The Long Eighth Century: Production, Distribution and Demand*, eds. I.L. Hansen and C. Wickham (Leiden, Boston, and Cologne: Brill, 2000), pp. 167–194.

Loveluck, C., *Northwest Europe in the Early Middle Ages, c. AD 600–1150: A Comparative Archaeology* (Cambridge: Cambridge University Press, 2013).

Löwe, H., "Regino von Prüm und das historische Weltbild der Karolingerzeit," *Rheinische Vierteljahrsblätter* 17 (1952), pp. 151–179.

Lugt, M. van der, "Tradition and Revision. The Textual Tradition of Hincmar of Reims' *Visio Bernoldi* with A New Critical Edition," *Bulletin Du Cange* 52 (1994), pp. 109–149.

MacGeorge, P., *Late Roman Warlords* (Oxford: Oxford University Press, 2002).

Mackay, C.S., "Lactantius and the Succession to Diocletian," *Classical Philology* 94, 2 (1999), pp. 198–209.

MacLean, S., *History and Politics in Late Carolingian and Ottonian Europe: The Chronicle of Regino of Prüm and Adalbert of Magdeburg* (Manchester: Manchester University Press, 2009).

"Insinuation, Censorship and the Struggle for Late Carolingian Lotharingia in Regino of Prum's Chronicle," *The English Historical Review* 124 (2009), pp. 1–28.

Ottonian Queenship (Oxford: Oxford University Press, 2017).

"Queenship, Nunneries and Royal Widowhood in Carolingian Europe," *Past & Present* 178 (2003), pp. 3–38.

"The Carolingian Response to the Revolt of Boso, 879–887," *Early Medieval Europe* 10, 1 (2001), pp. 21–48.

MacMaster, T.J., "The Origin of Origins: Trojans, Turks, and the Birth of the Myth of Trojan Origins in the Medieval World," *Atlantide* 2 (2014), pp. 1–12.

"The Pogrom that Time Forgot: The Ecumenical anti-Jewish Campaign of 632 and Its Impact," in *Inclusion and Exclusion in Mediterranean Christianities, 400–800*, eds. Y. Fox and E. Buchberger (Turnhout: Brepols, 2019), pp. 217–235.

Maissen, T., *Von der Legende zum Modell: Das Interesse an Frankreichs Vergangenheit während der italienischen Renaissance* (Basle: Helbing und Lichtenhahn, 1994).

Margolis, O., "The Gaulish Past of Milan and the French Invasion of Italy," in *Local Antiquities, Local Identities: Art, Literature and Antiquarianism in Europe, c. 1400–1700*, eds. K. Christian and B. de Divitiis (Manchester: Manchester University Press, 2019), pp. 102–120.

Markevičiūtė, R., "Rethinking the Chronicle: Modern Genre Theory Applied to Medieval Historiography," *The Medieval Chronicle* 13 (2020), pp. 182–200.

Martín, J.C. "Une nouvelle édition critique de la 'Vita Desiderii' de Sisebut, accompagnée de quelques réflexions concernant la date des 'Sententiae' et du 'De viris illustribus' d'Isidore de Séville," *Hagiographica* 7 (2000), pp. 127–180.

Martindale, J.R., *The Prosopography of the Later Roman Empire*, 4 vols. (Cambridge: Cambridge University Press, 1992).

Martínez Pizarro, J., "Images in Texts: The Shape of the Visible in Gregory of Tours," *The Journal of Medieval Latin* 9 (1999), pp. 91–101.

Masai, F., "La *Vita patrum iurensium* et les débuts du monachisme à Saint-Maurice d'Agaune," in *Festschrift Bernhard Bischoff zu seinem 65. Geburtstag*, eds. J. Autenrieth and F. Brunhölzl (Stuttgart: A. Hiersemann 1971), pp. 43–69.

Maskarinec, M., *City of Saints: Rebuilding Rome in the Early Middle Ages* (Philadelphia: University of Pennsylvania Press, 2018).

Mathey-Maille, L., "Mythe troyen et histoire romaine: de Geoffroy de Monmouth au 'Brut' de Wace," in *Entre fiction et histoire: Troie et Rome au Moyen Âge*, eds. E. Baumgartner and L. Harf-Lancner (Paris: Presses de la Sorbonne Nouvelle, 1997), pp. 113–125.

Mathisen, R.W., *Roman Aristocrats in Barbarian Gaul: Strategies for Survival in an Age of Transition* (Austin, TX: University of Texas Press, 1993).

"Sigisvult the Patrician, Maximinus the Arian, and Political Stratagems in the Western Roman Empire c. 425-4," *Early Medieval Europe* 8, 2 (1999), pp. 173–196.

McKitterick, R., "Charles the Bald (823–877) and His Library: The Patronage of Learning," *The English Historical Review*, 95, 374 (1980), pp. 28–47.

History and Memory in the Carolingian World (Cambridge: Cambridge University Press, 2004).

"Paul the Deacon and the Franks," *Early Medieval Europe* 8, 3 (1999), pp. 319–339.

Perceptions of the Past in the Early Middle Ages (Notre Dame, IN: University of Notre Dame Press, 2006).

The Carolingians and the Written Word (Cambridge: Cambridge University Press, 1989).

"The Illusion of Royal Power in Carolingian Annals," *English Historical Review* 115, 460 (2000), pp. 1–20.

"The Scripts of the Bobbio Missal," in *The Bobbio Missal: Liturgy and Religious Culture in Merovingian Gaul*, eds. Y. Hen and R. Meens (Cambridge: Cambridge University Press, 2004), pp. 19–52.

McNair, F., "Governance, Locality and Legal Culture: The Rise and Fall of the Carolingian Advocates of Saint-Martin of Tours," *Early Medieval Europe* 29, 2 (2021), pp. 201–224.

McRobbie, J., "Gender and Violence in Gregory of Tours' *Decem libri historiarum*," doctoral dissertation (University of St. Andrews, 2012).

Meens, R., "Opkomst en ondergang van de Karolingers. De kroniek van Regino van Prüm," *Millennium* 24 (2010), pp. 3–18.

"Politics, Mirrors of Princes and the Bible: Sins, Kings and the Well-Being of the Realm," *Early Medieval Europe* 7, 3 (1998), pp. 345–357.

"The Rise and Fall of the Carolingians: Regino of Prüm and His Conception of the Carolingian Empire," in *Faire lien. Aristocratie, réseaux et échanges compétitifs: Mélanges en l'honneur de Régine Le Jan*, ed. L. Jégou et al. (Paris: Sorbonne, 2015), pp. 315–323.

Mégier, E., "Karolingische Weltchronistik zwischen Historiographie und Exegese: Frechulf von Lisieux und Ado von Vienne," in *Diligens scrutator sacri eloquii: Beiträge zur Exegese- und Theologiegeschichte des Mittelalters: Festgabe für Rainer Berndt SJ zum 65. Geburtstag*, eds. H.P. Neuheuser, R.M.W. Stammberger, and M.M. Tischler (Münster: Aschendorff Verlag, 2016), pp. 37–52.

Mériaux, C., *Gallia Irradiata: saints et sanctuaires dans le nord de la Gaule du haute Moyen Âge* (Stuttgart: Franz Steiner Verlag, 2006).

"Parochiæ barbaricæ? Quelques remarques sur la perception des diocèses septentrionaux de la Gaule pendant le haut Moyen Âge," *Revue du Nord* 360–361 (2005), pp. 293–303.

Merrills, A., and R. Miles, *The Vandals* (Malden, MA, and Oxford: Wiley-Blackwell, 2010).

Meyers, J., "*Vitarum scriptor*: une analyse critique et litteraire de la methode hagiographique de Sigebert de Gembloux," in *Sigebert de Gembloux*, ed. J.-P. Straus (Barcelona and Madrid: Fédération Internationale des Instituts d'Études Médiévales, 2015), pp. 51–76.

Mintz-Manor, L., "The Discourse on the New World in Early Modern Jewish Culture," doctoral dissertation (Hebrew University of Jerusalem, 2011) [Hebrew].

Monod, G., "Les origines de l'historiographie à Paris," *Mémoires de la société de l'histoire de Paris et de l'Ile-de-France* 3 (1876), pp. 219–240.

Montesquiou-Fézensac, B. de, "Le tombeau de Charles le Chauve à Saint-Denis," *Bulletin de la Société des Antiquaires de France* (1963), pp. 84–88.

Moore, M.E., *A Sacred Kingdom: Bishops and the Rise of Frankish Kingship, 300–850* (Washington, DC: The Catholic University of America Press, 2011).
"The King's New Clothes: Royal and Episcopal Regalia in the Frankish Empire," in *Robes and Honor: The Medieval World of Investiture*, ed. S. Gordon (New York: St. Martin's and Palgrave, 2000), pp. 95–135.
Morelle, L., "Une somme d'érudition dédiée aux actes royaux mérovingiens," *Bibliothèque de l'École des chartes* 161, 2 (2003), pp. 653–675.
Morris, J., ed. and trans., Historia Brittonum, in *British History and The Welsh Annals* (London: Philimore, 1980).
Murray, A.C., "*Post vocantur Merohingii*: Fredegar, Merovech, and 'Sacral Kingship'," in *After Rome's Fall: Narrators and Sources of Early Medieval History*, ed. A.C. Murray (Toronto: University of Toronto Press, 1998), pp. 121–152.
Nason, C.M., "The Vita Sancti Arnulfi (BHL 689–692): Its Place in the Liturgical Veneration of a Local Saint," *Sacris Erudiri* 54 (2015), pp. 171–199.
Natunewicz, C.F., "Freculphus of Lisieux, His Chronicle, and a Mont St. Michel Manuscript," *Sacris Erudiri* 17 (1966), pp. 90–134.
Nauroy, M.G., "La Vita anonyme de Saint Arnoul et ses modèles antiques: La figure de saint évêque entre vérité historique et motifs hagiographiques," *Mémoires de l'Académie nationale de Metz*, a. 183, sér. 7, t. 15 (2002), pp. 293–321.
Nees, L., *Perspectives on Early Islamic Art in Jerusalem* (Leiden and Boston: Brill, 2016).
Nelson, J.L., *Charles the Bald* (London and New York: Longman, 1996).
"Gender and Genre in Women Historians of the Early Middle Ages," in *L'historiographie médiévale en Europe*, ed. J.-P. Genet (Paris: Editions du Centre National de la Recherche Scientifique, 1991), pp. 149–163.
"Queens as Jezebels: Brunhild and Balthild in Merovingian History," in *Medieval Women*, ed. D. Baker, Studies in Church History, Subsidia 1 (Oxford 1978), pp. 31–77, repr. in J. Nelson, ed., *Politics and Ritual in Early Medieval Europe* (London: Bloomsbury, 1986), pp. 1–48.
Neveu, B., "Histoire littéraire de la France et l'érudition bénédictine au siècle des Lumières," *Journal des savants* 2, 1 (1979), 73–113.
Niles, J.D., "Myths of the Eastern Origins of the Franks: Fictions or a Kind of Truth?," in *Origin Legends in Early Medieval Western Europe*, eds. L. Brady and P. Wadden (Leiden and Boston: Brill, 2022), pp. 385–404.
Nimmegeers, N., *Évêques entre Bourgogne et Provence: La province ecclésiastique de Vienne au haut Moyen Âge (V^e–XIe siècle)* (Rennes: Presses universitaires de Rennes, 2014).
Nora, P., "Between Memory and History: Les Lieux de Mémoire," *Representations* 26 (1989), pp. 7–24.
O'Brien, J.M., "Locating Authorities in Carolingian Debates on Image Veneration: The Case of Agobard of Lyon's *De picturis et imaginibus*," *Journal of Theological Studies* 69, 1 (2011), pp. 176–206.
O'Sullivan, D., "*Grandes chroniques de France*," *Encyclopedia of the Medieval Chronicle*, eds. G. Dunphy and C. Bratu (Leiden: Brill, 2016).
O'Sullivan, S., "From Troy to Aachen: Ancient Rome and the Carolingian Reception of Vergil," in *Inscribing Knowledge in the Medieval Book: The*

Power of Paratexts, ed. R. Brown-Grant et al. (Berlin and Boston: De Gruyter, 2019), pp. 185–196.

Oexle, O.G., "Die Karolinger und die Stadt des heiligen Arnulf," *Frühmittelalterliche Studien* 1, 1 (1967), pp. 250–364.

Olivier, S., "Clovis beyond Clovis: Individuality, Filiation, and Miraculous Intervention in the *Miracle de Clovis*," *European Medieval Drama* 22 (2018), pp. 127–148.

"La mémoire mérovingienne à travers ses réécritures. Dagobert et Saint-Denis: élaboration, circulation et instrumentalisation d'une association (IXe–XVIe siècle)," doctoral dissertation (University of Geneva, 2022).

Olivier-Martin, F., *Étude sur les régences: I. Les régences et le majorité des rois sous les Capétiens directs et les premiers Valois (1060–1375)* (Paris: Recueil Sirey, 1931).

Ottewill-Soulsby, S., "'Hunting Diligently Through the Volumes of the Ancients': Frechulf of Lisieux on the First City and the End of Innocence," in *Remembering and Forgetting the Ancient City*, eds. J. Martinez Jiménez and S. Ottewill-Soulsby (Oxford: Oxbow Books, 2022), pp. 225–245.

Palmer, J., "Defining Paganism in the Carolingian World," *Early Medieval Europe* 15, 4 (2007), pp. 402–425.

Pancer, N., "Le silencement du monde: Paysages sonores au haut Moyen Âge et nouvelle culture aurale," *Annales Histoire, Sciences Sociales* 72, 33 (2017) pp. 659–699.

Papaconstantinou, A., "Historiography, Hagiography, and the Making of the Coptic 'Church of the Martyrs' in Early Islamic Egypt," *Dumbarton Oaks Papers* 60 (2006), pp. 65–86.

Papenbroeck, D., *Propylaeum antiquarum circa veri discrimen in vetustis membranis* (Antwerp, 1675).

Patzold, S., *Episcopus: Wissen über Bischöfe im Frankenreich des späten 8. bis frühen 10. Jahrhunderts* (Sigmaringen: Jan Thorbecke Verlag, 2008).

Paxton, F., "Liturgy and Healing in an Early Medieval Saint's Cult: The Mass *in honore sancti Sigismundi* for the Cure of Fevers," *Traditio* 49 (1994), pp. 23–43.

"Power and the Power to Heal: The Cult of St. Sigismund of Burgundy," *Early Medieval Europe* 2, 2 (1993), pp. 95–110.

Penkett, R., "Perceiving the Other: Sensory Phenomena and Experience in the Early Medieval Other World," *Reading Medieval Studies* 25 (1999), pp. 91–106.

Peters, E.M., "Roi fainéant: The Origins of an Historians' Commonplace," *Bibliothèque d'Humanisme et Renaissance* 30, 3 (1968), pp. 537–547.

Shadow King: Rex Inutilis in Medieval Law and Literature, 751–1327 (New Haven, CT: Yale University Press, 1970).

Plassmann, A., *Origo gentis. Identitäts- und Legitimitätsstiftung in früh- und hochmittelalterlichen Herkunftserzählungen* (Berlin: Akademie-Verlag, 2006).

Pohl, W., *Die Awaren: Ein Steppenvolk in Mitteleuropa, 567–822 n. Chr.* (Munich: Beck, 1988), pp. 269–270, trans. into English in W. Pohl, *The Avars: A Steppe Empire in Central Europe, 567–822* (Ithaca, NY: Cornell University Press, 2018).

"Genealogy: A Comparative Perspective from the Early Medieval West," in *Meanings of Community across Medieval Eurasia: Comparative Approaches*, eds.

E. Hovden, C. Lutter, and W. Pohl (Leiden and Boston: Brill, 2016), pp. 232–269.
"History in Fragments: Montecassino's Politics of Memory," *Early Medieval Europe* 10, 3 (2001), pp. 343–374.
Poveda Arias, P., "Clovis and Remigius of Reims in the Making of the Merovingian Kingdoms," *European Review of History: Revue européenne d'histoire* 26, 2 (2019), pp. 197–218.
Priesterjahn, M., "Back to the Roots: The Rediscovery of Gregory of Tours in French Historiography," *Mittelalter: Interdisziplinäre Forschung und Rezeptionsgeschichte* 4 (2016).
Pringle, D., "King Richard I and the Walls of Ascalon," *Palestine Exploration Quarterly* 116, 2 (1984), pp. 133–147.
Prinz, F., *Frühes Mönchtum im Frankenreich: Kultur und Gesellschaft in Gallien, den Rheinlanden und Bayern am Beispiel der monastischen Entwicklung dargestellt* (Munich: R. Oldenbourg Verlag, 1965).
Prinz, O., "Die Überarbeitung der Chronik Reginos aus sprachlicher Sicht," in *Literatur und Sprache im europäischen Mittelalte: Festschrift für Karl Langosch zum 70. Geburtstag*, ed. A. Önnerfors (Darmstadt: Wissenschaftliche Buchgesellschaft, 1973), pp. 122–141.
Quast, D., *Das Grab des fränkischen Königs Childerich in Tournai und die Anastasis Childerici von Jean-Jacques Chifflet aus dem Jahre 1655* (Mainz: Verlag des römisch-Germanischen Zentralmuseums, 2015).
Quentin, H., *Les martyrologes historiques du moyen age* (Paris: J. Gabalda, 1908).
Raisharma, S., "Much Ado about Vienne? A Localizing Universal *Chronicon*," in *Historiographies of Identity, Volume 3: Carolingian Convergence and Its Later Uses*, eds. R. Kramer, H. Reimitz, and G. Ward (Turnhout: Brepols, 2020), pp. 271–290.
Ranum, O., *Artisans of Glory: Writers and Historical Thought in Seventeenth-Century France* (Chapel Hill, NC: The University of North Carolina Press, 1980).
Reimitz, H., "Die Konkurrenz der Ursprünge in der fränkischen Historiographie," in *Die Suche nach den Ursprüngen. Von den Bedeutung des frühen Mittelalters*, ed. W. Pohl (Vienna: Verlag der Österreichischen Akademie der Wissenschaften, 2004), pp. 191–209.
"Genre and Identity in Merovingian Historiography," in *Historiography and Identity II: Post-Roman Multiplicity and New Political Identities*, eds. G. Heydemann and H. Reimitz (Turnhout: Brepols, 2020), pp. 161–211.
"Historiography and Identity in the Post-Roman West: An Introduction," in *Historiography and Identity II: Post-Roman Multiplicity and New Political Identities*, eds. G. Heydemann, H. Reimitz (Turnhout: Brepols, 2020), pp. 1–26.
History, Frankish Identity and the Framing of Western Ethnicity, 550–850 (Cambridge: Cambridge University Press, 2015).
"The Early History of Frankish Origin Legends, c.500–800 C.E.," in *Origin Legends in Early Medieval Western Europe*, eds. L. Brady and P. Wadden (Leiden and Boston: Brill, 2022), pp. 156–183.

"The Early Medieval Editions of Gregory of Tours' *Histories*," in *A Companion to Gregory of Tours*, ed. A.C. Murray (Leiden and Boston: Brill, 2016), pp. 519–565.

'The Social Logic of Historiographical Compendia in the Carolingian Period', in *Herméneutique du texte d'histoire*, ed. O. Kano (Nagoya: Nagoya University Press, 2012), pp. 17–28.

"Social Networks and Identities in Frankish Historiography: New Aspects of the Textual History of Gregory of Tours' *Historiae*," in *The Construction of Communities in the Early Middle Ages: Texts, Resources and Artefacts*, eds. R. Corradini, M. Diesenberger, and H. Reimitz (Leiden and Boston: Brill, 2003), pp. 229–268.

"Transformations of Late Antiquity: The Writing and Re-Writing of Church History at the Monastery of Lorsch, c. 800," in *The Resources of the Past in Early Medieval Europe*, eds. C. Gantner, R. McKitterick, and S. Meeder (Cambridge: Cambridge University Press, 2015), pp. 262–282.

Reynolds, B.W., "The Mind of Baddo: Assassination in Merovingian Politics,"*Journal of Medieval History* 13 (1987), pp. 117–124.

Riché, P., *The Carolingians: A Family Who Forged Europe* (Philadelphia, PA: University of Pennsylvania Press, 1993).

Ristuccia, N., *Christianization and Commonwealth in Early Medieval Europe: A Ritual Interpretation* (Oxford: Oxford University Press, 2018).

Robinson, K., "The Anchoress and the Heart's Nose: The Importance of Smell to Medieval Women Religious," *Magistra* 19, 2 (2013), pp. 41–64.

Robinson, O.F., *Penal Practice and Penal Policy in Ancient Rome* (London and New York: Routledge, 2007).

Rognoni, L., and G.M. Varanini, "Da Verona a Parigi: 'Paulus Aemilius' autore del *De rebus gestis Francorum* e la sua famiglia," *Quaderni per la storia dell'università di Padova* 40 (2007), pp. 163–180.

Rosenwein, B.H., *Negotiating Space: Power, Restraint, and Privileges of Immunity in Early Medieval Europe* (Ithaca, NY: Cornell University Press, 1999).

"One Site, Many Meanings: St.-Maurice d'Agaune as a Place of Power," in *Topographies of Power in the Early Middle Ages*, eds. M. de Jong, F. Theuws, and C. van Rhijn (Leiden, Boston, Cologne: Brill, 2001), pp. 271–290.

"Perennial Prayer at Agaune," in *Monks and Nuns, Saints and Outcasts: Religion in Medieval Society. Essays in Honor of Lester K. Little*, eds. S. Farmer and B. H. Rosenwein (Ithaca, NY, and London: Cornell University Press, 2000), pp. 37–56.

Rotman, T., *Hagiography, Historiography, and Identity in Sixth-Century Gaul: Uncovering the Miracle Collections of Gregory of Tours* (Amsterdam: Amsterdam University Press, 2022).

Rouche, M., *Clovis* (Paris: Fayard, 1996).

ed., *Clovis, histoire & mémoire: la baptême de Clovis, son écho à travers l'histoire*, 2 vols. (Paris: Presses de l'Université de Paris-Sorbonne, 1997).

"Miracles, maladies et psychologie de la foi à l'époque carolingienne en France," in *Hagiographie cultures et sociétés IVe–XIIe siècles: Actes du Colloque organisé à Nanterre et à Paris (2–5 mai 1979)* (Paris: Études Augustiniennes, 1981), pp. 139–160.

Saito, S., "The Merovingian Accounting Documents of Tours: Form and Function," *Early Medieval Europe* 9, 2 (2000), pp. 143–161.
Sarti, L., *Perceiving War and the Military in Early Christian Gaul (ca. 400–700 A.D.)* (Leiden, Boston: Brill, 2013).
"Byzantine history and stories in the Frankish Chronicle of Fredegar (c. 613–662)," *Francia. Forschungen zur westeuropäischen Geschichte* 48 (2021), pp. 3–22.
Saucier, C., *A Paradise of Priests: Singing the Civic and Episcopal Hagiography of Medieval Liège* (Rochester, NY: University of Rochester Press, 2014).
Savigni, R., "Storia universale e storia ecclesiastica nel Chronicon di Frechulfo de Lisieux," *Studi Medievali* 28 (1987), pp. 155–192.
Scheibelreiter, G., "Fredegar – Chronist einer Epoche," in *The Medieval Chronicle: Proceedings of the 1st International Conference on the Medieval Chronicle Driebergen/Utrecht 13–16 July 1996*, ed. E. Kooper (Amsterdam and Atlanta, GA: Rodopi, 1999), pp. 251–259.
Schilling, B., "*Ansemundus dux*, das Ende des Burgunderreichs und der Senat von Vienne: Zur gefälschten Gründungsurkunde des Andreasklosters (Vienne)," *Archiv für Diplomatik* 46, 1 (2000), pp. 1–47.
"Zu einem interpolierten Diplom Ludwigs des Frommen für die Kirche von Vienne (BM^2 570)," *Archiv für Diplomatik* 57 (2011), pp. 63–104.
Schneidmüller, B., "Constructing the Past by Means of the Present: Historiographical Foundations of Medieval Institutions, Dynasties, Peoples, and Communities," in *Medieval Concepts of the Past: Ritual, Memory, Historiography*, eds. G. Althoff, J. Fried, and P.J. Geary (Washington, DC: German Historical Institute and Cambridge: Cambridge University Press, 2002), pp. 167–206.
Schoysman, A., "Jean Lemaire de Belges et Josse Bade," *Le Moyen Age* 112, 3 (2006), pp. 575–584.
Schreiner, P., "Eine merowingische Gesandtschaft in Konstantinopel," *Frühmittelalterliche Studien* 19, 1 (2015), pp. 195–200.
Schwedler, G., "Lethe and 'Delete' – Discarding the Past in the Early Middle Ages: The Case of Fredegar," in *Collectors' Knowledge: What Is Kept, What Is Discarded/ Aufbewahren oder wegwerfen: wie Sammler entscheiden*, eds. A.-S. Goeing, A. T. Grafton, and P. Michel (Leiden and Boston: Brill, 2013), pp. 71–96.
Screen, E., "Carolingian Fathers and Sons in Italy: Lothar I and Louis II's Successful Partnership," in *After Charlemagne: Carolingian Italy and Its Rulers*, eds. C. Gantner and W. Pohl (Cambridge: Cambridge University Press, 2021), pp. 148–163.
"Lothar I in Italy," in *Problems and Possibilities of Early Medieval Charters*, eds. J. Jarrett and A.S. McKinley (Turnhout: Brepols, 2013), pp. 231–252.
"Remembering and forgetting Lothar I," in *Writing the Early Medieval West*, eds. E. Screen and C. West (Cambridge: Cambridge University Press, 2018), pp. 248–260.
Sewell, Jr., W.H., "The Concept(s) of Culture," in *Beyond the Cultural Turn: New Directions in the Study of Society and Culture*, eds. V.E. Bonnell and L. Hunt (Berkeley and Los Angeles: University of California Press, 1999), pp. 35–61.
Shanzer, D., "Dating the Baptism of Clovis: The Bishop of Vienne vs the Bishop of Tours," *Early Medieval Europe* 7, 1 (1998), pp. 29–57.

"Gregory of Tours and Poetry: Prose into Verse and Verse into Prose," *Proceedings of the British Academy* 129 (2005), pp. 303–319.

"The *Cosmographia* Attributed to Aethicus Ister as *Philosophen-* or *Reiseroman*," in *Insignis Sophiae Arcator: Medieval Latin Studies in Honour of Michael Herren on His 65th Birthday*, eds. G.R. Wieland, C. Ruff, and R.G. Arthur (Turnhout: Brepols, 2006), pp. 57–86.

Sherer, I., "Joseph ha-Kohen, Humanist Historiography and Military History," *Journal of Jewish Studies* 69 (2018), pp. 86–108.

Shulvass, M.A., "To Which of Rabbi Joseph Hacohen's Works Had the Proof-Reader Written his 'Continuation'?," *Zion* 10 (1945), pp. 78–79 [Hebrew].

Simonsohn, S., "Joseph HaCohen in Genoa," *Italia: Studi e ricerche sulla cultura e sulla letteratura degli Ebrei d'Italia* 13–15 (2001), pp. 119–30.

Sivéry, G., *Philippe III le Hardi* (Paris: Fayard, 2003).

Smith, J.M.H., "Did Women Have a Transformation of the Roman World," *Gender & History* 12, 3 (2000), pp. 552–571.

"The Hagiography of Hucbald of St.-Amand," *Studi Medievali* 35 (1994), pp. 517–542.

Sluhovsky, M., *Patroness of Paris: Rituals of Devotion in Early Modern France* (New York, Cologne: Brill, 1998).

Sommers, G., "A Royal Tomb Program in the Reign of St. Louis," *The Art Bulletin* 56, 2 (1974), pp. 224–243.

Smith, K.A., "An Angel's Power in a Bishop's Body: The Making of the Cult of Aubert of Avranches at Mont-Saint-Michel," *Journal of Medieval History* 29, 4 (2003), pp. 347–360.

Sonzogni, D., "Un acte de vente inédit du chartrier de Saint-Denis (11 avril 702?)," *Bibliothèque de l'école des chartes* 159, 2 (2001), pp. 609–613.

Sot, M., "Le baptême de Clovis et l'entrée des Francs en romanité," *Bulletin de l'Association Guillaume Budé* 1 (1996), pp. 64–75.

Spiegel, G.M., "Genealogy: Form and Function in Medieval Historiography," *History and Theory* 22, 1 (1983), pp. 43–53.

Romancing the Past: The Rise of Vernacular Prose Historiography in Thirteenth-century France (Berkeley and Los Angeles, CA: University of California Press, 1993).

The Chronicle Tradition of Saint-Denis: A Survey (Brookline, MA, and Leiden: Brill, 1978).

"The *Reditus Regni ad Stirpem Karoli Magni*: A New Look," *French Historical Studies* 7, 2 (1971), pp. 145–174; repr. in *The Past as Text: The Theory and Practice of Medieval Historiography* (Baltimore, MD: Johns Hopkins University Press, 1997), pp. 111–137.

Stancliffe, C., "Columbanus and the Gallic Bishops," in *Auctoritas: Mélanges offerts au Olivier Guillot*, eds. G. Constable and M. Rouche, Cultures et Civilisation Médieval 33 (Paris: Sorbonne PUPS, 2006), pp. 205–215.

Staubach, N., "*Christiana tempora*. Augustin und das Ende der alten Geschichte in der Weltchronik Frechulfs von Lisieux," *Frühmittelalterliche Studien* 29 (1995), pp. 167–206.

Stegeman, H., "The Growth of an Austrasian Identity: Processes of Identification and Legend Construction in the Northeast of the *Regnum Francorum*, 600–800," doctoral dissertation (University of Groningen, 2014).

Stevens, C.E., *Sidonius Apollinaris and His Age* (Oxford: Clarendon, 1933).
Stoclet, A.J., *Fils de Martel: La naissance, l'education et la jeunesse de Pepin, dit le bref (v. 714–v. 741)* (Turnhout: Brepols, 2014).
Stone, R., "'Bound from Either Side': The Limits of Power in Carolingian Marriage Disputes, 840–870," *Gender & History* 19, 3 (2007), pp. 467–482.
"Kings Are Different: Carolingian Mirrors for Princes and Lay Morality," in *Prince au miroir de la littérature politique de l'Antiquité aux Lumières*, eds. F. Lachaud and L. Scordia (Mont-Saint-Aignan: Publications des Universités de Rouen et du Havre, 2007), pp. 69–86.
Stringer, G.P., "Book 1 of William the Breton's 'Philippide': A Translation," MA thesis (University of New Hampshire, 2010).
Summerfield, T., "Filling the Gap: Brutus in the Historia Brittonum, Anglo-Saxon Chronicle MS F, and Geoffrey of Monmouth," *The Medieval Chronicle VII* (2011), pp. 85–102.
Sunderland, L., *Rebel Barons: Resisting Royal Power in Medieval Culture* (Oxford: Oxford University Press, 2016).
Taayke, E., "Some Introductory and Concluding Remarks," in *Essays on the Early Franks*, ed. E. Taayke et al., *Groningen Archaeological Studies*, vol. 1 (Eelde: Barkhuis, 2003), pp. ix–xvi.
Tamás, H., and L. Van der Sypt, "Asceticism and Syneisaktism in Asterius' *Liber ad Renatum monachum*," *Zeitschrift für antikes Christentum* 17, 3 (2013), pp. 504–525.
Taranu, C., *Vernacular Verse Histories in Early Medieval England and Francia: The Bard and the Rag-Picker* (New York and London: Routledge, 2021).
Taylor, A.L., "Poetry, Patronage, and Politics: Epic Saints' Lives in Western Francia, 800–1000," doctoral dissertation (University of Texas at Austin, 2006).
Taylor, C., 'The Salic Law and the Valois Succession to the French Crown', *French History* 15, 4 (2001), pp. 358–377.
Theis, L., *Dagobert: Un roi pour un peuple* (Paris: Fayard, 1982).
Theurillat, J.-M., "L'abbaye de St.-Maurice d'Agaune: des origines à la réforme canoniale, 515–830 environ', *Vallesia* 9 (1954), pp. 30–84.
Theuws, F., "Maastricht as a Centre of Power in the Early Middle Ages," in *Topographies of Power in the Early Middle Ages*, eds. M. de Jong and F. Theuws (Leiden, Boston and Cologne: Brill, 2001), pp. 155–216.
Thomas, E.J., "The Second Jezebel: Representations of the Sixth-Century Queen Brunhild," doctoral dissertation (University of Glasgow, 2012).
Tiraboschi, G., *Storia della letteratura italiana* (Modena: Presso la Società Tipografica, 1792).
Touati, F.-O., "Faut-Il En Rire? Le Médecin Rigord, Historien de Philippe Auguste," *Revue historique* 305, 2 (2003), pp. 243–265.
Travassos Valdez, M.A., *Historical Interpretations of the "Fifth Empire": The Dynamics of Periodization from Daniel to António Vieira, S.J.* (Leiden and Boston: Brill, 2019).
Tyl-Labory, G., "Essai d'une histoire nationale au XIIIe siècle: la chronique de l'anonyme de Chantilly-Vatican," *Bibliothèque de l'école des chartes* 148, 2 (1990), pp. 301–354.

van Uytfanghe, M., "Hagiographie: un 'genre' chrétien ou antique tardif," *Analecta Bollandiana* 111 (1993), pp. 135–188.

Verweij, M., "Les manuscrits des œvres de Sigebert de Gembloux à la Bibliothèque royale de Belgique" in *Sigebert de Gembloux*, ed. J.-P. Straus (Turnhout: Brepols, 2015), pp. 91–116.

Vircillo Franklin, C., "Frankish Redaction or Roman Exemplar? Revisions and Interpolations in the Text of the *Liber pontificalis*," in *Inclusion and Exclusion in Mediterranean Christianities, 400–800*, eds. Y. Fox and E. Buchberger (Turnhout: Brepols, 2019), pp. 17–46.

Wagner, M., "Die Torci bei Fredegar," *Beiträge zur Namenforschung* 19 (1984), pp. 402–410.

Waha, M. de, "Sigebert de Gembloux faussaire? Le chroniqueur et les «sources anciennes» de son abbaye," *Revue belge de philologie et d'histoire* 55, 4 (1977), pp. 989–1036.

Wallace-Hadrill, J.M., *A Carolingian Renaissance Prince: The Emperor Charles the Bald* (London: British Academy, 1980).

"Fredegar and the History of France," *Bulletin of the John Rylands Library* 40, 2 (1958), pp. 527–550.

The Long-Haired Kings and Other Studies in Frankish History (London: Methuen, 1962).

Ward, G., *History, Scripture, and Authority in the Carolingian Empire: Frechulf of Lisieux* (Oxford: Oxford University Press, 2022).

"Lessons in Leadership: Constantine and Theodosius in Frechulf of Lisieux's *Histories*," in *The Resources of the Past in Early Medieval Europe*, eds. C. Gantner, R. McKitterick, and S. Meeder (Cambridge: Cambridge University Press, 2015), pp. 68–83.

"The Sense of an Ending in the *Histories* of Frechulf of Lisieux," in *Historiographies of Identity, vol. III: Carolingian Convergence and Its Later Uses*, eds. H. Reimitz, R. Kramer, and G. Ward (Turnhout: Brepols, 2021), pp. 291–315.

"The Universal Past and Carolingian Present in the Histories of Frechulf of Lisieux," doctoral dissertation (University of Cambridge, 2014).

Waswo, R., "Our Ancestors, the Trojans: Inventing Cultural Identity in the Middle Ages," *Exemplaria: A Journal of Theory in Medieval and Renaissance Studies* 7, 2 (1995), pp. 269–290.

Wasyl, A.M., "An Aggrieved Heroine in Merovingian Gaul: Venantius Fortunatus, Radegund's Lament on the Destruction of Thuringia, and Echoing Ovid's Heroides," *Bollettino di Studi Latini* 45, 1 (2015), pp. 64–75.

Weber, M.-L., "Die Merovingerkönigin Brunichilde in den Quellen des lateinischen Mittelalters," in *Nova de veteribus: Mittel- und neulateinsiche Studien für Paul Gerhard Schmidt*, eds. A. Bihrer and E. Stein (Munich and Leipzig: K.G. Saur, 2004), pp. 45–70.

Weidemann, M., "Zur Chronologie der Merowinger im 7. Und 8. Jahrhundert," *Francia* 25, 1 (1998), pp. 177–230.

Weiler, B., "Image and Reality in Richard of Cornwall's German Career," *English Historical Review* 113, 454 (1998), pp. 1111–1142.

Wemple, S.F., *Women in Frankish Society: Marriage and the Cloister, 500 to 900* (Philadelphia, PA: University of Pennsylvania Press, 1989).
Werner, K.F., "De Childéric à Clovis: antécédents et conséquences de la bataille de Soissons en 486," Actes des VIIIe journées internationales d'archéologie mérovingienne de Soissons (19–22 Juin 1986), *Revue archéologique de Picardie* 3–4 (1988), pp. 3–7.
"Die Legitimität der Kapetinger und die Entstehung der 'reditus regni Francorum ad stirpem Karoli'," *Die Welt als Geschichte* 12 (1952), pp. 203–225.
"Die literarischen Vorbilder des Aimoin von Fleury," in *Medium Aevum Vivum: Festschrift für Walther Bulst*, eds. H.R. Jauss and D. Schaller (Heidelberg, 1960), pp. 69–103.
"Zur Arbeitsweise des Regino von Prüm," *Die Welt als Geschichte* 19 (1959), pp. 96–116.
West, C., "Knowledge of the Past and the Judgement of History in Tenth-Century Trier: Regino of Prüm and the Lost Manuscript of Bishop Adventius of Metz," *Early Medieval Europe* 24, 2 (2016), pp. 137–159.
Wickham, C., *Framing the Early Middle Ages: Europe and the Mediterranean, 400–800* (Oxford: Oxford University Press, 2007).
Widdowson, M., "Merovingian Partitions: A 'Genealogical Charter'?," *Early Medieval Europe* 17, 1 (2009), pp. 1–22.
Wijnendele, J.W.P., "The Early Career of Aëtius and the Murder of Felix (c. 425–430 CE)," *Historia* 66, 4 (2017), pp. 468–482.
Wolfram, H., *History of the Goths* (Berkeley, CA: University of California Press, 1988).
Origo et religio: Ethnic Tradition and Literature in Early Medieval Texts," *Early Medieval Europe* 3, 1 (1994), pp. 29–38.
Wood, I.N., "Aethicus Ister: An Exercise in Difference," in *Grenze und Differenz im frühen Mittelalter*, eds. W. Pohl and H. Reimitz (Vienna: Verlag der Österreichischen Akademie der Wissenschaften, 2000), pp. 197–208.
Wood, I.N. , "Chains of Chronicles: The Example of London, British Library ms. add. 16794," in *Zwischen Niederschrift und Wiederschrift: Hagiographie und Historiographie im Spannungsfeld von Kompendienüberlieferung und Editionstechnik*, eds. R. Corradini and M. Diesenberger (Vienna: Verlag der Österreichischen Akademie der Wissenschaften, 2010), pp. 67–78.
"Defining the Franks: Frankish Origins in Early Medieval History," in *From Roman Provinces to Medieval Kingdoms*, ed. T.F.X. Noble (New York and London: Routledge, 2006), pp. 91–98.
"Deconstructing the Merovingian Family," in *The Construction of Communities in the Early Middle Ages: Texts, Resources and Artefacts*, eds. R. Corradini, M. Diesenberger, and H. Reimitz (Leiden and Boston: Brill, 2003), pp. 149–171.
"Entrusting Western Europe to the Church, 400–750, *Transactions of the Royal Historical Society* 23 (2013), pp. 37–73.
"Genealogy Defined by Women: The Case of the Pippinids," in *Gender in the Early Medieval World: East and West, 300–900*, eds. L. Brubaker and J.M. H. Smith (Cambridge: Cambridge University Press, 2004), pp. 235–256.

"*Gentes*, Kings and Kingdoms – The Emergence of States. The Kingdom of the Gibichungs," in *Regna and Gentes: The Relationship between Late Antique and Early Medieval Peoples and Kingdoms in the Transformation of the Roman World*, eds. H.-W. Goetz, J. Jarnut, and W. Pohl (Leiden and Boston: Brill, 2003), pp. 243–270.

"Gregory of Tours and Clovis," *Revue belge de philologie et d'histoire* 63, 2 (1985), pp. 249–272.

"The Bloodfeud of the Franks: A Historiographical Legend," *Early Medieval Europe* 14, 4 (2006), pp. 489–504.

The Christian Economy of the Early Medieval West: Towards a Temple Society (Binghampton, NY: Gracchi Books, 2022).

"The Fall of the Western Empire and the End of Roman Britain", *Britannia* 18 (1987), pp. 251–262.

The Merovingian Kingdoms, 450–751 (London and New York: Routledge, 1993).

The Modern Origins of the Early Middle Ages (Oxford: Oxford University Press, 2013).

"'There Is a World Elsewhere': The World of Late Antiquity," in *Motions of Late Antiquity: Essays on Religion, Politics, and Society in Honour of Peter Brown*, eds. J. Kreiner and H. Reimitz (Turnhout: Brepols, 2016), pp. 17–43.

Wood, S., *The Proprietary Church in the Medieval West* (Oxford: Oxford University Press, 2006).

Woodruff, J.E, "The Historia Epitomata (Third Book) of the Chronicle of Fredegar: An Annotated Translation and Historical Analysis of Interpolated Material," doctoral dissertation (University of Nebraska, 1987).

Woods, D., "Theophilus of Edessa on the Death of Constans II," *Byzantine and Modern Greek Studies* 44, 2 (2020), pp. 212–219.

Woolgar, C.M, "Medieval Smellscapes," in *Smell and History: A Reader*, ed. M. M. Smith (Morgantown, WV: West Virginia University Press, 2019), pp. 50–75.

Yavuz, N.K., "From Caesar to Charlemagne: The Tradition of Trojan Origins," *The Medieval History Journal* 21, 2 (2018), pp. 251–290.

"Late Antique Accounts of the Trojan War: A Comparative Look at the Manuscript Evidence," *Pecia* 17 (2014), pp. 149–170.

"Transmission and Adaptation of the Trojan Narrative in Frankish History between the Sixth and Tenth Centuries," doctoral dissertation (University of Leeds, 2015).

Yerushalmi, Y.H., "Clio and the Jews: Reflections on Jewish Historiography in the Sixteenth Century," *Proceedings of the American Academy for Jewish Research* 46–47 (1979–1980), pp. 607–638.

"Messianic Impulses in Joseph Ha-Kohen," in *Jewish Thought in the Sixteenth Century*, ed. B.D. Cooperman (Cambridge, MA: Harvard University Press, 1983), pp. 460–487.

Zale, S. "The French Kill Their King: The Assassination of Childeric II in Late-Medieval French Historiograph," *Fifteenth-Century Studies* 27 (2002), pp. 273–294.

Zangenberg, J.K., "*Scelerum inventor et malorum machinator*: Diocletian and the Tetrarchy in Lactantius, *De mortibus persecutorum*," in *Imagining Emperors in the Later Roman Empire*, eds. D.P.W. Burgersdijk and A.J. Ross, Cultural Interactions in the Mediterranean, vol. 1 (Leiden: Brill, 2018), pp. 39–62.

Zöllner, E., *Geschichte der Franken bis zur Mitte des sechsten Jahrhunderts* (Munich: Beck, 1970).

Index

Aachen, 81, 150
Abbo, abbot of Fleury, 5, 6
Abraham, patriarch, 141
  bosom of, 200
  timeframe, 272
Acta Sanctorum, 18, 239
AD 751, 3, 24, 25, 89, 262, 271, 275
Adalgisel, mayor of the palace, 195
Adam, first man, 258
Additamentum Nivialense de Fuillano, 237
Ado, archbishop of Vienne, 14, 15, 16, 17, 128, 133, 140–142, 272
  Chronicle, 23, 128, 129, 140–169, 225, 234, 276, 277
  Life of Theudarius, 17, 141–146
  Martyrology, 207, 209
  Suffering of Desiderius, 17, 165, 278
Aega, mayor of the palace, 53, 54, 166, 198, 203, 216
Aegidius, Roman general, 38, 40, 51–54, 78–80, 93, 98, 151
Aeneas, Trojan prince, 33, 48, 49, 60, 65, 67, 70
Æthelthrith, queen of Northumbria and abbess of Ely, 166
Aethicus Ister
  Cosmographia, 59
Aëtius, Roman general, 35, 78, 151
Africa, 151, 161, 166
Agilulf, king of the Lombards, 215
Agiulf, bishop of Metz, 60, 61
Aigulf, abbot of Saint-Denis, 199
Aimoin of Fleury, 5, 6, 32, 54, 181
  Gesta Francorum, 5–7, 9, 12, 54, 64, 67–69, 77–79, 82, 85, 87, 99, 100, 102, 105, 111, 133, 227, 233, 235, 239, 264, 273–277
  Life of St. Abbo, 6
  Miracles of St. Benedict, 6
Airlie, Stuart, 208, 219
Alamanni, 88, 95, 102, 109–114, 150, 151, 210, 245

Alamannia, 69, 71, 110, 126
Alani, 150
Alaric I, king of the Visigoths, 137
Alaric II, king of the Visigoths, 93, 96, 99, 106, 114, 115, 136, 137, 210
Albion. *See* Britain
Alcuin of York, 154
Alethius, patrician, 128, 188
Alguades, Meir, Jewish physician, 257
Allen, Michael, 131, 135
al-Mansura, Battle of, 82
Alpaida, wife of Pippin II, 250–252
Alphonse, brother of Louis IX, 81
Amalafrid, Thuringian prince, 52
Amalaric, king of the Visigoths, 118, 157, 210
Amalasuntha, queen of the Ostrogoths, 106
Amandus, bishop of Maastricht, 192, 212, 235, 241–243, 244
  Life, 192, 235, 241–243
Amatus, bishop of Sens, 248
Amazons, 43
Ammianus Marcellinus, historian, 33, 37, 100
ampulla, holy, 113
Amsivarii, Frankish tribe, 45
Anastasius, emperor, 116, 117, 152, 210
Angilram, bishop of Metz, 59, 76
Angoulême, 115
Anianus, bishop of Orléans, 78
Annales Lobienses, 243
Annales Mettenses Priores, 139, 218, 226, 239, 243
Annales regni Francorum, 58, 75, 208, 217, 219, 220, 222, 234, 243, 276
Annegray, monastery, 127
Ansbrand, king of the Lombards, 218
Anschises, the father of Aeneas, 60
Anschisus. *See* Ansegisel
Ansedunum, variant of Cosa, 73
Ansedunus. *See* Ansegisel
Ansegisel, father of Pippin II, 59, 60, 61–62, 73, 74, 235, 243, 245, 250

318

Index

Ansoald, bishop of Poitiers, 199–203
Antenor, Trojan prince, 46, 65, 69, 70
Antioch, 55
Antony, Egyptian monk, 160
Aquitaine, 152, 169, 176, 185, 186, 187, 189, 196, 210, 211, 253
Aramea, 258, 259
Arbogast, Roman general, 45
Arcadius, emperor, 133
Arians, 96, 97, 99, 107, 112, 116, 152, 160
Arles, 158
Arnoald, bishop of Metz, 60, 72, 73
Arnulf of Carinthia, emperor, 207, 215
Arnulf, bishop of Metz, 53, 60–62, 73, 74, 77, 84, 142, 171, 175, 177, 184, 185, 187, 188, 190, 207, 211–215, 219, 234, 240, 242, 246, 247, 250, 251, 274
  Life, 53, 61, 165, 207, 213–215, 221
Arnulfings, 235, 237, 276
Arras, 116, 210
Artogast, Frankish lawgiver, 148
Ascalon, 81
Ascanius, son of Aeneas, 65, 70
Ascension, 210
Ascyla, mother of Theudemer, 37
Asia Minor, 166
Athanagild, king of the Visigoths, 158, 160
Athanaric, king of the Goths, 94, 107, 151
Atticus, Titus Pomponius, 104
Attila the Hun, 36, 38, 51, 78
Auctor, bishop of Metz, 61
Audofled, queen of the Ostrogoths, 106, 135
Audoin, bishop of Rouen, 127, 172, 198, 242
Audovera, queen of the Franks, 158
Augustus, emperor, 137
Austrasia, 21, 50, 70, 159, 160, 185, 187, 192, 194, 195, 220, 249, 265, 266, 268
  elites, 184, 185, 188, 189, 220, 245
  kingship, 72, 74, 76, 195, 203, 233, 235, 236, 237, 244, 245, 247, 266, 268
  mythology, 68, 69
  Pippinids, 76, 190, 203, 211, 214
  subkingship, 166, 184, 185, 186, 212, 216, 220, 234, 242
Austrogoths, descendants of the Scythian Trojans, 66
Autbert, bishop of Avranches, 249, 250
Autun, 40, 144, 160, 187, 248
Auvergne, 33, 40, 96, 248
Auxerre, 187
Avars, 57, 126, 158, 170, 187, 194
Avignon, 256
Avitus, abbot, 155

Avitus, bishop of Vienne, 88, 96, 155
Avitus, emperor, 40
Ba'al, Canaanite deity, 270
Badius, Jodocus, publisher, 102, 103
Balthild, queen of the Franks, 72, 181, 246
barbatoria, 176
barons, 1, 78, 79, 80, 81, 82
Barontus, Vision of, 202
Basina, Merovingian princess, 125
Basina, queen of the Franks, 1–7, 11, 38, 84, 92, 275
Basques, 170
Bavaria, 126, 170, 194, 218
Bazas, 115
bear, 2, 3, 99
beasts, small, 2, 3
Beatrice, daughter of Raymond Berenger, count of Provence, 81
Beaujeu, Pierre de, regent of King Charles VIII, 99
Beaune, Colette, 86
Becket, Thomas, saint, 80
Bede, the Venerable, 100, 131, 207
  Ecclesiastical History, 100, 227, 233, 235
  Martyrology, 143
  On the Reckoning of Time, 131, 138, 151, 152, 207, 209–210
Begga, mother of Pippin II, 74, 235, 242, 251
bella civilia, 168, 249
Benedict of Nursia, 5, 6
Bernard, archbishop of Vienne, 144
Bernard, *dux* of Septimania, 177
Berthar, mayor of the palace, 249
Bertoald, Saxon chieftain, 189
Bertrude, queen of the Franks, 175
besant, 80, 82
Bethmann, Ludwig Conrad, 231, 233, 247
Bilichild, queen of the Franks, 50, 248
Biondo, Flavio, 87, 106, 107, 109, 112, 114
  Decades, 106, 109, 110
Bissinus, king of the Thuringians, 1, 38, 78, 93
Blithild, fictional Merovingian princess, 74–76
Bodilo, Neustrian noble, 178, 248
Boemus, Joannes
  Omnium gentium mores, leges, et ritus, 257
Bolland, Jean, 18
Bollandists, 18–19
Boniface IV, pope, 130, 133, 138
Boniface, archbishop of Mainz, 10, 74, 254
Bordeaux, 115
Boso, *dux* of Provence, 150, 158, 159

Boso-Landegisilus. *See* Landegisel, brother of Nanthechild
Bretons, 136, 137
Britain, 65, 70, 100, 166, 170, 209
Brittany, 10, 134, 137, 170
Brodulf, uncle of Charibert II, 185, 186–190, 212
Brunhild, queen of the Franks, 33, 161–165, 167, 169, 215
Brunulf. *See* Brodulf
Brussels, 239, 244, 254
Brutus, son of Silvius, 33, 65, 70
Buccelen, Frankish *dux*, 134, 138
Buchner, Max, 173, 177
Bulgars, 194, 216
Burchard, bishop of Würzburg, 218
Burgess, Richard W., 13
Burgundy
   Carolingian, 253
   Gibichung, 85, 88, 93, 94, 96, 105, 106–110, 115, 125, 131, 136, 151–152, 153, 155, 156, 157, 210
   Merovingian, 124, 160, 161, 162, 187–189, 216
Byzantium, 131, 161, 231, 234
   Frankish relations, 52, 54–57, 117, 170, 211, 262
   Jewish policy, 9
   other diplomatic ties, 202
   wars, 56, 166, 265

Cædwalla, king of the West Saxons, 247
Caesar, Julius, 117, 119, 261
Caesarea, city in Palestine, 132
Caesaria II, abbess, 158
Caesarius, bishop of Arles, 142, 144, 158
Cahors, 115, 171
Calvo, Minizio, publisher, 260
Cambrai, 98
Cannacarius. *See* Ragnachar
Capet, Hugh, king of France, 5, 271
Capetians
   dynasty, 3, 5, 6, 82
   kings, 1
   origins, 11, 68
   politics, 22, 81
   wars, 80
Carloman I, king of the Franks, 62
Carloman of Bavaria, king of the Franks, 215
Carloman, mayor of the palace, 57, 72, 128, 253, 269
Carolingians
   administration, 129
   decline, 206, 215, 219, 271, 276
   dynasty, 3, 6, 77, 129, 155, 167, 169, 215, 242, 243, 276, 278
   elites, 128, 167
   empire, 139, 140, 255, 273
   hagiography, 84
   historiography, 5, 30, 57–62, 75, 84–85, 87, 91, 148–150, 168, 172, 178, 179–183, 208–209, 217, 218, 225–228, 230, 231–232, 237, 243, 245, 246, 250, 251, 255, 268, 270, 271, 273, 276
   ideology, 131, 154, 168, 190, 271
   kings, 73, 139, 155, 173
   origins, 58, 70, 73, 76, 133, 139, 140, 142, 167, 169, 177, 194, 215, 217, 219, 221, 237, 238, 243, 246, 250, 255, 262, 271, 275, 279
   religious patronage, 154
   renaissance, 140
   wars, 187
Cassiodorus, 106, 114
   Variae, 106, 113, 136
Castille, kingdom, 257
Catalaunian Plains, Battle of, 35, 105
Catulliacus, village, 175, 182
chain chronicle, 4
Chalaronne, river, 160
Chalon-sur-Saône, 143, 187, 201
Chamavi, Frankish tribe, 45
Champagne, 249
Chararic of Cambrai, Frankish king, 90, 116
Charbonnière, forest, 45
Charibert I, king of the Franks, 158, 160, 162, 262, 263
Charibert II, king of the Franks, 184–187, 189–190, 192, 193, 212, 213, 242, 262
Charlemagne, emperor, 22, 60, 61–62, 73, 74, 77, 102, 131, 139, 149, 154, 190, 199, 209, 242, 243, 246, 252, 274, 276, 279
Charles I of Anjou, brother of Louis IX, 81
Charles Martel, mayor of the palace, 57, 58, 62, 70, 72, 73, 74, 102, 167, 169, 208, 217–218, 226, 231, 242, 250, 252, 253, 266, 271
Charles of Bourbon, cardinal, 99
Charles the Bald, emperor, 73, 91, 139, 140, 148, 149, 150, 155, 158, 159
Charles the Good, count of Flanders, 80
Charles the Young, king of Aquitaine, 159
Charles V, king of France, 270
Charles VI, king of France, 86
Charles VIII, king of France, 99, 261
Chatii, Frankish tribe, 45

Index

Chazan, Mireille, 230
Chelles, monastery, 246
chevalerie, 65
Chevalier, Pierre, director, 171
Childebert "the Adopted," king of the Franks, 21, 50, 235, 236, 244, 245, 255
Childebert I, king of the Franks, 104, 126, 135, 157, 210
Childebert II, king of the Franks, 56, 160, 161, 174, 211
Childebert III, king of the Franks, 72, 226, 249, 252, 253, 266, 267, 268, 269
Childéric de Saône, literary character, 279
Childeric I, king of the Franks, 1–2, 3–7, 20, 22, 29, 37–41, 66, 72, 92, 93, 98, 103, 105, 150, 151
  tomb, 55
Childeric II, king of the Franks, 50, 70, 72, 178, 237, 244, 247–248, 255, 265–266, 267, 268
Childeric III, king of the Franks, 20, 25, 57, 72, 73, 74–75, 79, 128, 194, 226, 253, 254, 268, 269, 270
Chilperic I, king of the Franks, 25, 48, 72, 143, 158, 160, 162, 180, 240
Chilperic II, king of the Franks, 72, 218, 226, 252, 253, 262, 266–269, 271
Chilperic, Burgundian prince, 108
Chilperic, Burgundian subking, 108, 109
Chilperic, son of Charibert II, 193, 213
Chimnechild, queen of the Franks, 50
Chloderic of Cologne, Frankish king, 90, 98, 111, 117
Chlodoald, Merovingian prince, 157
Chlodomer, king of the Franks, 85, 95, 104, 110, 125, 134, 136, 155, 156, 157, 210
Chlodulf, bishop of Metz, 234, 237, 251
  Life, 234, 235, 237
Chlothar I, king of the Franks, 72, 74, 75, 76, 104, 126, 127, 134, 136, 137, 157–158, 160, 210, 263, 277
Chlothar II, king of the Franks, 72, 124, 126, 134, 160, 163, 164, 165, 166, 174–176, 177, 180, 181, 183–185, 186, 187, 188–189, 211, 212, 215, 240, 263
Chlothar III, king of the Franks, 50, 72, 246, 247, 248, 265, 268, 275
Chlothar IV, king of the Franks, 72, 73, 253, 268
Chramn, Merovingian prince, 134, 137, 157, 277
Chrodegang, bishop of Metz, 61
Chrodoald, noble, 184
Chroma, Burgundian princess, 94, 109

Chunibert, bishop of Cologne, 188, 190, 195, 216, 234, 245
clergie, 65
Clermont, 40, 92, 96
Clichy, 185–186, 192, 241, 242, 254
  Council, 186
Clodio, king of the Franks, 37, 38, 44–49, 72, 77–78, 103, 104–105, 116, 117, 150, 271, 274
Clothild, Merovingian princess, 125
Clothild, queen of the Franks, 88, 94–95, 98, 101, 107, 109–110, 112, 114–115, 118, 125, 127, 151, 157, 167, 169
Clovis I, king of the Franks, 10, 17, 20, 21–23, 25, 32, 38–41, 55, 60, 68, 72, 75, 84–123, 125, 126, 128, 134, 135–137, 150–155, 159, 160, 167, 168, 169, 170, 180, 210–211, 225, 262, 271
Clovis II, king of the Franks, 11, 20–21, 24, 25, 54, 72, 127, 166, 195, 198, 203–205, 207, 216–220, 221–222, 233, 236, 242, 246, 247, 252, 255, 265, 268, 271, 275–276
Clovis III, king of the Franks, 226, 266, 268
Clovis, royal pretender, 248, 249
coat-of-arms, 113
Collins, Roger, 53
Cologne, 34, 36, 151, 159, 188, 207, 212, 216, 245, 250, 253, 259
Columbanus, abbot, 10, 127, 145, 146, 163, 215
  Life, 53, 144, 145, 146, 162, 163, 165, 171, 207
  monastic movement, 202
Commemoratio de genealogia domni Arnulfi, 76
Computus of 737, 253, 254
Conseil du roi, 261
conservatism, 8, 10, 83, 277
consilium, 54, 189, 193, 195
consors regni, 210, 240
Constans II, emperor, 202
Constantine, emperor, 38–41, 91, 95
Constantinople, 52, 54–56, 133, 213, 259
  Council of, AD 680–681, 133
Contreni, John, 173
Corbie, monastery, 246
Cornwall, 81
Creation, 130, 132, 141, 258, 272
Crescens, bishop of Vienne, 152
crown, 2, 116, 117, 197
Crusades, 81, 100
  first, 259
  seventh, 82

Cuenca, 256
Cunincpert, king of the Lombards, 247

Dagobert I, king of the Franks, 10, 14, 20, 21, 23, 24, 25, 54, 57, 65, 170–209, 211–217, 219–221, 227, 233–234, 235, 236, 239–242, 260, 262–265, 268, 275–276
  Gesta Dagoberti, 12, 14, 15–16, 24, 170–209, 211–217, 219–221, 225, 233–234, 275, 276, 278
  Inventio et translatio, 173
Dagobert II, king of the Franks, 125, 217, 236, 243, 245
Dagobert III, king of the Franks, 72, 226, 253, 266, 268
Dagobert, Merovingian prince, 72
Damascus, 259
Daniel, biblical book, 131, 229
Daniel, monk. *See* Chilperic II, king of the Franks
Danube, river, 43, 44, 66, 132
Dares of Phrygia
  Historia de origine Francorum, 59
De rebus gestis Francorum. See Emilio, Paolo: *De rebus gestis Francorum*
de Waha, Michel, 227
deer, 175, 176, 182
Deerhurst, estate of Saint-Denis, 81
Deluge, 141
Denis. *See* Dionysius
Desiderius, bishop of Cahors, 171
Desiderius, bishop of Vienne, 17, 141, 145, 146, 160–161, 162–165, 166, 169
Desiderius, king of the Lombards, 190
Devisse, Jean, 173
Dido, bishop of Poitiers, 124, 202, 236, 244
Dido, queen of Carthage, 65
Dijon, 187
Diocletian, emperor, 38–41
Dionysius, bishop of Paris, 11, 21, 65, 86, 116, 176, 179, 183, 189, 200, 204–205, 211, 212, 216, 217, 233, 255, 262, 265, 275
Dionysius Exiguus, monk, 232, 254
divisio regni, 186, 195, 216
Doda, wife of Arnulf of Metz, 234
Dodo, brother of Alpaida, 251, 252
dog, 2, 3, 175, 176
Dome of the Rock, 258
dove, 113
DRG. *See* Emilio, Paolo: *De rebus gestis Francorum*
Drogo, duke of Champagne, 249, 250
Drogo, son of Carloman, 62

duces, 44–47, 48, 53, 69–70, 76, 83, 132
Duisburg, 37

Ebbo, archbishop of Reims, 130
Ebroin, mayor of the palace, 202, 246, 247, 248–249, 266
Effros, Bonnie, 55
Egypt, 55, 82, 259, 267
Einhard, 75, 183, 199, 247, 255
  Vita Karoli, 57–58, 138, 139, 183, 199, 247, 276
Eleanor, daughter of Raymond Berenger, count of Provence, 81
Eleutherius, companion of Dionysius, 183, 189
Eligius, bishop of Noyon, 172, 189, 201, 242
  Life, 172, 189, 207
Emilio, Paolo, 6, 13, 14, 17, 18, 19, 20, 23, 87, 99–119, 277
  De rebus gestis Francorum, 6, 17, 23, 87, 101–119, 274, 277
England, 80, 81, 82, 202, 209, 229, 247
Enlightenment historiography, 19, 20, 124
Épinay, villa, 198
Erasmus, Desiderius, humanist scholar, 101
Erchinoald, mayor of the palace, 166, 203, 233, 246, 248
Eriugena, John Scotus, 149
Ermarius, partisan of Charibert II, 186
eschatology, 265
Esders, Stefan, 57
Eudo, duke of Aquitaine, 253, 266, 269
Eufrasius, bishop of Clermont, 96
Eugene III, pope, 244
Eusebius, bishop of Caesarea, 132
Eusebius, bishop of Vercelli, 143
Eusebius-Jerome, chronicle of, 39–42, 43, 92, 227, 229, 230, 231, 272, 273
Eustachius, martyr, 182
Eutharic, Ostrogothic prince, 106

Faramund, king of the Franks, 46, 71, 72, 86, 102, 103, 104, 148
Ferrières, 140
fideles, 55, 189
Filibert, abbot of Noirmoutier, 201–202
Fischer, Svante, 55
Fleury, monastery, 5–6, 9, 12, 32, 181
Floachad, mayor of the palace, 203
Flodoard of Reims
  History of the Church of Reims, 227, 233
Foillan, Irish monk, 237
fortuna, 112, 219

Index

Fos, 189
Fosses, monastery, 235
four kingdoms, historiographical model, 131
Francia, West, 5
Francio, mythological king of the Franks, 43, 44, 47, 48, 66–70, 132
Francis I, king of France, 229
Frechulf, bishop of Lisieux, 15, 128–140, 168–169, 225, 275
  Histories, 23, 84, 85, 128–140, 168–169, 272, 277
Fredegar, *Chronicle*, 4–5, 7, 9, 14, 15–16, 22, 23, 24, 25, 32, 34, 41–57, 58, 59, 67–69, 77–79, 82, 84–85, 87, 94, 99–102, 111, 125, 127–128, 135, 138, 151, 155, 163, 168, 172, 174–175, 184–199, 202, 203, 207, 212, 220–221, 227, 229, 233, 235, 239, 242, 245, 258, 261, 264, 273, 274, 278
  Book II, 134
  Book III, 4, 5
  Book IV, 4, 123, 215
  Continuations, 21, 58, 59, 227, 249, 253
  Scarpsum de Cronica Hieronimi, 48, 273
Fredegund, queen of the Franks, 158–159, 160–161, 165, 167, 240
Friga, mythological king of the Franks, 43–44, 47, 48, 67
Frisia, 126, 249, 253
Fulrad, *capellanus*, 218

Gaguin, Robert, French humanist, 100, 261–262
  Compendium de origine et gestis Francorum, 261, 268
Gallus, bishop of Clermont, 96
Gallus, hermit and disciple of Columbanus
  Life, 172
Galswinth, queen of the Franks, 158, 160, 167
Gascony, 5, 6, 118, 253, 266
Gaza, 258
Geary, Patrick, 3, 8
Genoa, 228, 256
Genobaud, Frankish *dux*, 35, 69–70
Genovefa of Paris, virgin, 98, 126, 179
  Life, 172, 233
genre theory, 12–14
Geoffrey of Monmouth, 33, 66, 70
  Historia regum Brittaniae, 66
Gepids, 117
Gerberding, Richard, 205
Gère, river, 144

Gerhard, duke of Provence, 141
Germania, Roman province, 34
Germanus, bishop of Auxerre
  Life, 233
Germanus, bishop of Paris, 158
Germany, 69, 71, 148, 261
Gertrude, abbess of Nivelles, 172, 234, 235, 237, 242, 246, 251
  Life, 235, 237
Geschichtsbewusstsein, 230
Gesta Dagoberti. See Dagobert I, king of the Franks: *Gesta Dagoberti*
Gesta Francorum. See Aimoin of Fleury: *Gesta Francorum*
Gesta Philippi Augusti. See Rigord of Saint-Denis: *Gesta Philippi Augusti*
Gibichungs, royal family, 94
Giles/Gilon. See Aegidius, Roman general
Godegisel, Burgundian king, 102, 108, 114–115, 153
Goderniaux, Alexandre, 250
Godfrey of Bouillon, ruler of the Kingdom of Jerusalem, 259
Godinus, son of Warnachar, 184, 185
Godomar, Burgundian prince, 108
Godomar, king of the Burgundians, 115
Goffart, Walter, 61–62
Göktürks, 55
Goldberg, Eric, 182
Gómara, Francisco Lopez de
  Historia general de las Indias, 257
Gomatrude, queen of the Franks, 184, 187, 188, 189–190, 192
Goths, 23, 35, 37, 92, 105, 131, 132, 168
Grandes Chroniques de France, 16, 18, 21, 77, 86, 100, 111, 119, 228, 229, 261, 263, 264, 268, 269, 273, 274–277
Greek, 61, 100
Greeks, 65, 117, 208
Gregory I, pope, 133, 138, 209
Gregory of Tours
  Excerpt in *Fredegar*, 43
  Histories, 4–5, 6–7, 15–17, 22–25, 32–41, 43–47, 50, 51, 53, 54, 55, 61, 78, 81–84, 87–128, 138, 143, 151, 153–155, 156, 164–165, 169, 203, 227, 233, 234, 272, 273, 274, 277, 278
  Other works, 17, 143, 233
  Six-book abridgement, 4, 5, 16, 273
Gregory VII, pope, 231
Grifo, son of Charles Martel, 62
Grimoald I, mayor of the palace, 21, 50–51, 62, 124, 185, 220, 226, 231, 235–237, 242–246, 251, 255, 278

Grimoald II, mayor of the palace, 249, 250, 252
Grimoald, king of the Lombards, 213
gubernator palatii, 186
Guenée, Bernard, 63, 127
Guenilo, archbishop of Sens, 141
Guinemenz. *See* Wiomad, *subregulus*
Gundioc, king of the Burgundians, 107, 108
Gundobad, king of the Burgundians, 41, 94, 96, 101, 102, 106, 107–109, 114–115, 118, 153, 210
Gundoin, mayor of the palace, 243
Gundolandus, mayor of the palace, 166
Gundovald, Frankish pretender, 56
Guntram, king of the Franks, 126, 127, 158, 159, 160, 167, 169

Ha-Kohen, Yosef, 9, 17–18, 20, 256–271, 272, 276, 278
 Divrei Hayamim, 12, 15, 17, 24, 229, 256–271
 Sefer Emeq Habakha, 257
 Sefer Fernando Cortez, 257
 Sefer India, 257
 Sefer Mekits Nirdamim, 257
 Sefer Metsiv Gevulot 'Amim, 257
Halsall, Guy, 55
Hebbo, bishop of Grenoble, 141
Hebrew, 15, 257, 259, 262, 266
Hebrews, 208
Hector, patrician of Marseilles, 248
Hector, son of Priam, 66
Hecuba, wife of Priam, 65
Helen of Troy, 43
Helenus, Trojan prince, 65, 70
Helisachar, chancellor, 130
Hempfer, Klaus, 13
Henry I, count of Salm, 244
Henry III, king of England, 81, 82
Henry IV, emperor, 231
Henry of Montaigu, canon and deacon, 251
Henschen, Gottfried, 18
Heraclius, emperor, 9, 56, 57, 193, 259, 263–264
Héristal, Pippin Arnulf literary character, 278, 279
Hermenfrid, king of the Thuringians, 157
Hermenigild, Visigothic prince, 133, 138, 209
Herod Antipas, son of King Herod, 147
Herod Archelaus, son of King Herod, 147
Hesbaye, 230, 254
Hilary, bishop of Poitiers, 97
Hilduin, abbot of Saint-Denis, 173–174, 183, 193, 207, 275

Hincmar, archbishop of Reims, 91, 173–174, 176, 178, 179, 193
 De regis persona et regio ministerio, 178
 Life of Remigius, 84, 113, 193, 233
 Histoire de France avant Clovis. *See* Mézeray, François Eudes de
 Histoire de France depuis Faramond jusqu'à maintenant. *See* Mézeray, François Eudes de
 Histoire littéraire de la France, 19, 20
 Historia Brittonum, 33, 34
 Historia vel gesta Francorum, 5, 58, 59, 85
Holy Apostles, church in Paris, 98, 103, 118
Holy Cross, nunnery in Poitiers, 125
Holy Sepulcher, church, 259
Honorius, emperor, 133
Hrabanus Maurus, 129
Hubert, abbot of Saint-Maurice d'Agaune, 159
Hubert, bishop of Liège, 182, 251
Hucbald of Saint-Amand, 251
Huete, 256
Hugh the Abbot, Welf noble, 155
Hugh the Great, duke of the Franks, 271
humanism, 6, 11, 13, 18, 19, 20, 64, 87, 100, 101, 105, 113, 114, 118, 229, 256, 261, 270, 274
Hungary, 39, 100
Huns, 35, 51, 54, 78, 105, 158, 229
hunting, 175, 179, 182–183, 191, 248, 266
Hydatius, chronicler, 42
Hypogoths, descendants of the Scythian Trojans, 66

Ibor, duke of the Sicambrian Trojans, 70, 71
idolatry, 95
imperium, 136, 232, 250, 255
Incarnation, 130, 132, 211, 215, 218, 240, 272
infanticide, 167
Ingomer, Merovingian prince, 95, 110
Innes, Matthew, 133
Inventio et translatio S. Dionysii tempore Dagoberti. *See* Dagobert I, king of the Franks: *Inventio et translatio*
Investiture Controversy, 231
Iran, 56
Ireland, 125, 202, 236, 244
Isabella, queen of Spain, 260
Israel, land of, 259
Italian, 260
Italy, 60, 65, 106, 115, 126, 131, 138, 139, 170, 171, 210, 247, 256, 260, 261, 262

Index

French occupation, 257
humanism, 229
Jews, 256
wars, 56, 126, 131, 133, 134, 137, 138, 140, 161, 211, 218
Itta, wife of Pippin I, 234, 235, 237, 246
iustitia, 188

Jerome, 42, 43, 229, 230
Chronicle, 39
Jerome-Gennadius
de viris illustribus, 143
Jews, 9, 42, 87, 196, 256–258, 259–260, 262–265, 267, 270
Jizya, tax, 259
John, abbot of Réomé
Life, 142, 165
John, bishop of Constantinople, 133
John, hermit, 199, 200
John, prior of Saint-Denis, 74
Jonas of Bobbio, 142
Life of Columbanus, 10, 53, 144, 145, 146, 162, 163, 165, 171, 207
Life of John, 142, 165
Jonas, bishop of Orléans, 182
De institutione laicali, 182
Jovenal, hermit of, 86
Judith, empress, 130, 139
Julian 'the Apostate', emperor, 229
Jumièges, monastery, 201
Jupiter, Roman god, 94
Justin I, emperor, 160, 161
Justin II, emperor, 161
Justinian, emperor, 136, 160, 161
Legal code, 100
Reconquest, 138

Kempf, Damian, 62
klosterpolitik, 203
Koziol, Geoffrey, 209, 219
Krusch, Bruno, 67, 144, 157, 164, 192, 205
Kulikowski, Michael, 13
Kurze, Friedrich, 207

Lake, Justin, 68, 77
Lambert, bishop of Tongres-Maastricht, 182, 244, 251–252
Life, 251–252
Lamourdedieu, Raoul, artist, 94
Landegisel, brother of Nanthechild, 194
Landeric, mayor of the palace, 159
Langres, 187
Lantechild, sister of Clovis, 112, 113
Lapidge, Michael, 173

Latinus, mythological king of the Latins, 65
laus perennis, 199, 203
Lavinia, daughter of King Latinus, 33, 65
Lefèvre d'Étaples, Jacques, French humanist, 100
Leodegar, bishop of Autun, 202, 244, 248
Suffering, 201, 249
leopard, 1
Lérins, monastery, 142
Leubovera, abbess, 125
Leudemund, bishop of Sion, 124
Leudesius, mayor of the palace, 248
Leuthar, duke of the Alamanni, 245
Levillain, Léon, 173, 177
Lex Baiwariorum, 171
Lex Salica, 75, 86, 138, 148, 170
Liber historiae Francorum, 13, 15, 16, 22, 24, 25, 32, 34, 46–47, 48–49, 51, 52, 54, 58–59, 67–69, 72, 77–78, 82–86, 101, 104, 105, 111, 112, 127, 128, 133, 138, 147–157, 163, 167–169, 171, 172, 175, 178, 189, 191, 204–205, 207, 209, 210, 211–212, 215, 217–218, 225–229, 230, 232–235, 237, 239–240, 244, 249, 252, 255, 258, 261, 273–278
Liber Pontificalis, 59, 207, 209, 234
Licinius, emperor, 39
Liège, 182, 251
Lifshitz, Felice, 16
Lind, Lennart, 55
lion, 1, 2, 3, 84, 179
Liuvigild, king of the Visigoths, 158
Lodoin. *See* Clovis
Loire, river, 109, 136, 164
Lombards, 23, 56, 129–133, 137–140, 157, 161, 168, 170, 194, 213, 215, 229
London, 180, 254
long-haired kings, 37, 41, 46, 47, 49, 103
Loseby, Simon, 202
Lothar I, emperor, 149, 177, 180
Lothar II, king of the Franks, 149, 159
Lotharingia, 149, 159, 206, 230
Louis 'the Child', king of the Franks, 207
Louis IV, king of the Franks, 214
Louis IX, king of France, 63, 80–82, 86
Louis the German, king of the Franks, 149, 150
Louis the Pious, emperor, 73, 129, 130, 137, 139, 144, 154, 173, 173, 177, 182, 183, 199
Louis V, king of the Franks, 5
Louis VII, king of France, 82
Louis XII, king of France, 99, 261
Louis XIV, King of France, 20

Lucofao, Battle of, 249
Ludovicus. *See* Clovis
Lunisolar cycles, 232
Lupus, abbot of Ferrières, 140, 150
Lutetia. *See* Paris
Luxeuil, monastery, 124, 127, 142, 247–248
luxure, 78
Lyon, 96, 134, 141, 150, 160, 163, 164, 189

Mabillon, Jean, 19
  De re diplomatica, 18
Macedonia, 44
Macedonians, 44
MacLean, Simon, 206, 208
Maeotian swamps, 68, 148, 150
maior domus. *See* mayor of the palace
Majorian, emperor, 38, 134, 135
Mamertus, bishop of Vienne, 152, 153, 210
Marcian, emperor, 55
Marcomer, Frankish *dux*, 34–36, 45, 233
Marcward, abbot of Prüm, 141
Margaret, daughter of Raymond Berenger, 81
Marius, bishop of Avenches
  Chronicle, 15, 88, 135, 136, 138, 168
Marquigny, Fernand, 93
Mars, Roman god, 94
Marseilles, 189, 248
Martin, bishop of Tours, 36–38, 39, 97, 152–155, 157, 164–165, 200, 207, 210, 216
Martin, bishop of Vienne, 152, 153
Martin, Frankish duke, 249
Mary, Virgin, 130, 144
Matthew of Vendôme, abbot of Saint-Denis, 63, 82
Maurice, emperor, 55–56, 161
Maurice, martyr, 144, 200, 216
Maurists, 18, 19, 20
mayor of the palace, 11, 53, 70, 73, 74, 166, 187, 198, 203, 211, 212, 214, 216, 228, 233, 234, 235–255, 266, 267, 271, 275, 279
Medard, bishop of Noyon, 157
Meersen, Treaty of, 149, 150
Memnon, mythological king, 43
Mercury, Roman god, 94
Merovech, king of the Franks, 22, 37, 38, 44–51, 67, 77–78, 103, 105, 116, 117, 134, 150, 239, 274
Merovech, Merovingian prince, 158, 162
Metz, 35–36, 59–61, 74, 75, 76, 84, 104, 125, 142, 149, 150, 171, 175, 177, 184, 185, 187, 190, 207, 211, 215, 216, 228, 234, 238, 240, 242, 244, 247, 251, 270
Meuse, river, 247
Mézeray, François Eudes de, 19, 20
  Abrégé chronologique de l'histoire de France, 19
  Histoire de France, 20
Michael, archangel, 247, 249
Migne, Jacques Paul
  Patrologia Latina, 152, 239
Milan, 261
Miracula S. Dionysii, 173
mirror of princes, 177, 178, 180
misericordia, 186
Modoald, archbishop of Trier, 234
Mont Saint-Michel, monastery, 250
Monte Cassino, 5
Monte Gargano, monastery, 250
Mucutima. *See* Chroma, Burgundian princess
Muhammad, prophet, 258
Murray, Alexander C., 48
Muslims, 9, 41, 56, 228, 258, 265

Nanninus, Roman military commander, 35
Nanthechild, queen of the Franks, 54, 187, 190, 192, 194, 198, 216
Narses, Byzantine general, 137, 138
Neustria, 25, 50, 155, 249, 255
  elites, 53, 58, 164, 167, 178, 189, 225, 274
  kings, 69, 70, 72, 76, 185, 268
  mayor, 166, 203
Neustria-Burgundy, kingdom, 50, 72, 195, 203, 216, 220
Nicaea I, council, 133
Nicene Christians, 91, 92
Nivelles, monastery, 172, 235, 237, 242
Noirmoutier, monastery, 201
Normandy, 102
Normans, 66
Notre Dame, church in Lyon, 99
Noyon, 172, 207, 242
nutritor, 54, 176, 241

Oexle, Otto Gerhard, 76
Old French, 1, 62
Olivier, Sarah, 174
origo gentis, 33, 41, 57, 59, 62, 66, 67, 133, 211, 232, 274
Orléans, 35, 78, 104, 114, 125, 150, 160, 182, 183, 192, 212, 242
  Council of, AD 511, 96, 98, 114
Orosius, Paul, 34, 35, 100, 107
Orvanne, river, 215

Index   327

Ostrogotho-Areagni, queen of the
  Burgundians, 106
Ostrogoths, 106, 109, 113–115, 118, 130,
  131, 134, 135, 137, 229
Otto I, emperor, 271
Otto, mayor of the palace, 245
Ottomans, 24, 227, 228, 257
Ottonians, dynasty, 231
Outremer, 81

paciencia, 54
paganism, 1, 32, 36, 37, 38, 48, 49, 68, 90,
  91, 94, 95, 110, 112
Pandrasius, mythological king, 65
Pannonia, 35–37, 50, 77, 126,
  148, 194
Pantheon, 130
Papenbroeck, Daniel, Bollandist scholar,
  18, 19
Paris, 66, 70, 71, 98, 99, 109, 125, 158,
  160, 175, 179, 185, 187, 188, 190,
  220, 233, 236, 262, 268, 270, 278
  books, 101, 103
  churches, 103, 104, 118, 126,
    157, 179
  inhabitants, 71, 104
  manuscripts, 69
  monasteries, 1, 247
  parliament, 261
  university, 261
Paris of Troy, 65
Paternus, legate, 213
Paul the Deacon, 15, 32, 62, 75, 148, 211,
  215, 217, 255, 276
  Gesta episcoporum Mettensium, 22, 59, 73,
    75, 133, 149, 207, 274
  History of the Lombards, 100, 210, 217,
    227, 247
Paul, apostle, 103
periodization, 3, 10, 11, 15, 16, 17, 18, 20,
  23, 24, 128, 131, 139, 168, 205, 219,
  221, 227, 229, 231, 265, 271, 275
Persians, 230, 258
Peter, apostle, 103
Philip Augustus, king of France, 1, 66, 71,
  73, 80
Philip III, king of France, 63, 80
Philipp, bishop of Vienne, 145
Philippide. *See* William the Breton
Philistines, 258
Phocas, emperor, 130, 215
Pippin I, king of Aquitaine, 177
Pippin I, mayor of the palace, 50, 77, 184,
  187, 189, 190, 191, 203, 211, 212,
  216, 234, 235, 240, 242, 246, 274

Pippin II, mayor of the palace, 58, 62, 70,
  73, 74, 75, 77, 166, 217–218, 226,
  231, 242, 249–252, 266, 267
Pippin III, king of the Franks, 57, 62, 72,
  73, 74, 77, 89, 128, 169, 218, 226,
  242, 252, 253, 254, 269, 274
Pippin IV. *See* Héristal, Pippin Arnulf
Pippinids, 11, 50, 58, 76, 85, 139, 182, 222,
  226, 234, 235, 237, 238, 242, 243,
  252, 255, 276
Placidas. *See* Eustachius, martyr
placita, 226
Plectrude, wife of Pippin II, 62, 250, 251
Poitiers, 97, 136, 196, 199, 201, 202, 210,
  236, 244
  Battle of, 167, 253, 269
  churches, 97, 199
  Holy Cross, 125
  inhabitants, 164
Poitou, 81
Pontius Pilate, Roman governor of
  Judaea, 147
Praejectus, bishop of Clermont, 248
Priam, king of Troy, 33, 43–44, 46–47, 49,
  65–71
Priam, mythological king of the Franks,
  68–70, 233
Primat, monk of Saint-Denis, 1, 3, 4, 6, 12,
  32, 71, 72, 85, 102, 274, 276
  Roman des rois, 4, 6, 9, 16, 22, 34, 62–69,
    77–83
principes, 46, 148, 165, 218, 243, 250, 251,
  252, 254, 255
prophecy, 3, 5, 7, 48
Provence, 81, 118, 141, 202
  parliament, 61
Prüm, monastery, 14, 16, 24, 133, 140,
  141, 174, 180, 205–208, 225, 234,
  272, 275, 276
Pyrenees, 69, 136

Quinotaur, 22, 47, 48–51
Quintianus, bishop of Rodez, 96–97
Quintinus, Roman military commander, 35
Quirinus, bishop of Siscia, 39

Radbod, *dux* of the Frisians, 249
Radegund, queen of the Franks, 52, 126
Radulf, *dux* of Thuringia, 245
Ragamfred, mayor of the palace, 218,
  252, 253
Ragnachar of Cambrai, Frankish king, 90,
  98, 116–117, 152
Ragnetrudis, queen of the Franks, 190–192
Ratbod, archbishop of Trier, 206

Ravenna, 109
Raymond Berenger, count of Provence, 81
Reccared, king of the Visigoths, 133, 158, 209
reditus regni ad stirpem Karoli Magni, 73, 85, 274
réécriture, 85, 146, 238
regales, 36, 46
reges criniti. *See* long-haired kings
Regino, abbot of Prüm, 14, 24, 174, 205–222, 225, 234, 272, 275, 276
 Chronicle, 14, 16, 24, 133, 174, 205–222, 275
Reimitz, Helmut, 34, 41, 58
Reims, 38, 86, 91, 95, 102, 105, 130, 180, 227, 233, 270
Remaclus, bishop of Tongres-Maastricht, 235, 245
 Life, 236, 237
Remigius, archbishop of Lyon, 141, 150
Remigius, bishop of Reims, 91, 94, 95, 97, 105, 107, 112, 180, 210
 Life, 113, 173, 193, 233
Renatus Profuturus Frigeridus, historian, 34, 35
renovatio, 10
Réole, La, priory of Fleury, 5
rex inutilis, 21, 79
Rhine, river, 33, 35, 43, 45, 69, 70, 108, 132, 148
Rhineland massacres, 259
Rhône, river, 33, 136, 144, 149, 164
Ricchar, Frankish king, 98, 152
Riccio, Michele, 261
 De regibus Francorum libri III, 261, 263, 265–269
Richard, duke of Cornwall, 81
Richild, empress, 158, 159
Richomeres, consul, 37
Ricimer, father of Theudemer, 37, 44, 45, 47
Rigord of Saint-Denis, 66, 82, 273, 274
 Courte chronique des rois de France, 74, 75
 Gesta Philippi Augusti, 63–77, 82
Rigunth, Merovingian princess, 158, 159
Risi, Dino, director, 171
Robert II, duke of Normandy, 102
Robert the Strong, 155
Robert, count of Hesbaye, 254
Rodez, 96, 115
rois fainéants, 23, 167, 279
Roman des rois. *See* Primat, monk of Saint-Denis: *Roman des rois*
Romaric, abbot of Remiremont, 142
 Life, 53

Rome
 empire, 20, 23, 31, 34, 35, 38, 43, 45, 48, 51, 52, 55, 70, 71, 93, 126, 129, 130–132, 134, 137, 139, 140, 148, 151, 160, 168, 179, 208, 229, 230, 231, 243, 250, 261, 276
 king, 81
 law, 196
 martyrs, 182
 origin, 43, 44, 48
 pantheon, 94
 popes, 14, 74, 160
 republic, 48
 troops, 38, 45
Romulus Augustulus, emperor, 137
Rosenwein, Barbara, 203
Rosweyde, Heribert, 18
Rouen, 127, 172, 198, 242
royal paternity, 46, 49–50, 77, 103, 105, 268
Rusticus, companion of Dionysius, 183, 189

Sabaria, 39
Sabino, Vittorio, 229
 Le vite de tutti gli Re di Francia, 260–271
sack of Rome, 41
Sadregisel, *nutritor* to Dagobert, 176–178, 181, 185, 189, 195–196, 202, 212, 221, 245
Saint John Lateran, church in Rome, 116
Saint John the Baptist, church near Alexandria, 160
Saint Vincent, tunic of, 157
Saint-Bertin, monastery, 173
Saint-Denis, monastery, 1, 5, 12, 21, 24, 32, 63, 64, 65, 73, 81, 82, 86, 170–174, 181–184, 189, 194–199, 203–205, 216, 217, 219–220, 221, 247, 262, 275–276
Sainte-Geneviève. *See* Holy Apostles, church in Paris
Saintes, 152
Saint-Germain, church in Paris, 104
Saint-Jean-de-Losne, 187
Saint-Lambert, church in Liège, 251
Saint-Martin, church in Tours, 98, 154, 155, 197, 199
Saint-Martin, monastery in Metz, 228, 238
Saint-Martin, monastery in Trier, 206, 207
Saint-Maurice d'Agaune, monastery, 155, 156, 159, 197, 199
Saint-Medard, church in Soissons, 126
Saint-Mihiel, monastery, 244
Saint-Trond, monastery, 254

Index 329

Saint-Vincent, church in Metz, 238
Saladin, sultan, 259
Salegast, Frankish lawgiver, 148
Salians, dynasty, 231, 250
Salic Law. *See* Lex Salica
Salm, 244
Samo, king of the Wends, 194, 242
Sanchia, daughter of Raymond
    Berenger, 81
Saône, river, 149, 164
Saracens, 57, 147, 213, 234, 253, 258, 269
Saragossa, 157
Sasanians, 55
Saturn, Roman god, 94
Saxons, 126, 136, 137, 175, 186, 189, 212
Saxony, 126, 134, 165, 170, 195
Scandinavia, 132, 133
Scanza. *See* Scandinavia
Scarpsum de Cronica Hieronimi. See Fredegar,
    Chronicle: Scarpsum de Cronica
    Hieronimi
scepter, 2, 175, 179–180, 192
Scythia Inferior, 66
Séguier, Pierre, chancellor of France, 19
Seine, river, 109
Sens, 141, 187, 248
Servatus, legate, 213
Severa, abbess in Trier, 234
Severinus, bishop of Cologne
    Life, 207
Severn, river, 81
Shakespeare, William
    Henry V, 75
Shapur, Persian king, 230
shards, 9, 263
Siagre. *See* Syagrius, ruler of Soissons
Sicambria, legendary city of the Franks, 66,
    69, 70, 71, 103, 110–111, 148, 261
Sicily, 81, 138, 199, 202
Sidonius Apollinaris, bishop of Clermont,
    40, 135
Sigebert of Gembloux, 13–15, 16, 17, 21,
    100, 227–256, 258, 272, 275–278
    Chronicle, 13, 16, 24, 227–256, 258, 272
    Gesta abbatum Gemblacensium, 228
    Liber Decennalis, 232
    Life of Sigibert III, 228, 238–246, 249
    Life of St. Lambert, 251–252
    Life of Theodoard, 244
    Vita Wigberti abbatum conditoris, 228
Sigibert 'the Lame'. *See* Sigibert of
    Cologne, Frankish king
Sigibert I, king of the Franks, 33, 34, 74, 75,
    76, 126, 127, 158–167
Sigibert II, king of the Franks, 162, 240

Sigibert III, king of the Franks, 17, 50, 166,
    184, 190, 191–192, 195, 198, 203, 213,
    216, 233, 235–238, 246, 252, 255, 278
    Life, 17, 238–246, 249
    translation of remains, 228
Sigibert of Cologne, Frankish king, 90, 98,
    111–112, 116, 117
Sigismund, king of the Burgundians, 93,
    106, 108, 115, 134, 136, 155–156
Suffering, 156, 180
Sigistrix, Burgundian prince, 156
Silvius, son of Ascanius, 65
simplicitas, 186, 189
Siscia, 39
Sisenand, king of the Visigoths, 216
Sithiu, monastery, 57
six-ages, 131, 132, 141, 147, 154
Sixtus IV, pope, 99
Slavs, 170, 187, 194, 216
Soissons, 32, 104, 126, 160, 205
    kingdom of, 38, 93, 106
    vase of, 90, 93, 107, 110
Solomon, biblical king, 171, 246
Song of Roland, 80
Soracte, mountain monastery, 269
Spain, 41, 102, 106, 126, 133, 157, 158,
    160, 170, 195, 207, 210, 211, 257, 260
    expulsion of AD 1492, 256
Spiegel, Gabrielle, 73
Stablo-Malmédy, monastery, 57, 144,
    235–236, 239, 245, 246
Steinbeck, John
    The Short Reign of Pippin IV, 278, 279
Stephen, bishop of Liège, 251
Stephen, bishop of Metz, 244
Stilicho, Roman general, 35
Stone, Rachel, 178
subregulus, 51, 53
Suevi, 266
Suger, abbot of Saint-Denis, 12, 66, 82
Sulpicius Alexander, historian, 34, 35,
    46, 53
Sulpicius Severus, hagiographer, 143
Sunno, Frankish *dux*, 35, 36, 45–48, 53,
    68–70, 148, 233
Syagrius, ruler of Soissons, 38, 81, 88, 90,
    93, 105–106, 151, 210
Sylvester, bishop of Rome, 91
Symphorian of Autun, martyr, 143
    cellula, 144
Syracuse, 202

Tacitus, Publius Cornelius, 100
Talmud, burning of, 258
Tassilo, duke of Bavaria, 211

330   Index

Teia, king of the Ostrogoths, 137
temperance, 1
Ten Books of History. See Gregory of Tours: *Histories*
Tertry, Battle of, 249
Teutberga, queen of the Franks, 158
Theodegotha, queen of the Visigoths, 106
Theoderic, king of the Ostrogoths, 101, 102, 106, 113, 114, 117, 134, 135
Theodisc nations, 132
Theodoald, mayor of the palace, 250–251, 252, 266
Theodoard, bishop of Tongres-Maastricht, 244
Theodulf, bishop of Orléans, 183
Theudarius, abbot, 17, 141–146
Theudebert I, king of the Franks, 126, 134, 136, 138, 157
Theudebert II, king of the Franks, 126, 159, 162, 214
Theudemer, king of the Franks, 37, 44, 45, 47
Theuderic I, king of the Franks, 93, 96, 104, 136, 157, 210
Theuderic II, king of the Franks, 126, 146, 159, 160, 161, 163, 165, 214, 215, 240
Theuderic III, king of the Franks, 72, 226, 247–249, 252, 265–269
Theuderic IV, king of the Franks, 57, 72, 74, 226, 253–254, 262, 265, 266–269, 271
Thrace, 66
Thuringia, 1, 37, 38, 51, 52, 78, 79, 105, 125, 126, 135, 157, 170, 195, 235
Tiberius II, emperor, 56, 161
Tolbiac, Battle of, 68, 110, 111, 115, 117
Torcoth, mythological king of the Turks, 44, 66–67
Toulouse, 115, 152, 186
Tournai, 55
Tours, 35, 92, 164
  bishops, 34, 40, 97, 152
  churches, 97, 98, 154, 197
  Trojan tradition, 33
  wars, 92, 97, 117
translatio generationis, 75
translatio imperii, 231, 255
Trier, 36, 206
  bishops, 234
  churches, 234
  imperial center, 35
  wars, 36, 150
Trinitarians, order, 261
Troilus, son of Priam, 66

Troy, 1, 21, 22, 31–34, 41–49, 52, 58–62, 64–71, 73, 77, 82, 83, 101, 232, 239, 273, 274
Tumba. See Mont Saint-Michel, monastery
Turcus. See Torcoth, mythological king of the Turks
Turks, 24, 44, 227, 257, 258
turmae, 197

Umar ibn al-Khattab, caliph, 258, 259, 260, 262
unicorn, 1, 2, 3
Uro, Austrasian noble, 245
utilitas, 139

Valence, 189
Valentinian I, emperor, 68, 69, 148
Valentinian III, emperor, 151
Vandals, 35, 66, 92, 105, 130, 134, 135, 140, 151, 161, 229
Vascosanus, Michael, publisher, 103
Vatican, 18, 239, 244
Vedast, bishop of Arras, 210
  Life, 207
Venantius Fortunatus, poet, 33
vendetta, 196
Verdun, 247
Vergil
  Aeneid, 94
Verona, 99, 103
Verus, bishop of Tours, 97
Verus, bishop of Vienne, 160
Verweij, Michiel, 255
Vézéronce, Battle of, 136
Vidomar. See Wiomad
Vienne, 14, 15, 16–17, 88, 96, 108, 115, 140–166, 210
Vienne, river, 164
Visigoths, 41, 78, 88, 92, 96–99, 106, 112, 114–116, 117, 126, 130, 131, 134, 136–137, 138, 151, 152, 157, 158, 170, 210, 229
vision, 1–4, 7, 13, 16, 20, 84, 127, 144, 156, 163, 167, 174, 183, 189, 199, 202, 207, 233, 249
Volusianus, bishop of Tours, 97
Vouillé, Battle of, 93, 96, 111, 114, 115, 117, 134, 136, 152

Walahfrid Strabo
  De imagine Tetrici, 183
Wallace-Hadrill, John Michael, 173, 184
Wandalbert of Prüm, monk
  Martyrology, 180
Wandregisel, abbot of Fontenelle, 171

Wascones, 187
Wends, 194, 195
Werner, Karl Ferdinand, 73
West, Charles, 219
William of Tyre, 100
William Rufus, king of England, 102
William the Breton, 64, 67, 82
  Philippide, 67, 71
Winomad. *See* Wiomad, *subregulus*
Wiomad, *subregulus*, 51–54, 78–80, 82, 98, 105
Wisogast, Frankish lawgiver, 148

Wisovast, Frankish lawgiver, 148
wolf, 2, 3, 99
Wood, Ian, 20, 38, 48, 49, 50, 97
Woodruff, Jane, 45, 46
World War I, 93
Wulfoald, mayor of the palace, 247

Zacharias, bishop of Vienne, 152
Zacharias, pope, 74, 218, 228, 269
Zavarisi, Daniel, protégé of Paolo Emilio, 103
Zwentibald, king of Lotharingia, 207

Printed by Printforce, the Netherlands